EXCAVATIONS AT THE MOLA DI MONTE GELATO

A ROMAN AND MEDIEVAL SETTLEMENT
IN SOUTH ETRURIA

This volume has been published with the help of a very substantial subvention from the Trustees of the British Museum, as well as with grants from the M. Aylwin Cotton Foundation and King Alfred's College, Winchester.

EXCAVATIONS AT THE MOLA DI MONTE GELATO

A ROMAN AND MEDIEVAL SETTLEMENT IN SOUTH ETRURIA

T.W. Potter and A.C. King

with

L. Allason-Jones, P. Arthur, D.M. Bailey, F. Fedeli Bernardini, A. Claridge, J. Conheeney, J. DeLaine, C.M. Gilliver, O. Gilkes, J. Giorgi, R.P.J. Jackson, F. Marazzi, J. Osborne, H. Patterson, J. Price, P. Roberts and D. Wilkinson

and

C. Cartwright, J. Cook, I.C. Freestone, R. Hobbs, K. Matthews, O. Murray, P. Parsons, B. West, D. Williams and R.J.A. Wilson

with drawings principally by

R.D. Andrews, S. Ashley, S. Cann, S. Gibson and T.W. Potter

principal photographs by

K. Warren

ARCHAEOLOGICAL MONOGRAPHS OF THE
BRITISH SCHOOL AT ROME
No. 11

Published by the British School at Rome London,
in association with
THE BRITISH MUSEUM

1997

ISBN 0 904152 31 6

Cover illustration: The mill and waterfalls on the river Treia at the Mola di Monte Gelato *(Photograph: Kate Warren)*

Typeset by Cristal, via degli Orti di Galba 24-26, 00152 Rome, Italy
and printed by Tipograf S.r.l., via Costantino Morin 26/A, 00195 Rome, Italy
Cover design by Silvia Stucky

This volume is dedicated to the memory of Molly Cotton,
an inspirational mentor during my early exploration
of southern Etruria

Contents

List of Figures

The following abbreviations have been used to indicate the artist, draughtsperson or photographer: RDA – R.D. Andrews; SA – Stephen Ashley; DB – Donald Bailey; SC – Sally Cann; AC – Amanda Claridge; SG – Sheila Gibson; RH – R. Hobbs; RJ – Ralph Jackson; ACK – A.C. King; KM – Keith Matthews; TWP – T.W. Potter; PR – Paul Roberts; AMS – Alastair M. Small; JBWP – John Ward-Perkins; KW – Kate Warren.

xiii

List of Tables

PREFACE

The excavations here reported form part of a long-standing investigation into the archaeology and history of the central part of the Ager Faliscus. It originated as a field survey, conducted by John Ward-Perkins and the British School at Rome in the 1950s, and by myself, for the School, in the later 1960s. In conjunction with this, I have in addition initiated a number of excavations in the area, aimed at setting in a sharper focus the results of the field survey. The present project forms part of this broader investigation, and the research design will be reviewed in the first chapter. Here it is necessary to make only three general points.

The first is to emphasize that most of these excavations arose from questions posed by study of the field-survey data. Conclusions derived from surface collections can be extremely informative, as Ward-Perkins demonstrated so magisterially in his work on the Ager Veientanus (Kahane, Murray-Threipland and Ward-Perkins 1968); but they also need testing and refining by the application of sophisticated techniques of excavation, as the Monte Gelato investigations have clearly demonstrated. The reading of the evidence acquired from surface inspection (set out in Chapter Two) in no way prepared one for the remarkable picture that emerged from our trenches, nor for the subtle nuances of the chronological sequence.

Secondly, it is pertinent to add that the site was to yield a range of artefacts that was by any standard exceptional. This turned what might have been a relatively small-scale enquiry (as was initially intended) into a major project, leading to a substantial publication. The wealth of sculpture, inscriptions, and objects in metal, bone, glass, pottery and other materials, together with critically important assemblages of animal, bird and fish bones, which poured forth on almost a daily basis, indeed remains an enduring memory. They allow for a much more sophisticated interpretation of the site's changing nature and status than is usually possible and, in turn, raise intriguing questions about the depositional factors that lie behind so rich a pattern of survival. These we are scarcely able to answer (and they are seldom addressed in classical archaeology, despite their prominence in prehistoric studies); but this is clearly an aspect of our results which merits further research.

Finally, it is pleasant to be able to record that, while the publication is largely in English, and produced in British institutions, the project as a whole was emphatically Anglo-Italian. This extended well beyond the composition of the team of archaeologists and specialists. Relations with the local community were close, and I recall with particular pleasure the visits of groups of children, organized by local schools. Their interest in the archaeology may have been nearly equalled by their fascination with the idiosyncratic Italian in which they were not infrequently addressed; but we very much welcomed these educational initiatives which, together with growth of true collaborative projects, represent a most welcome trend over recent years. We trust that this volume, together with the many discussions that have also appeared in Italian, will be seen as a further contribution to our understanding of the archaeology of a region with an especially rich and rewarding patrimony.

T.W. Potter

ACKNOWLEDGEMENTS

Monte Gelato was an extraordinarily pleasant and happy excavation, due in large measure to a first-class and highly dedicated team. Many began their archaeological careers as students of Dr King at King Alfred's College, Winchester, and have subsequently taken full-time employment in British archaeological units. For them, Monte Gelato was truly a 'busman's holiday', and we owe them a special debt of thanks for their loyalty to the project, which brought them back to the site year after year. We cannot, alas, mention all who worked with us – the list is far too long – but we would like to express our warmest gratitude to Oliver Gilkes, our chief supervisor throughout the project; to Robin Brunner-Ellis, Crispin Jarman, Nicki King, Sally Martin and David Wilkinson who also supervised; and to Martin Brown, Simone DeTurris, David Forster, Alan and Jane French, Douglas Hird, Tony Hurley, Federico Marazzi and Alex Turner, who were the most conspicuously long-term excavators. It is most striking that virtually all who were with us at the start of the project in 1986 were still digging at Monte Gelato in the last season of 1990.

We also gladly acknowledge Dr Simon James of the British Museum, who was the main site planner throughout the excavation, and thus deeply involved with interpreting a complex site; Mr Danny Andrews, ARIBA, who carried out the survey of the valley and the mill; and Dr Kate Gilliver, who ran the Finds Department with enormous efficiency, and who also coordinated the specialist study season at the British School at Rome in 1991.

The field team was accommodated in a *palestra* at Campagnano di Roma, and we are most grateful to the *Comune* and then mayor, Sig. Filippo Lorenzetti, for all manner of help, not least the provision of evening meals for some of the seasons: we were delighted and honoured when the *Comune* of Campagnano awarded the British School at Rome, as principal sponsor of the project in Italy, a gold medal. To the British School itself we are especially indebted. Here was accommodated the main post-excavation team, drawn principally from staff of the British Museum. These comprised Kate Warren (Photographic Division) who, between 1988 and 1990, did all the studio photography, as well as the majority of the photographs on site (and who gratefully acknowledges the loan of much equipment by Bronica Ltd); Sandra Smith (1988), Penny Fisher (1989) and Loretta Hogan and Denise Ling (1990), of the Museum's Conservation Department, who conserved the entire collection and, in 1990, joined the vessels from the huge second-century dump in a fish-pond (cf. Figs 216 and 217); and Janice Conheeney, who, as a museum assistant in my department, in 1988 organized the storage of the collections, before beginning an independent study of the human remains. The achievements of the British Museum staff will be obvious in the pages of this volume, and we are particularly grateful to them; and, too, to their respective Keepers for providing special leave, especially Dr Andrew Oddy, head of Conservation at the British Museum.

We also offer our sincere thanks to our principal illustrators, Stephen Ashley and Sally Cann. They carried out their excellent work at the British School, and rose to the challenge of drawing an extraordinarily diverse range of objects with commitment and great skill. All who worked in the School are extremely indebted to successive Directors, Professor Graeme Barker and Professor Richard Hodges, for their support; and especially to the then Assistant Director, Amanda Claridge, for aiding the project in every possible way, both academically and logistically. We would also like to acknowledge with warmth and affection the work of the School's staff, who so very unassumingly and yet so efficiently ease the path of those involved with projects like the one here described.

Likewise, the Italian authorities did everything they could to ensure that the excavation ran smoothly and without hindrance. I personally owe a deep and profound debt of gratitude to the former Superintendent of Antiquities for southern Etruria, Prof. Paola Pelagatti, for her support over many years; and now to her successor, Dott. G. Scichilone, for his warm encouragement. We also owe much to Dott.ssa Bruna Amendolea, of the office of the *Assessore della Cultura*, particularly in her attempts to improve the *mise-en-valeur* of the site. But our warmest thanks must be reserved for the region's inspector, Dott.ssa Clementina Sforzini, who has been unflagging in her efforts to help the project. Both by her work on the site and behind the scenes, she has been a true friend of the excavation, and we most genuinely appreciate it.

Our sponsoring bodies have been numerous. The British School has been more than generous in allocating funds and logistic support, while our biggest patron has been the British Museum, which provided financial help (and, as described above, much more) throughout, including the study season. We gladly thank the Trustees; the former Director, Sir David Wilson; the present Director, Dr Robert Anderson; and the Keepers of the various departments concerned (Prehistory and Roman Britain; Greek and Roman Antiquities; Medieval and Later Antiquities; the Research Laboratory and the Department of Conservation). I owe a very real personal debt of gratitude to the former Keeper of my own department, Dr Ian Longworth, for his unswerving support and encouragement; without it, the Monte Gelato excavation could hardly have happened. Likewise I owe a very deep debt of gratitude to Kate Down who, with the assistance of Judith Cash, both of my department, undertook the onerous task of preparing the typescript, not least a daunting array of tables, with astounding good cheer.

We were particularly delighted to receive a grant from the M. Alywin Cotton Foundation towards the costs of this volume, and take great pleasure in dedicating it to the memory of Molly Cotton; this is in tribute to her contribution to the work in South Etruria, and especially her guidance during my Ager Faliscus field survey in the later 1960s (in which she from time to time participated).

We are also extremely grateful to the British Academy, the Society of Antiquaries of London, King Alfred's College, Winchester, the Society for the Promotion of Roman Studies, and the Craven Fund of the University of Oxford, for their financial contribution to the project, which was conducted at a total cost of £51,000. Many individuals, far too numerous to name in their entirety, have also been free and generous in their help. We particularly thank the specialists who have contributed to this volume, not least scientists from the British Museum's Research Laboratory, who have examined problematic material; and would like to make special mention of those whose names do not necessarily feature in the text, but who have given us advice and help: Janet Ambers, Sheridan Bowman, Piero Brunetti, Andrew Burnett, Lucos Cozza, Paolo Delogu, Vincenzo Fiocchi Nicolai, Riccardo Francovich, Sheila Gibson, Karen Hughes, Catherine Johns, Enzo Litta, John Lloyd, Federico Marazzi, Lidia Paroli, Nicholas Purcell, Joyce Reynolds, Valerie Scott, Andrew Wallace-Hadrill, Susan Walker and Chris Wickham. Nor can we forget the friendly officials of the *Parco suburbano della valle Treja*; Giancarlo, the kindly proprietor of the much frequented Monte Gelato bar; and the contribution of my own family, especially my wife Sandra, who did a huge amount to aid the project, both in terms of organization (especially the travel arrangements) and in deeply valued moral support. Likewise, I owe much to my readers, especially Neil Christie (himself a Monte Gelato digger), who subjected the excavation text to ruthless scrutiny, to its great advantage; and to Gill Clark who, as the British School's Publications Manager, has made a decisive contribution to this volume, in an editorial role.

Finally, I would like to pay special tribute to the co-director of the project, Anthony King. It was he who directed work on site, and supervised the arrangements in Campagnano, and he brought to the project an enviable degree of archaeological expertise, and a very real flair for interpreting the evidence in the ground. He was also responsible for assembling the first-rate team. His many other duties have meant that he was unable to do as much for this volume as we had hoped, so that the report and illustrations of the excavations were largely drafted by myself; however, it is very much the fruit of extended discussion, and represents our joint views. We both, I fancy, enjoyed the project to the full but, without his talent and commitment, it would have been a shadow of what it was to become.

T.W. Potter

Chapter One

INTRODUCTION: THE NATURE OF THE PROBLEM

The Mola di Monte Gelato lies in the pleasantly wooded valley of the river Treia, about 34 km north from the heart of Rome. Until the creation in the early 1980s of a suburban park, extending down the Treia valley from the Mola to Mazzano and Calcata, this was a relatively remote and isolated spot. Yet its setting is known to millions, as a backdrop to the countless films that have been made there over the past 40 years or so. Attracted by charming waterfalls and the rustic remains of a medieval mill, bridge and tower, cinematic and television directors are still drawn to the Mola di Monte Gelato. So too, these days, are numerous weekend visitors, largely from Rome, who make the now easy drive from the city, up the Via Veientana, the modernized *superstrada* that has partly replaced and partly improved the Via Cassia. The city of Rome and its hinterland are thus integrated in a way unthinkable even twenty years ago, but a phenomenon which, as this volume will show, can be closely paralleled in the past. Indeed, the history of the Mola is in many respects a mirror of the changing fortunes of Rome itself.

The hill known as Monte Gelato lies in fact some 1,100 m to the east of the Mola (Fig. 1). For convenience, we have tended to call the site at the Mola 'Monte Gelato', and indeed wonder whether it is the seductive and creamy-cold texture of the waterfalls which provides an origin for the toponym. That, however, is speculation. What is not in doubt is that the place has an intriguing history, and a very rich archaeology, as the ensuing pages will attempt to show. But first we must set out something of the background to the project, not least to demonstrate how it fits into a relatively coherent and logical campaign of research into the archaeology of this region (Figs 2 and 3).

The Mola di Monte Gelato is situated in the southern part of the Ager Faliscus. This effectively corresponds with the drainage basin of the river

Fig. 1. The Mola di Monte Gelato in 1970, looking southeast across the terrace of the main site towards the mill and adjacent tower. *(TWP)*

1

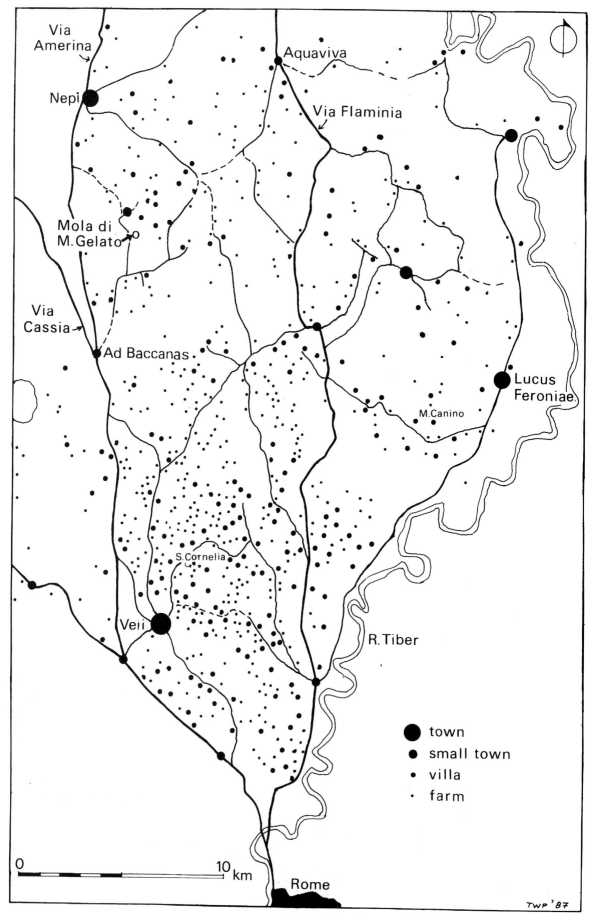

Fig. 2. South Etruria in the early Imperial period. *(TWP)*

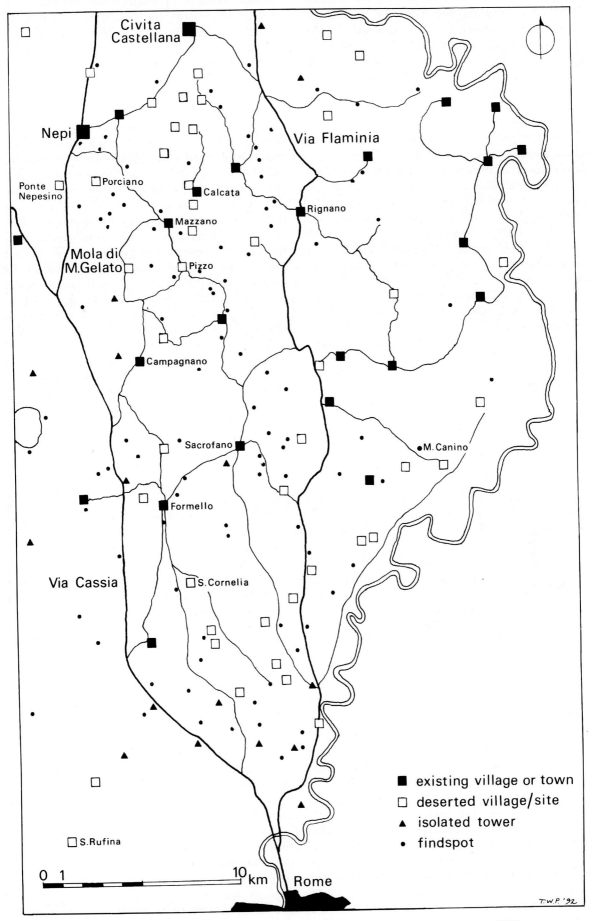

Fig. 3. South Etruria in the medieval period. (Lines are roads in use in medieval times.) *(TWP)*

Treia, and its tributaries, which flows in a northeasterly direction, entering the Tiber to the east of Civita Castellana, more or less opposite Poggio Sommavilla. It is a favoured and fertile land, occupied in pre-Roman times by the Faliscans, a people who, according to Strabo (v. 2.9), 'spoke a special and distinct language all of their own'. Although culturally close to the Etruscans, the Faliscan language appears to have been most akin to Latin, and it may be that the Latins and the Faliscans shared common roots.

The Faliscan region has been long studied. Fundamental was the work of Adolfo Cozza and Angelo Pasqui, together with Gian Francesco Gamurrini and Raniero Mengarelli, in the late nineteenth century, so splendidly presented by Cozza's grandson, Professor Lucos Cozza (1972: 429-30; 1981), in the relevant volumes of the *Carta archeologica d'Italia*. Similarly important are the studies of the great historian, Giuseppe Tomassetti (1913, republished with further commentary in 1979), with their detailed documentary and topographical discussions. All modern scholars are indebted to these pioneering works.

Hardly less influential was Thomas Ashby, Director of the British School at Rome between 1906 and 1925, whose studies of the Campagna (Ashby 1927; 1986) 'will always remain a treasured possession of any lover of the Roman countryside' (Ward-Perkins 1970: x). It was Ashby who properly established a British tradition of topographical studies in the environs of Rome, a mantle that was brilliantly assumed by John Ward-Perkins when he was Director of the British School, between 1946 and 1974. Of the South Etruria field survey, which he initiated and directed, it is hardly necessary to write. Its unique importance in the history of landscape studies is universally recognized, so much so that field survey is now a dominant theme of contemporary investigations. Even though methodologies have become ever more sophisticated, the value of the work in South Etruria – conducted as it was at a time when so many sites were in the process of being destroyed – remains. It is a point vividly made by survey in 1989 of the sector to the southwest of Campagnano di Roma, which painted a sorry picture of an archaeologically devastated landscape (King 1993). Whilst not all of the Roman Campagna has suffered in this way, the timeliness of Ward-Perkins's intervention is nevertheless obvious, as he himself clearly recognized (1955: 44).

My own involvement with the region began in 1966, when I was asked to survey some 200 square kilometres of the central and southern Ager Faliscus. These results, although available in typescript, have never been published in detail. This is because, when the manuscript was prepared in 1980-81, I was becoming increasingly uneasy about the accuracy of my pottery identifications, which I thought, upon reflection, to be overconfident. This is why there is currently a project underway to re-

examine (and computerize) the collections, with a view to reassessing the South Etruria survey as a whole. The results, we can be sure, will be intriguing.

Ward-Perkins always stressed the need to develop pottery chronologies by excavation of promising sites revealed by the survey. Thus we were to devote five seasons of work to the deeply-stratified bronze age and iron age site beside the river Treia at Narce, just a few kilometres downstream from the Mola di Monte Gelato. Discovered in the autumn of 1966, the site clearly had the potential to illuminate a crucial period of Faliscan pre- and proto-history. It was a complex and difficult site, but did indeed provide an important corpus of material, including faunal and floral assemblages, spanning the period between the latter part of the second millennium BC and about 250 BC (Potter 1976). Considerable light was shed upon the evolution of stock and arable economies. In the fourth and third centuries BC the site was used for tile manufacture, exploiting exposures of Pliocene clay which underlie the volcanics. This industrial tradition continued elsewhere along the Treia valley in Roman and medieval times, not least at the Mola di Monte Gelato, where Roman pottery wasters and an early medieval pottery kiln were discovered in the present excavations. Indeed, the question of local pottery manufacture in the Roman period has been greatly illuminated by Peña's study of a number of the kiln sites in the region (Peña 1987), which indicates widespread and relatively intensive rural production.

The other main direction of post-survey excavations in the Ager Faliscus has focused upon the transition from the dispersed pattern of rural settlement in the Roman period to the fortified and nucleated towns and villages (*castelli*) which dominated the medieval landscape. It had been long recognized that the documentary sources imply that these medieval sites were, in the main, creations of the tenth and eleventh centuries AD, which, as Toubert (1973) demonstrated, were often undertaken for economic reasons. Closer to Rome, in the Ager Veientanus, farming based on rural 'villas' carried on well into medieval times, as historical and archaeological research has shown (Kahane, Murray Threipland and Ward-Perkins 1968; Wickham 1978; 1979). It is a point most vividly made by the excavations at Santa Cornelia, the primary centre of the *domusculta* of *Capracorum*, founded *c.* 774-6, by Pope Hadrian I (Christie and Daniels 1991).

In the Ager Faliscus there seemed to be reasons for suggesting a rather earlier trend towards the occupation of defensible positions. The arguments need not be rehearsed again in detail, for they are familiar and in some respects flawed. They were proposed (Potter 1975) partly because forum ware, the lead-glazed pottery produced from the late eighth century in Rome, was conspicuously rare on the late Roman 'villas' (unlike the Ager Veientanus), but did occur on some of the defended medieval sites. Moreover, the Ager Faliscus had become, from the time of the Lombard invasion of 568, something of a frontier zone. Sutri, for instance, fell to the Lombards and was retaken soon after, in 592-3, and hostilities are frequently mentioned in the letters of Gregory the Great. Later, in the eighth century there was conflict between Rome and the Lombard king, Liutprand, as well as with local nobles like Duke Toto of Nepi. It did not seem implausible to correlate the archaeological and historical evidence, and to infer an earlier phase of medieval *castelli* than in some other regions.

Two excavations were made to test the point, one in 1971 at Mazzano Romano (Potter 1972) and the other in 1982 at Ponte Nepesino (Cameron *et al.* 1984), a now deserted promontory site, overlooking the Via Amerina, to the south of Nepi. Both yielded forum ware, in association with masonry structures (at Mazzano) and wooden buildings (at Ponte Nepesino); but radiocarbon dates from Ponte Nepesino suggested that occupation was unlikely to have begun before the later ninth century. There thus remained what seemed to be an archaeological gap between the apparent demise of the late Roman 'villas' – somewhere in the sixth century, to judge from surface finds – and the emergence of the medieval *castelli*, three to four centuries later.

The time was clearly ripe to examine the question from a different angle, by choosing a well-stratified Roman rural site, where there might be some possibility of occupation continuing into medieval times. The Mola di Monte Gelato was a prime candidate. Here was what appeared to be a large Roman villa, overlooking the Treia valley, and its waterfalls, with surface indications of both late Roman and medieval occupation. Moreover, nearby was a deserted medieval *castello*, known as Castellaccio, a juxtaposition that is not uncommon in the Ager Faliscus (Potter 1975; 1979: 165-7). It seemed to raise the possibility that there might have been movement from one to other, an intriguing thought that merited investigation.

Tomassetti (1882; 1913: 109-10) had long before recognized the potential importance of the site at the Mola. He identified it with the *castrum Capracorum* referred to in a bull of 1053, with its lands, vineyards and mill, together with a church of Saint John *que dicitur Latregia* (= Treia), 27 miles from Rome. He noted that the name *Capracorum* is preserved as *Crepacore*, one of the *quarti della tenuta Montegelato* (Tomassetti 1882: 147), also observing that it is half Greek and half Latin – a fascinating observation given that our excavations were to demonstrate the presence of Greek speakers at the site in Roman times. Moreover, he discussed in a summary fashion the results of excavations carried out between 1875 and 1877 by a Signor Giorgi, on

behalf of the *principe* Del Drago. Tomassetti must have seen some of this work on a visit to Mazzano in 1876 '*per dirigere alcune scavazioni di antichità*' (1882: 146). He recorded how Giorgi was spurred on by the discovery of very many fragments of marble, and found a '*cappella cristiana presso i piloni di un ponte romano diruto (sul Treia), con un piccolo sotteraneo (lunga m. 4×3,50)*'. There was a Latin cross in iron, and near the church a Christian burial with large tiles, gold earrings and glass *balsamarii*. There were in addition '*due torri cadute, un altro sepolcreto formato di loculi scavati nel tufo, donde la contrada trasse il nome di Scifelle (altro quarto di Montegelato)* [500 m to the south of the Mola]; *una vena d'acqua eccellente presso la collina e innumerevoli avanzi di stoviglie più o meno rozze*'.

Tomassetti (1877; 1882) also referred to an ancient Roman road, a *diverticolo della Cassia*, and inscriptions from nearby Monte Caio (below, Fig. 8: *CIL* XI 3207, 3228). Further light on these is shed by the archival research of Fiocchi Nicolai (1988: 235-7), who has published the transcription of three further inscriptions, made by the *guardiascavi* on the 21 December 1877. They are early Christian tombstones, one dated to AD 361, and a second, of *Iohannes* and others, to AD 407. The third, of Calvisius Mesalinus, is not dated, but is presumably of the same general period.

We will show below that Tomassetti was almost certainly correct in his correlation of the bull of 1053 with the site at the Mola di Monte Gelato; it is very plausibly identified as *castrum Capracorum*. We cannot convincingly locate all the features mentioned in his description, but there is a sufficient correlation between our results and those of Giorgi, as described by Tomassetti, to suggest that we were digging in the same place. The *piccolo sotteraneo*, in particular, eludes us (unless it is the rock-cut cave to the west of the church, although the dimensions do not match), as do the two collapsed towers (although it is clear that Tomassetti was describing a wide area, since he mentioned the zone known as Scifelle, which lies well to the south of the Mola). But the church, the paved road and the burials have all been relocated during our work.

The name *Capracorum* immediately links the site with the *domusculta* founded about 776 by Pope Hadrian I (772-95). The *Liber Pontificalis* states:

> The same most holy Pope [Hadrian I] created and founded four papal estates, of which one is called Capracorum, in the territory of Veii, about 15 miles out of Rome. Of this estate, the original farm of Capracorum together with several other farms adjoining it, was his own property, inherited from his family; and to it he added a number of other estates, giving just compensation for each to the persons from whom he bought them. This *domusculta* of Capracorum, with its *massae* [lands], *fundi* [farms], *casales* [farm buildings], vineyards, olive groves, watermills and all else appertaining to it, be established under apostolic privilege and with the sanction of solemn penalties, that it should for all

time continue to be applied to the use of our brothers in Christ, the poor; and that the wheat and barley grown each year in its fields should be carefully collected and stored apart in the granary of our holy church. The wine, too, and the vegetables grown each year in the domains and fields of the aforesaid *domusculta*, should similarly be diligently collected and stored separately in the storehouse of our holy church. And of the pigs which should each year be fattened in the *casales* in the said *domusculta*, one hundred head should be slaughtered and stored in the same storehouse.

(*Liber Pontificalis* (Duchesne) I, 501-2)

Once thought of as a continuous tract of land, it is now clear that the *domuscultae, Capracorum* included, consisted of a series of farms, with their own separate estates (Wickham 1978: 174). Moreover, their purpose, whilst overtly to feed the poor of Rome, had a political significance as well. Rome in the eighth century was a city under threat – from the Lombards (Liutprand had taken Sutri and its territory in 728-9) and from nobles like Duke Toto of Nepi, who in 768 was able to install his brother as anti-pope. The *domuscultae* were thus additionally intended to assert papal authority in the countryside around Rome (Christie 1991b).

We referred above to the site of Santa Cornelia, which excavation and documentary evidence together show was unquestionably the estate-centre of the *domusculta* of *Capracorum*. Although nothing is heard of the *domuscultae* after the mid-ninth century, it is clear on archaeological evidence that Santa Cornelia continued in occupation, and probably between 1026 and 1035 it was converted into a monastery. Tomassetti conjectured that the estate-centre passed from Santa Cornelia to the Mola di Monte Gelato although, in the absence of any evidence to show that the *domusculta* continued to exist after 846, this must remain in question – especially as no suitable buildings were identified in the present excavations. It is to these that we must now turn.

As chance would have it, attention had already been focused upon the Mola when, in 1983, widening of the road-cutting that leads down to the river Treia from the north brought to light burials, early medieval interlace sculpture, and Roman and medieval walls. The paved Roman road was also visible. These discoveries were recorded by the Superintendency inspector for the area, Dott.ssa Clementina Sforzini, and further damage was prevented. When our own programme of work was finally launched, in September 1986, this was clearly the place at which to begin.

The results were immediately fruitful (Fig. 4). Cleaning of the side of the modern road-cutting revealed part of a small early Imperial bath-house, with later structures above. A trench was therefore excavated on the east side of the road-cutting, and came down upon the remains of two superimposed churches, with associated burials. It was an auspicious start, and over the following four years a substantial area of the gently sloping ground to the north and east of the church was investigated. The preservation of structures and stratigraphy was very variable. The hillside had been terraced into at least three levels in Roman times, and structures and deposits on the lower terrace, immediately beside the modern road, had survived very well. The buildings on the upper terrace had suffered a fair amount of damage from ploughing, although there were intact deposits over most of the floors except within the church, where only one small area of floor remained. The top terrace, on the other hand, had been severely affected by modern agriculture, and only features that were deeply recessed into the bedrock were preserved. Even some *selce* blocks from the road paving had been pulled out by the plough, although covered by as much as 1.5 m of colluvium; further up the hillside a scatter of blocks on the surface shows that it must have been destroyed more or less completely.

This in itself amply illustrates the destructive effect of modern agriculture. However, we were in 1989 to meet the man who claimed to have first ploughed the site in the early 1950s, as part of the *Ente Maremma* scheme. He spoke of walls (including one in what was evidently *opus reticulatum*) which were then standing to a height of 2.0 m, as well as numerous large tufo blocks, of the sort utilized in the early medieval complex, to the southeast of the church. He also referred to a white marble statue, lacking only an arm. These structures were duly levelled. Furthermore, in 1976, as records in the Villa Giulia show, vine trenches were cut over much of the area. These penetrated to a depth of 1.4 m, with immensely destructive results. Thus, when we came to excavate in the central part of the site (below, Fig. 11, Trench H), and beside some still-standing masonry, in close proximity to a low cliff (Fig. 4, Trench K), we found that virtually no stratigraphy survived. It is clear therefore that much of the better-preserved parts of the main site have been examined, and that, while there is doubtless much more to be discovered, it would seem that the most fruitful areas have now been explored. Indeed, on the east side of the site, where a track now runs across the area and up the hill, bedrock outcrops at a number of points: whatever there may have been there has long since disappeared.

We call the site to the east of the modern road the 'main site' to distinguish it from work undertaken elsewhere in the valley. One focus of attention arose by chance rather than by design. In the spring of 1989, a local *azienda agricola* acquired the land on the south and west sides of the modern road, opposite the main excavation. This was covered with scrub, and comprised a low ridge, running parallel with the modern road, and flattish terrain, the old flood plain, extending down to the river Treia. The whole area was then systematically

MOLA DI MONTE GELATO 1986-1990

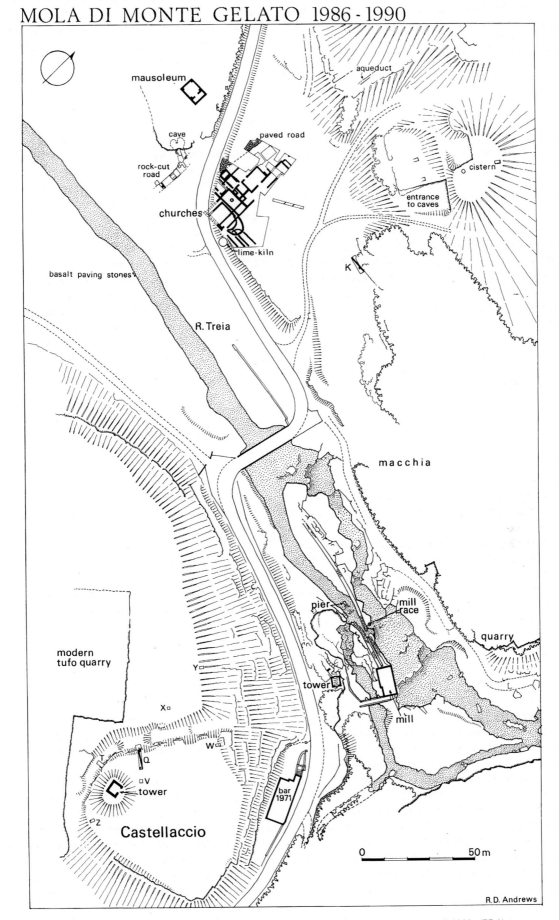

Fig. 4. The site and its known archaeological features, surveyed between 1986 and 1990. *(RDA)*

bulldozed and ploughed, and a deep drainage ditch was also cut. When word finally got out, the bulldozing was stopped, and we were asked to assess the damage to what proved to be a rich archaeological area. Immediately conspicuous was a brick-built mausoleum or temple-tomb of early Imperial date, on the crest of the ridge. This we surveyed and partially excavated in 1989 and 1990, and were able to show that it was the sole surviving feature on that part of the ridge. Also revealed was a rock-cut early medieval cave habitation, set into the ridge below the mausoleum. We investigated the entrance to the cave: we acquired dating evidence and identified a number of other features. Finally we examined the area below the cave, and uncovered some poorly-preserved Roman wall-footings, and a remarkable road-cutting, which reached a depth of nearly 4.0 m. It was clearly the precursor of the paved Roman road, and was filled with rich dumps of Roman-period refuse.

In addition to these excavations, a new survey of the valley was made, by Richard Andrews, who also prepared detailed drawings of the still-standing mill, bridge and adjoining tower. This was an important work of record, since plans were afoot to restore these buildings, thereby inevitably changing their appearance. The mill machinery, which was still operating in the 1950s, is very well preserved (cf. Figs 127 and 128), and we are delighted to include in this volume Dott.ssa Fedeli's study of the documentary and architectural evidence relating to the mill. To date, work has only been carried out on restoring the tower, but the plan is to have a small site museum, with information panels.

The final element of the project was to survey and acquire dating evidence from the castle site of Castellaccio. This had become extremely overgrown over the previous 25 years, but the remains of a tower were still visible, as well as a rock-cut ditch along the northwest side of the site. In 1990, therefore, seven small trenches were excavated, five on the castle itself and two on the flattish ground beyond the ditch. Although the density of trees precluded the recovery of building plans, both walls and an adequate collection of sherds were found, indicating that the site was first occupied (some prehistoric material apart) in the eleventh-twelfth centuries AD. Given that occupation had effectively ceased on the main site by about AD 1100, it is very reasonable to suppose that the castle was the successor of the valley-bottom settlement. If so, it was not apparently held for long. There is little material that post-dates the twelfth century, and the quantities of refuse are such as to imply that the population was never large. By the late thirteenth century, they may well have been moved to Mazzano, leaving only the mill complex as testimony to the valley's long and rich history.

It is perhaps ironic that this extended programme of investigation into the origins of *incastellamento* in the Ager Faliscus should weaken, if not destroy, the original proposition: the medieval nucleated settlements do seem to be mainly a late feature, and certainly on present evidence cannot be shown to pre-date the later ninth century. Yet the period between the late sixth and ninth centuries still remains archaeologically shadowy and elusive, even at a site like the Mola di Monte Gelato with its abundance of evidence. We shall show below that there is little stratigraphical evidence for activity on the site after a major collapse of roofs and walls, dated on good coin evidence to the mid-sixth century AD, at any rate before *c.* AD 800, and we certainly cannot assert that there was continuity of occupation between the later sixth and later eighth centuries.

It is the purpose of this volume, therefore, to present these findings in appropriate detail, as a contribution to an ongoing and stimulating debate. Its production was greatly facilitated by a study season in 1991, when a dozen specialists gathered at the British School to examine and catalogue the finds. This provided a forum for a fruitful dialogue and exchange of views, from which this volume has benefited greatly – as it has from the opportunity to present the findings at conferences in Siena, Rome, London and Nottingham and in many other public lectures.

Meanwhile, further work continues. In 1991 a team headed by Dr Simon Stoddart and Dr Caroline Malone then of the University of Bristol (now of the University of Cambridge), and with my general involvement, working in close collaboration with the Superintendency of Antiquities and other Italian archaeologists, began a programme of excavations within the old centre of the nearby town of Nepi. It is a place with a distinguished history, extending back into the pre-Etruscan period. Nepi and Sutri are together described by Livy (vi. 21.4) as '*loca opposita Etruria et velut claustra inde portae-que*', referring to a revolt by these cities in 386 BC, and a Latin colony was sent to Nepi in either 383 or 373 BC. Later a Roman *municipium*, it is described as a *frourion* (fortress) by Procopius (*De Bello Gothico* iv. 35), alluding to its strategic role on the Via Amerina in the sixth century AD. This role it maintained throughout medieval times. Duke Toto, as we have seen, was an aggressive leader in the eighth century, and the Borgia fortress (which overlies the still-standing Roman gate to the town) remained an imposing symbol of Nepi's military importance until recent times.

The excavations at Nepi (which are receiving very notable support from the *comune*) offer the prospect of complementing and calibrating the results from other excavations in the region, not least those at the Mola di Monte Gelato. Already rich sequences from the seventh century BC to Republican times have been discovered by the cathedral, and dumps of early medieval sculpture, of the same type and date as those found at Monte Gelato, bear witness to a doubtless splendid Carolingian *duomo*, the predecessor of the present Romanesque building. Here, if anywhere in the Ager Faliscus, we may expect archaeological work to cast further light upon the so-called 'Dark Ages', and provide the basis for a comparison between the rural sequence garnered from our work at the Mola di Monte Gelato and at a nearby urban counterpart. It is a logical sequel to the investigation here reported, and it is more than encouraging that the vitality which has, I think, attended the programme of survey and excavation in this part of Etruria is hardly abated. That is surely a tribute to the distinguished scholars, Italian and British, who long ago set an archaeological agenda for us to follow today.

Chapter Two

THE SETTING

GEOLOGY AND GEOMORPHOLOGY

The site rests on the volcanic deposits of the Pleistocene period. These constitute the landscape of the entire South Etruria region, and have had a profound influence on the pattern of human settlement and economy. The generally soft tufos laid down as an indirect or direct result of volcanic action have formed fairly level plateaux, which in due course have been deeply cut by river systems. Locally, the river Treia, although relatively small, has created a deep, steep-sided canyon system, with a number of superbly secure locations for defended settlements. Security was a prime consideration at various periods of the region's history, notably in the Faliscan period and at the time of medieval *incastellamento*. Pre-Roman centres, such as Narce, and medieval villages, like Mazzano Romano and Calcata, amply illustrate this in the Treia valley, as does the medieval site of Castellaccio at the Mola di Monte Gelato itself.

The river Treia runs in a palaeovalley cut into the *tufo leucitico del Fosso Treia*, which can be seen in the cliff face below the waterfall (Alvarez 1972: 165). Overlying this is the *tufo stratificati varicolori di Sacrofano*, a fairly soft tufo into which the palaeovalley is also cut, and which forms the sides of the valley in various places. Subsequently, a lava flowed down the palaeovalley. This is the hard *piperno di Mazzano*, a grey to bluish grey highly welded and resistant tufo of pyroclastic origin, with inclusions of collapsed *scoriae* (Mattias and Ventriglia 1968; 1970: 360-1; Gancarz 1970: 13-15). It derived from the Monti Sabatini (Alvarez 1972; 1973), and forms the hard shelf on which the main site was positioned. Some deep features, such as the limekiln (below, Fig. 64), were cut into the *piperno*. However, most rested upon, or were dug into, a soft, yellow-brown tufaceous deposit, that had formed over the bedrock. In places this appeared to cover artificially cut surfaces in the bedrock, implying a period of formation not long before the first occupation of the main site in Augustan times. It may well be the result of downslope erosion, brought about by agricultural activity over the previous millennium. Some was certainly water-lain, probably during the heavy rainstorms that are a feature of the region.

One other volcanic deposit is represented in the study area, namely a ridge of *tufo rosso a scorie neri*, which underlies the mausoleum or temple-tomb. This is a low density, soft reddish-brown tufo with buff and black *scoriae*, 0.15-0.2 m in diameter (Mattias and Ventriglia 1970: 348-9). It is easily excavated, and housed at least one cave habitation in medieval times (Fig. 4).

THE SITE

When first explored in the 1960s, the Mola di Monte Gelato was still relatively remote. Approached only by a *strada bianca*, it was very much a country preserve, in sharp contrast with today. However, the vegetation was much less dense (Fig. 1), and signs of antiquity were abundant. These were recorded initially by John Ward-Perkins, and supplemented by later visits. Hitherto unpublished, the field observations are cited here in a manuscript first drafted in 1972, since they shed interesting light on what was achieved by the South Etruria survey team, especially when it can be matched against the excavated record.

D7 (835737-8) An important multi-period complex at the Mola di Monte Gelato.

Pre-Roman:
A. A scatter of archaic tile and pottery on the low hill overlooking the Mola on the north side.
   Brown coarse-ware, with fingerprinted cordons, red burnished sherd, internal-slip ware.
B. A cuniculus-shaped tunnel, cut into the base of the cliff on the south side of the Mola, may also be pre-Roman in date. The tunnel extends for about 12.0 m, and is apparently unfinished. There are no traces of vertical shafts.

Roman:
C. The remains of a substantial Roman villa (*c.* 100 × 150 m), on the north side of the Mola. It is built on a low natural platform, which slopes down to within 30 m of the river. The remains of a *tufelli*-faced wall survive in the face of a low cliff at the north end of the platform. There are also traces of *opus quadratum* walling still *in situ*. The villa is situated near the point where paved Roman road crosses the river Treia. This road enters the valley of the Mola from the south and, after crossing the river, heads northwest, on the line taken by the modern road to the Via Cassia – Mazzano road. A section of *selce*-paved road, 6.0 m wide, is visible in the section of the modern road cutting. Other remains include tufo blocks and much tile, tufo *opus reticulatum*, various marbles (white Italian, *Africano*, *cipollino*, *corallina breccia*), white and basalt tesserae, red-painted wall-plaster, window-glass and fine glass. There is also a tufo moulding [cf. Fig. 161, below], and a quarry in the cliffs [cf. Fig. 22, below]. These quarries appear to have been producing

long tufo blocks, suitable for *opus quadratum*; but their date is uncertain. Ward-Perkins additionally recorded a tufo channel, probably from a water duct; and a tufo altar with traces of an inscription. He also mentioned post-Roman architectural remains, including a marble spiral colonnette and a marble slab with interlace.

Black glaze (three – all very abraded, and perhaps derived from site A); *terra sigillata* (eleven), African red slip ware (fifteen), second century AD, late second century AD, mid-late third century AD, mid-fourth century AD or later (as dated by John Hayes in 1968).

Colour coat, Hayes Form 197 (4), sherds with cogged decoration, flanged bowls, lamp fragment.

Medieval:

D. [Detailed records were also made of Castellaccio, the mill and the adjacent tower, which it is unnecessary to repeat here, as they are described in Chapter Three.]

The excavated evidence apart, there is little to add to the above account. Not noted were the caves in the northern part of the valley, nor the cisterns and aqueduct channel on the crest of the hill above; the latter may well not have been visible. The creation of the park in 1982 has resulted in some changes, especially the provision of car parks and the planting of trees (and of course a deluge of visitors). The unfortunate bulldozing of the area to the west of the main site has also greatly changed the appearance of the landscape.

THE PAVED ROMAN ROAD

The road referred to above was surveyed in 1967-68, and recorded in some detail. It proved to be one of the better-preserved Roman roads of the Ager Faliscus, a country route that ran more or less parallel with the Via Amerina (Fig. 5). Briefly noticed by Tomassetti (1882; 1913) and by Martinori (1930: 208), it still retained many stretches of paving and there were few points where its course could not be established with certainty. The function of the road is also clear; if the large number of villas and farms along its route provides any guide, then it must have come into use primarily as a service road for these sites. Indeed, the fact that it is the southern section that is paved would tend to suggest that the produce of these estates was intended principally for the markets of Rome.

The road originated as an unpaved track, which left the Via Amerina at Casale l'Umiltà (Fig. 5), a short distance to the south of Nepi. It then headed southeastwards, across the two plateaux divided by the Fosso di Ronci, and down into the valley of the Fosso Stramazzo. The paved road appears to have started within a large settlement (E21), which straddles the Fosso Stramazzo. The size of this site suggests that it may have been a *vicus*. The first section of intact paving, destroyed about 1970, lay in the side of a modern cutting for the Via Cassia – Mazzano road, some 200 m west of site E21. It was 1.9 m wide, with polygonal blocks set in make-up.

Beneath was the bedrock, in which deep ruts could be seen, belonging to an unpaved predecessor. This was precisely the sequence identified by excavation in 1970-71 of another stretch of paved road at Vallelunga, 3.5 km to the south (Potter 1979: 107; see below); here there were three pairs of ruts under the paved surface. It may be, therefore, that the rock-cut road excavated at the Mola di Monte Gelato relates to this early phase of road.

After the Fosso Stramazzo, the paved road (and doubtless its precursor) climbed the ridge to the south of the Mazzano road in a still prominent cutting, some 10.0 m wide. Its immediate destination was the crossing of the river Treia at the Mola di Monte Gelato where, according to Tomassetti (1882: 147), there was a bridge. The road then headed out of the valley, swinging first southwestwards to avoid the hill on which the medieval castle of Castellaccio stands, before turning back to take a more or less straight line south. Through the woods to the south of the Mola a good deal of paving still survived, but once out of the *macchia*, the surface had been destroyed and only the occasional block was to be found. Its general direction is nevertheless quite clear, as it headed down to a minor stream that drains into the Treia, the Fosso Sarnacchiola.

At this point, in the Valle del Pero, there was in effect a T-junction (Figs 5 and 6): while the main road turned west and then south, a branch road headed off towards the east. We shall describe this branch road first. Two features made its line immediately obvious. Initially, there was a long stretch of paving, resting upon an *agger*, immediately below site D5. Then, some 600 m east of the T-junction, the road entered a long cutting through a north-south ridge in the Valle del Pero. This cutting itself formed another junction, upon which no fewer than four ancient roads converged. The paved road immediately headed south, climbing out of the cutting and entering a substantial villa site, D10. The arrangement of levels was such as to suggest two constructional phases, with the cutting as the primary feature and the building of the paved road as a secondary stage. The paving itself was very clear at D10, showing that the road then struck southeastwards down the ridge. At 843716, close to sites M18 and M19, there was another long stretch of paving, 2.2 m wide, and the road apparently terminated at a substantial villa site (M21), covered (in 1968) by a derelict farm. We should not, however, exclude the possibility that the paved road once continued, for the terrain beyond M21 was heavily wooded and difficult to explore. There was certainly a seemingly old track which headed down to Campagnano, and a Roman origin is by no means improbable.

The branch road evidently acted as the focus for a radial network of communications, serving the dispersed sites of this area. The main road, on the other hand, was clearly designed to link up with the

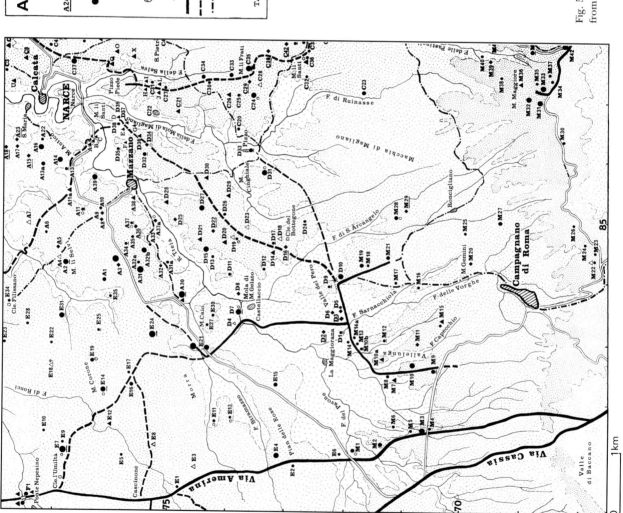

Fig. 5. The southwestern area of the Ager Faliscus, with data from field survey between 1966 and 1971. Part of a larger map, drawn in 1972. *(TWP)*

nearest trunk road, the Via Amerina. Its course was established at several points. It could first be seen just west of the Fosso Sarnacchiola, with paving set into a prominent shelf; then at Vallelunga (Fig. 7), where there was also a clearly marked ford across the stream, and subsequently at the Fosso Capecchio: here a cuniculus 87.5 m long facilitated the crossing of the stream. It then turned south down a ridge, its course marked by the occasional scatter of *selce* blocks (for example, at M10). These extended as far as the modern Via Cassia to Campagnano road. This area to the south was not surveyed in the 1960s, and when examined in 1989 (King 1993) proved to have been severely damaged by modern agriculture. However, it seems very probable that it swung southwestwards to join the Via Amerina, and thus the main trunk-road system down to Rome.

As noted above, the road was investigated by excavation in 1970 and 1971 when a stretch was uncovered during building work at the car racing track at Vallelunga (site M106). In 1970, only the visible remains were examined, but the following year the paving stones were lifted, under the supervision of Sig. A. Bracci, assisted by Miranda Buchanan and Graeme Barker, as I was unable to be present. This exposed completely the earlier wheel ruts visible in Figure 7. There were three pairs of ruts, and another at the edge of the excavated area (Potter 1979: fig. 31). Some 50 m away was a building, 13.0 m wide, recessed into the bedrock. Foundation trenches were recorded at both ends, as well as a central partition, resting on a low sill. No masonry survived *in situ* (although there were tufo blocks in the vicinity) and it may be that this was largely a timber structure. More probably, however, the blocks had been robbed out. In the fill over the floor were sherds of the second-first centuries BC, including black glaze, closely paralleled by the assemblage from near Sutri, published by Duncan (1965). Duncan's forms 7, 9, 20 and 38B, and a loom weight, Duncan form A131, were all represented in the finds from Vallelunga.

There can be no doubt that at least some of the ruts formed while the adjacent building was in occupation. The paved road, on the other hand, is certainly later, and may not have been laid much before the end of the first century AD; it is a matter considered in more detail in discussing the same road at Monte Gelato in the next chapter. It varied in width between 2.25 and 2.3 m, and on each side was a low kerb, made of carefully faced but otherwise irregular pieces of basalt, 0.1 m high. There were also two stones in the kerb with rounded profiles, which projected 0.25 m above the paving; placed precisely 20 Roman feet apart, they may

Fig. 6. Cuttings marking the T-junction of the Roman paved road in the Valle del Pero, to the south of Monte Gelato: see Figure 5. Looking southeast. *(AMS)*

Fig. 7. The Roman paved road at Vallelunga (Fig. 5, site M10), under excavation in 1970.
Note the earlier ruts. *(TWP)*

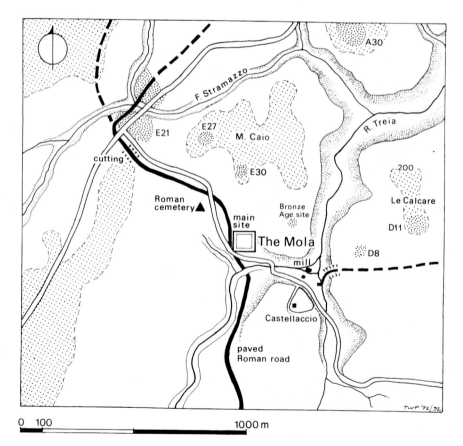

Fig. 8. The Mola di Monte Gelato in its local setting, showing ancient sites, roads and tracks
(dotted) identified mainly between 1966 and 1971. *(TWP)*

have been distance markers. Similar stones appear on some main highways, with a nearby example on the Via Amerina just to the north of the Settevene – Campagnano road (Frederiksen and Ward-Perkins 1957: 76 and pl. xviia).

The paving was neatly constructed with large polygonal blocks of *selce*, some over a metre in length. They were set into tufaceous make-up, so that the surface was 0.4 m above the bedrock. Parallel with the southeast side of the road was a retaining wall of long tufo blocks, some over 1.0 m in length, and 0.6 m high and 0.45 m wide: contemporaneity with the construction of the road is demonstrated by chips of *selce* in the foundation deposits. The blocks may well have derived from the adjacent Republican building.

The quality of the building work at Vallelunga requires emphasis, since it is in some contrast with that at Monte Gelato (below, Figs 17 and 18). There were no kerbstones at Monte Gelato, and the arrangement of the paving-stones was generally much more haphazard. However, it will be shown that some or all of the surface was relaid in late Roman and/or in early medieval times, albeit to an inferior standard. This was evidently not the case at Vallelunga, although this does not necessarily mean that it was abandoned. A recent study of the Via Flaminia at Malborghetto has clearly demonstrated its continued use in early medieval times (Bosman 1993), and durably made country roads like that at Vallelunga would have served for many centuries with minimal maintenance. The stretch at Monte Gelato, on the other hand, will have seen particularly heavy wear, running through a settlement, and its downhill course will have exacerbated this.

There is, however, an additional possibility, namely that the Vallelunga stretch did go out of use, and that the branch road replaced it as the main route to the south, heading down through the area where Campagnano was to grow up (Figs 3 and 5). There is some support for this in that three of five sites along its route yielded African red slip ware of the fifth and sixth centuries, whereas only one of seven sites along the Vallelunga section produced pottery of comparable date. The matter might have been clinched by the recovery of medieval pottery from the sites along the branch road, but none was identified, and the question can only be left open.

FIELD SURVEY IN THE VICINITY OF THE MOLA DI MONTE GELATO (FIGS 5 AND 8)

The following notes, prepared in 1972, describe the sites examined between 1966 and 1971 in the area shown on Figure 8. Some had also been looked at in earlier British School at Rome exploration, led by John Ward-Perkins in the late 1950s. In addition, a bronze age site, with a diameter of *c.* 30 m, was observed to the north of the Mola in

1990, and a recently looted Roman cemetery, with rock-cut tombs, was seen in the same year. The latter lies to the northwest of the main site, but was too overgrown to permit a proper record. It should also be noted that Peña (1987) has made a detailed study of the Roman pottery-producing centre at site A31 (Fig. 5), to the west of Mazzano.

A30 (838-9747)
An important site on the Ponte Maglianella ridge. At the west end there is a cemetery, which has been the focus of clandestine excavations (area A). Towards the east end is a building nucleus (area B), measuring about 100×70 m. There is a large dump of building rubble, including tufo blocks, *selce* lava fragments, a corner stone with a moulding in tufo, other architectural fragments and much tile and dolia. Other finds include white Italian marble, *opus spicatum* bricks, fragments of fine glass, and an inscribed tile base. There are also fragments of archaic tile.
Area A: painted Italo-Corinthian sherd (one), pre-Roman coarse-ware.
Area B: BG (9 – 4 misfired to a reddish colour); these include typical third-century BC pieces (including a stamp), as well as sherds more likely to be second or first century; also TS (two); ARS (five), two late second century AD; sherd with cogged decoration; Hayes 197; rouletted beaker; colour coat; lamp fragment; flanged forms; base in a brown burnished fabric, with a stamped reticulate motif.

D8 (838737)
A scatter of archaic tile and pottery on a low hillock.
Pre-Roman coarse-ware, fragment of a spindle-whorl.

D11 (841739)
A scatter of material, including archaic and later tile, dolia and pottery, ploughed out from a knoll on Le Calcare (the name meaning limekilns).
TS (three); ARS, second half second century AD (one).

E21 (828-9744-5)
A large and important site, which extends over both sides of the Fosso Stramazzo. To the south of the stream, there is an underground cistern and a scatter of tile and pottery on the hilltop. The main part of the site lies, however, on more level ground on the north side of the stream, beside the point where a minor tributary enters from the north. The importance of the site is underlined by the fact that the paved Roman road begins within the settlement. Its exact status – a village or a very large villa – is, however, unclear. There is a funerary inscription lettered in a style characteristic of the second or third centuries AD (Reynolds 1966: 65), and other remains include tufo blocks, much tile, Italian marble, *opus spicatum* brick, painted wall-plaster, basalt tesserae, window-glass and fine glass, and a fragment of bronze.
BG of the second or first centuries BC; TS (fourteen); ARS: most sherds are second or third centuries AD in date, but some are fourth and fifth centuries AD.
Colour coat, fine beakers, Hayes 197, sherds with cogged decoration, flanged forms.

E27 (833743)
A scatter of tile and pottery on the west slopes of Monte Caio.
ARS, mid third-mid fourth centuries AD (two), Hayes 197 (two).

E30 (834742)
A thin scatter of tile and pottery on the southern slopes
of Monte Caio.
TS (one).
Tomassetti (1877: 263) recorded two sepulchral inscrip-
tions from Monte Caio (*CIL* XI 3207, 3228).

These notes serve mainly to illustrate the rich
archaeological inheritance of this part of the Ager
Faliscus, at any rate as it survived in the 1960s. The
Mola di Monte Gelato was but one of many sites in
the region, and not a place of special consequence.
There were numerous other Roman villas around,
some apparently large and luxurious, and while
few, if any, manifest signs of early medieval occupation, this may be no more than a reflection of the
difficulties at the time of the survey in recognizing
the pottery (which was not identified in the surface
collections from the Mola di Monte Gelato).

Chapter Three

THE EXCAVATIONS

INTRODUCTION

As outlined in Chapter One, the excavations were spread over five seasons, which took place every September between 1986 and 1990 (Figs 9 and 10). Once it was established that there was a heavy overburden of plough-soil, considerable use was made of a mechanical excavator. This enabled the strippage of a comparatively large area, about 1,500 square metres in all. The site was backfilled yearly, to discourage vandalism and illicit *sondages*. Remarkably, there was very little of either, despite the accessibility of the site and a great deal of public interest.

For recording purposes, the site was divided into a number of areas, each of which was given a letter (Fig. 11). The contexts, 1,378 of which were allocated, were then listed by these areas, as A1, B1 etc. A full list is retained in the archive, but the original site references are used throughout the volume; the only exception is the burials, where it proved more convenient to renumber them in sequence (although here too the original references are cited, and are carried onto some of the drawings). The catalogue numbers cited in this section refer to the different categories of material (for example, small finds, ironwork, sculpture) described and discussed in Chapter Four.

The importance of the results was such that we gave high priority to publishing interim reports, nine of which were produced, mainly for Italian journals and conference proceedings. These were principally about the site, but did include articles about the freed-people tomb inscription (Gilliver 1990), and the inscribed Greek 'stork-vase' (Murray *et al.* 1991). Whilst a quite proper procedure, this does have the disadvantage of presenting interpretations which ultimately may turn out to be dubious or wrong when the evidence is assessed in its entirety. Thus initial attempts to postulate a degree of continuity between late Roman and early medieval times must now be treated with scepticism and, in all probability, rejected outright. Likewise, a structure that from the outset we regarded as a latrine (and is so labelled on many published plans) is, in reality, quite certainly a fish-pond, built to ornament an elegant Augustan complex. Similarly, DeLaine's work on the 'mausoleum' suggests that it is better termed a temple-tomb, while the features that we long considered to be oil-vats are in fact most probably water cisterns.

These matters are debated in the sections that follow; but they require emphasis here since some of the preliminary conclusions have already passed into the wider literature (for example, Christie 1991a: 356), as more or less established fact. Such certainty is rarely possible, and we have tried to examine a range of interpretations, before favouring one or the other. Erroneous readings of the data doubtless remain; but we hope that there is a sufficiency of detail in the ensuing analysis for these, in due course, to emerge.

THE EARLY IMPERIAL ROMAN COMPLEX (PHASES 1 AND 2) (FIGS 12 AND 13)

The evidence to be set out below will show how in Augustan times an elegant ornamental courtyard complex was laid out, facing a road. This was apparently not a working farm, although there could have been such a place nearby. It might have been a sacred site, although no temple was found; but it is more probable that the investigated early Imperial remains were above all decorative in purpose, and resembled in many respects Varro's villa near Casinum (*De Re Rustica* iii. 5.8).

Subsequently, in phase 2, a paved road, bathhouse, cisterns and a mausoleum (or temple-tomb) were added to the complex, all probably in the first half of the second century. Pottery was manufactured in the vicinity, and at least two of the potters were Greek. There was also wine production, the wine being transported in locally made amphorae. The majority of the buildings then seems to have been pulled down in the late second or early third century when, in all likelihood, the place was abandoned until around the mid-fourth century, in phase 3.

THE ROADS

Two roads were uncovered during the excavations. One was part of the well-known paved country route down to the Via Amerina or Via Cassia, described above in Chapter Two; the other was of earlier construction and hitherto unknown. It is referred to throughout the text as the 'rock-cut road', since this was the principal feature of its construction.

The rock-cut road (Figs 9, 14-16)

This was initially identified in the side of a modern drainage ditch, cut in 1989 at the eastern edge of the flood plain of the river Treia and at the foot of the rock scarp along the western side of the modern road. The scarp is some 2.5 m in height at this point, and steeply inclined, although it slopes away to nothing a short distance to the south. There must, therefore, have been a reason for taking this particu-

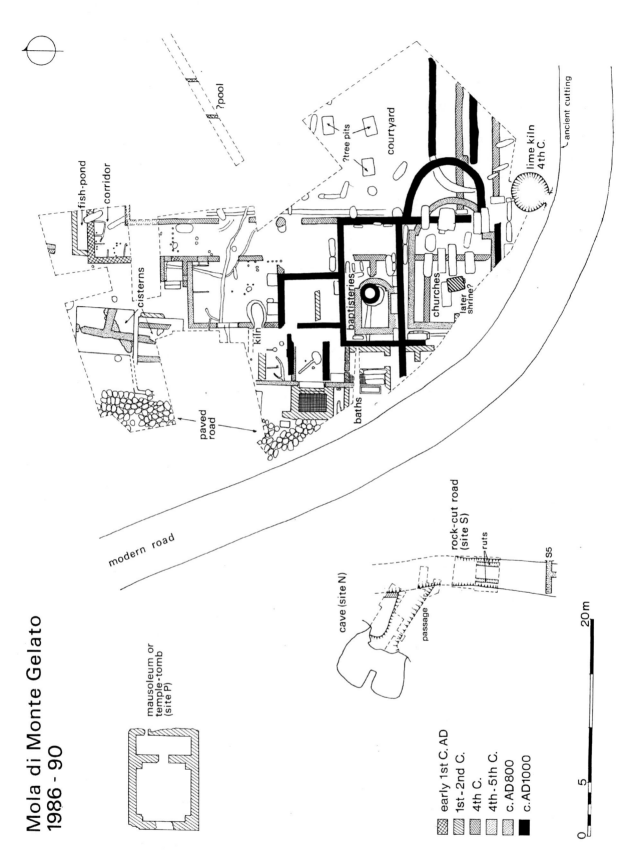

Fig. 9. General plan of the main site. *(TWP)*

Mola di Monte Gelato
1986 - 90

mausoleum or
temple-tomb
(site P)

early 1st C. AD
1st - 2nd C.
4th C.
4th - 5th C.
c. AD 800
c. AD 1000

cave (site N)

rock-cut road
(site S)

ruts

passage

S5

0   5   20m

?pool

fish-pond

corridor

cisterns

kiln

paved
road

baths

baptisteries

churches

later
shrine?

courtyard

?tree pits

lime kiln
4th C.

ancient cutting

modern road

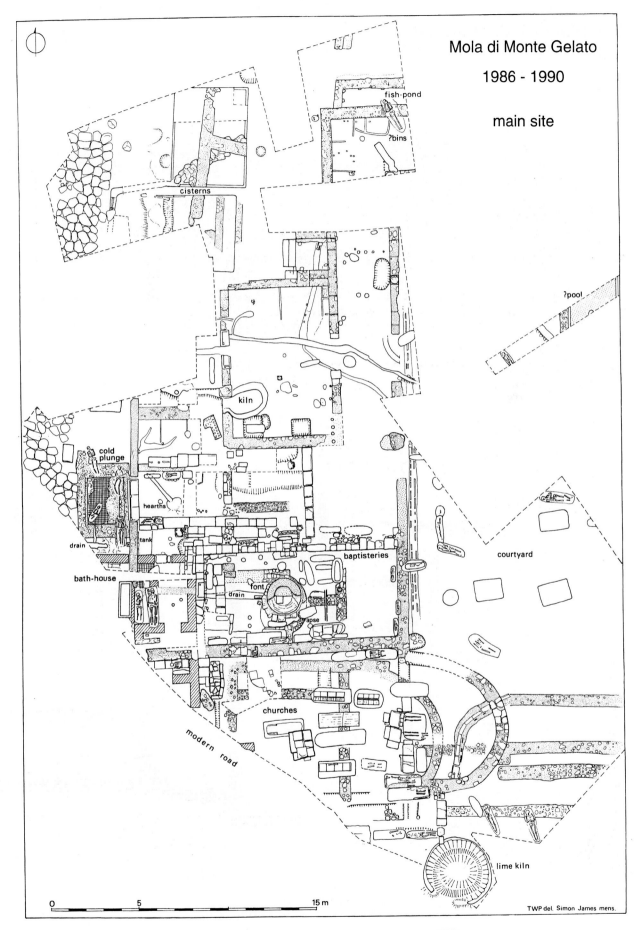

Mola di Monte Gelato
1986 - 1990
main site

fish-pond

?bins

cisterns

?pool

kiln

cold plunge

hearths

drain

tank

bath-house

baptisteries

font

drain

apse

courtyard

churches

modern road

lime kiln

0   5   15 m

TWP del. Simon James mens.

Fig. 10. Detailed plan of the main site, all phases. *(TWP)*

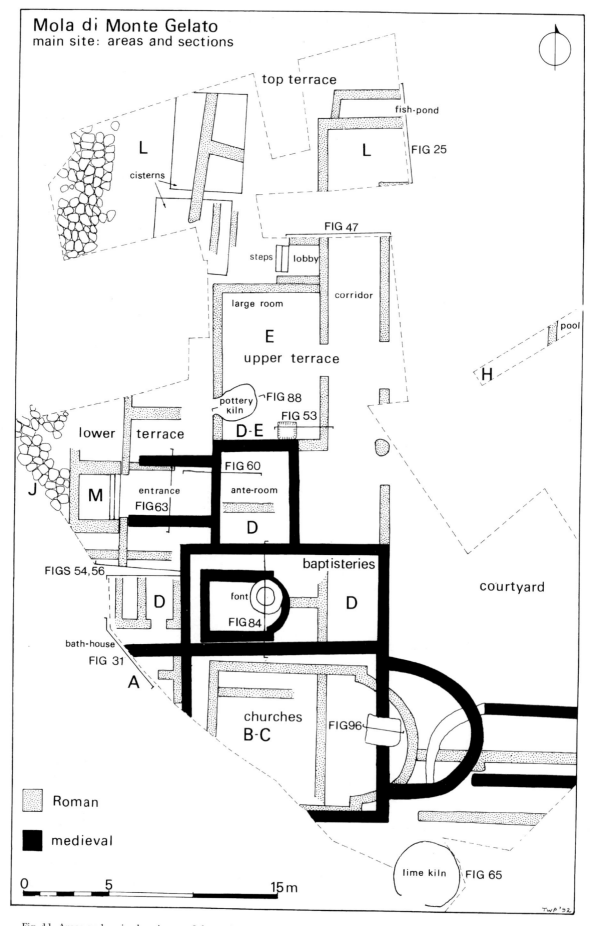

Fig. 11. Areas and main descriptors of the main site. For sites N, P and S see Figure 9; for site K see Figure 38. *(TWP)*

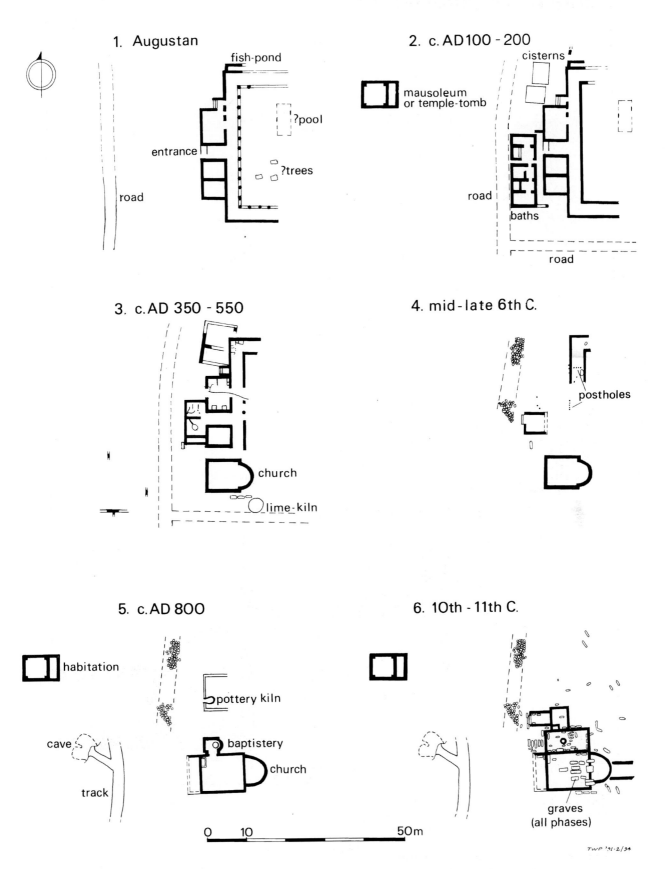

Fig. 12. Principal phases on the main site, excluding site K. *(TWP)*

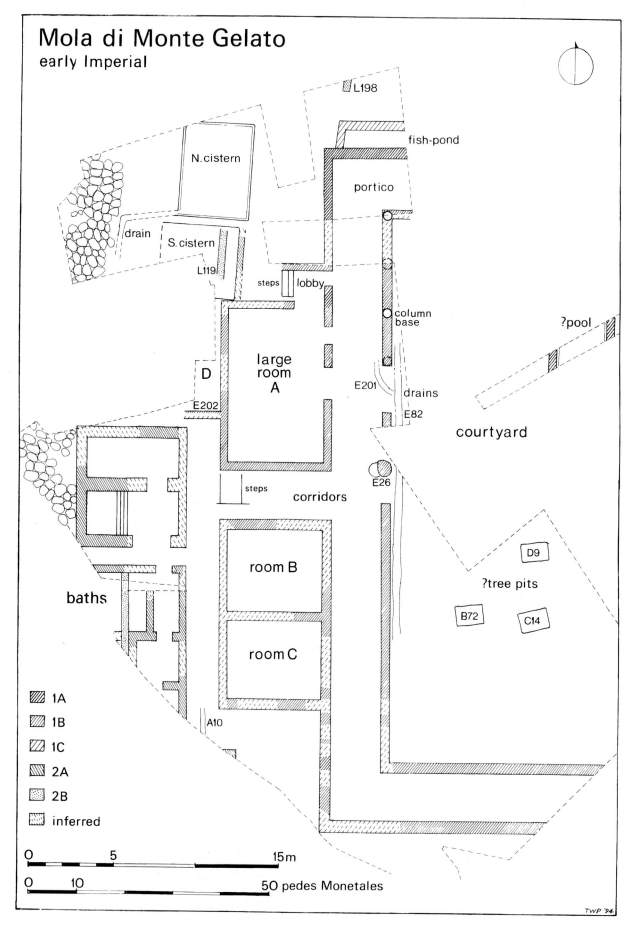

Mola di Monte Gelato
early Imperial

L198

fish-pond

N.cistern

portico

drain

S.cistern

L119

steps   lobby

column
base

?pool

large
room
A

D

E201

E202

drains

E82

courtyard

steps

corridors

E26

baths

room B

?tree pits

D9

B72

C14

room C

A10

1A
1B
1C
2A
2B
inferred

0   5   15m

0   10   50 pedes Monetales

TWP '94.

Fig. 13. Main site: phases 1 and 2. *(TWP)*

lar route, rather than the easier terrain later followed by the paved road. This must surely reside in the fact that an alignment parallel with that of the façade of the courtyard complex was considered of prime importance, despite the inconvenience of cutting through the scarp.

A trench was cut across the road where it intersected with the face of the scarp. A length of 2.3 m was exposed completely, and a further 2.3 m down to the basal silts (Fig. 15). The total depth of the incision into the bedrock was 3.5 m, and its width at the top was 2.65 m. The sides, however, tapered gradually, so that at the bottom of the cutting the width was reduced to 1.95 m. Two very pronounced wheel-ruts were scored into the bedrock. Between 0.3 and 0.35 m in depth, and some 1.4 m apart (measured from centre to centre), there were clear wheel-scuffing marks along the edges: they had evidently formed through the heavy passage of traffic, rather than being cut features, and had in fact been filled in with *selce* cobbles, presumably in an attempt to slow further down-cutting (Fig. 16).

As noted in Chapter Two, wheel-ruts were a conspicuous feature of the precursor to the paved road at Vallelunga (the onward continuation of the paved road at Monte Gelato). There were three pairs, with widths of 1.38, 1.4 and 1.5 m (Potter 1979: 107-8, where, however, the drawn scale is incorrect). These are a little on the wide side for a vehicle, but allowance must be made for the tendency of tufo, normally a soft rock, to wear very rapidly. By way of comparison, Ward-Perkins (1961: 19) recorded an average figure of 1.24 m at the northeast gate of Veii, and Chevallier (1976: 89) suggested 1.3 m as a standard axle-width in antiquity, and 1.45 m in the Middle Ages. The measurements at Monte Gelato and Vallelunga are therefore not significantly outside the range.

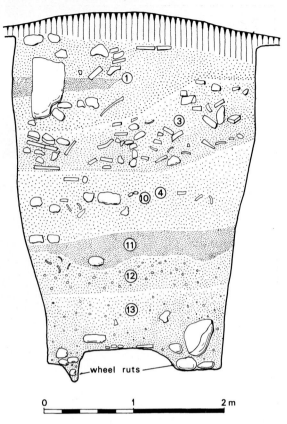

Rock-cut road, site S

Fig. 14. Deposits in the rock-cut road; for description of the layers, see text. *(TWP)*

Fig. 15. North section of the rock-cut road, excavated in steps. *(KW)*

Fig. 16. The ruts at the base of the rock-cut road, with the cobble fill partly removed. *(KW)*

The line of the road was established in all for a distance of 16.0 m, sufficient to confirm its north-south orientation. To the south it presumably headed across the flood plain to a bridge across the river Treia, while to the north it skirted the eastern side of the low ridge (below, Fig. 89) where later a mausoleum or temple-tomb was to be built. It then climbed the hill in the cutting which today carries the modern road.

Although the style of the road, with its great depth, is manifestly Etrusco-Faliscan, it does not seem to have been the result of successive lowerings of the surface, as the soft rock became too rutted for use: the sides were smoothly cut, with no traces of the earlier working levels customary with such roads (Frederiksen and Ward-Perkins 1957: 186). Given that its orientation is precisely that of the adjacent Augustan complex, along the cardinal points, it may well be that both were part of a unitary design, with the rock-cut road passage as a feature of that layout. Archaic in style, it harks back to older traditions, the signs of which are still so conspicuous in the surrounding countryside, not least around the former Faliscan centre at Narce (Potter 1976: pl. IIb).

It is not easy to say when the road went out of use. The bottom metre was filled with silts and sands of waterlaid appearance (Fig. 14, units 12 and 13), but contained no datable material. Above was a series of dumps with much second- and early third-century pottery, building materials, slag and a number of small finds. These included bone needles and pins (cat. 112, 115, 119, 123), some fine glass, and part of a jet bracelet (cat. 147). The deposit in many respects resembles others, described below, filling the feature interpreted as a fish-pond, and also a cistern. However, some well-stratified sherds indicate that the dumps cannot have been made before the fifth century AD (cf. below), so that this section of the road cutting at least must have been a prominent feature for much of the Roman period. Doubtless it served as a convenient short cut from the main site down to the valley bottom.

The paved road (Figs 9, 17-18)

Two areas of this road, the overall course of which was described in the previous chapter, were uncovered. It took a much easier line that diverged from the north-south orientation of the rock-cut road, and its onward route up the hillside could be seen as a gently curving hollow way, littered with *selce* paving-stones (Fig. 4). It is not clear at which point it descended onto the flood plain of the river Treia, but a scatter of paving-stones on the far side of the river may indicate the position of the crossing. There is, however, no trace of the bridge referred to by Tomassetti (1882: 147).

The surviving paving was rather irregular and haphazard, and not at all like the neat work revealed further south at Vallelunga (Fig. 7). There were no kerbstones, and only in the northern part of Trench L was there the semblance of a properly laid edge (Fig. 18). There was, however, an *a cappuccina* roadside drain along part of this stretch (Fig. 17 and below, Fig. 23,b), fed from a nearby cistern. The drain was not traced further south, and almost certainly relates to the bath-house, constructed *c.* AD 100.

With a width of *c.* 3.2 m, the road was both wider and different in character from the sections examined at the Fossa Stramazzo and Vallelunga (cf. Chapter Two). This is explained by the fact that the blocks were partly or wholly

Fig. 17. The drain on the east side of the paved road: see Figure 23b. *(KW)*

Fig. 18. The road in the northern part of site L, sealed beneath colluvium. *(KW)*

re-laid, possibly both in late Roman and medieval times. This was very evident in the section adjoining the bath-house, where the blocks overlapped the footing of the demolished *piscina*, and sealed a third-century coin (cat. 6). There was also pottery of the late eighth and early ninth centuries in some deposits below the paving, confirming the re-laying of at least part of the road. This renders extremely difficult the dating of the original construction, for which there is little real evidence. One deposit beneath the paving (M104) did yield sherds broadly assignable to *c.* AD 100, and the alignment of the northern stretch with the cisterns, and the southern part with the bath-house, may be an indication of a general contemporaneity. Moreover, this would not be inconsistent with the finds from beneath the road at Vallelunga, and recalls the sequence of road surfaces at Podere Sant'Angelo, on the country route between the Via Flaminia and the Monti Sabatini (Kahane, Murray Threipland and Ward-Perkins 1968: 127): here the paving was laid at some point after the mid-first century AD, and may have used *selce* from the nearby quarry at Monte Maggiore, the focus of a considerable number of well-appointed villas, occupied throughout Imperial times (Potter 1979: 135-6).

The building of this paved stretch of road at Monte Gelato may have been part of a general attempt to upgrade a much frequented route from the rich farmland of the central Ager Faliscus down to the trunk roads that led to Rome. It was lined with substantial sites, the owners of which presumably paid for the work – for example, T. Humanius Stabilio, who in the first century AD built a road bridge at his own expense in the adjoining Ager Veientanus (Guzzo 1970). Certainly the new section of road at Monte Gelato must have been altogether more practicable than its rock-cut predecessor, and forms one of a number of signs of change in the nature of the site around the beginning of the second century AD.

THE COURTYARD (FIG. 13)

The gently sloping hillside to the east of the roads was terraced into three levels (Fig. 19). The lowest, and smallest, lay immediately beside the paved road, and was cut to a depth of some 2.0 m, to accommodate a small bath-house, probably built around the beginning of the second century AD. Above lay an extensive main, or upper, terrace, while to the north was a third, or top, terrace. There may have been still higher terraces beyond the excavated area, and there

were certainly structures on the crest of the hill above the valley (Fig. 4). These include a rock-cut channel, probably part of an aqueduct (Fig. 20), and also cisterns (Fig. 4), and it is easy to imagine that the entire northern hillslopes were eventually built up. It is all the more unfortunate that plough damage in this area has been so severe.

The main upper terrace was occupied by a large courtyard, bounded by a portico. The whole of the west side of the courtyard was uncovered, as well as parts of the north and south ranges. The eastern side was not located, but there is adequate space for a square arrangement, as suggested below for phases 3 and 4 (Fig. 38). Alternatively, if the pool in the courtyard lay centrally, a rectangular layout is implied.

It is quite evident that the courtyard was set out in *pedes Monetales* (hereafter *p.M.*). Thus the portico corridor measured 2.96 m internally, or 10 *p.M.*, while the length of the north-south portico is very close to 110 *p.M.* (32.85 m = 110.9 *p.M.*). Likewise, the two surviving column bases are 20 *p.M.* from centre to centre, suggesting that columns were placed at intervals of 10 *p.M.* Other instances of Roman mensuration will be cited below. There is, of course, nothing surprising in this, for careful surveying was a commonplace in early Imperial times (see, for example, Duncan-Jones 1980); but it is an illustration of the attention that was lavished upon the layout of the complex.

The interior of the courtyard was only explored in part, and most extensively in the southwestern corner. Ploughing had removed any trace there may once have been of a surface, and features were notably sparse. However, there were three closely grouped and evenly spaced rectangular pits (B72, C14, D9) (Fig. 13), each measuring *c.* 1.7 × 1.2 m (that is, close to 6×4 *p.M.*). As they survived, all were fairly shallow, with depths ranging from 0.1 to 0.25 m; but ploughing had bitten deeply into the subsoil, so that they must originally have been much deeper. Their fills were of soft tufaceous earth, containing a few small fragments of pottery: those sherds from pit C14 were tentatively assigned a date in the late Republican-early Imperial period, indicating that the pits (which are surely of the same period) should be contemporary with the courtyard.

The grouping of the pits suggests that there was probably another in the unexcavated northwest corner, making a cluster of four in all. Their function is more problematic, for they were clearly not intended for refuse. However, their context does provide an important clue. As will be seen, the courtyard was embellished with a pool, a marble *labrum* and

Schematic section, M, E and L

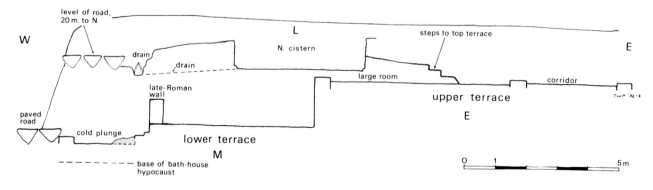

Fig. 19. Section showing the relative levels in different parts of the site. *(TWP)*

Fig. 20. The rock-cut aqueduct channel on the ridge to the north of the main site, looking south. *(KW)*

statuary, indicating a place of some elegance. It would therefore be entirely consistent with this picture were the pits to have contained trees or shrubs, as part of an ornamental garden. This would certainly have befitted the beautiful setting, adjacent to the river Treia with its attractive sequence of waterfalls, and is in harmony with the apparent absence of functional, agricultural buildings on the site at this time.

The laying out of a garden is hardly surprising, in the light of the evidence of the Vesuvian region (Jashemski 1979; MacDougall and Jashemski 1981). At the San Marco villa at Stabia, to cite but one instance, trees flanked a pool in a courtyard surrounded by a portico (De Vos and De Vos 1982: 323; Mielsch 1987: 168), and recent botanical studies have amply illustrated the wide range of species that might be grown in such gardens (Mastroroberto 1990). Groves of trees were also planted in the Latian temple complexes, in Hellenistic tradition (Caroll-Spillecke 1992; Coarelli 1993). At Gabii the pits were 1.5-1.6 m across in the first phase, and 1.2-1.3 m across in a second replanting, figures comparable with the Monte Gelato examples. While the three pits hardly constitute a grove, clumps of trees in the courtyard seem an entirely reasonable interpretation.

The pool referred to above was identified in a narrow exploratory trench (H) in the northern part of the courtyard (Figs 11 and 13). Modern ploughing and vine-trenching (to a depth of 1.4 m) has had a ruinous effect upon the archaeological deposits, but the very bottom of the feature did survive (Fig. 21). This comprised a grey *cocciopesto* floor with much wear in the centre; piercing it was a circular hole 0.28 m in diameter which, if not a later feature, may

have been for drainage. It was flanked by walls, 0.5 m in width, made of rubble and mortar, lined with pale yellow tufo blocks on the inside. A quarter-round moulding sealed the junction between the walls and the floor on both sides.

The internal width of the pool was 2.9 m (9.79 *p.M.*), and it was probably intended to have been 10 *p.M.* across. Although its north-south dimensions were not established, it was a substantial feature. That it was decorative, rather than functional, in purpose is, however, a matter of inference, based upon its position within the courtyard, and the items of sculpture referred to above. Likewise, there was no direct dating evidence for the construction of the pool, although there was late Roman pottery in the silty and loamy fills above it, which mark its disuse. It does not, however, lie in an obviously measured position in *p.M.* within the courtyard, and may not therefore have been part of the initial design. On the other hand, there is no real reason to doubt that it belongs within the first main phase of the site's history.

THE PORTICO (PHASE 1A)

Little that was original remained of the phase 1 portico. This is due to the fact that it was later converted into an enclosed corridor, and only two column bases survived. One lay in the northwest corner, where traces of curvature in the footing left little doubt that there had been an emplacement for a column resting on a very low stylobate (Fig. 13). The other was 20 *p.M.* (centre to centre) to the south, and was much clearer. A circular base, 0.4 m in diameter, was

Fig. 21. Site H: the base of an *opus signinum* pool in the courtyard. *(KW)*

edged with small orange *tufelli*, set in grey-white mortar; this was cemented onto a block of grey tufo, 0.5 m square. The base stood only 60 mm above the adjacent *cocciopesto* floor of the portico, an additional indication of the low height of the stylobate. There may also have been another column base still further to the south, where there were two successive, roughly circular, pads of grey mortar (Fig. 13; D26). However, these do not fit the mensuration in Roman feet, and are more likely to belong to a later door emplacement.

The original back wall of the portico survived only in the northwest corner (cf. below, Fig. 42). Standing to a height of between 0.6 and 0.75 m, it owed its preservation to the fact that it had been recessed into the tufo that underlies the top terrace. The wall was made of *opus reticulatum*, with *tufelli* that averaged 0.1 × 0.1 m in size, cut from a hard brownish tufo. This is not unlike the leucitic tufo which was quarried from the cliffs below the waterfalls (Figs 4 and 22) and, in all probability, they were manufactured locally. There was also a very small section of *opus reticulatum* a short distance to the south, adjoining the lobby (below, Fig. 40,b). Although complicated by the later blocking of a door, this stretch appeared to terminate with tufo quoins. If so, this is a pointer to the work being of Augustan date (Blake 1947: 274; Lugli 1957: 506), with the farm at Monte Forco in the Ager Capenas providing a good local parallel (Jones 1963: 150). The relatively large size of the *tufelli* is also consistent with this date, and is in harmony with the ceramic record from the site (Roberts, this volume), which effectively begins with material of the Augustan period, especially *terra sigillata*. While none was stratified in primary contexts, there is little real difficulty in regarding the first phase of the courtyard complex as a creation of the early decades of the first century AD.

The floor of the portico survived only as a *cocciopesto* surface, laid on a variable amount of make-up (Fig. 23,a). Even though it was to remain in use for four to five centuries, there were few signs of repairs or replacement, and it must be seriously doubted whether the existing floor was the original one. Indeed, the evidence from adjoining rooms is for a white tessellated surface in this period, and it would be surprising if this had not extended into the portico. The inside walls of the portico were certainly rendered in plaster, to judge from a small surviving section, painted in now very faded red, against the base of the *opus reticulatum* opposite the lobby. One drain of the period was identified, being a U-shaped gully that debouched into the courtyard from the western portico (Fig. 23,a, E201). This presumably marks one of the entrances through the portico, and indeed lies opposite a doorway into a room in the western range.

THE WESTERN RANGE

There were several rooms adjoining the western portico. They are denominated as phase 1B in Figure 13, to reflect the fact that the surviving walls were largely rebuilt in the late Roman period. However, there was a sufficiency of *opus reticulatum tufelli* from fallen sections of wall (particularly from the lower terrace) to suggest that these later footings

Fig. 22. Tufo quarry in 1970 for *opus quadratum* blocks; cf. Figure 4 for location. *(TWP)*

mainly followed lines established at the beginning of phase 1. This conclusion finds support from the fact that Roman feet were used to measure out many of the main elements.

Almost exactly central to the range was a corridor, 10 *p.M.* wide, leading from the portico down to the lower terrace and the road. Very eroded wide steps were cut down into the subsoil at the western end of the corridor (see below, Fig. 60), although these appeared to have been placed only in the northern part, thus leaving a passage at the level of the upper terrace. This is puzzling, but the explanation may be that it led to structures laid out at that level, which were later destroyed when the lower terrace and bath-house were inserted. Alternatively, and more probably, it provided passage to some ornamental feature, such as a garden, which occupied the area between the façade and the road.

To the north of the corridor was room A, which we have tended to describe as the 'large room' (Fig. 13). This measured internally 5.8 × 8.65 m (19.59 × 29.22 *p.M.*), which is sufficiently close to 20 × 30 *p.M.* to imply that these were the intended figures. There seem to have been two entrances onto the portico in this period, as well as a small lobby or vestibule to the north. This lobby provided access both to the portico and, via a flight of rock-cut steps, to the top terrace. A small fragment of white mosaic survived *in situ*, set in pale mortar upon the bedrock (into which the lobby and the north end of the large room had been recessed). There were also many white tesserae, of similar size and appearance, incorporated into a secondary drain in the large room (cf. phase 3, below). This was surely also floored in mosaic,

although the resemblance between this tessellated surface and that in the later bath-house may suggest that the work could belong to the late first or early second centuries, rather than to the Augustan period. However, whatever the date, there was apparently extensive use of mosaic, matching other indications of an elegantly laid-out complex.

There were two further rooms, B and C, to the south of the corridor. Of almost equal size, they were also 20 *p.M.* internally, although the total internal length, 9.65 m (32.6 *p.M.*) is a little more than that of room A. This may be explained by the fact that the overall arrangement of the west range allows for very nearly identical spacing between (a) the north wall of the lobby and the north end of the portico and (b) the south wall of room C and the south end of the portico. In other words (and best seen on the phase plan, Figure 12,1), the rooms of the western range projected centrally, leaving virtually symmetrical empty spaces in the northwest and southwest corners. It can hardly be doubted that this was intentional, especially as the façade fronted onto the road. Given that the stylobate and colonnade opposite the east end of the corridor, between the façade and the courtyard, were completely rebuilt in the late Roman period, obliterating the earlier layout, it is reasonable to conclude that the original arrangement was that of a relatively formal and prestigious entrance. Against this is a lack of really substantial foundations for such a structure; but, with so much subsequent architectural intervention, it would be optimistic to pretend that unequivocal evidence would survive (and, indeed, the area was not completely investigated).

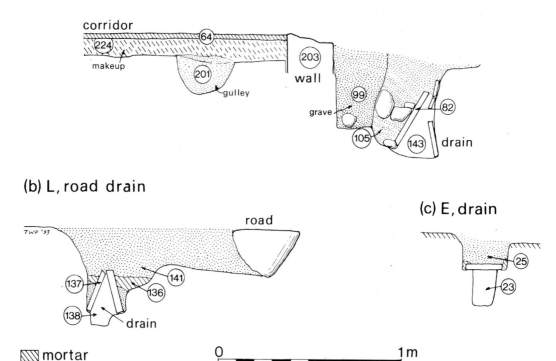

Fig. 23. Sections across drains:

(a) E64: *cocciopesto* floor. E224: mortary make-up. E201: gully for drain with yellow-brown sandy silt fill; first century AD. E99: brown loam fill. Drain along edge of courtyard: E82: tiles. E143: silts within drain, with mid-Imperial pottery. E105: fill of grey-brown soil, with tufo packing, and second- to early third-century pottery.

(b) L141: grey-brown silt, with a ?fifth-/sixth-century coin, and mid to late Imperial pottery. L136: yellow-grey mortar capping. L137: tiles (averaging 0.19 x 0.22 m). L138: grey-brown fill, with second- to early third-century pottery.

(c) E25 (also E26, E76, E78): brown-black silt, with fifth-/sixth-century pottery. E23: rock-cut drain, with tile cover, sealed by mortar. *(TWP)*

THE NORTHERN RANGE: THE FISH-POND (FIGS 24 AND 25, AND BELOW, FIG. 41)

The only phase 1 structure to be identified on the north side of the portico was a rectangular feature, built up against the back wall of the corridor. Although only a part was uncovered, it was at least 3.5 m in length, measured internally, and between 0.95 and 1.0 m in width. The walls were solidly constructed, varying in width from 0.46 to 0.56 m; and the structure was recessed into the bedrock to a maximum depth of 1.6 m below the highest surviving point of the surrounding walls. These extended to the base of the feature on the north and west sides, but below the *opus reticulatum* wall to the south it was the tufo that formed the side. The tufo had been cut as a gentle slope which descended towards a relatively flat bottom, although with a slight downward slope to the east. There was no evidence for any sort of lining, although the tufo would have been relatively impermeable.

The masonry belongs to more than one phase. The original build was in well-cut blocks up to 0.5 m in length, and with course heights of 0.12 m. As Figure 40,c, below, makes very clear, the upper part of the west wall had, however, been rebuilt in much smaller and less regular blocks, with variable courses of 60-100 mm. Similar repairs had been carried out on the north wall and, at its eastern end, it had been completely refaced over its whole height in a crude style that distinctly recalls *opus incertum* (below, Fig. 40,d).

One notable feature of the walling is the heavy and careful application of mortar to the joins, doubtless with the intention of making them watertight. This is explained by the fact that four *tubuli* fed into the structure, two at the west end and two along the north side. They were 0.14 m in diameter, with a bore of 90 mm, and were angled downwards, showing that they carried water into the feature. The trenches by which they had been inserted into the subsoil to the west and north were not visible, and the layout of these conduits could not, therefore, be established; but they could have formed part of an underground system of aqueducts, with the rock-cut channel on the crest of the hill to the north (Figs 4 and 20) perhaps being part of it.

The walls butted against the *opus reticulatum* wall of the corridor, and thus post-date it; they are accordingly denominated as phase 1C on Figure 13. However, there were sherds of Augustan type in the foundation trench, and the walls cannot be very far separated in time, despite their different construction. The repairs must also all belong within the first century AD, since the primary silt, which formed after the latest rebuild (Fig. 23, unit L184), contained pottery of the late first or early second centuries. This was a dark grey-brown deposit, some 0.15 m deep, and with relatively few finds: it is the sort of sediment that might well have accumulated at the base of a water-filled feature.

The primary silt was in turn covered by two successive dumps, L165 and L105. Although separated only by a thin and discontinuous lens of what appeared to be white plas-

Fig. 24. The fish-pond looking west; note the pipes. To the left: the northwest corner of the portico. *(KW)*

L, east section

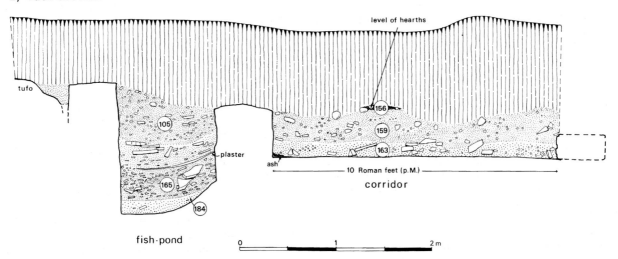

Fig. 25. Section across the fish-pond and portico corridor:

Fills in fish-pond: 105: upper fill, late second century. 165: lower fill, early second century. 184: primary silt, dark grey-brown colour, late first- to early second-century pottery.

Layers over corridor: 156: interpolated hearth from just to the west; a related nearby hearth yielded fifth- to sixth-century pottery. 159 (= 157): rubble, wall fragments with tile, *opus reticulatum*, statue of Venus, and pottery of early to mid fifth century. 163: red-brown silt, with little rubble and few finds; at the base, some ash on the floor. *(TWP)*

ter, the finds suggest that the lower (L165) belongs to the early second century and the upper to the later second century. It is extremely curious that the intervening deposit should be so ephemeral, and it may be that the dumps were in fact contemporaneous, but derived from different sources of refuse. On the other hand, despite the difficulty in excavation of distinguishing precisely between the two deposits, joins were limited to sherds from just two lamps and one colour-coated vessel. A much greater degree of mixing should be expected were the dumps made at the same time, and it is perhaps best to take the evidence at face value and regard the deposits as the result of two separate actions, which took place some 50-70 years apart (see Roberts, this volume, for the dating evidence).

Where this rubbish was generated is unclear, for the adjoining courtyard complex seems an unlikely source. Most probably it came from buildings higher up the hillside to the north, although a slightly more distant origin is not impossible. Interestingly, the dumps included a significant number of wasters (the 'stork-vase' (Figs 239-42, below) amongst them), and wine amphorae of local origin (type P105: Arthur, this volume). The wasters are closely paralleled by finds from a site with pottery kilns just 2.0 km to the northeast (Fig. 5, A31 – Peña 1987: site 9) and certainly imply another production centre. This was quite probably at the Mola di Monte Gelato itself, where later, pottery of early medieval date was also to be manufactured (see below).

The range and quantity of the pottery was remarkable (cf. below, Figs 216 and 217). There were over 400 vessels in the two deposits, varying in size from small drinking cups to large flagons and amphorae, and in quality from elegant green-glazed dishes to kitchen-wares. A few were complete, with just some slight damage, but many could be largely restored. This was also the case with the glass vessels, many fine examples of which were found (Price, this volume). The pottery and glass together provide a further argument for suggesting that the material in the deposits had not been transported over any great distance.

The other finds are listed in Table 1, which reveals some interesting differences between the two groups. Common to both are some fine items of jewellery, and a remarkable array of bone needles and pins. Also noteworthy are many elements from a bone fan (cat. 100), a rare and luxurious object. The later deposit (L105), however, does in addition include a substantial proportion of building materials. Apart from many fragments of roof tile, there are pieces of box flue (one largely complete), a fragment of white mosaic floor and much *opus sectile*, as well as a large part of a marble *labrum* (below, Fig. 144), and the complete neck of an ornamental crater (below, Fig. 146), also in marble. Here is unambiguous testimony of the pulling down of buildings, and the breaking up of elegant decorative furnishings. These must surely relate to the adjoining courtyard complex, and the significance of this will be considered further below. There were also the remains of two articulated skeletons of dogs, both working animals who had sustained some injuries (King, this volume).

Two other points about the contents of the deposits require emphasis. One is the presence of a few graffiti (below, Fig. 140) in both Latin and Greek. They derive from the later second-century dump, except for the 'stork-vase' (Murray *et al.* 1991, and this volume), signed by Abaskantos and Epinikos, which came from the early second-century layer. This is the cup of a drinking club and, being a very cracked waster, must have been made locally: together with the graffiti, it is compelling evidence for the presence of Greeks at Monte Gelato. They were presumably slaves although, as Murray has shown (Murray *et al.* 1991), of a highly literate and educated kind, as the motto on the cup makes clear.

The other significant conclusion derives from a study of the organic remains. Despite sieving 55 litres of soil, plant remains were disappointingly sparse; however, the animal bones more than compensate for this. Apart from normal domestic species, and a number of chickens, these include edible dormice; toads (one from the primary silts); fourteen fish bones (see below); and a large number of bird bones, of which those of a tawny owl, jays, thrushes, blackbirds and chaffinches could be readily recognized. There were also tentatively identified bones of ducks, and two oyster valves.

Table 1. Small finds from the fish-pond (catalogue numbers in parentheses).

	early second century (L165)	later second century/early third century (L105)
copper alloy	Aucissa brooch (3)	bracelet (8), two needles (18, 19), box fitting (28), two strips (42, 44)
lead		?net weight (49)
bone	three needles (17, 108, 111), strip inlay (135)	fan (100), handle (102), inlay (103), four needles (106, 109, 110, 114), fourteen pins (116-18, 120-2, 124-5, 128-33)
glass	melon bead (138)	two glass counters (142, 143)
stone		weight (149)
iron	key (1), six nails	key (2), hook/hinge staple (4), T-clamp (5), three pieces of binding (8-10), stud (11), 22 nails
marble sculpture		*labrum* (4), complete neck of crater (5)
building materials	much tile	much tile, including many pieces of box flue, fragment of mosaic (limestone), 124 pieces of marble veneer

Thrushes, blackbirds and chaffinches are of course common garden birds; but tawny owls and jays require a secluded woodland environment, where they can find adequate protection. This allows for the intriguing possibility that there may have been an aviary, perhaps in the adjacent courtyard. The raising of birds, especially fieldfares (a thrush, *Turdus pilaris*), for the table was a profitable business (Varro, *De Re Rustica* iii. 2.15; Toynbee 1973: 277-8); but they were additionally kept for pleasure. Varro has provided a detailed description of the aviary in his villa near Casinum (*De Re Rustica* iii. 5.8-17). He kept chiefly songsters, such as nightingales and blackbirds, which lived amongst the colonnade of a portico and in trees planted in a courtyard. There were also ponds for fish and ducks, making an ambience that so vividly recalls the description of the above pages as to be remarkable. Indeed, one might wonder whether the stork on the 'stork-vase' – although convincingly linked by Murray (Murray *et al.* 1991: 102) with the name of a pottery vessel (*pelargos*) – could not also be an allusion to an aviary on the site.

This in turn brings up the question of the function of a building that, from the moment of its discovery, we regarded as a latrine. This interpretation depended essentially upon its long rectangular plan, and the provision of water pipes to flush out the tank. Against such a view are: (a) the absence of a floor, even though the *opus reticulatum* wall stands to a height of 0.75 m above the corridor; (b) the absence of any lavatory seat emplacements in the back wall, which rises still higher; (c) the lack of any deposits, especially in the primary silts, which resemble an accumulation of human waste. Moreover, the plans of latrines in Italian villas are usually of much more conventionally proportioned rooms, rather than long, narrow structures (cf., for example, Rossiter 1978).

The true purpose of the structure was only realized, however, at a relatively late stage in the preparation of this report. Both the literary and the archaeological sources indicate that tanks or ponds provided with vessels such as amphorae or *tubuli* were used to house fish; the vessels created places for the fish to breed, and Higginbotham (1991; forthcoming), who has produced an authoritative survey of the subject, illustrates a fish-pond with eels swimming in and out of *tubuli* arranged almost exactly like the Monte Gelato example (Higginbotham 1991: fig. 104). This in itself would be suggestive enough, but confirmation that the structure was indeed an eel pond came with the identification of a vertebra of *Anguilla anguilla* (and also two fish spines) from the lower fill. Shad was represented in the upper layers, but this is more likely to be food refuse (there were eleven fish bones, mostly unidentifiable), than an indication of the pond's inhabitants.

Fish-ponds were probably not uncommon in the Roman Campagna (Thomas and Wilson 1994: 164-7), and certainly could be a profitable enterprise. Eels were particularly popular from the first century BC, and were raised in enormous quantities, fetching high prices (e.g. Pliny, *Naturalis Historia* ix. 170-1). But, as Pliny also informed us, they were also kept as pets, and even decorated with jewellery, an ornamental role I have already alluded to in discussing Varro's villa near Casinum. Varro told us that he had 'two oblong fish-ponds, not very wide, facing the colonnades' (*De Re Rustica* iii. 5.12), a description which fits the Monte Gelato example very closely. Certainly the modest dimensions of the pond would appear to rule out commercial production of eels, and it is best seen as a harmonious ornamental addition to an elegant porticoed courtyard, with trees, a nymphaeum (below, Fig. 142), statues, a fountain (below, Fig. 144), pools and an aviary.

THE SOUTHERN RANGE AND SIDE ROAD

Only a limited area was investigated beyond the south portico, since outcrops of bedrock indicated that little could have survived. Moreover, a large late Roman limekiln had cut away any earlier features. There would have been space for a series of rooms for there is a 6.0 m gap between the portico and a steep-sided and certainly ancient cutting into the bedrock. This cutting, which still carries the modern road, follows an alignment that is parallel with the south portico (Fig. 12,2), and may be contemporary with it; but there is no direct evidence for its date, and the overall layout of the Augustan complex (Fig. 12,1) rather suggests that this remained vacant ground at this time (and quite possibly later).

PHASE 1: THE OTHER FINDS

No refuse deposits of the first century AD were encountered in the excavations, and the small quantities of pottery of this date all occurred in residual contexts (Roberts, this volume). This is further confirmation of the non-functional aspect of the investigated area at this time, although the second-century finds from the deposits in the fish-pond must imply that there was a substantial villa nearby. No traces of buildings were discovered in the very thick *macchia* overlooking the waterfalls, although there is one possible ancient footing exposed in the surface of the track that runs along the southeastern side of the river Treia. However, the most obvious possibility must be the area to the north of the courtyard complex, where the ground rises gradually to the ridges that surround the valley. While the vestiges of only one footing, perhaps of this period, were identified (see below, Fig. 41, L198), there is ample space here for a considerable range of buildings, although little is likely to have survived the effects of modern ploughing.

It is the sculpture, architectural elements and inscriptions which otherwise shed most light on the site at this period. They are discussed in detail in the catalogues, but a few summary words will be appropriate here. Mention has already been made of the marble crater and *labrum* (usually, but not always, associated with the *caldarium* of a bathhouse). To these may be added the lower half of a nymph, reused in a late Roman floor; a weathered male head (?Ganymede) from a medieval context; and a statue of Venus, two-thirds life-size, from a late Roman fill over the portico corridor (Claridge, this volume). An early Imperial date would not be inappropriate for any of them. The identifiable architectural fragments are not numerous, but include an architrave, two sections of a cornice and a block with a decorative moulding, all again quite possibly of early first-century AD date. A pilaster capital was also found, with a parallel of the late Republican-early Augustan period; it may derive from a small temple or funerary monument (DeLaine, this volume). In short, these finds certainly do not contradict an Augustan date for the complex, and amply support the notion of a graciously embellished place.

The assumption here is that all these items were part of the phase 1 complex, and not later introductions to the site, as often happened (for example, Santa Rufina: Reynolds 1991: 301; Santa Cornelia: Reynolds 1991: 137). The inscriptions are more problematic, especially the important tomb monument of four freed-people, including C. Valerius Faustus, cattle merchant and *magister* of the *Augustales* at Veii

(Gilliver 1990; this volume). Almost certainly Augustan in date, it was found in a late Roman limekiln, but had survived incineration (Figs 135 and 136). Faustus's spouse would appear to have been a lady called Hilara, with an extremely rare *nomen*, Aesconius. This may indicate a family relationship with an Augustan veteran equestrian officer, Aesconius Capella, who was a *duumvir* of Veii (Gilliver 1990). All the other inscriptions are also funerary, except for that on a fragment of local *peperino*, also from the limekiln. It reads *fa*]CIVND[*um curavit* on one line, and]S.ET.HILA[on the next, and Purcell (1988a: 286) has suggested that it records the work of *curatores fani* or *magistri pagi* or *vici*, in late Republican or Augustan times.

There was a substantial village-like settlement at the Fosso Stramazzo (Fig. 8, E21), less than a kilometre to the north, from which the inscription could derive. Alternatively, it may indeed be from the Mola di Monte Gelato itself although, as will be seen in the discussion, below, a context is not easy to identify. For the funerary inscriptions there are, however, good local contexts. There is the second-century mausoleum or temple-tomb on the ridge opposite the main site (cf. DeLaine, this volume), and a Roman cemetery, ravaged by the *clandestini*, some 200 m to the northwest, by the paved road. Tomassetti (1877) records sepulchral inscriptions from Monte Caio (Fig. 8), including one of the *praetor* Q. Petronius Urbanus (*CIL* XI 3207; see also 3228), and there is a further funerary text from the Fosso Stramazzo site (Reynolds 1966: 65, no. 18). There is no real need, therefore, to invoke the cemeteries of Rome as the source of these inscriptions, and an origin in the vicinity of the Mola di Monte Gelato is entirely plausible. If so, the strong onomastic links with Veii and Rome that the inscriptions record is of considerable interest. One, for example, bears the name Herennia (below, Fig. 139), which recalls M. Herennius Picens, consul in AD 1 and patron of Veii (*CIL* XI 3797). Settlement in the towns and countryside of South Etruria by people from Rome was a well-defined phenomenon from Augustan times onwards (Potter 1991: 176-7; Purcell 1983: 161, 166), and would help to explain the apparent urban connections of the complex at the Mola di Monte Gelato.

THE PHASE 2 DRAINS

From the late first or early second centuries AD there were significant modifications to the complex. Some were minor, like the provision of an *a cappuccina* tile drain (E82) along part of the west side of the courtyard (Figs 13 and 23,a). This cut across the phase 1 drain (E201) from the portico, and contained second-century pottery in its fill. It was recessed into the natural subsoil to a depth of 0.5 m, and flowed from north to south. Although the full extent did not survive at either end, its sealed nature means that it was not intended as an eaves-drip. The idea may have been to carry away, down hill, storm water, although it would appear to have become rapidly choked with silt.

One other drain (A10) of this period lay on the lower terrace (Fig. 13), parallel with the east wall of the bath-house (cf. below). Only a short length was exposed, due to the overlay of later features; but it was 0.22 m wide and cut 0.42 m into the bedrock. Presumably it once held a terracotta or lead pipe. There were a few sherds of early Imperial date in its fill, and there is no reason to doubt its association with the bath-house.

ROOM D

It is also possible that a room (D) was added to the west of the large room (A) in phase 2, at the level of the upper terrace. In the limited area that was excavated, there was a *cocciopesto* floor, at the edge of a shallow foundation trench (E202), running east-west and parallel with the southern edge of the upper terrace (Fig. 13). In the late Roman period there was a door threshold in the western wall of the large room, but this was clearly a late insertion. However, it is possible that this represents a replacing of a much earlier doorway.

THE CISTERNS (FIG. 26)

In the northwest area of the excavation were two adjacent cisterns. Both showed the same broad alignment, although this differed slightly from that of the main complex, instead following that of the paved road. There is no very obvious reason for this, unless it was dictated by a higher ridge of bedrock between the cisterns and the northwest corner of the courtyard.

Plough damage had been severe, and had removed all traces of the wall around the north cistern. What remained was a rectangular tank, 5.46 × 4.24 m, and with a maximum surviving depth (at the north end) of 0.9 m. There seems to be no real correspondence with *p.M.* here (18.44 × 14.32), unless there was a general intention to make it 20 × 15 *p.M.* The floor was made up of a somewhat coarse *cocciopesto*, with clear signs of differential wear. There was a well-made quarter-round moulding around the base of the walls, which were lined with whitish *opus signinum*. This had been applied in two stages, an initial coarse mixture and then a smooth surface, giving a total thickness of 20 mm. There had been difficulties in the coating of the tufo, however, and in places nails had been driven into the rock, to aid the keying. This was not entirely successful, and the west face had partly fallen away. Much of what remained had also become detached on that side, giving the impression of a job that was poorly done (cf. Vitruvius viii. 6.14, on the lining of cisterns).

The base of the adjoining south cistern was 0.3 m (perhaps, therefore, one *p.M.*) higher, and much less well preserved. No superstructure survived, and part of the floor had been ploughed away. There was a gap of 0.46 m between the two cisterns, and the overall internal dimensions of the south cistern were *c.* 4.5 × 4.2 m, so that it was smaller and squarer in shape. Traces could be seen of a wall footing, 0.4 m wide, along the east side, but it consisted of no more than tufo rubble set in a bluish grey mortar. It was not, however, precisely aligned with the north cistern, a disparity of layout which seems somewhat curious. Possibly they represent two separate periods of construction.

Neither cistern was completely excavated, and the manner in which they were fed is unclear. A drain was, however, identified in the southwestern corner of the north cistern. It consisted of a U-shaped cut into the bedrock, down to just below the base of the cistern, and headed towards the paved road; there were traces of what appeared to be a mortar capping. The channel then debouched into an *a cappuccina* drain, running along the east side of the paved road (Fig. 23,b).

The whole channel of the cistern drain was not fully excavated, and the feature is not easy to understand in detail. It seems a rather crude device for draining the cistern and,

Fig. 26. The north cistern, and later Roman footings, looking southwest. The scant remains
of the south cistern are on the left. *(KW)*

given that the channel was apparently cut through the *opus signinum* lining, must be regarded as a secondary construction. This in turn raises the question of function. We have tended to regard these features as water cisterns, whilst recognizing that they might also have served as vats for the separation of oil or the fermentation of wine. It could indeed be that a complex of presses lies just outside the excavated area, to the north. However, given the proximity of the bath-house (DeLaine, below), which lies at a much lower level (Fig. 19), it does seem much more plausible to regard them as cisterns, constructed specifically to service the baths.

There is no direct evidence with which to date the building of the cisterns, although they were manifestly inserted into the Augustan complex and aligned on the paved road. They are thus most probably to be assigned to phase 2 which, to judge from the evidence of the bath-house, may have begun *c.* AD 100. Subsequently, a wall-footing (Fig. 13, L119) was built on the floor of the eastern part of the south cistern. Whether this represents a modification of the cistern or belongs to a period after its abandonment is, however, uncertain, in the absence of proper stratification (cf. Fig. 39).

The backfilling of the north cistern, where there was a good depth of deposits, appears to have taken place rapidly. There was a very thin layer of grey-brown silt on the floor, not more than 20 mm thick, and then a dump of loose rubbly fill, 0.4 m deep. Above this was a layer with less rubble and more colluvium, but with a sufficiently homogeneous character to suggest that it was not a natural accumulation. This conclusion is supported by the finds, which indicate

that the backfilling took place in the late second or early third century. This is close in time to the final dump in the fish-pond, and also the date of virtually all of the refuse in the rock-cut road: the Severan period, therefore, would seem to mark something of a watershed in the site's history.

The other finds from the north cistern include some pieces of bronze and lead sheet (cat. 26, 27, 87), an iron hook (cat. 3) and two iron rings (cat. 6, 7). There was also much wall-plaster, all of it very fragmented, but with some traces of faded painted decoration. Recognizable were yellow and white flowers and green vegetation, while other pieces bore purple and red paint. Tile and lumps of mortar also occurred in significant proportions, and a tufo cornice of late Republican or early Imperial date (below, Fig. 161) had been thrown into the upper fill, where it had come to rest diagonally, along a tip line. Another section of this cornice was recorded as a surface find in 1970.

THE BATH-HOUSE (FIGS 27 AND 28), by J. DeLaine

On the western edge of the main site, next to the paved Roman road, were discovered the remains of a small bath building, the heated part of which came to light during the widening of the modern road in 1983 (Fig. 29) and was investigated during the first two seasons of excavation (DeLaine in Potter and King 1988: 263-6). This was followed by the

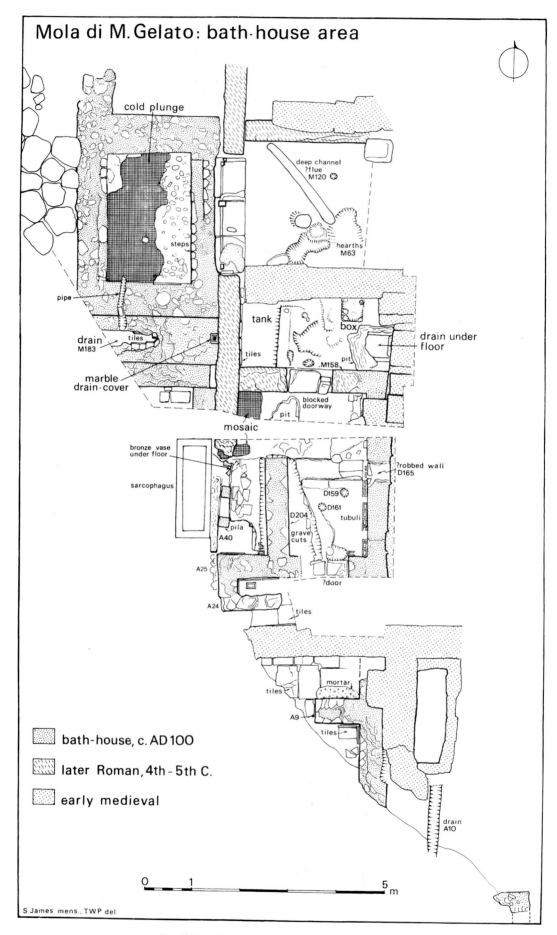

Fig. 27. Detailed plan of the bath-house area. *(TWP)*

bath-house: reconstructed plan

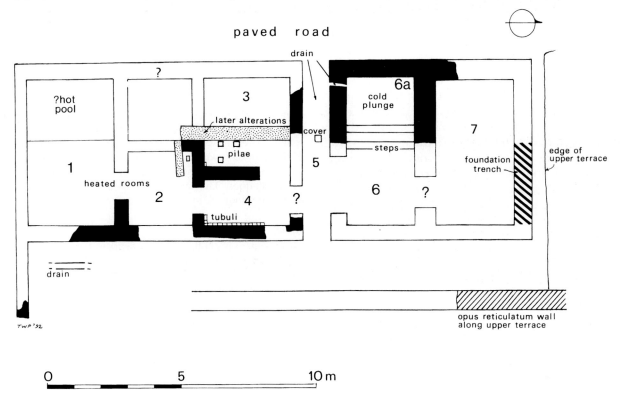

Fig. 28. Bath-house plan. *(TWP)*

Fig. 29. The southern part of the bath-house and later features. The section to the left is drawn in Figure 54. *(TWP)*

discovery of the cold section during the 1990 excavation season (Fig. 30). Unfortunately the southwest corner of the building appears to have disappeared during the construction of the modern road, while much of the northeastern section was deliberately demolished in Antiquity to make way for later Roman and early medieval structures. It is not, therefore, possible to recover the complete plan of the baths, although the main lines are clear. The bath building appears to have consisted of a simple rectangular block, approximately 6.5 × 19.3 m, containing at least seven rooms. There were four (or possibly five) heated rooms in the southern half, separated by a narrow corridor from an unheated room with a cold plunge pool and with one large or two smaller rooms to the north of the pool.

Heated areas (rooms 1 to 4) (Figs 27 and 28)

Rooms 1 and 2

Only the northeast corner of room 1 remains, although the line of the south wall of the room can be inferred from the short section of wall appearing in the modern road cutting. This appears to form the southern limit of the bath block. Both the northwest and southeast corners of room 2 are preserved, defining a room c. 2.5 m square. There is no evidence to indicate whether or not there was a further room to the west of room 2.

The surviving walls of the two rooms have a maximum height of 0.5 m and enclose the hypocaust space. Both floor and walls of the hypocaust preserve extensive traces of a tile lining, formed predominantly from reused roof tiles of minimum dimensions 0.48 × 0.69 × 0.025 m with their flanges removed, but including a few standard *bipedales* (Figs 29 and 31). One jamb of an opening between the two hypocausts is preserved, which may indicate that there was also a door between the two rooms at this point. No *tubuli* from the wall heating remain in place, although there is a single *tubulus* mortared vertically into the sub-floor in the northwest corner of room 2. It is hard to see how this *tubulus* may have functioned in relation to the bath, since it is too far from the wall to have been part of the heating system and could not have acted as a drain for a pool as it had no outlet at the base. It is more likely to be related to a later use of the area which involved building a rough wall which sits on the hypocaust sub-floor and runs parallel to the north wall of room 2. The northeast corner of the room remained concealed by a baulk, but there appears to have been a doorway into room 4 in the centre of the north wall.

Room 3

Although part of the north and east walls remains to a maximum height of nearly 1.0 m above the sub-floor of the hypocaust, the original arrangement of the room is rather obscured by later phases, including late Roman walls and early medieval burials. There appears to have been a door into room 4 at the north end of the east wall, but the south wall has been truncated and the jamb does not survive. Both walls are of concrete construction, but the upper part of the north wall appears to incorporate a tufo ashlar block which is difficult to interpret. It is unlikely to have functioned as a threshold, as the top of the block is 0.2 to 0.4 m higher than the floor levels of the rooms on either side, while the use of solid tufo door jambs in an otherwise brick-faced concrete construction has few parallels.

In the eastern section of the room, part of the hypocaust remains intact (Fig. 32). Tiles line the floor and walls of the hypocaust as in rooms 1 and 2, with those on the wall appearing to support the inner edge of the wall tubes, one of which remains in place in the southeast corner of the room. The hypocaust *pilae*, 0.39 m high, are composed of eight courses of *bessales* of average dimensions 0.2 × 0.2 × 0.034 m. The *pilae* are covered by standard *bipedales* which support the floor of the room. As well as the floor packing, which remains over most of the east end of the room, small areas of white mosaic, with tesserae averaging 10 mm square, survive in places at an average height of 0.71 m above the hypocaust sub-floor. The hypocaust appears to have continued under the doorway to room 4.

Room 4

This room, only c. 1.6 m wide, appears to form a heated passage linking rooms 2 and 3. The north wall has been much altered in the late Roman period by the cutting through and later blocking of a doorway, but sufficient of the Roman structure survives to suggest that there was originally no opening between this and room 6. The floor of the room is reasonably well preserved, being broken through to the hypocaust space only in the opening between rooms 3 and 4. A row of *tubuli* extending below floor level remains along the southern half of the east wall and as far as the opening to room 2.

All the visible walls of these heated rooms are of brick-faced concrete with a tufo rubble core, except for the tufo ashlar block mentioned above. The bricks are predominantly regular triangles of average length along the face of 0.26 m within the range 0.23-0.28 m, and of average thickness either 33 mm in the range 30-35 mm, or 38 mm in the range 38-40 mm, suggesting that they were cut from a mixture of *bessales* and *bipedales*. The horizontal mortar joints are irregular but mostly fall within the range 20-24 mm, although they can be as wide as 30 mm. The modulus of five rows of brick and five of mortar averages 0.29 m. The bricks are yellow to salmon-pink in colour and of a uniform consistency.

The Cold Rooms (Rooms 5-7) (Figs 27 and 28)

Room 5

This is a narrow space, 0.95 m wide, defined by the north wall of room 3 and the south side of the pool room 6a. There does not appear to have been a wall to the west, which would suggest that this room formed an entrance passage from the Roman road which ran along the west side of the bath block. A large drain of *a cappuccina* type runs under the floor of the room, in an east-west direction, into which runs a rough drain from the pool (Fig. 33). Only the tufo rubble and mortar packing of the floor remains, except at the east end where a white marble drain cover connecting with the drain survives, set into what may be a later concrete floor some 0.24 m above the level of the mosaic floors in the heated rooms. The same large drain reappears further to the east, on a line with the outer east wall of the heated rooms. This whole area east of the corridor and the pool was greatly altered in later phases, so that it is no longer possible to tell whether the corridor also continued straight across, or whether this area formed part of room 6. In either case there must have been a doorway in the east wall corresponding to that in the west.

Fig. 30. The plunge bath (Fig. 28, no. 6a) looking south, with to the left late Roman walls and the entrance to the baptistery complex. *(KW*

Section in modern road cutting, A

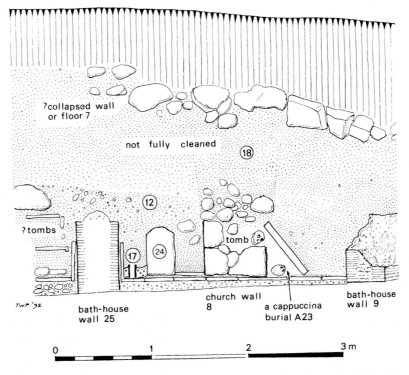

Fig. 31. Section of the southern part of the bath-house, overlain by the churches, and with burial no. 26 (A23).
7: tufo blocks and lumps probably from the latest floor of the church (or its wall). 18: darkish fill; traces of a demolition or robber trench down to the church wall, 8, are indicated by a discrete cluster of tufo lumps. 12: layer with building material and human bones. 17 (=19): loose grey layer with fifth- to sixth-century pottery. 24: wall built of roughly-shaped blocks and lumps of tufo, resting on a thin layer of soil; beside it is a *tubulus* set in mortar. *(TWP)*

Fig. 32. The bath-house, second baptistery west wall, and overlying deposits (Figs 54 and 72).
In the foreground, the sarcophagus of burial no. 61. *(TWP)*

Fig. 33. The bath-house drain (Fig. 28, no. 5) looking east. *(KW)*

Room 6a

The cold plunge pool (Fig. 30), which measures 1.78 × 2.6 m, is one of the best preserved parts of the bath block. The white mosaic floor is in good condition (and is made with small tesserae averaging 8.0 mm square), although the eastern side is concealed by later rubble concrete. The north, south and west sides, defined by a wall 0.6 m thick of tufo rubble concrete faced with tufo blocks, survive to only a few centimetres above the floor of the pool, except in the north-west corner. On the east the wall forms two steps, the lower complete step being 0.24 m wide and 0.31 m high; the risers are also faced with tufo blocks. The outer east edge of the pool is concealed by the later threshold block, but it is clear from the shallowness of the resulting pool that there must have been a stepped ledge dividing it from the rest of room 6, a common method of constructing such pools.

Rooms 6 and 7

Very few traces of these rooms were preserved. The east wall of room 6 was completely obliterated by a later concrete floor, and it can only be assumed that it followed the line of the hot rooms. A rough and shallow concrete foundation, which continues the line of the west boundary of the pool northwards, is the only surviving structure relating to room 7 and even this may be a later addition as there appears to be a join at this point. A trench for another shallow foundation runs parallel to the edge of the upper terrace and close to it, and this presumably denotes the northern boundary of room 7. It is also possible that the later Roman walls which start at the northeast corner of the bath-house – one running north-south cutting room 7 in two, and the other east-west continuing the line of the north wall of the pool – reflect the arrangement of the earlier structure.

DISCUSSION

Although the basic linear arrangement of this small bath building, with unheated rooms to the north and heated rooms to the south, is clear, a number of features require further comment. From its location at the end of a series of heated rooms, it can be assumed that room 1 was the *caldarium* and a hot pool can be restored on the west, or, less probably, on the south. The poor state of preservation of the remaining three or four heated rooms makes it difficult to identify the function of each or to determine the circulation pattern, although the wall heating in room 4 precludes this being a *tepidarium* in the strictest sense (Rebuffat 1991: 7). This would make room 3 the only possible candidate for a *tepidarium*, with access from room 5, as well as suggesting that room 2 functioned as a *sudatio*. Since no evidence was found on the east side for the *praefurnia* of the heated rooms, these are most likely to be sought to the west of rooms 1 and 2. Room 6 is clearly a *frigidarium*, with a cold plunge pool, and this would suggest that the ill-defined room 7 to the north, if belonging to the bath at all, might have acted as an *apodyterium*. The corridor room 5 appears to have allowed access to the baths from the road as well as from an area between the upper terrace of the complex and the

east side of the block; it is no longer possible to determine whether there was also access into rooms 6 or 7 from the east.

With the exception of the area around Vesuvius buried in the eruption of AD 79, baths belonging to rural villas in Italy have been little studied and parallels are few. On the whole, the early examples gathered by Fabbricotti (1976) have at most two heated rooms, as have the late Republican-early Imperial examples from *villae rusticae* at Scansano, near Grosseto (Del Chiaro 1989; 1990), and Petraro, near Stabiae (De Caro 1987). It appears that the multiplication of heated rooms in otherwise unpretentious rural bath-houses should be seen as a later phenomenon, one which presumably follows the better-documented development of elaborate public and urban bath buildings under the influence of the Imperial *thermae* (cf. DeLaine 1992). The same has been suggested for the appearance of bath-houses as independent structures in rural villas rather than integral parts of the *pars urbana* (Rossiter 1978: 37); the small third-century bath-house of the villa at Crocicchie is a case in point (Potter and Dunbabin 1979).

In the absence of any datable finds relating to the construction phase, the bath can only be dated broadly on the basis of its plan and the type of construction. Its independent structure, the increased number of heated rooms, and the incorporation from the start of a cold plunge, together suggest a *terminus post quem* for the Monte Gelato bath towards the end of the first century AD. The use of brick-faced concrete for the heated areas, and the cutting of the facing bricks into triangles, would also suggest a date not before the later part of the first century and more probably in the second; the quality of the brickwork should preclude a date after the middle of the third century. The use of tiles to line the walls as well as the floors of hypocausts has a number of parallels, for example the late first- to early second-century baths at Massaciuccoli (Levi 1935: 218-19, figs 3-5), but is unlikely to have any value as a chronological indicator.

The location of the Monte Gelato bath-house, next to the *diverticulum* and with access from it as well as presumably from the rest of the complex on the terrace above, must raise the question of what clientele the building was intended to serve. Nothing is known about the provision of baths for rural workers, including small tenant farmers and day labourers, who would have had no such facilities at home. With baths becoming an increasingly fundamental part of daily life for urban dwellers under the Empire, it would be surprising if the rural population had recourse only to the public baths in the nearest town or *vicus* on market-days and holidays. One possibility is that public baths were sometimes provided by rural villas. This seems to be the context of two very similar inscriptions from rural areas, one from near Ficulea (*CIL* XIV 4015), and the other from near Bologna (*CIL* XI 1 712), which advertize refined or commodious urban-style baths – 'more urbico' – on private estates. Too few mid-Imperial villas with baths have been fully excavated and published to allow us to identify with any certainty those which might have served a wider clientele than the villa owners and *familia*, but it could be plausibly suggested that those like Monte Gelato, with more developed facilities in a separate bath block and access to a public road, should be high on the list of potential candidates.

THE TEMPLE-TOMB OR MAUSOLEUM (FIGS 34-7), by J. DeLaine

Remains of a rectangular structure, *c.* 6.8 m wide and 10.6 m long, with walls of brick-faced concrete, were identified and partially excavated on the top of a small ridge on the west side of the Roman and modern roads. The ridge is about 6.0 m above the roads, so that the building would have been particularly prominent. It is divided into two unequal parts, with a small chamber facing almost due east, overlooking the road, and a larger one, cut into the hillside behind.

The main chamber is almost square and has reinforcing piers 0.56 m square in each corner, suggesting it was originally roofed with a cross-vault. The smaller chamber, 1.73 m wide, was reached from the main chamber through a narrow doorway 0.88 m wide. An area of possibly medieval

rebuild in the centre of the rear (west) wall of the main chamber may indicate the location of an original access door, but further excavation would be necessary to confirm this. Excavations in both chambers failed to uncover any trace of a built floor, although the presence of a slightly projecting brick course forming a narrow ledge on the south wall of the smaller chamber at the same level as the sill of the door may suggest that an original floor at that level was removed at some later period. The natural tufo in the main chamber is 0.42 m lower than the door sill and shows signs of levelling in addition to a number of ruts and irregular depressions, relating to later use of the structure in early medieval times.

The walls, 0.71 m thick, survive to a maximum height of 1.0 m. They have no separate foundations but sit directly on the natural tufo. In the main chamber the underlying tufo appears to have been cut back at the rear (west) to create an artificial platform and levelled to form a uniform bedding for the walls. The internal face of the walls in the smaller chamber follows the irregularities of the underlying tufo. A rough drain passes through the foot of the south wall of the main chamber. A layer of mortar and tufo rubble, extending for up to 0.24 m beyond the outer wall of the smaller chamber, was used to level the irregularities in the natural tufo, and the outer face of the wall above it rests on a levelling course of *bipedales* of dimensions in the range 0.56-0.6 m long and 40-45 mm thick.

All the walls are of brick-faced concrete construction with a core of irregular *tufa caementa*. The bricks are mainly light yellow to pale salmon-pink in colour, with noticeable inclusions of red and black angular fragments and some small nodules of darker orange-red terracotta. Where visible in the top of the wall the bricks are mainly neat triangles with

Fig. 34. The mausoleum or temple-tomb, looking southwest. *(KW)*

Fig. 35. Excavated southeast quadrant of the mausoleum. *(KW)*

some irregular trapezoidal pieces. Brick measurements were taken from the exposed interior faces of the walls only. A *bessalis* of sides 0.197 m and 36 mm thick was used in the door jamb, and some of the facing pieces appear also to be cut from *bessales* of uniform thickness within the range 30-38 mm. These are combined in the facing with thinner bricks (18-30 mm thick), which may be cut from roof tiles, and with bricks of variable thickness generally within the range 38-46 mm but with some up to 60 mm thick, presumably cut from *bipedales* or *sesquipedales*. The mortar joints are variable within the range 9-30 mm, with most falling within the range 13-21 mm and having a median of 17 mm. The modulus of five courses of brick and five of mortar ranges from 0.27 to 0.305 m. The strong, hard mortar consists of a grey, rounded fine aggregate in a fairly clean white matrix.

On the outer face of the west wall of the building, at the highest point of the surviving structure, traces remain of a decorative brick moulding consisting of a half-round 42-6 mm thick over a deep fillet 60 mm tall, the total height of the moulding being 0.12 m. The half-round mouldings appear to be formed from *bipedales* 0.590-0.595 m long, cut in four to produce rectangles 0.14 m wide. It is possible that bricks with a bevelled edge found in the fill of the rock-cut road, and perhaps the fragments of brick columns and capitals/bases found elsewhere on the main site, are also to be related to this structure.

Discussion

Despite the fact that little more than the plan of the building survives, it is clear that the remains are

to be identified as the substructures of a small temple or temple-tomb on a high podium, which can probably be restored as prostyle and either tetra-style or distyle *in antis*, reached by a set of frontal steps across the full width of the pronaos.

Although brick-faced concrete tombs enjoyed a particular vogue in Rome and its hinterland during the second and early third centuries AD (Blake and Bishop 1973: 117-38), few examples of true temple-tombs, distinguished by a separate pronaos, survive. In addition, the distinction between temple and temple-tomb is not an easy one, as can be seen from the various interpretations given to structures such as Sant'Urbano alla Caffarella, the so-called 'Tomb of Annia Regilla' or 'Temple of Deus Ridiculus' (Kammerer-Grothaus 1974: 154-87), the 'tempietto' forming part of the Villa dei Sette Bassi (Lupu 1937: 179-83), and the structure from the Villa del Torraccio di Torrenova reconstructed in the Museo delle Terme (Quilici 1974: 583-7; Pensabene 1985), which form the closest parallels to the building under consideration. In the absence of evidence for either arcosolia or columbarium niches, the existence of a lower chamber or chambers within the podium of the building is inconclusive: as appears to have been the case with the so-called 'Tomb of Annia Regilla', the vaulted chambers in the podium may have functioned only as substructures, the actual tomb chamber being the

Mola di M.Gelato: mausoleum or temple·tomb

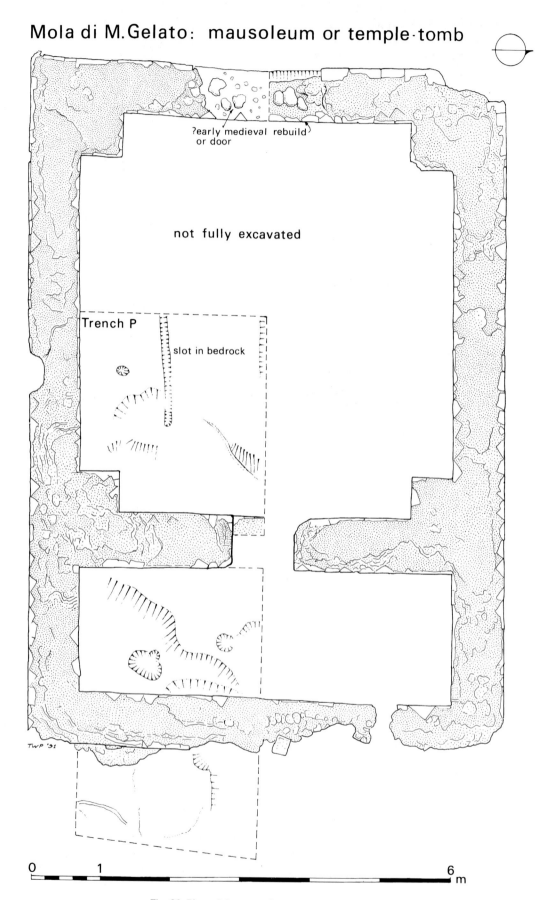

?early medieval rebuild
or door

not fully excavated

Trench P

slot in bedrock

TWP '91

0   1   6
                                                 m

Fig. 36. Plan of the mausoleum or temple-tomb. *(TWP)*

cella above. The location of the structure parallel to and overlooking the road, and its eastern orientation, are also ambiguous. It should also be borne in mind that there is not necessarily any relation between this structure and the villa and baths on the opposite side of the road.

In the absence of any clear archaeological evidence, only general indications of the date of the structure can be given on stylistic grounds. Most of the parallels cited above are thought to be Hadrianic to Antonine in date, and the use of brick facing even within the podium chambers would tend to suggest a date later rather than earlier in this period, certainly closer to Rome.

DISCUSSION OF PHASES 1 AND 2

The analysis of the first two phases of the site's history reveals a place of some pretensions, with a population of presumed urban origin, especially Veii and Rome, and sophisticated taste. As originally envisaged in the Augustan period, it was provided with relatively grand architecture, accompanied by some handsome sculpture, ornamental trees, an aviary, a fish-pond for eels, and a pool. It was, in short, a place built to grace a lovely setting.

While the excavations were in progress, we were reluctant to describe the site as a villa, although this was the preferred interpretation at the outset of the investigation. The misgivings arose partly through the discovery of the inscription in the limekiln which Purcell (1988a: 286) thought might refer to the work of *curatores* of a *fanum* or magistrates of a *pagus* or *vicus*. But they also stemmed from the failure to identify any traces of a residential area or a *pars rustica*. As excavation and study proceeded, the notion that the original site was a religious complex gained ground (although no temple was found in the main complex), as did the idea that it may have been a *vicus*.

These uncertainties would now seem to be resolved. There seem to be an insufficiency of buildings for it to have been a *vicus*, and the *fanum* hypothesis is likewise difficult to sustain. On the other hand, the identification of the Augustan complex as part of a villa gains credence in the light of the remarkably close analogy drawn above with Varro's Casinum villa, and with some features of the Vesuvian gardens. The presence of a Campanian-style country house, with luxurious elements like the keeping of songbirds and eels, would be entirely appropriate in a place with attractive waterfalls and much natural woodland along the valley slopes. There may indeed have been no attached farm at this time, as would appear to be the case with the contemporary villa of the Volusii at Lucus Feroniae (Moretti and Moretti 1977).

Who then was its owner? Here we must stress again the epigraphic links with Veii and Rome (Gil-

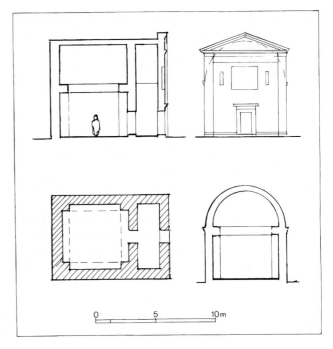

Fig. 37. A possible reconstruction of the mausoleum or temple-tomb. *(SG)*

liver 1990; this volume), which surely hint at a wealthy *dominus* mainly based in either, or both, places. Indeed, one is bound to wonder whether the recovery of the Augustan tomb monument of C. Valerius Faustus, a *mercator bovarius* and a *magister Augustales* at Veii, does not by extraordinary chance reveal the owner of the place. Cattle merchants were prosperous people, to judge from the ancient sources (Gilliver 1990: 195 n. 9): to take one example, C. Caecilius Isodorus, *libertus*, left 3,600 pairs of oxen, 257,000 other cattle, and also 60 million sesterces in cash when he died in 8 BC (Pliny, *Historia Naturalis* xxxiii. 135). Faustus, an important public official, was also doubtless a wealthy man. Naturally, it is very speculative to suggest this correlation; but the fact that most of this very large funerary monument was found suggests that it cannot have been brought far, and we have shown that the area was a focus for tombs. At the very least, the possibility should not be ignored.

Around the Trajanic or Hadrianic period (and the fragility of the dating evidence requires emphasis), there are manifest signs of change. The original phase 1 entrance was blocked by a bath-house, a new paved road was constructed, and for the first time significant quantities of rubbish were being generated, albeit much of it of high quality. Later a temple-tomb of some elegance was built on the ridge overlooking the main complex and, to judge from the absence of any features in the surrounding bedrock, stood in isolation. We may reasonably infer that Monte Gelato remained a favoured place in the Antonine period, whose inhabitants ate much pork, young and tender chickens, and delicacies such as dormice and thrushes. Educated Greek slaves numbered amongst them, as the signed drinking vessel (the 'stork-vase') and various graffiti attest, and it may be significant that more than a quarter of the second-century wine amphorae derive from Greek-speaking parts of the east Mediterranean, especially from the island of Kos (Arthur, this volume). It is probable, however, that a working farm now lay nearby. Although the plant remains do not suggest crop growing in the immediate vicinity, the amphorae include a locally produced type, P105, which accounts for ten per cent of the wine amphorae in the early second century, and 65 per cent in the later second century. When coupled with other evidence for pottery production, amongst which is the signed drinking vase (an unusable waster), it is clear that the manufacture of ceramic vessels, including wine containers and, presumably, the making of the wine itself, was an important industry in the region. Pottery-production sites are indeed known nearby (Peña 1987), and the site at the Mola di Monte Gelato is likely to have been a particular focus for this activity. To infer that a *pars rustica* had been added to the *pars urbana*, if so far unlocated, has decided attractions.

The demise of the villa was, on the other hand, almost certainly abrupt. The evidence is set out in more detail in the next section, but consistently presents a picture of torn-up mosaics, demolished walls and hypocausts and the smashing of sculptures and architectural elements. Much was thrown into features like the cisterns and fish-pond. While a crude tile floor in the lobby may belong to this period, much of the complex must have become ruinous and, we suspect, abandoned.

The dating evidence indicates that this probably took place in the Severan period (although the bath-house may have been properly demolished in the fourth century, as will be shown). Whether this was a single event is not clear, for it is possible that there was a slight time difference between the material filling the top of the fish-pond and that in the north cistern. Yet it is inherently more plausible to suppose that the destruction was contemporaneous, and seemingly wanton (although there is nothing to indicate that the buildings were burnt down).

It would be easy to read too much into these observations. Many villas entered a period of demise around this time, not least in South Etruria (see, for example, Kahane, Murray Threipland and Ward-Perkins (1968: 152) on the Ager Veientanus), and broader economic and social factors certainly played their part. The demolition may have been no more than a prelude to a planned rebuilding of the complex which, in the event, did not materialize. Nevertheless, it is striking that this site, which was clearly patronized by high-ranking people, should have been so systematically destroyed, probably in an epoch of considerable political upheaval. Severus's purges of the aristocracy became notorious (Birley 1971: 279-80), and many will have owned land near Rome; indeed, the grandfather of Severus had a property *in solo veiente* (Statius, *Silvae* iv. 5), on the Via Cassia, only some 2.0 km to the south of the Baccano crater (Becatti *et al.* 1970), or a mere 7.0 km from Monte Gelato. It does not, therefore, seem otiose to offer the suggestion that the Roman complex at the Mola di Monte Gelato might at this time have been the possession of an aristocratic Roman citizen, who fell into disfavour in the Severan period. The slighting of his villa may have seemed a just dessert.

THE LATE ROMAN SETTLEMENT (PHASE 3) (FIGS 38 AND 39)

Following the apparently drastic work of demolition at the end of phase 2, it is likely that occupation ceased altogether. Six third-century coins were found, but hardly any identifiable pottery of the period between *c.* AD 225 and 325/50. This may simply be accounted for by the fact that rubbish was being dumped elsewhere; but this does not seem a very satisfactory explanation, and a sharp reduction in activity, and probably abandonment, seems a preferable interpretation. Only in the lobby to the north of the large room (A), where a tile floor and drain may have been laid at this time, is this picture contradicted; but these may well have been short-lived alterations.

Reoccupation, accompanied by extensive building-work, probably began in the second quarter of the fourth century, and certainly by *c.* AD 350. Coin-loss was thereafter quite prolific and, despite the absence of any large dumps of refuse, like that which filled the fish-pond, there were considerable quantities of late Roman pottery. This makes the dearth of third-century material all the more striking. Likewise, there is little that is identifiable which post-dates the mid to late sixth century, until the construction of the early medieval ecclesiastical buildings in about AD 800: the implications of that are explored in the next section.

The complexity of the late Roman features and stratigraphy is such that each area requires detailed discussion. Most have a number of sub-phases, which are not always easily related across the site: no comprehensive matrix is feasible, although an attempt to compare the absolute chronologies of each part of the site is made at the end of this section.

BUILDING TECHNIQUES

The Roman walls display a wide variety of constructional techniques, brought together for comparative purposes in Figure 40. The work of the early

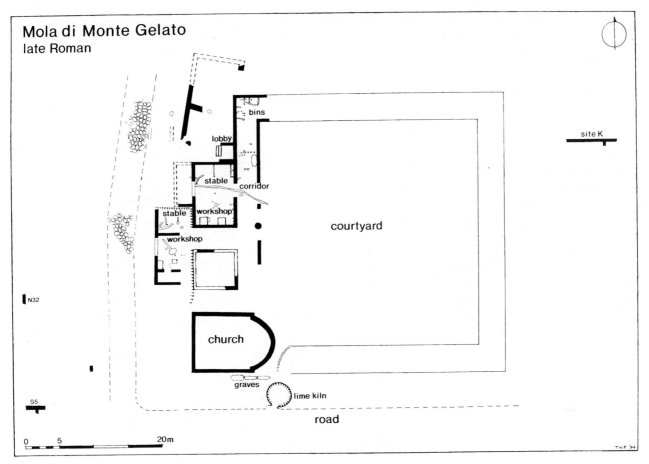

Fig. 38. General plan of the late Roman features of phases 3 and 4. *(TWP)*

Imperial period, when *opus reticulatum* and then brickwork were employed, stands out as sophisticated and urban; just the fish-pond, constructed in the first century AD with *tufelli* (albeit rather neatly), looks like the addition of a local jobbing builder. The *opus reticulatum* was well-preserved only in the northwestern corner of the corridor, but was extensively used, as a spread of its distinctive blocks all across the main site clearly shows. Brickwork, discussed above by DeLaine, was confined to the bath-house and the mausoleum or temple-tomb. This is an indication that building-work was on a comparatively limited scale in the later first and second centuries and, the bath-house apart, involved no additions or alterations to the main complex.

The remaining walls (Fig. 40,g-l) were all constructed with *tufelli*, whether with or without tile courses. The *tufelli* can be divided into three main types: (a) with very neatly cut blocks, 80 mm in height; (b) being rather less tidy work, but also with course heights of 80 mm; and (c) where the blocks are much less regular, and have course heights of 0.13 m. Wall M22 (Fig. 40,k), which stood to a considerable height, used string tile courses, although in an untidy way so that they were rarely flush with the *tufelli*. The other walls were much less well preserved, and the use of tile courses cannot therefore be excluded.

The majority of these walls appear to have been built in the fourth century, as will be shown below. The only relative sequence is found on the lower terrace, where wall M40 (Fig. 40,j) butted against wall M22 (Fig. 40,k), and was clearly later, and conceivably of the fifth century. Likewise of later date was a rough foundation of tufo, tile and mortar, overlying a bath-house wall (Fig. 27 and, below, Fig. 59 (M158)); this could also belong to the fifth century, although only the crudeness of the work commends the date. Otherwise it is hard to know what significance should be attached to these relatively slight variations in style. They may reflect the use of different builders, or small differences in date. The availability of materials may also have been a factor.

With no good evidence in the late Roman period for the use of wall-plaster, and fairly unsophisticated building techniques (including much use of wood), one is left with the clear impression that this was local work of a very functional kind. Indeed, a collapsed section of walling, described below in connection with the large room (A), presented a very heterogeneous mixture of materials, quite possibly as a result of later repairs. As we shall see, this is entirely consistent with the equally functional interpretation that can be placed upon the use of the various areas and rooms. The late Roman building techniques employed at Monte

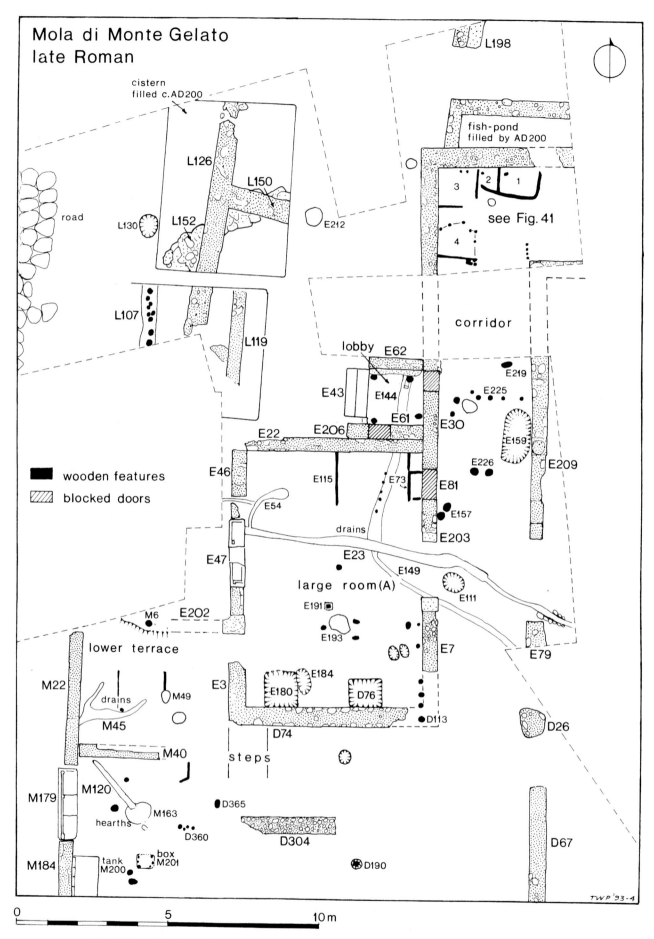

Fig. 39. Detailed plan of late Roman features in the northern and central part of the main site. *(TWP)*

Gelato are thus a useful yardstick of rural styles in this area of the Campagna, and may in time help to shed light on how the local building industry operated in late Antiquity.

THE CORRIDOR

The better-preserved sections of corridor, around the northeastern side of the courtyard, yielded considerable evidence for structural additions in wood in the late Roman period. Most striking was a series of timber features in the northwest corner (Figs 41-3). Made up of narrow slots and stake-holes, cut into the *cocciopesto* floor, they appear to represent four small bin-like structures, built up against the *opus reticulatum* wall which forms the back of the corridor. The constructional details are as follows (Fig. 41).

(1) This bin measures 1.2×0.9 m, with continuous slots on three sides (L179D). The slots varied in depth from 50 to 100 mm. In the wall face above the western slot was a socket, 0.24 m in width and 0.14 m in depth; it presumably held a horizontal pole as part of the superstructure, and probably had a counterpart on the eastern side, where the wall had been cut away (Fig. 43). There was one possible stake-hole.

(2) This structure is 0.75×0.6 m. On the west side was a free-standing slot (L179C), 1.0 m long and 80 mm deep; above it there was a further socket, 0.2 m in width and 0.11 m in depth, for a horizontal pole. The southern slot curves inwards in a curious manner, terminating so as to leave a small gap between it and L179C. One small stake-hole was identified.

(3) In the corner of the corridor, slot 179C combined with another slot (L179B) to enclose an area 1.2 m square, but with an entrance 0.5 m across. Slot 179B was 0.77 m long, and only 30 mm deep. There was a possible socket in the wall face above it, but other holes in the north face of the reticulate may not be deliberate (Fig. 43). There were two possible stake-holes.

(4) A feature, made up of a slot (L179A) and stake-holes, measured $1.2 \times c.$ 1.0 m. The slot was 40 mm deep, and with three stake-holes at the end, 90-150 mm in diameter and 90-150 mm in depth. Two lines of stakes made up the north and east sides (L181): these ranged from 90 to 130 mm in diameter, and 80 to 140 mm in depth.

There was also a line of stake-holes, running north-south, to the east of feature 4.

Function and date

The shallowness of the slots and stake-holes shows that these structures cannot have stood to any great height: these features served to anchor the footings rather than to provide vertical stability. As such they would have been well suited for wickerwork screens, which may have been permanent, or moved at will. Wickerwork structures are well known from waterlogged Roman military sites in the northern provinces, where they served a wide variety of purposes: in addition to buildings, they included the lining of pits and wells, and features such as animal pens (for examples, McCarthy (1991: 19-20)).

The Monte Gelato structures seem too small to have been pens, and we might tentatively suggest that they were built as bins, for the storage of agricultural produce. They may again appear rather small for such a purpose; but they would have afforded a measure of protection for sacks of,

for example, grain or olives. Certainly an agricultural purpose seems the most appropriate interpretation of these features.

A spread of ash suggests that these structures were eventually burnt, although not apparently *in situ*, for there was no charcoal in the slots or stakeholes. Above was a layer of silt, and then a deposit of rubble (Figs 25 and 44); this included the statue of Venus (below, Fig. 141), and much *opus reticulatum* and wall fragments in brick, and a partially articulated piglet. There was also an ARS stamp of the late fourth to mid-fifth century, and colour coated ware and coarse-ware (cat. 157, 170c, 173) probably of comparable date. This was in turn covered by a plough-damaged layer with traces of hearths, burnt red in colour, as well as post-holes (e.g. L161), some 0.5 m above the *cocciopesto* floor of the corridor. One hearth, in the northwest corner, yielded pottery of fifth- to sixth-century date (L144, L145). This area of the corridor would therefore appear to have become ruinous in the fifth century, perhaps implying a fourth-century date for the wooden features. There was, however, clearly some reoccupation after the collapse of the walls.

THE CENTRAL AREA OF THE WEST CORRIDOR (FIGS 39 AND 45)

The wall (E209) bordering the east and north sides of the corridor saw considerable modification during its lifetime. It would seem to have begun as a colonnade, to which a dwarf wall was subsequently added. It was then enlarged to a width of 0.48 m (the commonest module on the site), by the addition of *tufelli* type B (Fig. 40,h), and some tiles.

The corridor floor in the northern part of site E was notably worn, much more so than in the section with the wooden (?)bins. It was also cut by a number of pits, post-holes and stake-holes, as follows (Figs 39 and 46).

(a) E219. An isolated post-hole, 0.22 m diameter, 0.12 m deep.
(b) E225. An east-west partition wall, made up of six post- or stake-holes, averaging 0.1-0.12 m in diameter. They were relatively shallow, and were probably inserted from a higher level. Immediately to the south was the base of a shallow pit, 0.12 m deep, and another post-hole.
(c) E159. A large pit, 1.88×0.8 m, with straight sides and a depth of 0.33 m. It had a silty red-brown fill, with charcoal, tile fragments and sherds of the later fifth and sixth centuries (cat. 169, 185).
(d) E226. Two adjacent post-holes, each some 0.35 m in diameter, in the centre of the corridor. Since only the bases remained, they were probably cut from a higher level.
(e) E157. Two post-holes by the corridor wall; diameters 0.17 and 0.22 m; depths 0.18 and 0.19 m.

On the floor was an accumulation of dark deposits, including a succession of hearths, burnt to a bright red colour (Fig. 47). These lay mainly in the area of the large pit (E159), although the area to the south was sufficiently damaged by ploughing to have removed any comparable traces: but no post-holes were identified in this area. Pottery of the fifth-sixth centuries was associated with these hearths.

These vestiges suggest that part of the corridor was used for domestic occupation, sufficient to cause severe wear to the *cocciopesto* floor. Wooden structures were put up in what

was probably a delapidated Roman building, and eventually the floor became buried beneath refuse. Subsequently, as the section (Fig. 47) clearly shows, this was engulfed by fallen wall (including *opus reticulatum*) and rubble, in the latter part of the sixth century, or later.

STRUCTURES OVER THE CISTERNS

The pottery from the north cistern leaves little doubt that it was filled in in the late second or early third century (although see below). There must have been extensive demolition at the time, for the fill included many fragments of wall-plaster, mostly very small, but bearing traces of purple, yellow, green and red paint: some appeared to show yellow and white flowers, with green stems. There was also a fragment of a tufo cornice, probably of late Republican or early Imperial date, from the top fill (below, Fig. 161).

The much shallower south cistern, only the base of which survived, is likely to have been filled in at this time too (as was the nearby fish-pond). Indeed, it may already have seen some modification for on its eastern side were the vestiges of a footing (Fig. 39, L119), 0.43 m wide, on the same alignment as that of the cistern wall. It survived only as lumps of tufo, set in a poor mortar, and there was a spread of mortar to the west. No onward continuation of the wall was noted outside the cistern (although plough damage had been severe), and, as already noted in the previous section, it may therefore be part of a modification or refurbishment in phase 2. Alternatively, it may belong to a later structure, all other elements of which have been destroyed.

Quite certainly later than the cisterns is a complex of wall-footings, again preserved only within them (Figs 26 and 48). These take a quite different alignment from that of the cisterns or main Roman buildings, quite possibly because of variations in the level of the bedrock, which rises to a prominent (and very plough-damaged) hump between the eastern and western sides of site L. Stratigraphically, the earliest footing was a crudely built mass of bluish grey tufo lumps (including some broken-up pieces of masonry blocks), laid out in a northeast-southwest direction across the bottom of the north cistern (Fig. 39, L152). Bonded with some mortar, this would seem to be an inelegant attempt to lend stability to the footings that were built across it. Indeed the base of the wall L126 partially lay on fill, rather than on the cistern floor; 0.51 m in width, it comprised roughly-shaped pieces of tufo, together with fragments of tile, set in a grey-buff mortar. Coursing was negligible, as with the footing for wall L150, which was laid out across the foundation (L152), at a somewhat approximate right angle to L126, heading east.

Traces of wall L126 were apparent on the floor of the southern cistern, and a large post-hole (E212) could mark the onward continuation of wall L150. However, the rest of the building had been largely destroyed. The only hint may

be a two-phase foundation (L198), where one wall had been added to another, to the north of the fish-pond. As with the foundations built across the cistern, this was aligned slightly to the east of north, in contrast to the other Roman buildings. All may therefore have belonged to the same structure, although its overall plan must remain conjectural.

Dating evidence is not abundant. The only clues are provided by a possibly fourth-century coin (cat. 31), not more closely datable, and two pieces of fourth-century glass (cat. 83, 85). All were in the upper fill of the cistern, adjacent to the walls, but a direct association cannot be asserted. Otherwise, the only other late Roman material was a small group of sherds (L146) from the top fill of the cistern in the northeastern corner. They belong to the fifth-sixth centuries, and may have been deposited in an area of subsidence.

One other feature requires mention. This is a shallow, flat-bottomed trench, 0.4-0.5 m in width, running in a north-south direction, and cut into the floor of the southern cistern (Fig. 39, L107). On the base were traces of what may have been impressions of wooden posts, quite closely spaced. The trench proved to be on the same alignment as a large possible post-hole (L130, although this yielded only Republican pottery), and, 9.0 m to the south, with another post-socket (M6), 0.15 m in diameter, and only 0.1 m deep. It is possible, then, that there was a wooden fence, bordering the road, along the top and upper terraces.

THE LOBBY

The so-called lobby, or vestibule, which gave access to the top terrace, underwent a series of major changes in the later Roman period. Originally floored in white mosaic, this was largely broken up, and a drain (E144) was laid north-south across the room (Figs 39, 47, 49). Its northern limits are unknown, but to the south it took a line across the large room, out through the doorway and across the corridor into the courtyard. The lobby drain consisted of a gully, 0.3 m wide, containing a *tubulus*, 0.11 m in diameter; one length of *tubulus* was preserved *in situ* (Fig. 50), but the rest had been subsequently stripped out. The drain was then filled in with earth and debris (including many fragments of tesserae from the mosaic floor), and sealed with concrete. Given that the lobby was recessed into the tufo, its purpose must have been to reduce the build-up of water behind the north wall of the room.

Covering the drain was a tile floor, a small part of which survived intact (Fig. 51). It included two complete tiles, one 0.39 m square, the other 0.42 m square, and many smaller fragments. A wall 0.43 m in width (E61) was built across the southern entrance and the drain, leaving a narrow doorway, 0.66 m in width. It butted against the corridor wall (E30) to the east, and against the rock-cut wall (E206) to the west. The construction utilized an irregular combination of pieces of tufo blocks and fragments of tile, set in a grey mor-

---

Fig. 40. Masonry styles. (a) *Opus reticulatum*, Augustan, site L. Scale division: 0.5 m. (b) Wall E30, west side of corridor, *opus reticulatum* and *tufelli* quoins, Augustan. Scale divisions: 0.1 m. (c) Fish-pond, west face, original masonry (?Augustan) and upper repair. Scale divisions: 0.5 m. (d) Fish-pond, north face, latest repair. Scale divisions: 0.5 m. (e) Mausoleum, west wall, probably Antonine. Scale division: 0.5 m. (f) Bath-house, wall A9, probably early second century. Scale exvisions: 0.1 m. (g) Blocked doorway (E81) in west side of corridor wall (E30). *Tufelli* type A, fourth century. Scale divisions: 0.5 m. (h) Northeast corner of corridor, wall L196. *Tufelli* type B. Fourth century. Scale division: 0.5 m. (i) North wall (E62) of lobby. *Tufelli* type B. Fourth century. Scale division: 0.5 m. (j) Wall M40, beneath baptistery entrance wall. *Tufelli* type B. Fourth century. (k) Wall M22, on lower terrace. Fourth century +. Scale divisions: 0.1 m. (l) North wall (E22) of large room. *Tufelli* type C. Fourth century +. Scale divisions: 0.5 m. *(KW/TWP)*

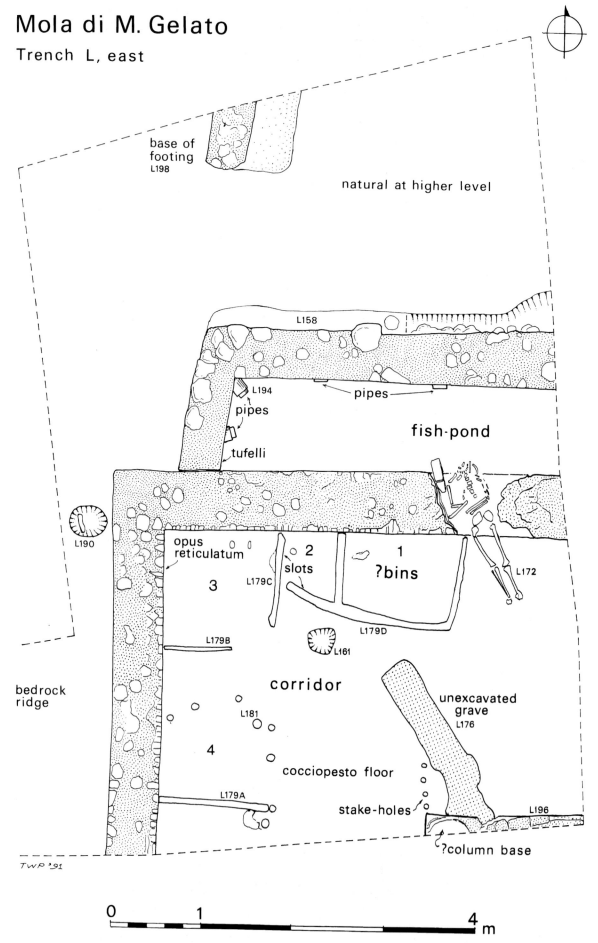

Mola di M. Gelato

Trench L, east

base of
footing
L198

natural at higher level

L158

L194

pipes

pipes

tufelli

fish-pond

L190

opus
reticulatum

3

2
slots

1
?bins

L179C

L172

L179D

L181

L161

corridor

unexcavated
grave
L176

bedrock
ridge

4

cocciopesto floor

stake-holes

L179A

L196

?column base

TWP '91

0   1   4 m

Fig. 41. Features in the northwest corner of the corridor around the courtyard. *(TWP)*

Fig. 42. The northeast corner of the corridor, with the fish-pond beyond, looking northwest. Also visible are the grooves for late Roman bins and a medieval grave: cf. Figure 44. *(KW)*

Fig. 43. As Figure 42, showing the holes for horizontal timbers of the bins cut into the reticulate walls. *(KW)*

Fig. 44. Fill with fifth- and early sixth-century pottery over the corridor in site L; the ranging pole rests on hearths. *(KW)*

Fig. 45. The western corridor and the large room (left) at the end of excavation, looking north. *(KW)*

Fig. 46. View looking southwest across site E, with the lobby (right) and the large room (left). In the foreground is the corridor, pit E159 and post-holes and stake-holes of late Roman date. *(KW)*

tar, an uncharacteristically shoddy piece of work for this site. It must have stood, however, to some height, since two contiguous post-holes (E177, C178) would appear to have supported scaffolding.

The north wall of this phase was totally obliterated by a later rebuild, described below. Nothing can therefore be said of its position or character. There was, however, some stratified datable pottery. The tile floor sealed sherds of the first-second centuries, while the fill of the gully for the drain contained pottery broadly describable as mid-Imperial. Whether these are contemporary or residual is not clear, for building-work at this time is contradictory to the general

impression of widespread demolition in the Severan period, followed by little or no occupation. It is an enigma that is not really resolved.

A post-hole (Figs 47 and 50 (E155)) was subsequently cut through the drain, making a large hole in the pipe. With a maximum diameter of 0.18 m, and a depth of 0.3 m, it held a fairly substantial post, and was matched by a second post-hole (E161), 0.17 m in diameter and 0.45 m in depth, a short distance to the west (Fig. 49). Both were in close proximity to wall E62, built along the north side of the lobby, and may have held scaffold posts. The wall (Fig. 49) rested on a conspicuous offset (E93), 0.4 m high, which projected

E, north section

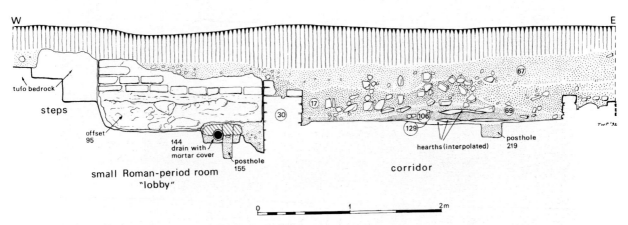

Fig. 47. Section across the lobby and corridor.
For the features in the lobby, see text. Layers over corridor: 67: grey-brown silty loam. 17: a layer of rubble, including *opus reticulatum* and wall-plaster, presumably collapse from wall 30. 69: dark grey silt with late Roman pottery. 106: dark grey-brown silt, with sixth-century pottery, underlying a hearth. 129: red-brown layers of hearths, with fifth- to sixth-century pottery. 219: post-hole with dark brown fill. *(TWP)*

Fig. 48. Late Roman walls built into the north and south cisterns, looking north. Note the modern plough grooves under the ranging pole. *(KW)*

Fig. 49. The lobby looking east. *(KW)*

Fig. 50. The pipe, cut by a post-hole (E155), in drain E144 in the lobby, looking north. *(KW)*

Fig. 51. The tile floor covering the drain in the lobby, with the large room beyond, where a wooden partition (E115) is visible running under the ranging pole. Looking southwest. *(KW)*

some 0.3 m beyond the line of the wall; it was roughly built with lumps of orange tufo, set in a grey-white concrete. Above was the wall itself, with fairly regular *tufelli* (type B), also in orange tufo and with courses of 80 mm. The offset partially blocked the lowest rock-cut step, and is thus clearly later. The wall, on the other hand, was built flush with the northern end of the stairway, showing that it must have continued in use.

The doorway in the corridor wall was blocked up, also using orange *tufelli* in a grey-white mortar, and with courses of 80 mm. This is likely, therefore, to be contemporary with the north wall of the lobby, E62. In addition, the door in the south wall was filled in with tufo lumps, tile and greyish mortar, and a second wall (E22) built against it, as the north wall of the adjoining large room. The construction consisted of somewhat irregular, roughly faced *tufelli* (type C) in a yellow tufo, with course heights of 0.13 m, and a width of 0.47 m.

Although the masonry style of the north and south walls of the lobby differ, they would appear on stratigraphical grounds to have been built at the same time. It may be, therefore, that it was the availability of materials that dictated the form of construction: reuse of older masonry was, after all, a commonplace of the period. This does not, however, explain the doubling of the width of the south wall of the lobby, which is not repeated elsewhere in the large room that adjoins it. The answer may well be that the inner wall, E61, was partially demolished to make an offset that matched that on the north wall: these offsets would then have provided supports for a wooden floor, as their common level also implies.

No doorway into the large room or the corridor was found but, with a raised wooden floor, these would have been at a level that would have been destroyed by ploughing. Indeed, it is the absence of a door threshold that increases the likelihood of a floor of planks, raised some 0.4 m above the earlier floor surfaces. The fill over the tile floor, but beneath the level of the offsets, yielded two coins of AD 353-8 (cat. 14, 15), and pottery of broadly similar date. A mid to late fourth-century date is thus implied for the construction. In the latest fill were sherds of the fifth-sixth centuries, although again with no associated floors.

THE LARGE ROOM (A)

Whilst this room always retained its plan as a substantial enclosed space (measuring 5.7 × 8.18 m in its final phase), the walls underwent considerable modification. This may have been of a rather piecemeal nature, however, since fallen sections of *opus reticulatum* (in places with *tufelli* additions) in the lower terrace to the southwest indicate that some of the original masonry did remain into late Roman times. The details of the walls are as follows (Fig. 39).

North wall (E22)

As described above, this was rebuilt, probably in the mid to late fourth century, in irregular *tufelli*, apparently in front of the original wall, although at floor level (Fig. 40,l). Little trace remained of the first wall, since this end of the room had been recessed into the bedrock; this was badly damaged by ploughing over the higher shelf where the original wall had stood. Towards the east end, the tufo had been shaped into a masonry block, 0.46 m in width (E206); but nothing else survived.

West wall

This was poorly preserved, and consequently difficult to divide into phases. The northerly section (E46) was cut out of bedrock, on the top of which were traces of tile and mortar, which gave the appearance of a rebuild of an earlier footing, 0.46 m in width. A drainage channel, running westwards from drain E54, had later been cut through it. The wall adjoined a threshold (E47) of grey tufo, 2.18 m in length; the blocks had been recessed so as to leave a rim on three sides, and there were two sockets for the doors to swing on. This would appear to have been inserted, since it overlay drain E23 (itself quite a late feature, as will be shown). The central part of the threshold had subsequently been cut away.

To the south of the threshold, the wall continued as a footing 0.47 m in width, with two courses, 80 mm high, of *tufelli*, and a course of tile. It thus resembles wall M22, on the lower terrace (below, Fig. 55), which is of fourth-century date. It terminated in a block of upstanding bedrock, 0.65 m in width, so that it projected to the west, where wall E202 continued that line. There was mortar and tile on top, and it seems probable that this was the jamb for a doorway that provided access to the lower terrace. In the fill over the terrace, immediately to the west of the large room and close to this doorway, there was a fallen section of masonry with an opening for a door (or possibly a window). The opening was at least 0.7 m in height, and the wall was built with irregular *tufelli*, with course heights of 80-100 mm, together with pieces of tile (Fig. 52). Its appearance is thus somewhat different from the neater construction seen in the footings of the wall to the north of the jamb, described above.

After a gap of 1.0 m, suitable for such a door, the wall (E3) continued as a rock-cut foundation, with some mortar and tile on top. This was a rather wider foundation, 0.55 m across, and was of one build with the south wall, D74.

South wall (D74)

The footing was built of tufo lumps and mortar, 0.55-0.6 m across, and, together with E3, would appear to be relatively early in the sequence. Its foundations were fairly shallow, with a depth of 0.2-0.3 m. Indeed, the east end of the wall, together with the southern end of the east wall (E7), had disappeared completely. That this is not due to modern agriculture is clear from the fact that a line of six small post-holes (D113) ran down the west side of wall E7 and across the foundations of D74. Averaging 0.15 m in diameter, they were mostly rather shallow (Fig. 53 shows the shallowest), and were probably therefore cut from a higher level, which had been destroyed by ploughing.

East wall

A small section of the east wall, opposite the lobby, retained its original *opus reticulatum* construction with traces of red-painted plaster (Fig. 40,b); but the rest of the wall was constructed in different techniques, representing subsequent rebuilds. The neatest masonry lay on either side of a tufo threshold block (E81), in the northeast section of the wall (Fig. 40,g). The block measured 1.02 × 0.46 × 0.29 m, and was flanked by carefully cut *tufelli*, with course heights of 80 mm. Four courses were preserved, two being at foundation level. The doorway was subsequently blocked, although only a layer of grey-white mortar survived as evidence of this.

Fig. 52. The upper and lower terraces, showing the fallen door (or window). Left: pit E180 (fill: E179) at the south
end of the large room, and the early medieval pottery kiln. *(KW)*

Almost exactly in the centre of the wall (taking wall E61 as the original northern limit) was a second entrance, 1.8 m in width. This was opposite a still wider entrance from the courtyard, and these spacious dimensions may well imply that they were intended to allow access to carts (which, on the evidence of the ruts in the rock-cut road, had axle widths of about 1.2 m), or large animals like horses and cows. Indeed, given the absence of threshold blocks in either case, these may have been arched entrances, without a permanent door. Both features seem to be original, since there were no traces of earlier foundations although, given their shallowness, one cannot be certain.

The entrance had, however, undergone modifications, for the southern jamb, a concrete block, 0.58 × 0.5 m, and a tufo block beyond, were both very clearly later insertions, overlying drain E149. Further to the south, little of the wall (E7) remained, apart from some mortar, and it then petered out completely, to be replaced by the line of posts referred to above (D113).

The interior of the large room

A number of white tesserae, incorporated in later features, shows that the room probably was once paved with a mosaic: subsequently it was provided with a *cocciopesto* floor. In the northern part, this was laid directly on bedrock and, in places, had worn completely away. To the south, where the bedrock sloped down, there was a variable amount of make-up, incorporating pottery of the later second to early third century (E130). Overlying this were at least two phases of flooring, albeit of a rather patchy nature. However, close to the south wall, there was a clear sequence (Fig. 53). Three pits had been cut into the bedrock, all being dug subsequent

to the construction of the wall (Fig. 39). Two adjoined the wall, and were carefully made with an almost square plan. Pit E180 measured 1.13 × 1.18 m, and was 0.98 m in depth; pit D76 measured 1.19 × 1.28 m, and was 0.8 m in depth. They both were filled with a brown tufaceous soil, somewhat darker at the bottom, and contained considerable quantities of tile and other building material. Pit E180 (fill: E179) also yielded a glass jug of late first- to mid second-century date (cat. 26), smashed upon the floor, and much other glass of a similar period, as well as some pottery of the fifth century. The sherds from pit D76 appeared somewhat later, and probably belong to the earlier part of the sixth century.

Both these pits were sealed by the second phase of *cocciopesto* flooring, grey in colour (Fig. 53). There was some make-up, and over pit D76 this included the statue of a nymph (below, Fig. 142), which had been placed upside-down, so as to utilize the flat surface of her base. This work must have taken place, on ceramic evidence, in the sixth century. Later, pit E184 was cut through the floor and part of pit E180. Measuring 0.9 × 0.7 m, and 0.69 m in depth, it yielded some late Roman material in the upper fill, and was certainly prior to the early medieval pottery kiln, built in the late eighth or early ninth century.

Near to these pits was a hearth (E193), surrounded by a cluster of post-holes. One of these, E191, was particularly well made, being carefully packed around with a square arrangement of tiles; the post-pipe was especially clear, 0.12 m square and 0.27 m deep. The other post-holes were smaller, ranging in diameter from 0.1 to 0.16 m, and in depth from 0.13 to 0.21 m; one had tile packing. Evidently there was some sort of wooden structure around the hearth, although interpreting its nature from these vestiges is not possible. However, it is worth noting that there was bronze-

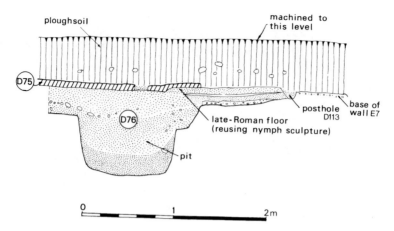

Fig. 53. Section across a late Roman pit, D76, and the southeast end of the large room.
D75: grey *cocciopesto* floor, with some layers of makeup. D113: one of a line of post-holes cutting the wall footing. E7: mortar base of east
wall of large room. D76: pit with brown tufaceous fill, darker at the bottom; much building material and sherds of the sixth century. *(TWP)*

casting waste (cat. 41) in the overlying fill, and also a lead
ingot (cat. 90). Metalworking is probable, and it may be that
the two pits, E180 and D76, were connected with this. They
would certainly have been capable of holding water, being
rock-cut, although other functions such as storage cannot
be ruled out. Indeed, it is not impossible that the glass from
pit E180 was intended for recycling.

In the northern part of the room there were some other
features, including two drains. The earlier (E144, E149) is
the same as that already discussed in connection with the
lobby. There was a section of collared pipe, of the same type
as that found in the lobby, and also white mosaic tesserae in
the fill. It was clearly built before the reconstruction of the
north end of the east wall (E7), but cannot be dated closely.

Cutting across the earlier drain was drain E23. This ran
east-west across the large room, and out through the main
entrance into the courtyard. It comprised a rock-cut trench,
some 0.2 m deep, and sealed by a tile and concrete cover
(Fig. 23,c). This lay at the base of a larger channel, of variable width, which appears to have functioned as an open
drain. A shallower drain (E54) fed into it from the north,
and there was also another narrow channel which headed
westwards through wall E46.

Drain E23 was evidently laid out prior to the construction
of the wide threshold (E47) in the west wall, and also cut
across the *a cappuccina* drain (D11; Fig. 23,a, E143) bordering the courtyard. It relates, therefore, to the last main
period of use of the large room, and its fill contained sherds
of the fifth-sixth centuries, confirming its late date.

There were also wooden features in the northern part of
the room. A slot (E115) that ran southwards for 1.85 m
from the north wall, must surely have held some sort of timber partition. It was 80 mm in width, and 0.11 m in depth
and, perhaps coincidentally, was aligned with a stake-hole to
the south of the late drain (E23), and the possible metalworking hearth. In addition, in the northeast corner of the
room was an arrangement of slots, averaging 0.11 m in
width and 0.12 m in depth. Together they form two rectangular boxes, measuring overall 1.4 × 0.4 m (E73). They are
thus not dissimilar to the supposed wooden bins in the
northwestern part of the corridor, although more regularly
laid out, and may indeed have been for storage. However,
they are just as readily explained as the foundations for animal feeding troughs, especially if the partition was for a
stall. This would also make sense of the considerable provision of drains, and of the worn nature of the floor in this

part of the room. In short, we might suggest that here was
a stable (or perhaps a byre for cows), to which there was
easy access through the wide entrance from the corridor.
Indeed, Amanda Claridge noted that all the many pieces of
marble veneer from the room were covered with some sort
of concretion, perhaps deriving from urine.

As a whole, therefore, the room appears to have been
adapted as a stable in the northern part, and a workshop
area to the south. This also provides a context for a number
of iron tools, found both in the room and just to the south.
These included a pruning or reaping hook and a linch pin
(cat. 23, 25) from within the room, and a metalworking
hammer and two axe-adzes (probably for woodworking)
from just outside (cf. cat. 12-17); there was also a bronze
harness mount (cat. 25). Coin evidence indicates a sixth-
century date for these objects. Here would seem to be
ample evidence to sustain the functional interpretation
advanced above.

Chronology

On the evidence already set out, the large room saw modifications to the north wall in the second half of the fourth
century, and repairs to the floor in the south part of the
room in the sixth century. Deposits on the floor yielded two
coins of fourth- to fifth-century type (cat. 34, 35), a lamp
(cat. 59) of *c.* AD 450-550, and pottery of late fourth- to mid
sixth-century type (e.g. cat. 163, 171). Occupation, albeit
increasingly squalid, must have continued to at least the
mid-sixth century. Still later may be the line of posts (D113)
cut across the totally demolished wall-footings in the southeast corner; for these, however, direct dating evidence is
wholly lacking.

THE LOWER TERRACE

The stratigraphy over the lower terrace was deep, and largely undisturbed by modern intervention. It was, however,
extremely complicated, and not every question can be satisfactorily resolved, partly because of the overlay of later foundations, but also because it was never possible to expose the
whole complex either in one operation, or completely. Nevertheless, the overall sequence is clear, and mirrors a change
from a bath-house, to rooms serving agricultural/industrial
purposes and, ultimately, to ecclesiastical structures.

The abandonment and destruction of the bath-house

In common with the entire site, from the bath-house there was virtually no pottery and only five coins which can be dated to the period between *c.* AD 225 and 325. As stressed earlier, with so few rubbish deposits, this may not be significant; but, on the face of it, there was a considerable scaling down in activity for most of the third century, and the bath-house is likely to have gone out of use during this period. The detailed evidence is as follows (cf. Fig. 28 for the room numbers).

Room 1

The hypocaust had been removed to the sub-floor level, over which was late fourth- to mid sixth-century pottery (cat. 156).

Room 2

Prior to the removal of the hypocaust, there were some alterations, including the insertion of a roughly built length of wall of tufo and mortar (Fig. 27; A24), possibly as a floor support. A further stretch of wall (Fig. 27 and below, Fig. 54; A40), was also inserted, and ran northwards through the hypocaust in room 3. It was made up of tile and mortar, and faced in places with tile. The hypocaust was then stripped out to sub-floor level, on which was a fourth-century lamp (cat. 54), and fifth- to sixth-century coarse-ware (cat. 162, 178a).

Room 3

A *tubulus* was inserted as an additional floor support, apparently after the deposition of a coin (cat. 10) perhaps of third- or fourth-century date. Part of the upper floor of the hypocaust was then dug away and, in the fill between the *pilae*, were coins of AD 330-5 and 353-8 (cat. 12, 13). There was also a copper-alloy vase of fourth- to fifth-century type (cat. 15), laid on its side in earth by a *pila*, and well under the floor. Although lacking a handle, and slightly damaged, this handsome object (below, Fig. 170) must still have been of value, and was surely concealed rather than being a casual loss.

Room 4

The hypocaust remained intact (but without a mosaic, a fragment of which survived in room 3). A wall-trench perhaps for a sill-beam (Fig. 27, D165) contained a coin probably of the fourth century (cat. 28), and there was another coin of fourth- to fifth-century date (cat. 41) from the room.

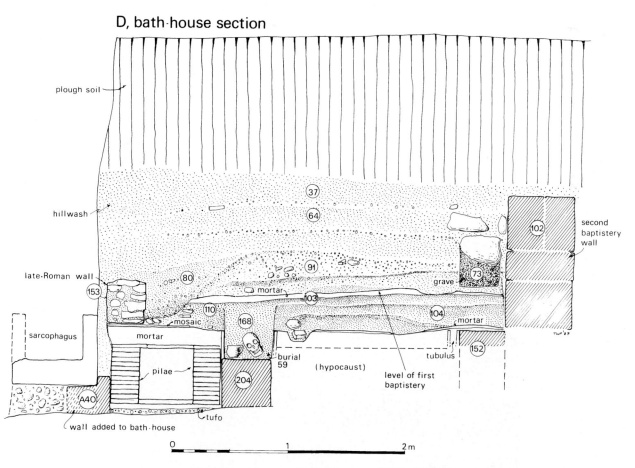

Fig. 54. Deposits over the bath-house, as in Figure 32.

37: hillwash. 64: dark brown hillwash with sixteenth-century pottery. 73: burial with a few very mixed bones. 80: a probable robber trench cut down to the late Roman wall; brown-grey silt fill, and sherds of the eleventh century; it would appear to pre-date the cutting of burial no. 73, but this may not be a correct reading of the sequence. 91: brown-yellow tufaceous fill with a grey silt lens in the middle: this might represent a turf-line. Some ninth- to tenth-century pottery. 103: surface of whitish mortar, of the same appearance as that used in the floor of the first baptistery which is on the same level. 104: layers of grey soil with ash and burnt orange clay; within the deposit were areas of tread; fifth- to sixth-century pottery. 110: soil and rubble beneath 103. 168: burial no. 59, of the late sixth to early seventh centuries, cutting the late Roman deposits, and sealed by the first baptistery surface. 153: late Roman wall on the bath-house mosaic; = M184/22, to the north. 152, 204: bath-house walls. A40: wall (or feature) of broken tile and mortar; a later Roman insertion, but not closely datable. *(TWP)*

Corridor and drain, Room 5

The drain had been broken open at two points, and contained a fourth- to fifth-century coin (cat. 39), and coarseware of the fifth and/or early sixth centuries (including cat. 179).

Room 6

The cold plunge mosaic was partially covered by a cement foundation, over which was a coin of AD 364-78 (cat. 18), and pottery of the fifth-sixth centuries (cat. 176, 180B; amphora cat. 47). Features in the floor to the east contained fourth- (cat. 16) and fourth- to fifth- (cat. 42) century coins, as did the overlying layer (cat. 21, 33, 38, 43).

Room 7

To the west, the *cocciopesto* floor had been largely stripped out, and covered with a dump of pottery probably of the mid-fourth century (M87: pottery Group 4 (see below), cat. 126-31). To the east, the north wall was completely demolished, and there was a coin of AD 249-50 (cat. 4) in the fill.

Whilst it is possible that room 7 (the *apodyterium?*) may have been pulled down before other parts of the bath-house, the evidence suggests that most of the demolition work took place in the earlier part of the fourth century (although allowance must be made for the lengthy period of circulation of fourth-century coins, often well into the fifth century: Reece 1984).

The late Roman building (Fig. 39)

The structure that followed was built over the northeastern part of the bath-house, and consisted of perhaps three rooms or enclosed spaces. The main wall (M22, M184) ran

for a minimum distance of 10.3 m, in a north-south direction. It was 0.4 m in width, and stood to a maximum height of 0.76 m. It was constructed with one or two courses of *tufelli*, with course heights of 70-80 mm, separated by a single course of tile (Fig. 55); these jutted out conspicuously, especially on the external side of the wall. There was no foundation trench, the wall being built either upon the bath-house mosaic, where it survived (Fig. 56; Fig. 54, D153), or upon the bath-house *cocciopesto* floor. Approximately in the centre was a tufo threshold, 2.3 × 0.65 m, with a deep groove and three sockets for door pivots (Fig. 57). Interestingly, the steps which once went down into the cold plunge of the bath-house, were now reused to gain access to the road. Part of the mosaic was mortared over to make a bottom step, covering what had once been a fine and carefully laid floor. This seems evocative of changed priorities.

The northern end of the wall (M22) terminated against the bedrock forming that end of the cut for the lower terrace. There was no trace of a return to the east, unless the east-west wall (E202) along the edge of the upper terrace could have been utilized (although, with no foundations, we might wonder whether wall M22 could have stood that high). There was, however, a southern east-west wall close to the door threshold (M40): 0.4 m in width, and up to 0.4 m in height, it was built of *tufelli* (type B: Fig. 40,j), resembling those of wall M22. But there was no use of tile coursing, and the walls butted rather than being bonded; two phases of construction are implied, with M40 apparently being the later.

The eastern end of this room was not completely excavated, and it is not clear whether there was a wall here; but no traces of such a wall were identified to the south, and the face of the cutting may have served instead. If this was also the case with the north wall, then it is possible that this was

Fig. 55. Late Roman wall (M22) on the lower terrace, looking west. *(KW)*

M, south section

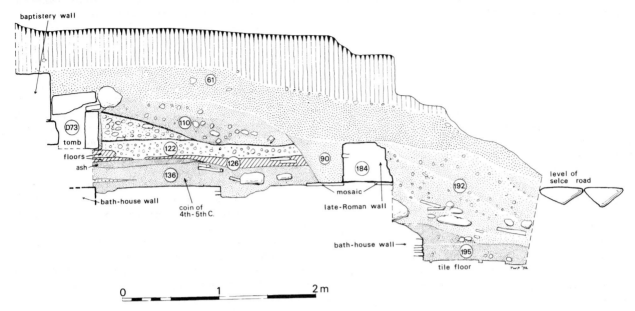

Fig. 56. Section across room 3 of the bath-house.

This section in most respects mirrors that on the north side of D (Fig. 54). 61: hillwash with much residual material as well as sixteenth-century pottery. 90: trench cut down to the wall, presumably to rob it. 110: brown tufaceous tips, with mortar. 122: layers of pale yellow-brown soil with much tufo rubble, probably connected with the construction of the second baptistery; cut by burial D73. 126: rough floor surfaces with yellow mortar; on the level of the first baptistery floor, and probably connected with it. 136: thick deposit of grey-brown silt, with ash and a mortary lens; late Roman pottery and coin. 184: fourth-century wall, built on bath mosaic of *c.* AD 100. 192: tips of brown tufaceous silty fill. 195: dark grey ashy silt, over the sub-floor of the bath-house. *(TWP)*

Fig. 57. View looking south down the late Roman complex on the lower terrace. Note the drains, partitions and post-holes, probably a stable, cut into the floor in the foreground, and the threshold for the doors beyond. *(KW)*

an unroofed enclosure, *c.* 4.5 × 3.5 m, presumably with an entrance at the unexcavated eastern end of wall M40. More probably, however, it was provided with a relatively simple cover of wood or thatch.

Within this enclosed space were a number of features, cut into the floor. There was one distinct north-south slot, terminating in a substantial post-hole (M49), with another large post-hole, *c.* 0.3 m deep, nearby (Fig. 57). There were also traces of a second parallel groove, 1.5 m away, with a post-hole 0.18 m deep nearby. Shallow channels led from the compartments created by these slots, and became part of a larger drain (M45), whose outlet was a hole, cut through the base of wall M22, at some point after its construction. The whole arrangement is therefore reminiscent of the features in the northern part of the large room on the upper terrace, and interpreted as a stable for horses or mules, or perhaps a byre for cows or oxen.

To the south was a second room where access was provided by the wide threshold (M179) in the western wall. Evidence for an eastern wall was lacking, although this is the area where there appears to have been a staircase of wide steps to the upper terrace (Fig. 39), albeit now very eroded. The south wall appears to have reused a bath-house wall, on which was grafted a rough foundation of tufo, tile and mortar (Fig. 27, M158). This is quite the crudest Roman masonry on the site, and should represent an alteration that is significantly later than the period of construction of the walls described above. Even so, a doorway, 0.9 m across, was subsequently inserted into the middle of the wall, and later blocked up. This implies modifications to the building over a not inconsiderable period of time.

The evidence therefore indicates that this was probably a roofed room, which measured internally some 4.5 m square. The floor also preserved a number of features. Most conspicuous was a narrow trench (Figs 39 and 58), 2.0 m in length, 0.25 m in width and 0.3 m in depth (M120). It was placed diagonally across the northern part of the room, and

the fill contained much ash and burnt tufo, as well as a coin of AD 355-63 (cat. 16). It was flanked by two post-holes, one very shallow and probably later, and the other 0.2 m in diameter and 0.3 m deep. At the southeast end (where the trench became shallower) was a sunken area containing burnt material from a large hearth (M163), including some slag. This has not been analysed, but is characteristic of metalworking. This suggests that the trench may have been designed as a flue for a metalworking hearth. Indeed, in related deposits were found bronze-casting waste and offcuts, including one from a mirror (cat. 12).

In the southern part of the room, the floor was very worn, and contained two possible post-holes (Fig. 59). However, the most prominent feature was a slightly recessed rectangular area, 1.25 × 0.8 m (M200), in the southwest corner of the room. It had an unworn concrete floor, and a tile lining, 0.2 m high, on the west side. We would suggest that this was the base of a tank, probably for water, used in connection with the metalworking. It also yielded a coin, of the fourth-fifth centuries (cat. 42). There was in addition another, less well defined, rectangular feature, *c.* 0.5 × 0.4 m, nearby (M201). There appeared to be posts around the sides, and it probably held a timber-lined box.

A few other features were observed on the east side of the room, although the pattern of excavation meant that these were not fully exposed. These included a post-hole and three stake-holes in a line (D360), another post-hole (D365) and a short length of slot (Fig. 39). Whatever their function, they are witness to a space that was used intensively.

Reference has already been made to the iron tools found in a sixth-century context in the corridor on the upper terrace, which led to this room. These included what is probably a metalworking hammer, and axe-adzes or mattocks, perhaps for woodworking. From the lower terrace rooms, in late Roman contexts, came two chisels (cat. 20, 21), a punch/point (cat. 22), a spoon auger for drilling holes in wood (cat. 19) and a joiner's dog (for clamping timber

Fig. 58. The central part of the lower terrace with the entrance to the baptistery complex, overlying a late Roman room with a workshop and, beyond, the bath-house plunge and paved road. *(KW)*

Fig. 59. The southern part of the lower terrace, showing the baptistery entrance wall (right),
and tank (M200) and the late Roman wall M158. Looking west. *(KW)*

together) (cat. 27), as well as a pruning knife (cat. 23) and
a knife (cat. 24). Such finds are in harmony with the structural remains, and leave little doubt that adjoining a stable
(or byre) was a workshop (where carpentry was clearly practised), as in the larger room on the upper terrace. The
emphasis on woodworking is especially interesting in view of
the widespread use of timber structures on the site, and
there are also signs that bone objects were also being made,
to judge from characteristic offcuts.

Much less can be said about the possible room to the
south. The southern end of the western wall had been cut
away although, as noted above, an east-west return in wood
may be represented by a shallow trench, D165 (Fig. 27).
This would have created a space with a width of less than
1.5 m, indicating that it was little more than a lean-to, built
up against the workshop. There were two post-holes on the
south side of the wall (Fig. 27, D159, D161), but no other
signs of construction (although this area was much disturbed by early medieval walls and burials).

Deposits over and adjacent to the late Roman rooms

In the north room, or stable/byre, the stratigraphical
sequence was relatively simple (Fig. 60). The floor was
covered with a thin deposit of soil, up to 40 mm thick, which
was in turn buried beneath a loose mass of collapsed wall
(some with plaster, retaining faded traces of paint), and tile
(Fig. 61). Up to a metre in depth at the eastern end, this
included both *opus reticulatum* and *tufelli*, and the section of
door or window from the large room (Fig. 52). Two of the
complete iron tools (cat. 19, 24), were found in this deposit and another collection of iron objects in comparable
condition came from the tile collapse over the steps. A mid-
sixth-century date is evident from the finds (see below).

Whatever caused this collapse, it seems clear that the
stable or byre was functioning until that date, since one
would otherwise expect a much deeper accumulation over
the floor. The sequence from the adjoining room, the workshop, was quite different, however (Figs 62 and 63). Here
deposits began to accumulate rapidly, especially in the centre
of the room over the area with the presumed metalworking hearths. A layer of dark silt (M97), some 0.2 m thick,
overlay the floor, and included a series of hearths within it.
It also yielded a coin of AD 364-78 (cat. 21), and two other
coins, probably of the fourth-sixth centuries (cat. 38, 47).
This was in turn sealed by an area of floor (M94), with a
coin of the fourth-fifth centuries (cat. 36), above which
were further hearths and a dark ashy layer (M93); these
were associated with fifth- to sixth-century pottery (cat.
170b, from an adjacent area to the north). These were also
covered over by a layer of make-up for a floor (M86), which
yielded fifth- to sixth-century pottery (cat. 167b), and a
lamp (cat. 60), which may date to the seventh or eighth century. However, there was also kiln waster material of the
ninth century, which, together with stratigraphical considerations, indicates that this floor (which was not continuous
over the whole area) should relate to the construction of
the medieval entrance to the baptistery. This suggests that
the late Roman deposits may have been truncated (see
below).

To sum up, therefore, the workshop remained in constant use well into the sixth century, causing a significant
build-up of hearths and deposits in the centre of the room.
Whether it retained its original function is uncertain, but
the iron tools suggest that it did. There are indications that
the door may have been narrowed, for there was a thick
layer of mortar over the southern threshold block; this
would be consistent with the alterations to the south wall of
the room, described above.

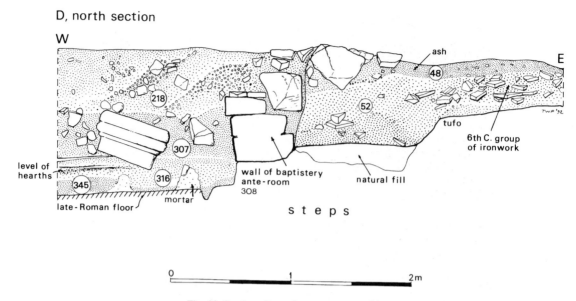

D, north section

W

ash
48

E

218

52

tufo

307

6th C. group
of ironwork

level of
hearths

316

wall of baptistery
ante-room
308

natural fill

345

mortar

steps

late-Roman floor

0   1   2m

Fig. 60. Section along the entrance corridor.

right: 48: an ashy layer, with remains of a collapsed wall (D247) at the west end; sixth-century pottery. 52: a layer with a collapsed tile roof in the upper eastern part, with mid-sixth-century pottery and coins; below was a homogeneous fill over a staircase of wide steps leading to the lower terrace.

left: 218: tips of tufaceous soil, rubble and tile, and much residual kiln waster material. 307: dark grey-brown fill, with masonry and rubble; lamp of *c.* tenth-century. 308: wall of *c.* AD 1000. 316, 345 (also including 337, 339): a complex series of deposits with fifth- to sixth-century material, and hearths (338) just to the south of the section, here interpolated; there is a stratigraphical gap between these layers and those of the tenth century + above. The upstanding lumps of mortar on the floor appeared to belong to some sort of sub-circular feature (364). *(TWP)*

Fig. 61. Section of fallen wall, *c.* AD 550, over the lower terrace. Note the peeling wall-plaster on the left-hand side. *(KW)*

Fig. 62. The entrance to the baptistery complex looking east over the Roman door threshold.
Compare with Figure 63. *(KW)*

Between the building and the road, there was also a steady accumulation of silts, containing pottery and coins datable to between the mid-fourth and mid-sixth centuries. There is nothing, however, to suggest that the road went out of use, and a coin of AD 268-70 (cat. 6) from beneath the paving may hint at repairs, as does a fifth- to sixth-century coin (cat. 52), and pottery of the same period (L138) from the upper fill of the roadside drain in site L to the north (Fig. 23, b). Other coins associated with the road include two fourth-century issues (cat. 17, 19), and four other fourth-century coins (cat. 24-7) which, although technically unstratified, had been dropped on or beside it.

The destruction of the building

As described above, the northern area of the lower terrace was filled with collapsed walls and roofing tiles, which had fallen from the upper terrace above. The deposit did not extend into the adjoining workshop to the south, although a collapsed roof did cover a large part of the corridor leading to the upper terrace (Fig. 60). As has been shown, both this layer and the debris over the northern part of the lower terrace yielded complete iron tools in identical condition, and the two deposits are surely contemporary.

The deposit over the lower terrace yielded sherds of fifth- to sixth-century type. The tile layer in the corridor contained two coins of Justinian I (AD 527-65, cat. 54, 55) with medium wear, and a coin of fourth- to sixth-century type (cat. 49) from an ashy layer immediately above. There was a further coin of Justinian I and one of Baduila (Totila) (AD 541-52) in later, but nearby, deposits, in the baptistery (cat. 56, 57). There was also a useful group of pottery (Group 5, cat. 132-44), of the early to mid sixth century. We can therefore infer that the collapse took place around AD 550 or

perhaps a little later, to allow for the moderate wear on the coins.

One other deposit is relevant to this discussion, namely a pit in the later baptistery (below, Fig. 84, D86). Although stratigraphically later than features of the ninth century, it was partially filled with large sherds, used as packing in a post-hole. These form a homogenous group of the mid-sixth century or later (pottery Group 6, cat. 145-53), and there are even joins with sherds from the collapsed roof. One can only suppose that this was refuse dug up in the course of later construction work, which was then reburied in this pit.

THE LATE ROMAN LIMEKILN (FIGS 64 AND 65)

In 1987, the edge of what was eventually revealed as a large limekiln was identified at the southern end of the main excavation. It bordered, and had partly been cut away by, the modern road, itself probably a widened version of a Roman predecessor. The kiln had thus been set into a sloping bank of tufo. This was an expedient that was not uncommonly adopted – for example, at Saint-Martin-du-Tertre (Coudray 1951) or at Brugg in Switzerland (Gessner 1907) – and helped to protect the kiln from the wind (cf. Cato, *De Agricultura* xxxviii), as well as facilitating the loading of the stone, and the unloading of the lime.

The work in 1987 was confined to cutting a section on the northeast side of the kiln. Amongst other things, this brought to light undamaged fragments of inscriptions and the head of the freedman C. Valerius Zetus. Given that other fragments of what turned out to be the great funerary monument of four freed-people were visible, but inaccessible, in the section, and that time was running short, it was decided

M, east: chronology

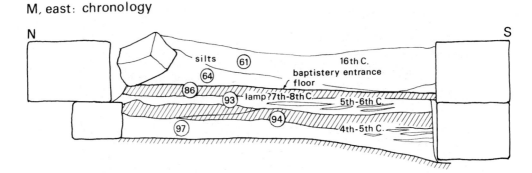

M, part of east section

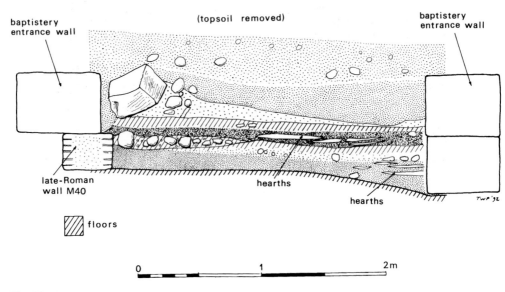

Fig. 63. The deposits and their chronology in the area of the baptistery entrance, over the lower terrace.
61: hillwash with much residual material and sixteenth-century pottery. 64: pale tufaceous rubbly tip, from the north. 86: floor and make-up in an orange-brown tufaceous deposit; late Roman pottery, a lamp of the ?seventh-eighth centuries and kiln waster material of the ninth century. 93: grey, ashy deposit with a series of hearths, burnt orange-red; fifth- to sixth-century pottery. 94: two phases of floor, in a pale brown-orange tufaceous material, with some mortar and rubble; one fourth- to fifth-century coin. 97: grey-brown silt, with a series of hearths, burnt orange, at the south end; one fourth- and two fourth- to fifth-century coins, and late Roman pottery. 40: wall, resting on the late Roman *cocciopesto* floor. *(TWP)*

to backfill the excavation as securely as possible, and reopen it in 1988. Security was naturally a worry and, when the investigation was resumed, it had to be carried out as speedily as possible, to avoid drawing attention to the find. In this we were successful, but it did mean that it was not practicable to cut a full half-section across the deposits filling the kiln. Although this would have been desirable, in the event it hardly mattered, for the fill divided essentially into three layers.

(1) (C51) The upper fill comprised a deposit over 1.0 m deep of soft, loose brown loamy silt. It contained much tile and tufo lumps and broken blocks, and also fragments of *selce*. The other finds included the tufo inscription F]ACIVND[VM (cat. 2); a possible piece of medieval sculpture (cat. 16); a clay mould (cat. 144); a lead dolium tie (cat. 54); and nails, wall plaster, glass (cat. 135, 136) and pottery of the early to mid fifth century.

(2) (C59) The main fill of the kiln consisted of a soft light grey brown deposit, nearly 3.0 m in depth. Laboratory

examination by Dr I. Freestone showed that it was made up largely of friable fired white lime, with sparse fine charcoal inclusions. In this deposit were the pieces of the tomb monument. It had been broken into about 32 large fragments, with some twenty more much smaller lumps. Most of the inscription and a considerable part of the upper section, including two of the four heads, were present (below, Figs 135 and 136), but they exhibited no fire damage. They were found in the area between the stokehole and the centre of the kiln, but not towards the other side. Here were numerous compacted lumps of heavily burned marble, including one piece which resembled a fragment of statue with a raised arm. It is possible, therefore, that the last firing was localized and thus incomplete; certainly, it was not wholly successful. Otherwise, the only finds were some broken column tiles, again not damaged by fire, and some pottery, also unburnt, of the fourth century.

(3) (C69) At the base of the kiln was a layer of fine black ash, between 50 and 70 mm in depth.

Fig. 64. The limekiln at the end of excavation, looking north across the stoke-hole. *(KW)*

The structure of the kiln

The kiln was circular in shape, with a diameter of 3.9-4.0 m (to include a slight undercutting). Its maximum surviving depth was 4.0 m, with a rather conical profile. The stoke-hole lay on the road side of the kiln, as one would expect, but nothing was preserved of it except for a U-shaped cut into the tufo. It lay some 2.0 m above the base of the kiln.

At the level of the flue was a damaged but still prominent ledge, known as a *fortax* (Dix 1981). Built on a rock-cut shelf, on average this was about 0.3 m in height, and consisted of an underpinning of tufo and limestone blocks or lumps, surmounted by horizontal tiles, set in grey mortar. At its maximum, it projected out some 0.25 m, but much of the ledge, as it survived, was much narrower. In places, it appeared to have been patched with tufo lumps.

The purpose of this ledge, as excavations of the legionary lime-plant at Iversheim in Lower Germany clearly showed (Sölter 1970), was to support a wooden framework, probably held in place with vertical props. Over this was placed the charge of stone to be burnt, laid as a rough arch (Sölter 1970: fig. 4). When the wooden framework had burnt away, the charge became self-supporting. The fire pit below also became the repository for the ashes (as recommended by Cato, *De Agricultura* xxxviii), and acted additionally as a 'turbulence domain', to enhance the efficiency of the firing (Dix 1982: 336). The considerable depth of the pit (nearly 2.0 m in the case of the Monte Gelato example) served to prevent the ash from impeding the burning of the lime, or from contaminating it: the ancient authors were at pains to stress the dangers of introducing impurities, especially through using unsuitable stone (Vitruvius, *De Architectura* ii.

5.1; Pliny, *Naturalis Historia* xxxvi. 53), and it was clearly desirable to avoid mixing the lime and the ash.

Kilns of this sort are described as 'periodic' or 'flare' kilns, where burning was not continuous. The lime was generally produced by means of radiant heat (Dix 1982), and temperatures of between 900° and 1,100° C were required to achieve the process of calcination, depending on the type of stone. Research has shown that the walls of the kiln were sometimes hardened before use to cope with these high temperatures (Jackson, Biek and Dix 1973: 135). This would appear to have been the case in the Monte Gelato example, for much of the wall of the fire pit was coated with a very hard, pale grey tufaceous concretion, which had the appearance of a mortar lining. This also covered the lower part of the ledge in places.

Comparatively speaking, the kiln is on the large size. Cato (*De Agricultura* xxxviii), who has provided the only detailed description of lime-burning, suggested that a kiln should be 10 [Roman] feet wide, 20 feet deep and reduced to a width of 3 feet at the top. With the *p.M.* this would be the equivalent of 2.97 m wide and 5.94 m deep. Most known lime-kilns of Roman date are in fact about 3.0 m in diameter (Saguì 1986: 351), although an example at Ostia stands 6.0 m high and is 4.5 m in diameter (Pavolini 1982: tav. XI, fig. 15), and three very large kilns have recently been excavated near Lucus Feroniae; situated close to the Tiber, they may have provided lime for Rome itself (Gazzetti 1992: 43).

It is uncertain how high the Monte Gelato kiln may have stood, although it is likely to have had a built superstructure which, on Cato's dimensions, could have risen 2.0 m or more above ground. The capacity of the surviving firing chamber is in the order of twenty cubic metres, but this

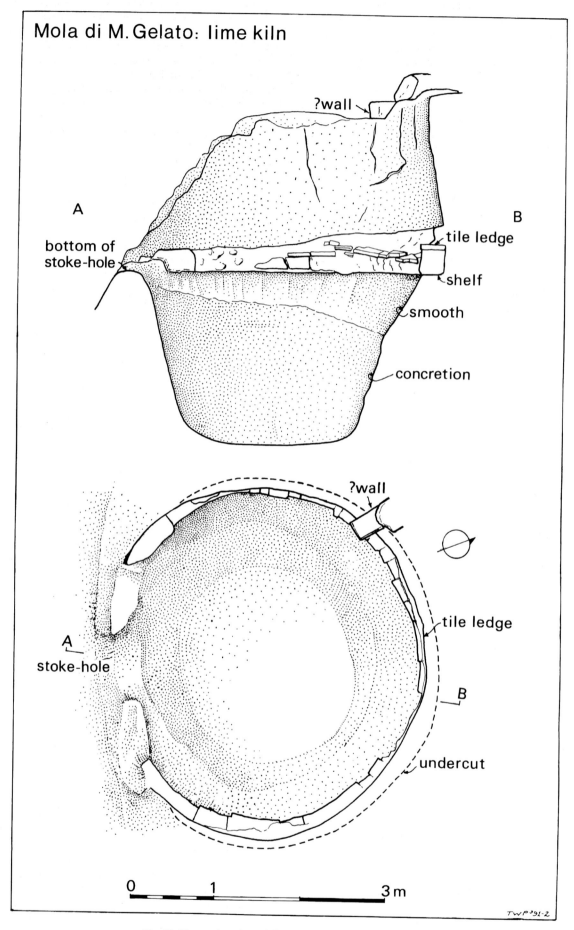

Fig. 65. Plan and section of the fourth-century limekiln. *(TWP)*

could easily have been doubled by the addition of a built top to the kiln. Calculations as to the operating times for kilns of this sort vary. Baradez (1957: 293) estimated twelve days for the kilns at Tipasa (Algeria), including the loading and unloading; but experimental work at Iversheim suggested a longer period of three weeks (Sölter 1970: 39-40).

The Monte Gelato kiln had plainly been used quite often. The ledge in particular was heavily damaged and patched, and the appearance of the walls of the kiln suggested heavy use. The kiln does, however, seem to have stood in isolation. The rest of the rock-face bordering the road was carefully searched for another kiln, but the only possible cut proved to be illusory. This would appear to have been quite normal on country estates (Dix 1982: Saguì 1986: n. 10); indeed, where they are known, banks of kilns were probably employed for specific major building projects, such as the construction of the town walls between AD 145 and 147 at Tipasa (Baradez 1957), and the legionary fortress at Bonn (the Iversheim kilns: Sölter 1970).

The lime had a variety of uses, other than for building (Dix 1982): for tanning, for medicines, and especially for marling clayey land (hence Cato's inclusion of a section about limekilns in his *De Agricultura*). However, the fertile volcanic soils that surround the Mola di Monte Gelato are hardly likely to have required much marling, and it is more probable that the lime was produced for the building industry, especially of Rome itself, with which there were such good road communications.

Rome in late Antiquity was certainly in need of lime. There were several magistrates responsible for maintaining public buildings, and various guilds of workmen, including lime-burners (*calcis coctores*) and carters (*vectuarii* or *vectores*). Jones (1973: 708) noted that the lime needed for these works came from certain specified estates in the provinces of Campania and Tuscia, and that an edict of AD 365 (*Codex Theodosianus* xiv. 6.1, 359) stipulated that the annual requisition should not exceed 3,000 cart-loads, half of which were to be used for the repair of the aqueducts. The workmen were paid one *solidus* per load by the landowners of the estates furnishing the lime (as was their obligation: Jones 1973: 462), although the state contributed a quarter of the sum, and the landowners gained tax exemption.

There can have been no shortage of old monuments of marble and stone to pull down for lime-burning in the Monte Gelato region. Field survey shows that sites abound (Fig. 5), one, probably significantly, bearing the place-name Le Calcare (Fig. 8). There was no prohibition on destroying these structures (*Codex Theodosianus* xiv. 6.3) and, obligations to the state apart, it may have been a not unprofitable sideline on an agricultural estate.

Dating

Some pottery was found, albeit in small quantities. In the top and overlying fills were an ARS fabric C sherd and coarse-ware of the late fourth to early/mid sixth century (cat. 155, 158, 167a, 170a). Given that the sherds are of quite large size, it seems reasonable to take this evidence at face value, and regard the limekiln as a fourth-century feature, with production probably ceasing by the end of that century.

THE LATE ROMAN CHURCH (FIGS 66 AND 67)

A significant addition to the complex in the late Roman period was a church, situated in the southwest corner of the site. It was very poorly preserved, but its ground-plan, with an apse to the east and a nave, is unmistakably ecclesiastical. Its overall dimensions were in the order of 12.4 × 7.6 m externally, the approximate element deriving from the vestigial nature of the footings on the west and south sides. Where they had survived what seems to have been a deliberate razing of the footings when the early medieval church was built, the Roman walls comprised lumps of grey and brown tufo, set in a friable grey mortar. The average width was between 0.55 and 0.6 m, and was thus fairly substantial. A relatively high building may be envisaged, as shown in Sheila Gibson's reconstruction (Fig. 67); this also suggests that there may have been a porch (see also below, Fig. 70, although there is no direct evidence for this, and the fall in the ground to the west may in fact exclude this possibility.

The orientation diverged very slightly from that of the main complex, although whether this was an error or a deliberate feature is a matter for conjecture. The construction of the church certainly resulted in a radical remodelling of the southwest corner of the courtyard complex, obliterating part of the corridor, and an earlier room (Fig. 38). A tile drain (C13) to the east of the apse (Figs 66 and 68) must also belong to this period, as it respects the line of the apse and is cut by the footings of the later church. It was a box drain, made of reused tiles set in a grey mortar. Only the base remained over the surviving part of its course, an indication that all trace of the original floor level had been removed.

The interior of the church had likewise lost every sign of floors and internal fittings. It is impossible therefore to say anything about the nature or quality of its decorations. Similarly, the removal of all deposits associated with the construction of the building rules out any attempt to assign it a close date. The only clue comes from three graves along the southern wall (B24, B26, A16 (Fig. 66) = burials nos. 105-7) which, from their position, may have been contemporary. One (B26) contained a complete pottery vessel (cat. 186), which is likely to be of the second half of the fifth century (or possibly very early sixth century). This is a pointer towards a late Roman date for the church, although no other graves of the period were identified. It is a matter that is considered further in the discussion below.

THE EAST SIDE OF THE SITE (SITE K)

Some 50 m to the east of the corridor, the natural tufo rises in a low cliff, approximately 2.0 m high. In places this had been dressed roughly flat, and in front was visible a short stretch of Roman walling, still standing up to 1.46 m in height (Fig. 69). There was one course of squared *tufelli*, averaging 0.2 × 0.8 m; but most of the wall, as it survives, consists of irregular lumps of tufo and some pieces of tile, bonded in a sandy mortar. The facing has evidently, however, been lost.

The standing wall may be the same as a stretch seen (by TWP) in undergrowth in this area in 1967, but then much better preserved. Photographs show that it had fairly regular coursing of *tufelli* (type A), with course heights of about 80 mm. The construction is thus closely similar to some of the late Roman masonry on the main site, such as the north wall of the large room (Fig. 40,l, E22). Clearly, there were buildings across much of the gently rising plateau in this period.

Excavation (site K: Fig. 38) showed that a length of footing, 0.6 m wide, survived to the west of the standing stretch. This was on a broadly east-west alignment, although there had been some slippage on the sloping bedrock. There were also vestiges of a second wall, laid out at right angles and running southwards.

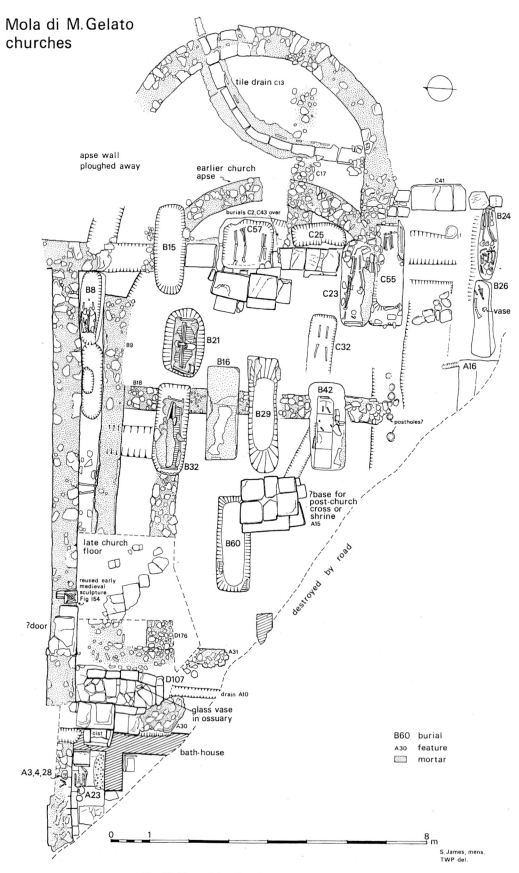

Mola di M.Gelato
churches

tile drain C13

apse wall
ploughed away

earlier church
apse

C17

C41

burials C2, C43 over

B15

C57

C25

B24

B8

C23

C55

B26

vase

B9

B21

C32

A16

B18

B16

B42

B29

postholes?

B32

?base for
post-church
cross or
shrine
A15

late church
floor

B60

reused early
medieval
sculpture
Fig 154

?door

D176

A31

destroyed by road

D107

drain A10

glass vase
in ossuary

A30

cist

bath-house

A3,4,28

A23

B60 burial
A30 feature
mortar

0   1   8 m

S.James, mens.
TWP del.

Fig. 66. Plan of the churches and other features.
Concordance with catalogue of burials: A3:26; A4:26; A16:107; A23:26; A28:26; B8:18; B15:1; B16:12; B24:105; B26:106; B29:13; B32:11; B42:14; B60:17; C2:2; C23:7; C25:3; C32:9; C43:2; C55:8; C57:2; D107:24. (TWP)

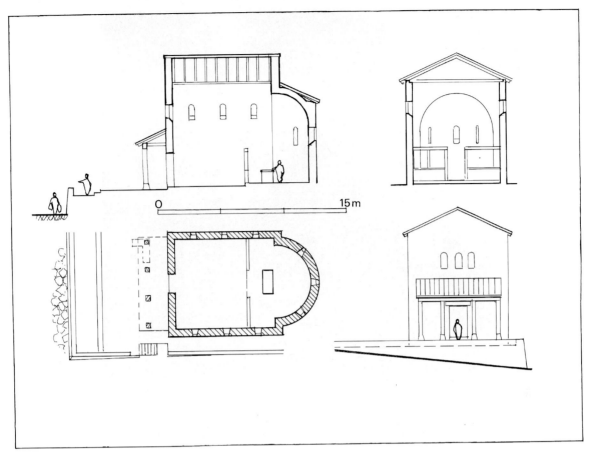

Fig. 67. Reconstructed plan and elevations of the late Roman church. *(SG)*

Fig. 68. The late Roman drain (C13) to the east of the first church; in the foreground, the apse wall of the early medieval church. *(KW)*

Fig. 69. Late Roman wall in site K, looking north; beyond is the natural tufo. *(KW)*

Virtually no stratigraphy was preserved, save for some fallen masonry and rubble, and an area of grey ash and burnt debris (K103), some 80 mm thick. This probable hearth yielded a coarse-ware bowl (cat. 164) of late fourth- to mid sixth-century date. The other datable pottery, from a small assemblage, was as follows: from the topsoil (K101) – ARS 'D', forms 61B (*c.* 380-450) and 67 (*c.* 360-470); two sherds of ARS 'D'; two coarse-ware bowls, late fourth to mid-sixth centuries (cat. 154, 181); two cooking vessels, late fourth- to mid-sixth centuries (cat. 174-78b): layer of rubble and hillwash (K102) – Spatheion amphora, late fifth-early sixth centuries; coarse-ware bowl (cat. 165) and lid (cat. 182), fifth-sixth centuries.

On the basis of this very small sample, occupation in this area belongs almost exclusively to the late Roman period, focusing mainly upon the fifth century, although probably extending into the sixth century. Given that the hearth rested upon sterile deposits, earlier buildings are unlikely ever to have been present, at any rate within the very restricted area that was investigated. However, it should be added that a small intrusion cut into the bedrock a few metres to the southwest did yield some sherds of the second century or later, attesting some earlier activity.

THE WEST SIDE OF THE PAVED ROAD (SITES S AND N)

The lower part of the rock-cut road was filled with a coarse, gravelly silt-sand (Fig. 14, units 12 and 13). It contained few finds, and was almost certainly water-laid. Above it was a layer (11) with much ash, and slag from metalworking. This was in turn covered with a deposit with some rubble, much pottery and window-glass (units 4 and 10), and then layers of rubble, tile, *tufelli* and tufo blocks (units 1 and 3). There was also a dump of ash in these upper layers.

The vast proportion of the pottery from the layers above the water-laid deposits dated between the mid-late second century and the early third century. It is thus of the same period as the dumps filling the north cistern, and the upper part of the fish-pond. However, sherds of ARS form 50A in layers 3 and 10, and forms 58 and 67 in layer 4, show that the dumping cannot have taken place before the early fifth century (and such sherds can hardly have been intrusive in so deep a feature).

The reason for the levelling-up of this area may well reside in the building of one or more late Roman structures, a few traces of which were identified. One wall (Fig. 38, S5) straddled the road fill, on an east-west alignment. In width it was 0.39 m, and was built with a course of tiles (0.45 × 0.39 × 0.025 m), and two courses of roughly shaped *tufelli*; it is thus of similar construction to wall M22 (Fig. 40,k) and clearly late Roman in date. There were traces of another wall at right angles, but it was badly disturbed by ploughing, and nothing can be made of the overall plan.

One other section of walling was found along the western lip of the rock-cut road (Fig. 38 and, below, Fig. 90, N32). Also 0.39 m in width, it too was constructed with long tiles (0.59 × 0.39 × 0.04 m), and courses of *tufelli* (80 mm in height); it is likely to be more or less contemporary with wall S5, and was associated with pottery of the fifth to early sixth centuries. To the west of it were some steps, cut into the bedrock (below, Fig. 90); but its function is wholly unclear, unless it was constructed as a revetment prior to the back-filling of the road. There were also traces of walling in the side of a modern drainage cut, to the east of the rock-cut road, apparently made with *tufelli*.

Although comparatively little excavation took place in this area, it is nevertheless clear that there was occupation, quite possibly on an extensive scale, in the late Roman period. The indications are that the north-south orientation of the main complex was followed, a degree of planning that is perhaps surprising, given the relatively humble use to which the other buildings were put. However, the structures on the west side of the paved road are unlikely to have been any more elegant. Not only were they in a low-lying, uncongenial setting, but there was a complete absence of anything more than the most basic building materials, and altogether very few finds. A utilitarian function is extremely probable.

DISCUSSION

Phase 3 evidently marks a period of renewed activity, on an extensive scale. The bath-house was immediately dispensed with (it may well have been in a ruinous state, after more than a century of neglect), and was partially built over, with a workshop and, in all probability, a stable. The large room was likewise converted into a stable and workshop, bins were inserted into part of the corridor, and a substantial building was placed over the cisterns. A limekiln was also constructed, with a capacity in excess of most known examples, and the paved road was repaired.

The evidence tends to converge upon the mid-fourth century for the beginning of this phase. This is not to say that every building or feature was constructed at the same time (slight differences in masonry techniques perhaps support this); but a broad contemporaneity is indicated. In addition, the evidence of inscriptions on gravestones, found in the excavations of 1875-77, shows that a Christian cemetery was in existence in the vicinity by AD 361 (the earliest dated inscription: Fiocchi Nicolai 1988: 235). There is also an inscription of AD 407, and several more which cannot be closely dated.

The buildings were notably bare and functional, and a far cry from those of a well-appointed villa. It seems reasonable to suggest that this was a settlement of *coloni*, engaged in agricultural, industrial and artisan activities (including the raising of sheep for wool: King, this volume). Indeed, they may have been slaves. We know, for example, that the aristocratic lady, Melania, owned a *massa* near Rome, on which were 62 hamlets, each with about 400 slaves involved in agricultural pursuits (Jones 1973: 793). Even the Church had slaves to run some of its estates, which multiplied enormously in the fourth century. Constantine was particularly generous to the churches of Rome, endowing them with lands which yielded over 400 pounds of gold a year (*Liber Pontificalis* I, 170-201; Jones 1973: 90). Some were in the territory of Veii and some near Nepi (Marazzi, this volume). Given Monte Gelato's

subsequent history as a papal farm, it is legitimate to wonder whether it did not come into Church hands in the fourth century. This would help to account for what seems to be a deliberate repopulation of the site, and is also supported by the fact that a late Roman church was subsequently added. A Christian private owner can hardly be excluded; but to infer that it was an estate developed and administered by the Church has decided attractions (see further Chapter Six).

When the first church was built is, as we have seen, impossible to say, with only a burial containing a fifth-century jar, in a seemingly contemporary relationship, as a pointer (although the demise of the adjacent limekiln, c. AD 400, might be relevant). In Rome, however, the pace of church-building accelerated significantly in the late fourth and early fifth centuries (Krautheimer 1980), and there is no reason to think that this did not extend to the Campagna. Examples may indeed be cited at nearby *Ad Baccanas* (Sant'Alessandro: Fiocchi Nicolai 1988: 106-13), and at the fifth mile on the Via Aurelia, where the church of Santi Nazario and Nabore was constructed in AD 404 (Fiocchi Nicolai 1988: 25-9, 363). The Christian community at Monte Gelato may well have presented itself as an obvious place for a church, especially if already in ecclesiastical ownership. Whilst the dearth of hard archaeological evidence must be stressed, a date of around AD 400 for its construction is at the very least plausible.

Sheila Gibson's intriguing reconstruction of this phase is shown in Figure 70. Whatever the details of the church's superstructure, its symbolic importance is immediately apparent. Whether some of the adjacent buildings really had two storeys is a matter for conjecture; but they would have provided living areas which are otherwise strangely lacking. The overall image, it might be argued, is perhaps too grand in appearance, given the functional activities that went on inside. But, even in Britain, simple fourth-century agricultural buildings could be provided with elaborately decorated façades, as at Meonstoke (King and Potter 1990), and the complex at Monte Gelato may likewise have presented a more elegant façade than the surviving evidence implies.

There were other changes around the end of the fourth century. The limekiln went out of use, leaving part of its last load unburnt, especially the tomb monument of four freed-people (Figs 135 and 136, below). The bins were demolished, and deposits which included a number of hearths began to accumulate in the corridor and large room, and in some areas of the lower terrace. However, both the far eastern side of the site (K), and the area to the west of the paved road (sites S and N), saw the erection of new buildings, probably around this time. Although so little of their plan was recovered that virtually nothing can be said about them, the implication is that the population

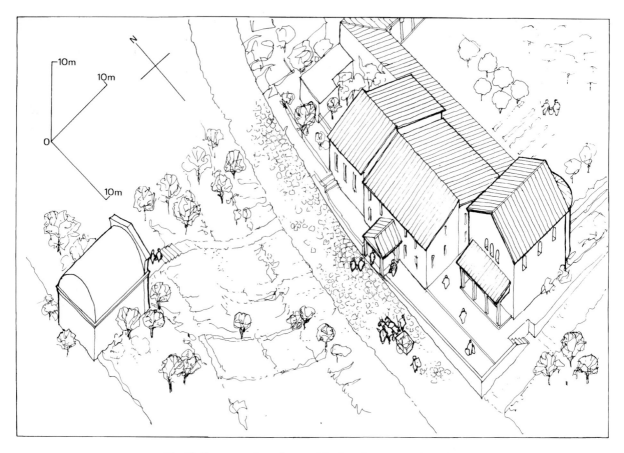

Fig. 70. Reconstruction of part of the late Roman complex. *(SG)*

was expanding, rather than contracting. This was quite possibly as a result of the construction of the church, which may plausibly be seen as an incentive towards enlarging the settlement.

That occupation continued unbroken well into the sixth century is implicit from the finds. There are 24 coins of the late Roman period, four definitely of sixth-century date (three of Justinian I and one of Totila). However, few fine-ware vessels reached the site after about AD 500, although several amphorae of late fifth- to sixth-century type were found. Features in wood, especially partitions and also individual post-holes, often of uncertain purpose, are represented in most areas. While no major structural elements were built in timber, at any rate at ground level, the use of wood was clearly extensive, in marked contrast with the buildings of the early Imperial period. The overriding impression is of a relatively basic existence, perhaps not far removed from subsistence level, for the majority of the population.

There are signs, indeed, that some parts of the building complex may have become ruinous even in the earlier part of the fifth century. Fallen masonry was associated with pottery of this date in the northern part of the corridor, and the deposit was overlain by hearths, probably of the sixth century, and cut by at least one post-hole. Here, therefore, is a clear sign of decay, followed by occupation

of a very run-down kind. The main period of wall-collapse took place, however, around the middle of the sixth century. It is best illustrated by the fallen roof and walls over the north part of the lower terrace, and the collapsed roof in the corridor to the south of the large room. But there was also fallen masonry in the corridor to the east of the large room, overlying deposits with sixth-century pottery, and heavy ploughing may have removed similar layers elsewhere. Only in the workshop on the lower terrace were there no signs of collapsed walls or roof.

There is a temptation to attribute large areas of fallen masonry to a natural disaster such as an earthquake, especially in a region prone to such phenomena. One might recall that tremors of the Tuscania earthquake of 6 February 1971 were felt quite strongly in the Mazzano area, and that Rome has a long history of seismic activity. However, no earthquake is recorded for the mid-sixth century in central Italy (Guidoboni 1989), and there is an absence of tell-tale signs, such as lesions in the walls and floors, at Monte Gelato. Moreover, the areas of wall-collapse do not form a continuous blanket such as occur at, for example, the villa of Patti Marina in Sicily (Voza 1989). We should therefore reject the idea that an earthquake caused the collapse of the buildings at Monte Gelato, and suggest instead that natural decay was entirely responsible.

It is, however, impossible to say how far the church survived these processes, but, with a falling population around, it is unlikely that even this spiritual base could have persisted. As we shall see, when a new church was constructed *c.* AD 800, it was an entirely new building that was erected.

THE SUB-ROMAN PERIOD (PHASE 4)

It is extremely hard to know what happened to the inhabitants of the site at Monte Gelato in the period immediately after the mid-sixth century. There are a few signs of activity, but of so vestigial a kind as to suggest more or less total abandonment. The evidence, such as it is, may be summarized as follows.

(1) A burial (no. 59; below, Fig. 94) contained a vessel of the late sixth or early seventh century (cat. 187), and a radiocarbon date from the bones yielded a calibrated range of AD 565-635 (one sigma: BM-2862).

(2) The collapsed masonry and tile filling the northerly room of the lower terrace was levelled to form a rough *battuto*, in which were visible two probable post-holes (Fig. 71). This surface cannot, however, be closely dated, and could belong to the period of the *domusculta*.

(3) The line of post-holes, D113 (Fig. 39), in the southeast corner of the large room, described in the previous section, clearly belongs to a period when the walls existed as no more than footings.

Yet they perpetuate the line of the Roman walls along the east side of the room, indicating a measure of continuity, although their relative shallowness suggests that they were cut from a higher level. They should belong, therefore, to the period after the mid-sixth century.

(4) The partition (Fig. 39, E225) in the corridor may, likewise, be a very late feature, cut from a higher level.

(5) As noted in the previous section, the workshop on the lower terrace yielded no fallen building rubble, and the south wall (Fig. 27, M158; Fig. 59) was reconstructed in very crude masonry. A lamp (cat. 60), possibly of the seventh or eighth century, was also found in the deposits over the late Roman levels. It is therefore conceivable that occupation may have continued in this room for a time.

(6) In the well-dated stratigraphical sequences (Figs 54, 56, 63, 72), there are no indications of a hiatus between the late Roman and early medieval deposits, such as a turf line. However, the very absence of layers which could belong to the seventh or eighth centuries may in itself be an argument for abandonment, even though one might expect some accumulation of silt on a hillside site.

To these observations must be added the fact that, burial no. 59 and the lamp apart, no pottery of the seventh or early to mid eighth centuries was identified, despite a search made in the light of typologies established for this period by the Crypta Balbi excavations in Rome (for example, Paroli 1992a; Romei 1992; Patterson, this volume). Unless

Fig. 71. Trodden surface with post-holes over the northern part of the lower terrace; the top of the late Roman wall (M22) is visible to the right. *(KW)*

D, bath-house section: chronology

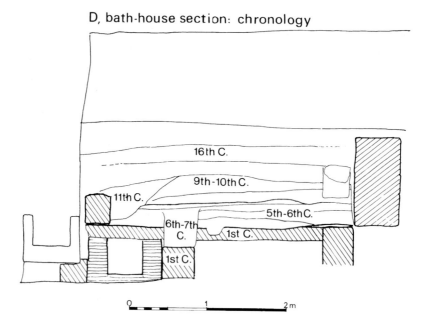

Fig. 72. Chronology of the section in Figures 32 and 54. *(TWP)*

the population at Monte Gelato was by now so destitute that even coarse pottery was beyond its means, it is hard to avoid the conclusion that the site was little, if at all, frequented. This would be a more satisfactory inference if one had any idea where the people might have gone – ironically, since this is one of the questions that the excavation hoped to resolve. But the only alternative is to propose a model where a diminutive population eked out a miserable existence amongst the ruins. For this, as we have seen, there is some very slight structural evidence, but hardly sufficient to make any real case.

THE EARLY MEDIEVAL COMPLEX

INTRODUCTION

Excavation of the main site in the valley bottom brought to light an extensive early medieval settlement. It comprised (1) a church and baptistery, built about AD 800 (our phase 5), and rebuilt and extended about AD 1000 (phase 6); (2) a considerable cemetery, which yielded a minimum of 243 individuals; (3) a pottery production site, albeit of a single kiln, of the late eighth to early/mid ninth centuries; (4) at least one cave habitation, together with others perhaps used for storage; and (5) reuse of the Roman mausoleum, possibly for animals. The Roman road was also repaved, and the existing mill, which is certainly of medieval date, most probably had one or more precursors, given the exceptionally advantageous configuration of the river at this point.

The sculptural finds show that the phase 5 church, of *c.* AD 800, was decorated to the best stand-

ards of the day, and there are other indications that this was a 'high-status' place in this period, with close connections with Rome. It does not seem, however, to have been a nucleated, village-type settlement, and the church probably served a largely dispersed rural community. This role may have been enhanced in the late tenth and early eleventh centuries, when the baptistery was greatly enlarged, the church partially or wholly rebuilt, and other structures added. If so, considerations were by now entirely parochial, and practices, such as the baptismal rite, deeply rooted in tradition. A significant proportion of individuals was probably related, and study of the human remains suggests that this was a hard-working, peasant population. Likewise, the remodelled ecclesiastical buildings would appear to have been plainly constructed, and apparently without internal embellishment.

The ecclesiastical complex was subsequently demolished in a very thorough way, and the main site abandoned. The evidence of the pottery places this around AD 1100, and later material is virtually absent; there is, for example, not a single sherd of archaic maiolica. Only some burials, cut into the ruins, at the base of what may have been a shrine or monument (attributed to phase 7) show that the place was not immediately forgotten. However, by this time occupation had probably begun on the castle site of Castellaccio, built on a hill overlooking the mill complex at the southern end of the valley. The style of the masonry of the mill suggests that this may have been constructed in the twelfth century and, on the evidence of limited trenching, this was also the main period of settlement of Castellaccio (although there is later pottery). It seems entirely reasonable to infer that the population served by the ecclesiastical complex at the Mola di Monte Gelato was moved to Castellaccio, as part of the well-attested phenomenon of *incastellamento* or *accentramento*.

The evidence to support these conclusions is set out in detail in the sections that follow. As with any archaeological interpretation, there are weaknesses and ambiguities in the data, which we shall attempt to identify. Moreover, it is inevitably coloured by Tomassetti's correlation, discussed in Chapter One, between the Mola di Monte Gelato and the *castrum Capracorum* of a bull of 1053, '*cum terris, vineis ... et molaria sua cum ecclesia sancti Iohannis que dicitur Latregia ... positam territorio Vegetano miliario ab urbe Rome plus minus vicesimo septimo*', and with a document of 1128 which describes the church of Saint John as *diruta*.

The likelihood of this correlation is everywhere supported by the evidence assembled in this volume, whether archaeological, art historical (Osborne, this volume), or documentary. Where we must disagree with Tomassetti is in supposing that the estate-centre of the *domusculta* of *Capracorum*, founded by Pope Hadrian I in *c.* 774-6, was shifted from Santa Cornelia, near Veii, to the Mola di Monte Gelato, when Santa Cornelia became a monastery in the early eleventh century. Instead, we shall suggest that our site was part of Hadrian's original foundation, one of a series of farms within the *domusculta* (Wickham 1978: 174), which in this case came eventually to acquire the name of the whole estate. This may in itself be a measure of the relative importance of the foundation at the Mola di Monte Gelato.

The excavations at Santa Cornelia, now fully published (Christie and Daniels 1991), enormously illuminate the archaeology and history of the *domusculta*, and provide important comparative material. Interestingly, our expectation that Monte Gelato would yield a nucleated farm, resembling that at Santa Cornelia, proved to be wholly in error. The ecclesiastical element apart, the two sites were quite differently organized, and the huddle of buildings, many reused from Roman times, around the ninth-century church of Santo Stefano, near Anguillara, provides a closer parallel (Van de Noort and Whitehouse 1992). The histories of Santa Cornelia and the Mola di Monte Gelato would seem, however, to be closely linked. Although for various reasons the *domuscultae* did not apparently survive for long – the last reference to that of *Capracorum* is in 846, when men from the estate worked on the building of the Leonine Wall around the Vatican – both Santa Cornelia and Monte Gelato continued in occupation. However, at Santa Cornelia, although a campanile was added to the church *c.* 875-900, the so-called administrative quarter was burnt down (or so it would seem) in the same period, and lacks evidence of replacement. By the early eleventh century, when a new church was constructed, the site was probably in an advanced state of decay (Christie and Daniels 1991: 186-7). Only with the founda-

tion of a monastery, in *c.* 1035-41, did its fortunes properly for a time revive.

The site at the Mola di Monte Gelato may, likewise, have entered a period of decline after the collapse of the *domusculta*, although there is no specific evidence for this. But it is striking that, as at Santa Cornelia, there was extensive rebuilding of the ecclesiastical complex around AD 1000. It is not impossible that the two events were related, given the similar history of the two sites, and the references in the papal bulls of 1053 and 1128 (if correctly linked with our site) suggest an active and prosperous agricultural community.

There are manifest dangers in approaching archaeological evidence with so conscious a historical model in mind, and this we clearly recognize. On the other hand, it would be foolish wholly to ignore the broader documentary and archaeological background, when it seems to be of such demonstrable relevance. But first the material findings require careful examination, and it is to these that we must now turn.

THE SECOND CHURCH (FIGS 66 AND 73)

The early medieval church was on a slightly different orientation from that of its late Roman predecessor, being aligned more or less exactly east-west. Prior to its construction, the Roman church was razed to its lowest footings, almost obliterating the wall lines in places, especially to the south. As a result it is impossible to say whether the older church was still standing and in use, since its floor and associated levels had been entirely cleared away. Given the lack of diagnostic seventh- and eighth-century material from the site, it may well have been in ruins, unless maintained by a dispersed community, which left little refuse around the church.

The new church was substantially larger than its predecessor. It had a deep apse to the east, internally 4.7 m in length, which was separated from the nave by a cross-wall. The nave measured 10.5 × 8.75 m internally, and was thus relatively squat in plan. There was, however, what we have interpreted as a narthex, or porch, to the west, which was at least 2.8 m in length. Neither the west nor south walls of the narthex survived, so it is impossible to work out its full dimensions; but it would have given a more balanced shape to the building. Yet this interpretation may not be correct. At Santa Cornelia there was no porch, but what may have been a large walled atrium or forecourt in front of the first church (Christie and Daniels 1991: 183 and figs 32 and 33). The nave here was also very squat in plan, measuring internally 13.5 × 14.5 m, and the church at Santo Stefano, near Anguillara, where there may also have been an atrium, is also comparable (Van de Noort and Whitehouse 1992) (Table 2). It is therefore feasible to postulate a similar arrangement at Monte Gelato although, given the way that the ground slopes down to the road in front of the church, a narthex would seem to be the more likely explanation (Fig. 73).

The walls of the church were quite substantial, averaging 0.7 m in width. The foundations were, however, of variable depth. Those of the apse and the south wall were especially shallow, and part of the apse footings had been completely

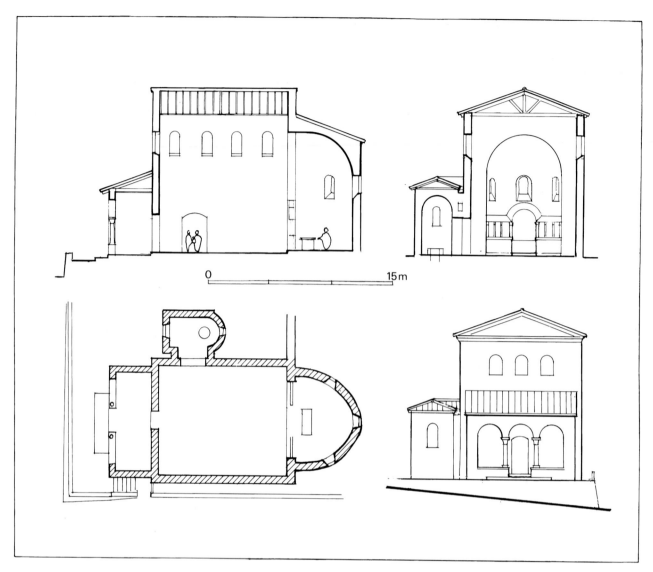

Fig. 73. Reconstructed plan and elevations of the church and baptistery of c. AD 800, phase 5. *(SG)*

ploughed away. The north and west walls were more deeply set, partly to take account of the fall-away in ground level over the lower Roman terrace. The footings mostly comprised irregular pieces of tufo, set in a yellow-grey mortar, now of a rather crumbly appearance. However, the whole area has clearly been subject to constant downslope water percolation since the abandonment of the site; this has had the effect of reducing much of the white marble from the church to a friable texture, and probably affected the mortar in the same way. On the whole, the foundations were well laid, and over the bath-house were taken down to the lowest Roman floor, at least 1.5 m below the probable level of the church floor.

The superstructure is likely to have comprised tufo blocks of variable sizes; some could have derived from a quarry once visible in the cliff face near the mill (Fig. 22). Blocks were certainly used in the footings of the west wall of the nave where it was built against and over an earlier bathhouse wall (Fig. 31); and in the wall that divided the nave from the apse. Here, they were employed to revet a raised presbytery, and also probably supported a chancel screen (see below). Within the apse (which gives the impression of being laid out in a series of almost straight sections, perhaps five in all), no floor survived. The main feature was the base

of a tile box-drain, set in mortar (Figs 66, and 68, C13); this must, however, be of earlier date, and is fairly certainly to be associated with the late Roman church, whose apse it respects. Otherwise, earlier footings apart, there were only a series of burials, all cutting or beside the cross-wall, a matter to which we shall return below.

Within the nave, the archaeological picture is more complex. Only in the northwest corner was there any area of preserved flooring, and this, as will be shown below, belongs to a late episode of rebuilding. Elsewhere, there was upwards of 1.0 m of plough-disturbed deposits, overlying natural tufaceous colluvium. Cut into the colluvium were a number of older footings, and a series of graves (below, Fig. 98). There was no sign of any earlier archaeological intervention, as might be expected from Tomassetti's description of Giorgi's excavations on the church at Monte Gelato (although there was what seemed to be a recent pit in the adjoining baptistery: below, Fig. 84). Either Giorgi's clearance was rather superficial, or it was another church that was investigated, however implausible that may sound.

The graves within the church are discussed in detail in a subsequent section. Here we may note that they were almost all of elaborate construction, when compared with those elsewhere on the site. Of the most imposing, two lay more

Table 2. Internal floor area of the naves of ninth-century churches.

site	nave, internal dimensions (m)	floor area	reference
Santa Cornelia	13.5 x 14.5	195.75	Christie and Daniels 1991
Santo Stefano, Anguillara	13.0 x 12.5	162.5	Van de Noort and Whitehouse 1992
San Liberato	13.35 x 8.05	113.5	Christie, Gibson and Ward-Perkins 1991
Monte Gelato	10.5 x 8.75	91.9	
Santa Rufina (?)	13.0 x 5.9	76.7	Cotton, Wheeler and Whitehouse 1991
Sant'Ilario	8.6 x 5.0	43.0	Fiocchi Nicolai 1988-89

or less centrally within the nave (Fig. 66, B16, B29 = below, Fig. 94, nos. 12 and 13), while one (Fig. 66, C57 = below, Fig. 94, no. 2) lay in a position that must have been close to, or under, the altar. Radiocarbon dating indicates that the two primary burials in this grave were in all probability relics. Certainly there can be no doubt from the position of the grave within the church that it was constructed after the second church had been built.

As noted above, no floor level can be associated with the majority of these graves. There were, however, a number of pieces of marble veneer and paving in secondary contexts, mainly relating to the final destruction of the church, which may derive from a floor. These included a number of thick slabs of greyish white marble, and pieces in *bardiglio fiorito*, *cipollino*, *portasanta* and *rosso antico*, as well as in a pink-white limestone breccia. All would seem to comprise reused Roman material, which must have occurred in abundance both at Monte Gelato and on nearby villa sites.

These admittedly slight signs of a not un-elaborate floor are matched by a greater wealth of evidence to show that the church was provided with some rather splendid internal architectural decoration. All of the sculpture was found in secondary contexts, and some of it had been built into walls and other structures during an extensive refurbishment of the complex around the end of the tenth century. Datable on stylistic grounds to around AD 800, the pieces included substantial, highly decorated fragments from a chancel screen or iconostasis, with octagonal colonnettes, several sections from pilasters (or architrave), and fragments from the end of an architrave or cornice. Some pieces bear the stylistic 'signature' of an individual carver or workshop, including the finest example of early medieval sculpture from the site (cat. 1). Described by Osborne (this volume), as 'a true masterpiece of the age ... [with] ... few equals', it shows the Agnus Dei in front of the Cross (below, Fig. 152). It may well have embellished the altar, and was indeed found reused in a tomb beneath (below, Fig. 96); the small socket at the centre of the Cross could have been intended to hold a jewel, a further indication of its importance. But it is the imagery that is most intriguing. As Osborne reminds us, below, the portrayal of Christ as the sacrificial lamb of God derives from the words of Saint John the Baptist (John 1.29, 36). Although well represented in early Christian art, the lamb disappeared from usage during the eighth century, and it has been argued that it was reintroduced during the pontificate of Pope Paschal I (817-24) (Nordhagen 1976: 165-6; Davis-Weyer and Emerick 1984: 27-8).

This is fascinating for two reasons. In the first place, it recalls the inscriptions of Pasqualis (*sic*) from Santa Corne-

lia, which may refer to activities or benefactions by that pope (Reynolds 1991: 137, 178). It could be, therefore, that this pope, who was actively involved in the building or restoration of churches in Rome (Krautheimer 1980: 122-3), was no less active in the Campagna. Secondly, the special link between the Agnus Dei and Saint John compellingly recalls Tomassetti's demonstration of a probable association between the Mola di Monte Gelato and the *Castrum Capracorum*, with its church of Saint John, of later Papal bulls (Tomassetti 1882: 146; 1913: 112). The altar front (if that is what it is) would thus appear to offer extraordinary confirmation of Tomassetti's brilliant deduction.

Little more that is concrete can be said about the internal arrangements or decoration of the church. Fragments of columns, and a column base, found in unstratified deposits over the church, may be no more than chance introductions, and there is certainly no evidence to indicate that the nave was divided into aisles. Likewise, the few fragments of painted plaster, although mainly from grave fills, are insufficient to demonstrate beyond dispute that the church was decorated in this way. Mural embellishment of this sort might be expected (Krautheimer 1980: 128; Christie and Daniels 1991: 178); but there is no real case for it here, just as a vault mosaic must be ruled out on the same grounds. Only the very damaged nature of the church precludes absolute certainty about the extent of its decoration.

The first period of the second church: dating evidence

As with the late Roman church, the chronological evidence for the building of the second church is not abundant. There was no usefully stratified pottery or coins associated with its construction, nor contemporary nearby occupation deposits. The church is, nevertheless, clearly coeval with the first baptistery (described below), because the two buildings share a common alignment (Fig. 73), an orientation that, as we have seen, differs a little from that of the first church. On independent evidence from the baptistery area, this points to a date of around AD 800 for the building of the complex.

In support of this, the following indicators can be cited from the church.

(1) All the early medieval sculpture from the site, although in no instance in its original position, is stylistically characteristic of the so-called Carolingian renaissance (Osborne, this volume). This is a phenomenon that is extremely well represented in southern Etruria (Christie

1991b; Van de Noort and Whitehouse 1992), most recently confirmed by the discovery of similar sculpture in secondary deposits beside the cathedral at Nepi (unpublished).

(2) The tomb (C57; Fig. 66 and below, Fig. 94, no. 2) which, from its position and elaborate structure, must have been the main focus of veneration, close to or beneath the altar, yielded a radiocarbon date for a primary interment which, when calibrated, gave values of AD 545-630 (one sigma), or AD 450-650 (two sigma, or 95% probability). This provides a useful *terminus post quem*, especially as the bones were almost certainly deposited as relics.

(3) Burial 24 (Fig. 66, no. D107; cf. Fig. 94), an ossuary that was built and filled prior to the construction of the latest floor, contained glass of the fifth to seventh centuries or later, as well as an early sherd of forum ware. Other graves also yielded fragments of glass vessels and lamps of late Antique/early medieval type (cf. Price, this volume). A period of deposition in the eighth and/or ninth centuries would seem entirely appropriate.

Both the documentary evidence, which suggests that Monte Gelato was one of Pope Hadrian's foundations of the *domusculta* of *Capracorum*, and the archaeological indications concur therefore that a date of *c.* AD 800 would well suit the construction of the first phase of the second, larger church (and baptistery). This may seem rather late for the use of *a cappuccina* tombs, which occur mainly in late Roman contexts, although there may have been some in the *domusculta* phase at Santa Cornelia (Christie and Daniels 1991: 182; cf. generally Blake (1983)). However, it is difficult to see the *a cappuccina* burials in the nave as pre-dating the second church, with the extensive building-work that this involved, and a date of AD 800+ is to be preferred for them.

The second church: the later phases (6 and 7)

The church appears to have remained unaltered for some two centuries, before undergoing what was probably a major reconstruction. At the same time, the first baptistery was pulled down, and rebuilt on a much larger scale, and ancillary structures added to the north. The most unequivocal sign of this was the dismantling, and breaking up, of the early medieval sculptural fittings. Many of the fragments were then incorporated into the new structures, such as a substantial piece of chancel screen and column, which was built into the foundations of the north wall of the church (Fig. 74), by a presumed door.

Whether all the walls were rebuilt to this extent is uncertain. What is clear is that the main grave under the altar was extensively reconstructed. It had originally been provided with a vault, which subsequently collapsed into the tomb, sealing the primary inhumations (below, Fig. 96). The upper part of the west end of the grave was then rebuilt, using tufo blocks, pieces of a Roman strigillated sarcophagus (below, Fig. 138) and the marble slab with the Agnus Dei. A disorganized series of burials was introduced into the tomb, possibly as relics, since all the bones were disarticulated. Two nearby *a cappuccina* graves (Fig. 66, C23, C55/C56; below, Fig. 94, nos. 7 and 8) may belong to this phase, since they appeared to cut the foundations of the apse. However, this area was sufficiently disturbed to render any chronological inferences uncertain, and it is quite possible to suppose that they had been built into the structure of the apse, rather than through it.

One small area of flooring was preserved, in the northwest corner of the nave (Fig. 74). It comprised irregu-

Fig. 74. Fragment of an early medieval chancel screen or iconostasis (cat. 2), reused in a ?doorway from the church to the baptistery (cf. Figures 66, 78, 151 and 152). In the top left is the latest floor of the church, *c.* AD 1000. *(TWP)*

Fig. 75. Reconstruction of part of the site *c.* AD 800. *(SG)*

larly shaped slabs of tufo, set in a rather random pattern, although quite neatly jointed. The overall effect, however, was quite rough and ready, and this is matched by a total lack of evidence for any internal embellishment. The walls do not seem to have been plastered and, unless decorated with portable fittings of textiles, wood or metal, the church would seem to have been very plainly finished.

No very useful dating evidence was found for these alterations. It is nevertheless evident that they were put in hand at the same time as the rebuilding of the baptistery (which shared the north wall of the church). We shall show below that this belongs to the period around AD 1000, a time when there was a significant reorganization of the whole complex, not least, as we shall see, in the provision of a greatly enlarged baptistery. It is interesting, therefore, that the church remained the same size. This was probably because the *domusculta*-period church was laid out with reasonably generous dimensions, as is clear from an analysis of the size of some other recently studied ninth-century churches in the Roman Campagna, especially southern Etruria.

It should be noted that Hadrian I's church at Santa Cornelia was, according to the *Liber Pontificalis*, intended to be lavishly decorated; indeed, all of the Roman clergy and Senate (that is, the nobility) were invited to its dedication. It is not, therefore, surprising that its floor area within the nave was more than double that of the church at Monte Gelato. Nevertheless, even at half the size of the church at Santa Cornelia, that at Monte Gelato will still have been imposing and impressive (Fig. 75), and capable of serving a relatively large congregation. By contrast, when the chapel was built for the now deserted medieval village at Castel Porciano, to the southeast of Nepi, it was provided with a nave with an internal floor area of as little as 40 square metres

(Mallett and Whitehouse 1967: fig. 7). It is a measure of the relative spaciousness of the church at Monte Gelato and, in the context of the late tenth/early eleventh centuries, when *incastellamento* was so prevalent, perhaps an indication of the not inconsiderable size of its *pieve*.

The destruction of the second church

That the church, and the adjoining buildings, were eventually systematically demolished is not in doubt. There was no fallen masonry and, in places, there were signs of robber trenches (for example, Fig. 31, unit 18). Demolition was everywhere thorough, systematic and efficient, leaving only empty wall-trenches in some sections. Presumably much of the material was reused at Castellaccio.

As will be shown below, many of the graves in the church were also emptied of their bones, and then in some cases rebuilt. This must be an indication both of the high status, and perhaps sanctity, of these individuals, and of the continued veneration of the site. Indeed, elsewhere on the site burials continued to be made, although not demonstrably within the church (phase 7). One structure was, however, built here (Fig. 66, A15; Figs 76 and 77). Approximately rectangular in shape, *c.* 1.5 × 1.35 m, it was built of roughly shaped tufo blocks, all reused. Amongst them was a Roman tombstone, where an inscription had apparently been chiselled off. The foundation stood two courses high, some 0.8 m in all, and was raised prominently above the surrounding footings. Given that it was quite certainly the latest feature in the area (and overlay one of the emptied graves), it seems plausible to suppose that it supported some sort of monument, perhaps a cross. Alternatively, it may have formed part of a wayside shrine, since the road certainly re-

Fig. 76. The base of the structure built after the final demolition of the medieval church,
perhaps for a shrine. *(TWP)*

mained in use, only its line being altered slightly over the
centuries (Fig. 4). The ubiquity of such shrines in the Campagna today, often in seemingly remote and unfrequented
places, adds credence to this explanation.

The finds from the site as a whole show that this work of
demolition took place around AD 1100. There is virtually no
pottery later than this date, apart from a few sherds stratified in the wash deposits over the bath-house, which document the gradual covering over of the structures during
later medieval and post-medieval times (Fig. 72). The papal
bull of 1128, which describes the church of Saint John as
diruta, demolished, is entirely consistent with the archaeological evidence from the site.

Post-church monument, W. face

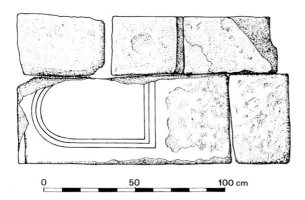

Fig. 77. The post-church structure, incorporating a Roman tombstone. *(TWP)*

THE BAPTISTERIES (FIGS 73 AND 78), by O. Gilkes and T.W. Potter

There were two superimposed baptisteries, both adjoining
the north side of the church. Orientated east-west, they
were built on ground which sloped gradually towards the
west, before descending to the lower terrace, cut for the
Roman bath-house. No stratigraphy was preserved at the
eastern end of the larger, later, baptistery; but to the west
there was an accumulation of nearly 1.0 m over the earliest
baptistery floor. It is therefore possible to reconstruct the
building sequence in some detail.

Underlying Roman remains were scant. The east wall of
the Roman-period corridor served as a foundation for the
east wall of the later baptistery, and the very lowest part of
the footing for the west corridor wall (D101), and a partition (D195), also survived. But virtually all of the Roman
floors, as well as associated deposits, had been stripped off
when the first baptistery was constructed. This may simply
have been for the reuse of these materials; however, the
work of demolition was so thorough as to suggest that the
site may have been deliberately 'cleansed' before the new
work began. This would have been a fitting symbolic act
before constructing a building where ritual purification was
of such immense significance.

The first baptistery (Figs 73 and 78)

This was a small apsidal structure, measuring, overall,
5.15 × 4.2 m externally. This is about half the size of the probably contemporary baptistery at Santa Cornelia, which was
about 11.5 × 8.5 m externally, a clear indication of the relat-

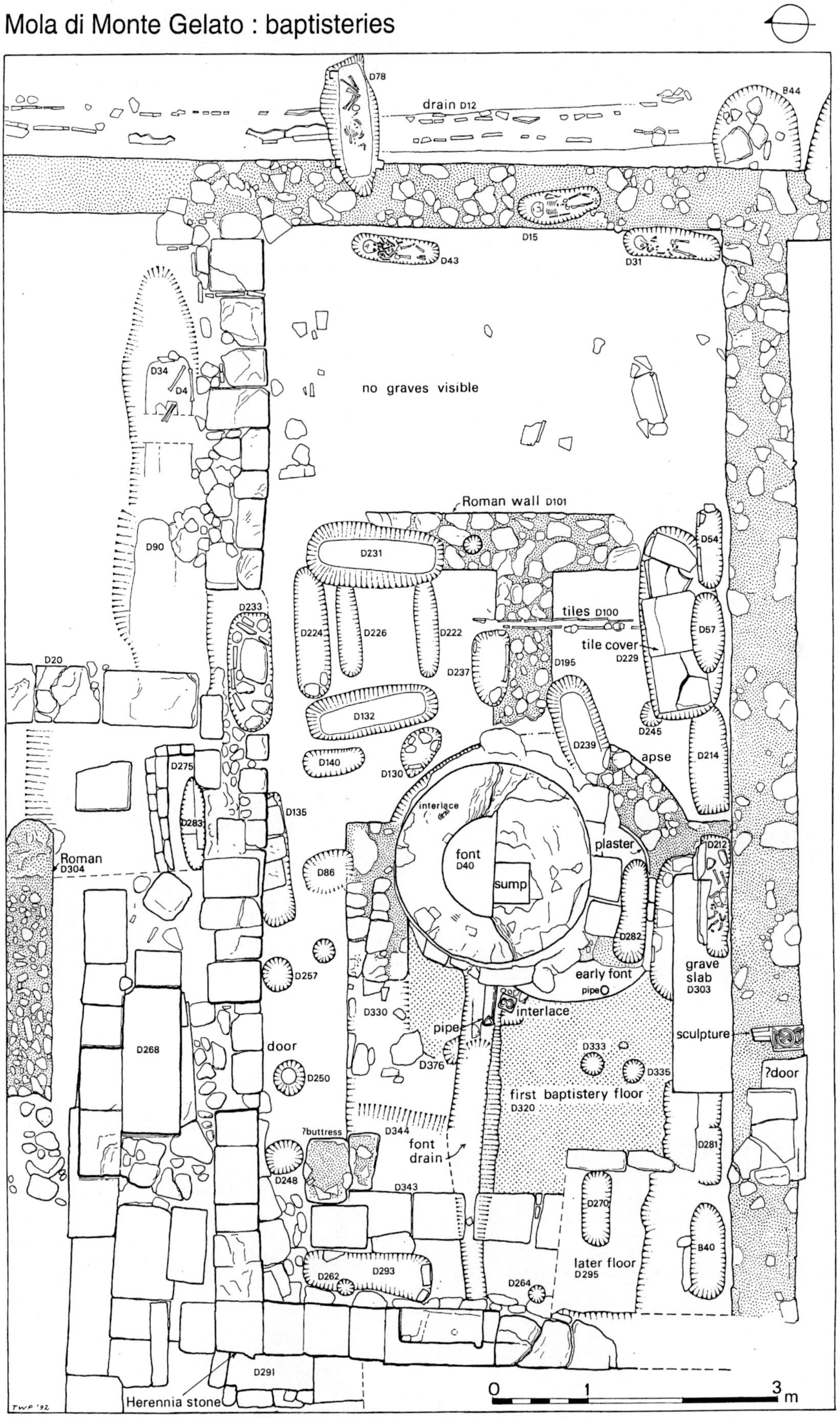

Mola di Monte Gelato : baptisteries

Fig. 78. Plan of the baptisteries.

Concordance with catalogue of burials: B40:52; D4:95; D15:28; D31:29; D34:95; D43:27; D54:38; D57:39; D78:97; D90:96; D132:41; D135:43; D140:42; D212:47; D214:40; D222:34; D224:32; D226:33; D229:37; D231:30; D233:31; D237:35; D239:36; D268:71; D270:51; D275:67; D281:50; D282:46; D283:68; D291:54; D293:53; D303:48. *(TWP)*

ive importance of the two foundations (Christie and Daniels 1991: 16-17). Unlike Santa Cornelia, where the baptistery was a free-standing structure, located to the northwest of the church, that at Monte Gelato lay immediately beside the church, and was almost certainly conjoined with it: Figures 73 and 75 provide possible reconstructions, by Sheila Gibson. It is instructive to compare these with her reconstruction of the church and baptistery at Santa Cornelia (in Christie and Daniels 1991: 177), which again underlines the altogether more modest appearance of the ecclesiastical complex at Monte Gelato. Although the presence of a baptistery indicates that this was a parish church or *pieve*, serving the local community, architecturally it took second place to the centre of the *domusculta* of *Capracorum*.

Many details concerning the layout of the first baptistery are, however, unclear, due to the overlay of later structures and graves. Nevertheless, a certain amount can be said about its construction. The north wall (D330) was built upon a shallow foundation of roughly shaped tufo lumps and pieces of tile, bonded with a yellowish mortar. The foundation was 0.74 m in width, while the wall was narrower, being 0.64 m across. The apse was of similar construction, and included a large block of tufo, thickly covered with mortar, where it joined with the north wall of the church; this was presumably to take the weight of the vault. Inside the southeastern corner of the apse was a layer of fine white plaster rendering, although without obvious signs of paint.

The west wall (D343) was of different construction, being built of large squared tufo blocks, averaging 0.6 × 0.45 m, resting upon the tufo bedrock. Pieces of tile were packed between them in places, but there was little or no use of mortar. At first sight, this variation in construction technique might suggest a secondary phase of building; but there was no other evidence for this, and it is more likely to reflect the fact that the ground slopes away at this point, creating problems of stability. A more substantial foundation was thus required, an inference which helps to explain the subsequent addition of what appears to be a buttress at the northwest corner of the baptistery. This was made of tufo, tile and marble fragments, consolidated with a rough greyish mortar.

A substantial area of floor (D320) was preserved in excellent condition (Fig. 79). It was made of very hard pale grey-white mortar, at least 80 mm thick, laid directly onto the tufo bedrock. It had cracked at only one point, and showed surprisingly few traces of wear and none of patching. It may possibly have been covered over with carpets or rugs. In the eastern half of the baptistery the floor ran up to, and lipped around, a semicircular mortar foundation, 0.4 m across. Although mostly obscured by the later font, there seems very little doubt that this was also a font. It was set off centre, in the southeast side of the baptistery, and had been sunk into the floor. The depth could not be established; but, with an estimated internal diameter of between 1.0 and 1.5 m, was evidently a *piscina* for semi-immersion, resembling (on a smaller scale) that at Santa Cornelia (Christie and Daniels 1991: 180). A terracotta pipe, 0.1 m in diameter and set vertically into the mortar surround, may have been something to do with the water supply (it can hardly have been for drainage), while the lipping upwards of the floor shows that the font was surrounded by a parapet.

Fig. 79. The baptistery, looking east, at the end of excavation; note the finely preserved floor of the first baptistery of *c.* AD 800, to the bottom right of the font. *(KW)*

Fig. 80. The second baptistery looking southwest. To the right is a probable built tomb (no. 71). *(KW)*

Christie and Daniels (1991: 180-1) have usefully summarized the evidence for the use of fonts in the early Middle Ages. Although there was a general trend from the ninth century for baptism to take place in a standing tub, often placed in the north aisle of the church, Italy was somewhat conservative in this respect, preferring the rite of immersion. Yet Pope Leo IV (847-55) recommended that every church should have a standing font, and at Santa Cornelia the baptistery was demolished, possibly in the mid-ninth century (Christie and Daniels 1991: 181). However, as we shall see, the use of a semi-immersion built *piscina*, and a separate baptistery, continued throughout the lifetime of the ecclesiastical complex at Monte Gelato, until *c.* 1100. This is a remarkable comment upon the insular character of this community, a matter that is reflected in many other ways, not least by the physical remains of those buried in the cemetery, which suggest close family relationships.

The first baptistery: dating evidence

None of the finely decorated early medieval sculpture can be directly associated with this baptistery, although such ornamentation is to be expected. Normally, there was an altar within the baptistery, where the newly baptized might take the first communion; but space for this is lacking, unless it lay in the northeast corner of the apse (which could explain why the font was positioned off-centre).

There was also a dearth of datable pottery from deposits relating to the construction of the buildings, apart from a few sherds of early medieval type. However, to the west of the baptistery was a spread of friable whitish mortar, which may derive from the work of plastering the walls and, perhaps, the preparation of the pale grey-white mortar for the floor. This layer was also clearly identifiable in the trench over the bath-house, further to the west, where it was firmly stratified between deposits of the sixth-seventh centuries and those of the ninth-tenth centuries (Figs 54 and

72, layer 103). This is satisfactorily consistent with the proposal that the first baptistery was constructed around the time of Pope Hadrian I, when he created the *domusculta* of *Capracorum* in the late eighth century. The ninth-century coin from burial 43 (below, Fig. 168, no. 58) also tends to support this view; but this is as far as one can go.

The second baptistery (Fig. 80)

Like the church, the first baptistery appears to have remained in use for about two centuries. It was then demolished to the lowest courses, and replaced with a much larger rectangular structure, without an apse. Its internal measurements were 10.8 × 4.9 m, so that the floor area was over four times as great as that of the first baptistery. This should indicate that the community that it served had increased substantially, as indeed a good deal of other evidence implies.

The structural sequence is, however, complex, reflecting some modifications made during the lifetime of the building. As with its predecessor, the baptistery was built up against the north wall of the church, and now extended for the entire length of the nave. There was what appears to have been a doorway towards the west end, on the level of the latest floor in the church. As noted above, beside it, and built into the fabric of the wall, was an elaborately carved element from a screen, with a column, decorated with interlace (cat. 2; Fig. 74, and below, Figs 153 and 154); it clearly illustrates how the decorative elements from the Carolingian church had been pulled down, and methodically reemployed as building material.

The east wall reused the line of the west wall of the Roman-period corridor, but only its lowest foundation, made of mortar and tufo lumps (like the church walls), survived. The north and west walls were much better preserved, in places to three courses of tufo blocks (Fig. 32). The quality of workmanship was very variable, and probably reflects

Fig. 81. The Herennia tombstone (Fig. 139), reused in the northwest corner of the second baptistery (Fig. 78) *(KW)*

The only difficulty with this interpretation is that the top of the foundation trench for the west wall did yield some sherds of sparse glaze ware, which are best dated to the late eleventh or early twelfth century. This might suggest a phase of repair or rebuilding, especially to the superstructure. However, given that the bulk of the evidence points to c. AD 1000 for the construction of the second baptistery, and that there is little evidence for occupation after the early twelfth century, it is more likely that these sherds relate to the demolition of the building. It is indeed possible that the top of the foundation trench was re-excavated, to facilitate the removal of the blocks, and that the scaffolding poles also belong to this episode.

The latest floor surface of the baptistery had been completely destroyed; as in the church it may well have consisted of slabs of tufo, which were taken up when the building was demolished. There was, however, a clearly marked doorway in the western section of the north wall, providing access into the ante-room beyond. The foundation for its threshold lay at the level of the offset blocks, referred to above, and a small part of the door jamb had been left standing when the baptistery was pulled down, and had subsequently fallen inwards (Fig. 82); it is notable that there was no trace of any plaster rendering, suggesting that the building was not elaborately decorated inside. There was also a threshold block placed rather off-centre in the west wall (Figs 78 and 82). At first sight, this might be taken to imply that there was a doorway leading through into a narthex beyond. However, there was no sign of a north or west wall for such a narthex, nor any trace of a floor. On balance, we are now inclined to think that this remained open ground, leaving the baptistery as a single-cell structure. This rather suggests that the threshold in the west wall occurred coincidentally, and was reused from a Roman building merely as a block of masonry.

Within the later baptistery, the main internal feature was a substantial font (Figs 83 and 84). The northern half was well-preserved, but the southern half had been largely demolished. It had a total diameter of 2.0 m, an internal diameter of 1.0 m, and still stood to a height of 0.48 m. It partially overlay the font of the earlier baptistery, and its base had been underpinned by tufo lumps and blocks, raising it some 0.25 m above the level of the floor of the first baptistery. The font itself was built of roughly coursed tufo, tile and marble, bonded with mortar; the retention of an impression of early medieval interlace on the top of the font (Fig. 78) shows that these decorative fittings had already been broken up for reuse. The exterior was heavily grouted with two layers of coarse, pinkish mortar, while the interior was also lined, but with much more care, to produce a smooth finish. There was no trace of marble veneer, as at Santa Cornelia (Christie and Daniels 1991: 18).

The surviving part of the font floor was made up of a single well-dressed slab of tufo, with a rebated edge; it was probably a reused piece. It formed part of the edge of an almost square sump, measuring 0.38 × 0.4 m, and 0.7 m in depth. Its sides were lined with pieces of reused marble veneer and fragments of tile, and there was a *tubulus*, 90 mm in diameter, on the western side, which served as a drain. This fed via a constricted passage into a channel which cut through the first baptistery floor, and led down to and through the west baptistery wall (Fig. 85).

The drain apparently did not work well. It was twice recut, and in the final phase a part of a late Roman amphora (cat. 50), 0.12 m in diameter, was cemented into the outlet on the west side of the font (Fig. 85). Included in this was a fragment of marble with an early medieval interlace design

more than one period of construction. The easterly stretch of the north wall used an irregular series of tufo blocks, together with tile and pieces of a marble sarcophagus, set in a shallow foundation trench. This left a ragged edge on the northern side, where the footing was recessed into a bank. The top course of the westerly stretch was more neatly jointed, as was that of the west wall. Included in the northwest corner was the cut-down tombstone of Herennia (Fig. 81). The lower courses were much less regular and, in some cases, offset (Fig. 82); they clearly lay below floor level, and the offsets may have supported the floor.

The only detectable foundation trench for the western and northwestern stretches of wall lay at a high level, namely that of the top of the course of offset blocks. It had thus been dug through the dumps of material that buried the first baptistery, and which were intended to bring the level of this lower ground up to that of the natural soil at the east end of the baptistery. There was a good deal of Roman building material in these dumps, including *opus reticulatum*. There was also an area of flooring, made up of tile fragments and plaster, revetted by two tufo blocks, which was stratified within the dumps (Fig. 78, D295). At first sight, this might appear to be a remnant of an earlier floor of the second baptistery; but its extent was limited, and it was of relatively slight construction. It is probably best interpreted as a working surface, created when the lowest courses of the western wall of the second baptistery were being built. The rest of the floor make-up was then laid, and the superstructure put up. Indeed, a series of post-holes, running along the inner line of the western and northwestern walls (Fig. 78, nos. D257, 250, 248, 262, 264), must surely relate to the use of scaffolding.

Fig. 82. The northeast corner of the second baptistery showing the fallen door jamb, the offset supporting the floor and the reused threshold (left). *(KW)*

(Fig. 86). It can probably be assumed that pipes carried the water down the entire length of drain, although these have now disappeared.

It may well be that the font drain followed the line of that laid out for the first baptistery, explaining the near super-imposition of the two fonts. Certainly, the later font was of broadly similar type, set some 0.25 m into the floor and with a parapet around, and thus suited for a semi-immersion baptismal rite. There could indeed have been steps leading into it from the south side, somewhat resembling the ar-rangement at Santa Cornelia, although here there were two flights (Christie and Daniels 1991: 20). Given the evidence for the abandonment of this type of font from the ninth century or before, this is again remarkable evidence for the conservatism of tradition at this rural site, even though it lay relatively close to Rome.

Fig. 83. The second font, looking north. *(KW)*

D, baptistery section

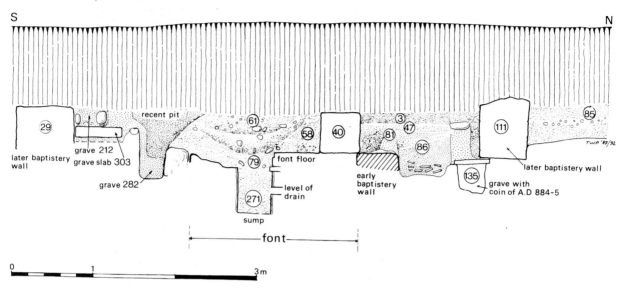

Fig. 84. Section across the baptisteries. Note: pit 85 contains pottery of the mid-sixth century, but this is clearly residual. *(TWP)*

The parapet was normally intended to support a colonnade, surmounted by a canopy. Curtains were then hung between the columns, so that the catechumen could be baptized in privacy (Bond 1908). No such colonnade survived at Monte Gelato (although, with such extensive demolition, this is not surprising), nor was there any sign of a base for an altar, where the newly baptized person could take the first communion. There were, however, a number of post-holes ringing the font, which might have supported such a structure. These include four (Fig. 78, D86, D376, D333 and

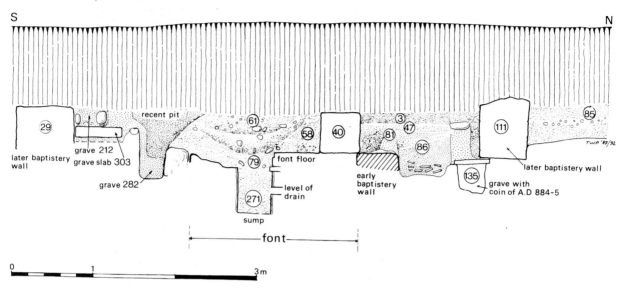

Fig. 85. The second font drain, cutting through the plaster floor of the first baptistery (right). *(KW)*

D335) which clearly post-date the first baptistery, and two (D130, D245) which probably do. They were well founded (D333 was at least 0.4 m in depth), and D86 had been packed with large sherds of the later sixth century, although it is clearly later than the first baptistery (Fig. 84). D130 was likewise well packed with stone and tile. If this interpretation is correct (and it is necessarily very speculative), it must have been a rudimentary structure, although curtains would have concealed something of that. But the whole appearance of the second baptistery, lacking even the traditional apse, must have been rustic and bare, symbolizing a rather poor and ruralized community.

The evidence for burials is discussed below. Here we may note that the majority is likely to belong to the period of the later baptistery, and that most were of infants and juveniles. It is unfortunate that it was impossible readily to identify most of the grave cuts in the area to the north of the Roman corridor wall, D101. Further excavation would surely have revealed a similar pattern to the area immediately to the west, namely a relatively dense, neatly ordered cemetery, with remarkably little intercutting. Individual graves, once dug, were clearly remembered and respected, unlike those in many other parts of the site.

The second baptistery: dating evidence

The reuse of pieces of early medieval sculpture, of later eighth- or early ninth-century date, provides a firm *terminus post quem* for the building of the second baptistery. There was also a certain amount of datable pottery. Much of it comprised residual Roman sherds and wasters from the nearby late eighth-/early to mid ninth-century pottery kiln, described below. There was also some contamination, introduced by a large pit (D300), some 2.5 × 1.7 m in size, dug to the west of the font. Although the exact level from which it was cut was not very clear, it contained sparse glaze of the late eleventh or early twelfth century, and was very probably part of the demolition process.

Otherwise, the sherds from the layers of make-up with datable material (D41, 47, 244, 266, 277 and 319) present a completely consistent picture: the latest finds are all fragments of forum ware or sparse glaze, together with domestic

Fig. 86. The fragment of early medieval interlace, cemented into the foundations of the second font. *(KW)*

wares. These are datable, according to Helen Patterson, to the late tenth or early eleventh century. With so many make-up layers for the floor of the second baptistery producing these chronologically identical results, we can therefore be fairly certain that the second baptistery was built in the decades either side of AD 1000. This is also consistent with the results from the trench to the west of the baptistery. Here, although the line of cut for the foundation trench of the baptistery wall was not as clear as one would like, it was probably dug through a layer with pottery of the ninth and tenth centuries (Fig. 72). Interestingly, the same layer was also cut through by a robber trench, dug down to one of the late Roman walls. It contained sherds of the eleventh century, and may well indicate that material was being removed for the construction of the second baptistery.

THE ANTE-ROOM

To the north of the baptistery was a room (or, less plausibly, a walled space), with internal measurements of 4.1 × 5.0 m. The east wall was made up of tufo blocks, some 0.55 m wide, and of variable length, set in a shallow foundation trench. It butted up against the north wall of the second baptistery, with which it is stylistically similar, and it seems certain that the two are coeval. The north wall was founded on an old Roman footing, and no obviously medieval work was preserved. The west wall, on the other hand, was all of medieval date, and was deeply recessed through late Roman deposits to the natural soil, at a level that is close to that of the floor level of the lower Roman terrace (Fig. 60).

No floor survived within the room, although there were late Roman deposits (including the sixth-century deposit of roof tile). Plough damage had, however, been considerable,

and had deeply scored the top of the western wall. In the southwest corner of the room was a curious masonry structure, which extended beyond the line of the western wall, filling the area between the baptistery and the south wall of the entrance (described below). The highest block, which measured 1.4 × 0.6 m, had been placed more or less opposite the doorway leading northwards out of the baptistery, and was some 0.4 m above the foundation for the threshold. There was one very narrow intermediate step between the two, and it is difficult not to interpret the arrangement as a rather rough and ready staircase. The remaining blocks were at a slightly lower level, and formed an approximate rectangle, parallel with the side of the baptistery, and some 5.0 × 2.0 m in extent. It is probably best interpreted as some kind of tomb (or tombs), which perhaps incorporated part of the west wall of the ante-room in its structure (Fig. 80 and, below, Fig. 94, no. 71).

There was another built tomb, with two successive interments, against the north wall of the baptistery (below, Fig. 94, nos. 67 and 68), but otherwise only a few disarticulated remains (nos. 69 and 70), some certainly much older. The ante-room was not, therefore, a focus for burials, unlike the adjoining baptistery, an absence that is surely meaningful. We might therefore propose that this room provided accommodation for the clergy. This would be entirely consistent with arrangements at contemporary monastic sites, such as Santa Cornelia, where there was also an 'ante-baptistery room', possibly to be interpreted as a guest-room, or as an additional dining-room for use by the abbot (Christie and Daniels 1991: 197). Given that Monte Gelato was a much more rustic ecclesiastical establishment, this simple provision of living space seems entirely in accord with the character of the site. By the early eleventh century (and probably well before), considerations were entirely parochial, and this is clearly reflected by the architecture.

THE ENTRANCE

Adjoining the west side of the ante-room was a rectangular structure, measuring internally 4.8 × 2.7 m. The north and south walls were made up of large blocks of tufo, up to 1.5 × 0.6 m in size. The south wall was the more neatly built, and stood two courses high to a height of 0.95 m (Figs 62 and 63). The north wall was more shoddily constructed, with blocks of variable width, although the inner face was quite tidily aligned. It partly rested on a Roman wall, just as the southern wall was founded on the Roman floor, with some fill to level it up. The blocks of the western wall had been removed, but it would seem that the Roman threshold was retained in use in this period. The floor then sloped gently upwards towards the east, being well preserved at this point (Fig. 63). In the more easterly part of the room, however, no trace of the floor remained, and it had presumably been dug away; the area was subsequently filled in with tips of tufaceous material (Fig. 60, unit 218). No threshold for a doorway between the entrance and the ante-room was discovered, but this too had probably been removed.

Whether this room served any function other than as a back entrance to the ecclesiastical complex is uncertain. Some burials (below, Fig. 94, nos. 76 and 77) were later introduced into it, and there were multiple interments in a grave, no. 75, cut into the south wall after its partial demolition. Dating evidence was, however, sparse. It is nevertheless reasonably certain that the entrance was constructed at the same time as the second baptistery and the ante-room, around AD 1000, and was demolished a century or so later.

THE EXTERIOR OF THE ENTRANCE AND THE PAVED ROAD

Outside the entrance the Roman levels were sealed by a series of tips. These were not easy to differentiate, but they contained vast quantities of very small sherds of *acroma depurata*, as well as much ash, derived from the pottery kiln of the late eighth to mid-ninth centuries. There was also a number of tufo slabs, which may represent an attempt to provide some rough paving of what must have frequently become a muddy, downslope area.

It is also clear that the road was repaved at this time. This is evident not only from the haphazard arrangement of the *selce* blocks (in marked contrast to the neat work of predecessors of the classical period), but also from the pottery in the make-up. These included many waster sherds from the kiln, thus establishing a firm *terminus post quem*. There is nothing surprising in this. Recent work at Malborghetto has shown how the paving of the Via Flaminia was maintained into the Middle Ages (Bosman 1993) and the same is probably true of the Via Appia (Quilici Gigli 1990). At the Mola di Monte Gelato, the ascent up the hill to the north is relatively steep, about 1 in 7, and it would thus have been effectively impassable for wheeled vehicles during the wet autumn and winter months, without a proper surface. By this time, the old Roman road was nearly a millennium old, and was probably in a poor state. Re-laying of the paving-stones may well have been deemed expedient, probably as part of the building operations in the late tenth or early eleventh century.

Some burials were introduced into the area outside the entrance (below, Fig. 94, nos. 78-81), but were stratigraphically quite late. All were simple graves, with the exception of no. 79, which was a built structure, immediately outside the door.

THE POTTERY KILN (FIGS 87 AND 88)

In the southwest part of the former Roman 'large room' was a simple pottery kiln. It had a single oval chamber, 1.95 × 1.3 m in size internally, and was recessed into the *cocciopesto* floor and overlying deposits, to a depth of at least 0.3 m. There was a flue, properly termed a fire tunnel, cut through a Roman wall to the west and, beyond, a stoking area on the sloping ground covering the lower terrace.

The kiln was provided with a substantial fired clay lining, baked to a reddish orange colour, and containing tile and stone inclusions. It was between 0.2 and 0.4 m thick, and had been given one major relining of the interior and some later patching. Within the chamber was a series of black and grey ashy fills, separated by layers of brown loam. If each deposit of ash represents a separate firing, then together they register the final two episodes of use of the kiln.

There was no evidence for supports for a raised floor, either of a permanent or a temporary nature. Nor were there any fragments of fire-bars in the fill. Temporary kiln furniture may have been used, and removed completely; alternatively, resort may have been made to a floor made up of inverted pottery vessels (themselves usually wasters: Swan 1984: fig. II ii; 114), since there were sherds, albeit of small size, in the deposits.

Kilns of this single-chamber, single-flue type normally had a permanent clay dome, with an exhaust vent at the top. The flue served as a furnace, the heat being drawn upwards through the load, while the gases escaped through the vents (Swan 1984: 114). Such kilns were widespread in the ancient world, and clearly worked very efficiently.

That this was a pottery kiln is not in doubt, since there were vast spreads of ash and small waster sherds all over the adjacent slopes to the west, and also on the ground to the south. So numerous were the wasters, and so extensive the deposits, that a not inconsiderable scale of production is implied, albeit using only a single kiln. The wares mainly comprised vessels for domestic use, although some of the larger ones could have been used for transport. Patterson (this volume) dates them to the late eighth to mid-ninth centuries (or possibly a little later), on the basis of comparable examples from the Crypta Balbi in Rome. Not only does this further underline the close links between the city and its farms at this time, but it suggests that the official purpose of the kiln may have been to supply pots for transporting the produce of the *domusculta* to Rome. Yet it is also easy to imagine how a consignment of vessels for domestic use might have been slipped onto a cart of agricultural produce, and sold off privately. Pottery production, utilizing the excellent local clays, was of long standing in this region, including Monte Gelato and its environs (Peña 1987), and ceramics are still made today, especially around Civita Castellana. This could well have been a factor in placing one of the centres of the *domusculta* of *Capracorum* at this site, but it was also an incentive to private enterprise.

Kilns of comparable date are so far not documented in Italy. Circular stone-built pottery kilns with raised floors, and belonging to the seventh century, have been found at Otranto in Apulia (Arthur *et al.* 1992), and would seem to represent a more elaborate scale of production; but, as Patterson shows (this volume), little is known about pottery manufacture of the early medieval period in the Rome area, or elsewhere in the peninsula. It may well have been quite organized. The related tile industry certainly continued under papal encouragement, as brick stamps (including some of Pope Hadrian I) attest. Manufacture also took place in monasteries and in some Lombard centres (Paroli

Fig. 87. The late eighth- to mid-ninth-century pottery kiln, looking east, in the southwest corner of the large Roman room. *(KW)*

early medieval pottery kiln

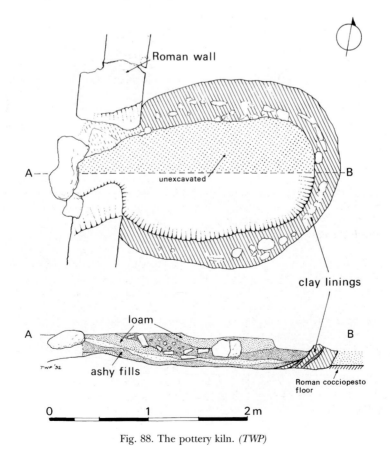

Fig. 88. The pottery kiln. *(TWP)*

1991; Arthur and Whitehouse 1983). But the small pottery kiln at Monte Gelato so far stands alone as a record of a modest rural industry, perhaps started with papal support, but which may have developed private sidelines. The silver *denarius* of Hadrian III (AD 884-5) from burial 43 (D135) in the baptistery may indeed be a hint of some commercial success.

It should be added that, although no traces of unequivocal workshop activity were found around the kiln, the ruinous area of the Roman 'large room' may well have provided such a space. The early medieval floor did not survive, and no features of the period were identified; but the ample dimensions of the room, some of whose walls may still have been standing, would have been most suitable for a workshop – a continuity of function from late Roman times which is striking, if, one must suppose, coincidental.

THE CAVES

The cave, site N

Amongst the features brought to light by bulldozing work on the southwest side of the modern road in 1989, was a rock-cut cave. It had been hollowed out of the tufo face at the head of the long spur that borders the modern road (Figs 9 and 89), and was immediately recognizable as a typical component of medieval sites in the Roman Campagna. Although the dangerous state of the roof precluded investigation within the cave, the entrance was partially excavated.

Internally, the cave measured about 6.0 × 5.0 m, a not inconsiderable floor area (Fig. 90). It was partially divided into two equally-sized rooms by an unexcavated wall of rock, which originally extended nearly half way across the cave. In the more northerly room was a shaft in the ceiling, now choked with soil and vegetation; it measured *c.* 1.2 × 0.7 m, and presumably served as a chimney. Other rock-cut features frequently encountered in medieval cave habitations of this sort, such as beds, benches, niches and mangers, were in this case not visible; but there was a deep accumulation of debris and soil over the floor, which would have concealed most elements of this sort. Cave houses are easy to construct in the soft volcanic tufo, and the tradition of carving furniture out of the rock was of great longevity, as so many Etruscan tombs – to name the most obvious example – clearly show.

The excavations in the entrance showed that the cave was provided with a rock-cut passage, leading up from the early Imperial Roman rock-cut road (site S, above). The road had survived as a hollow way, heading down the slope towards the river, and would have provided a convenient route up and down a cliff some 3.5 m in height. The passage was not fully exposed, but was a minimum of 1.5 m in width, and cut nearly 1.0 m deep into the bedrock, with fairly straight sides. It had also been dug through a Roman wall of *tufelli* and tiles, built along the top of the older road, and there was a post-hole, 0.55 m in diameter but only 0.2 m deep, at the mouth. This may have been for a gate. At the entrance to the cave, the north side of the passage had been cut back at the base, forming a rectangular recess, 0.15 m high. There was also a square socket at the centre. The equivalent area on the south side of the entrance was not investigated, but there can be little doubt that these were housings for a

Fig. 89. The cave habitation, looking northwest. *(KW)*

Cave, site N

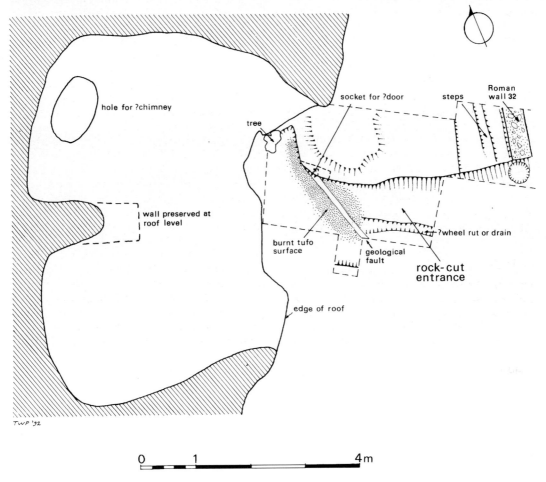

Fig. 90. Cave habitation cut into the ridge to the west of the main site. *(TWP)*

door, probably with a wooden sill beam across the passage. The rest of the façade was presumably filled in with wood or other building materials, perhaps with windows on either side of the door, for which there was ample space. Cave storage rooms with simple façades of this sort abound to this day in local villages of medieval origin, like Mazzano and Calcata, and many were undoubtedly once lived in.

Along the centre of the entrance passage was a rock-cut drain, 0.2 m wide and 0.1 m deep, and there was also a diagonal fissure, of natural origin. This latter area had been the focus of an intense fire, which had burnt the tufo to a deep hue of red. This can hardly have been a fireplace, although the localized nature of the burning shows that the conflagration was carefully controlled; it may relate to the abandonment of the cave. Above this was a fine silt wash, and then dumps of pulverulent, tufaceous soil, together with lumps of tufo, fragments of tile and *selce*, as well as a certain amount of pottery.

An examination of the sherds by Helen Patterson indicated that only one was typical of the ninth century, while the rest belonged to the tenth and eleventh centuries. These must therefore mark the abandonment of the cave, and should imply that its main period of use belonged to the ninth and tenth centuries. It is possible that occupation extended well into the eleventh century, since sherds of this period occurred throughout the fill, but the precise period of abandonment must remain uncertain.

Other caves

The dense vegetation along the sides of the spur, where the cave described above was located, precluded the identification of other rock-cut dwellings in this area. Their existence certainly cannot be ruled out. Moreover, other caves are to be found in the upper hillslopes, some 60 m to the northeast of the main site (Fig. 4). These were not investigated in detail, but the main features were quite clear. There was a long entrance, some 20.0 m in extent, with well-cut straight sides. This gave access to a rectangular chamber, again carefully shaped (Fig. 91). It was 9.0 m long, 4.5 m wide and, although the floor was covered with fill, at least 2.4 m high. From it led a smaller chamber, measuring 4.0 × 3.5 m, and of the same height as the main cave.

No excavation was carried out, and there were insufficient surface finds to provide an indication of their date. However, there must be a very high chance that they were cut during the early medieval period. Their large size, and the quality of the work, argue for an organized effort of construction, and they are wholly atypical of medieval rock-cut dwellings. They would, however, have been ideal for the storage of produce, and it is tempting to suppose that they were made for this purpose during the period of the *domusculta* of *Capracorum*. It is certainly the most plausible context, and helps to explain why no other storage building was identified in the excavations.

Fig. 91. Cave on the east side of the main site (see Figure 4). *(KW)*

THE REUSE OF THE MAUSOLEUM (SITE P)

The fill in the excavated areas of the mausoleum (or temple-tomb) was exclusively of early medieval date, as the pottery made clear. It comprised some 0.75 m of loose pulverulent soil, together with tufo rubble, tile and other Roman building material, but without any very obvious stratification. It overlay the natural bedrock which, in the main chamber, was relatively flat, except to the east. In it was cut a narrow, flat-bottomed slot, some 0.13 m deep at maximum, and a single post-hole, 0.14 m in diameter, and 0.15 m deep (Figs 36 and 92). There was also a possible second slot, at the edge of the trench. In the smaller room, the bedrock shelved down to the east, and had been roughly levelled up with tufo blocks and lumps. There were also the bases of what may have been two post-holes.

Although only part of the fill was excavated, it seems reasonably certain that the mausoleum was used as some form of habitation or byre, with some internal fittings of wood. In addition, there was what seems to have been a doorway, cut through the west wall, but later filled in; and also a roughly made drain, inserted through the base of the south wall in the larger room. The drain, if of this period, may be a pointer that animals were housed here, rather than people, just as the slots could have been for wooden stalls.

It is reasonable to assume that the mausoleum still retained its vaulted roof, as do so many at, for example, the Isola Sacra at Ostia. Such robust structures will have provided more than adequate shelter, and in this instance on a spacious scale – a further indication, perhaps, that it was utilized for agricultural rather than domestic purposes. It should also be noted that when the mausoleum was first exposed by bulldozing work in 1989, the adjacent rock surface was scraped clean over a wide area. This was closely scrutinized for features, especially post-holes and pits, but in

the event, not a single constructional element was identified. There was also a dearth of pottery. Thus, unless very superficially built, we can be reasonably certain that occupation was here confined to the mausoleum.

The sherds from the fill suggest that this occupation spanned the late eighth to late eleventh centuries. In the apparent absence of floor levels within the fill, it must be assumed that the deposits represented accumulated refuse, which was eventually dumped inside the mausoleum. Alternatively, the fill may have been in some way reworked when the building was finally pulled down, at some unspecified date, and the remains carted away. This must have been a considerable operation, but the complete absence of collapsed masonry or vault shows that, like the rest of the complex, the mausoleum was also very largely systematically demolished.

THE AREA TO THE EAST AND SOUTH OF THE CHURCH

Two footings (C15 and C18) in this area belong to the medieval period (below, Fig. 94). C18 was the more substantial, with a width of 0.7 m and a maximum surviving depth of 0.3 m. It was made of tufo lumps, set in a greyish mortar, and ran parallel with C15, the two walls being 3.25 m apart. C15 was narrower, some 0.55 m across, but otherwise of similar construction. Both terminated just before the apse of the second church, indicating that they post-dated it.

No other walls could with certainty be attributed to the early medieval phases in this area, and plough damage was such that the footings were all but destroyed at the eastern edge of the excavation (Fig. 93). Beyond, the tufo bedrock outcropped in such a manner as to suggest that little had

Fig. 92. Slots and post-hole of early medieval date in the tufo bedrock at the base of the mausoleum or temple-tomb (see Figure 36). *(KW)*

Fig. 93. View looking west towards the churches. The left-hand footing (C18) is of early medieval date, the right-hand one (C17) is the north wall of the southern corridor around the Roman courtyard. *(TWP)*

survived in this area (although there are reports of the ploughing up of large tufo blocks in this part of the site). It is not, therefore, possible to provide any definitive interpretation of these remains. At first sight, the larger wall, C18, might be seen as a perimeter to the complex, with a room built up against it; but, in the absence of any indication of a return, that must remain conjectural. Nevertheless, if the remains are those of a perimeter wall of the *domusculta* period, it would be of extreme interest. Santa Cornelia was provided with a boundary wall, enclosing a trapezoidal area *c.* 65 × 75 × 50 m, in the period *c.* 815-50 and, although only 1.0 m thick, and apparently lacking either towers or a ditch, must have afforded a measure of protection (Christie and Daniels 1991: 184-5). Santa Rufina may also have been similarly enclosed around this time, while radiocarbon dates place the first occupation of the defended promontory at nearby Ponte Nepesino, near Nepi, in the mid to late ninth century (cf. Chapter One). The causes are not hard to seek. Hostility from noble Roman landowners, seemingly threatened by the foundation of the papal *domuscultae*, ran deep: in 816 they organized a systematic torching of the farms. Later in the century, Arab war-bands ran amok, forcing the construction of the Leonine Wall around the Vatican, with the help of men of *Capracorum*, in 846. The Ager Faliscus did not escape, and the territories of Nepi and Sutri were plundered. The site at the Mola di Monte Gelato, although well away from the main roads, was nevertheless a papal show-piece; defences, perhaps never completed, will surely have seemed desirable, for it must have been a prime target. If so, definite archaeological evidence for any such attack is lacking, as is the provision of an *enceinte* against marauders. Yet the possibility must be borne in mind.

Only one other feature in this area requires mention, namely a short length of tufo blocks, which extended southwards from the church apse, over the top of the limekiln (Fig. 66, C41; Fig. 65). Whether this really constituted a wall is quite unclear; but it is clearly late in the sequence and, if not part of a makeshift structure, might belong to a stockpile of blocks, assembled during the demolition of the church.

THE LATE ROMAN AND EARLY MEDIEVAL CEMETERY

A total of 107 certain or probable graves was excavated, yielding the remains of 159 individuals. Parts of at least 84 further skeletons were found in unstratified contexts, so that the minimum population was 243. Given the concentration of interments in and around the ecclesiastical complex (Fig. 94), this is likely to be a significant proportion of those who were buried at the site, suggesting that it was not a particularly large community. Certainly there would seem to be grounds for some valid generalizations regarding this population.

Human remains were encountered in all five seasons of excavation but expert study only began in the third. Some recording errors were therefore unavoidable, compounded by the fact that skeletons, once discovered, could not be left *in situ* overnight. Mistakes were not, however, numerous, and are unlikely to have an affect on the validity of the conclusions. More problematic is the nature of the burials. Multiple burials were the rule rather than the exception, and it is clear that many individuals were unceremoniously shoved aside when a new body was introduced into the grave. Bones thus came to be scattered, rendering the identification of individual graves extremely difficult at times. Moreover, grave cuts were in places very hard to pick out. Cemetery excavations are rarely easy; and at Monte Gelato the task was indeed difficult, a factor that should be borne in mind when assessing the results.

Nevertheless, the archaeological and osteological studies have, in combination, arrived at some striking conclusions. Although assigning the graves to phases has proved far from easy – most are effectively unstratified – typological and spatial analyses have proved particularly illuminating. What emerges is a picture of a closely-related, working, rural community, but with a clear social hierarchy. This conforms most convincingly with the other archaeological and historical inferences and, given the rarity of full studies of cemeteries in Italy of this period (Ginatempo 1988), encourages as detailed a presentation of the evidence as possible.

GRAVE MORPHOLOGY

There proved to be a clear grave typology, which responds well to spatial analysis (Fig. 95). The details of the more elaborate tombs are summarized in Table 3; they belong to three main classes.

Elaborate tombs

Three fall into this category. One was the largest grave on the site (no. 2), and probably lay beneath the altar (Fig. 94 and, below, Fig. 96). It contained fragments from a collapsed mortar vault in the middle fill, perhaps from a structure over the altar, or from an internal feature, and had been later partly rebuilt; included in this was part of a decorated screen from the first early medieval church. The position of the grave makes it fairly certain that it belongs with the second church and, in its original form, was coeval with the foundation of the *domusculta* estate-centre in the late eighth century. It was certainly in a suitable position for a reliquary, and in fact contained two articulated primary burials, one of an adult (the sex could not be established) of about 22 or more, and the other of a female of about 24 or more. Radiocarbon dating of the adult yielded a result of 1480 ± 45 BP (BM- 2861) which calibrates to AD 545 to 630 (one sigma) or, at two sigma (or 95% probability), to AD 450 to 650. Assuming that the tomb was constructed at the time of the foundation of the *domusculta*, this implies that the bodies were at least 150 years old when buried in the grave, suggesting that they may well have had the status of saintly relics. It is a little puzzling that the bones excavated were articulated, but it is possible that they were preserved in a shroud or coffin (although no traces of these were detected). However, it should be pointed out that only the eastern part of the burials could be uncovered, since the western half lay beneath a later structure: one cannot therefore be certain that all the bones remained in articulation.

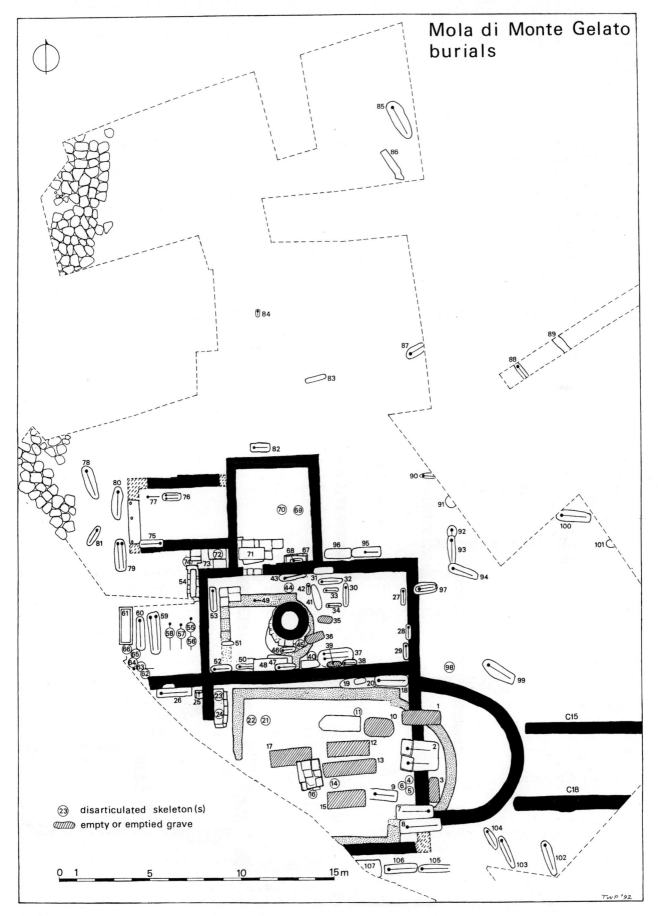

Fig. 94. Distribution of burials by catalogue number. *(TWP)*

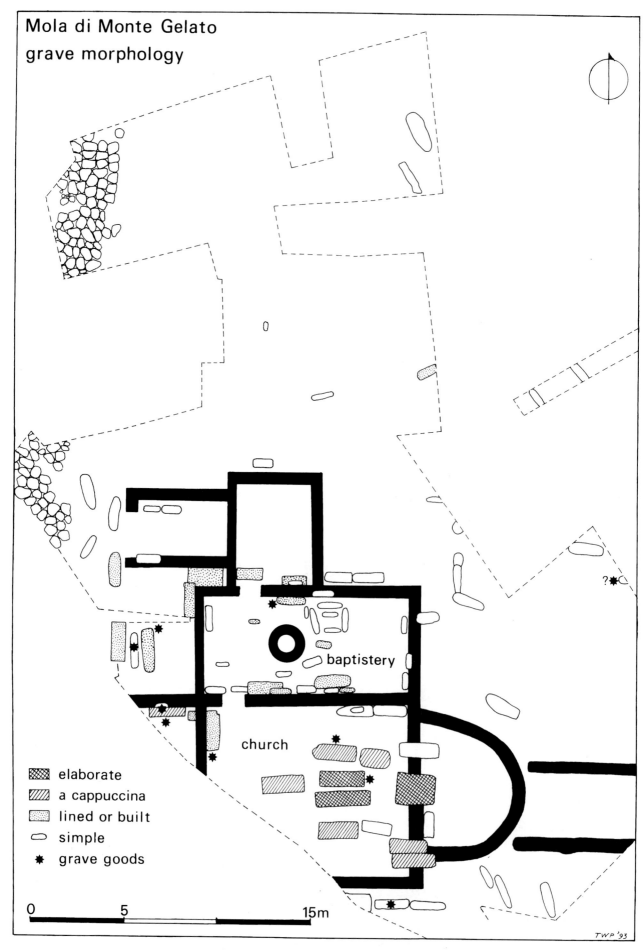

Fig. 95. Distribution of grave types. *(TWP)*

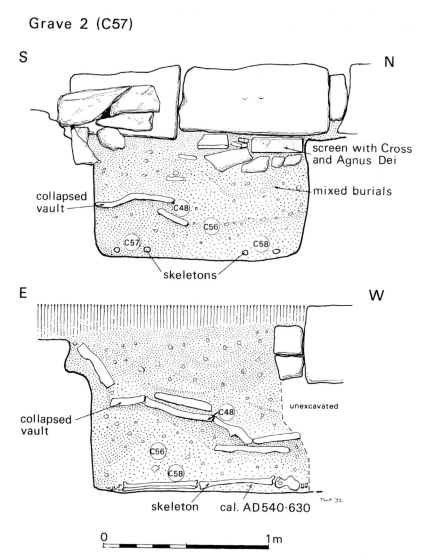

Fig. 96. Sections across the grave in the church that probably lay underneath the altar. *(TWP)*

The translation of relics to newly founded churches was, of course, a phenomenon of the age. When the estate-centre of the *domusculta* of *Capracorum* was built, the church became home to the remains of four popes, three of the second century and one of the early fifth century. All the Roman clergy and Senate were invited by Pope Hadrian I to attend the dedication (Christie and Daniels 1991: 6, 178). Normally these holy relics were displayed, although it is hard to see how this was done at Monte Gelato, at least for the primary interments; it is not impossible, however, that the collapsed vaulting in the tomb derived from a structure that made visible the remains of suitable relics.

The other two 'elaborate' graves, nos. 12 and 13, lay more or less centrally within the nave of the church. Both had been emptied of their bones (assuming that they had once contained interments), a measure of the importance of these individuals. No. 12 was covered by a tufo grave slab, which rested upon six pillars, set into the side of the tomb (Figs 97-9); this may have been to facilitate the raising of the lid. There was mortar on the lid, possibly a symbolic sealing of the tomb. There were tufo lumps at the east end, which may have been for a headrest. If so, this would be one of only four burials from the site with the head at that end; one (no. 7) was also in the church and the other two came

from a multiple burial in the entrance (no. 75). It has been suggested that these could be the graves of priests, enabling them to face their normally west-east flocks (Rahtz 1977: 59, n. 2); the question of orientation is taken up further below.

Beside grave no. 12 was no. 13, a much longer tomb. This contained some fragments of mortar, bearing timber impressions, again implying some sort of built structure. Exactly what form this may have taken is impossible to say, but the centrality of the grave indicates that it held the remains of an important individual, buried in an elaborate tomb.

A cappuccina tombs

While only seven of these pitched tile-built graves were found, it is immediately striking that six were in the church nave and one (a simpler structure) in the church narthex. This is suggestive of high status, as is the fact that all but two had seen the subsequent removal of the bones. Interestingly, two (nos. 10, 11: Figs 97, 100, 101) had apparently been rebuilt, and sealed with mortar. Assuming that they did once hold interments, it would seem that the graves continued to be venerated, a matter for which there is corroborative evidence, discussed further below.

Table 3. The 'high-status' tombs.

no.	location	state	structure	orienta-tion	sex and/or general age category	age	coffin nails	lead	other finds	phase
ELABORATE TOMBS										
2	church	in situ primary burials	vaulted	W-E	adult F	>22 y <24 y	yes	-	glass	5 (cal. AD 545-630) 1-sigma
12	church	emptied	stone slab on pillars	W-E			yes	yes	glass vessel fragments	5
13	church	emptied	mortar with timber impressions	W-E			-	yes	-	5
A CAPPUCCINA TOMBS										
7	church	partly intact	a cappuccina	E-W	F	25-35 y	yes	-	glass, plaster	6-7?
8	church	most bones removed	a cappuccina	W-E	adult infant infant	>17 y 0-6 mon. 4-5 y	yes	yes	glass	6-7?
10	church	empty	a cappuccina (child-sized)	W-E	infant below floor		-	-	glass	5-6
11	church	empty; bones beneath floor	a cappuccina	W-E	infant below floor adult below floor	1.5-2.5 y <22 y	-	yes	fourth-century coin, glass	5-6
15	church	empty, disturbed	a cappuccina	W-E	few infant bones	0-1 y	yes	-	-	5-6
17	church	empty	a cappuccina	W-E	few infant bones	0-1 y	yes	-	-	5-6
26 (1)	church narthex	intact	a cappuccina against wall	W-E	juvenile adult	12-13 y ?	-	-	fourth-century coin, glass	5-6
OTHER BUILT TOMBS										
24	church	intact	ossuary	N-S	M M F F adult juvenile juvenile juvenile juvenile	c.50 y 30-40 y 17-25 y adult adult ? 20-4 y 10-15 y 5-10 y 5-10 y	-	yes	glass flask	5
25	church narthex	intact; few bones	tile and tufo cist	N-S	infant infant adult	3-9 mon. 2-3 y ?	-	-	-	6

no.	location	state	structure	orienta-tion	sex and/or general age category	age	coffin nails	lead	other finds	phase
35	baptistery centre	empty	tile and marble lining	W-E				-	-	-	6
37	baptistery	in situ	tile seal	W-E	juvenile infant infant	8-9 y 3-4 y 3.5-4.5 y	Yes	-	-	6
38	baptistery	in situ	tile lining	W-E	infant	0.6 mon.	-	-	-	6-7
43	baptistery	in situ	tile cover	W-E	juvenile	6-8 y	-	-	coin of AD 884-5, iron boss	5
47	baptistery	in situ	some tile lining	W-E	infant	3.5-4.5 y	-	yes	-	6
49	baptistery	disturbed	some tile on sides and bottom	W-E	?	?	-	-	-	6
54	baptistery ?narthex	largely in situ	tufo lining and cover	N-S	M M	17-25 y 17-25 y	-	-	-	6-7
59	baptistery ?narthex	in situ	some tile lining	N-S	M M	33-45 y 17-25 y	yes	-	pottery cup	4 (cal. AD 565-635 1 sigma)
61	baptistery ?narthex	empty	tufo sarcophagus	N-S			-	-	-	?4-5
67	ante-room	empty; previously excavated	tufo blocks	W-E	a few infant bones	3-7 y	yes	-	-	5-6
79	outside entrance	in situ	tufo block walls, tile floor	N-S	M F	25-35 y 33-45 y	-	-	-	5-6
87	to north of building	in situ	tile and tufo lining	SW-NE	infant	0.5-1.5 y	-	-	-	3+

KEY: N – north; S – south; E – east; W – west; F – female; M – male; mon. – months; y – years

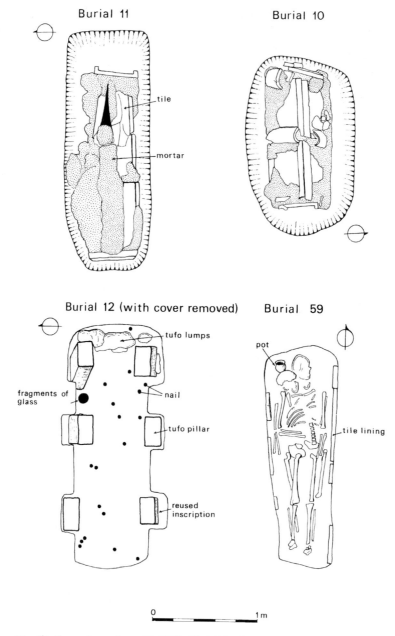

Fig. 97. Grave plans of nos. 10 (B21), 11 (B32), 12 (B16) and 59 (D168). *(TWP)*

Most of the graves yielded a scatter of infant bones, as well as an articulated juvenile of 12-13 years, and an articulated female of 25-35 years. Two other adults could not be assigned a sex. There were also bones beneath the floor in two cases, including two infants and an adult. It is clear, therefore, that these tombs were not restricted to adult males (one, indeed, is child-sized: no. 10) from, say, the priesthood. Perhaps they were members of influential local families. But it is notable that there are so few of these *a cappuccina* graves: it may be that they too in some cases contained the bones of people with saintly status or associations, which merited removal when the church was deconsecrated and pulled down about AD 1100. If so, it is noteworthy that Conheeney's study (below) of the human bones that remained in the church shows that, like all the individuals from the site, they bear the signs of a life of strenuous toil.

One further observation may be added. It is possible that two other graves, nos. 1 and 3, were *a cappuccina*, since they

too had been thoroughly emptied of their contents. Similarly, burial no. 9 was severely damaged (although there were some *in situ* bones), and may have had a more elaborate structure than the surviving evidence implies. It underlines the point that ordinary burials were extremely rare within the church (Fig. 95). There were some in the northeast corner of the nave (nos. 18-20), and groups of disarticulated bone; but the impression is that this *ad sanctos* area was essentially reserved, at any rate in a formal sense, for individuals who were accorded privileged status, whether for religious or for social reasons.

Other built tombs

At least fourteen other tombs exhibited special constructional features. They lay mainly in or near the baptistery and, although often very simply built, may be an indication of higher status. The most remarkable was an ossuary, made of

Fig. 98. Church nave: burial no. 12 with the cover *in situ*; burials nos. 10, 11 and 13 fully excavated; and the post-church monument base. *(ACK)*

small tufo blocks and with a tile floor (no. 24). It contained the bones of three males, two females, an adult and four juveniles, and was tucked into the northwest corner of the church nave. There was also a fine glass pilgrim's flask (cat. 115, below, Fig. 190), placed at the top of the deposit. There were no osteological signs that this was a family tomb, but this possibility cannot be excluded. It would seem that the remains were collected together from elsewhere, probably in a single operation, and that the flask was placed as a parting gift once the bones had been deposited in the ossuary.

Of similar construction was a tomb, no. 54, outside the northwestern corner of the baptistery. It contained the remains of two males, one disarticulated and the other articulated, representing successive interments. The tomb had been sealed with tufo slabs but, curiously, the skull of the later interment had been removed. This may be reminiscent of the emptying of other apparently 'high-status' graves elsewhere on the site. Also of similar construction, and likewise empty of human remains, except for a few infant bones, was a tomb, no. 67, in the ante-room to the north of the baptistery.

The other built tombs mainly consisted of tile-lined grave pits, sometimes with a tile floor and, in a few cases, with a tile cover (Fig. 102). The standard of construction ranged from the quite neat to the very crude, but in each instance would seem to represent an attempt to make a rather more elaborate grave. They were built for men, women and children and, in one case (no. 79), osteological considerations suggest a family relationship between the female and younger male buried in the tomb (below, Fig. 109).

Four other probable burials in this category require mention. One is a tufo sarcophagus (no. 61) in the area to the west of the baptistery, the possible narthex. This lay in the side of the modern road cutting (cf. below, Fig. 107), and

Fig. 99. Burial no. 12 with the covering slab removed (seen resting against the back section). *(ACK)*

Fig. 100. Burial no. 10 (B21) in the church nave. Scale: 0.2 m. *(TWP)*

Fig. 101. Burial no. 11 (B32) in the church nave. Scale: 0.2 m. *(TWP)*

Fig. 102. Burial no. 37 (Fig. 78, D229) with its tile cover. *(KW)*

had long since been emptied; but there seems no reason to doubt that it once held a burial, presumably of an important individual. It is likely to be a reused Roman sarcophagus, although it had not been embellished in any way. In a similar category is no. 48, an adult-sized tufo grave slab along the inside of the south wall of the baptistery. The grave itself was not investigated further, but virtually every other burial in the baptistery was of an infant or juvenile, making this probable tomb particularly unusual. Finally, there were two areas with tufo block structures, which may well have been tombs. One, no. 71 (Fig. 80), lay to the north of the entrance leading from the baptistery to the ante-room, and possessed what looked like a grave cover; the other (no. 73) was tucked into the alcove between the baptistery and the entrance. It was not possible to take apart these structures; but it is hard to explain them unless they were tombs.

Ordinary tombs

The remaining 80 identifiable tombs were simple affairs, dug into the subsoil or, where it outcropped, the rock. The line of three tombs, nos. 105-7, cut into the tufo just outside the south wall of the church, might be considered to be of higher status, both from their position, and from their well-made appearance. But these are exceptions (and are all likely to be of late Roman date). Thus, possible coffin nails were found in only three of these graves but, with just one nail in each grave, can hardly constitute evidence for the use of coffins in these burials. A priori, one would suppose that these are in the main the graves of the ordinary mem-

bers of the community, especially those buried *sub divo*, far from the church. It is symbolized by a man of 45 or more from a simple earthfast burial (no. 78) by the road (below, Fig. 108): he had lost his upper teeth and the cavities had fused over, and he had suffered (and survived) appalling injuries to his ribs. He is an evocative reminder of the traumas of peasant life.

GRAVE ORIENTATION

Measurement was possible for only 62 burials, with the following results.

Feet to:		
	south	20
	southwest	1
	west	3
	northeast	1
	east	29
	southeast	8

These results are set out diagrammatically in Figure 103, where it is possible to incorporate the deviations from the main compass points. The pattern is remarkably clear. East-west and north-south alignments occur in almost equal measure, when slight divergences are included, and it seems evident that, for this population, there was no predominant rule in the way of death. The main determining factor was probably the alignment of the nearest wall, although even that generalization is not wholly valid. The organization is, understandably, at its neatest in the church nave and bap-

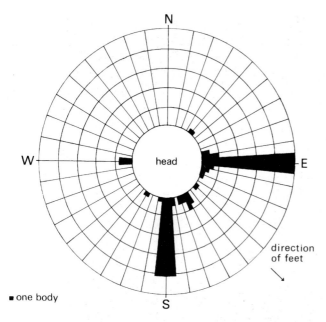

Fig. 103. Orientation of the skeletons. *(TWP)*

tistery, and at its most chaotic in the area to the west of the baptistery, where there may have been a narthex. For those buried *sub divo*, outside the buildings, in most cases alignment hardly mattered: here are further hints that these were the graves of individuals who were towards the bottom of whatever social hierarchy may have existed.

We have already referred to the few individuals who faced the west (burials 7, (?)12, 75). Two are 'high status' graves, and the argument that these were priests facing their flock has its attractions (Rahtz 1977). But burial 7 is that of a woman, ruling out that explanation in this case, and it is perhaps more likely that these were simply mistakes.

POSITION OF BODY

The bodies were generally interred supine, but in a variety of postures, listed in Table 4. The level of disturbance is such that the figures cannot be pressed at all hard for the sample is far too small. The most prevalent practice was to bury the individual with arms folded across the body, and straight legs, in a Christian manner. However, there is a considerable range of variations, and certainly no standard procedure. It may be that these different positions did have some meaning (or, less probably, chronological implications); but no pattern emerges from this fairly small group.

COFFINS AND GRAVE-GOODS

Nails were found in twelve graves, but were only numerous in three, all important burials in the church nave: nos. 2 (fourteen nails), 8 (sixteen nails) and 12 (sixteen nails). There were three from the disturbed grave no. 7, but the remaining tombs yielded only one, or, in one case, two nails; it is hard to suppose that there were coffins in these graves. Fragments of lead were also found in twelve tombs, and might in some instances have been coffin fittings, although only a piece from burial no. 2 appeared convincing.

Certain or possible grave-goods were found in ten tombs (Table 5). Of immediate interest is the fact that two with fourth-century coins, burials nos. 26 and 60, have osteological traits suggesting that the two individuals were related (Conheeney, below). Only one other tomb (no. 11) contained a Roman coin (and that in the fill, where it may have been introduced accidentally); thus it would seem that the inclusion of the coins with the bones (one was in the mouth) in burials 26 and 60 can hardly be fortuitous. The coins must have been many centuries old when buried and, being of bronze, of no value; but they hint at the continuation of an old pagan practice which was perhaps traditional in this family.

A silver *denarius* of AD 884-5 was placed with a child in burial 43, and a finger-ring, perhaps of sixth-century date, with a disarticulated female in burial 26. Otherwise gravegoods were confined to two pots, a glass vessel (and many fragments) and, much less certainly, an iron knife. The date ranges are listed in the table; it is notable that the range for the vessel from burial 59 is matched by a radiocarbon assessment of cal. AD 565-635 (one sigma), suggesting that the vessel was not old when it was placed in the grave.

The grave finds recall Tomassetti's record of a Christian burial, with large tiles, gold earrings and *balsamarii* of glass (Tomassetti 1882: 146). It was apparently situated outside the church, and should therefore belong with the more elaborate burials recorded in the present excavations. Indeed, there is a clear relationship between these built tombs and the occurrence of grave-goods, suggesting that even a simple pottery vessel (or its contents) was a mark of status. As Table 5 shows, men, women and children were distinguished in this way. It was not, therefore, a clerical hierarchy that was being singled out, but rather members of particular families, whose status was further enhanced by being buried in or close to the church.

OTHER SPATIAL CONSIDERATIONS

Although discussed in detail by Conheeney, below, it is worth stressing here that the burials in the baptistery were almost all of infants and children. They were also found in other parts of the site, often in disturbed contexts; but the concentration in the baptistery and the neat organization of these graves imply that special factors were operating. At first sight, it might appear that these were children who had yet to be baptized: but the age range is against this, since there is a wide span (Table 6).

It is notable, too, that the baptistery includes a number of more elaborate tombs, one with a silver *denarius* of Pope Hadrian III (AD 884-5), a rare issue and the only medieval coin from the excavations. Moreover, two of the graves (nos. 36 and 39) had been subsequently emptied of their bones, like many of those within the nave of the church. The implication is that the child burials within the baptistery may reflect higher social ranking within the community, as with those in the church. Interestingly, there is some evidence to suggest that a similar practice may have been followed at Santa Cornelia, particularly after the baptistery had gone out of use (Christie and Daniels 1991: 198). The analogy is particularly apt since, at Monte Gelato too, some of the child interments in the area of the baptistery clearly post-dated the demolition of the building (for example, Fig. 94, nos. 28, 31, 97). Evidently, the site of the baptistery retained a symbolic importance, as did the church, if the monument base (Figs 76 and 77) marking its site is any guide.

Table 4. Body positions.

arm positions	
both straight	six (two males, four infants)
right across body, left straight	four (one male, one female, one juvenile, one infant)
left across body, right straight	one (infant)
both folded across body	twelve (six males, four females, one juvenile, one infant)
left arm folded across body, right arm pointing to right shoulder	two (females)
both arms flexed	two (infants)
	TOTAL: 27

leg positions	
broadly straight	31
flexed	three (infants)

Table 5. Burials with grave-goods (certain or possible).

no.	type	location	sex	age	object	date of object
11	*a cappuccina*	church	adult infant	<22 yr 1.5-2.5 yr	coin (in fill) base of glass vessel	fourth century ?
12	elaborate	church	-	-	glass fragments	?
24	ossuary	church	M M M F F juvenile juvenile juvenile juvenile	c. 50 yr 30-40 yr 17-25 yr adult adult 20-4 yr 10-15 yr 5-10 yr 5-10yr	glass flask	?sixth to eighth centuries
26 (1)	*a cappuccina*	church narthex	juvenile adult	12-13 yr adult	coin glass fragments	fourth century
26 (2)	bag of bones	church narthex	F	25-35 yr	finger-ring	?sixth century
43	tile-covered grave	baptistery	juvenile	6-8 yr	coin, iron boss	AD 884-5
59	tile-lined	baptistery ?narthex	M M	17-25 yr 33-45 yr	pottery cup	later sixth to early seventh centuries
60	simple	baptistery ?narthex	juvenile F	7-9 yr 17-25 yr	coin glass fragments	fourth century
101	simple	courtyard	-	-	iron knife	?
106	rock-cut	south of church	F	17-25 yr	pottery vessel glass fragments	later fifth to early sixth centuries

Note: glass fragments were also found in burials nos. 2, 7, 8, 10, 39, 55, 77, 81, 93, 95 and 99, but whether these are coincidental or broken grave-goods is unclear.

Table 6. Approximate ages at death of children buried in the baptistery.

years	0	<1	1-2	2-4	3-4	4-5	6-8	8-9
number of individuals	1	3	2	4	5	1	2	1

THE PHASING

The phasing of the cemetery has been referred to little in the preceding discussion. This reflects the fact that, in many areas of the site, it was difficult or impossible to arrive at a satisfactory verdict, certainly within any very close limits. Few graves could be dated stratigraphically, and relative sequences were not easy to establish. Nevertheless, some general observations can be made.

The earliest datable grave is probably no. 106, one of three rock-cut examples just outside, and parallel with, the south walls of the churches. No. 106 contained a pottery vessel datable to the second half of the fifth century (cat. 186); if not old when it was buried, which seems unlikely, it ought to be a good indication of the date of the grave. On the other hand, no other burial is demonstrably of this period, and it seems certain that the excavated area was not the focus of a late Roman cemetery.

A Roman cemetery has been located by *clandestini*, some 200 m to the northwest of the main site (Fig. 8). It is extremely overgrown, but contains rock-cut tombs, associated with Roman pottery. It is not, however, clear what its chronological limits may have been. Excavations in 1877 did, however, yield three early Christian tombstones. Two can be dated, one to AD 361 and the other to AD 407 (Fiocchi Nicolai 1988: 235-7). The exact provenance of these finds is unknown, but it was these investigations which yielded a Christian church which we assume, but without corroborative evidence, to be the same as that excavated by us. It is, of course, possible that these tombstones had been brought from some other location but, without knowing more of their context, that must remain uncertain. All that can safely be said is that there was an early Christian cemetery in the vicinity of our main excavations.

As we have seen above, the late Roman church cannot be dated closely. The probability is that it was constructed in the early fifth century, to serve this rural community and surrounding sites. If this is the case, it does not, however, appear immediately to have been the centre for burials. Apart from burial 106 (see above), there were human remains incorporated into a sixth-century deposit (no. 69), and burial 59 is dated both by a pottery vessel and by a radiocarbon date to the late sixth or early seventh century; but no other interments can be assigned with certainty to this phase. There are certainly insufficient grounds for suggesting a late Roman cemetery church.

Indeed, it seems fairly clear that the main period of the cemetery belongs to the three centuries between about AD 800 and 1100. With a minimum total of only 243 individuals in all, this implies a fairly small community, perhaps as few as 30, at the roughest of guesses. There may, of course, have been peaks and troughs in the size of the population over this period, and there is some evidence to suggest that more burials belong to the tenth and eleventh centuries or later, than to the ninth century. This is certainly the case in the deeply stratified deposits to the west of the baptistery. At least 32 individuals were buried here and, while many of these graves were heavily disturbed, it is none the less clear that the majority occurred in fairly late contexts (Fig. 54).

Within the baptistery, no burials can be associated with confidence with the early baptistery, except for burial no. 43. This partly underlay the wall of the later baptistery, and contained a coin of AD 884-5. There were, however, sherds of the late ninth and/or tenth centuries in the fill of burial 33, probable tenth-century sherds in burial 32 and possible eleventh-century material in no. 46. Other burials, as pointed out above, post-date the demolition of the building. It

may be, therefore, that the majority of these interments should be assigned to a late period in the site's history.

Within the church, the ossuary (burial 24) was sealed by a small surviving area of the latest flooring of the second church; it should thus pre-date the late tenth century (as the associated glass vessels also imply). Beneath the floor of the ossuary were bones of a juvenile and two infants (no. 23), which must again be relatively early in the sequence. Likewise, there were disarticulated bones of an adult, a juvenile and an infant (nos. 21 and 22) in the adjoining make-up for the second church floor; whether these represent disturbed *in situ* burials, or bones brought in from elsewhere during the building work is open to question.

Another relatively early burial is no. 26, an *a cappuccina* grave placed against the second church wall in the narthex (Figs 31 and 104). The sequence of interments is complex, and the grave cuts were difficult to identify; but, stratigraphically, this burial (which lies at a depth of 0.72 m below the floor of the ossuary (no. 24)) is likely to be contemporary with the first phase of the second, that is the early medieval, church. As we have seen, two late Roman objects, a coin and a finger-ring, were associated with these burials, and *a cappuccina* graves are a recognized late Roman tradition. It follows that the other *a cappuccina* burials within the church nave should be of similarly early date, together with the three 'elaborate' graves (nos. 2, 12 and 13). The only real difficulty is posed by burials 7 and 8 (C23, C55), which seem to have been cut through both church apses (Figs 66 and 94). However, this part of the site had been severely damaged by the plough, and little reliance can be placed upon apparent stratigraphical relationships in this area. It may well be that they were in fact built into the structure of the first early medieval church and perhaps destroyed during the refurbishment of the church and baptistery in the late tenth or early eleventh century.

The fills of three of these graves did yield datable pottery. No. 12 contained a sherd possibly of the tenth century in the lower fill, and another of the eleventh or twelfth century in the upper fill. No. 13 produced a late tenth-century sherd, and no. 17 material of the late tenth or eleventh century. However, each of these burials seems to have been emptied of the bones when the church was pulled down and it is therefore probable that this pottery relates to that phase, rather than the primary period of interment.

Unlike the baptistery, most burials within the church are therefore likely to belong to the first early medieval period, namely the ninth-tenth centuries. The main exceptions are nos. 18, 19, and 20 which were tucked into the northeast corner of the nave, parallel with the north wall. On stratigraphical grounds, these should be late interments, and no. 18 did indeed yield a sherd of tenth-century date. There were also the bones of three infants, one juvenile, five females and five adults in plough-disturbed deposits over the church; these must also represent burials of the last period of the building or, perhaps, graves dug subsequent to its demolition.

Outside these areas, it is more difficult to determine the date of the burials. The group nos. 102, 103 and 104, to the southeast of the church, would seem to be quite late, on stratigraphical grounds. Interestingly, two skeletons (nos. 102 and 103) exhibit osteological characteristics which suggest that they were related. Likewise, the burials between the entrance and the road (nos. 78-81) were inserted into deposits containing wasters from the late eighth- to mid ninth-century kiln, providing a firm *terminus post quem*; these also include a family group (no. 79). Otherwise, there is

Fig. 104. Left: the *a cappuccina* burial no. 26 (A23); right: the northeast corner of bath-house room 1 (wall A9). Cf. Figures 27, 28, 31 and 66. *(TWP)*

only a subjective impression that this seemingly random series of interments, mostly in shallow graves, belongs mainly to the later phases of the graveyard.

The final period (phase 7) of the cemetery is of some interest. As already noted, a number of graves appear to have been emptied of their bones, seven in the nave of the church and two in the baptistery. In at least three cases, the grave structure was then replaced, suggesting continued veneration of the site. This is supported by the fact that burials continued to be made after the demolition of the church and baptistery. This is evident from the fact that some were cut through the wall footings, and adds support to the identification of the rectangular footing in the church nave (Figs 76 and 77) as the base of some sort of memorial or shrine, erected when the ecclesiastical complex was taken down. The site, although largely abandoned, did not lose its sanctity for the local populace: some 600 years of Christian burial and tradition was not easily forgotten. In all probability, it was only when Castellaccio was finally abandoned, probably by the late thirteenth century, that veneration lapsed and the church and baptistery dwindled into folk memory.

CATALOGUE OF BURIALS

In the following catalogue, for ease of reference the graves have been renumbered (cf. Fig. 94). The original site references are, however, used on the other plans, and are also included here. It should also be noted that it was not always possible to draw plans of all the skeletons *in situ*. This was because, once found, it was necessary to excavate and lift a skeleton within the day, due to the threat of vandalism. This was particularly the case in the baptistery, where there was a very high density of burials.

The suggested phasing, itself very approximate, is as follows – phase 3: late Roman; phase 4: late sixth-seventh centuries; phase 5: late eighth to late ninth centuries; phase 6: tenth-eleventh centuries; phase 7: twelfth century or later.

THE CHURCH (FIGS 66 AND 94)

Burial 1 (B15). Rectangular west-east grave, 2.18 × 0.8 m; depth 0.86 m. It cut the second church cross-wall, but the bones had been largely removed; a few adult bones remained. Phase 6.

Burial 2 (C57). Fig. 96. A complex and important tomb which probably underlay the altar. It comprised a rectangular pit of *c.* 1.4 × 1.9 m, with a depth of 1.08 m. Two primary inhumations of an adult and a female (C57, C58), west-east, were found at the bottom, and had not been disturbed. The tomb had a vault in or above it, the mortar remnants of which had partially collapsed into the tomb, when it had half filled with soil; some retained impressions of wood. There were further disarticulated burials, including a male and an adult (C2, C26, C43, C47, C48), above this. At the west end were blocks of tufo which covered that end of the tomb; built into this was the decorated screen with the Cross and the Agnus Dei (cat. 1). Six strips of lead were found (cat. 71, 72, 74), possibly from coffin fittings, and there was a total of fourteen iron nails. There were also three pieces of glass, one handle and two bases, all from lamps (cat. 145b, 148, 149). The primary burial, C57, yielded a radiocarbon date of 1480 ± 45 BP (BM-2861), which calibrates to AD 545-630 (one sigma). Phase 5/6.

Burial 3 (C25). Sub-rectangular north-south grave, 1.35 × 0.58 m; depth 0.25 m. Set beside the second church cross-wall in the apse of the first, late Roman church, it had a large block of tufo in the fill, but no articulated bones; there were a few adult bones in the fill. Phase 6.

Burial 4 (B53). Disturbed infant burial by the second church cross-wall. Phase 6.

Burial 5 (C42). Juvenile and infant bones in a layer near and over the second church cross-wall. Phase 6.

Burial 6 (C47). Disturbed infant burial in fill by the cross-wall of the second church. Phase 5/6.

Burial 7 (C23). A west-east *a cappuccina* burial, 2.1 × 0.86 m; depth 0.39 m. It contained a partially intact male inhumation, with the head to the east. There was a tile and mortar cover, broken at the top. There were also three iron nails in the fill, a piece of painted plaster and a fragment of glass base (cat. 155) by the head. The grave appeared to cut the apses of both churches, and the adjoining grave, 8. ?Phase 6/7.

Burial 8 (C55). A west-east *a cappuccina* burial, 2.3 × 0.8 m; depth 0.3 m. It had vertical sides and a flat bottom, but the tile and mortar structure had been largely removed, as had most of the skeleton. Some foot and lower leg bones of an adult remained *in situ*, at the east end of the grave. There were also bones of two infants. In the fill were sixteen coffin nails, a piece of lead, a fragment of painted plaster and five pieces of glass (cat. 81, 130, 130a, 135b, 138). The grave appeared to cut the apses of both churches. ?Phase 6/7.

Burial 9 (C32). Rectangular west-east burial in the nave, the west end of which had been removed; 0.6 m wide. Some leg bones of an adult survived at the east end of the grave. A whetstone was found in the fill (cat. 150). Phase 5/6.

Burial 10 (B21). Figs 97 and 100. A west-east tomb, *a cappuccina*, in the nave. The tomb itself, which measured 1.34 × 0.6 m, and 0.66 m in depth, was made of four pitched tegulae, with imbrices over the joins. The ends were sealed by tegulae, and the structure was partially covered with mortar. The tomb was contained within an ovoid pit, 1.66 × 1.0 m. The fill of the tomb was of clean silt, disturbed by rodents. Its base consisted of two unmortared tegulae, but there were no traces of bones and, given its sealed character, it is not clear whether it ever held a corpse (which, from the dimensions, would have been either that of a child or disarticulated). There were two glass bases and a rim (cat. 109, 114, 135c). Beneath the tile floor were the disturbed bones of an infant, not further recorded (B36). Phase 5/6.

Burial 11 (B32). Fig. 97. A west-east tomb, *a cappuccina*, in the nave. The sub-rectangular grave pit was 2.26 × 0.8 m; depth 0.68 m; and the tomb itself was 1.74 × 0.6 m. It was made of four pitched tegulae, and sealed with tegulae at either end, and then partially covered with mortar. In the fill were mixed human bones of an infant over a marble floor, as well as residual Roman sherds, a piece of lead (cat. 67) and a coin of Valentinian II (AD 375-8) (cat. 23). Beneath the marble base was a disturbed skeleton of a young adult (B49), and the lower body, stem and base of a glass vessel (cat. 150) and the rim of a glass flask (cat. 154). Phase 5/6.

Burial 12 (B16). Figs 97-9. An important west-east grave in a more or less central position in the early medieval church. It was covered with a tufo slab, 2.3 × 0.82 m, and 0.1 m thick. There were areas of mortar on the slab, although whether this merely 'sealed' the tomb, or supported a higher structure, is unclear. The slab itself was held up by six tufo supports, 0.45 m high, and recessed into the side of the tomb; one was originally a Roman tombstone, that had been cut in half (below, Fig. 133). The grave was filled with a loose loamy soil, but it contained only a few scraps of adult and infant bone. There were also sixteen iron nails, scattered over the bottom of the grave, pieces of lead (cat. 51, 98) and many fragments of glass (cat. 122, 127d, 140f, 140g, 147, 152i, 154a, 156a). There were in addition some tufo

lumps at the east end, perhaps a headrest. Presumably the body, or bodies, had been removed, and the grave slab replaced. There were sherds of the tenth to twelfth centuries. Phase 5/6.

Burial 13 (B29). Fig. 98. A deep sub-rectangular west-east grave in the nave, 1.8 × 0.54 m, but enlarged at the top to 2.8 × 0.7 m; depth 0.16 m. Lumps of mortar, some with timber impressions, indicate the former existence of a tomb structure. However, no human bones were found, and had presumably been removed. There was a piece of lead (cat. 66) and a sherd of the late tenth century. Phase 6/7.

Burial 14 (B34). A few scraps of human bone in a fine silty fill over destruction rubble. Phase 6.

Burial 15 (B42). A west-east *a cappuccina* burial, badly disturbed, in the nave. Only the base of the tomb survived, comprising four square tiles measuring in total 1.74 × 0.43 m. A few bones still lay upon them, but most of the roof structure had been destroyed. The overall grave pit was *c.* 2.2 × 0.9 m. Phase 5/6.

Burial 16 (B66). Adult bones in the foundation trench for the post-church monument or shrine base (A15). Phase 7.

Burial 17 (B60). A west-east *a cappuccina* burial in the nave, 2.32 × 0.84 m. Only two pieces of the tile structure survived, and the grave may have been deliberately emptied, although there were some infant bones present. The upper fill of the grave contained much rubble, and it is patently earlier than the post-church monument or shrine base (A15). One iron nail and sherds of the late tenth or eleventh century were found. Phase 5/6.

Burial 18 (B8). A complex series of burials, west-east, 1.8 × 0.6 m, tucked in the gap between the north walls of the two churches. There was one articulated male skeleton, articulated west-east but lacking the head and most of the lower limbs. There were also remains of another adult and an infant, and from the lower fill (B22), two adults and one juvenile. Two pieces of lead (cat. 50, 65) were found, as was a tenth-century sherd. Phase 6/7.

Burials 19 and 20. Further graves to the west of no. 18: west-east, 1.8 × 0.5 m, cut by an infant burial. Details of the skeletons were not recorded. Phase 6/7.

Burial 21 (D96). Juvenile and infant bones, disarticulated, in the make-up for the latest floor of the second church nave. Phase 6.

Burial 22 (D108). Adult bones, not articulated, in lower make-up deposits for the latest church floor. Phase 6.

Burial 23 (D123). Burial of two infants and a juvenile under the ossuary, burial 24, below. Phase 5.

Burial 24 (D107). An ossuary built of tufo blocks and with an irregularly laid tile floor, set into the northwest corner of the second church nave. It was sealed by make-up for the second church floor, but there was no trace of a lid. It was orientated north-south, with maximum dimensions of *c.* 2.2 × 1.05 m. The structure stood to a height of 0.41 m, and its floor was about 1.0 m below the latest floor of the second church. Apart from a mass of unarticulated human bone, it contained a fine glass flask (cat. 115) and other fragments (cat. 110), and three pieces of lead (cat. 73, 75, 76). The bones included the remains of three males, two females, one adult and four juveniles. Phase 5.

Burial 25 (D173). Infant, north-south with head to the north, in a small tufo and tile cist, in the narthex to the church. There were also bones of another infant and an adult. Phase 6.

Burial 26 (A23, A3, A4, A28). Figs 31 and 104. A complex sequence of interments in the church narthex, and partly cutting into its north wall (here built upon Roman bathhouse foundations), which are not easy to interpret in detail. They include the following. (1) A west-east *a cappuc-cina* tomb (A23), comprising mortared tiles, had been placed at an angle against the stub of a bath-house wall, and was sealed by a tegula. The body of a juvenile was laid out with the head to the west, and a coin of Honorius (AD 410-23) was placed in the mouth (cat. 46). There were also some adult bones. The floor of the tomb was made up of the tiled surface at the base of the bath-house. (2) Burial A28, which was thought to be earlier than A23, consisted of a group of disarticulated bones of a female, perhaps deposited in a bag or a box. They included a finger bone with a copper alloy ring (cat. 6) of late Antique type. (3) There was a skull and other disarticulated bones of an infant (A3). (4) An infant burial, partly beneath A3, was broadly orientated west-east (A4).

The adult in (1) may have been related, on osteological grounds, to a female in burial 60; both graves also contained Roman coins. Two fragments of glass (cat. 126i) were found. ?Phase 5/6.

Other burials in the church area

There were some disturbed burials, presumably of quite late date, in the plough-soil over the church, including B1, C1, C3, C27 and D94. These are not recorded on the plan, as they were not *in situ*. They included three infants, one juvenile, five females and five adults.

THE BAPTISTERY (FIGS 78 AND 94)

Burial 27 (D43). North-south infant burial, with head to the north, beside the east wall of the second baptistery. 0.92 × 0.26 m; depth 0.27 m. Phase 6.

Burial 28 (D15). North-south infant burial, with head to the north, cut into the second baptistery east wall. 0.86 × 0.34 m; depth 0.13 m. Phase 6/7.

Burial 29 (D31). North-south infant burial with head to the north, in the southeast corner of the second baptistery. 1.0 × 0.3 m; depth 0.23 m. Phase 5/6.

Burial 30 (D231). A north-south infant burial, in the eastern area. 1.42 × 0.64 m. Phase 6.

Burial 31 (D233). Fig. 105. A west-east grave, set into the north wall of the baptistery. It was filled with lumps of tufo and tile, and was not excavated further. 1.18 × 0.48 m. Phase 7.

Burial 32 (D224). A west-east grave, close to, and at right angles to, burial 30, with the head of an infant to the west, and the right arm across the chest. 1.32 × 0.34 m; depth 0.6 m. Phase 6.

Burial 33 (D226). A west-east grave, parallel with burial 32, containing an infant, the head being to the west. 0.92 × 0.24 m; depth 0.35 m. Phase 6.

Burial 34 (D222). A west-east infant's grave, parallel with burial 33, with the head towards the west. Buried in a semi-sitting position, with the head against the side of the grave, the left arm across the body and the right arm by the side. 0.96 × 0.26 m; depth 0.3 m. Phase 6.

Burial 35 (D237). A west-east grave close to the second font, partially lined with tile and marble, but containing no burial. It had probably been emptied. 0.78 × 0.4 m. Phase 6.

Burial 36 (D239). A northeast-southwest grave, cutting the earlier baptistery apse but containing no burial. It had probably been emptied. 1.04 × 0.48 m. Phase 6.

Burial 37 (D229). Figs 102 and 106. A substantial west-east grave near the south wall. 1.94 × 0.84 m. There was a large amount of broken tile and marble in the upper fill. Below, at a depth of about 0.4 m, was a tile cover, comprising two

Fig. 105. Burial no. 31 (Fig. 78, D233) cut into the north wall of the second baptistery, looking west. *(KW)*

Fig. 106. Burial no. 37 (Fig. 78, D229) in the baptistery with its cover removed, comprising
the bones of two infants and a juvenile. *(KW)*

more or less square tiles (0.585 × 0.57 × 0.04 m) and three broken pieces. This sealed two extended burials, of an infant and a juvenile, with the heads at the west, and the bones of a third infant. One iron nail was included. Phase 6.

Burial 38 (D54). A west-east grave, partly lined with tiles, cut into burial 37. It contained the disturbed remains of an infant, with the head towards the west. 0.80 × 0.26 m. Phase 6/7.

Burial 39 (D57). A west-east infant-sized grave, but without any bones. Like burial 38, it was cut into burial 37. 0.8 × 0.36 m. Phase 6/7.

Burial 40 (D214). A west-east grave, with three disarticulated skeletons, one of a very young infant and two of older infants. Cut by grave 37. 1.12 × 0.4 m; depth 0.34 m. It included an iron nail. Phase 6.

Burial 41 (D132). A northwest-southeast grave, of an infant, close to the second font. 1.4 × 0.48 m. Phase 5/6.

Burial 42 (D140). A north-south grave by burial 41, with traces of a burial, very poorly preserved. 0.8 × 0.36 m. Phase 5/6.

Burial 43 (D135). A west-east grave which partly underlies the north wall of the second baptistery; it is, however, not entirely clear from where it was inserted (Fig. 84). The grave was covered with three tiles, beneath which was a cavity some 0.8 × 0.4 m, and about 0.35 m deep. It was virtually free of fill, and contained the bones of a juvenile, 6-8 years old, with the head to the west, and the hands crossed over the lower torso. There was a silver coin of Pope Hadrian III (AD 884-5) with the body (cat. 58; below, Fig. 168), and an iron boss (cat. 33). Phase 5.

Burial 44 (D86). Some infant bones in a pit by the second font. ?Phase 5.

Burial 45 (D287). A possible grave to the south of the second font. Bones not located. Phase 5/6.

Burial 46 (D282). A west-east infant burial, badly disturbed, but with the head to the west. It lay on the east side of the second font, and may belong to the period after the demolition of the baptistery. 1.04 × 0.3 m? Phase 6/7.

Burial 47 (D212). A west-east burial, containing the disturbed remains of an infant, possibly once oriented with the head to the west. The grave was lined with tile on one side and had the south wall of the second baptistery on the other. It was filled with broken tile. There was also a piece of lead (cat. 52). 1.32 × 0.35 m; depth 0.20 m. Phase 6.

Burial 48 (D303). A rectangular west-east grave slab in blue-grey tufo, partly inset into the south wall of the second baptistery. When lifted the underside was found to be slightly concave. The grave itself was not excavated, but appeared to cut an earlier grave. 1.2 × 0.62 m. Phase 6.

Burial 49 (D332). Traces of the burial of an infant, cutting the north wall of the first baptistery, placed west-east with some broken tiles along the sides and beneath. The full grave cut was not defined. Phase 5/6.

Burial 50 (D281). Very poorly preserved west-east infant burial, in an ill-defined grave, and resting upon the plaster floor of the first baptistery. *c.* 0.6 × 0.3 m. Phase 6.

Burial 51 (D270). A probable west-east grave, not further investigated, cutting the west wall of the first baptistery. *c.* 0.78 × 0.3 m. ?Phase 6.

Burial 52 (B40). A west-east infant burial, with the head to the west, in the southwest corner of the second baptistery. 1.0 × 0.38 m. Phase 6.

Burial 53 (D293). A north-south grave in the northwest corner of the second baptistery. It contained the skeleton of a juvenile, with the head to the north, and also a few adult bones. 1.38 × 0.36 m; depth 0.5 m. ?Phase 7.

Other burials in the baptistery

Unstratified burials in the plough-soil include D33 and D38 – they are not recorded on the plan. They contained bones of an infant, two juveniles and an adult.

THE AREA TO THE WEST OF THE BAPTISTERY (?NARTHEX) (FIGS 78 AND 94)

As noted previously, this area comprised either a narthex to the second baptistery or, perhaps, merely open ground.

Burial 54 (D289, D291). A north-south tomb, built of tufo blocks against the northwest external corner of the second baptistery. Close to the northwest corner of the tomb (which resembles the ossuary, burial 24), were the skull and some disarticulated bones of a male (D289), which may have been disturbed when the tomb was built. The tomb itself contained the skeleton of another male, oriented north-south, with the arms crossed across the chest. The skull had been removed in Antiquity, and the tomb resealed with roughly shaped tufo slabs. *c.* 1.6 × 0.5 m (full dimensions not exposed); depth 0.35 m. Phase 6/7.

Burial 55 (D92). Disturbed burials near the west wall of the second baptistery, including remains of two males, two females and five infants. At least one appeared to be a north-south interment, with the head towards the north. The burials were superimposed upon each other, and there were no clear grave cuts. One iron nail and a glass base (cat. 152d) were found. Phase 6/7.

Burial 56 (D91). A very disturbed burial near no. 55 of a juvenile and two females, with no articulated remains. Phase 6/7.

Burial 57 (D95). Two disturbed burials, beside no. 56, one an infant and one a juvenile. What survives suggests that they followed a north-south orientation, with the heads to the north. Phase 6/7.

Burial 58 (D133). Disturbed bones beside no. 57, apparently aligned north-south, with the skull to the north, of an adult, together with some bones of two juveniles. Phase 6.

Burial 59 (D168). Figs 97 and 107. A north-south grave beside no. 58, containing two male inhumations, one on top of the other. Both had their heads to the north, and the lower skeleton had extended arms, while the upper had his right arm folded across the torso. The grave was partly lined with tile. A small single-handled jar (cat. 187) had been placed by the heads, although with which interment is uncertain; it probably dates to the late sixth or early seventh century AD (see Roberts, this volume). 2.0 × 0.6 m; depth 1.0 m. Two iron nails were found. The eastern skeleton yielded a radiocarbon date of 1460 ± 40 BP (BM-2862), which calibrates to AD 565-635 (one sigma). Phase 4.

Burial 60 (A13, A34). Two burials parallel with no. 59, of which the lower (A34), of a female, was relatively undisturbed. The other was of a juvenile. Both were north-south, with the heads to the north. A coin of Gratian, AD 367-83 (cat. 22), was included. The female may, on osteological grounds, have been related to an adult in burial 26; both graves contained Roman coins (cf. cat. 46). There were also five pieces of glass (cat. 120g, 125, 141, 152e and 152k). ?Phase 6.

Burial 61. Figs 32, 54, 107. Tufo sarcophagus, projecting into the modern road cutting and damaged on the west

Fig. 107. Burial no. 59 (D168) to the west of the baptistery. It contained two male adults, one with a pot (arrowed) of the late sixth or early seventh century, by the head. Beyond is the sarcophagus, burial no. 61. *(TWP)*

side. Oriented north-south, it had been already emptied of its contents. 2.0 × 0.7 m; internal depth: 0.4 m; total height: 0.6 m; wall width: 0.1 m. ?Phase 4/5.

Burial 62 (A5). Disarticulated adult bones in the fill over the bath-house. Phase 7.

Burial 63 (A12). Disarticulated bones of two adults and one juvenile in the hillwash over the bath-house. Phase 6.

Burial 64 (A35). Highly disturbed adult bones in destruction deposits over the bath-house. ?Phase 5 (or later).

Burial 65 (A2). Bones from disturbed burials over the bath-house, including the remains of two adults and one juvenile. Phase 7.

Burial 66 (A21). Bones of a juvenile in the fill over the bath-house. Phase 5/6.

Other burials in this area

There were a number of other very disturbed skeletons in the upper fills. These were so mixed that they have not been put on the plan. They comprise D64, D73, D80, and included an infant, a juvenile and three adults.

ANTE-ROOM TO THE NORTH OF THE BAPTISTERY (FIGS 78 AND 94)

Burial 67 (D275). A built tomb, west-east, against the north wall of the baptistery. It had quite neatly made walls of tufo blocks, two courses wide on the north side. No interment was found, except for a later grave (burial 68), and a few other infant bones. 1.24+ (full length not established) × 0.5 m. One iron nail was found. Phase 5/6.

Burial 68 (D283). A west-east oval grave containing the body of an infant, cut into burial 67 (which may have been emptied at the time). The body rested upon a floor of marble, and was extended with flexed arms. A piece of lead was found (cat. 92). 0.74 × 0.26 m. Phase 6.

Burial 69 (D52). A rib bone, possibly from a juvenile, in the tile collapse associated with mid-sixth-century coins (phase 3). Although very inadequate evidence, this may be an indicator that burials were being made in the area in this period. Phase 3.

Burial 70 (D51). Adult bones in an occupation deposit. Phase 5+.

Burial 71 (D268). Fig. 80. A rectangular slab of grey-blue tufo, 1.44 × 0.6 m, associated with other large blocks of tufo. Although these were not lifted, it seems probable that they represent some sort of tomb structure. Phase 6.

Unstratified burials

There was just one disturbed burial in the plough-soil, D6 (unidentified).

THE SPACE BETWEEN THE BAPTISTERY, ANTE-ROOM AND ENTRANCE (FIG. 94)

Burial 72 (D296). The disarticulated remains of a female and a young juvenile. Osteological study suggests that the two were related. ?Phase 7.

Burial 73 (D286) A structure of tufo blocks somewhat resembling those of burial 71 (although without an obvious grave slab). It seems likely that this too is a grave structure, although it was not further investigated. Phase 6.

Burial 74 (M76). A collection mainly of skulls and long bones placed with no ceremony into gaps between tufo blocks in this corner. They included two males, one female and an adult. Phase 6/7.

THE ENTRANCE TO THE ANTE-ROOM (FIG. 94)

Burial 75 (M61, Sk. 5 and 5a). Two partially articulated male skeletons oriented east-west, with heads to the east. They appear to represent successive burials, the earlier with arms across the chest. There were also bones of another male, a female and two adults. The grave cut was not really clear, but the tomb was *c.* 1.5 m long, and overlay the south wall of the entrance. Phase 6/7.

Burial 76 (M69, Sk. 4). A west-east grave close to the north wall of the entrance, with two infant inhumations, one much disturbed. The heads are to the west. Shallow grave pit, *c.* 1.1 × 0.4 m. Phase 6/7.

Burial 77 (M72, Sk. 6). Poorly preserved west-east infant burial near no. 76, much damaged by later activity. Head to the west. It included a fragment of glass (cat. 107). *c.* 0.71 × 0.32 m. Phase 6/7.

THE AREA BETWEEN THE ENTRANCE AND THE PAVED ROAD (FIG. 94)

Burial 78 (M33, Sk. 1) Fig. 108. A shallow northwest-southeast grave beside the road, containing the skeleton of a male with the head towards the north. The left arm was folded across the stomach and the right arm pointed towards the right shoulder. There was no very clear grave pit, and the body was in a layer of debris from the early medieval kiln. *c.* 1.7 × 0.5 m. Phase 5/6.

Burial 79 (M112, Sk. 8 and 9). Fig. 109. A north-south grave by the southwest corner of the entrance. It was lined with tufo blocks, and with a tile at the north end, and pieces of tile to form a floor. It contained two successive burials, one female and one male: the bones of the earlier (the male) had been pushed on one side to make way for the later burial. Both heads were to the north, and the arms of the later skeleton were folded across the chest. Osteological study suggests that the two were related. 1.6 × 0.65 m; depth 0.3 m. Phase 6.

Burial 80 (M18, Sk. 3). A north-south grave close to the door threshold, containing a female skeleton with the head to the north, and the arms folded across the torso. *c.* 1.8 × 0.6 m, depth 0.4 m. Phase 6.

Burial 81 (M16, M88, Sk. 2). A northeast-southwest grave close to the road, with a disturbed skeleton with the head to the northeast. *c.* 1.2 × 0.35 m. Phase 6.

OVER ROMAN ROOMS TO THE NORTH OF THE CHURCH COMPLEX (FIG. 94)

Burial 82 (E4). Badly disturbed west-east grave beyond the north wall of the ante-room. 1.0 × 0.45 m. Phase 5/6.

Burial 83 (E57). Grave-shaped pit, west-east (approximately), 1.1 × 0.38 m. No bones were found, however. Phase not certain.

Burial 84 (E39, E40). Infant burial, probably north-south. *c.* 0.4 × 0.22 m. ?Phase 5/6.

Fig. 108. Burial no. 78 (M18), an adult female, buried in a simple grave by the road. *(KW)*

Burial 85 (L172). A northwest-southeast grave, cutting a Roman wall (Fig. 41). It contained the skeleton of a male with the head to the northwest, and arms folded across the torso. There were also some infant bones. *c.* 2.25 × 0.75 m. One iron nail was found. Phase 6/7.

Burial 86 (L176). A northwest-southeast grave, with a sharply rectangular plan. *c.* 1.4 × 0.35 m. Traces of human bone were seen, but it was not excavated. Phase 6/7.

BURIALS IN THE COURTYARD (FIG. 94)

Burial 87 (E99). An oval southwest-northeast grave, containing an infant, with a lining of irregular humps of tufo, and pieces of tile. The skull was to the southwest. 1.08 × 0.5 m. Phase 3 or later.

Burial 88. (H16). A northwest-southeast grave, containing the burial of an infant, with the head to the northwest. 1.0+ (full length not established) × 0.4 m. This grave included one iron nail. Phase 6/7.

Burial 89 (H21). A northwest-southeast grave, parallel with and of similar size to burial 88. Not excavated, but a few adult bones were recorded. Phase 6/7.

Burial 90 (D36). A west-east burial; width 0.45 m, full length not established.

Burial 91 (D84). The west end only of a grave. ?Northeast-southwest. Phase 5/6.

Burial 92 (D18). The north end only of a north-south grave of a female, the rest being cut away by burial 93. The skull lay to the north, and the arms were folded across the chest. Width 0.42 m. Phase 6.

Burial 93 (D5). A north-south burial of a female, with the head (which is missing) to the north. The arms were folded across the chest. One piece of lead was found (cat. 70) and a piece of fourth-century glass (cat. 77). Cuts burial 92. 1.78 × 0.48 m. Phase 6.

Fig. 109. Burial no. 79 (M112), a stone-lined grave with successive interments of a male and female, who were probably related. *(KW)*

Burial 94 (D32). A northwest-southeast burial of a female, with the head to the northwest. The torso is badly crushed. Cuts burial 93. 1.65 × 0.45 m. Phase 6.

Burial 95 (D4, D34). A complex series of west-east infant graves along the exterior of the north wall of the second baptistery. D4 was oriented with the head to the west. Width 0.7 m. Length not properly established. A fragment of glass (cat. 140i) was found. Phase 6/7.

Burial 96 (D90). A poorly defined west-east grave, extending west from burial 95. Dimensions not properly established. Phase 6.

Burial 97 (D78). A west-east infant grave, cutting across the east wall of the second baptistery. The skeleton was oriented with the head (which is missing) to the west. 1.2 × 0.55 m (grave proper 1.1 × 0.32 m); depth 0.42 m. Phase 7.

Burial 98 (B2). Plough-damaged burial of an adult, possibly with a west-east orientation. Phase 6.

Burial 99 (B4). Disturbed northwest-southeast graves, containing some articulated and some disarticulated bones. These include a male burial, with the head to the northwest, and bones of two other males, and five adults. Included was a fragment of glass (cat. 126d). 2.0×0.4 m. Phase 6.

Burial 100 (D63). A west-east burial of a female, with the head at the west. The arms were folded across the chest. 1.8 × 0.48 m. Phase 5/6.

Burial 101 (D69). The edge of what is possibly a west-east grave. Unexcavated. An iron knife was found here (cat. 32). ?Phase 5/6.

Human bones in the topsoil over the courtyard

There were two significant clusters, D9 and D21; one adult was identified.

BURIALS TO THE SOUTH AND SOUTHEAST OF THE CHURCH (FIG. 94)

Burial 102 (C29). A northwest-southeast grave of a male, with the skull to the northwest, and with the arms across the torso. There were also some disarticulated bones. 1.85 × 0.5 m. Cuts Roman wall C34. Phase 6/7.

Burial 103 (C160). A northwest-southeast grave of a female, with the skull at the northwest end. The arms were folded across the chest, with the right arm pointing to the right shoulder. 1.7 × 0.42 m. Cuts Roman wall C34. Phase 6/7.

Burial 104 (C39). Infant burial, northwest-southeast. The grave dimensions were not properly established, but it cut Roman wall C34. Phase 6/7.

Burial 105 (B24). A west-east rock-cut grave, sealed by a tufo slab, containing two adults, one a male and one a female, and two infants, with the heads at the west. The male had his arms folded across his stomach. 1.8 × 0.5 m; depth 0.45 m. ?Phase 3.

Burial 106 (B26). A west-east rock-cut tomb. There were some *in situ* bones of a female in the east end of the grave, indicating that the head had been at the west. There was also a complete pottery vessel, of fifth-century date (cat. 186), and two pieces of glass (cat. 117, 129). The other bones may well have been deliberately removed, as with some burials within the church (which is immediately adjacent). 1.9 × 0.5 m; depth 0.5 m. Phase 3/4.

Burial 107 (A16). The eastern part of a west-east rock-cut grave, the rest having been destroyed by the modern road. It had been emptied completely prior to the excavation. Depth 0.6 m. ?Phase 3.

THE HUMAN BONE, by Janice Conheeney

INTRODUCTION

A minimum of 243 individuals was represented in the human bone. This total includes remains from *in situ* burials, from disturbed burials, and from disturbed and fragmentary deposits of disarticulated bone. The *in situ* burials contained remains of 159 individuals, and it is these that form the basis for this report.

In some ways the analysis has been disappointing, as the fragmentary nature of the remains has meant that much information normally contained in the skeleton has been lost. However, some very interesting patterns emerged in the spatial organization of the burials, which may allow inferences about the social attitudes of the people burying their dead at this site. At the present time little has been published in a comparable way, although many important sites in Italy have yielded human remains. Monte Gelato cannot, therefore, be set into a wider context and has been analysed in isolation.

Composition of the sample

The sample was recovered from ten areas of the site: (1) the church; (2) the baptistery; (3) the possible narthex to the west of the baptistery; (4) the ante-room to the north of the baptistery; (5) the space between the baptistery, ante-room and entrance; (6) the entrance to the ante-room; (7) the area between the entrance and the paved road; (8) over the Roman rooms to the north of the church complex; (9) the courtyard; and (10) to the south of the church.

One hundred and seven burials containing the 159 bodies included in this analysis were excavated within these areas. The number of individuals recovered from burials in each area and the phasing of these burials is given in Table 7 (whilst Table 8 gives additional details of age, sex and condition). The ten groups of bodies as defined by these areas were analysed separately, in order to investigate any spatial differences in the type of person buried. With regard to phasing, it was decided to include all the burials together. This decision was felt to be justified as the majority of burials came from phase 6e. Any further subdivision would have meant that the group sample size would have been so small as to be without meaning. In any case of pathology or possible genetic relationship, where phasing could have a particular importance, the phasing of the body involved was checked.

A further thirteen contexts contained evidence of disturbed burials. These remains produced a minimum body count of 26 individuals. However, they are not included in the analysis as they cannot be phased. This is not a great loss, as the majority of individuals in this category were represented by very small amounts of bone (Table 9), and so would have provided very little additional information.

Table 7. Individuals per area and phasing.

area	no.	phasing
church	51	principally phase 6, some 5/6 and two x 6/7
baptistery	24	principally phase 6, some 5/6 and 6/7
northern or open ground west of baptistery	32	mostly 6/7, some 6 and 5/6, one possible 4/5
ante-room north of baptistery	4	5/6 and 5+
space between baptistery, ante-room and entrance	6	7?
entrance to antechamber	8	6/7
area between entrance and paved road	5	5/6
over Roman rooms to north of church complex	3	5/6, 6/7
courtyard	18	principally 6, some 6/7, one x 5/6, one x 7
south of church	8	6/7 and 6
total	159	

Thirty-seven contexts held disarticulated human bone. These deposits were composed of a minimum of 58 individuals (Table 10).

Representativeness of sample

Since most of the graves date to the early medieval period, the skeletons recovered should give a fair representation of those buried in each area. The baptistery, the ante-room, the space between the baptistery, ante-room and entrance, the entrance to the antechamber and the area over the Roman rooms were excavated in full, so all burials contained there should have been recovered (except in one area of the baptistery: Fig. 78). Most of the narthex and the area between the entrance and road was excavated, and about three-quarters of the church. The courtyard and the area to the south of the church are likely to be the least representative, as little of these areas was uncovered, and the proportion that the excavated part forms of the whole area is not known. This means that for the majority of the ten areas any introduced bias to the sample should be restricted to the, effectively, random disturbance and destruction of some burials in the years between the cessation of burial at the site and recovery today. The 'secondary' bias unavoidable at the majority of sites, where due to practical restrictions only certain areas of a burial sample can be excavated, has been avoided here, with the exception of the courtyard and the area to the south of the church.

It should be stressed, however, that the sample, although now established as 'potentially well representative', in fact only includes those people who were selected for burial within the complex by whatever criteria were operating amongst those living at the site at the time. The sample does not represent the contemporary early medieval population as a whole; merely a predetermined fraction of it. This need not be as negative as it at first appears, as the analysis undertaken here will establish what type of person that fraction was composed of, and so allow conjecture on the selection criteria that may have been in operation.

Limitations to the analysis

The scope of the analysis was limited by four factors: the size of sample; the fragmentary nature of much of the remains; the time span over which stages of the work were completed; and the lack of comparative data.

Although the total sample size is reasonable, the sample size of each of the ten groups, when considered separately, is too small for any statistical analysis. However, given the lack of detailed human bone data available for Italian sites at the present time, it was still considered worthwhile to conduct a detailed analysis, even if this could only be couched in general terms. The majority of the data recorded has been included in the tables and appendix, as too often such data are confined to inaccessible archive reports.

The disturbed and fragmentary nature of many of the remains means that approximately a third of the contexts containing human bone could not be included in the analysis. The fragmentary condition of many individuals is also of consequence as this could have affected many areas of the analysis. Besides limiting the demographic and metrical information retrievable, surprisingly little evidence of pathological change was present. This could be due to the high level of fragmentation and the small proportion present of many of the skeletons.

The cleaning and recording of the material took place in Rome over a period of eleven weeks between 1989 and 1991. The limited time available meant that there had to be restrictions on the amount of information recorded: for example, a selected range of non-metric traits was scored for rather than including all possible traits. Moreover, the analysis of human bone has progressed in the five years [at the time of writing] since the project began, and certain categories of information which the author would wish to record now were not then obvious – for example, calculation of prevalence rates for certain types of pathology. It should also be noted that it was not possible to gain a second opinion on any of the pathology, nor were radiographic facilities available. These would have helped to confirm some of the pathology, and X-rays would have allowed examination for the presence of Harris lines in those individuals exhibiting conditions also associated with stunted growth.

Finally, the lack of comparative material is a particular problem, as the significance of the burials recovered from Monte Gelato will have to be considered in isolation for the time being. This means that unusual features of the Monte Gelato sample relative to elsewhere in Italy will not be apparent until other sites are published in a comparable way.

Table 8. Gender, age and preservation data for *in situ* burials.

CHURCH

BURIAL	CONTEXT	SEX	AGE	AGE GROUP	% PRESENT	CONDITION
1	B15	3	adult	7	2	2
2	C57	3	>22	7	40	3
	C58	4	>24	7	45	2
	C2	1,3	2x adult	7,7	40,40	3,3
3	C25	3	25-35	4	1	2
4	B53	inf	<5	1	5	2
5	C42	juv, 3	5-10, adult	2,7	5,1	3,3
6	C47	inf	3-4	1	2	1
7	C23	5	25-35	4	40	2
8	C46	3, 2x inf	>17, 0-6mths, 4-5	7,1,1	40,2,5	3,3,3
9	C32	3	adult	7	5	3
10	B21	no bones				
11	B32(B49)	inf, 3	1.5-2.5, <22	1,3	30,20	3,3
12	B16	stone context				
13	B29	no bones				
14	B34	?	?	?	2	3
15	B42	?	?	?	5	3
16	B66	3	adult	7	5	3
17	B60	inf	0-1	1	10	2
18	B8	1,2,juv	25-35,30-40,10-15	4,5,2	85,30,35	1,2,2
	B22	3,3,juv	25-35,17-25,<15	4,3,2	15,10,10	3,3,3
19	?					
20	?					
21	D96	inf,juv	?,<15	1,2	1,5	3,3
22	D108	3	adult	7	10	3
23	D123	2x inf,3	0-5,0,adult	1,1,7	10,50,50	3,3,3
24	D107	1,1,1,5,5,3, 4x juv	30-40,c50,17-25,2x adult,20-24, 10-15, 2x 5-10,?	4,6,3,7,3,2, 2,2,2	c50	2
25	D173	2x inf,3	3-9mths,2-3,adult	1,1,7	5,5,5	3,3,3
26	A23	juv,3	12-13,adult	2,7	50,30	2,3
	A3	inf	3-4	1	20	2
	A9	not bone				
	A28	5	25-35	4	70	1
	A4	inf	2-3	1	50	2

BAPTISTERY

BURIAL	CONTEXT	SEX	AGE	AGE GROUP	% PRESENT	CONDITION
27	D43	inf	1,5-2	1	95	1
28	D15	inf	12-18mths	1	95	1
29	D31	inf	3-3.5	1	95	1
30	D231	inf	0-5	1	50	3
31	D233	no bones				
32	D224	inf	4-5	1	90	2
33	D226	inf	6-9mths	1	75	2
34	D222	inf	2-4	1	95	2
35	D237	no bones				
36	D239	no bones				
37	D229	juv,2 inf	8-9,3-4,3.5-4.5	2,1,1	95,95,30	1,1,1
38	D54	inf	0-6mths	1	75	2
39	D57	no bones				
40	D214	3x inf	0-6mths,2.5-4.5,1.5-4.5	1,1,1	60,60,40	2,2,2
41	D132	inf	2-4	1	85	1
42	D140	3	adult	7	20	2
43	D135	juv	6-8	2	95	1
44	D86	inf	?	1	5	3
45	D287	no bones				

BURIAL	CONTEXT	SEX	AGE	AGE GROUP	% PRESENT	CONDITION
46	D282	inf	0	1	80	2
47	D212	inf	3.5-4.5	1	95	1
48	D303	no bones				
49	D332	no bones				
50	D281	inf	3-4	1	10	3
51	D270	no bones				
52	B40	inf	<5	1	5	2
53	D293	juv,3	6-8,adult	2,7	95,5	1,3

NARTHEX OR OPEN GROUND TO WEST OF BAPTISTERY

BURIAL	CONTEXT	SEX	AGE	AGE GROUP	% PRESENT	CONDITION
54	D289,D291	2,2	17-25,17-25	3,3	30,20	2,2
55	D92	5x inf,4,1,2,5	3x 0-6mths,0.5-1.5,3-4, 25-35,20-40,50,40-50	1,1,1,1,1,4,4, 6,6	scraps	2
56	D91	juv,4,5	10-18,>19,33-45	2,3,5	20,30,30	2,2,2
57	D95	juv,inf	6.5-7.5,3.5-4	2,1	95,60	1,2
58	D133	3,2x juv	17-25,<19,?	3,2,2	5,2,2	3,3,3
59	D168	1,1	17-25,33-45	3,5	80,30	3,3
60	A13,A34	juv,5	7-9,17-25	2,3	10,90	2,1
61	no bones					
62	A5	3	adult	7	1	3
63	A12	juv,3,3	<15,>15,>18	2,3,3	5,10,10	3,3,3
64	A35	3	adult	7	2	3
65	A2	juv,3,3	<15,2x adult	2,7,7	15,20,50	3,3,3
66	A21	juv	6-10	2	10	2

ANTE-ROOM

BURIAL	CONTEXT	SEX	AGE	AGE GROUP	% PRESENT	CONDITION
67	D275	inf	3-7	1	1	3
68	D284	inf	1.5-2.5	1	95	1
69	D52	juv?	?	2?	1	3
70	D51	3	>15	adult	5	3
71	D268	no bones				

SPACE BETWEEN BAPTISTERY, ANTE-ROOM AND ENTRANCE

BURIAL	CONTEXT	SEX	AGE	AGE GROUP	% PRESENT	CONDITION
72	D296	juv,5	4-8,21-25	2,3	60,90	2,2
73	D286	no bones				
74	M76	1,1,5,3	17-25,3x adult	3,7,7,7	scraps	3

ENTRANCE TO ANTE-ROOM

BURIAL	CONTEXT	SEX	AGE	AGE GROUP	% PRESENT	CONDITION
75	M61	2,2,2,4,3,3	17-25,2x 25-35,17-21, 15-21,17-25	3,4,4,3,3,3	c50	2
76	M70	inf	1.5-2.5	1	95	1
77	M72	inf	6-12mths	1	40	2

AREA BETWEEN ENTRANCE AND PAVED ROAD

BURIAL	CONTEXT	SEX	AGE	AGE GROUP	% PRESENT	CONDITION
78	M33	1	>45	6	90	1
79	M112	5,1	33-45,25-35	5,4	95,30	1,1
80	M18	5	25-35	4	90	1
81	M16,M88	5	25-35	4	20	1
82	E4	no bones				

OVER ROMAN ROOMS

BURIAL	CONTEXT	SEX	AGE	AGE GROUP	% PRESENT	CONDITION
83	E57	no bones				
84	E39,E40	inf	0	1	40	2
85	L172	inf,1	0,25-35	1,4	5,65	3,3
86	1176	no bone				

COURTYARD

BURIAL	CONTEXT	SEX	AGE	AGE GROUP	% PRESENT	CONDITION
87	E99	inf	0.5-1.5	1	80	1
88	H28	inf	4-5	1	70	1
89	H21	3	adult	7	1	3
90	D36	no bones				
91	D84	no bones				
92	D18	4	>45	6	30	1
93	D5	5	35-45	5	80	1
94	D32	5	45-50	6	50	3
95	D4,D34	inf	0	1	30	2
96	D90	no bones				
97	D78	inf	4-5	1	95	1
98	B2	3	adult	7	15	3
99	B4	1	25-35	4	30	2
	B4A	2,1,juv,3	22-25,adult,juv,adult	4,7,2,7	75,30,2,10	1,3,3,3
	B4B	3,3,3	>25,>18,>15	4,3,3	20,10,5	2,2,2
100	D63	5	25-30	4	95	1
101	D69	no bones				

SOUTH OF CHURCH

BURIAL	CONTEXT	SEX	AGE	AGE GROUP	% PRESENT	CONDITION
102	C29	1	25-35	4	95	1
103	C160	5	25-30	4	95	1
104	C39	inf	6-9mths	1	20	3
105	B24	2x inf,5,1	2-3,6-12mths,25-35, 17-25	1,1,4,3	60,30,95,95	1,3,1,1
106	B26	5	17-25	3	30	3
107	A16	no bones				

Table 9. Gender, age and preservation data for burials not *in situ*.

AREA	CONTEXT	SEX	AGE	AGE GROUP	% PRESENT	CONDITION
Church	B1	inf,4,3,3	2.5-3.5,22-25,2x adult	1,3,7,7	10,40,10,10	3,3,3,3
Church	C1	5,3,4,3,2x inf, juv	25-35,adult,2x 17-25, 2x 0-6mths,10	4,7,3,3,1,1,2	35,10,5,10,15 5,10	3,3,3,3,3,3,3
Church	C3	4	17-25	3	20	2
Church	C27	4	>25	7	30	2
Church	D94	3	adult	7	1	2
Baptistery	D33	inf,juv	5,12-17	1,2	10,5	3,3
Baptistery	D38	juv,3	5-10,adult	2,7	10,2	3,3
Narthex	D64	juv	?	2	1	3
Narthex	D73	inf,3	?,adult	1,7	5,10	3,3
Narthex	D80	3,3	<25,adult	3,7	1,10	3,3
Ante-room	D6	?	?	?	2	3
Courtyard	D9	?	?	?	2	3
Courtyard	D21	3	adult	7	10	3

Table 10. Gender, age and preservation data for residual human remains.

CONTEXT	SEX	AGE	AGE GROUP	% PRESENT	CONDITION
B12	juv,3,3	<15,adult, elderly	2,7,8	10,10,10	3,3,3
B28	inf,3	2-4,adult	1,7	5,2	3,3
B36	inf	2-4	1	20	3
B49	2x juv,5	7-15,6-10,22-30	2,2,4	20,70,30	3,3,3
B54	3	>19	7	15	2
B73	inf	0-6mths	1	5	2
B80	inf,3	?,?	1,7	5,5	3,3
CD1	>6x3	>6x adult	>6x7	scraps	3
D1	spoil:- could be any number, counting as one adult				
D2	4	33-45	5	30	2
D3	?	?	?	2	3
D45	3,3,1	>16,>17,>17	7,7,7	5,5,5	2,1,1
D61	3	adult	7	5	3
D73	1	17-25	3	50	2
D80	inf,juv,4	0-6mths,5-15,40-50	1,2,5	10,5,10	3,3,3
D125	1	>25	7	75	1
D73/125	3	>22	7	20	2
D125	3	adult	7	1	3
D192	3	adult	7	1	3
D219	inf,3	<5, adult	1,7	20,20	3,3
D220	inf,3	?,adult	1,7	5,1	3,3
D244	inf,3	<1,adult	1,7	5,1	3,3
D301	inf,3	c1,adult	1,7	10,1	3,3
D316	3	adult	7	1	3
E19	3	14-22	3	15	3
E23	3	adult	7	20	3
E49	3	adult	7	1	3
E67	3	adult	7	5	3
H29	3	>15	7	1	3
L163	3	adult	7	2	3
M1	4	>25	7	5	3
M3	3	adult	7	1	3
M10	3	adult	7	5	3
M14	3	adult	7	1	3
M64	3	adult	7	5	3
M106	juv,2x adult	?,?,?	2,7,7	scraps	3,3,3
R1	3	adult	7	1	3

METHODS

Preservation of remains (Appendix)

Preservation was recorded by the surviving skeletal elements, and by the condition of the bone on a scale of good, average or poor. The percentage of the skeleton present was estimated.

Dentiton was catalogued on the standard chart of Brothwell (1981: 53). In addition to tooth and alveolar bone presence or absence, the chart records the health status of each tooth.

Separation of multiple burials

Generally it was quite simple to separate the remains of several individuals by comparing size, stage of development or age, condition, colour and so on, and confirming by check-ing articulation. In the case of large deposits of disarticulated bone, which were not included in the final analysis beyond a body count, the remains were treated in the same way as an animal bone sample, with no attempt to reconstruct the individuals. Anything of note on each bone was recorded separately, and the minimum number of individuals present was established by the number of the most frequent bone present.

Age estimation

At any point where age is discussed in this report the estimates given are of developmental or relative age and not of absolute, chronological age. This must always be the case when age estimates are obtained by comparing the degree of skeletal development of one individual to standards for expected skeletal development by a given age as derived from a larger sample. Given the controversy surrounding ageing techniques, the preferred method of age estimation would have been to arrange all the individuals into a series of advancing age from the youngest person present to the oldest. Demographic statements would then be made based on proportions of this series, rather than by referring to individuals as of a definite age. Unfortunately, time restrictions did not permit this, and the usual age groupings have been retained.

Individuals who are still developing provide the most accurate age estimates (Bass 1987: 12), particularly in the most active phases of dental eruption before about ten years of age (Ubelaker 1989: 63-4). After about 25 years of age, when maturity is reached and development ceases, age estimates are based mainly on the progress of degenerative processes, the rate of which tends to be far more variable between individuals and therefore more unreliable. Consequently, infants, juveniles and adolescents are considered in year by year detail in parts of the report, whereas adults are considered in groups of ten year intervals, and in many cases have been simply classed as adult.

A variety of ageing methods was employed for the infants and subadults, applying the principle that it was better to arrive at an age estimate based on as diverse a basis as possible. This avoids errors that may arise when using only one category of development, due to potential inter-individual variability in the rate of that category. This included assessment of the development of the dentition (Schour and Massler 1944), the length of the diaphysis (Johnston 1962; Sundick 1978), stage of epiphyseal fusion, and appearance and fusion of other elements (Salter 1984).

Adults, that is those individuals with a complete dentition and all epiphyses fused, were also subjected to a combination of methods, following the advice of Lovejoy, Meindl and Mensforth (1985). Dental attrition was assessed by comparison with Brothwell's (1981: 71-2) chart of wear stage by age. Although this would not be applicable to a sample which had experienced a soft diet, and therefore little tooth wear, previous studies (Moore and Corbett 1973; Tattersall 1968) have already demonstrated that people of this period were exposed to quite a coarse diet, producing the wear required for this method. Of course, the degree of this wear could still vary between samples, causing some error in the evaluation. It would have been preferable to calibrate the adult dental wear from wear on more reliably aged immature individuals as described by Miles (1978); unfortunately, time did not allow. Age-related changes to the pubic symphysis in the few cases where this was possible were evaluated using the McKern and Stewart method (1957) for males, and the Gilbert and McKern method (1973) for females. Advance of cranial suture obliteration with age was not included, as it is extremely variable between individuals, and therefore notoriously unreliable.

Sex estimation

Estimation of sex was based largely on the dimorphic characteristics of the skull and pelvis, with most weight given to the pelvis. Five grades were assigned: female, probably female, indeterminate, probably male, and male. These are denominated as 1-5 on Tables 8-10.

Skull dimorphism was assessed following Ascadi and Nemeskeri (1970), Ferembach, Schwidetzky and Stloukal (1980) and Brothwell (1981: 90-8).

Observations were made on the pelvis following the Phenice system (1969), and further suggestions by Ascadi and Nemeskeri (1970). The measurements suggested by Ferembach, Schwidetzky and Stloukal (1980) were not implemented as they proved to be unrepeatable on this sample. Scarring of the pelvis due to parturition has been demonstrated as unreliable as a guide to sex (Kelley 1979; M. Cox pers. comm.), and so has been excluded from the analysis. Sacral dimorphism was judged with reference to Brothwell (1981: 61).

Where morphological characteristics were ambiguous, metrical data were used as a sexing tool. Only those individuals who, through incomplete data sets, could not be included in the later analysis to establish the degree of dimorphism in this sample could be sexed in this way. Otherwise, to include individuals sexed by metrical information would have created a circular argument.

It is generally accepted that immature individuals cannot be reliably sexed. Ubelaker (1989: 52-3) has suggested that rates of developmental progress differ between males and females, and could possibly be used for sexing. This is not possible here as a subsequent part of the analysis indicated that there was stunted growth in adolescents relative to developmental age in this sample; the developmental data are, therefore, unreliable for sexing purposes. The canine has been shown to be dimorphic even in deciduous dentitions in some cases (Rosing 1983), and dental development is least affected by any impediment to growth. In this case, only the permanent canine was used as this is more reliable, and is in place by 11-12 years. The mesiodistal and buccolingual diameters were taken following the definitions by Hillson (1986: 233) and plotted against each other to observe any grouping.

Metrical data

Forty-five cranial and 46 post-cranial measurements were recorded for each individual when the relevant skeletal elements were in sufficiently good condition. They were taken following the conventions laid out in Brothwell (1981: 77-87) and Bass (1987). Any skeletal landmarks referred to in the text follow the definitions given in those works or in that of McMinn and Hutchings (1977). More measurements were taken than are used in this analysis, but this was necessary for future comparisons with samples from other sites as the skeletal metric data for Italy grow.

Stature was calculated from the length of the long bones, using the regression formulae of Trotter and Glesser (1952; 1958). Indices calculated were restricted to the cranial index and the meric and cnemic indices (Brothwell 1981: 87); these are the most commonly quoted indices in reports, and are some of the most useful in describing the physique of the individual.

Evidence for stunting of growth in immature individuals was tested for by comparing estimates of age by diaphysis length to age estimates derived by developmental observations (either tooth development or sequence of fusing, as described above). Corroborating evidence was also gathered by comparing this data to those individuals suffering from hypoplasia, cribra orbitalia or cribra femoralis, or cranial hyperostosis. An explanation of this relationship is given below. Only immature individuals were included, as it has been demonstrated that, after periods of childhood stunting, there is often a rapid growth spurt and the adult section of the population will present no evidence of reduced stature (Clegg 1978; Harrison et al. 1983).

Metrical data were also used to examine the degree of dimorphism present in the humerus, femur and palate, by plotting head diameter against epicondylar width, and length against breadth respectively. Limb asymmetry of the upper and lower arms and legs was noted to investigate the possibility of handedness in the sample.

Non-metric data

Non-pathological variability of specific traits was recorded in order to test for a genetic component to the distribution of burials. In the long term, this will also allow comparison to other sites in order to comment on the 'genetic distance'. Twenty cranial and 22 post-cranial traits (Berry and Berry 1967; Finnegan 1978) were scored as present, absent or data missing. This is a rather restricted number of traits, but included the most commonly used, and the most useful. Occurrences of the traits were plotted on to plans of the burials and particular attention was given to those clusters of individuals presenting more than one trait in common. The data were also examined for patterns of recurring traits, following the study by Saunders (1989) on occupationally related skeletal modification.

Dental pathology

Caries prevalence was recorded by location on a particular tooth. Abcess and ante-mortem loss were recorded by tooth. Calculus, alveolar recession and periodontal disease were recorded on a severity scale of 0-3. The grading for calculus was after Brothwell (1981: 155) and Ramfjord, Kerr and Ash (1966). The normal position of the alveolar crest was taken to be 2.0 mm below the cemento-enamel junction (Barker 1975). Alveolar recession was recorded if this distance had increased. Periodontal disease was recorded as 0 for healthy alveolar; 1 for slight pitting of the crest around the tooth as a possible indicator of inflammation of the soft tissue; 2 for definite remodelling of the bone, particularly of the interdental septa; 3 for severe disease and the presence of infrabony pockets (Conheeney, forthcoming a). The distinction was made between alveolar recession and periodontal disease as it is accepted that some recession may be due to continual eruption of the teeth, even in cases where there appears to be little wear on the occlusal surface (Whittaker *et al.* 1990).

Dental non-metric traits, including third molar agenesis, malocclusion, crowding of teeth and general pathology were also recorded.

Skeletal pathology

Each individual was examined for evidence of pathology. Osteoarthritis was only diagnosed when the criteria put forward by Rogers *et al.* (1987) were met. Location of vertebral osteophytes was, unfortunately, only recorded by the areas cervical, thoracic and lumbar and severity, as were Schmorl's nodes and intervertebral disc disease. If carrying out the study today, it would be preferable to record location by specific vertebrae and position on each vertebra. Infections and other pathology were assigned to a most probable cause, following the definitions laid down in standard reference works (Steinbock 1976; Ortner and Putschar 1981; Rogers and Waldron 1989). The levels to which prevalence rates were calculated are included in the relevant analysis section, as the degree of detail of this varies with the type of pathology and skeletal element. The prevalence data is of value in this study as the majority of burials took place over a period of about 300 years. This is a tighter chronological denominator than at some sites (Waldron 1991).

PRESERVATION OF REMAINS (TABLES 11 AND 12)

The macroscopic condition of the bone varies between areas. No microscopic survey was carried out. Survival of the skeleton as a unit tended towards a small proportion of the body being present (Table 11). The total number of bodies in Table 11 is 134 rather than 159, the true total, because several multiple burials were summarized as one entry or body. Considering the total percentage column and row, the remains show a definite skew to poor condition and to poor survival. Forty-four per cent of bone was in poor condition, 30.6 per cent moderate and only 25.4 per cent good. At sites where there are no unusual conditions of preservation, a roughly normal distribution with most bone in the moderate category could be expected. At Monte Gelato 69.5 per cent of skeletons had less than 50 per cent present and 35.1 per cent had less than ten per cent present. Again, in a normal distribution, only 50 per cent of skeletons should be less than 50 per cent represented, and there should not be over 35 per cent of bodies in the smallest category. This would seem to indicate poor preservation for the site as a whole. This is important, and should be noted, as it affects the amount of information available at several stages of the analysis. The poor condition is in part due to the tufaceous soil of the site, which tends to acidity and erodes the bone. That so little of many skeletons survived is probably due to three factors. Firstly, during excavation it was found that several tombs had been cleared intentionally in Antiquity; secondly, graves near to the ground surface were badly damaged and disturbed due to deep ploughing; thirdly, if the majority of bone was already in a poor condition, smaller bones would suffer particularly badly and may disintegrate and be lost.

It is harder to explain why the condition varies between areas. In the church, narthex, ante-room and the area over the Roman rooms, the majority of bone was in poor condition. Other areas were more mixed, except for the baptistery and area between the entrance and road, which were in moderate/good and good condition respectively. Only two bodies were recovered from the latter area, so the good condition of both could be an artifice of the small sample size. The baptistery contained mainly infant burials, and it is generally accepted that small infant bones are fragile and have a lesser chance of survival than robust adult bones. However, there was relatively little intercutting of these graves, unlike adjoining areas.

This phenomenon of variable preservation is more apparent when the cells of the 'areas totalled' section of Table 11 are split into their component parts of male, female, juvenile and infant (Table 12). The pattern that would be expected if age and sex were responsible for differential preservation is for fragile, easily damaged infants to fall into the upper left-hand corner of the table; relatively robust males into the lower right-hand corner; and females and juveniles to be spread in between. Instead, the infants form the majority of those in the 'good' category, and of those in the 'over 90 per cent present' category. Also, there are equal numbers of males and females in the 'good' category, and four females compared with two males with over 90 per cent of the body surviving. Whilst caution is necessary as the figures involved are so small, this would seem to rule out age and sex as the major factors affecting condition and survival of the remains. Much more significant is the fact that burials close to the church, the baptistery apart, were frequently disturbed to introduce new interments.

The relative rates of survival of elements of the skeleton were much as expected. In Table 11 the percentage of predicted numbers gives the number present of a particular

Table 11. Preservation of remains.

	<10	<20	<30	<40	<50	<60	<70	<80	<90	<100	total
CHURCH											
poor	17	2	2	4	2						27
mod.	4	1	2	1	4						12
good	1						1		1		3
total	22	3	4	5	6	0	1	0	1	0	42
BAPTISTERY											
poor	3				1						4
mod.	1	1		1		2		3	1	1	10
good			1						1	8	10
total	4	1	1	1	1	2	0	3	2	9	24
NARTHEX											
poor	8	2	1		1			1			13
mod.	3	1	2		1	1					8
good									1	1	2
total	11	3	3	0	2	1	0	1	1	1	*23
ANTE-ROOM											
poor	3										3
mod.											0
good										1	1
total	3	0	0	0	0	0	0	0	0	1	4
SPACE BETWEEN ANTE-ROOM, BAPTISTERY AND ENTRANCE											
poor	1										1
mod.						1		1			2
good											0
total	1	0	0	0	0	1	0	1	0	0	3
ENTRANCE TO ANTECHAMBER											
poor											0
mod.				1	1						2
good										1	1
total	0	0	0	1	1	0	0	0	0	1	3
AREA BETWEEN ENTRANCE AND ROAD											
poor											0
mod.											0
good		1	1						2	1	5
total	0	1	1	0	0	0	0	0	2	1	5
OVER ROMAN ROOMS NORTH OF CHURCH											
poor	1						1				2
mod.				1							1
good											0
total	1	0	0	1	0	0	1	0	0	0	3
COURTYARD											
poor	3	1	1		1						6
mod.	2	1	2								5
good			1				1	3		2	7
total	5	2	4	0	1	0	1	3	0	2	18
SOUTH OF CHURCH											
poor		1	2								3
mod.											0
good						1				4	5
total	0	1	2	0	0	1	0	0	0	4	8
AREAS TOTALLED											
poor	36	6	6	4	5	0	1	1	0	0	59
mod.	10	5	7	4	5	4	0	4	1	1	41
good	1	1	3	0	0	1	2	3	5	18	34
total	47	12	16	8	10	5	3	8	6	19	**134

KEY:

* nine short of 51 as Burial 24 ten individuals summarized for condition as 1. Burial 55 summarized, Burial 74, Burial 75

** not to true total of burials as several multiple burials summarized as one

Table 12. Preservation of remains split by age and sex for all areas.
Burials nos. 24, 55, 74 and 75 have not been included as they are multiple burials summarized for preservation and condition.)

	split	<10	<20	<30	<40	<50	<60	<70	<80	<90	<100
poor	inf / juv	10	7 1		1 2			2			
	♂ / ♀				2	1 1			1	1	1
	indeterminate	18	4		1		3	2			
moderate	inf / juv	3	2 1		1 1	3	1 1	1 3	1	3	1
	♂ / ♀		3		3		1 2	1			1
	indeterminate	3	3								
good	inf / juv	1			1			1	1	1	8	4
	♂ / ♀		1		1	1			1 1	1 3	1 2	4

Key to split:-

inf.	juv.
♂	♀
indeter-	minate

element as a percentage of the number of that element if all individuals were complete (following Mays 1991a; 1991b). Looking at the 'total' column, the percentage of an element recovered appears to be related to its size and possibly to its appearance. Small bones such as the carpals fall below five per cent recovery and the patella, which is not so small but is perhaps not so easily distinguishable as a bone, has around ten per cent recovery. The poor representation of smaller bones, such as those of the hand and foot, relative to larger bones, should be noted, as this could compromise the pathological data. Attribution of cause for much pathology depends on its distribution throughout the body, so, if sections of the skeleton are consistently absent, some pathologies could be missed. When the data are broken down by area in the body of the table, it is apparent that the level of recovery of each element conforms to the varying preservation present in the areas, whilst retaining the overall pattern. This means that the varying levels of preservation of skeletons in each area is not caused by any unusual recovery rates of particular elements. (The catalogue of skeletal parts present for each individual is given below, in the Appendix.)

DEMOGRAPHY

Eighty-three adults, 23 juveniles and 51 infants were re-covered from the intact burials (where infants are defined as nought to five years and juveniles as six to fifteen years). Of the adults, 24 were male or possibly male; 23 were female or possibly female; and 36 were of indeterminate sex. The high number for whom sex could not be determined was due to the fragmentary nature of much of the remains. Of these indeterminates, 82.9 per cent were composed of bone in poor condition, and all of them had less than 50 per cent of the skeleton present; 60 per cent had less than ten per cent (Table 8).

Sex composition

The sex ratio over the whole site was practically equal, with 25 males and 23 females (1.09:1). With a few exceptions, namely the baptistery, ante-room, entrance to the ante-room and over the Roman rooms, this was reflected by most of the areas of the site (Table 13). It should be borne in mind that very small numbers are involved, so that a differ-ence of one between the sexes, in areas of the site with few burials, can have a disproportionate effect on the ratios. However, a possible explanation of the exceptions could be seen when the sex composition was broken down by area (Table 14).

The baptistery contained two adults out of 24 skeletons and the ante-room one adult amongst four skeletons; all were of indeterminate sex. Rather than being something unusual in the sex composition, something unusual had affected the age structure across the site and, therefore, indirectly affected the sex composition. This is examined in the next stage of analysis, dealing with age. The area over the Roman rooms yielded only three skeletons, two of which were infants and one a male – hence the apparent male skew to the ratio in Table 13, when it was, in reality, the age structure that was more influential again. The only ratio which cannot be explained away easily is that for the entrance to the ante-room. Here three out of eight burials were male, and there was one female and two infants. It is very difficult to say whether this may have a true cause con-nected in some way to the location within the site complex, or whether it is an artificial phenomenon associated with the small sample size.

If it is accepted that the sex ratio is approximately equal for all areas of the site where adult burials take place, two inferences are possible. Firstly, neither sex was being reared to adulthood at the expense of the other sex. Secondly,

males and females were treated similarly in death. For example, if the church was the preferential place for burial, both sexes were present in almost equal numbers. Burial no. 2, which may have been beneath the altar, contained a female and an adult of indeterminate sex as the primary burials, and a male and second indeterminate in the com-plex of burials on top of the primary ones. This seeming equality of treatment was also borne out by looking at the burials which had grave-goods. Burial no. 24, also within the church, and with a glass beaker, contained three males, two females and one indeterminate. Burial no. 26, likewise within the church, had a bronze ring and was a female. Burial no. 59 held two males with a cup between their heads. Burial no. 106, south of the church, contained a female with a complete pottery vessel. The combination of these two inferences makes it tempting to suggest an egalit-arian society with regard to sex. However, this data, ex-tracted as it is from burials, need not necessarily mean that the sexes were treated equally in life. A woman may have few rights in many societies but be accorded an élite burial because of the status or wealth of her husband.

One other small point of note is that amongst all the areas of adult burials shown in Table 14, with the exception of the entrance to the ante-room, more bodies were as-signed to a positive sex than to a possible sex category. This could suggest that there was marked dimorphism in this sample. This is explored further below.

Age composition

The predicted death curve for a pre-modern society is given in Figure 110. Deaths would be high in those less than one year old, falling off through infancy with a trough in later childhood and adolescence, and then gradually climbing again with increasing age (Clegg 1978: 182). The age struc-ture across the whole site by ten-year groupings is presented in Table 15. This roughly conforms to the predicted curve (the six to fifteen years group is fairly high because of the under tens rather than the older children), except that the number in each age category decreases with increasing age, rather than increasing again after young adults. This can be ignored, as it is a function of the inadequacy of the most commonly used ageing techniques for dry skeletons. At pres-ent, the usefulness of these methods tails off rapidly after the age of 45, and they are often not reliable before that age; hence the 18.5 per cent classified only as 'adult' in Table 15. For the same reason the average age of death for the site has not been calculated as this is fairly meaningless, although it is quoted in many reports.

Table 13. Sex ratios by area (combining possible and definite of each sex).

	♂	♀	Ratio (♂ : ♀)
church	6	5	1.2 : 1
baptistery	0	0	-
narthex	6	5	1.2 : 1
ante-room	0	0	-
space between baptistery and ante-room	2	2	1 : 1
entrance to ante-room	3	1	3 : 1
area between entrance and road	2	3	1 : 1.5
over Roman rooms	1	0	1 : 0
courtyard	3	4	1 : 1.3
south of church	2	3	1 : 1.5
TOTAL	25	23	1.09 : 1

Table 14. Sex composition by area.

KEY: 1 = male; 2 = possibly male; 3 = indeterminate; 4 = possibly female; 5 = female; juv. = juvenile (6-15 years); inf. = infant (0-5 years). Burials nos. 14 and 15 have been excluded as no details are available.

(a) numbers in each area

	1	2	3	4	5	juv.	inf.	total
church	5	1	16	1	4	9	13	49
baptistery	0	0	2	0	0	3	19	24
narthex	3	3	7	2	3	8	6	32
ante-room	0	0	1	0	0	1	2	4
space between baptistery and ante-room	2	0	1	0	2	1	0	6
entrance to ante-room	0	3	2	1	0	0	2	8
area between entrance and paved road	2	0	0	0	3	0	0	5
over Roman rooms to west	1	0	0	0	0	0	2	3
courtyard	2	1	6	1	3	1	4	18
south of church	2	0	0	0	3	0	3	8
TOTAL	17	8	35	5	18	23	51	157

(b) numbers expressed as percentages of the total number per area

	total number	1	2	3	4	5	juv.	inf.	total
church	49	10.2	2.0	32.7	2.0	8.2	18.4	26.5	100
baptistery	24	0	0	8.3	0	0	12.5	79.2	100
narthex	32	9.4	9.4	21.9	6.3	9.4	25.0	18.8	100.2
ante-room	4	0	0	25.0	0	0	25.0	50.0	100
space between baptistery and ante-room	6	33.3	0	16.7	0	33.3	16.7	0	100
entrance to ante-room	8	0	37.5	25.0	12.5	0	0	25.0	100
area between entrance and paved road	5	40.0	0	0	0	60.0	0	0	100
over Roman rooms to north	3	33.3	0	0	0	0	0	66.7	100
courtyard	18	11.1	5.6	33.3	5.6	16.7	5.6	22.2	100.1
south of church	8	25.0	0	0	0	37.5	0	37.5	100
	157								

Whilst the age structure for the site as a whole was very much as expected, more unusual patterns were apparent when age composition was considered by area (Table 16). The baptistery, ante-room and the area over the Roman rooms are composed almost completely of under fifteen year olds: 22 out of 24 burials for the baptistery; three out of four for the ante-room; and two out of three for the area over the Roman rooms. This is even more apparent when the cumulative totals of the number dead by each age group, for each area, are considered (Table 17). Of those in the baptistery, 79.2 per cent were dead by the age of five, and 91.7 per cent by fifteen years of age. In the ante-room, 50 per cent were dead by five years, and 75 per cent by fifteen years of age. Over the Roman rooms, 66.7 per cent were dead by five years, but there were no further deaths until the 25-35 age group. The phenomenon is therefore most marked in the baptistery area. To some extent, the figures for burials over the Roman rooms could be disregarded as the product of chance, as there are so few burials in that area. The ante-room is more difficult to explain away in this fashion and, without a doubt, some factor seems to be preferentially selecting infants for burial in the baptist-

ery. This may be related to the recent christening of the infants, or perhaps their unbaptized status, and might also apply to the ante-room next door to the baptistery.

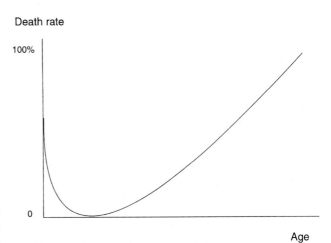

Fig. 110. Death-rate curve, after Clegg (1978).

Table 15. Number in each age group as a percentage of total of whole site (excluding burials nos. 14 and 15).

age	no.	%
0-5	51	32.5
6-15	23	14.6
16-25	22	14.0
26-35	20	12.7
36-45	5	3.8
>45	6	3.8
adult	29	18.5
total	157	100%

teen, the deaths conformed to a tripartite pattern common in other samples (Brothwell 1981; Manchester 1983). Of the immature deaths, 70.4 per cent occurred before the age of five, and 23.9 per cent before one year.

Considering the total figures in Table 18, the large number of deaths, seventeen, before one year of age was probably because of the high immediately postnatal risk to the baby of infection and complications. There was then a trough between one and two years with only four deaths present. Age two to three showed an increase to twelve deaths, age three to four maintained this level with eleven deaths, then the rate falls again to six deaths in age four to five. Although the figures must not be pressed too far, given the small numbers involved, the most likely explanation of

Table 16. Age composition by area.

area	years																		
	0-5	5-15	16-25			26-35			36-45			>45			adult		
			♂	♀	I	♂	♀	I	♂	♀	I	♂	♀	I	♂	♀	I
church	13	9	0	1	3	1	2	2	2	0	0	1	0	0	1	3	11
baptistery	19	3													0	0	2
narthex	6	8	3	1	4	1	1	0	1	1	0	1	1	0	0	1	3
ante-room	2	1													0	0	1
space between baptistery, ante-room and entrance	0	1	1	1	0										1	1	1
entrance to ante-room	2	0	1	1	2	2	0	0	0	0	0	0	0	0	0	0	0
area between entrance and paved road	0	0	0	0	0	1	2	0	0	1	0	1	0	0	0	0	0
over Roman rooms	2	0	0	0	0	1	0	0									
courtyard	4	1	1	0	1	1	1	2	0	1	0	0	2	0	1	0	3
south of church	3	0	1	1	0	1	2	0									
totals	51	23	7	5	10	8	8	4	3	3	0	3	3	0	3	5	21
totals when areas are combined	51	23	22			20			6			6			29		

Table 17. Cumulative percentage in each age group in each area.

area	by 5	by 15	by 25	by 35	by 45	>45	adult
church	26.5	44.9	53.1	63.3	67.3	69.4	30.0
baptistery	79.2	91.7					8.3
narthex	18.8	43.8	68.8	75.0	81.3	87.5	12.5
ante-room	50.0	75.0					25.0
space between baptistery, ante-room and entrance	0	16.7	50.0				50.0
entrance to ante-room	25.0	25.0	75.0	100.0			0
area between entrance and paved road	0	0	0	60.0	80.0	100.0	0
over Roman rooms	66.7	66.7	66.7	100.0			0
courtyard	22.2	27.8	38.9	61.4	66.7	77.8	22.2
south of church	37.5	37.5	62.5	100.0			

When deaths occurring before 25 years of age, that is, before adulthood, were examined year by year (Table 18), a series of clusters of deaths could be seen. The cluster at 21 years in several of the areas is artificial, as the average age of those placed in the age group 17-25 by tooth wear was used in the plot, creating the false impression that all these individuals were 21 years of age. Ages younger than this group, where tooth eruption could assign ages more finely, could be more reliably considered. Below the age of seven-

this rise between two and four years is the cessation of breast-feeding with the associated nutritional and environmental stress. This stress would be in the form of poor diet after weaning, or illness brought on by insanitary feeding methods. Indeed, the diet described by Wickham (1981: 94) for the early medieval rural population of corn, oil and wine, supplemented by small amounts of beans and fruit, would not appear to be very suited to the needs of a child immediately post-weaning. Iron deficiency due to nutritional stress, or to chronic diarrhoea, causes bony changes which could also support this suggestion. This is examined in the pathology section, below.

In the deaths between five and fifteen years, there was an unusual, slight cluster between twelve and thirteen years. There are no obvious reasons for this; but the most likely explanations are either pathology which targets the early teens, or increased stress at the onset of puberty, tipping the balance between life and death. The first cause may be apparent in the pathology, but only if it was of a type which caused bony changes. There would have to be extremely arduous conditions for the second cause to be possible, but it could be evidenced by signs of nutritional deficiency. Both were tested for in the pathology section below.

When the age and sex composition were considered together (Table 16), there was a very even split between the sexes in all age groups in the total row. To a slightly lesser degree, this held for all the areas with adult burials. This is very interesting as it would appear that childbirth, the most important factor in early female death, had little influence here.

PHYSIQUE

The raw data for this section are presented in Tables 19 and 20. The mean measurements are not presented in the text as the usefulness of this practice seems questionable.

Stature

The statures calculated for all those adults with the required long bones are presented in Table 21. Reading across the stature estimates for each individual, the arm bones appear to produce somewhat greater statures in some cases than the leg bones. This is interesting, as during the recording, it was noted that lower arm measurements tended to underestimate the age of children by one or two years, relative to dental development. Dental development is the most accurate of ageing techniques as it is least affected by nutritional and other hardships. Presumably, then, this deficit in arm length was being caught up by adulthood and in some cases even surpassed. A genetic cause rather than environmental would seem most likely, as other child limb measurements were not affected.

The stature values were plotted for each area. The smallest and tallest males both occurred in the area south of the church at 1.66 m and 1.82 m respectively, although the tall male appeared to be unusual for the site. The females ranged from 1.55 m in height in burials to the south of the church to 1.6 m in those in the courtyard. The average stature for each area is given in Table 22. The male figures were not very different from the modern male average stature of 1.74 m. However, the females of all areas were well below the modern female average of 1.66 m. This deficit in height could explain the dimorphism evident in the sample. Nutritional deficiency can result in reduced stature, and marked sexual dimorphism in a sample can also indicate the presence of nutritional hardship, because much of the female's energy goes into reproduction, thus causing the female to be more compromised in height (T. Molleson, pers. comm.).

None of the areas contained strikingly tall or short individuals compared to the others. In several sites in London,

(St Mary Graces – Waldron, forthcoming; St Mary Spital – Conheeney, forthcoming b) probable privileged burials were within the normal range of statures expected for the period, but all tended to fall towards the top of the range. Other areas of burials would produce a wider spread. This did not appear to be the case at Monte Gelato; if the church, for example, was an area of preferential burial, then data for stature did not reveal any difference from other areas of the site.

Indices

The cranial, meric and cnemic indices were calculated for all individuals for whom the required measurements were recordable. This proved to be an extremely limited number. Therefore, although site areas were considered separately initially, further division into age and sex was not practical.

Cranial shape

The shape of the skull, as determined by its length relative to breadth, is described by the cranial index (Brothwell 1981: 87). The closer this approaches to 100 per cent, the rounder the skull anterioposteriorly (brachycranial), rather than being long and narrow (dolichocranial). The skulls were assigned to categories using the ranges for each cranial type set out by Wells (1982) and the results are presented in Table 23.

The numbers involved were so small as to be virtually meaningless. Long, narrow skulls were most frequent with three skulls, followed by mesocranial with two. The least frequent type was rounded skulls, represented by just one individual. This differs completely from pooled data from medieval sites in Britain, which show that brachycranial skulls were the most frequent type (Brothwell 1972).

Meric index

The meric index reflects the anterioposterior flattening of the femur in the region just inferior to the sub trochanter. As values for the index decrease from 100 per cent, they indicate increased flattening. Right and left femurs were analysed separately to test for differences according to side, and the values were assigned a category according to those set out by Wells (1982).

The marked tendency for the site as a whole (and for all areas taken individually except over the Roman rooms) was for eumeric femurs on both sides, with 76.2 per cent of right femurs eumeric and 81.3 per cent of left (Table 24).

Various explanations for this flattening of the femur have been advanced, although so far no definitive cause has been agreed. Generally, it is accepted that there is a remodelling of the femur in order to cope with stresses imposed on the neck in the most mechanically economic way (Brothwell 1981: 88-9). The suggested sources of these stresses have ranged through vigorous activity over rough ground, strain on the immature femur, calcium deficiency or nutritional stress or, in later life, as being linked in some way to arthritis (Cameron 1934; Buxton 1938; Lovejoy, Burstein and Heiple 1976). Dawes and Magilton (1980) have suggested that in extreme cases of rickets, the meric index may be affected, with individuals presenting a high degree of flattening. In less extreme cases, individuals may still have a tendency towards eurycnemia of the tibia. The roundedness of most femurs at Monte Gelato, therefore, could be taken to indicate a freedom from any of these conditions, if any

Table 18. Age composition of those < 25 years per area.

Church

0	1	2	3	4	5	6	7	8	9	10	11	12	13	14	15	16	17	18	19	20	21	22	23	24	25
			x																						
			x					x		x		x													
			x	x				x		x		x									x				
	x	x	x	x	x			x		x		x							x		x	x			

Baptistery

0	1	2	3	4	5	6	7	8	9	10	11	12	13	14	15	16	17	18	19	20	21	22	23	24	25
	x		x	x																					
	x		x	x			x																		
	x x		x x	x	x		x		x																

Narthex

0	1	2	3	4	5	6	7	8	9	10	11	12	13	14	15	16	17	18	19	20	21	22	23	24	25
	x																				x				
	x			x				x				x									x				
	x		x	x			x	x				x		x							x				
												x									x				

Ante-room

0	1	2	3	4	5	6	7	8	9	10	11	12	13	14	15	16	17	18	19	20	21	22	23	24	25
		x			x								x												

Space between baptistery & ante-room

0	1	2	3	4	5	6	7	8	9	10	11	12	13	14	15	16	17	18	19	20	21	22	23	24	25
						x															x		x			

Entrance to ante-room

0	1	2	3	4	5	6	7	8	9	10	11	12	13	14	15	16	17	18	19	20	21	22	23	24	25
	x	x																			x				
																		x	x		x				

Courtyard

South of church

TOTALS

Table 19. Adult skull measurements.

sex	burial	context	L	B	H	PBH	NH	NB	GB	J	G1	G2	LB	GL	FL	FB	TFH	GH	S1	S2	S3
5	7	C23																			
3	18	B8a																			
3		B8b																			
5	26	A28	173.5	130.5	129.0	88.2	51.0	/	86.0	/	44.8	39.2	94.5	87.3	32.8	26.9	/	69.5	122.0	120.0	116.0
2	54	D289																	128.0	98.0	
2	54	D291																			
5	56	D91																			
1	59	D168																			
5	60	A34	169.5	126.0	124.5	88.0	48.3	23.9	88.2	123.5	43.2	40.3	100.5	97.4	36.0	29.3	107.4	65.9	116.0	112.0	106.0
5	72	D296																			
5	81	M16																			
1	85	L173																			
4	92	D18																			
5	94	D32																			
1	99	B4																			
1,3	99	B4A																			
5	100	D63	178.5	132.5	131.0	94.0	51.9	24.1	91.4	/	43.4	40.1	98.0	86.5	36.3	28.3	117.6	72.8	122.0	128.0	115.0
1	102	C29a	192.5	138.0	130.5	127.5	49.5	/	/	/	58.7	/	104.5	99.4	38.0	31.7	123.8	70.4	117.0	128.0	122.0
5	103	C160	/	/	/	/	49.4	25.6	101.4	91.0	49.4	38.0	/	/	/	/	108.2	66.3	/	/	/
	105	B24																			
5	79	112(8)	180.0	141.0	125.0	123.5	50.0	24.0	118.7	87.9	52.5	38.5	96.5	92.0	37.2	30.6	114.3	65.1	127.0	121.0	113.0
1	79	112(9)	178.0	144.5	127.5	126.0	47.7	20.6	124.0	89.5	47.8	42.2	90.5	87.5	/	/	107.4	63.2	120.0	115.0	/

sex	burial	context	S1'	S2'	S3'	DA	DC	BQ	SC	09L	U	B'	RORbB	LORbB	ROL	LOL	GoGo	HI	ML	WI	RCH
5	7	C23																			
3	18	B8a																			
3		B8b																26.0			
5	26	A28	108.3	108.9	96.3	40.0	19.8	206.5	10.3	71.5	482.5	88.5	35.9	34.2	34.9	36.0	101.4	29.0	94.0		56.52
2	54	D289	106.4	90.5													102.2	29.7	98.0	114.5	
2	54	D291																			
5	56	D91															96.9	28.9	100.1	127.1	72.0
1	59	D168															91.5	25.8	98.0	117.0	54.7
5	60	A34	102.1	100.7	88.3	49.0	22.8	196.0	10.3	70.0	482.0	89.7	37.2	39.8	34.3	33.9		26.2			57.0
5	72	D296															92.6	30.5	93.5	118.0	62.5
5	81	M16																			
1	85	L173																			
4	92	D18															96.6	29.0			
5	94	D32																			
1	99	B4															45.1	30.9	98.5	111.7	69.5
1,3	99	B4A																			

sex	burial	context																				
5	100	D63	105.9	115.3	92.7	46.5	23.7	232.0	7.9	75.4	493.0	96.3	36.0	/	32.5	/	30.2	86.3	104.5	115.5	62.0
1	102	C29a	111.1	115.4	99.8	/	/	/	/	/	/	/	39.5	/	31.0	/	29.9	113.2	120.0	/	66.0
5	103	C160	/	/	/	46.0	22.6	/	/	/	/	90.6	39.5	37.9	32.2	34.8	27.8	89.8	103.5	124.5	/
	105	B24															31.5	94.8			70.0
5	79	112(8)	109.9	110.2	91.7	45.0	22.6	305.0	/	/	520.0	95.8	33.8	34.9	33.9	33.4	27.1	89.6	95.0	/	62.0
	79	112(9)	103.9	108.0	/	40.0	22.0	298.0	/	/	/	96.7	34.4	36.0	30.0	29.5	26.0	107.5	/	/	64.0

sex	burial	context	LCrH	RM1/2	LM1/2	RRB'	LRB'	RM2	LM2	ZZ	UCBL	UCMD	LCBL	LCMD
5	7	C23								40.5	7.8	7.2	7.7	6.4
3	18	B8a							17.5		8.3	7.7	7.9	6.5
3		B8b	57.0	28.1	26.9	34.6	31.6	18.2	15.8		7.0	6.4	6.3	5.5
5	26	A28		25.5	26.9	32.2		17.2			8.0	7.2		
2	54	D289								45.8	8.6	7.0		
2	54	D291			47.7	37.4	36.6			43.9	8.6	7.0	9.0	7.1
5	56	D91	55.5	46.5		32.3	31.1	15.9	16.3		9.0	7.8	8.2	6.8
1	59	D168	56.0	22.4		29.6	28.5	13.7	13.9		7.9	7.4	7.5	6.2
5	60	A34	62.0	28.2	28.1	28.2	29.6				8.2	7.7	7.7	
5	72	D296									7.0	8.1	6.7	7.1
5	81	M16									8.7	7.3	8.9	7.6
1	85	L173		27.0	27.4	33.4	33.4	15.4	14.1		6.8	6.8	6.8	6.3
4	92	D18		49.9	47.7	29.9	30.2				7.2	6.4		7.1
5	94	D32		20.0	21.0			12.4	13.6		1			
1	99	B4				31.9	32.0	17.4	17.4		7.9	6.9	7.7	7.1
1,3	99	B4A		30.0	28.3	29.6	33.4	17.6	16.1		8.8	8.0	7.4	6.3
5	100	D63	62.5	30.6	28.9	30.4	30.7	14.8	14.9		8.0	7.2	7.5	7.0
1	102	C29a	65.5	26.8	23.7	25.2	26.5	13.0	13.8		7.4	6.6	7.4	6.3
5	103	C160	61.5	26.0	/	34.7	35.1	18.7	16.9		8.0	7.8	/	6.6
	105	B24	72.0	30.8	33.4	32.0	31.9	19.0	18.6		8.8	7.8	/	6.7
5	79	112(8)	61.5	27.8	27.3	29.9	31.9	18.7	19.9		9.4	8.0	8.6	7.2
1	79	112(9)	/	24.2	24.3									

Table 20. Adult postcranial measurements.

burial	context	RFdl	LFHd	RFE	LFE	RHHd	LHHd	Atld	RScB	LScB	RCLL	LCLL	SB	SL	Sbdy	RHuL	LHuL	RHuC	LH
2	C57																		
2	C58		43.8																
18	B81	45.6	45.2	/	84.5	46.1	45.9	/	28.0	/	136.5	139.0	/	/	119.0	303.5	301.0	62.0	64.0
26	A28	/	42.8	/	67.8	40.5	38.9	70.5	/	/	/	134.5	/	/	/	302.0	297.5	58.0	57.5
54	D291			70.0	69.5	48.8	/	79.0	27.0	27.8	/	/	/	/	/	329.0	/	79.0	/
56	D91(2)	/	38.3						25.7	/									52.0
59	D168	46.1[1]	41.8[2]																61.5
60	A34	42.1	40.9	67.6	/	42.3	/	70.5	24.2	24.3	125.5	132.0	115.0	113.5		292.0	296.0	55.0	54.0
72	D296(1)	43.9	44.2	/	/	43.9	/	/	26.8	25.4	/	/	/	/	/	30.1	/	57.0	/
78	M33																		
80	M18/81	39.3	39.9	68.5	70.0	/	37.4	/	/	24.5	/	141.0	121.0	108.0	/	/	287.5	64.0	64.0
85	L173	46.8																67.0	/
92	D18	/	/	/										/	/				
93	D5	42.6	42.1	75.0	72.6	39.0	39.5	/	26.0	25.6	120.0	137.0	/	/	/	29.9	300.0	60.0	58.0
94	D32	42.9	42.9	/	75.9	40.1	41.0	/	24.4	24.8	/	/	/	/	/	297.0	290.0	56.0	57.0
99	B4	/	/	/	79.9	/	/	88.0	/	25.6									
99	B4A	49.4	/	81.7	/	46.4	48.8	/	/	/	150.5	153.5	/	/	/	316.0	313.0	66.5	64.5
99	B4B	/	44.6	/		/	38.7												
100	D63	43.7	44.3	70.5	72.1	40.7	43.3	/	24.6	25.6	141.0	120.0	120.0	99.0	/	311.5	305.0	61.5	61.5
102	C29(I)	51.1	/	85.6	84.3	49.2	/	/	28.2	29.8	153.0	161.0	125.0	115.5	/	332.0	327.0	65.5	65.0
	C29(II)					/	41.9												
103	C160	39.6	40.9	66.5	66.8	37.9	/	/	22.6	22.6	/	131.0	121.0	/	/	287.5	294.0	58.0	57.0
105	B24	44.4	40.4	68.7	70.6	41.0	40.4	/	23.1	24.4	/	143.0	121.0	129.5	52.2	/	303.0	55.5	54.0
	B24(II)	50.8	51.3	/	77.9	/	47.0	/								/	341.0	61.0	57.5
79	M112(8)	41.2	39.0	72.8	72.0	38.0	38.6	/	/	25.6	131.0	131.0	106.0	104.0	/	291.0	287.5	59.0	59.0

burial	context	RRaLi	LRaLi	RUL	LUL	RFeL1	LFeL1	RFeL2	LFeL2	RFeED1	LFdD1	RFeD2	LFeD2	RFeD3	LFeD3	RFeD4	LFeD4	RTiL1	LTiL1	RTiL2
2	C57																			
2	C58									25.0	30.3	32.8	32.5	28.6	28.0	26.7	25.8	/	335.0	339.0
18	B81	244.5	247.5	266.0	266.0		421.0	418.0	417.0	30.3	27.2	31.4	29.9		29.6		27.8	/	377.0	/
26	A28			240.0	243.5		436.0		436.0	25.4	26.4	30.4	26.1		25.7		26.2	/	350.5	/
54	D291						422.0		417.0		24.4									
56	D91(2)				236.0															
59	D168	237.0				422.0				22.8		29.4								
60	A34	226.5	221.5		241.5	410.5	411.0	407.5	406.5	31.2[1]	29.5[2]	32.8[1]	27.4[2]	24.9	25.1	24.8	25.5			
72	D296(1)	225.0	/							24.8	23.9	26.2	26.2							
78	M33									23.2	23.5	30.6	32.7					364.0	/	/
80	M18/81	229.5	225.0	247.0	244.0	418.0	417.5	416.0	415.0	25.5	24.5	27.3	28.7	27.0	26.5	26.3	26.0	/	364.0	358.0

Upper table (measurement column headings not printed):

burial	context																			
85	L173							409.0			24.8	31.3						383.0	/	379.0
92	D18					414.0				23.1	24.2	28.1	26.9	25.6	24.3	24.6	24.3			
93	D5	214.0								26.3	25.9	28.7	28.9					329.0	/	324.0
94	D32	215.0					414.0											339.0	341.0	335.0
99	B4						414.0											362.5	357.5	
99	B4A																			
99	B4B																			
100	D63	230.0	224.0	250.5	241.5	428.5	435.0	425.0	432.5	26.5	26.0	28.6	29.3	28.3	28.3	27.7	27.7	358.5	361.0	355.5
102	C29(I)	237.5	240.0	257.0	258.0	431.0	/	424.5	/	29.9	26.5	28.0	26.6	25.1	27.3	26.1	26.2	338.0	341.0	338.0
	C29(II)																			
103	C160	219.0	221.0	237.5	241.0	409.0	420.5	407.0	418.5	25.6	28.8	24.6	24.4	24.1	24.9	28.5	26.4	353.0	355.0	349.0
105	B24		233.0			413.5	473.5	410.5	470.0	27.0	28.8	26.4	26.1	28.0	29.8	25.9	26.3	352.0	361.5	345.5
	B24(II)					/		470.0		26.7	27.6	27.3	27.7		29.4		26.2	413.0	/	408.0
79	M112(8)					424.5	427.0	424.0	423.0	24.6	22.6	28.6	29.0	27.6	26.2	23.7	24.7	342.0	340.0	335.5

Lower table:

burial	context	LTiL2	RTiD1	LTiD1	RTiD2	LTiD2	RFiL1	LFil	RFeC	LFeC	RPatL	LPatL	RPatB	LPatB	RC	LC	RT	LT
2	C57		35.0	35.8	24.5	22.4				87.0								
2	C58			30.0		24.3			89.0									
18	B81	370.5	/	35.0	/	26.8	/	/			44.4	/	48.0	/	86.0	85.5	60.0	64.0
26	A28	347.0	29.7	31.0	22.7	21.9	/	/			/	44.4	/	/	/	73.0	56.0	56.5
54	D291						/	/										
56	D91(2)							/										
59	D168			33.2	21.5	25.9		/										
60	A34	/	27.3	28.7	/	20.1	/	/										
72	D296(1)							/										
78	M33	360.0	30.5	31.8	24.0	25.6	353.0	354.0							82.8	81.0	60.0	60.4
80	M18/81	/		30.7		22.4	/	/										
85	L173	/	32.4	31.9	25.4	25.7	363.0	/			45.8	/	47.3		/	78.7	/	59.3
92	D18																	
93	D5	/	28.6	27.0	23.9	23.1	/	318.0			36.2	37.7	39.8	39.1	52.3	53.3	52.0	52.1
94	D32	335.0	30.6	30.8	22.5	22.5	330.0	328.0			38.0	39.7	39.7	40.0	52.3		74.5	71.2
99	B4										43.3	42.9	43.7	43.2			/	/
99	B4A	354.0	35.2	34.2	24.7	24.7	352.5	348.5							80.5	80.5	59.0	62.0
99	B4B																	
100	D63	358.0	29.6	29.3	24.1	24.7	345.5	345.5			41.0	41.4	43.4	44.0	51.0	51.5	74.0	74.5
102	C29(I)	336.0	31.5	30.7	24.6	24.1	334.0	331.0			47.7	48.1	43.4	/	76.5	/	61.0	59.5
	C29(II)																	
103	C160	349.0	27.4	25.7	21.3	20.3	/	/							70.5	70.8	48.9	48.0
105	B24	356.5	32.8	32.3	24.3	23.0	/	/			42.1	43.5	44.4	44.2	81.0	80.5	55.0	56.0
	B24(II)	/	34.2	32.3	26.5	26.4	/	/							89.0	90.0	66.5	65.5
79	M112(8)	336.0	31.0	29.8	22.1	22.8	327.0	/			42.1	43.5	44.2		72.9	72.8	51.2	50.2

Table 21. Stature.

burial	context	area	R fem.	L fem.	R tib.	L tib.	R hum.	L hum.	R rad.	L rad.	R uln.	L uln.
4 2	C58	church	158.3	158.1		158.7						
1 18	B8 (1)	church		166.7		173.2	166.0	165.1	172.3	173.4	175.6	175.6
3 26	A28	church										
2 54	D291	narthex or open ground to west of baptistery					173.2					
5 56	D91 (2)	narthex or open ground to west of baptistery										158.5
1 59	D168	narthex or open ground to west of baptistery							169.2			
5 60	A34	narthex or open ground to west of baptistery	155.6	155.6			156.1	157.4	162.5	160.2		161.1
5 72	D296 (1)	space between baptistery, ant-room and entrance					159.1		161.6			
1 78	M33	area between entrance and paved road			170.0	170.0		154.7				
5 79	M112 (8)	area between entrance and paved road	159.1	159.6	160.7	160.1	155.7					
5 80	M18/81	area between entrance and paved road	157.3	157.3				154.7	164.0	161.6	163.2	161.9
1 85	L173	over Roman rooms			174.6							
4 92	D18	courtyard					158.4	158.8				
5 93	D5	courtyard	156.4	156.4	156.9		157.8	155.4	156.4	156.8		
5 94	D32	courtyard			159.8	160.4						
2 99	B4A	courtyard			169.8	168.6	169.4	168.6				
5 100	D63	courtyard	160.1	161.5	165.6	166.2	162.8	160.5	164.0	161.1	164.9	161.1
1 102	C29 (1)	south of church	165.5		163.7	164.5	174.0	172.6	169.6	170.4	172.2	172.6
5 103	C160	south of church	155.1		163.9	164.5	154.7	156.8	158.7	159.7	167.5	160.7
5 105	B24	south of church	156.4	158.1	163.6	166.5		159.8		165.4		
1	B24 (11)	south of church		175.5	181.9			176.6				

Table 22. Average stature by area.

area	no. of ♂	average ♂ stature	no. of ♀	average ♀ stature
church	1	166.7	1	158.3
baptistery	0	-	0	-
narthex	2	171.2	2	157.1
ante-room	0	-	0	-
space between baptistery, ante-room and entrance	0	-	1	159.1
entrance to antechamber	0	-	0	-
area between entrance and road	1	170.0	2	158.2
over Roman rooms	1	174.6	0	-
courtyard	1	169.8	4	158.7
south of church	2	170.5	2	155.8

Table 23. Cranial index.

	range	dolichocranial	mesocranial	brachycranial
church	75.2		1	
narthex	74.3	1		
area between entrance and road	78.3-80.9		1	1
courtyard	74.2	1		
south of church	71.7	1		

Table 24. Meric index.

burial	context	R femur				L femur			
		AP	ML	index	interpretation	AP	ML	index	interpretation
CHURCH									
2	3 C57	25.0	32.8	76.2	platymeric	-	-	-	
2	4 C58	30.3	31.4	96.5	eumeric	27.2	32.5	83.7	platymeric
7	5 C23	22.8	25.0	91.2	eumeric	20.6	23.3	88.4	eumeric
8	3 C46	-	-	-		-	-	-	
18	8 (1)	25.4	30.4	83.6	platymeric	26.4	29.9	88.3	eumeric
18	8 (11)	29.8	30.7	97.1	eumeric	-	-	-	
18	3 B22	-	-	-		-	-	-	
23	3 D123	25.3	27.3	92.7	eumeric	-	-	-	
26	5 A28	-	-	-		24.4	26.1	93.5	eumeric
NARTHEX									
56	D91 (2)	22.8	29.4	77.6	platymeric	-	-	-	
59	1 D168	31.2	32.8 (1)	95.1	eumeric	29.5	27.4 (2)	107.7	eumeric
60	5 A34	24.8	26.2	94.7	eumeric	23.9	26.2	91.2	eumeric
SPACE BETWEEN BAPTISTERY AND ENTRANCE									
72	5 D296 (1)	23.2	30.6	75.8	platymeric	23.5	32.7	71.9	hyperplatymeric
AREA BETWEEN ENTRANCE AND ROAD									
80	5 M18/81	25.5	27.3	93.4	eumeric	24.5	28.7	85.4	eumeric
OVER ROMAN ROOMS									
85	1 L173	24.8	31.3	79.2	platymeric	-	-	-	
COURTYARD									
93	5 D5	23.1	28.1	82.2	platymeric	24.2	26.9	90.0	eumeric
94	5 D32	26.3	28.7	91.6	eumeric	25.9	28.9	89.6	eumeric
100	5 D63	26.5	28.6	92.7	eumeric	26.0	29.3	88.7	eumeric
SOUTH OF CHURCH									
102	1 C29 (1)	29.9	28.0	106.8	eumeric	26.5	26.6	99.6	eumeric
103	5 C160	25.6	24.6	104.1	eumeric	28.8	24.4	118.0	eumeric
105	5 B24	27.0	26.4	102.2	eumeric	28.8	26.1	110.3	eumeric
105	1 B24 (11)	26.7	27.3	97.8	eumeric	27.6	21.7	99.6	eumeric
106	5 B26	25.3	27.3	92.7	eumeric	-	-	-	
AREA BETWEEN ENTRANCE AND ROAD									
79	5 M112 (8)	24.6	28.6	86.0	eumeric	22.6	29.0	77.9	platymeric

Table 25. Meric index by area.

	R femur				L femur				how many cases differ between sides
	range	hyp	plat	eum	range	hyp	plat	eum	
church	76.2-97.1		2	4	83.7-93.5		1	3	2/3
narthex	77.6-95.1		1	2	91.2-107.7			2	0
space between baptistery, ante-room and entrance	75.8		1		71.9	1			1/1
area between entrance and road	86.0-93.4			2	77.9-85.4		1	1	1/2
over Roman rooms	79.2		1						-
courtyard	82.2-92.7			3	88.7-90.0			3	0
south of church	92.7-106.8			5	99.6-118.0			4	0
totals		0	5	16		1	2	13	
KEY: hyp = hyperplatymeric; plat = platymeric; eum = eumeric									

Table 26. Cnemic index.

burial	context	R tibia				L tibia			
		AP	ML	index	interpretation	AP	ML	index	interpretation
CHURCH									
2	3 C57	35.0	24.5	70.0	eurycnemic	35.8	22.4	62.6	platycnemic
2	4 C58	-	-	-		30.0	24.3	81.0	eurycnemic
7	5 C23	23.8	19.6	82.4	eurycnemic	25.1	19.3	76.9	eurycnemic
8	3 C46	38.0	26.4	69.5	mesocnemic	36.6	25.5	69.7	mesocnemic
18	B8 (1)	-	-	-		35.0	26.8	76.6	eurycnemic
18	3 B22	32.2	24.1	74.8	eurycnemic	-	-	-	
26	5 A28	29.7	22.7	76.4	eurycnemic	31.0	21.9	70.6	eurycnemic
NARTHEX									
59	1 D168	-	-	-		33.2	25.9	77.1	eurycnemic
60	5 A34	27.3	21.5	78.8	eurycnemic	28.7	20.1	70.0	eurycnemic
AREA BETWEEN ENTRANCE AND ROAD									
78	1 M33	30.5	24.0	78.7	eurycnemic	31.8	25.6	80.5	eurycnemic
79	5 M112 (8)	31.0	22.1	71.3	eurycnemic	29.8	22.8	76.5	eurycnemic
80	5 M18/81	-	-	-		30.7	22.4	73.0	eurycnemic
OVER ROMAN ROOMS									
85	1 L 173	32.4	25.4	78.4	eurycnemic	31.9	25.7	80.6	eurycnemic
COURTYARD									
93	5 D5	28.6	23.9	83.6	eurycnemic	27.0	23.1	85.6	eurycnemic
94	5 D32	30.6	22.5	73.5	eurycnemic	30.8	22.5	73.1	eurycnemic
99	3 B4B	35.2	24.7	70.2	eurycnemic	34.2	24.7	72.2	eurycnemic
100	5 D63	29.6	24.1	81.4	eurycnemic	29.3	24.7	84.3	eurycnemic
SOUTH OF CHURCH									
102	1 C29 (1)	31.5	24.6	78.1	eurycnemic	30.7	24.1	78.5	eurycnemic
103	5 C160	27.4	21.3	77.7	eurycnemic	25.7	20.3	79.0	eurycnemic
105	5 B24	32.8	24.3	74.1	eurycnemic	32.3	23.0	71.2	eurycnemic
105	1 B24 (11)	34.2	26.5	77.5	eurycnemic	32.3	26.4	81.7	eurycnemic

Table 27. Cnemic index by area.

	R tibia					L tibia					how many cases differ between sides
	range	hyp	plat	meso	eur	range	hyp	plat	meso	eur	
church	69.5-82.4			1	4	62.6-81.0		1	1	3	1/4
narthex	78.8				1	70.0-77.1				2	0
area between entrance and road	71.3-78.7				2	73.0-80.5				3	0
over Roman rooms	78.4				1	80.6				1	0
courtyard	70.2-83.6				4	72.2-85.6				4	0
south of church	74.1-78.1				4	71.2-81.7				4	0
totals				1	16			1	1	17	
KEY: hyp = hyperplatymeric; plat = platymeric; meso = mesocnemic; eur = eurycnemic											

of these explanations are accepted. However, until a larger body of comparative material is available it is difficult to comment on the meaning or significance of this index.

Where both left and right femurs survived there was often a difference in the category of index between sides. This may indicate a lack of stability in the index between sides (below, Table 28).

One interesting point is that comparison of the actual values for the index for each individual showed that three of the five individuals in the area south of the church had exceptionally high index values for the sample (Table 25). These were two females from burials 103 and 105 and a male from burial no. 102. The possibility of a familial link is examined in the spatial analysis section below.

Cnemic index

The cnemic index reflects the degree of mediolateral flattening of the tibia in the region of the nutrient foramen. As the index decreases away from 100 per cent, the degree of flattening of the bone increases. Individuals were assigned to categories of the index as set out by Wells (1982).

The most common tibia type was eurycnemic, with 94.1 per cent of right and 89.5 per cent of left tibiae eurycnemic for the site as a whole (Table 26). Again, many explanations of this index have been put forward, but its meaning remains as unclear as the meric index. There was much less difference in the index between sides, with only one pair differing (below, Table 28). Whatever was causing this category of index in the tibiae, therefore appears to have been much more constant between sides than was the cause of the meric index amongst the femurs. Values for the three unusual individuals in the area south of the church appear no different from the others (Table 27). This would tend to support the idea that the femurs were affected by a quite separate factor from that influencing the tibiae.

Limb asymmetry or sidedness

It has been suggested that the dominant side in use, that is in most cases the right arm and left leg, are frequently found to be the larger side in a sample. Whether this is the result of preferential usage, or is in fact determined in the foetus, has been discussed by Mays (1991a; 1991b). The humerus head diameter and length, combined radius and ulna length, femoral head diameter and length, and the tibia length, were examined for signs of this tendency.

The arm measurements showed very little pattern, with the right greater in thirteen cases and the left also greater in thirteen cases (Table 28). A possible explanation of this was supplied by the leg-bone measurements, where four cases were identical between left and right, while in a further five cases there was very little difference. This would seem to suggest that the people in this sample were not favouring either limb over the other.

Sexual dimorphism

The existence of dimorphism in the sample has already been shown by the clear division in stature range. It was further investigated by looking at regions of the body known to differ in average size between the sexes. This included the length and breadth of the palate, the length and breadth of the skull, the dimensions of the canine, and the femoral head diameter against epicondylar width (Figs 111-15).

As expected, each of these plots demonstrated the presence of dimorphism; but, interestingly, the different body parts exhibit this to varying degrees. The cranial and palatal dimensions are difficult to comment on as so few male individuals possessed the required data; but in each case (Figs 111 and 112) the males were distinct from the females at the greater end of the axes. The canine was more

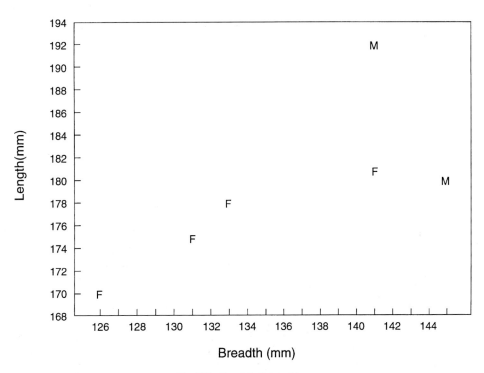

Fig. 111. Cranial dimorphism.

Table 28. Sidedness in different areas.

	right greater	left greater	same	no. in sample
HUMERUS HEAD				
church	2			2
area between entrance and road		1		1
courtyard		4		4
south of church	1			1
HUMERUS LENGTH				
church	2			2
narthex		1		1
area between entrance and road	1			1
courtyard	3	1		4
south of church	1	1		2
RADIUS AND ULNA				
church		2		2
narthex	1			1
area between entrance and road	1			1
courtyard	1	1		2
south of church		2		2
FEMUR HEAD				
church	1	1		2 (but very little in it)
narthex	2			2
space between baptistery, ante-room and entrance		1		1
space between entrance and road	1	1		2
courtyard	1	1	1	3 (right one is almost equal)
south of church	1	2		3
FEMUR LENGTH				
church	1			1
narthex		1		1 (but practically same)
area between entrance and road	1	1		2 (right very little in it)
courtyard		1	1	2
south of church		1		1
TIBIA AND FIBULA				
space between entrance and road	1	1		2 (L is virtually same)
courtyard	1	1	1	3
south of church		2	1	3
TOTAL	23	27	4	54

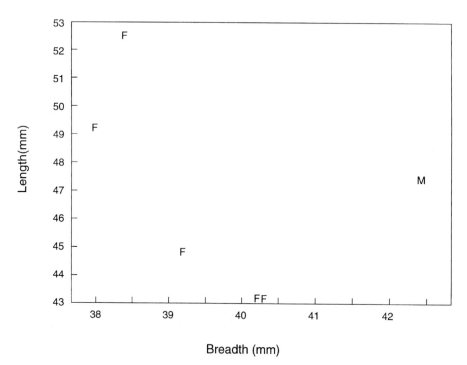

Fig. 112. Palatal dimorphism.

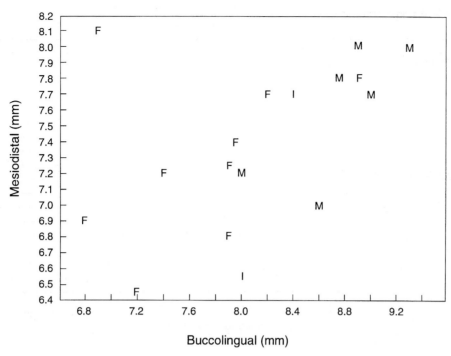

Fig. 113. Dimorphism of upper canine.

informative as more males could be included in the plots. This was very interesting as the division between the sexes was much less distinct for the upper canine (Fig. 113) than for the lower canine (Fig. 114). The most marked split of all was in the plot for the femoral dimensions (Fig. 115), although it is possible that this has an exaggerated appearance because of the scarcity of males. As more Italian sites become available for comparison, it will be possible to see if this is a characteristic of the populations of the period or whether the dimorphism was particularly strong at Monte Gelato.

Certainly from the few individuals that it was possible to include here, with the exception of the upper canine, there was unexpectedly little overlap between the sexes. It seems likely, therefore, that some other factor was acting on the living population to affect their growth potential, and that this factor appears to have had a worse effect on the females than the males. The most likely would be nutritional hardship, compounded by the energy requirements of childbirth. It will have to remain as supposition but, if the tentative suggestion concerning late weaning around two and a half to three and a half years was correct, this may

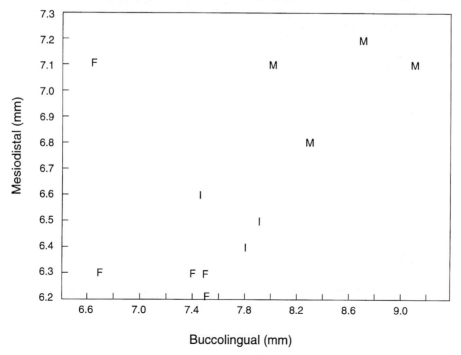

Fig. 114. Dimorphism of lower canine.

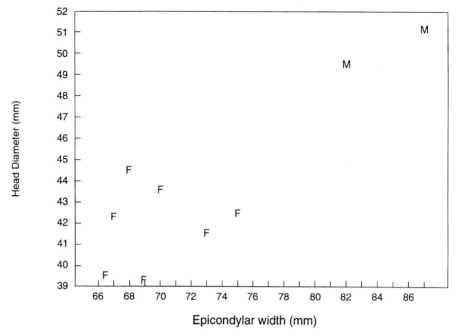

Fig. 115. Dimorphism of the femur.

well support this theory. Mothers would breast-feed longer to cut down demands on other food supplies and possibly to increase the spacing of pregnancies.

DENTAL PATHOLOGY

Deciduous or mixed dentitions were excluded from the following calculations of prevalence. In many parts of this analysis the sample size is so small that the inclusion of one individual may result in a 25 per cent prevalence rate. Working with this sample size appears unreliable on first consideration. However, if only four individuals are present in an area and one has a dental complaint, it is probably reasonable to assume that the complaint is fairly common in that population. Care is necessary not to overinterpret the data; but the evidence is still worth examining. The teeth present for each individual are listed in Table 29.

Wear data has not been included in the analysis. The sample showed evidence of wear at a rate which was roughly in accordance with that set out by Brothwell (1981: 71-2), and this is to be expected for this period.

Congenital complaints

The individuals who presented possible congenital conditions are listed in Table 30. There was only one case of crowding, normally quite a common complaint, and this affected the anterior teeth. It appears to be associated with rotation of the same teeth. In all there were eight individuals with teeth rotated out of the normal tooth row. There was quite a number of malformed teeth. Both lower canines of burial no. 54 had enamel extension down the roots (this was a very common trait at this site, but it was not until the later part of the fieldwork that it was recorded). Conversely, all four third molars of burial no. 81 were shaped from cementum, with just 1.0-2.0 mm of enamel on the tips. Burial no. 105, an infant, had a very oddly shaped upper left

canine, peg-shaped but with three equal cusps, and only a short stubby root about half normal length. There were five other peg teeth amongst four individuals and one taurodontic tooth. Peg teeth are fairly infrequent phenomena in most samples (Mays 1991a; 1991b). Six people had overbite, two markedly so. These were the possibly related individuals in the double burial (79) between the entrance and the road. They also had a palatal torus in common, and a very odd tooth row which raised up the lower anterior teeth in a curve. Two other individuals from burials 26 and 60 have very similar looking, unusual, teeth with short stumpty roots. They also have slender skeletons, whilst the majority from the site appear quite stocky and robust. In addition, burial no. 26 had a three cusped lower left premolar. The possibility of any of the congenital conditions reflecting familial relationships, including these apparent ones, is tested in the spatial analysis below.

Acquired pathology

Caries

Only three children from the whole site suffered from caries. Burial no. 68 was unusual, having two occlusal caries on the lower first molar. This was probably due to the cusp form, and/or little wear, allowing food to get trapped in the fissures. Burials 28 and 72 were more usual in suffering from interproximal caries. Burial no. 28 had only one, but burial no. 72 had four, ranging from slight to moderate severity. This child was buried with a female with notably poor dental health, and it is tempting to suppose that the two could be related and that she may have passed on weak enamel.

The prevalence of adult caries was calculated as the proportion of teeth present which had carious lesions. The prevalence rate by particular tooth for each area is shown in Table 31. Teeth from the baptistery, the ante-room, the entrance to the ante-room and the area over the Roman rooms had no adult caries. These were all areas, however,

Table 29. Teeth catalogue, maxilla.

(a) adults

individual	8	7	6	5	4	3	2	1	1	2	3	4	5	6	7	8
MAXILLA																
AREA BETWEEN ENTRANCE AND ROAD																
79 M112 sk. 8	NP	Y	Y	Y	Y	Y	/	Y	N	Y	Y	Y	Y	Y	Y	NP
79 M112 sk. 9	Y	Y	Y	Y	Y	Y	Y	Y	Y	Y	Y	Y	Y	Y	Y	Y
CHURCH																
7 C23	NP	Y	Y	Y	Y	Y	-	-	-	-	Y	Y	Y	Y	Y	Y
	9	9	9	9	Y	9	9	9	9	9	9	9	9	9	9	9
18 B8 (1)	-	-	-	-	Y	Y			Y		Y	Y		Y	Y	Y
18 B22 (1)	-	-	-	-	-	-	-	-	-	-	-	-	-	-	-	-
18 B22 (11)	-	-	N	N	Y	/	/	/	/	/	/	Y	N	N	-	-
26 A28	N	Y	Y	Y	Y	Y	NP	N	Y	Y	Y	Y	Y	Y	Y	Y
NARTHEX																
54 D289			Y	Y	Y	Y	NP	/	/	/	/	/	/	Y		
54 D291	9	9	9	9	9	9	9	9	9	9	9	9	9	9	9	9
56 D91 (3)	9	9	9	9	9	9	9	9	9	9	9	9	9	9	9	9
59 D168	-	-	Y	Y	Y	Y	Y	Y	Y	Y	Y	Y	Y	Y	-	Y
60 A34	NP	Y	Y	Y	Y	Y	Y	Y	Y	Y	Y	Y	Y	Y	Y	Y
SPACE BETWEEN ANTE-ROOM, BAPTISTERY AND ENTRANCE																
72 D296 (1)	Y	Y	N	/	Y	Y	Y	Y	-	Y	Y	Y	Y	Y	Y	Y
AREA BETWEEN ENTRANCE AND ROAD																
81 M16	Y	Y	Y	Y	Y	Y	/	Y	Y	Y	Y	/	Y	Y	Y	Y
OVER ROMAN ROOMS																
85 L173	Y	Y	Y	Y	Y	Y	Y		Y					Y	Y	Y
COURTYARD																
92 D18	NP	Y	Y	Y	Y	Y	Y	?	Y	Y	Y	Y	Y		Y	
94 D32			Y	Y	Y		.		Y	Y	Y					
99 B4													Y	Y	Y	Y
(99 B4 a)																
99 B4 A	Y	Y	Y	Y	/	/	/	/								
100 D63		Y	Y	Y	Y	Y	Y	Y	Y	Y	Y	Y	Y	Y	Y	
SOUTH OF CHURCH																
102 C29	9	N	N	N	/	Y	Y	Y	/	/	/	Y	-	-	-	9
103 C60	Y	Y	Y	Y	Y	Y	Y	Y	/	/	Y	Y	Y	Y	Y	Y
105 B24 (1)	Y	?	Y	Y	Y	Y	?	Y	Y	Y	?	Y	Y	Y	?	Y
105 B24 (11)	-	Y	Y	Y	/	Y	Y	/	/	Y	Y	Y	Y	Y	Y	/
106 B26	-	-	N	Y	Y	Y	-	-	-	Y	Y	Y	Y	-	-	?
MANDIBLE																
AREA BETWEEN ENTRANCE AND ROAD																
79 M112 sk. 8	Y	Y	Y	Y	Y	Y	/	/	/	Y	Y	Y	Y	Y	Y	?
M112 sk. 9	Y	Y	Y	Y	Y	Y	Y	Y	Y	Y	Y	Y	Y	Y	Y	Y
CHURCH																
7 C23	NP	-	-	N	/	Y	Y	-	-	-	-	Y	N	Y	Y	NP
	9	9	9	9	9	9	9	9	9	9	9	9	9	9	9	9
18 B8 (1)	Y	-	-	-	-	Y			Y				Y		Y	Y
18 B22 (1)	-	N	Y	Y	Y	Y	/	/	/	/	Y	Y	Y	N	-	-
18 B22 (11)	/	Y	/	-	-	-	-	-	-	-	-	-	-	-	-	-
26 A28	Y	Y	Y	Y	Y	Y	Y	N	N	Y	Y	Y	Y	Y	Y	N
NARTHEX																

individual	8	7	6	5	4	3	2	1	1	2	3	4	5	6	7	8
54 D289	9	9	9	9	9	9	9	9	9	9	9	9	9	9	9	9
54 D289	Y	Y	Y	Y	Y	Y	Y	Y	Y	Y	Y	Y	Y	Y	Y	Y
56 D91 (3)	NP	Y	N	N	Y	/	N	N	N	N	/	/	/	N	N	NP
59 D168	Y	Y	Y	Y	-	Y	Y	Y	Y	Y	Y	Y	Y	Y	Y	Y
60 A34	NP	Y	Y	Y	Y	Y	Y	Y	Y	Y	Y	Y	Y	Y	Y	NP
SPACE BETWEEN ANTE-ROOM, BAPTISTERY AND ENTRANCE																
72 D296 (1)	Y	Y	N	Y	Y	/	/	/	/	/	/	/	/	N	N	N	Y
AREA BETWEEN ENTRANCE AND ROAD																
81 M16	Y	Y	Y	/	Y	Y	Y	Y	Y	Y	Y	Y	Y	Y	Y	Y
OVER ROMAN ROOMS																
85 L173		Y	Y	Y	Y	Y	Y				Y	Y	Y	Y	Y	Y
COURTYARD																
92 D18	Y	?	N	Y	Y	Y	Y	Y	?	Y	Y	Y	Y	Y	Y	NP
94 D32	9	N	N	Y	/	/	Y	-	-	Y	/	Y	Y	N	N	9
99 B4				Y	Y	Y	Y	Y	Y	Y	Y	Y	Y			
(99 B4 a)				Y	Y				Y		Y	Y	Y			
99 B4 A	Y	Y	Y	/	/	Y	/	/	/	/	/	/	/	/	Y	Y
100 D63	Y	Y	Y	Y	Y	Y	Y	Y	Y	Y	Y	Y	N	Y	Y	Y
SOUTH OF CHURCH																
102 C29	9	N	N	Y	Y	Y	Y	Y	Y	Y	Y	Y	Y	Y	N	9
103 C60	Y	Y	Y	Y	Y	Y	Y	Y	Y	Y	Y	Y	Y	Y	Y	Y
105 B24 (1)	Y	Y	Y	Y	Y	Y	Y	Y	Y	Y	Y	Y	Y	Y	Y	Y
105 B24 (11)	Y	Y	Y	Y	Y	Y	Y	/	/	/	Y	Y	Y	Y	Y	-
106 B26	-	-	Y	/	Y	-	-	/	Y	Y	Y	Y	Y	Y	Y	-

(b) infants

individual	5	4	3	2	1	1	2	3	4	5	
					MAXILLA						
18 B8(III)	-	- Y	-	- Y	-	Y	-	-	-	-	perm
27 D43	O Y	Y	O Y	Y	Y	Y	Y	O Y	Y	O Y	
28 D15	V Y	Y	/	Y	Y	Y	Y	V23 /	Y	V Y	
29 D31	Y	Y	/	- Y	- Y	/	/	/	Y	Y	jaw not lost
32 D224　V 16	Y	Y	Y	Y	Y	/	Y	/	Y	Y	V 26
33 D226	V 55 -	-	V 53 -	V 52 -	O 51 -	O 61 -	V 62 -	V 63 -	V 64 -	V 65 -	
34 D222　V 16	Y	Y	Y	Y	Y	Y	Y	Y	Y	Y	V 26
37 D229 V 17 16	Y	Y		0 12	11	/	0 22		Y	Y	V 26 27 mixed
37 D229(11) V 16	Y	Y	Y	Y	Y	Y	Y	Y	Y	Y	V 26
37 D229(1)					Y	Y	Y	Y	Y		
38 D54		V Y		V Y	V Y	V Y			V Y		
41 D132　V 16	Y	Y	Y	/	Y	/	TY	Y	Y	Y	V 26
43 D135 O 16	Y	Y	/	Y	Y	Y	/	Y	Y	Y	26 O

individual	5	4	3	2	1	1	2	3	4	5	
47 D212	Y	Y	Y	V 12	V 11	Y V 21	V 22	Y	Y	Y	V 26
53 D293 V 17 16	Y	O 14 Y	V 13	12		21		V 23	Y	Y	26 V Mixed. 27
57 D95 16	y	/	/	/	/	/	/	/	/	Y	26
57 D95 II	Y	Y	/	Y	/	/	Y	Y	Y	Y	V 26
60 A13											
66 A21											
68 D284 V 16	Y O	Y	/	Y	Y	Y	/	/	Y	Y O	V 26
72 D296(11) 16						21		24 V Y	25 V Y	26	V 27 Mixed
76 M70 16 V	Y O	Y	Y O	Y	Y	Y 21 V	Y	Y O	Y	Y O	26 V
77 M72	55 Y	54 Y	53 Y								
97 D78 O 16	Y	Y	Y	/	/	/	/	Y	Y	Y	O 26
105 B24 (III)							Y	Y	Y	Y	

MANDIBLE

individual	5	4	3	2	1	1	2	3	4	5	
18 B8(III)	-	-	-	-	-	-	-	-	-	-	
27 D43	O Y	Y	O Y	Y	Y	Y	Y	O Y	Y	O Y	
28 D15 46 V	V Y	Y	V Y	Y	Y	Y	Y	V Y	Y	V Y	36 V
29 D31 46 V	Y	Y	Y	Y	/	/	/	Y	Y	Y	36 V
32 D224 47 46 V V	Y	Y	Y	Y	Y	/	Y	Y	Y	Y	36 37 V V
33 D226 46 V -	Y V	Y V	Y V	Y V	Y V			Y V	Y V	36 - V
34 D222 46 V	Y	Y	Y	Y	Y	/	/	Y	Y	Y	36 V
37 D229 V 47 46	Y	Y	/ 43	42 O	41	91	32 O	Y 33 V	Y	Y	36 37 V
37 D229(11)	-	Y	Y	Y	Y	Y	/	Y	Y	Y	
37 D229(1) 46 V	Y	Y	Y	Y	Y	/	Y	Y	Y	Y	
38 D54	V Y	V Y		V Y	V Y	V Y			V Y	V Y	
41 D132 46 V	Y	Y	Y	Y V 42	V 41	Y	/	Y	Y	Y	36 37 V V
43 D135 O 46	Y	Y	Y	Y	Y	Y	Y	Y	Y	Y	36 O

individual	5	4	3	2	1	1	2	3	4	5	
47 D212　46 V	Y -	Y	Y	Y	Y	Y	Y	Y	Y	Y	36 V
53 D293 47 46 V	Y		V 43	42		31	32	33 V	Y	Y	36 37 V Mixed
57 D95 (I) 46	/	/	/	/	/	31 O	/	/	Y	Y	36 Mixed
57 D95 II	Y	Y	Y	Y	Y	Y	Y	/	Y	Y	
60 A13　48 V	Y 47 V 46	/	/	/	/						Mixed
66 A21			Y V/O	Y	Y	Y	Y	Y V/O			
68 D284　V 46	Y O	Y	/	Y	/	Y	Y	/	Y	Y O	V 36
72 D296(a) 46	Y	Y 44 V		42 V	41 V				Y	Y	
76 M70　46 V	Y O	Y	Y O	Y	Y	Y	Y	Y O	Y	Y O	36 V
77 M72											
97 D78　O 46	Y	Y	/	/	/	/	/	/	Y	Y	36 O
105 B24 (III)		N	N	N	N	N	N	N	Y	Y	

with very few adults. This fact, combined with the low prevalence of childhood caries in general, suggests that caries was a disease associated with ageing, and the prolonged exposure to carious agents that greater age would mean, rather than a feature of the population itself, or of the diet. If either of the latter circumstances were the cause of caries, the children would also have been affected.

In all of the areas yielding teeth with caries, the incisors were not affected. Apart from one canine from a burial in the church, caries were restricted to teeth posterior to the premolars, which would agree with modern incidence patterns. The maxilla appeared to be slightly worse affected than the mandible, and people buried within the church were slightly worse affected than those in other areas. On the whole, however, there were few noteworthy differences between the areas, either in prevalence rates or in areas of the mouth affected.

The sites on the tooth attacked by caries, and the frequencies, are set out in Table 32. Of all caries, 44 per cent were cervical, and just over a quarter, 26 per cent, were interproximal. The real rate of cervical caries was higher than this, as many were also interproximal and only scored in that category. The most likely explanation of this type of caries would be natural sugars in the food, combined with poor hygiene, and soft, pulpy food as a secondary factor. Sugars released from food, if not cleaned away, will sit in the saliva around the neck of the tooth just above the gum. This area is therefore most at risk from caries. The interproximal area is also at risk when soft, pappy food becomes

trapped in gaps between the teeth. This attracts and feeds cariogenic bacteria which may result in caries formation. The relatively low rate of occlusal caries was produced by only three individuals, two of whom were the double burial (79) between the entrance and the road. This low prevalence would be due to tooth wear which would flatten out the fissures in the complex cusped posterior teeth, where occlusal caries would be most likely to occur. Only twelve per cent of all caries were gross, meaning that caries was not a severe problem at this site. This was confirmed by the low number of abcesses, only six for the whole sample. Whether this was because the diet was generally healthy, and took a long time to cause caries, or because people were dying early is impossible to demonstrate.

Abcesses

The prevalence rate was calculated by the number of abcesses as a proportion of the surviving tooth sockets (Table 33). As noted in the previous section, the prevalence of abcesses was very low for the whole site, and they were attested in only three areas: the space between the ante-room, baptistery and entrance; the area between the entrance and road; and the courtyard. Again, the maxilla appeared to be slightly worse affected than the mandible. This would follow, as caries attacked the maxilla to a greater extent than the mandible, and the most common cause of abcess is apical infection following exposure of the pulp cavity due to caries or excessive wear. Alternatively, the difference could

Table 30. Dental non metric.

indiv.	tooth rot^n	over-bite	pal torus	crowding	fen^n	peg.	PE	chip
79 M112 sk. 9	13, 31, 32, 41-42	very	slight	Ant. mand. very	17, 16, 13, 26, 27, 18			
79 M112 sk. 8		raised/ curved ant. teeth	✓		16, 17, 26, 27, 36, 37, 46, 47			
7 C23	28					28	26, 36	36 ling ant. cusp
18 B8 (1)						14, 27		
26 A28	14, 24					(12 NP) 22		
54 D291	0	✓	0	0	0	0	0	32
56 D91(3)								44
59 D168	43						46, 36	
60 A34		✓			14, 26, 34			
72 D296 (1)							25, 26	
81 M16							36, 46	38, 11
92 D18	13	✓				48		15, 16, 25
94 D32							14, 15 24, 35	
99 B4a					26-28			turned into 36
100 D63	43, 33, 12	✓			14, 18, 22			22
102 C29							11	
103 C60	42				33, 43			
105 B24 (1)								14
105 B26	34				14, 24			14

KEY: tooth rot^n = tooth rotation; pal torus = palatal torus; fen^n = fenestration; PE = pulp exposure

INFANT AND JUVENILE DATA

individual	incisor form
18 B8 (111)	groove on permanent incisors
27 A43	deep groove of wear on 51, none on other incisors
68 D284	55 and 65 something similar to Carabelli's cusp
105 B24 (11)	very old canine – fully circular and three similar size cusps. Root only formed to *c.* ½ length and still open. Polish wear – peg tooth probably but has three cusps

---

NOTES TO TABLE 30

26 A28	21 not developed. 23 position has lump lingually and over it – could be unerupted 23 but no x-ray.
	12 is very peg-like. 21 and canines normal. Both lower canines very small, almost peg-like.
	All teeth very short roots and skeleton as whole slender – very similar to A3. 34 almost 3 cusped.
54 D291	Both lower canines enamel extends down roots and heavy ridges on crown.
59 D168	Fold in lingual upper 1st incisors.
60 A34	Very short and stumpy roots and very slight skeleton.
81 M16	All four 3rd molars shaped from cementum with 1-2 mm of enamel on top.
85 L173	M2 and M3 have the very elongated cusp form.
102 C29	Calculus deposit so solid has made block of teeth and goes onto occlusal surfaces – could it be endocrinal problem? As well as resorbed sockets, there is alveolar resorption all round remaining teeth but especially severe in left side mandible where all from I to M probably held by tissue only as only just in place now. So wobbly – difficulty eating – could he have died from fever? Gets progressively worse from I to M. Also maxilla looks affected but alveolar is damaged.

be a function of the thinner bone in the walls of the maxilla compared with that in the mandible. Only those abcesses which penetrated the alveolar were scored, in the absence of an X-ray programme to detect those contained inside the alveolar. Given the greater fragility of the maxilla, more abcesses may successfully perforate the wall than in the thick plate of the mandible. Anterior teeth were not affected; this corresponds with the caries pattern, suggesting that the observed difference is accurate (despite the lack of X-ray analysis). The high rate in the space area is deceptive, as it is caused by three abcesses, all in the same female, burial no. 72. This was the female buried with the child with very unusual caried dentition.

Ante-mortem loss

The prevalence rate was calculated by the number of teeth lost ante-mortem as a proportion of all the possible sockets present. The rates for each tooth are given in Table 34. The two main causes of ante-mortem tooth-loss are caries or periodontal disease. Given the generally low incidence of severe caries (or abcesses), periodontal disease appeared the more likely cause. In any case, as all three conditions progress with age, it is likely that a relationship will be apparent between them. Four areas yielded individuals with affected maxilliae: the church; the space between the entrance, ante-room and baptistery; the area between the entrance and the road; and the area to the south of the

Table 31. Caries prevalence by area.

MAXILLA

	8	7	6	5	4	3	2	1	1	2	3	4	5	6	7	8
church		1/3	1/3	1/2	2/4	1/3						1/5	2/2	2/2		
narthex	1/2		1/1	1/1										1/3	3/4	
space between entrance, baptistery and ante-room	1/1	1/3												1/3	1/3	
area between entrance and road	1/2				1/4							1/3	1/4	1/3		
courtyard		1/3	1/2	1/3										2/3	1/1	1/2
south of church														2/5		

MANDIBLE

	8	7	6	5	4	3	2	1	1	2	3	4	5	6	7	8
church		7	6	5	4	3	2	1	1	2	3	4	5	6	7	8
narthex		3/4	1/3	1/3	1/3							1/3	1/3	1/3	1/3	
space between entrance, baptistery and ante-room	1/3	1/3													1/1	
area between entrance and road																
courtyard				1/3										2/3		1/2
south of church														2/5		

MAXILLA

	8	7	6	5	4	3	2	1	1	2	3	4	5	6	7	8
church		7	100	100	20.0	33.3					33.3	50.0	50.0	33.3	33.3	50.0
narthex		75.0	33.3													
space between entrance, baptistery and ante-room	100												100	100		
area between entrance and road	50.0															
courtyard			33.3	25.0	33.0							25.0		50.0	33.3	50.0
south of church													33.3	66.6	33.3	50.0

MANDIBLE

	8	7	6	5	4	3	2	1	1	2	3	4	5	6	7	8
church		7	6	5	4	3	2	1	1	2	3	4	5	6	7	8
narthex		33.0	33.0	33.0	33.0							33.0	33.0	33.3	33.0	
space between entrance, baptistery and ante-room	33.0	33.3													33.3	
area between entrance and road																
courtyard				33.3									33.3	66.6	100	50.0
south of church														40.0		

Table 32. Caries by location on tooth.

	occlusal	inter-proximal	cervical	gross	abcess	comments
church	0	5	8	1	0	
baptistery	0	0	0	0	0	
narthex	0	3	7	0	0	
ante-room	0	0	0	0	0	
space between baptistery, ante-room and entrance	0	2	4	0	3	D296 (78) all one individual. ♀ with child
entrance to ante-room	0	0	0	0	0	
area between entrance and road	5	0	3	0	2	The two related in double grave and rare occlusion
over Roman rooms	0	0	0	0	0	
courtyard	4	1	0	5	3	
south of church	0	2	0	0	0	
total	9	13	22	6	8	
% of total caries (total caries = 50)	18	26	44	12	-	

church. Individuals buried within the church were most affected (as they were by abcesses and caries).

There is a striking difference in the prevalence of tooth-loss between the mandible and maxilla. Anterior teeth were affected in both the lower and upper dentitions; but in the mandible both central and lateral incisors were missing, whereas in the maxilla only central incisors had been lost. Periodontal disease is likely to have been responsible as caries have been shown not to affect these areas in this sample.

Non-eruption of teeth

The prevalence rate for each tooth type was calculated by the number of unerupted teeth, as a proportion of surviving corresponding alveolar regions. The result was predictable, with the majority of teeth comprising the third molar (Table 35). It is more surprising that agenesis of the third molar on mandibles was found in burials from only three areas of the site: the church, the narthex and the courtyard. On the maxilla, it occurs in a single burial in the area between the entrance and the road. As this is an inherited trait, it is tempting to assume that it was a sign of familial relationships. However, a far more probable explanation is that the areas with predominantly deciduous dentitions had a much lesser chance of including an affected individual; these include four of the unrepresented areas. Two unerupted right upper lateral incisors are also interesting, since these are more unusual and could indicate a family relationship. However, one came from a burial in the church and one in the narthex, rather than being in close proximity.

Calculus

The severity of calculus is shown in Table 36. The areas not represented include the baptistery, the ante-room and the entrance to the ante-room – all sectors dominated by child interments, where less calculus would be expected given that it is another age-related condition.

In burials elsewhere, 43.5 per cent had slight or moderate calculus on the maxilla, but in only 8.7 per cent of cases could it be classed as severe. By contrast, there was severe calculus on sixteen per cent of mandibles. This agrees with the difference between the two dentitions apparent in the ante-mortem loss and supports the suggestion that

periodontal disease (in which calculus is a factor) was a greater cause of tooth loss than caries in this sample.

Periodontal disease

The occurrence of periodontal disease is detailed in Table 37. The three areas that were unaffected by calculus were also unaffected by periodontal disease, as could be predicted, given the contributory relationship of calculus to this disease. Again there was no observable pattern in the variation between areas. There was a major difference between upper and lower dentitions. The mandible was more affected than the maxilla, with 33.3 per cent of dentitions presenting signs of severe periodontal disease, as opposed to 18.8 per cent in the maxilla. This suggests that periodontal disease was a major problem in the people of this sample. However, 49.9 per cent of the stratified, recordable, maxilla dentitions and 38.9 per cent of the mandibles had no periodontal disease whatsoever. If all the unstratified dentitions were included, the percentages free of disease would be higher still. In a modern society practically all adults are affected by periodontal disease, at least in its preliminary stages of gingivitis; even this shows up as bony changes on the alveolar. The lack of hygiene indicated by the caries rate makes it more likely that this low rate of periodontal disease was due to firm textured food. This requires mastication, and therefore stimulates the alveolar and keeps it healthy, rather than rigorous hygiene controlling the incidence (Conheeney, forthcoming a).

Alveolar recession

The distribution of alveolar recession followed the prevalence of periodontal disease very closely (Table 38). Given the interrelatedness of these two conditions this was to be expected (Conheeney, forthcoming a). As with periodontal disease, the distribution of individuals across the severity categories may indicate the relative ages of those buried in different areas of the site, since both conditions are age-related. For example, prevalences in the church were limited to the severe category, which may suggest that the burials here contained the older elements of the sample. However, this relies on just two cases, and cannot be considered in isolation.

Table 33. Abcess prevalence by area.

MAXILLA	8	7	6	5	4	3	2	1	1	2	3	4	5	6	7	8
space between baptistery, ante-room and entrance					1/1								1/1	1/1		
area between entrance and road		1/3												1/3		
courtyard													1/2			
MANDIBLE	8	7	6	5	4	3	2	1	1	2	3	4	5	6	7	8
space between baptistery, ante-room and entrance																
area between entrance and road		1/3											1/5	1/5		
courtyard																
MAXILLA	8	7	6	5	4	3	2	1	1	2	3	4	5	6	7	8
space between baptistery, ante-room and entrance					100								100	100		
area between entrance and road													50.0	33.3		
courtyard																
MANDIBLE	8	7	6	5	4	3	2	1	1	2	3	4	5	6	7	8
space between baptistery, ante-room and entrance																
area between entrance and road		33.3											20.0	20.0		
courtyard																

Table 34. Ante-mortem loss prevalence by area.

MAXILLA	8	7	6	5	4	3	2	1	1	2	3	4	5	6	7	8
church	1/2		1/3	1/3					1/2				1/3	1/3	1/3	
space between entrance, baptistery and road			1/1											1/1		
area between entrance and road									1/3							
south of church		1/3	2/4	1/4									1/4			

MANDIBLE	8	7	6	5	4	3	2	1	1	2	3	4	5	6	7	8
church		1/3	1/3	1/4				1/2	1/2				1/4	1/3	1/3	
space between entrance, baptistery and road			1/1					1/4	1/4					1/1		
narthex							1/4	1/4	1/4	1/4			1/4	1/4	1/4	
south of church		1/5											1/5	1/5	1/5	
courtyard		1/5	2/4										1/5	2/4	1/5	

MAXILLA	8	7	6	5	4	3	2	1	1	2	3	4	5	6	7	8
church	50.0		33.3	33.3					50.0				33.3	33.3		
space between entrance, baptistery and road			100													
area between entrance and road									33.3							
south of church		33.3	50.0	25.0									25.0			

MANDIBLE	8	7	6	5	4	3	2	1	1	2	3	4	5	6	7	8
church	33.3	33.3	100	33.3				50.0	50.0				25.0	33.3	100	33.3
space between entrance, baptistery and road																
narthex			25.0				25.0	25.0	25.0	25.0				25.0	25.0	
south of church		25.0	20.0											20.0	20.0	
courtyard		20.0	50.0										20.0	50.0	20.0	

Table 35. Prevalence of unerupted teeth by area.

MAXILLA

	8	7	6	5	4	3	2	1	1	2	3	4	5	6	7	8
church	1/2															1/2
narthex																1/2
area between entrance and road	1/3															1/3
courtyard																2/3

MANDIBLE

	8	7	6	5	4	3	2	1	1	2	3	4	5	6	7	8
church	1/4															1/4
narthex	2/4															2/4
area between entrance and road																
courtyard	1/3															

MAXILLA

	8	7	6	5	4	3	2	1	1	2	3	4	5	6	7	8
church	50.0															50.0
narthex																50.0
area between entrance and road	33.3															33.3
courtyard																66.6

MANDIBLE

	8	7	6	5	4	3	2	1	1	2	3	4	5	6	7	8
church	25.0															25.0
narthex	50.0															50.0
area between entrance and road																
courtyard	33.3															

Table 36. Calculus prevalence rates by area.

	total no. that can be scored for this condition	grade 1		grade 2		grade 3	
		no. of sufferers	as a % of total	no. of sufferers	as a % of total	no. of sufferers	as a % of total
MAXILLA							
church	4	2	50.0	2	50.0		
narthex	4	2	50.0	1	25.0		
space between entrance, baptistery and ante-room	1	1	100.0				
area between entrance and road	3			3	100.0		
over Roman rooms	1			1	100.0		
courtyard	5	2	40.0	2	40.0	1	20.0
south of church	5	3	60.0	1	20.0	1	20.0
total	23	10	(43.5%)	10	(43.5%)	2	(8.7%)
MANDIBLE							
church	5	2	40.0	2	40.0		
narthex	4	1	100.0	3	75.0		
space between entrance, baptistery and ante-room	1			3	100.0		
area between entrance and road	3			1	100.0		
over Roman rooms	1	2	33.3	1	16.7	3	50.0
courtyard	6	3	60.0	1	20.0	1	20.0
south of church	5						
total	25	8	(32.0%)	11	(44.0%)	4	(16.0%)

Table 37. Periodontal disease prevalence by area.

	total no. that can be scored for this condition	grade 1		grade 2		grade 3	
		no. of sufferers	as a % of total	no. of sufferers	as a % of total	no. of sufferers	as a % of total
MAXILLA							
church	2					1	50.0
narthex	2						
space between entrance, baptistery and ante-room	1			1	100.0		
area between entrance and road	3					1	33.3
over Roman rooms	1						
courtyard	4	1	25.0	2	25.0	1	25.0
south of church	3			1	33.3		
total	16	1	(6.3%)	4	(25.0%)	3	(18.8%)
MANDIBLE							
church	3					1	33.3
narthex	4	1	25.0			2	50.0
space between entrance, baptistery and ante-room	1			1	100.0		
area between entrance and road	3	1	33.3			1	33.3
over Roman rooms	1						
courtyard	3			1	33.3	2	66.6
south of church	3			1	33.3		
total	18	2	(11.1%)	3	(16.7%)	6	(33.3%)

Table 38. Alveolar recession prevalence rates by area.

	total no. that can be scored	grade 1		grade 2		grade 3	
		no. of sufferers	as a % of total	no. of sufferers	as a % of total	no. of sufferers	as a % of total
MAXILLA							
church	3					2	66.6
narthex	1						
space between entrance, baptistery and ante-room	1			1	100.0		
area between entrance and road	3			1	33.3	1	33.3
over Roman rooms	1						
courtyard	3	1	33.3	1	33.3		
south of church	4	1	25.0				
total	16	2	(12.5%)	3	(18.8%)	3	(18.8%)
MANDIBLE							
church	3					2	66.6
narthex	3	1	33.3	1	100.0		
space between entrance, baptistery and road	1						
area between entrance and road	3	1	33.3	1	33.3	1	33.3
over Roman rooms	3	1	33.3			1	33.3
courtyard	3					1	33.3
south of church	4	1	25.0			1	25.0
total	17	4	(23.5%)	2	(11.8%)	5	(29.4%)

Table 39. Hypoplasia prevalence rate by area.
(There were also three infant cases, two in the baptistery and one in the narthex.)

	total no. that can be scored for this condition.	grade 1		grade 2		grade 3	
		no. of sufferers	as a % of total	no. of sufferers	as a % of total	no. of sufferers	as a % of total
MAXILLA							
church	3						
narthex	2	1	50.0				
space between entrance, baptistery and ante-room	1						
area between entrance and road	2	1	50.0				
over Roman rooms	1						
courtyard	4			1	25.0		
south of church	4			1	25.0		
total	17	2	(11.8%)	2	(11.8%)	0	0
MANDIBLE							
church	4	1	25.0				
narthex	3	1	33.3				
space between entrance, baptistery and ante-room	1						
area between entrance and road	3	2	66.6				
over Roman rooms	1						
courtyard	4			1	25.0		
south of church	4	1	25.0	1	25.0		
total	20	5	(25.0%)	2	(10.0%)	0	0

Hypoplasia.

The prevalence of hypoplasia is given in Table 39. The mandible was again more severely affected, which is difficult to explain: an individual would be affected in upper and lower dentitions, if suffering from true hypoplasia. Perhaps a congenital defect was imitating the appearance of hypoplasia.

This condition is an interruption of the normal development of the tooth enamel, usually attributed to bouts of childhood illness (Hillson 1986: 127-40; Johnston and Zimmer 1989). The surprising factor is that 23.6 per cent of adult maxillary dentitions were affected, and 35 per cent of the mandibular ones. By contrast, only around thirteen per cent of child dentitions were affected. It is possible that children were sometimes dying before or during the severe disease episodes that would cause the condition, whereas adults with the condition represented those children who had survived the disease. The only conclusion that can be inferred from the data was that about 23 per cent, or roughly one quarter of the adults with surviving dentition, had undergone serious episodes of illness during childhood. (The lower figure is used because of the possibility of overestimation in the mandible.)

SKELETAL PATHOLOGY

Congenital pathology

Vertebral defects

Defects around the junction of the lumbar and sacral vertebrae are common because of the instability of this region (Ortner and Putschar 1981; Waldron, forthcoming). Monte Gelato was no exception to this (Table 40).

A male of 25-35 years from the area south of the church (burial no. 102) had an imperfectly closed sacral canal on the dorsal surface. The level of closure can vary, but is normally fused over from the level of the first and fifth bodies. This case does not qualify as true spina bifida occulta, as the canal was not completely open. Modern frequencies for this complaint are not well known, because the sufferer would probably be unaware of the condition and so would not present at the doctor's surgery. The same probably applies to all the vertebral defects discussed here.

Occasionally the fifth lumbar vertebra has a sacral appearance, or the first sacral vertebra has the appearance of a lumbar vertebra. Burial no. 59, a male of 17-25 years in the narthex, had the former condition, and a female of 25-30 years in the courtyard (burial no. 100) had the latter (with both first and second sacral vertebrae affected).

Various oddities of vertebral form occur which cannot be readily classified. Burial no. 105 from south of the church, a 17-25 year old male, was one such case. The lower articular facets of his fourth lumbar vertebra were crumpled, and the upper facets of the fifth matched and fitted with these.

Other pathology

Two individuals had unusual congenital defects (Table 40). Burial no. 56 in the narthex had the styloid process missing from the left ulna. Burial no. 102 from south of the church had a double facet on the left radius distal facet. The facets were very smooth with no sign of osteoarthritis or trauma.

It is interesting that, with the exception of burial no. 100 from the courtyard, all the congenital defects came from individuals buried in the narthex or from the area south of the church. A familial relationship between these burials is tested for in the spatial analysis section below.

Acquired pathology

Degenerative defects

In common with most archaeological samples, degenerative defects, along with dental disease, were the most frequent pathology. Prevalence rates were calculated as the number of individuals suffering from the complaint as a proportion of the number of individuals in an area of the site.

Osteoarthritis was only scored for those individuals who satisfied the criteria laid down by Rogers et al. (1987). The frequencies are given in Table 41. The four areas composed mainly of children (the baptistery, the ante-room, the entrance to the ante-room and the area over the Roman rooms) recorded no sign of the condition, as would be expected since it is associated with ageing. The prevalences in the other areas also closely reflected the age composition of the sample. The church, with 44.9 per cent dead by fifteen years, had only two per cent with indications of the complaint. Similarly, the narthex, with 45.2 per cent dead by a similar age, had no sufferers. The area between the entrance and the road had the highest proportion of sufferers, at twenty per cent, but contained nobody who had died before the age of 25 years. More females than males were affected, but this could simply be due to the small figures available.

The most commonly affected parts of the skeleton were the acetabulum and femur head, the lumbar vertebrae, the cervical vertebrae, and the wrist and foot bones. In modern populations the large weight-bearing joints are most fre-

Table 40. Congenital defects.

1. INCOMPLETE CLOSURE OF SACRAL CANAL				
south of church	burial no. 102	♂	25-35 years	open to bottom of second segment from top
2. SACRILIZATION/LUMBARIZATION				
narthex	burial no. 59	♂	17-25 years	fifth lumbar sacralized
courtyard	burial no. 100	♀	25-30 years	first and second sacral lumbars with intact spines and marked depression between
3. VERTEBRAL ODDITIES				
south of church	burial no. 105	♂	17-25 years	fourth lumbar lower articular facets crumpled and fifth's upper match
4. ANY OTHER				
narthex	burial no. 56	♀	33-45 years	left ulna styloid process missing
south of church	burial no. 102	♂	25-35 years	left radius distal facet 'double-faceted' but still very smooth

quently affected in clinical populations (Ortner and Puts-char 1981). In archaeological samples, however, it is not uncommon to find the signs in smaller joints (Mays 1991a; 1991b). Osseous indicators of the disease are symptomatic of the deterioration of the cartilage between the joint artic-ular surfaces, to such an extent that bone articulates with bone, in some cases producing a polished surface or ebur-nation. It may be extremely painful when it has progressed this far. The difference between modern and archaeolo-gical distribution of the condition is probably because the disease would be most troublesome and debilitating in the large joints, and therefore these are most frequently pre-sented for attention, whereas the archaeological samples are possibly identifying cases which may never come to the attention of a modern clinician. The affected individuals would have felt some pain and lack of mobility of the joint. The female in burial no. 79 with severe osteoarthritis of the hip might have been a candidate for hip replacement today. The other cases varied in severity.

The majority of people in a modern population are affec-ted by vertebral osteophytes by about 45 years of age (Bass 1987: 18-21), and there has been much debate as to the extent of stress-related occupational factors on this age-rela-ted phenomenon (Ortner and Putschar 1981). The relative frequencies of osteophytes in the different areas at Monte Gelato again reflected the age composition of the samples in the same way as osteoarthritis, but not quite so obviously (Table 41). This was probably because osteophytosis is a far more common condition and would affect a greater age-range of people. Females were more affected than males in every area except that to the south of the church. If the con-dition is related to physical stress, this could mean that the females were working harder manually than the males, rel-ative to their physique and strength. The areas of the skel-eton most affected were the vertebrae and foot bones. The condition of the vertebrae could be predicted, but that of the foot bones was more unexpected. Changes of this type are often attributed to frequent mobility over rough ground, as in the case of an agricultural worker. What is most interesting is that this distribution was also true for the burials in the church. Despite the fact that these graves are the most elaborate on the site, the evidence of the osteo-phytes would seem to indicate that at least some of those buried in the church were engaged in similar activities to those buried elsewhere.

The prevalence of intervertebral disc disease in the differ-ent areas of the site was much more similar to the rates for osteoarthritis (Table 41), and again probably age-dictated. Males and females were equally affected, suggesting that the variation between the sexes apparent for osteophytosis was genuine. The most obvious indication of this disease is ero-sion and deposition of bone on the body end plates of the vertebrae, as a result of degeneration of the disc. The suf-ferers would probably have experienced stiffening and lessening mobility of the joints.

Ossification of the ligamentum flavum again corres-ponded to the age composition of the various areas. The thoracic vertebrae were mostly affected and some lumbar vertebrae. This is similar in most samples. This would have had no great effect on the living person.

The distribution of bony exostoses and entheses else-where in the body was also recorded. Various workers have tried to relate these changes to occupational stress (Saun-ders 1989). In this sample, hand and foot phalanges were widely affected in all the adult burial areas of the site, including the church (Table 42). This may mean active use of the hands and feet. The next most frequently involved

Table 41. Frequency of osteoarthritis (OA), osteophytes (OP), intervertebral disc disease (IVD) and ossification of ligamentum flavum (LF).

	OA					OP					IVD					LF				
	J	♂	♀	?	total	J	♂	♀	?	total	J	♂	♀	?	total	J	♂	♀	?	total
church	0	0	0	1	2.0%	0	1	3	3	17.1%	0	1	0	0	2.0%	0	0	1	0	2.0%
narthex					0	0	0	2	0	6.5%					0	0	0	1	0	3.2%
space between baptistery, ante-room and entrance					0	0	0	1	0	16.7%					0					0
area between entrance and road	0	0	1	0	2.00%	0	2	3	0	100%	0	1	1	0	40.0%	0	0	2	0	40.0%
courtyard	0	0	2	0	11.1%	0	2	4	1	38.9%	0	1	0	0	5.6%	0	2	0	1	16.7%
south of church	0	1	0	0	12.5%	0	1	1	0	25.0%	0	0	1	0	12.5%	0	1	1	0	25.0%

NOTES: The total for the church uses 41 as the total buried there rather than 51 as in Table 7 as the ten people from the ossuary have been excluded. Locations most affected are:
OA – acetabulum and femoral head, lumbar vertebrae, cervical vertebrae, wrist and feet bones. OP – vertebrae and feet bones. IVD – mainly cervical and lumbar. LF – mostly thoracic, some lumbar.

Table 42. Entheses.

B1 B15	raised on phalange (only phal)
79 M112 sk. 8	fourth metatarsal, proximal hand phalange base, phal. flex, grade 2 on R and L ulnae, R first rib
2 C58	see OP sheet as very advanced
7 C23	L foot phalange (though not on tarsals) though R calcaneum superior facet rough and pitted
8 C46	fourth R metatarsal and metacarpal R and L calcaneum posterior and inferior and R and L talus; tibiae and fibulas proximal ends
18 B8 (1)	L humerus medial distal, R humerus deltoid, R radius
24 D107 (ossuary)	R femur ossified ligament half way down shaft
26 A28	finger phalanges (though note that the skeleton is slight and the feet are not robust)
65 A2	very marked linea aspera and L tibial insertions
78 M33	calcaneum
92 D18	hand phalanges
93 D5	phalanges; both lateral clavicles
94 D32	raised on hand phalanges
100 D63	R and L humeral lateral epicondyles
102 C29	both tibiae marked soleal lines and on inferior surface of clavicles

bone was the humerus, possibly suggesting strenuous physical activity of some sort. The majority of skeletons was robust and stocky, with well-marked muscle attachment sites. A small number was noticeably slender and slight. This included burials 63 and 65 from the narthex and burial no. 94 in the courtyard. Burial no. 63 was particularly interesting as it contained two individuals: a mature adult who was very small and slender, with no muscle markings; and a second adult of more average build, but with non-craggy feet bones (unlike the majority), and no raised flanges on the hand phalanges.

Trauma

The fractures present in the sample are described in Table 43. The most striking feature of the list is that all affect the ribs, and the majority were well healed (although some were slightly misaligned, and one may have had some infection). This suggests that the people frequently received blows of some sort to the trunk. Only adults were affected, but this included males and females equally, so, whatever the cause, both sexes were exposed to it. The good level of alignment does not mean that the rib cage was necessarily bound in some way, as the intact ribs would have braced the

fractured ones. The low level of infection means either that the wounds did not penetrate the surface; or, that they were kept clean; or had occurred a long while before death and any infection had had a chance to clear. The most striking case was an elderly male buried next to the road (burial no. 78) whose entire rib cage was crushed. The ribs were fractured in a line near their necks, and on their shafts near to the sternal end. Somewhat surprisingly, the man had survived, and the ribs had healed well, although misaligned and with much ossification of the connecting soft tissue. The man's breathing must have been impaired to some extent by this unnatural rigidity of the rib cage, and he was extremely fortunate not to have sustained fatal internal injuries to organs such as his spleen.

The only other type of trauma in this sample was Schmorl's nodes. Schmorl's nodes are interpreted as the result of herniation of the intervertebral disc into the end plate of the vertebral body due to overlifting by a young person. At Monte Gelato the highest prevalence of this condition was in the burials in the courtyard, where over a fifth of the sample was affected (Table 43). There was one case from the church and one from the narthex. The most commonly affected vertebrae were the lower thoracic and the lumbar, which is usual as these bear the most weight.

Table 43. Trauma.

area	burial	sex	age	location	frequency of individuals with fracture
FRACTURES					
church	18	♂	22-35	rib band - healed well	2/51 – 3.9%
church	24	?	adult	rib neck - healed, misaligned	
narthex	56	♀	33-45	ribs both sides, bony spurs	1/31 – 3.2%
area between entrance and road	78	♂	adult (elderly)	crushed rib cage, healed but misaligned and massive ossification of connecting soft tissue	1/5 – 20.0%
courtyard	93	♀	33-45	2nd and 3rd R ribs and a L rib well–healed though possibly some infection	1/18 – 5.6%
SCHMORL'S NODES					
church				T5 inferior surface	1/51 – 2.0%
narthex				inferior surface L1 or 2	1/31 – 3.2%
courtyard				lower thor.; lumbar	4/18 – 22.2%

Table 44. Nutritional disorders.

	cribra orbitalia			cribra femoralis			cranial hyperostosis		
	slight	moderate	severe	slight	moderate	severe	slight	moderate	severe
church (inf)				1/26					
baptistery (10 inf, 1 juv) %	2/19 10.5	3/19 15.8	1/19 5.3	1/26 3.8	1/26 3.8	3/26 11.5	2/19 10.5		2 cases of hypoplasia
narthex (1 inf, 2 juv, 1 adult) %	2/14 14.3				2/17 11.8		3/14 14.3		1 case of hypoplasia
ante-room (inf) %		1/1 100.0		1/1 100.0					
space between baptistery, entrance and ante-room (juv adult) %	1/6 16.7		1/6 16.7						2/6 33.3
entrance to ante-room (inf) %					1/9 11.1				
courtyard (2 inf, 2 adult) %	1/9 11.1		1/9 11.1		1/12 8.3				
south of church (inf, adult) %	1/7 14.3				1/7 14.3				

Nutritional deficiencies

The prevalence rates of those conditions associated with nutritional deficiency are given in Table 44. Two areas had none of the conditions present, the area between the entrance and the road and the area over the Roman rooms. There appears to be no simple explanation for this, other than the effect of the small sample size. Of the areas with cases, the church yielded the fewest, with no cribra orbitalia or cranial hyperostosis, and just one out of 26 femurs with slight cribra femoralis. Perhaps this is an indication that more privileged burials were placed within the church; but this is very tenuous given the absence of other physical indicators of status, such as attainment of the maximum stature in the range for the sample.

These lesions are generally accepted as indicative of iron deficiency anaemia during childhood, either because of illness or nutritional compromise (Stuart-Macadam 1989). Table 44 shows that most cases came from burials in the baptistery (the ante-room prevalence rate being the result of a sample of one). Cribra orbitalia in particular tends to occur in two age groups: infants, because of the stress of weaning; and adolescents, because of stress around puberty. A glance (Table 44) at those affected reveals that most were infants (hence the high rate in the baptistery). More interestingly, only four juveniles were affected, compared with seventeen infants. This could mean that there was no nutritional stress by the age of puberty; but this seems unlikely given other indicators, already discussed, such as the reduced stature of female adults. This lack of instances in juveniles seems, therefore, to support the tentative suggestion, made above (p. 131), that the slight peak of deaths around 12.5 to 13.5 years could be due to stress around puberty.

Stunted growth can be another indicator of nutritional compromise. This was tested by comparing dental development age (which tends to be more stable) with age by epiphyseal union and by diaphyseal length, which are affected by adverse environmental conditions (Table 45). On the whole, dental age agreed very well with growth age. This is peculiar given the small female stature, which suggested stunting. It may be that an effort was made to provide well for children; more stress occurred later, between childhood and puberty, resulting in the deaths of a proportion of teenagers. Of those that survived, the females then underwent the additional stress of childbirth, thus never reaching their true growth potential. However, at this point, with such scant data, this can be no more than very tentative supposition.

Infectious disease

Most interestingly, with the exception of one case of a pair of femur heads, all cases of infection involved the bones of the feet, tarsals, metatarsals and phalanges (Table 46). This supports the suggestion made above that frequent cases of osteophytosis of the feet bones may indicate that the people were moving about on rough ground surfaces, as this could have caused frequent small injuries to the feet, with the risk of infection.

It was surprising that there were no instances of periostitis, but this could be due to the erosion of the surface of much of the bone.

Circulatory disorders

Five cases of osteochondritis dissecans were recorded (Table 47). This condition usually occurs on the articular surface of the long bones, when a small piece of bone atrophies and ultimately detaches away from the remainder

because of poor blood supply (Manchester 1983). A small pit is left in the bone, though this may eventually heal. The condition is fairly common in both modern and archaeological populations, so its occurrence here is no surprise.

Other pathology

Miscellaneous observations which cannot be assigned to a particular category are listed in Table 48. The most noteworthy of these was burial no. 100, a female of 25-30 years. The woman had a large bony growth in her nasal cavity, described in detail in the table. The most likely diagnosis is a polyp (D. Brothwell, pers. comm.). A child of about eight years was remarkable in having no sagittal suture, and no sign of it. This would not necessarily be detrimental to the development of the child in later life, as the brain is practically adult in size by this age, and any expansion could still take place laterally or posteriorly. Ultimately this produces a slightly oddly shaped head, but is in no way fatal.

SPATIAL ANALYSIS

Frequency of multiple burials

Organization of the burials is largely dealt with elsewhere (above, pp. 98-109). However, when the remains from each burial were separated into individual bodies, it was interesting to note that there did seem to be a difference in the incidence of multiple burials between the different areas. The pattern is merely described here as no explanation is immediately apparent.

The number of multiple burials and their number expressed as a percentage of total burials with bones for each area is given in Table 49. Burials 8 and 53 were excluded from this analysis as the proportions of skeleton present suggested that there was one principal body and just scraps of others. Only those burials with similar percentages of bone per individual were included, with the exception of burial no. 85, which may have contained a single adult, together with scraps of a child; alternatively, it may have been a joint burial with poor preservation.

The baptistery and the ante-room to the north of the baptistery had the fewest multiple burials. It is of note that these were the areas almost exclusively reserved for infant burial. This might suggest that the infants placed in these areas were treated differently from the infants and juveniles interred elsewhere. Of the two areas with the highest rates of multiple burials, the narthex (with 75 per cent multiple), and the space between the entrance and baptistery (with 100 per cent), eight out of nine of the multiple burials in the former area and one out of the two in the latter area involved infants or juveniles.

In the church and the area south of the church, the multiple burials also comprised infant and adult bones, mixed together. Elsewhere, the multiple burials were composed of adults alone, except for burial no. 85. That almost half of the burials within the church were multiple may suggest the presence of family graves. Certainly the double burial (79) in the area between the entrance and the road appeared to have contained two related bodies.

Related graves

Apparent relatives (Fig. 116)

Some skeletons immediately stood out in the osteological analysis as being very similar. Burial no. 72 contained a

Table 45. Infant age estimation.

individual	epiphyseal union	diaphysis length	dental
8 B 8 (III)	10-15	> 5	12 yrs ± 30 mths
26 A4	< 7	2-3	-
27 D43	1-3	1.5-2.5	18 yrs ± 6 mths
28 D15	> 1	1-1.5	1 yr - 18 mths
29 D31	1-5	2.5-3.5	3 yrs ± 12 mths
32 D224	< 5	3.5-5.5	4 - 5
33 D226	tiny	0.5-1	6-9 mths ± 3 mths
34 D222	0-5	2.5-3.5	3 yrs ± 12 mths
37 D229	5-10	c. 9	6-10
37 D229 (II)	0-5	4-5	-
37 D229 (I)	0-5	3-4	3-4
38 D54	0-5	0-0.5	0 ± 2 mths
40 D214A	near birth	newborn-0.5	-
40 D214B	2.5-4.5	0-5	-
40 D214C	0-5	1.5-2.5	-
41 D132	0-5	2.5-3.5	3 yrs ± 12 mths
43 D135	c 7	6-10	7 yrs ± 2 yrs (* small compared to dental and fusion)
46 D282	0	foetal-newborn (nearest to newborn)	-
47 D212	0-5	3.5-4.5	3-4
53 D293	5-10	6-8	6-10
57 D95 I	7-15	c. 6.5	6.5-7.5
57 D95 II	3-7	3.5-4	4 yrs ± 12 mths
60 A13	> 7	-	7 yrs ± 24 mths
66 A21	< 10	-	8 yrs ± 2 yrs
68 D284	c. 5	1.5-2.5	1.5-2.5
72 D296a	c. 5	-	4-8
76 M70	1.5-2.5	1-5	2 yrs ± 8 mths
77 M72	c. 1	0.5-1.5	9 mths ± 3 mths
87 E99	0-3	0.5-1.5	-
88 H28	0-5	4-5	-
95 D34	< 3	0	-
97 D78	3-8	4-5	5 yrs ± 16 mths
105 B24 (III)	< 3	c. 2.5	2-4

Table 46. Pitting or infection.

individual	area	sex	age	
18 B(1)	church	♂	25-35	L 1st metatarsal head; R 1st metatarsal and proximal phalange on plantar surfaces; 2nd unaffected; 5th base slightly pitted; pitting over L calcaneum, talus and navicular, cuboid and 1st cuneiform
54 D291	narthex	♂	17-25	possible infection of proximal 1st phalange of foot; possible trauma or infection as very pitted and spicules of bone; possibly just very strong flex
94 D32	courtyard	♀	45-50	raised roughening and pitting on femur heads

female and child both with very poor dentitions. Given the rarity of caries in children in this sample, it is reasonable to assume that a child with severe caries, in a burial with an adult with exceptionally bad dental health, was probably related to that adult. They could have had weak enamel or an inherited metabolic disorder. Burial no. 79 contained a female and a younger male. These two shared so many unusual characteristics that they were almost definitely related. Both had an oddly shaped line of occlusion; occlusal caries when these were the least common type of caries in the sample; a palatal torus each – a quite unusual trait in any case, and the only two found in this sample; the same pattern with regard to the parietal foramen; and similar skulls. These two cases would clearly seem to indicate that members of families were being buried together in the same grave. Likewise, burials 26 and 60 each contained an adult with very similar teeth of very odd appearance, being exceptionally short rooted and stumpy. These were the only two cases in the sample, and so similar as to suggest some relationship. In addition, the two individuals had very slight and slender post-cranial skeletons when virtually all other skeletons recovered from the site were fairly stocky and robust. It therefore seems quite probable that these two were related in some way. This was interesting, as burial no. 26 was in the church and burial no. 60 in the narthex. If the two were related, this means related burials were taking place both in the same grave and separated in different parts of the site.

Age and sex

Apart from the clustering of infant graves in the baptistery, very little patterning was apparent when age and sex data were added to the site plan.

Indices

The cranial index could be calculated for very few individuals. When plotted on the site plan, these few data produced no pattern at all.

The cnemic index was similarly unhelpful. The meric index, however, revealed a cluster of extremely high values of the index in the area south of the church in burials 102, 103 and 105.

Non-metric traits

The only traits of all those recorded for the skull and the post crania (Table 50) that produced any clustering were the supraorbital foramen and parietal foramen. These are fairly common traits and so, perhaps, should not be accorded too much weight. However, there were few cases as a whole at the site, and those that did occur appear to be in clusters, possibly suggesting related burials. Burials 54, 57, 60 and 79 all had supraorbital foramen and were all in close proximity, although there were other graves between them. There was also a cluster of infants very close together in the baptistery with this type of foramen: burials 32, 33 and 41 and, slightly further away, burial no. 29. Two of the adjacent graves with high meric indices, 102 and 103, also had parietal foramen in common.

Dental non-metric traits

The dental traits are particularly interesting as they are thought to be more strongly genetically controlled than skeletal traits, and there were two unusual characteristics present here. This would suggest possible family relationships even though the burials presenting them were scat-

Table 47. Osteochondritis dissecans.

individual	area	sex	age		
42 D140	baptistery	indet.	adult	L foot proximal 1st phalange – centre of base diameter 3 x 1.5 mm	4.2%
26 A28	church	♀	25-35	L and R 1st proximal phalange foot	2.0%
54 D291	narthex	♂	17-25	R glenoid fossa	
60 A34	narthex	♀	17-35	L glenoid fossa, both femoral medial condyles; tibia medial condyle; phals 6/20 had pits in head, 1/20 in head and base, 1/20 in base; very gracile hands and skeleton	6.5%
100 D63		♀	25-30	R glenoid fossa 3 x 1.5 mm	5.6%

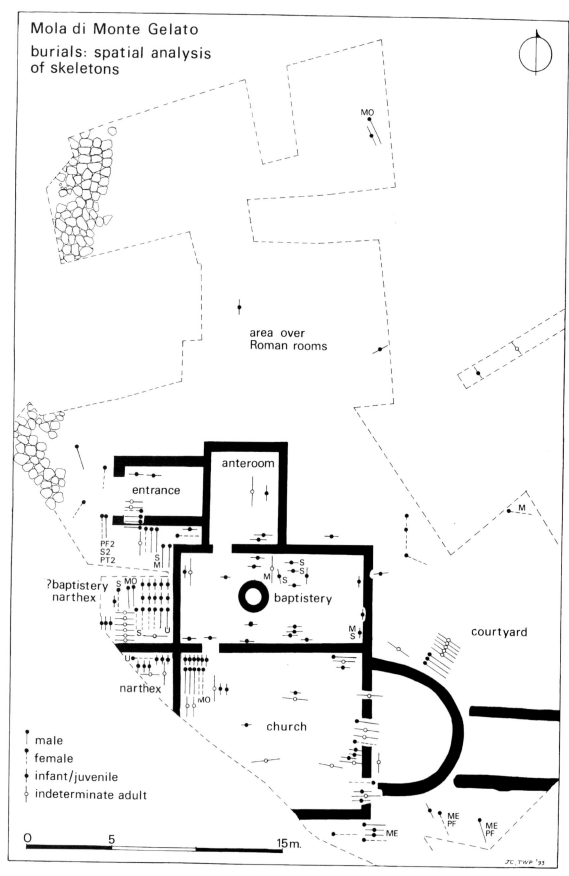

Fig. 116. Distribution of skeletons by age and sex. The letters refer as follows: M, metopic; ME, meric index; MO, oddly formed molar; PF, parietal foramen; PT, palatal torus; S, supraorbital foramen; U, unerupted lateral incisors. *(TWP)*

Table 48. Miscellaneous pathology and observations.

42 D140	patellae, hands and feet and bits of rib only surviving – precisely bits missed in excavation – were graves being emptied on purpose
44 D86	infant has foramen in form of slit *c.* 3 mm above auditory meatus
79 M112 sk. 8 & 9	very similar wear patterns except 8 slightly older probably due to similar cusp patts; think related – anterior teeth have raised occlusal line, they have same parietal foramen pattern, skull shape, cusp form similar, sagittal suture in 9 depressed along length, 8 depressed rear 2/3
79 M112 sk. 9	18 erupted distally
79 M112 sk. 8	elderly female – possible osteoporosis of proximal humeri and femurs – has OA as well
26 A 28	green stain all around phalange probably of L4th metacarpal – matches colour of stain on thoracic vertebra – not on base or head of phalange – could be from a ring finger
27 D43	frontal bone reaches a point where metopic suture would have been on this 2 yr old
43 D135	noted odd found no hypoplasia when such severe cribra orbitalia and cribra femoralis; this applied generally not just to this one
	N.B. lower arm bones consistently gave age 1 yr lower than all other estimates
53 D293	*c.* 8 yrs yet no sagittal suture and no sign of it; bregma asymetric towards left but lambda central; ectocranially double ridge running along where sagittal suture should be
54 D291	thoracic spines twisted to L; probably occurred am as C 3-7 more developed on L and twisted; slightly narrowed lumbar spine
55 D92	omitted as the four adults and five infants were too jumbled to catalogue; no non metric to link elsewhere
59 X D168	5th L vertebra sacralized fully at back, partially on front
60 A34	L superior articular facet of atlas trying to split into double; very very slight ossification of ligamentum flavum, spreading articular facets and odontoid peg – but on whole far healthier spine than majority, i.e. not labourer??
63 A12	adult > 15; very small and slender and no muscle markings adult > 18 more average build but feet not craggy like majority and hand phals no raised flanges
65 A2	indivdual 1 very marked linea aspera and muscle insertion on back L tibia and bones robust individual 2 very slender, even toes not gnarled
94 D32	despite raised finger flanges rest of skeleton quite dainty and no OA
95 D34	could this be twins stillborn? as two infants of very similar appearance – indeed practically indistinguishable, foetal to newborn; also rib and long bone fragment of an adult
99 B4	double L occipital condyle; quite slight for a ♂
100 D63	very bent sacrum – this is sometimes attributed to rickets although this is debatable; foramen of Huschke both sides; large bony 'polyp' in nasal cavity 38 mm AP, 12 mm across and 25 mm top to bottom; smooth surface with striations, flat bottomed with a few pits; has pushed nasal bones to side (and parts of ethmoid); hard up against maxillary bone at side and joining into bone at top of cavity; see plate; slight depression at lambda: L arm markedly shorter than R though L does not appear wilted in any way just shorter; all ribs oddly bowed – could possibly be rickets like sacrum; 1st two bodies of sacrum lumbarized with intact spines and marked depression in artic surf between the two; all bones have bright pink hue, very unusual, only skeleton like this at Monte Gelato
103 C60	very noticeably healthy – even no osteophytes etc. on spine odd; that mandible affected with hypoplasia yet maxilla not, yet the two definitely fit together

Table 49. Frequency of multiple burials per area.

area	no. of multiple burials	total burials	empty burials	total with bones	multiples as % of those with bones
church	10*	26	4	22	45.5
baptistery	2¶	27	8	19	10.5
narthex/open ground	9	13	1	12	75.0
ante-room north of baptistery	0	5	1	4	0
space between baptistery, ante-room and entrance	2	3	1	2	100.0
entrance to ante-room	1	3	0	3	33.3
area between entrance and paved road	1	4	0	4	25.0
over Roman rooms to north of church complex	poss. 1§	5	3	2	33.3
courtyard	2	15	4	11	18.2
south of church	1	6	1	5	20.0
total	29	107	23	84	

*Burial 8
¶ Burial 53 omitted as percentage of bones present suggests one principal body and scraps of others not true multiple burial – i.e. only those with similar percentages of bone per individual are include
§ L172 possibly a single adult burial but possibly including an infant

tered across the site. Burial no. 26 in the church and burial no. 58 in the narthex had unerupted lateral incisors. Burials 24, 59 and 85 had an unusual molar form; elongated and narrowed as though stretched out. These three burials came from the church, the narthex and the area over the Roman rooms respectively.

SUMMARY

There were 107 relatively intact burials which provided parts of 159 skeletons. The great majority of these burials belongs to the period between c. AD 800 and 1100. There were also 26 individuals from disturbed, unphased burials, and at least 58 individuals represented by disarticulated bone. The analysis reported here is restricted to the undisturbed, phased burials. The sample has been considered in isolation because of the lack of comparative material.

The bone tended to be in poor condition and often only a small proportion of the skeleton survived. Thus, 40.4 per cent of bone was classed as poor and only 25.4 per cent as good. 35.1 per cent of skeletons were less than ten per cent complete and 69.5 per cent had less than 50 per cent of the skeleton. The condition varied between areas; however, the bones from the baptistery and the area between the entrance and the road were in relatively good condition.

Of the 157 individuals from relatively intact burials, 83 were adults, 23 juvenile and 51 infants; infants are classed as nought to five years, and juveniles as six to fifteen years. Of the adults, 25 were male, 23 female and 35 of indeterminate sex. The sex ratio of male to female was therefore 1.09:1, and this equality was true of all areas of the site where adults were not in the minority. This suggests that neither sex was being reared to adulthood at the expense of the other sex, and that males and females were being treated equally in death. This includes the interior of the church. However, it must be remembered that this was treatment in death, and the idea of an egalitarian society in life cannot necessarily be extrapolated from this evidence. A woman may be buried in a way dictated by the wealth of her partner, rather than in a style reflecting her own status.

There was much more differentiation of burials across the site when age was considered rather than sex. Of those in the baptistery, 79.2 per cent were dead by five years of age and 91.7 per cent by fifteen (there was one adult burial in the baptistery). There was a similar composition in the ante-room, and in the area over the Roman rooms (though less marked). Here, however, the sample size was very small. The baptistery appears to have been reserved for infant burials, and it may be that this area held those individuals who had died before baptism.

The infant deaths followed a tripartite pattern, with 23.9 per cent of deaths in those aged less than 25 years occurring before one year and 70.4 per cent before five years. The peak of deaths before one year was probably due to the immediate postnatal risk of infection or complications. A second lesser peak, between two and a half and three and a half years, may reflect a late age for weaning, and the nutritional stress that weaning could cause if the diet available was unsuitable. The theory of late

Table 50. Cranial non metric.

individual	metopic	coronal	sagittal	lamboid	sphenoid	other	pariet for	sup orb
79 M112 sk. 9	0	✓	✓	✓		temporal	symmetrical; left stronger; 1 each	symmetrical,1 each
79 M112 sk. 8	0	✓	✓	✓			both, left slightly stronger	very slight both sides
18 B8 (1)			✓					
24 D107 ossuary	1 adult	also very misshapen molar – very similar to one found in D168 – also D168 similar folds in canine as loose canine in D107						
29 D31	✓							infant
32 D224				✓				infant
33 D226	½ metop							infant
41 D132	✓							infant
54 D289	✓	0	0	0		possibly an inca	0	R and L
57 D95 11				✓				infant
59 D168	0	none						
60 A34	0	✓	0	✓				R
72 D296 (1)	0			✓				
81 M16				✓				
100 D63	✓	✓		✓				
102 C29	0	✓ multiple on lateral ⅓s	0	✓ multiple on lower ½s		1 right squamous	1 each side	
103 C60	0	0	0	0		0	1 each side	9

individual	mylo hyoid groove	calc doub/abs	talus double	atlas pb lb hum SA	stern A
79 M112 sk. 9	both sides				
79 M112 sk. 8	both sides				
2 C58		R	R (triple)		
7 C23	L				
8 C48			L		
18 B8 (1)		both			
18 B22 (1)	both				
54 D291	both			L atlas	
56 D91 (3)	both				
59 D168		both			
72 D296 (1)		both		L atlas R db fac	
78 M33		both			
80 M81					✓
81 M16	both				
92 D18	both				
93 D5		R			
99 B4				✓ lat br	
99 B4A		R			
100 D63		R, L almost		atlas db fac	both pats very slight vastus
102 C29	both				
103 C60	both				
104 B24 (1)		both			
105 B24 (11)		both		Atlas db fac both/SA both	very slight vastus notch both sides

KEY TO TRAITS: parietal for – parietal foramen; sup orb – supra orbital foramen; calc doub/abs – calcaneus facet double or absent; talus double – talus facet double; atlas pb lb – atlas posterior bridge or lateral bridge; hum SA – humerus septal aperture; stern A – sternal aperture lat br – lateral bridge; db fac – double facet; pats – patellae

weaning was to some extent supported by evidence of possible nutritional hardship amongst the adult females. There would also be an increased risk of infection from contaminated feeding utensils.

There was also a slight increase in deaths around twelve to thirteen years. A possible explanation is that the onset of puberty, and the stresses imposed by this on the body, were sufficient to tip the balance between life and death. This would suggest that conditions were very arduous indeed. Although tenuous, this argument is supported, to some extent, by the evidence for nutritional deficiencies.

Amongst the adults, there was an even split between the sexes in all age groups, suggesting that death by childbirth did not have a great effect on the sample.

In terms of physique, there was a lack of length of the lower arm in infants compared with the rest of the long-bone lengths (although this was caught up by adulthood). This may be a local phenomenon; future studies will clarify this. There was pronounced dimorphism in stature, where there was no overlap between male and female ranges. The male range was 1.66-1.82 m (the tallest man was unusually tall for this site). The female range was 1.55-1.6 m. The male range was similar to that of modern males, where the average is about 1.74 m. The females from all areas of the site fell well below the modern female average of 1.66 m. This may be due to nutritional hardship, as this can produce stunting in a group. As females are particularly susceptible to deficiencies because of the direction of so much of their energy into childbirth, they may be more prone to stunting and therefore pronounced stunting results.

Occasionally, an area of a particular site may contain individuals who are all at or close to the maximum stature within the stature range for the site; in conjunction with other evidence, this may indicate burials of elevated status. There was no such evidence at Monte Gelato.

The most common skull shape was long and narrow; but there were so few that could be assessed that this is probably not reliable. Most femurs were eumeric, meaning that they were rounded rather than flattened: 76.2 per cent of right femurs and 81.3 per cent of left were in this category of the index. The tendency for rounding rather than flattening was even more pronounced in the tibiae, where 94.1 per cent of right and 89.5 per cent of left tibiae were eurycnemic. Whatever the cause of this phenomenon, it was more constant in the tibia than the femur, as there were more differing values of the meric index between sides in the femur than there were for the cnemic index in the tibia.

There was virtually no sidedness between the arms and even less difference in size between the right and left leg. This could mean that the people were not favouring either limb over the other in everyday activities.

Parts of the skeleton were dimorphic in the same way as stature. The most dimorphic measurements were those of the lower canine and the femur, and seemed so distinct that there was probably more than a simple genetic cause. The most likely candidate would be nutritional deficiencies.

Only three children suffered from caries. One of these was probably related to the female with which it was buried, as she had exceptionally bad dental health. The most common type of caries amongst the children was interproximal. Occlusal caries were rare because of the wear, even on young dentitions, at this site. As only three children were affected, it is suggested that in this sample caries attack was either a disease of ageing, rather than a result of diet, or a genetic characteristic of the sample. This may indicate that there were many elderly people amongst the burials that ageing techniques are, at present, incapable of identifying.

Amongst the adults, 44 per cent of caries were cervical and 26 per cent interproximal (some of which would be cervical). Occlusal caries were rare. Only twelve per cent were gross, suggesting that caries was not a severe problem. This is confirmed by the low number of abcesses, only six throughout the sample. It suggests that the diet was generally a healthy one. However, natural sugars, combined with poor hygiene, would cause the cervical caries, and some proportion of soft, pulpy food would cause attack in the interproximal area.

Ante-mortem loss of teeth was generally more severe in the mandibles than in the maxilliae. This followed the pattern of periodontal disease, rather than that of the caries, again suggesting that caries was not a major problem in this sample. Similarly, there were almost twice as many cases of severe calculus deposits in the mandibles than the maxilliae. This would also correspond with the prevalence of periodontal disease, given the interrelationship of these two conditions. A third of those individuals suffering from periodontal disease were severe cases. This indicates that this was a major problem for the population and the principal reason for tooth-loss, rather than caries. This would also support the suggestion that a substantial proportion of the sample was elderly, as this is very much a disease which progresses with age. However, a substantial proportion was unaffected. As this is not attributable to good hygiene (as the caries prevalence demonstrates), there must have been a good, textured diet, which would require mastication and would thus stimulate the gums and keep them healthy. Individuals buried in the church appeared to suffer more heavily from both caries, periodontal disease and alveolar recession (another age-related condition), suggesting, perhaps, that there was a greater proportion of elderly people buried here than in other areas.

Hypoplasia on the teeth showed that approximately a quarter of the adults had probably undergone bouts of serious childhood illness.

Along with dental disease, degenerative changes to the skeleton were the most common pathology. There were signs of osteoarthritis which were largely age-related. Osteophytes on the vertebrae and elsewhere were more widespread, but still followed the ageing pattern to some extent. Females were more affected by osteophytes than males. If it is accepted that their development may be partly stress-related, this could suggest that the females were working physically harder than the males, relative to their physique and strength. The vertebrae and foot bones were most affected. The changes to the feet may indicate repetitive mobility over rough ground. Findings were similar for all parts of the site, suggesting that there was no overall division of physical labour between the sexes, nor any indication of different status from one area to another.

The great majority of skeletons were of stocky, robust individuals, with well-marked muscle insertions particularly on the humerus and hands. This may be the result of hard, physical work. Only three skeletons were slender or slight, two in the narthex and one in the courtyard.

All fractures present involved the ribs, and only adults were affected. It is impossible to say whether these presumed blows to the torso were the result of accidents or of violence. However, the prevalence was equal between males and females, and there was no evidence for parry fractures, the most common fracture received in violence. Accidental cause seems, therefore, most likely. Schmorl's nodes, perhaps indicative of carrying heavy loads from an early age, were most common in skeletons found in the courtyard.

Signs of nutritional deficiency were most apparent in infants, as could be predicted because of the difficulties associated with weaning and with childhood illness. Very few teenagers, the other group which could be expected to present cribra orbitalia, exhibited signs of nutritional deficiency, although there was a small peak in deaths around this age. The lack of stunting in small children suggests that an effort was made to provide for children; this, however, may not have extended past puberty, since there were a number of teenager deaths. Moreover, the surviving females were stunted compared to the males, due to the additional stress of childbearing.

Nearly all cases of infection involved the feet, again pointing to frequent walking over rough ground. There were five cases of osteochondritis dissecans, which would, however, have had little effect on the individual.

The analysis of non-metric dental and skeletal traits, and of age, sex and physical characteristics, demonstrates that some individuals may have been related. Some were buried in the same grave or in graves in close proximity, but others were found in quite different parts of the cemetery.

INTERPRETATION

The people buried at Monte Gelato were generally robust and physically active, probably from an early age. The role of the site as an early medieval farm is borne out by the higher prevalence of infection and degenerative changes to the feet than any other part of the skeleton, excluding the vertebrae. Although not exclusively pointing to this same conclusion, the restriction of traumatic injury to the ribs would support a physical activity where blows to the torso would be received frequently.

It was probably a hard life, principally because of poor or limited diet and sickness. Almost a quarter of adults presented signs of having suffered severe bouts of disease in childhood. Many infants died at what could be a late weaning age, around two and a half to three and a half years, and another batch died at around the start of puberty. If this second batch was not due to some disease, which targeted this age group, and they did die solely from inadequate nutrition, conditions must have been very hard indeed. Those females who did survive to adulthood were of reduced stature compared to the males, probably because of the additional demands imposed by childbirth. If the suggestion of late weaning is correct, it suggests that they were attempting to prolong the gap between children as long as possible.

In osteological terms, it seems to have been an egalitarian society, for no groups of skeletons were found with characteristics that could be interpreted as indicative of higher status. Practically all the skeletons had a similar physique, suggesting that everybody had to work physically for a living. The same was true between the sexes; males and females were equally robust, and suffered similar degenerative disease. Both therefore presumably participated in the physical work. Interestingly, the 'high-status' graves contained both males and females. This may suggest that 'higher status' was enjoyed equally by men and women. Certainly, both sexes survived equally into adulthood, indicating that neither sex was reared at the expense of the other.

Any division that there was in burial organization seems to have been dictated more by the age of the person than by differing lifestyles or sex. The baptistery was reserved almost exclusively for the burial of young children and, to some extent, this was also true of the ante-room next door. The other areas were more mixed, but there was a slight hint, from the dental evidence, that the church may have held a greater proportion of older people than other areas. Periodontal disease, a disease of advancing age, was more of a problem than caries, and the caries themselves appear to have required a long onset, perhaps confirming that a large proportion of the sample was elderly.

There was also a distinction in burial practice between the baptistery and the rest of the site, with the majority of infant burials in the baptistery being single interments, whilst elsewhere children were buried together or with adults. It seems most likely that children who qualified for burial in the baptistery were viewed or treated differently for some reason. It has been suggested elsewhere that the reason may be that they died before being baptized. Elsewhere, burial seems to have quite often been in family groups. There also appears to have been an element of interrelation across the site which would not be altogether unexpected in a small, isolated community such as Monte Gelato probably was.

All the interpretation advanced here must be viewed with considerable caution as the sample was very fragmentary, and sample size was often very small, once spatial or other divisions were taken into account. The suggestions that are made are those that best fit the evidence; but the evidence itself is not particularly strong in some aspects. When more data for Italian sites become available, it may be possible to confirm or refute some of these ideas.

Acknowledgements
I am very grateful to Dr Tony Waldron for his comments on this paper, and to Mrs Kate Down for her painstaking work in organizing the tables.

EXCAVATIONS AT CASTELLACCIO, 1990, by David Wilkinson

THE SITE

Castellaccio (literally 'nasty castle') lies some 250 m to the southeast of the main excavation area, occupying a now heavily-wooded bluff on the west side of the river Treia (Figs 4 and 117). The present-day tree cover means that all sense is lost of what must have once been a series of commanding views over the mill, the ecclesiastical complex and the surrounding countryside. On top of the bluff, a sub-triangular area of *c.* 0.25 ha is defined to the west and northwest by a wide rock-cut ditch, with traces of a curtain wall on its inner edge. The ground beyond the ditch remains relatively flat. In contrast, the ditch appears as little more than a narrow terrace to the south, where the ground falls away quite sharply, and is apparently absent from the very steep and rocky eastern side. It is difficult to define any entrances precisely, though one may have existed at the northern corner of the enclosure. There is a gap through the rock terraces at this point, but the slope here is very steep, and would have required steps or other structures to create a usable route. Otherwise, the most prominent feature of

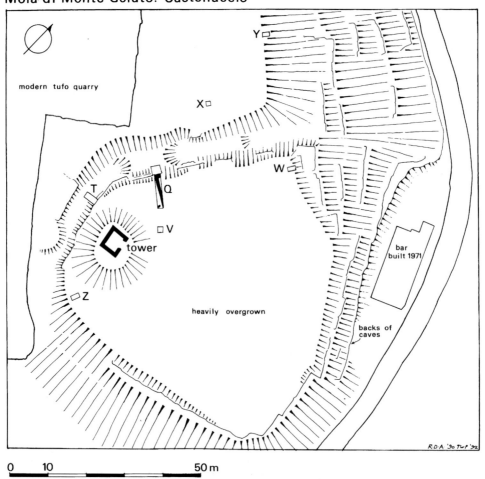

Fig. 117. Plan of the trenches at Castellaccio. *(RDA/TWP)*

APPENDIX: SKELETAL COMPONENTS

For key, see page 180

SKELETAL COMPONENTS

	church	baptistery	narthex	ante-room	space	entrance	area between entrance and road	over Roman rooms	courtyard	south of church	total
1	50	23	28	3	6	8	5	3	18	8	152
2	30	19	14	1	6	5	5	2	9	7	98
3	11	17	15	1	4	8	4	2	8	6	76
4	188	225	161	14	33	94	85	23	115	125	1052
5	10	74	38	1	7	14	22	5	44	19	264
6	98	120	81	12	13	15	32	1	83	52	507
7	46	38	39	5	5	6	15	0	40	20	214
8	8	7	8	0	2	2	3	0	6	5	41
9	0	1	0	0	0	0	0	0	0	1	2
10	10	14	8	1	2	6	2	1	8	4	56
11	11	16	6	1	2	2	3	2	7	3	53
12	6	16	13	1	2	5	2	1	7	4	57
13	12	17	13	1	2	3	3	1	8	5	65
14	18	18	13	1	2	13	3	2	8	8	86
15	16	17	11	1	4	4	3	0	9	5	70
16	11	15	11	1	2	8	4	1	10	6	69
17	12	10	12	1	3	6	3	1	11	5	64
18	15	14	13	1	3	5	4	2	10	5	72
19	13	11	10	1	2	4	3	1	13	7	65
20	7	5	5	0	2	1	1	2	19	11	53
21	12	5	3	0	0	0	2	2	11	10	45
22	44	81	25	9	5	12	6	3	37	15	237
23	32	11	12	0	5	7	10	2	16	13	108
24	62	87	34	13	13	38	21	0	88	42	398
25	7	0	0	0	0	0	0	7	0	0	14
26	13	17	8	1	4	2	4	1	10	6	66
27	13	17	12	1	1	7	3	1	9	6	70
28	26	17	17	1	5	9	3	1	10	7	96
29	25	16	12	1	6	7	3	2	12	7	91
30	4	1	1	0	1	0	1	1	4	2	15
31	6	2	1	0	0	0	0	1	4	2	16
32	21	17	11	2	8	5	3	1	8	5	81
33	17	14	8	1	6	9	3	1	6	6	71
34	14	9	6	1	5	6	3	1	8	6	59
35	14	11	6	1	2	5	2	1	8	5	55
36	41	16	5	1	3	9	11	1	29	24	140
37	38	14	4	1	2	7	11	1	28	25	131
38	41	49	26	9	8	19	10	0	39	17	218
39	37	10	17	0	3	1	13	0	20	24	125
40	40	21	10	9	1	15	15	0	43	35	189
41	3	5	2	0	0	0	2	0	7	2	21
42	74	128	115	11	9	40	29	7	83	34	530
43	63	96	21	11	8	29	30	5	67	40	370
44	6	5	3	0	1	1	3	0	5	2	26

PREDICTED NUMBERS OF EACH SKELETAL ELEMENT

	church	baptistery	narthex	ante-room	space	entrance	area between entrance and road	over Roman rooms	courtyard	south of church	total
1	50	23	28	3	6	8	5	3	18	8	152
2	50	23	28	3	6	8	5	3	18	8	152
3	50	23	28	3	6	8	5	3	18	8	152
4	/	/	/	/	/	/	/	/	/	/	/
5	350	161	175	21	42	56	35	21	126	56	1064
6	600	276	336	36	72	96	60	36	216	96	1824
7	250	115	140	15	30	40	25	15	90	40	760
8	50	23	28	3	6	8	5	3	18	8	152
9	50	23	28	3	6	8	5	3	18	8	152
10	50	23	28	3	6	8	5	3	18	8	152
11	50	23	28	3	6	8	5	3	18	8	152
12	50	23	28	3	6	8	5	3	18	8	152
14	50	23	28	3	6	8	5	3	18	8	152
15	50	23	28	3	6	8	5	3	18	8	152
16	50	23	28	3	6	8	5	3	18	8	152
17	50	23	28	3	6	8	5	3	18	8	152
18	50	23	28	3	6	8	5	3	18	8	152
19	50	23	28	3	6	8	5	3	18	8	152
20	400	184	224	24	48	64	40	24	144	64	1216
21	400	184	224	24	48	64	40	24	144	64	1216
22	250	115	140	15	30	40	25	15	90	40	760
23	250	115	140	15	30	40	25	15	90	40	760
24	1400	644	784	84	168	224	140	84	504	224	4256
25	1400	644	784	84	168	224	140	84	504	224	4256
26	50	23	28	3	6	8	5	3	18	8	152
27	50	23	28	3	6	8	5	3	18	8	152
28	50	23	28	3	6	8	5	3	18	8	152
29	50	23	28	3	6	8	5	3	18	8	152
30	50	23	28	3	6	8	5	3	18	8	152
31	50	23	28	3	6	8	5	3	18	8	152
32	50	23	28	3	6	8	5	3	18	8	152
33	50	23	28	3	6	8	5	3	18	8	152
34	50	23	28	3	6	8	5	3	18	8	152
35	50	23	28	3	6	8	5	3	18	8	152
36	350	161	196	21	42	56	35	21	126	56	1064
37	350	161	196	21	42	56	35	21	126	56	1064
38	250	115	140	15	30	40	25	15	90	40	760
39	250	115	140	15	30	40	25	15	90	40	760
40	1400	644	784	84	128	224	140	84	504	224	4256
41	1400	644	784	84	128	224	140	84	504	224	4256
42	600	276	336	36	72	96	60	36	216	96	1824
43	600	276	336	36	72	96	60	36	216	96	1824
44	50	23	28	3	6	8	5	3	18	8	152

COMPONENTS PRESENT AS PERCENTAGE OF PREDICTED NUMBERS

	church	baptistery	nrthex	ante-room	space	entrance	area between entrance and road	over Roman rooms	courtyard	south of church	total
1	/	/	/	/	/	/	/	/	/	/	/
2	60.0	82.6	50.0	33.3	100	62.5	100	66.7	50.0	87.5	64.5
3	22.0	73.9	53.6	33.3	66.7	100	80.0	66.7	44.4	75.0	50.0
4	/	/	/	/	/	/	/	/	/	/	/
5	11.4	46.0	21.7	4.8	16.7	25.0	62.9	23.8	34.9	33.9	24.8
6	16.3	43.5	24.1	33.3	18.1	15.6	53.3	2.8	38.4	54.2	27.8
7	18.4	33.0	27.9	33.3	16.7	15.0	60.0	0	44.4	50.0	28.2
8	16.0	30.4	28.6	0	33.3	25.0	60.0	0	33.3	62.5	27.0
9	0	4.3	0	0	0	0	0	0	0	12.5	1.3
10	20.0	60.9	28.6	33.3	33.3	75.0	40.0	33.3	44.4	50.0	36.8
11	22.0	69.6	21.4	33.3	33.3	25.0	60.0	66.7	38.9	37.5	34.9
12	12.0	69.6	46.4	33.3	33.3	62.5	40.0	33.3	38.9	50.0	37.3
13	24.0	73.9	46.4	33.3	33.3	37.5	60.0	33.3	44.4	62.5	42.8
14	36.0	78.3	46.4	33.3	33.3	162.5	60.0	66.7	44.4	100	56.6
15	32.0	73.9	39.3	33.3	66.7	50.0	60.0	0	50.0	62.5	46.1
16	22.0	65.2	39.3	33.3	33.3	100	80.0	33.3	55.6	75.0	45.4
17	24.0	43.5	42.9	33.3	50.0	75.0	60.0	33.3	61.1	62.5	42.1
18	30.0	60.9	46.4	33.3	50.0	62.5	80.0	66.7	55.6	62.5	47.4
19	26.0	47.8	35.7	33.3	66.7	50.0	60.0	33.3	72.2	87.5	42.8
20	1.7	2.7	2.2	0	4.2	1.6	2.5	8.3	13.2	17.2	4.4
21	3.0	2.7	1.3	0	0	0	5.0	8/3	7.6	15.6	3.7
22	17.6	70.4	17.9	60.0	16.7	30.0	24.0	20.0	41.1	37.5	31.2
23	12.8	9.6	8.6	0	16.7	17.5	40.0	13.3	17.8	32.5	14.2
24	4.9	13.5	4.3	15.5	7.7	17.0	15.0	0	17.5	18.8	9.4
25	/	/	/	/	/	/	/	/	/	/	/
26	26.0	73.9	28.6	33.3	66.7	25.0	80.0	33.3	55.6	75.0	43.4
27	26.0	73.9	42.9	33.3	16.7	87.5	60.0	33.3	50.0	75.0	46.1
28	52.0	73.9	60.7	33.3	83.3	112.5	60.0	33.3	55.6	87.5	63.2
29	50.0	69.6	42.9	33.3	100	87.5	60.0	66.7	66.7	87.5	59.9
30	8.0	4.3	3.6	0	16.7	0	20.0	33.3	22.2	25.0	9.9
31	12.0	8.7	3.6	0	0	0	0	33.3	22.2	25.0	10.5
32	42.0	73.9	39.3	66.7	133.3	62.5	60.0	33.3	44.4	62.5	53.3
33	34.0	60.9	28.6	33.3	100	112.5	60.0	33.3	33.3	75.0	46.7
34	28.0	39.1	21.4	33.3	83.3	75.0	60.0	33.3	44.4	75.0	38.8
35	28.0	47.8	21.4	33.3	33.3	62.5	40.0	33.3	44.4	62.5	36.2
36	11.7	9.9	2.6	4.8	7.1	16.1	31.4	4.8	23.0	42.9	13.2
37	10.9	8.7	2.0	4.8	4.8	12.5	31.4	4.8	22.2	44.6	12.3
38	16.4	42.6	18.6	60.0	26.7	47.5	40.0	0	43.3	42.5	28.7
39	14.8	8.7	12.1	0	10.0	2.5	52.0	0	22.2	60.0	16.4
40	3.1	4.0	1.5	10.7	0.6	6.7	12.1	0	9.9	16.5	4.9
41	/	/	/	/	/	/	/	/	/	/	/
42	12.3	46.4	34.2	30.6	12.5	41.7	48.3	19.4	38.4	35.4	29.1
43	10.5	34.8	6.3	30.6	11.1	30.2	50.0	13.9	31.0	41.7	20.3
44	12.0	21.7	10.7	0	16.7	12.5	60.0	0	27.8	25.0	17.1

SKELETAL COMPONENTS PRESENT

CHURCH

burial	context	2	3	4	5	6	7	8	9	10	11	12	13	14	15	16	17	18	19	20	21	22
1	B15	1																				
2	C57	1									1							1	1	1		2
	C58	1			1																	
	C2	2				1				1						1						
3	C25	1		1																		
4	B53	1		1										1								
5	C42	2																				
6	C47	1																				
7	C23	1	1	14		6	5	1										1	1			
8	C46	3	1	6		1	1					1										
9	C32	1			1									1	1		1					1
10	B21	no bones																				
11	B32(B49)	2	1											1								3
12	B16	stone context				6																
13	B29	no bones																				
14	B34	1																				
15	B42	1																				
16	B66	1																				
17	B60	1															1	1				
18	B8	3		21	4	12	5	1		1	1	1	2	1	2	1	2	1	2	3	3	6
	B22	3	2	11		3											1					2
19	?																					
20	?																					
21	D96	1																				
22	D108	3																				1
23	D123	10	3	37	19	1	1			1		2	1	2		1	1		1			
24	D107	3		5	1	43	24	4		4	5	1	6	8	10	5	3	6	1	3	1	16
25	D173	2	1	36	7	1	5	1		1	1	1	2	1	1	1	1		4		6	6
26	A23	2		5		12												2	2		1	
	A3	1																				
	A9	not bone	1	26																		
	A28	1	1					1		1	1	1	1	1	1	1	1	1			1	
	A4	1																				
27	D43	1	1	24	7	12	5			1	1	1	1	1	1	1	1	1	1			7

CHURCH CONTINUED

burial	context	23	24	25	26	27	28	29	30	31	32	33	34	35	36	37	38	39	40	41	42	43	44
1	B15							1			1	1											
2	C57	1	2				1					1		1	4	1	4	2	1		2		
	C58	1		1	1	1	1	1			1	1	1	2		1	1	2	1				
	C2						2	2															
3	C25							1															
4	B53																				4	5	
5	C42																						
6	C47					1	1	1		1	1	1			1	2		1	1	1	1		
7	C23					1	1	1			1	1			5	3		2					
8	C46		1		1	1	1	1			1	1	1	1	2		8						
9	C32								1														
10	B21	no bones				1	1								1	1							
11	B32 (B49)																						
12	B16	stone context																					
13	B29	no bones																					
14	B34										1										1		
15	B42						1				1												
16	B66																						
17	B60																						
18	B8	10	15		1	1	1	1	1		1	3	2	3	6	5	6	9	16	1	8	10	1
	B22	2	1		1		2	3		1	2	1			1	5	3	5	3		1		
19	?						2	3															
20	?																						
21	D96						1	1					1		1			1			1		
22	D108				1	2	1	5													7		
23	D123	11	34		4	1	7							6	1		1		1		24	25	3
24	D107								1	3	8	4	6	6	17	15	14	10	15		1	1	1
25	D173	4	11		1	1	1	1	1						1				1		13	12	
26	A23																						
	A3	not bone			1	1		1			1	1	1										
	A9	3			1	1	1	1		1	1	1	1		2	5	4	5	1	1			1
	A28				1	1	1	1			1	1	1										
	A4			6										1									
27	D43																				11	9	

BAPTISTERY

burial	context	1	2	3	4	5	6	7	8	9	10	11	12	13	14	15	16	17	18	19	20	21	22
28	D15	1	1	1	21	6	12	5	1		1	1	1	1	1	1	1	1	1	1			6
29	D31	1	1	1	11	6	12	5			1	1	1	1	1	1	1	1	1	1			5
30	D231	1	1	1		5	4	5			1	1	1	1	1	1	1	1	1	1	1		
31	D233	no bones																					
32	D224	1	1	1	23	6	2	1	1		1	1	1	1	1	1	1	1	1	1			6
33	D226	1	1	1	18	3					1										1		1
34	D222	1	1	1	20		12	5			1	1	1	1	1	1	1	1	1	1			7
35	D237	no bones																					
36	D239	no bones																					
37	D229	3	3	3	48	8	7	1			1	3	2	3	3	3	2	1	2	1		1	10
38	D54	1	1	1	12	2	12	2			1	1	1	1	1	1	1	1	1	1			9
39	D57	no bones																			2		
40	D214	3	3	2	16	15	19	4	2		3	3	3	2	3	2	1	1	2	1	1	1	13
41	D132	1	1	1		2					1	1	1	1	1	1	1	1	1	1	1	2	
42	D140	1				1																	4
43	D135	1	1	1	22	7	12	5	1		1	1	1	1	1	1	1	1	1	1			8
44	D86	no bones																					
45	D287	1	1			4				1	1	1	1	1	1	1	1	1	1	1			2
46	D282	1	1	1	20	6	9	5	1		1	1	1	1	1	1	1	1	1	1			3
47	D212	1	1				12				1				1					1			
48	D303	no bones																					
49	D332	mine says none															1						
50	D281	1	1																				2
51	D270	no bones																					
52	B40	1	1								1									1			
53	D293	2	1	1	14	2	7	5	1		1	1	1	1	1	1	1	1	1	1	1		5

BAPTISTERY CONTINUED

burial	context	23	24	25	26	27	28	29	30	31	32	33	34	35	36	37	38	39	40	41	42	43	44
28	D15		5		1	1	1	1	1		1	1	1	1	2	2	6		1		43	42	44
29	D31		9		1	1	1	1	1		1		2	2	1					11	11	11	
30	D231				1	1	1	1	1		1			1	2	2				1	1	2	
31	D233																						
32	D224		9		1	1	1	1	1		1	1		1	1	2		3	4	11	9	
33	D226		2		1	1	1	1	1		1					6	1		2	1	
34	D222				1	1	1	1	1	1	1	1							11	11	11	
35	D237																					
36	D239																					
37	D229	4	13		3	3	3	3	3	1	3	2	2	4	2	3	7	4	3	10	10	11
38	D54		8		1	1	1	1	1		1	1	1							10	5
39	D57																					
40	D214		14		3	2	2	2	2		2	2	1		1	1	9	2	1	23	23	18
41	D132				1	1	1	1	1		1	1	1							2	2	4	
42	D140	2	6														1			1	1	
43	D135		7		1	1	1	1	1	1	1	1	1	2	1	2	7	2	4	11	11	10
44	D86																					
45	D287																					
46	D282		6		1	1	1	1	1		1	1	1			1	9	1		11	7	8
47	D212				1	1	1	1	1		1		1		1	1				5	10	11
48	D303																					
49	D332						1		1		1						1					
50	D281															1						
51	D270																					
52	B40		8		1	2	1				1	1	2	3	2	4	4		8	8	
53	D293	5			1	1	1				1	1	1			7	8		11		

NARTHEX

burial	context	1	2	3	4	5	6	7	8	9	10	11	12	13	14	15	16	17	18	19	20	21	22
54	D289,D291	2	1	1	22	7	8	4	2		1	1	1	1	1	1	1	1	1	1	1		3
55	D92	9	5	4	32	11	13	8	1		2	1	5	5	3	1	4	3	4	2			7
56	D91	3	1	1	2		17	10	2		2	2	3	2	3	2	2	2	3	1			6
57	D95	2	2	2	27	11	18	5						1	2	2	2	2	1	1			
58	D133	2	2	2	34	2	4	5	1		2	1	2	1	1	2	1	1	2	2	4		1
59	D168	2	1	2	33	6	16	7	2		1	1		1	1	1	1	2	1			2	5
60	A13,A34	2	1																				
61	no bones																						
62	A5	1																					
63	A12	3	1	1	3	1	3							1									
64	A35																						
65	A2	3	1	1	2		1						1	1	2	1			1			1	3
66	A21	1		1	6		1							1		1				1			

NARTHEX CONTINUED

burial	context	23	24	25	26	27	28	29	30	31	32	33	34	35	36	37	38	39	40	41	42	43	44
54	D289,D291		2		1	1	6	5			4	2	3	3	2	2		2	2	1	8	8	1
55	D92		5		2	3	2	1			1	2	1			2					86	4	1
56	D91	2				2	2	2			2						6				7		
57	D95		6		2	2					1	2	1		2	3	6	3	2		3	6	1
58	D133				1	2	2	2			1	1				1		1					
59	D168				2	2	1	2			1												
60	A13,A34	4	20						1	1	1	2	1	4			4				2	2	
61	no bones																						
62	A5															4			2				
63	A12		1				1							2		5	10	5	6	1	2		
64	A35																						
65	A2										1										9		
66	A21	6					3																

ANTE-ROOM

burial	context	1	2	3	4	5	6	7	8	9	10	11	12	13	14	15	16	17	18	19	20	21	22
67	D275	1	1				12	1			1	1	1	1	1	1	1	1	1	1			
68	D284	1	1	1	14			4															9
69	D52																						
70	D51	1																					
71	D268	no bones			1																		

ANTE-ROOM CONTINUED

burial	context	23	24	25	26	27	28	29	30	31	32	33	34	35	36	37	38	39	40	41	42	43	44
67	D275		12		1	1	1	1			1	1	1	1	1	1	9		9		11	11	9
68	D284																						
69	D52		1								1												
70	D51																						
71	D268																						

SPACE BETWEEN BAPTISTERY AND ANTE-ROOM AND ENTRANCE

burial	context	1	2	3	4	5	6	7	8	9	10	11	12	13	14	15	16	17	18	19	20	21	22
72	D296	2	2	2	28	7	13	5	2		2	2	1	1	1	2	2	2	2	2	2		5
73	D286	no bones																					
74	M76	4	4	2	5		3	4					1	1	1	2		1	1				

SPACE BETWEEN BAPTISTERY AND ANTEROOM AND ENTRANCE CONTINUED

burial	context	23	24	25	26	27	28	29	30	31	32	33	34	35	36	37	38	39	40	41	42	43	44
72	D296	5	13		2	1	2	2	1		2	2	2	1	3	2	7	3	1		9	8	1
73	D286																						
74	M76				2		3	4			6	4	3	1			1						

ENTRANCE TO ANTECHAMBER

burial	context	1	2	3	4	5	6	7	8	9	10	11	12	13	14	15	16	17	18	19	20	21	22
75	M61	6	3	6	74	6	1	1	1		4	1	3	1	11	2	6	4	3	2	1		2
76	M70	1	1	1	20	7	12	5	1		1	1	1	1	1	1	1	1	1	1			2
77	M72	1	1			1	2	1			1		1	1	1	1	1	1	1	1			10

ENTRANCE TO ANTECHAMBER CONTINUED

burial	context	23	24	25	26	27	28	29	30	31	32	33	34	35	36	37	38	39	40	41	42	43	44
75	M61	7	25		1	6	7	5			4	7	5	4	9	7	9	1	9		23	12	1
76	M70		13		1	1	1	1			1	1	1	1			10		6		10	10	
77	M72						1	1				1									7	7	

AREA BETWEEN ENTRANCE AND PAVED ROAD

burial	context	1	2	3	4	5	6	7	8	9	10	11	12	13	14	15	16	17	18	19	20	21	22
78	M33	1	1	1		7	12	5	1		1	1	1	1	1	1	1	1	1	1			
79	M112	2	2	2	56	11	11	5	1		1	1	1	1	1	1	2	1	2	1	1	2	5
80	M18	1	1					5	1			1	1	1	1	1	1	1	1	1			1
81	M16,M88	1	1	1	29	4	9	5				1	1	1	1	1	1	1	1	1			

AREA BETWEEN ENTRANCE AND PAVED ROAD CONTINUED

burial	context	23	24	25	26	27	28	29	30	31	32	33	34	35	36	37	38	39	40	41	42	43	44
78	M33	5			1	1	1	1	1		1	1	1	1	6	5	5	5	8		12		
79	M112	5	16		2	1	1	1			1	1	1		5	5	5	4	7	2	9		1
80	M18	5	5		1	1	1	1			1	1	1	1		1		4			8		1
81	M16,M88				1	1	1	1			1	1	1										1

OVER ROMAN ROOMS

burial	context	1	2	3	4	5	6	7	8	9	10	11	12	13	14	15	16	17	18	19	20	21	22
82	E4	no bones																					
83	E57	no bones																					
84	E39,E40	1	1	1			1				1	1	1		1		1		1		2	2	
85	L172	2	1	1	23	5						1	1	1	1			1	1	1	2	2	3
86	L176	no bones																					

OVER ROMAN ROOMS CONTINUED

burial	context	23	24	25	26	27	28	29	30	31	32	33	34	35	36	37	38	39	40	41	42	43	44
82	E4			7																	3		
83	E57																				4	5	
84	E39,E40	2													1	1							
85	L172							1	1	1	1	1	1	1	1	1							
86	L176				1	1	1	1															

COURTYARD

burial	context	1	2	3	4	5	6	7	8	9	10	11	12	13	14	15	16	17	18	19	20	21	22
87	E99	1	2	3	4	5	6	7			1	1	1		1	1	1	1	1	1	5	1	22
88	H28	1	1	1		6	9	4	1		1	1		1	1	1	1	1	1	1	5	6	10
89	H21	1				6	8	5													2	3	6
90	D36	no bones																					
91	D84	no bones																					
92	D18	1	1	1	23	6	10	5			1	1	1	1	1	1	1	1	1		5	5	1
93	D5	1			5	5	12	5	1		1	1		1	1		1	1	1		5	5	5
94	D32		1	1	13	1							1								2		
95	D4,D34	1	1	1																			
96	D90	no bones																					
97	D78	1	1		14	7	12	5	1						1		1	1	1		5	7	8
98	B2	1	1		20	4	2	4	1				1	1	1	1	1	1	1		4	1	
99	B4	4	1		11	1	12	5			1	1	1	1	1	1	2	1	1	1	1	1	3
99	B4A	4	1	2		1	6	2					2	1		1		1	1	3	2		4
99	B4B	3				7	12	5												1	1		
100	D63	1	1	1	29	7		5	1		1	1	1	1	1	1	1	1	1	1	4	1	1
101	D69	no bones																					

COURTYARD CONTINUED

burial	context	23	24	25	26	27	28	29	30	31	32	33	34	35	36	37	38	39	40	41	42	43	44
87	E99	5	5		1	1	1	1			1	1	1	1			4				11	11	
88	H28	5	13		1	1	1	1	1		1	1					1				11	9	1
89	H21	3																					1
90	D36																						
91	D84																						
92	D18		11		1	1	1	1	1	1	1	1	1	1	4	6	5	4	1		9	10	1
93	D5		20		1	1	1	1	1	1	1	1	1	1	7	7	4	5	4			6	1
94	D32		8					1						1					9		1		
95	D4,D34																						
96	D90		9												2	2	9	2	8		1	10	1
97	D78				1	1	1	1	1	1	1	1	1	1							11	12	1
98	B2				1	1	1	1	1		1	1	1	1							11	1	1
99	B4	3	11		2	1	2	2	1	1	3	1	1	2	3	2	4	2	6	2	11	12	1
99	B4A		2			1		2		1			2	1	3	4	5	2	3	5	6		1
99	B4B							1							5	7	2	5	1		12		
100	D63	5	9		1			1	1	1	1	1	1	1	5		5		11			6	1
101	D69																					12	1

SOUTH OF CHURCH

burial	context	1	2	3	4	5	6	7	8	9	10	11	12	13	14	15	16	17	18	19	20	21	22
102	C29	1	1	1	16	7	12	5	1		1	1	1	1	1	1	1	1	1	1	5	5	5
103	C160	1	1	1	30	3	12	5	1		1	1	1	1	1	1	1	1	1	1	2		1
104	C39	1	1		1		1								1				1				
105	B24	4	1		6	1	6			1													
—			1	1	5	6	12	5	1		1	1	1	1	1	1	1	1	1	1	2	3	5
—				1	28	2	9	5	1		1		1	1	1	1	1	1	1	1	2	2	4
—				1	23																		
106	B26	1	1	1	16				1														

SOUTH OF CHURCH CONTINUED

burial	context	23	24	25	26	27	28	29	30	31	32	33	34	35	36	37	38	39	40	41	42	43	44
102	C29	5	17		1	1	1	1	1	1	1	1	1	1	6	6	4	5	14		11	10	1
103	C160	1	6		1	1	1	1					1	1	4	5	2	4	4		3	9	1
104	C39		1																		1	1	
105	B24		1		1	1	1	1	1		1	1	1	1							6	9	
—		3	10		1	1	1	1	1		1	1	1	1	7	7	5	5	8		9	10	
—			7		1	1	1	1	1		1	1	1		7	7	5	5	8	2	4	1	
—					1	1			1		1	1	1	1			1	5	1				
106	B26	4								1													

KEY: 1) number of individuals; 2) skull; 3) mandible; 4) teeth; 5) cervical vertebrae; 6) thoracic vertebrae; 7) lumbar vertebrae; 8) sacrum; 9) coccyx; 10) right clavicle; 11) left clavicle; 12) right scapula; 13) left scapula; 14) right humerus; 15) left humerus; 16) right radius; 17) left radius; 18) right ulna; 19) left ulna; 20) right carpals; 21) left carpals; 22) right metacarpals; 23) left metacarpals; 24) right phalanges; 25) left phalanges; 26) right innominate; 27) left innominate; 28) right femur; 29) left femur; 30) right patella; 31) left patella; 32) right tibia; 33) left tibia; 34) right fibula; 35) left fibula; 36) right tarsals; 37) left tarsals; 38) right metatarsals; 39) left metatarsals; 40) right phalanges; 41) left phalanges; 42) right ribs; 43) left ribs; 44) sternum.

the site is the ruined stone tower just inside the western ditch (Figs 118 and 119).

Two sides of the hill have suffered some damage in more recent times: from a tufo quarry on the west, and from landscaping for the modern road and bar on the east, where some traces of the backs of caves, of unknown date, still remain. In general, however, the topography suggests that the modern cuttings have encroached little, if at all, onto the medieval site.

EXCAVATION STRATEGY

Extensive excavation on the heavily-wooded Castellaccio site was neither practical nor desirable: tree felling could not be countenanced within a park and nature reserve. It was therefore only possible to excavate small trenches within natural clearings, and the aims of the excavation had to be limited accordingly. Broadly speaking, data were sought on the character and, particularly, the dating of the settlement; it was, however, appreciated from the outset that any data being retrieved from such limited excavation would always have to be interpreted with caution.

Seven trenches were excavated on the site during the three week season in 1990. The main trench Q, measured 10.0 × 1.5-2.0 m, and was sited in a natural clearing where the remains of a perimeter wall were visible on the inner edge of the ditch. The trench was intended to examine the curtain wall, and any structures built up against it. Other smaller trenches also took advantage of small clearings: V was positioned so as to examine the interior of the settlement close to the tower, W and Z the periphery of the site. Trench T was laid out to provide a section across the ditch, while X and Y tested for occupation on the flat area beyond the north ditch (Fig. 117).

THE RESULTS

The area beyond the northwest side of the main enclosure

Trench Y
Size: 2.0 × 1.0 m. Orientation: northeast-southwest. Position: 18.0 m northwest of the main enclosure, on the edge of the scarp.

The tufo bedrock, which was irregular, fissured and degraded, was encountered at 2.18 m below ground level. Above the tufo was a compact, dark brown, tufo-flecked loam (Y4), 0.6 m deep; it contained four sherds of pre-Roman coarse-ware, not more closely datable. This was overlaid by 0.5 m of a very similar deposit (Y3), slightly lighter in colour, but containing 27 sherds of pre-Roman coarse-ware (? bronze age). The remaining stratification consisted of clean, yellow sand (Y2: 0.9-1.0 m deep), covered by loose brown loam and leaf litter (Y1: 0.1-0.3 m deep).

Trench X
Size: 1.0 × 1.0 m. Orientation: northeast-southwest. Position: 6.0 m northwest of the main enclosure, on level ground.

Tufo bedrock lay 0.8 m below ground level, and was covered by one deposit only, a loose grey-brown loam with sparse tufo fragments. No finds were recovered from this trench.

Trench T and the enclosure ditch

The ditch on the west side of the enclosure remains to this day a substantial feature. It varies in size from 5.0 to 12.0 m in width, and is cut deeply into the natural rock. However, neither the actual depth nor the complete profile of the ditch could be ascertained.

Trench T
Size: 1.5 × 3.5 m. Orientation: east-west. Position: within and across the enclosure ditch, at a point opposite the tower.

The trench was excavated to a depth of 1.4 m from the present (relatively flat) ditch bottom. The ditch is thus at least 3.0 m deep, but may well be considerably deeper, given that the side of the ditch as seen in the excavated trench section remained vertical, with no sign of it bottoming-out. The fills, T6 to T1 in order of deposition, proved to be a series of layers of tufo rubble, 0.2 m to 0.4 m deep, in a matrix of either fine loam (T6, T5, T2) or white, decayed mortar (T3). The rubble comprised pieces of brown tufo including, in the case of T3, some fairly large squared blocks, up to 0.3 × 0.44 m. Occasional pieces of dark tufo and *selce* were also present. The white mortar layer additionally contained fragments of a harder, coarse grey mortar.

Two anomalies were noted within the ditch sequence. Firstly, the rubble fills were interrupted by layer T4, a loam, 0.34 m deep, with fine grit and small tufo fragments (pieces larger than 10 × 10 mm were very rare). Secondly, at the top of the sequence, the rubble layer T3 appeared to have been cut away towards the middle of the ditch, and the resultant hole filled by another rubble deposit, T2. The upper surface formed by these two layers sloped only slightly towards the ditch centre, and was relatively flat. Finally, the sequence was completed by T1, a humic, brown loam up to 0.38 m deep.

A few sherds were recovered from layers T4 and T5, ranging in date from the twelfth to the late thirteenth or early fourteenth centuries. Whilst little can be made from what may well be – given the type of context – redeposited material, a piece of archaic maiolica from layer T5 gives a *terminus post quem* of the late thirteenth to early fourteenth centuries for these fills.

Trenches Q, V, W and Z – the curtain wall and the interior of the enclosure

Trench Q
Size: 10.0 × 1.5-2.0 m. Orientation: northwest-southeast. Position: north of the tower, at right angles to and across the perimeter wall.

The first phase of the curtain wall
Excavation of the ditch in Trench Q consisted only of the clearance of vegetation and topsoil, and the excavation of a small amount of rubble. This revealed part of the inner rock-cut edge of the ditch which rose steeply to the foot of a 2.2 m wide ashlar wall foundation, Q15 (Fig. 120). It was faced in neatly-squared tufo blocks, which averaged 0.45-0.5 m in width, and 0.3 m in height. The blocks were tightly fitted, with no visible mortar between the joints. A coarse white mortar was, however, used in the wall core, which consisted of rough tufo fragments of all sizes up to 0.4 × 0.28 m. Wall Q15 survived to a maximum height of 1.36 m on the outer face.

The lowest layer, which butted against wall Q15, was a clean yellow-brown loam containing very sparse tufo frag-

Fig. 118. Castellaccio seen from the west, in the 1960's, across a modern tufo quarry
(JBWP)

Fig. 119. Castellaccio, the tower in 1970. *(TWP)*

Fig. 120. Castellaccio, Trench Q; the first phase of curtain wall. *(KW)*

ments (Q21). On the south side of wall Q4 (which, being later, was left *in situ*, effectively dividing the trench diagonally: Fig. 121), the tufo bedrock was overlain by Q9/10: this was a layer similar and probably equivalent to Q21, and contained two sherds of either Roman or medieval coarse-ware. Within Q9/10 were thin layers of small tufo rubble, beneath which was a deposit of dark grey-brown loam which also butted against wall Q15. The total depth of these deposits was 0.9 m.

The second phase of the curtain wall

A metre in front of wall Q15, and on the same line, was a later perimeter wall, Q3, with a foundation in rough tufo fragments up to 0.32 × 0.2 × 0.2 m high, set in hard, coarse grey mortar with small black inclusions (Fig. 122). Above this two courses survived of the inside face, made up of roughly-shaped tufo blocks up to 0.6 × 0.35 × 0.5 m in height, and set in the same mortar. Much of the wall core and all of the outer face had been robbed or had fallen, so that the original width of Q3 could not be determined. A shallow layer of fine, light yellow-brown loam (Q18) overlay wall Q15 and butted against wall Q3.

The internal walls

Layers Q18 and Q9/10 were cut by a 0.3 m deep foundation trench, Q11, which was only 50-80 mm wider than the wall, Q4, which was constructed within it. Wall Q4 followed a northeast/southwest alignment, being roughly at right angles to, and butting up against, the curtain wall Q3. A length of 7.4 m was revealed, consisting of four courses of roughly-shaped tufo pieces up to 0.4 × 0.3 × 0.25 m, standing to a total height of 0.75 m, and 0.43-0.51 m in width (Fig. 121). These tufo pieces were laid in two lines within a loose, grey mortar but with no true wall core, although some smaller tufo fragments were packed in between. The upper two courses were more clearly faced than those below, which were largely within the foundation trench; these lower courses were also offset by *c.* 0.1 m at the east end of the wall. The fill of the foundation trench was a friable dark grey-brown loam, which contained a single residual sherd of pre-Roman coarse-ware (probably iron age).

On the north side of wall Q4 was a deep layer of large tufo rubble up to 0.35 × 0.26 m, set in a matrix of soil and grey mortar. Many of the tufo pieces were roughly dressed. To the south of Q4, and again butting the wall, was a fine, light-brown silty loam (Q2), with sparse tufo fragments up to 40-80 mm. This layer, which was only 0.1-0.15 m deep, was cut by the vertical-sided foundation trench (Q23) for the stub of another wall, Q8. The wall was of identical construction to Q4, and survived to the same height. It emerged from the south section of the trench, running for only 0.64 m at approximately right angles to wall Q4. The fill of the foundation trench was a loose mid-brown loam (Q22).

A layer of dark grey-brown loam (Q1) covered the entire trench. This layer contained a few small fragments of tufo and tile, and fourteen sherds, of which the earliest were two fragments of sparse glaze, one late eleventh- or twelfth-century, and the other twelfth-century. The remaining sherds were as follows: seven medieval coarse-wares and domestic ware – probably twelfth to thirteenth/fourteenth centuries; two probable *ceramica laziale* – thirteenth century; one archaic maiolica – fourteenth century; one maiolica – late fifteenth century onwards; one yellow glaze – sixteenth-seventeenth centuries.

Trench V

Size: 1.5 × 1.5 m. Orientation: northwest-southwest. Position: 12.0 m northeast of tower.

The hard, clean surface of the tufo bedrock was reached at a depth of 0.7-0.9 m. The deeper part of the trench consisted of a shallow cut, V5, across the northwest half of the trench, of which only a right-angled corner was seen, on a north-south/east-west orientation; it measured 1.0 × 0.8 m. This cut had vertical sides and was filled by fine sandy loam (V4) with sparse tufo fragments up to 30 by 50 mm. It contained a single fragment of medieval coarse-ware, *c.* twelfth century.

Fig. 121. Castellaccio, Trench Q. View looking northwest towards the curtain wall and ditch; in the foreground internal walls Q4 (right) and Q8 (left). *(KW)*

In the east corner of the trench was a second right-angled cut, 0.2 m deep, into the bedrock (V8). It followed the same orientation as V5, while the near-vertical sides fell in two stages to a narrow step and then to a rounded bottom. The fill was similar to V4, but contained several irregular fragments of *selce* up to 0.13 × 0.08 m. No pattern could be observed in their placement.

Overlying the fills of both cuts was a compact, yellow-brown fine sandy loam with sparse small tufo fragments (V3). This layer was 0.2 m deep, and covered the whole trench; it contained the following pottery sherds: three probable *ceramica laziale* (thirteenth century); five medieval coarse-ware and eleven medieval domestic ware (all twelfth, thirteenth or fourteenth centuries). The layer above V3 was a mid grey-brown loam, 0.18-0.25 m deep, containing tufo rubble of various sizes, including some squared blocks, averaging 0.3 × 0.3 × 0.15 m, as well as fragments of fine, white mortar with tiny dark inclusions. It contained the following pottery fragments: two medieval coarse-ware and fourteen medieval domestic ware (all twelfth, thireenth or fourteenth centuries); one archaic maiolica (late thirteenth to early fourteenth centuries) and one lead-glazed kitchen-ware (late fourteenth to fifteenth-sixteenth centuries).

The uppermost layer in the trench was a mid-brown loam, 0.25-0.3 m deep, containing small tufo fragments and roots; it contained no finds.

Trench W

Size: 2.0 × 1.0 m (reduced to 1.0 × 1.0 m because of tree roots). Orientation: northeast-southwest. Position: north corner of the enclosure, on the inside edge of the ditch.

A very compact yellow sandy soil (W2) was the lowest context excavated in this trench. It was not the natural subsoil, as it contained the following pottery sherds: two probable Roman domestic ware; ten coarse-ware (not medieval); one probable *ceramica laziale* (thirteenth century). Cut into W2 was a small sub-circular post-hole, which was steep-sided, 0.22 m in diameter and 0.14 m deep. It was filled by loose brown loam, containing a single sherd of Roman coarse-ware, and overlain by an identical layer, which was 0.3-0.45 m deep, and again yielded a single Roman coarse-ware sherd.

Trench Z

Size: 2.0 × 1.0 m. Orientation: northeast-southwest. Position: south of tower, on the edge of scarp.

Fig. 122. Castellaccio, Trench Q. The second phase of curtain wall, seen from
the ditch. *(KW)*

The irregular, hard clean surface of the natural tufo lay at a depth of 1.17 m below ground level. In the south corner of the trench was a single post-hole, which was 0.22 m in diameter, 0.24 m in depth, and had regular, near-vertical sides sloping to a rounded bottom; it was filled with a very friable, light yellow-brown tufo rubble. Above was a very compact yellow-brown tufo rubble with charcoal flecks (Z7). This layer, which was 0.2 m in depth, was relatively rich in finds, including tile fragments, animal bone and a total of 56 sherds. There comprised 33 medieval domestic wares (one possibly eleventh century, while the others could be of the eleventh, twelfth or thirteenth centuries); thirteen sparse glaze (first half of twelfth century) and ten pieces of medieval coarse-ware (*c.* twelfth century). This was cut by Z6, a shallow sub-circular scoop, 0.68 m wide and 0.12 m deep. It was filled with a fairly compact yellow-brown rubble, consisting of small fragments of travertine. It contained a single sherd of medieval coarse-ware of the twelfth century. This was sealed by a very hard-packed tufo rubble floor, 0.51 m in depth, which was itself covered by a second similar floor of smaller rubble, 0.28 m deep. This yielded two sherds of medieval domestic ware (twelfth, thirteenth, fourteenth centuries) and two sherds of medieval coarse-ware (*c.*

twelfth century). Finally, a thin lens of grey-white mortar with minute black inclusions overlay these floors, although only at the north end of the trench.

The tower (Figs 117 and 119)

The surviving structure of the tower rises some 10.0 m above a distinct mound, much of which is undoubtedly made up of rubble fallen from the walls. The building measures 6.0 by 5.0 m externally, has walls 0.75 m thick and is oriented north-south/east-west. The lower half of the tower is very roughly faced, using mainly pieces of fairly hard, dark tufo, but also some *selce*; these range from 0.15 × 0.07 m to 0.2 × 0.09 m, and are set in a good-quality grey to off-white mortar with coarse tufo inclusions. Some of the *selce* fragments are smooth on one side and may have been taken from the paving blocks of the nearby Roman road. The wall core is constructed of similar material to the faces, but also contains some softer, brown tufo.

The upper half of the tower is built in the same mortar as the lower section but, with very few exceptions, using a softer brown tufo. The individual stones are generally larger, up to 0.25 by 0.1 m high, and the impression is of a partial rebuild of the structure. The height of the surviving stonework, and the placement of the putlog holes, indicate that there must have been several storeys, and the location of the tower on the highest point of the hill suggests that surveillance of the surrounding landscape was its major role. In this, it contrasts with the setting of nearby villages like Mazzano Romano and Calcata, which were built on spurs in the Treia valley, well below the level of the countryside around. Unlike Castellaccio, they were thus invisible from a distance (cf. Potter 1979: 157).

DISCUSSION

Prehistoric and Roman occupation

The discovery of sherds of bronze age or iron age date at Castellaccio is not in itself surprising. It occupies a high, easily defended hill, with a large area available for settlement. As such, it resembles some of the other pre-Roman centres of the Ager Faliscus, such as Narce, Nepi or Torre dell'Isola (Frederiksen and Ward-Perkins 1957: 92-3), so many of which were reoccupied in medieval times.

It is not, however, clear how extensive the pre-Roman settlement at Castellaccio may have been. The small and undiagnostic sherds came principally from Trench Y, where they were found within the upper of two loam layers, which together were 1.1 m in depth. This seems a very substantial deposit to have survived on the very edge of the ridge, but it was sealed by a further 1.0 m of clean sand. The two well-mixed loam layers could be interpreted as cultivated soils (explaining the abraded nature of the sherds), and the sand layer as a windblown deposit which formed after agriculture had ceased; but it is difficult to see how either could have formed to such a depth unless they had built up against some feature, such as a wall, which was either not revealed by excavation, or has since been destroyed. In short, there are traces of a buried prehistoric landscape at Castellaccio; but its nature and significance is currently elusive.

Roman finds at Castellaccio were limited to a few sherds of coarse-ware from Trench W and a possible sherd from Trench Q. It is also noteworthy that no Roman building materials were found in the excavations, and that the only Roman material reused in the tower was basalt, presumably robbed from the road below. The evidence points therefore to little or no use of the site during the Roman period.

The medieval origins of Castellaccio

Any discussion of the origins of Castellaccio, when derived from such a small body of data, requires an approach tempered with caution. Above all, the possibility must always be borne in mind that earlier material exists, but was not recovered. That said, some tentative conclusions can still be drawn.

No medieval pottery which could be dated earlier than the eleventh century was found. Forum ware, which could indicate activity in the tenth century or before, was conspicuous by its absence, as was any of the *ceramica acroma* from the late eighth-/early ninth-century pottery kiln found on the main excavation. If we compare this with the way that small quantities of prehistoric and Roman pottery *did* find their way into the excavated medieval contexts at Castellaccio, it seems reasonable to attach some weight to the negative evidence for occupation before the eleventh century. Indeed, the earliest pottery which can be dated with confidence consisted of sparse glazed ware of the first half of the twelfth century. A total of fifteen sherds was found, almost all from layer Z7, where they were associated with charcoal and animal bone (cf. King, this volume). Also from Z7 were 33 sherds of medieval domestic ware and ten sherds of medieval coarse-ware, none of which would be out of place in a twelfth-century context, although one fragment could be of the eleventh century.

The limited evidence for wooden structures is mainly associated with the early medieval pottery described above. This applies particularly to a post-hole, cut into the bedrock in Trench Z, and sealed by layer Z7. If we accept that the most likely *terminus post quem* for the deposition of Z7 is the first half of the twelfth century, then the post-hole must have been cut before this. Furthermore, provided the post-hole represents something durable (and not, say, just a scaffolding post), we should allow a sufficient period for the use, and decay or destruction, of a wooden structure. The evidence from Trench Z can be supplemented by that from Trench V, where the right-angled corners of two cuts in the bedrock, V5 and V8, were found. The latter contained fragments of *selce*, perhaps the remains of packing for wooden posts, while V5 produced a single fragment of twelfth-century coarse-ware.

None of the foregoing could be described as compelling evidence, but it does suggest the probability that wooden structures were being built on the site in the later eleventh or early twelfth century. Given that occupation ceased about AD 1100 on the site in the valley, it is more than reasonable to suppose a transfer of the population from there to Castellaccio. Equally, the case for identifying Castellaccio with the *castrum Capracorum* of the bull of 1053, as discussed in the introduction to this volume, finds not insignificant archaeological support. Whilst it would be desirable to have more diagnostic eleventh-century pottery from the castle site, the findings of the very modest investigation tend to sustain rather than refute this correlation with the documentary evidence.

The ditch and the extramural area

Although the cross-section (Trench T) could not be fully excavated, it is clear that the ditch was a substantial feature, 5.0 to 12.0 m wide and over 3.0 m deep. It would be difficult, then, to ascribe it anything other than a defensive purpose, and the vertical inner face is also consistent with this interpretation. The ditch would also be the logical source for much of the stone used in building Castellaccio (although the main site must also have been a useful quarry), so that it may, to some extent, have grown with the settlement. Of the fills which were excavated, the lowest to contain datable sherds, T5, formed during or after the late thirteenth to early fourteenth centuries. The nature of the fills shows them to be a mixture of rubble and masonry from the curtain wall, with one deep loam layer, T4, representing a gap in the process. In its current form, the ditch is noticeably flat-bottomed, giving rise to the suggestion that it may later have served as a track, perhaps when the hilltop was being used for agriculture. If the ditch was so used, this might explain the infilling of a cut in layer T3 to create a level surface.

Two trenches (X and Y) excavated outside the ditch disclosed no traces of medieval occupation, and the extramural terrain is very flat, showing none of the tell-tale humps and platforms which are evident in the enclosed area. Settlement would appear never to have expanded beyond the defences, a conclusion that is consistent with a settlement occupied for a relatively short period by a small population.

The curtain wall

The first phase of the curtain wall (Q15) cannot be independently dated as no diagnostic material was recovered from the foundation deposits. A broad clue may be found, however, in the type of stonework, which is characterized by the neatness of the tightly-fitted ashlars on the inner face, with courses 0.3 m high. The recurrence of this unit of measurement, which is probably a medieval foot, and more or less corresponds to the Roman foot (0.297 m), has already been noted in Lazio, and the phenomenon has been discussed by Andrews (1978). His study has suggested that the change to masonry cut to this module occurred at around AD 1100-50, while both the lengths of the blocks in the Castellaccio example and the neatness of the work would place it between his periods 1 and 2 in the Viterbo sequence. This would suggest a date in the late eleventh or early twelfth century (Andrews 1978: 396-400). However, while such comparisons are worthwhile, it is necessary to be cautious: masonry styles can be highly regional in character, and Monte Gelato lies towards the southern edge of the area which Andrews has discussed. The curtain wall, it should be added, was built directly onto the tufo bedrock, so that some prior clearance of the site must have taken place. The deposits which overlay the bedrock, and butted against the wall, included small tufo fragments and may well relate to the

construction of the wall. No trace was found of any structures against the inside of the first phase of the curtain wall, and the presence of a thick loam layer would also indicate that the space was kept open.

The construction of a second phase of curtain wall (Q3), which uses Q15 as a foundation, also cannot be dated. The construction technique is altogether cruder, and more varied, and it is not really possible to fit it within the sequence proposed by Andrews. Perhaps the only useful observation which can be made is that the first phase wall had been reduced to a few courses, suggesting either a period of decay or, more probably, a major collapse.

Internal structures

A single, rough tufo wall, Q4, to which another, Q8, was later added at right angles, was built against the second phase curtain wall. The presence of structures against the inside of the curtain wall is a commonplace in medieval hilltop villages, for example at nearby Castel Porciano (Mallett and Whitehouse 1967), and needs little comment. No floor levels were found in association with these walls, but wooden floors could have existed, perhaps at first-floor level, leaving a dirt-floored room below. It is unfortunate that the lack of material recovered from Trench Q meant that the structure cannot be dated. Indeed, the only datable building activity within the settlement was identified in Trench Z, where there was a dump of the twelfth century, covered by two hard-packed tufo floor surfaces.

The stone tower is another common feature of medieval hilltop villages of the region. The difficulty at Castellaccio is to establish the date of the tower when, in the absence of other archaeological data, we are again left with only the style of the masonry. This comprises small tufo fragments, somewhere between *tufelli* (small, neat tufo blocks) and *selcetti*-type work. A similar building technique was employed for the defensive tower (below, Fig. 126) in the valley below. Andrews (1978: 406) discussed the possible chronologies of both *tufelli* and *selcetti*-type work, but it is evident that in the state of current knowledge they can only be regarded as very broad clues: that the tower was built somewhere between 1150 and 1250 is most likely, but a date outside this range cannot be excluded.

The end of the settlement

The evidence discussed above suggests that a walled settlement, built at least partly in stone, existed by the first half of the twelfth century, with the tower, or at least the phase of the tower that is now visible, being built somewhat later. Occupation was never, however, heavy or prolonged. Pottery which dates to between the thirteenth-fourteenth centuries and the fifteenth-sixteenth centuries was recovered from destruction layers in the ditch, as well as near the tower. Post-medieval pottery, on the other hand, was found only in the topsoil, and then in very small quantities. On balance, then, Castellaccio probably had a relatively short life, and is likely to have been abandoned by the late thirteenth century. Whether the population was transferred to Mazzano Romano is a matter of conjecture: but it remains the most plausible possibility, especially as the mill, traditionally worked by the people of Mazzano, remained in use.

LA TORRE O SIA NOVA MOLA: IL MULINO DI MONTEGELATO (FIG. 123), di Franca Fedeli Bernardini

Il marchese Urbano del Drago Biscia Gentili, antico feudatario di Mazzano, il 9 ottobre 1830 scrive al Tesoriere Generale dello Stato Pontificio, Mario Mattei, per attivare gratuitamente un nuovo mulino nella tenuta di Montegelato, fatta salva l'osservanza delle leggi sul Dazio del Macinato. Tale mulino 'privativo', in contrasto con le disposizioni di Pio VII, per le facoltà accordate da Leone XII nel 1827 si giustificherebbe, nelle parole del 'barone', con l'antico diritto statutario[1] di costruire mulini, con l'assenza di mole 'camerali' cui farebbe concorrenza e di altre fabbriche cui toglierebbe l'acqua, e soprattutto con la necessità di farina della capitale. A partire dall'autorizzazione del 30 ottobre concessa dal Pubblico Erario, per quanto di propria competenza, il 18 novembre il Presidente della Comarca si rivolge alla Sacra Congregazione delle Acque 'che deve giudicare la libera defluenza' e predisporre un'idonea ispezione sul fiume. Inizia in tal modo un lungo e complesso iter burocratico per ottenere l'autorizzazione definitiva dalla Sacra

Congregazione delle Acque che emette infine apposito decreto il giorno 19 maggio dell'anno successivo.[2]

LA TENUTA DI MONTEGELATO A MAZZANO

Elisabetta Pucci, vedova del marchese d'Elci che aveva acquistato Montegelato dai conti Gallo nel 1813,[3] dopo aver affittato la tenuta ad Arcangelo Sansoni, dal 30 settembre 1827 al 30 settembre 1830, ed avergli rinnovato l'affitto per un altro anno,[4] inizia contestualmente le pratiche, per la vendita o la cessione enfiteutica, seguite dai patteggiamenti con Urbano del Drago,[5] che culminano con l'atto di compravendita il 29 marzo 1837.[6]

Tale tenuta di 240 rubbie si situa in una posizione territorialmente strategica al confine dei distretti di Roma e di Viterbo, tra il territorio dei comuni di Campagnano, Mazzano, Calcata, presso l'antica strada 'comunitativa' detta Logajo che entra nel territorio di Nepi ed incrocia la strada di Campagnano. Il marchese tesse in tal modo una politica di accorpamento e di espansione territoriale attorno ai tre principali nuclei iniziali di possidenza: frammenti di pascolo e di bosco ceduo proprio in località Montegelato, l'antica 'molina' in contrada Le Ripe e la tenuta di Ronciglianello (Figs 124 and 125).[7]

L'intento di sfruttare al massimo le potenzialità del territorio e della tenuta che vuole acquistare[8] è del resto evidenziato, oltre che dall'acquisizione della privativa sui mulini del paese, dalla creazione di un mulino, da affittare dietro corresponsione in denaro contante, e dal progetto di edificazione di una ferriera presso le cascate.

Con la costruzione di tali strutture, che sfruttano la forza motrice generata dalla caduta dell'acqua, il barone intende ribadire e rafforzare i centri delle possidenze passate e future. Inoltre la presenza nella tenuta di una antica calcara,[9] sfruttata almeno

[1] Archivio di Stato di Roma (ASR), Archivio del Drago (ADD), fascc. 12-13-14, n. 289: lo statuto è del 1536. La copia conservata in ASR, Statuti, Mazzano 652 è del 1542; cfr. libro V, cap. XXXXI; cfr. inoltre ASR, Camerale II-Molini, b. 26, fasc. 315 (1806). Si ringraziano la dott.ssa M. Pieretti che sta riordinando l'Archivio della famiglia Del Drago per l'indispensabile aiuto fornito nella consultazione dei materiali inediti, gli architetti A. Rebecchini e F. Avarini per ricerche, confronti e consigli, il dott. G. Guaita per indicazioni sulle cave e sulle rocce utilizzate per materiale da costruzione, e la dott.ssa C. Sforzini.

[2] ASR, Sacra Congregazione delle Acque (SCA), b. 138, fasc. 397.

[3] ASR, Congregazione del Buon Governo (CBG), S. II, b. 2319.

[4] ASR, ADD, Cass. Azz. 56, 373, 374.

[5] ASR, ADD, Cass. Azz. 58, p. 90 del 24/6/1831; riprese nel 1833, pp. 103-4.

[6] ASR, CBG, b. 2319.

[7] ASR, Brogliardo del Catasto Gregoriano, Comarca 50, 1819. Montegelato: ppcc: 563, 564; Le Ripe: ppcc: 448, 449, 450, 459, 460; AAD, Cass. Azz. 58, fasc. 51:la tenuta di Montegelato 'confinante nei suoi lati con la tenuta di Roncigliano grande spettante alli Monaci di S. Paolo, di Ronciglianello spettante all'Ill.mo Sr Marchese del Drago, con il territorio di Nepi e con li Beni del Beneficio della Madonna' (1789).

[8] 1679: scudi 230 (ASR, ADD, Cass. Azz. 57, n. 145); 1706-8: scudi 396:04 (ASR, Camerale III, Comuni, b. 1321); 1708-9: scudi 154:15 (ASR Camerale III, Comuni, b. 1321); 1709-10: scudi 205:45 (ASR Camerale III, Comuni, b. 1321); 1710: scudi 132:40 (ASR Camerale III, Comuni, b. 1321); 1714: scudi 197:10 (ASR Camerale III, Comuni, b. 1321); 1743: scudi 242:33 (ASR, ADD, Cass. Azz. 56, pos. 59, n. 8); 1779: scudi 375 (ASR, CBG, S. II, b. 2319); 1785-90: scudi 375 (ASR, CBG, S. II, b. 2319); 1805 ricavo dichiarato all'atto di vendita a Antonio Ciai per 14591:25 scudi di scudi 450.95; proprietà di rubbie 133.3 'solita a affittarsi un anno per l'altro scudi 450' (ASR, CBG, S. II, b. 2319); 1827-30 scudi 325 annui (ASR, ADD, Cass. Azz. 56, n. 374).

[9] La comunità affitta la tenuta, nel 1679, con la calcara per 230 scudi (ASE, ADD, Cass. Azz. 57, n. 40) 'fatto obbligo a mantenere li stradoni', a concedere il passo e il pascolo al bestiame, a permettere di cesare 'spallette e spallettoni', nonché cavare calce che necessitasse ai priori. Nell'affitto per scudi 242:33:24 del 1743 la comunità si riserva la calcara di calce (ASR, ADD, Cass. Azz. 56, pos. 59, n. 8); la tenuta è affittata per il quinquennio 1785-90 per 375 scudi l'anno 'che non possa esser Padrone ... detta Pietra da calce, ne della Cava della Pietra d o Peperino, ma queste restino a favore della Com tà' (ASR, CBG, S. II, b. 2319).

Fig. 123. The mill and waterfalls, looking southwest. *(KW)*

dal XVII secolo, di cave di peperino e di tufo giu-
stificano pienamente l'acquisizione. Entrato in possesso della tenuta, il tentativo immediato di libe-
rarla dagli antichi usi civici e consuetudinari, e di
recintarla, porta il marchese a scontrarsi, subito,[10]
con la Comunità di Mazzano per tentare, poi, un
faticoso compromesso con la stessa frutto di due
transazioni nel 1841 e nel 1843.[11] Il barone che,
con l'entrata in funzione del mulino, paga tramite
l''Esattore Giovanni Cesarone scudi dieci quali
sono per il canone della torre di Monte Gelato e
questi per il primo anno maturato a tutto Aprile
1832',[12] con la transazione del 1843 ottiene dalla
Comunità l'abbuono della corrisposta dovuta 'per
cagione della mola di Mte Gelato dietro il libero

pascolo del bestiame. Se infine intende ristringere
tutte le dette Tenute in detto caso l'annua corrisposta come sopra ceduta di Scudi dieci tornerà a
beneficio della Comunità'.

LA COSTRUZIONE DEL MULINO (FIG. 126)

Il barone inizia la costruzione del mulino a partire
da preesistenze: una vecchia torretta ed una torre
sulla penisola formata dai due rami del Treja, iden-
tificabili probabilmente con i 'fienili' di Montegelato danneggiati dai 'terrazzani' di Mazzano nel
1808.[13] La prima torre segue le sorti della tenuta
agricola e si ritrova menzionata come 'casa diroca-

[10] ASR, CBG, S. II, b. 2319.
[11] ASR, CBG, S. II, b. 2319.
[12] ASR, ADD, Cass. Azz. 55.
[13] ASR, ADD, Cass. Azz. 58, n. 40.

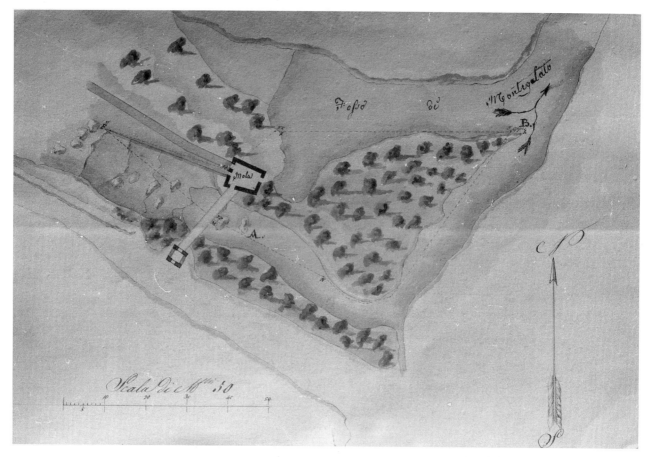

Fig. 124. Plan of the mill and tower in 1831 (Archivio di Stato di Roma).

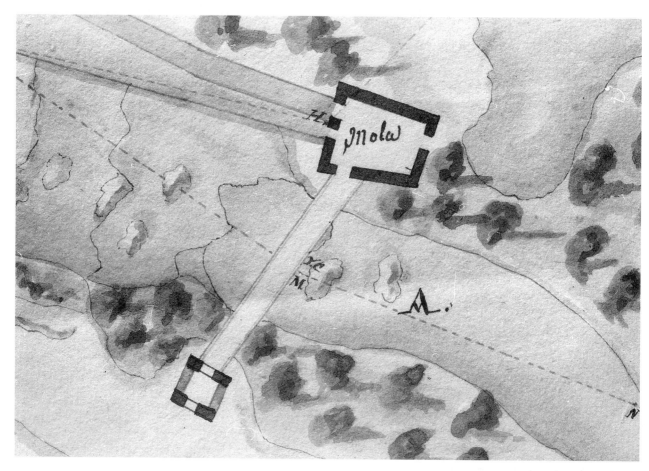

Fig. 125. Plan of the mill and tower in 1831 – detail (Archivio di Stato di Roma).

Fig. 126. The mill (right), bridge and tower in the 1960s. *(JBWP)*

ta', di proprietà degli Elci, nel brogliardo del catasto gregoriano del 1819; la seconda torre, a differenza della prima, non viene catastalmente menzionata.

Le preesistenze, da una parte, e la posizione topografica dall'altra, con la torretta prospiciente la strada che porta alle calcare e la torre presso la cava e 'la caduta' del fiume, finiscono per rendere i due edifici strettamente complementari, anche dal punto di vista costruttivo.

Il marchese, già in evidenti trattative per l'acquisizione della proprietà, decide d'iniziare, prima di richiedere la necessaria autorizzazione governativa per l'impianto del mulino, costosi lavori di restauro alle 'torri di Montegelato' attestati dai primi pagamenti noti a 'Sante di Stefano scudi Sette quali sono per le pietre che il Medemo cava' e 'allo muratore della Torre di Montegelato Michele de quarto dico scudi sei', annotati negli 'esiti' dell'amministratore del mese di maggio dell'anno 1830.[14] Solamente alla fine dell'anno sono 'pagati a Santo di Stefano Scudi Sei sotto il di 14 xbre 1830 quali sono per conto della nuova mola a retricine che si deve fare nella Torre di Montegelato'. Questo mandato di pagamento assume una particolare importanza in relazione alla menzione di una torre preesistente da adattare a mola e alla costruzione avanzata di un mulino, prima dell'espletamento delle pratiche burocratiche.

IL CANTIERE

Negli 'esiti' degli anni 1828-29 di Francesco Mostarola, amministratore locale del principe,[15] vengono liquidati, a partire dal 30 maggio 1830, i primi mandati di pagamento allo scalpellino Sante di Stefano per tre diverse operazioni: 'le pietre che il Medesmo cava per le torri' (scudi 7), 'le lastre che li a nova nelle Torri' (scudi 6) e 'le lastre che cava alla torre' (scudi 30). Contestualmente Mostarola paga l'impresario, il capo mastro muratore Michele de Quarto di Ponzano, con sei scudi per lavori di muratura alla torre e i calciaroli Giacomo Spunta di Rignano, Leone Pelegrini e Agostino Palazini con scudi 1:60 'per sprozzatura di calcio a Monte gelato compreso vino e Cortesia, che era in tempo di mietitura'.

Nei mesi di giugno, luglio e agosto, oltre ai regolari pagamenti di 6 scudi mensili a mastro Michele, vengono emessi più mandati a diversi calciaroli e trasportatori: Antonio Chiani di Campagnano e Giuseppe Morotti 'per some 43 di calce fornita' e 'per la calcie prese a Montegelato', Pietro Barberi e Alessandro Spalone 'per avere smorzata la calcio a Monte Gelato', Antonio Chieni e Nicola Giulianelli 'per vetura di somaro per carigiatura di calcie a Monte Gelato' e Giovanni de Luca 'per una giornata Fra essere il Somaro a carigiar la calcie a Montegelato'.

[14] ASR, ADD, Cass. Azz. 55, pos. 35, n. 16.
[15] ASR, ADD, Cass. Azz. 55, pos. 35, n. 16.

Nel mese di ottobre vengono emessi pagamenti per il falegname di Vigniano per l'acquisto e il trasporto di '16 tavole e cinque pezzi' alla Torre di Montegelato, necessarie per la messa in opera delle travi pontaie o del ponticello.

Il lavoro del muratore, rallentato durante l'estate, riprende a pieno ritmo in autunno come attestato dal pagamento in novembre di ben 38 scudi in tre mandati; contestualmente, tra ottobre e inizi di dicembre, vengono liquidati allo scalpellino oltre 57 scudi a saldo dei lavori fatti.

A partire dal mese di dicembre sembrerebbero ultimati i lavori esterni e iniziano i lavori interni alla mola che proseguono in gennaio con la costruzione 'delli scalini' 'o siano scale per la torre' e l'intaglio della 'nova Macina': in tale fase di particolare lavoro Sante di Stefano si fa aiutare, in maniera marginale, dal fratello Matteo.

Lavori di falegnameria per la mola e la porta vengono ultimati nell'aprile del 1831; il fabbro di Ronciglione per 'tramaglie Inferre e Cassone e tutto altrove compresi altri viatamenti fatti' viene liquidato nel mese di luglio[16] e successivamente[17] il ferraro di Campagnano nel mese di ottobre. Nell'esito dal 23 ottobre 1831 apprendiamo che vengono pagati scudi 1:30 per la benedizione della nuova mola data in affitto a Gervasio Conti per 7 scudi nel primo semestre che va dal 24 ottobre 1831 al 6 maggio 1832.

Attraverso i mandati di pagamento è possibile seguire i tempi di 'costruzione' del mulino e l'organizzazione del cantiere. In un primo momento, nella primavera del 1830, fervono i lavori per l'approvvigionamento dei materiali: calce della calcara trasportata alle 'torri' dai 'calciaroli' e dai 'somarari' per essere spenta sul luogo. Già prima lo scalpellino inizia a cavare pietre e a ridurle in 'lastre'. Contestualmente viene pagato, con la somma più alta mai ricevuta di 30 scudi, 'per le lastre che cava alla torre di Montegelato'. Tale 'cavare', all'inizio dei lavori, da precedente costruzione sembrerebbe connesso ad un restauro esterno del paramento murario della torre, da adibire a mulino, particolarmente sconnesso.

L'approvvigionamento dei primi materiali, con la prosecuzione del lavoro dello scalpellino, sembrerebbe rallentare il lavoro del muratore che riprende a pieno ritmo dopo l'estate.

L'entità relativamente scarsa dei mandati di pagamento del muratore e dello scalpellino, la quasi totale assenza di mandati di pagamento per trasportatori, falegnami e carpentieri in presenza di edifici coperti a volte, il tempo relativamente ridotto di costruzione, contro la notevole mole dell'edificio, fa decisamente propendere per il restauro di una costruzione preesistente, organicamente collegata all'antistante torre, realizzata riattivando la cava di peperino su cui insiste.

ITER BUROCRATICO (FIGG. 124 E 125)

Il mulino, dato provvisoriamente in gestione a Gervasio Conti nell'ottobre del 1831,[18] è praticamente ultimato già dall'aprile quando l'ingegnere Provinciali, incaricato il 18 novembre 1830, e risollecitato il 28 febbraio 1831, compie finalmente l'ispezione richiesta dal Presidente della Comarca, indispensabile per l'emissione del decreto di autorizzazione per la sua costruzione. L'eco di tale ispezione si ritrova in un mandato di pagamento[19] emesso dall'amministratore del marchese di 65 baiocchi 'pagati per spedizione alle Pauone con due Cavalli, e un uomo a prendere l'architeto il Sig.e Poleti, e l'inginiere per rivedere i lavori a Monte Gelato Come per commando di sua Eccellenza'. Sollecitato due volte a compiere l'ispezione, l'ingegnere accampa scuse, che si possono giustificare solamente con la conoscenza della costruzione in atto. In data 3 marzo scrive al Presidente della Comarca, descrive la situazione naturale, ma non compie il sopralluogo giudicando inutile rilevare di nuovo le piante e accedere al luogo poiché la domanda del marchese e il progetto dell'ingegner Poletti 'lasciano le cose nello stato attuale'.[20] Unisce altresì, alla relazione inviata alla Sacra Congregazione delle Acque del 5 marzo, 'tipi' ed allegati del tecnico del marchese non personalmente verificati.

Tale caparbia, giustificata solo in parte dal prestigio del Poletti[21] e dall'imbarazzo a denunciare l'operato del barone, viene spezzata da una terza ingiunzione del 31 marzo del Presidente della Comarca che denuncia l'insufficienza della relazione inviata.

Il 26 aprile l'ingegner Provinciali ispeziona la zona ed esegue i richiesti rilievi 'del Tratto del Fosso di Montegelato nel punto ove deve costruirsi la mola'[22] allegati alla relazione del 3 maggio 1831. Nel profilo del ramo destro prende come punto di riferimento la torre minore e disegna il profilo della torre maggiore dallo spiccato di fondazione 'del masso ove poggia la Fabbrica' fino al tetto con la 'soglia del sottarco della porta della mola', il fondo e il pelo d'acqua dopo la caduta.

---

[16] ASR, ADD, Cass. Azz. 56, n. 438: pagamento di scudi 2:50 a Giuseppe Rossi 'per porto delle Macine di Montegelato'.
[17] ASR, ADD, Cass. Azz. 59, pos. 66, nn. 44 e 45.
[18] ASR, ADD, Cass. Azz. 59, n. 38.
[19] ASR, SCA, b. 138, fasc. 397; ASR, ADD, Cass. Azz. 55, pos. 35, n. 16.
[20] ASR, Mulini, b. 26, fasc. 315.
[21] ASR, SCA, b. 138, fasc. 397; per l'abilità di rilevatore di Luigi Poletti cfr., Tosti (1835).
[22] ASR, SCA, b. 138, fasc. 397.

Tale implicito riconoscimento dell'esistenza del mulino non impedisce tuttavia che venga emesso il decreto di autorizzazione in data 19 maggio dalla Sacra Congregazione delle Acque 'Con condizione che la Fabrica si costruisca inferiormente alla caduta, e che il muro per riunire l'acqua nel ramo destro non oltrepassi con la sua altezza le ordinarie piene medie, e si lascino nel medesimo li opportuni incastri, e scarico per aprirli in caso di bisogno'.[23]

Il marchese, che aveva dichiarato in data 26 aprile al Tesoriere Generale di richiedere l'autorizzazione 'solo' per la costruzione di un mulino a grano, ottenuta tale autorizzazione, l'11 luglio presenta nuova istanza alla stessa congregazione per costruire 'inferiormente' una ferriera, ossia un opificio ad uso di fonderia e lavorazione del ferro, 'prevalendosi dell'avanzo dell'Acque che serve già ad un suo mulino a grano'.[24]

Il permesso viene accordato prontamente in data 8 ottobre, vista la nuova relazione con pianta dell'ingegnere Provinciali e 'risultando che l'opificio da costruirsi non può recare alcun pregiudizio nè superiormente, per la sensibile declività del Fosso, e perché l'unico opificio Superiore è il Molino costrutto dal Medesimo Sig e M se del Drago, nè inferiormente perché la Ferriera si costruisce nel tratto della caduta terminata la quale le acque dopo di aver fatto il loro officio vengono a porsi nello stesso livello in cui ordinariamente si trovano ed in fine considerando che niun danno può accadere lateralmente alle Campagne perché le sponde sono alte'.[25]

Alla relazione dell'ingegnere del 3 maggio, oppure a quella dell'8 ottobre 1831, è probabilmente allegata la pianta non datata,[26] conservata presso l'Archivio di Stato di Roma. Risultano immediatamente visibili, per l'uso di diversi colori, i due livelli dell'antica torretta, attraversata inferiormente da un passaggio come avviene attualmente, e superiormente connessa, tramite un ponticello di legno appoggiato su massi rocciosi, con la mola. Si comprende così l'importanza iniziale del restauro che coinvolge contestualmente il complesso delle due 'Torri'.

LE TRASFORMAZIONI DEL MULINO E DELLA 'FERRIERA' (FIGG. 127–9)

Il nuovo mulino è costruito 'in un punto nel quale viene animato dalla naturale cadente delle Acque, senza bisogno di costruir chiusa per elevarle superiormente, regolarizzando soltanto i scaglioni naturali di masso, e raccogliendole nel canale artificiale FH ad uso dell'Opificio. Il Muraglione poi BH munito di saracinesche da manovrarsi in occasione di piene fa si che queste potendo liberamente espandersi, come per lo innanzi, non può il corso d'acqua soffrire rigurgito a danno dei terreni superiori'.[27]

Alle spalle del mulino situato su una penisola, trasformata oggi in isolotto con la riattivazione della cava di peperino, si trova 'la muraglia', munita di saracinesche per il 'troppo pieno', del serbatoio. Tale 'rifolta' triangolare a monte raccoglie l'acqua e la immette a grande velocità, data la pendenza, nel 'carcerario del ritrécine' attraverso un canale, originariamente di quercia, facendo muovere la ruota orizzontale, inizialmente di legno, collegata alla macina superiore, mobile.

Le piene del fiume finiscono per rendere quasi subito necessari lavori di restauro: l'alluvione del 1835[28] porta via le pale della ruota, quella del 1839 'sfalda' il ritrécine,[29] quella del 1844-45 rende necessario costruire 'Una legata ... per allacciare tutta l'acqua che conduce alla mola e sia libero il passo per Monterosi e Trevignano', ripristinare le pale e il ponticello.[30] L'alluvione del 1848-49 rende nuovamente necessario l'intervento del 'Facocchio di Campagnano per riatto del ponte di legno alla mola', quella del 1849 il rifacimento della 'Retreggine' (intero ingranaggio composto da ruota, palo, distanziatori, cerchioni e tre macine – provenienti, in due giorni di 'barrozza', dalla cava di Settevene) e, soprattutto, del ponte.[31] L'inagibilità della mola per lunghi periodi e il grave pericolo per persone ed animali, evidenziato dal rischio di annegamento dell'affittuario Giuseppe Beni di Campagnano e del suo garzone nel 1848, accelerano la decisione di ricostruire stabilmente il ponte.

[23] ASR, SCA, b. 138, fasc. 397.

[24] ASR, SCA, b. 138, fasc. 397.

[25] ASR, SCA, b. 138, fasc. 397.

[26] ASR, SCA, b. 138, fasc. 397.

[27] ASR, SCA, b. 138, fasc. 397.

[28] Per l'alluvione del 1832 o 33: ASR, ADD, Cass. Azz. 56, n. 466; per l'alluvione del 1835, ASR, ADD, Cass. Azz. 55, Esiti anno 1835.

[29] Per l'alluvione del 1839 'che a Sfondato il Ritrecine': ASR, ADD, Cass. Azz. 57, n. 83.

[30] ASR, ADD, Cass. Azz. 55, n. 37; tra l'altro vengono pagati al muratore Antonio Marconi nel 1844 scudi 8.50 'per chiudere due vani sotto la torretta per rimettere i giumenti ad uso di stalla' e scudi 2.50 per 'due stipiti di peperino nella porticella (probabilmente posteriore) della mola'.

[31] ASR, ADD, Cass. Azz. 55, n. 16: scudi 3.35 'per ristauro al Ponte della Mola'; ASR, ADD, Cass. Azz. 55, n. 5; ASR, ADD, Cass. Azz. 58, n. 145. 'Il molinaro di Monte Gelato ha dovuto fare riattare il ponte di legno perchè era affatto intercettato l'ingresso nella mola per le correnti del fosso, chè mancò poco ad annegarsi il padrone Beni col garzone, vi sono voluti i travicelli nuovi, i tavoloni perchè portati via dalle acque' (9 dic. 1848).

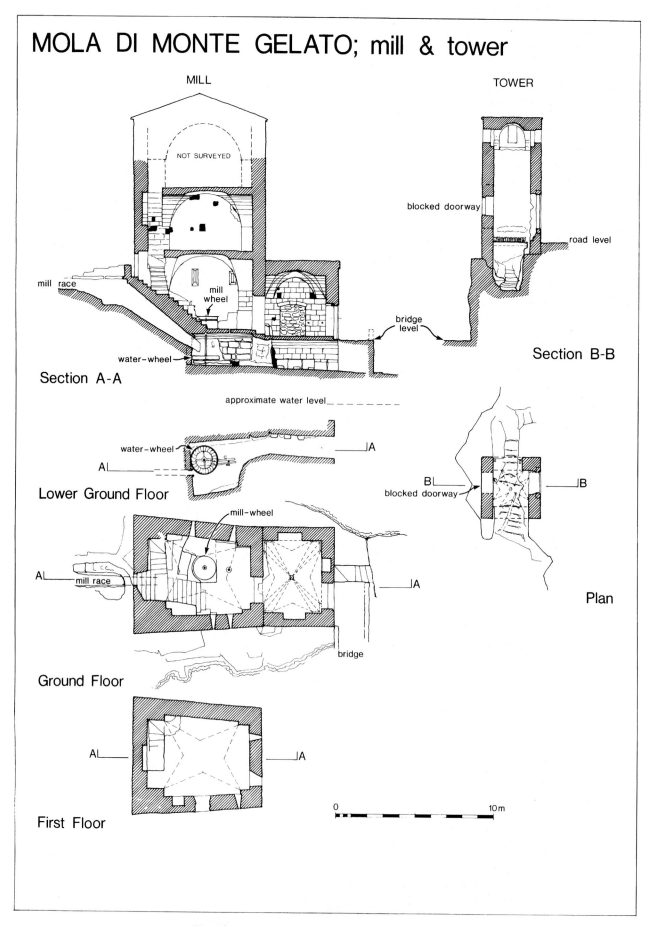

Fig. 127. Plans and sections of the mill and tower. *(RDA)*

Fig. 128. The mill-wheel and steps leading to the first floor. *(KW)*

Fig. 129. The vault of the room with the mill-wheel. *(KW)*

Il muratore Antonio Marconi riceve da Giuseppe Pizzuti, amministratore del barone, il 20 settembre 1850,[32] in saldo lavori la somma di scudi 71:70 per il ponte nuovo della mola di Montegelato 'Cioè per fattura, sassi, fattura e servitù sc.50 calce some 32 compreso la smorzatura sc.16:70 Pozzolana cavata e trasportata sc.03:00'. Tale ponte, iniziato dopo il mese di ottobre 1849, viene costruito impiegando in parte materiale di recupero.

L'esame comparato del menzionato disegno e della situazione topografica evidenzia come il ponte di legno collegasse il piano di calpestio della torretta con il primo piano della mola, come è possibile notare dalla nuova porta in peperino della torretta su via delle Calcare, dall'apertura, successivamente richiusa, sulla parete prospiciente e dalla tagliata sulla roccia in corrispondenza del lato lungo del mulino. Il ponte, fatto di passoni e travicelli era probabilmente irrigidito da un rompitratta su banco roccioso. Un ponticello all'imboccatura del canale del serbatoio, portato via dalla piena del 1861 e successivamente ricostruito, collegava la sponda opposta del Treja alla zona di molitura. Il ponte attuale in muratura, più spostato sulla destra e a un livello più basso, viene costruito utilizzando banchi rocciosi preesistenti per le fondazioni. La nuova posizione comporta la trasformazione in finestra della originaria porta d'ingresso al mulino al primo piano e la modificazione del nuovo accesso principale, in corrispondenza del piano di molitura, sul lato corto attraverso il basso edificio antistante.

Tale trasformazione funzionale finisce per liberare i due livelli superiori del mulino che diverranno alloggio del mugnaio, per trasformare definitivamente in stallette i due locali sovrapposti della torretta[33] e per modificare l'uso del basso edificio antistante. Tale costruzione inizialmente con accesso uguale all'attuale, forse collegata con stretta apertura alla zona di molitura, non era originariamente servita dal ponte di legno, situato ad una quota più alta, bensì da un sentiero che la collegava all'altra sponda del fiume. Osservando il disegno ottocentesco si può infatti notare come esistesse un passaggio molto più ampio dell'attuale sul ramo del fiume e che in corrispondenza di questo vi fosse una porta, oggi tamponata, sul corpo antistante. Sicuramente con la costruzione del ponte in muratura il basso edificio finisce per diventare l'anticamera del mulino, come dimostrato dall'apertura a strappo molto ampia, che sostituisce probabilmente una piccola apertura di comunicazione.

I documenti menzionati del 10 ottobre 1831 avevano autorizzato il barone a costruire una ferriera nell'area antistante il mulino, sfruttando la stessa forza motrice dell'acqua che muoveva la ruota. Tale edificio che 'si costruisce nel tratto della caduta terminata la quale le acque dopo di aver fatto il loro officio vengono a porsi nello stesso livello in cui ordinariamente si trovano'[34] non può che essere l'edificio antistante con nicchia trasformata in camino e contestualmente 'rifoderata'. In una lettera, inviata al Principe Del Drago da Giuseppe Fornaciani nel 1841, in cui si elencano lavori urgenti e necessari da eseguire alla mola, si ricorda che 'Anche la parete nuova dove stà il camino è in sommo pericolo' per infiltrazioni d'acqua.[35]

Non sappiamo se la ferriera abbia mai funzionato per la scarsa forza motrice dell'acqua che deve muovere prima la ruota orizzontale del mulino, sicuramente lo stato di degrado dopo soli dieci anni dell'intero complesso (ferriera e mulino) è prova indiretta delle difficoltà di avvio. La ricostruzione del ponte dà comunque una nuova destinazione all'edificio che accoglie persone ed animali (come dimostrato dai fori nelle pietre per il passaggio delle corde) in attesa della molitura.

I MUGNAI

Con l'uso privativo dei mulini il marchese mette in atto due diverse forme di conduzione; il primo mulino vicino al paese, che serve principalmente gli abitanti di Mazzano, continua ad essere ceduto ad affittuari, spesso mugnai 'locali' consorziati (gli Scatena di Vetralla, i Conti di Magliano, i Santarelli di Fermo domiciliati a Campagnano, i Belli ugualmente di Campagnano, i Mancinelli), che lo prendono tradizionalmente in affitto ogni anno dietro corrisposte variabili in grano (da quindici a venti rubbie, eccezionalmente 40). Il nuovo mulino, viceversa, che dovrebbe servire più comunità, viene principalmente affittato agli stessi affittuari, spesso mugnai locali, con offerte annuali che vedono tuttavia il concorso di mugnai 'forestieri' 'itineranti', che corrispondono al marchese non più quote di grano da trasportare sul mercato granaio di Roma, bensì consistenti quote in denaro (da meno di 100 a 240 scudi).[36] In aste, generalmente annuali,[37] viene aggiudicato l'affitto del mulino, in relazione all'offerta più vantaggiosa. In alcuni anni gli stessi mugnai riescono ad affittare i due mulini pagando le rate in maniera diversa in denaro e in natura. Mentre tuttavia il vecchio mulino continua ad avere la propria clientela in paese, il nuovo mulino, collegato alle due sponde del fiume Treja, stenta economicamente a decollare come risulta anche

---

[32] ASR, ADD, Cass. Azz. 55, n. 9.
[33] ASR, ADD, Cass. Azz. 55, n. 37.
[34] ASR, SCA, b. 138, fasc. 397.
[35] ASR, ADD, Cass. Azz. 58, pos. 124 (1841).
[36] ASR, ADD, Cass. Azz. 55, pos. 32, n. 8; ASR, ADD, Cass. Azz. 55, pos. 33-7.
[37] ASR, ADD, Cass. Azz. 61, pos. 125, n. 1.

dalla variazione delle quote annuali e dal libro dei debitori del marchese che annota spesso o puntualmente mugnai e affittuari di Montegelato.[38] Il mulino può essere affittato ad affittuari 'andante e macinante', con tutti i propri 'stigli'[39] annotati puntualmente in verbali, dietro corrisposta in denaro, da pagare generalmente in due semestri. L'affittuario a sua volta dovrà pagare il mugnaio con scudi 4:70 mensili provvedendo a far eseguire piccole riparazioni dietro rimborso, mentre i grandi lavori sono a carico del proprietario.

Laddove, solitamente, l'affittuario è il mugnaio stesso questo verserà ugualmente la quota, trattenendo per sè la paga, eseguendo spesso, da solo, piccole riparazioni dietro rimborso, fenomeno che attesta la grande abilità raggiunta e lo scambio d'opere tra mugnai. Tale quota può essere ridotta se il mugnaio, particolarmente abile, come Giuseppe Scatena, provvede da sè alle piccole riparazioni.[40] Quest'ultimo, già affittuario del mulino vecchio,[41] riceve dall'amministratore del marchese 'Scudo 1,40 per sette pale nove messe nella mola Monte Gelato per Comissione del Molinaro Domenico Santarelli a cui la piena portò via come da sua ricevuta sotto il di 13 marzo 1836'. Il mugnaio, se non è forestiero, non risiede normalmente nel mulino ad eccezione di momenti di particolare carico di lavoro. Del resto le precarie condizioni dell'edificio, spesso abbandonato, sono evidenziate già nel 1841 quando 'Occorre di far accomodar le pietre della Tore, perché ogni volta che piove cadendo le acque dentro restano pregiudicanti li muri delle volte'.[42]

La nota dei lavori di restauro dell'intero edificio fatta nel gennaio del 1858, e del prezziario dell'architetto Salvatore Bianchi, testimonia infatti[43] il rifacimento dell''attuale canale di quercia lung. pmi 31' con 'pmi 25 di pietra di Montegelato, e pmi 6 di quercia', della 'Macina[44] di pietra di due pezzi di Monte Gelato', delle camere superiori alla mola[45] 'l'una sovraposta all'altra da destinarsi per il Molinajo', entrambe mattonate, con chiusura delle travi pontaie, delle finestre 'con telaro e sportello' ed infine del tetto a quattro falde. La sostituzione delle 'lastre' in pietra di Montegelato con più funzionali tegole alla romana, previa impermeabilizzazione in cocciopesto, testimonia ancora una volta una tecnica costruttiva originariamente del tutto simile a quella impiegata nella torretta, ancora esistente fino ai recenti lavori di restauro.

LA TORRE, IL MULINO E LA FERRIERA: PROBLEMI CRONOLOGICI E COSTRUTTIVI

'Per avere anche sempre inteso dire che di loro Antichi Antenati, che la Tenuta detta di Montegelato sia stata ceduta a questa Comunità da quei Particolari, che erano nel Castello, che esisteva in detta Tenuta dopo che il medesimo Castello, fù diruto come l'è al presente, con patti, e condizioni che sù quella entrata si dovesse fabricare, e mantenere questa chiesa Parrocchiale, far mantenere le Mura Castellane della Terra di Mazzano, Strade publiche, fonte della Treja, Fontana, così ancora pagare tutti i Provjjgiamenti, come anche ciò costa da qualche Libro de Consigli, benché li primi antichi di tali Istituzioni non più esistono per essere andati a fuoco in un Incendio di questo archivio.'

Questo interessante documento del 1802[46] teso a dimostrare, attraverso la testimonianza orale dei priori, un mitico e immemorabile possesso della tenuta di Montegelato da parte della Comunità, incorporata 'ingiustamente' dalla Sacra Congregazione, rammenta, attraverso il 'dono' degli antichi abitanti trasferitisi a Mazzano, l'esistenza, ancora viva nel ricordo, dell'antico castello abbandonato. La ricostruzione della storia del mulino è avvenuta finora considerando solamente i documenti d'archivio, a prescindere dalle preesistenze che complicano ulteriormente il quadro di intervento.

I diversi corpi di fabbrica presso il fiume e la cascata (torre, mulino e corpo antistante), sono situati nell'area della domusculta di Capracorum presso la chiesa di San Giovanni, già diruta nel 1158. Il passaggio dall'insediamento sparso (curtis) all'insediamento fortificato (castrum), è attestato dalla bolla di Leone IX del 1053 che menziona il 'Castrum Capracorum cum terris vineis, fundis, casalibus, montibus, collibus, plagis, planitiis, molendinis et molaria sua cum ecclesia Sancti Johannis que dicitur delatregia, cum cellis, terris, vineis et cum omnibus ad eandem ecclesiam pertinentibus, positam territorio Vegentano, miliario ab urbe Rome plus minus vicesimo septimo' (Tomassetti 1883: 137 e sgg.).[47] Il castrum, non più menzionato nel corso del secolo XIII (Conti 1980), viene precocemente abbandonato e la popolazione confluisce nei centri vicini, come rimane nel ricordo. Con l'abbandono e l'ampliamento dei confini castrali l'area di pertinenza del castrum diruto entra a far parte del territorio del comune di Mazzano, sotto forma di grande tenuta, e viene venduta, dopo al-

[38] ASR, ADD, Cass. Azz. 58, n. 53: 'Prima Nota dei Debitori di Mazzano a settembre 1853'.

[39] ASR. ADD, Cass. Azz. 59, pos. 75, n. 4 (1852); per la vecchia mola: ASR, ADD, fascc. 143-4 (1780).

[40] ASR, ADD, Cass. Azz. 55, doc. 1.

[41] ASR, ADD, Cass. Azz. 55, doc. 16.

[42] ASR, ADD, Cass. Azz. 58, n. 124 (1841).

[43] ASR, ADD, Cass Azz. 59, pos. 81, n. 1.

[44] ASR, ADD, Cazz. Azz. 59, pos. 81, n. 3.

[45] ASR, ADD, Cazz. Azz. 59, pos. 81, n. 1.

[46] ASR, CBG, S. II, b. 2319.

[47] Tale domusculta darà vita, dal secolo X al fenomeno complesso dell'incastellamento particolarmente precoce nella zona (945: Mazzano; 974: Calcata; 996: Sorbo; 998: Faleria ...). Vedi anche Liber Pontificalis I, 501-21, CCXXXIV.

Fig. 130. The tower looking southeast in the 1960s. *(JBWP)*

terne vicende, dall'abate di San Gregorio al Celio a Giovanni Battista Anguillara per 12.000 scudi nel 1527 (Tomassetti 1913: v. III, 120 e sgg.) e dal conte nel 1581 alla Comunità di Mazzano.[48] A seguito del Motu Proprio di Pio VII del 1801, la proprietà divenuta demaniale verrà venduta nel 1805 al Signor Antonio Ciai,[49] e rivenduta nel 1813 agli Elci.[50] In tale complessa ed esemplare stratificazione storica (il centro tardo-antico, la domusculta, la *curtis*, il castello poi desertificato, la grande tenuta) si ubica il mulino e il corpo antistante e la torretta, separati dal fiume.

LA TORRETTA (FIGG. 130 E 131)

La prima menzione di una torre si ha in un documento del 1037 riportato da Kehr (1907: v. II Latium, pp. 25 e sgg., docc. 4075–110) in cui si menziona, tra i confini di proprietà, la 'turre de Capra-

corio' sede di 'militia', non identificabile con la torre di Montegelato. La torre in esame, con paramento esterno e interno in 'selcetti' regolari di 60-80 mm e giunti stilati, può essere datata, in relazione agli studi sulle murature (Serafini 1927; Bertelli, Guiglia Guidobaldi e Rovigatti Spagnoletti Zeuli 1976–77; Avagnina, Garibaldi e Salterini 1976–77), alla metà del secolo XII. La costruzione, originariamente più alta, viene successivamente tagliata e coperta da volta unghiata con bel rosone in chiave; tale volta è impostata su piedritti in pietra, su preesistente paramento, e viene realizzata con conci lapidei accuratamente tagliati. La torre non presentava aperture sull'attuale fronte strada e già in antico poteva essere collegata con l'antistante struttura tramite un ponte.

IL MULINO E IL CORPO ANTISTANTE

Il toponimo 'Torri di Montegelato', che si riscontra nella tradizione ottocentesca, presuppone l'esistenza di più strutture fortificate a protezione del guado sul fiume.

La prima menzione di una mola si ha nella citata bolla di Leone IX del 1053; anche in questo caso tuttavia la mola menzionata non sembra corrispondere al mulino esistente, come risulta dall'esame delle murature. Tutt'ora si conserva nella costruzione bassa, antistante la mola vera e propria, un bel paramento murario di tufo perfettamente squadrato a ricorsi di circa 0,32 metri, costruito secondo una tecnica muraria simile a quella usata nel viterbese. Tale datazione, che potrebbe risalire al secolo XI secondo l'Andrews (1982: 7, fig. 7)[51] contestabile cioè alla menzione della bolla, sembrerebbe tuttavia smentita dalla notevole omogeneità costruttiva di tutto il piccolo edificio coperto con volta unghiata, che presenta un rosone intagliato in chiave, del tutto simile a quella che copre la torretta antistante.

La torre del mulino, slittata rispetto all'avancorpo, è costituita da un sistema di tre volte sovrastanti anch'esse unghiate; tali volte sono realizzate con tecnica costruttiva a blocchi regolari, analoga a quella usata per la costruzione di tutte le altre volte, e sono impostate su pilastri in ottima pietra da taglio, di dimensioni simili a quelle usate nel corpo antistante. Tuttavia mentre l'avancorpo risulta omogeneamente realizzato con una doppia fodera di pietra da taglio regolare, con grande stranezza costruttiva le parti esterne di 'tamponamento' del mulino sono realizzate con scheggioni irregolari messi in opera con l'uso di molta malta.

[48] ASR, CBG, S. II, b. 2319.
[49] ASR, CBG, S. II, b. 2319.
[50] ASR, CBG, S. II, b. 2319.
[51] La muratura in tufelli e selcetti si ritrova in un raggio di 30-40 kilometri da Roma con un limite che passa per Cerveteri, Trevignano, Montegelato, Rignano. Montegelato si costituisce pertanto come zona di confluenza della tecnica costruttiva a selcetti e a blocchi di tufo.

Fig. 131. The interior of the tower. *(KW)*

I due edifici sono separati da una rozza muratura a scheggioni di tamponamento che alloggia un doppio arco di scarico, parzialmente occluso, su cui s'incuneano i conci delle volte appositamente tagliati. L'unitarietà e la continuità della struttura che si appoggia e si aggrappa sul preesistente muro è data dai pilastri del corpo antistante e del mulino che sembrano pensati senza soluzione di continuità.

Le volte unghiate, in pietra da taglio regolare farebbero presupporre una struttura più antica di notevole importanza su cui s'imposta la muratura ottocentesca per la ricostruzione della mola. L'esame sistematico dei mandati di pagamento dei muratori e dei trasportatori di pietre definisce del resto l'entità dei lavori intrapresi.

L'esame della cartografia pone tuttavia alcuni problemi rispetto a tali ipotesi poiché solo la torretta è menzionata nella mappa del catasto del 1819; il mulino, ricordato come 'Torre' nei documenti del 1830, viene disegnato solo nella menzionata pianta della zona del 1831 che tuttavia non graficizza il corpo antistante; quest'ultimo, in contraddizione con quanto detto, dovrebbe pertanto essere stato costruito dopo tale data.

Tuttavia se ricordiamo che il brogliardo del catasto menziona solo edifici con proprie funzioni come la torre (impiegata fino a pochi anni prima come fienile e poi diroccata), resterebbe da spiegare il silenzio circa il corpo antistante nella mappa del 1831.

L'autore di tale mappa è probabilmente l'ingegnere Provinciali che, o rileva direttamente la zona, oppure riporta disegni precedenti dell'architetto Poletti. Ricordando il comportamento non proprio lineare del marchese e tantomeno dell'ingegnere in esame, la mappa potrebbe volutamente ignorare l'esistenza di un edificio, preesistente, prima della concessione dell'autorizzazione richiesta in quanto rudere privo di funzione.

I MATERIALI IMPIEGATI

L'ipotesi, non suffragata da grafici esistenti, di preesistenze medioevali si fonda, oltre che sulla critica delle fonti, sull'esame dei materiali con cui le 'Torri' vengono costruite provenienti, quasi tutti, dalle vicine cave di peperino di Montegelato e di tufo di Castellaccio.

La torretta, appoggiata sulla viva roccia tagliata dalla cava, viene realizzata con 'selcetti' di tufo e peperino locali, mentre la volta in pietra da taglio è realizzata in tufo biancastro di provenienza non identificata con certezza. L'edificio antistante il mulino è costruito nella bella pietra tufacea di Castellaccio, mentre le volte del mulino stesso sono realizzate con materiale tufaceo non immediatamente identificabile per le intonacature e rasature successive. Sicuramente gli scheggioni di pietra delle pareti del mulino sono della cava di peperino locale, come originariamente era la copertura a lastroni del mulino e della torretta antistante.

L'analisi dei materiali sembrerebbe evidenziare con costanza la presenza di volte costruite in ottima pietra da taglio tufacea impostate su paramenti di diverso tipo.

Due gruppi di elementi fanno propendere per una stratificazione storica di tali strutture: i caratteri costruttivi difformi e coesistenti, le diverse tecniche e i materiali (selcetti regolari con stilature di giunti; decorazioni floreali e conci perfettamente tagliati; scheggioni rozzamente lavorati e materiali di spoglio impiegati nei lavori sicuramente ottocenteschi) e gli elementi archivistici (lavori alle torri, estrazione di pietre alle torri, carenza di spese di trasporto per materiale lapideo).

Se non si hanno dubbi sull'antichità della torretta, l'assenza del mulino nella cartografia del primo ottocento può generare incertezze sull'antichità della struttura. Il piano seminterrato detto 'carcerario', che conteneva l'ingranaggio, è coperto da volta a botte in tufo che si restringe in corrispondenza del corpo antistante. La presunta contemporaneità delle due volte realizzate in tufo, al di là dei restauri resi necessari dall'alluvione del 1861,[52] fa apparire probabile una più antica utilizzazione a mulino della parte bassa dell'edificio.

Inoltre se si esamina la muratura della rifolta triangolare questa è realizzata in blocchi di tufo simili a quelli del bel paramento murario, restaurata con l'aggiunta di speroni più tardi, quasi sicuramente ottocenteschi.

Il primo intervento del marchese si limiterebbe pertanto al restauro del paramento, del tetto e della rifolta, alla costruzione del ponte di legno, delle scale in muratura e dell'ingranaggio. Meno convincente appare l'ipotesi di una costruzione interamente ottocentesca dell'antistante corpo e del mulino, realizzato con una 'struttura a scheletro' di ottimo paramento e tamponamento a scheggioni. Avvalorando tale ipotesi si avrebbe una realizzazione ricca di suggestioni mediate da *revival* stilistici; le tecniche di costruzione nell'ottocento per edifici utilitaristici tuttavia non sembrano in genere presupporre simili e raffinati trattamenti del paramento. Il ruolo dell'architetto Poletti, a giudicare dalle registrazioni delle spese e dagli altri documenti d'archivio, si limiterebbe a rilevazioni dell'area e a una visita al cantiere soprattutto a lavori ultimati.[53]

L'ambigua descrizione del Coppi (1847: 30) che visita la zona attorno al 1814, meglio riferibile a Montegelato che non al possedimento della Maggiorana, menziona 'una antica torre sopra quel mulino' della Comunità tra ruderi di antiche fabbriche che erano visibili nella zona di Montegelato fino a qualche decennio fa. La presenza dell'antistante mulino diruto potrebbe giustificare del resto la somma di 10 scudi che il barone deve pagare alla Comunità dal momento dell'avvio dell'attività, per l'uso privativo che intende farne dopo il restauro intrapreso. Reinterpretando pertanto i dati a disposizione, il corpo antistante almeno e la rifolta sembrerebbero coevi e, per quanto detto, non anteriori alla fine del XII secolo.

L'atto del 1154 in cui la badessa Agnese del monastero di San Biagio di Nepi loca per tre generazioni a Gregorio de Senebaldo romano '*molendinum unum ante dirutum, sed a te voluntate nostra raedificatum in plano de Mazzano. Ipsum tibi, concedo cum rotalibus eius et omnibus suis utilitatibus, a tribus lateribus cuius Treia currit, a quarto est molaria antiqua; sic tamen ut liceat mihi meisque successimis domum ibi edificare et animalia quecumque abebimus ille habere ...*', sembra attestare l'esistenza di un vecchio mulino a Montegelato, ricordato un secolo prima e restaurato attorno al 1150 (Hartmann 1895–1901: v. III, p. 30, doc. 183). Il mulino quale appare oggi, con la retrostante torre, simile a quello della Maggiorana, sembra infine tipologicamente affine ad un gruppo di mulini romani 'a torre' (mola di San Sisto Vecchio e moletta dei Frangipane al Circo Massimo) risalenti alla prima metà del secolo XIII, ma molto rimaneggiati successivamente (Bianchi 1989).

---

[52] ASR, ADD, Cass. Azz. 61, pos. 123, n. 1: rapporto dell'agrimensore Luigi Sarmienti del 12 febbraio 1862 sui danni dell'alluvione dell'anno precedente. 'Caduta una parte della volta del Carcerario, è stato trasportato dall'acqua il ponticello di materiale, all'imboccatura del canale, al muro della mola apparisce qualche lesione, lo sperone esistente nell'angolo ove sorte l'acqua del ritricine, in parte è caduto, ed il restante scatenato, oltre altri danni di minore conto.'

[53] ASR, ADD, Cass. Azz. 59, n. 45: esiti dal 23 ottobre al 6 maggio 1831-32 'per spedizione con l'architetto'.

Chapter Four

THE FINDS

INTRODUCTION

The richness and variety of the artefact record will have become apparent in earlier pages. The finds do not, however, in the main derive from rubbish pits or middens of a sort commonly encountered on Roman sites in northern Europe. Rather, they come from dumps in features, especially the fish-pond, the north cistern and the rock-cut road. The late Roman limekiln also yielded important discoveries, while some Roman inscriptions and sculpture were incorporated into later buildings. Likewise, some of the Carolingian decorative stone elements were built into the remodelled church and baptistery of c. AD 1000, and survived the subsequent demolition. The graves also produced a few significant items, while the collapsed walls and roofs of the mid-sixth century contained a good deal of material, not least some well-preserved iron tools. Surprisingly, there were no signs of later scavenging in these deposits, very possibly a reflection of the sanctity of the site, at any rate from the late Roman period.

There were episodes of stratigraphical build-up (other than make-up levels), notably in the late Roman period. Moreover, discarded wasters and ash deposits from the early medieval kiln created extensive tips. However, the quantity of refuse was relatively small, a point underlined by the paucity of plant remains and, given the size of the excavated area, animal bones. The implication is that there was a system of rubbish disposal rather unlike that of, for example, Roman Britain, where objects usually proliferate in such layers.

Questions of this sort, concerning the deposition and survival of artefacts and other material, are of some importance. Monte Gelato appears at first sight somewhat unusual in its wealth of finds, but it must be stressed that the majority derives from dumps in a few contexts, rather than through casual loss. This does not account for the exceptional preservation of the objects, many of which are substantially complete, if found in fragments; but this does suggest that this was rubbish generated close to the place of deposition, and ought to relate to the lives of the occupants of the site.

THE INSCRIPTIONS,[54] by C.M. Gilliver

TEXTS AND COMMENTARY

1. [D   ]   M
    [   ]ME ET
    [   ]FAVST
    [CO^]NIVGI
    [   ]BENE
    [   ]TIBVS FE

Figs 132 and 133. A tombstone of the *D(is) M(anibus)* type. Letter size: 22-9 mm. Small Find no. (SF) 37. Reused as a support for the grave slab in burial 12.

It probably commemorates two people, as is shown by the plural ending in line 6, which with the end of line 5 may be restored as *bene merentibus*. The name of the builder would probably have been included in line 5 and since there is no space for the *tria nomina* of a citizen, Reynolds (1988: 284-5) has suggested that the builder may have been of low status, possibly a slave. The identity of the pair mentioned in lines 2 and 3, and the person to whom the tombstone was set up, is unknown.

2. [F]ACIVND[   ]
    [   ]VS•ET•HILA[R   ]

Fig. 134. An inscription on a fairly rough block of local nenfro, 0.285 m high, and broken at both ends. Letters: l1 - 90 mm; l2 - 72 mm. SF 165. Found in the late Roman limekiln.

The inscription is dated to the late Republic or early Empire by the simple letterforms, use of shading, and the content. The first line has been restored by Purcell (1988a: 285-6) as *faciendum curaverunt*, or a variation thereof, the plural form because of the two individuals mentioned in the second line. Purcell has restored the name of the second as Hilario in the light of inscription cat. 3, and suggested that the use of *cognomina* only indicates slave status or freedmen with a common *praenomen* and *nomen*. In the light of the other epigraphic evidence from the site, this argument is plausible. The inscription may record the dedication of some kind of public building by officers of a local temple or community, possibly a bridge over the Treia or a shrine. Purcell has suggested that the officials may be associated either with a *vicus* at Monte Gelato or with the settlement at Monte Caio to the north; but the interpretation of a *vicus* at Monte Gelato now seems less likely.

---

[54] No. 1 has been discussed previously by Reynolds (1988: 284-5) and nos. 2-5 by Purcell (1988a: 284-91). The complete text of no. 3 was first published by Gilliver (1990).

Fig. 132. Tombstone (inscription no. 1). *(KW)*

Fig. 133. Detail of inscription no. 1. *(KW)*

3. C•VALERIVS•C•L AESCIONIA• •L C•VALE-
   RIVS•C•L C•VALERIVS•C•L
   ZETVS [HI]LARA FAVSTVS HILARIO
   MERCATOR BOVARIVS MAG•AVG•VEIS

Figs 135 and 136. An inscription from a large tomb monument of fine-quality marble (cf. Claridge and Matthews,
below). The whole inscription is on thirteen fragments of

marble from a single slab that was originally 2.65 m long.
Above this was another block with four roundels and
sculpted heads of those commemorated (Claridge, this
volume, cat. 6). Letters: l1 - 65 mm; l2 - 45 mm; l3 - 28 mm.
The reading [Hi]lara is preferred to a shorter name, such
as [C]lara, on the grounds of spacing. The inscription may
be dated by letterforms and content to the early Imperial
period. From the late Roman limekiln.

The four individuals mentioned are all freed slaves (*liber-
tini*), and the monument as a whole is typical of those set
up by groups of freedmen and freedwomen in the late
Augustan and early Julio-Claudian period (cf. Kleiner 1977:
cat. nos. 20, 48, 78; Frenz 1985: cat. nos. 52, 135; Claridge,
this volume). The principal figure of the inscription is C.
Valerius Faustus, the freedman of a C. Valerius; and
[Hi]lara, whose patron was a woman of the *gens Aescionia*, is
possibly his wife. The inscription does not clarify the relationships between the individuals commemorated, though
the two other C. Valerii may be either *conlibertini* of Faustus
or, perhaps more likely, freedmen of Faustus himself.

Fig. 134. Inscription no. 2. *(KW)*

Faustus is described as being involved in the cattle trade, a fairly lucrative business,[55] and an official of the Imperial cult at Veii, 18 km to the south of Monte Gelato, probably at some time between *c.* 12 BC and AD 14.[56] The connection with Veii appears to be strengthened through the very rare *nomen* of the woman [Hi]lara. An Aescionius Capella was honoured under Augustus or Tiberius by the *municipes extramurani* and *Augustales* of Veii, and a link between the two Aescionii seems likely. Faustus therefore appears to have connections with Veii through the office he held and through the family of his wife's *patronus*. For further discussions of links between the site at Monte Gelato and Veii, see below.

4. [   ]IO FER[   ]
       DVLCISSIM[   ]
   [   ]ACHILL[   ]

Fig. 137. Inscription on three fragments of greyish white marble, possibly Proconnesian, with the remains of three lines, badly damaged in places by weathering. The letters of the first line cannot be established with certainty. Height of letters in two remaining lines: 72 mm. The letterforms suggest possibly a mid-first century AD date. SF 40, 92. Incorporated in later deposits in the baptistery.

The discovery of the third fragment of this inscription has proved Purcell's suggestion (1988a: 288-9) of the superlative form of *dulcis* in the second line, and the third refers to a name connected with the Greek ʼΑχιλλεύς. The inscription is clearly a funerary dedication, though it is not known whether Achill[was the deceased or the dedicator. The name is relatively common in Rome.

5. [   ]IS

Fig. 138. Inscription on a fragment of a strigillated sarcophagus in poor-quality coarse-crystalled greyish white marble, rapidly decomposing. SF 180. Incorporated into the structure of burial 2.

Only the letter S, 30 mm high, is visible on a smoothed panel, probably in the centre of one side. The previous letter may have been I. The sarcophagus probably dates to the late second or third century.

6. D [   ]
   V [   ]
   D [   ]

A roughly worked piece of volcanic tufo, with traces of a red painted text. B1. From the plough-soil over the church.

The D in line 1 is the only clearly visible letter and suggests that the inscription may have been a tombstone of the *D(is) M(anibus)* type. However, nothing further can be argued from the remaining fragments of text.

7. DIS   •   M
   HERENNIAE
   ]VIDI

Fig. 139. An inscription on a fairly rough block of local volcanic tufo with the first two lines and fragments of the third line surviving. (No number assigned.) Found built into the northwest corner of the baptistery, where it remains. Letters: l1 - 55 mm; l2 - 50 mm. A tombstone of the *Dis M(ani-*

[55] Cf. C. Caecilius Isidorus, also a freedman, who died in 8 BC, leaving 3,600 pairs of oxen, 257,000 other cattle and 60 million sesterces (Pliny, *Naturalis Historia* xxxiii. 135); Columella and Cato both stated that cattle farming was an extremely profitable enterprise (Columella, *De Re Rustica* vi. pref. 3-5; Cato, in Cicero, *De Officiis* ii. 89).

[56] Faustus is described as a *Magister Augustalis*, the only known holder of this office in Veii. All references to *Magistri Augustales* that can be dated are Augustan and they seem to have been replaced by the *Seviri Augustales* and *Augustales*. For the development of the different offices of the Imperial cult, see Taylor (1914).

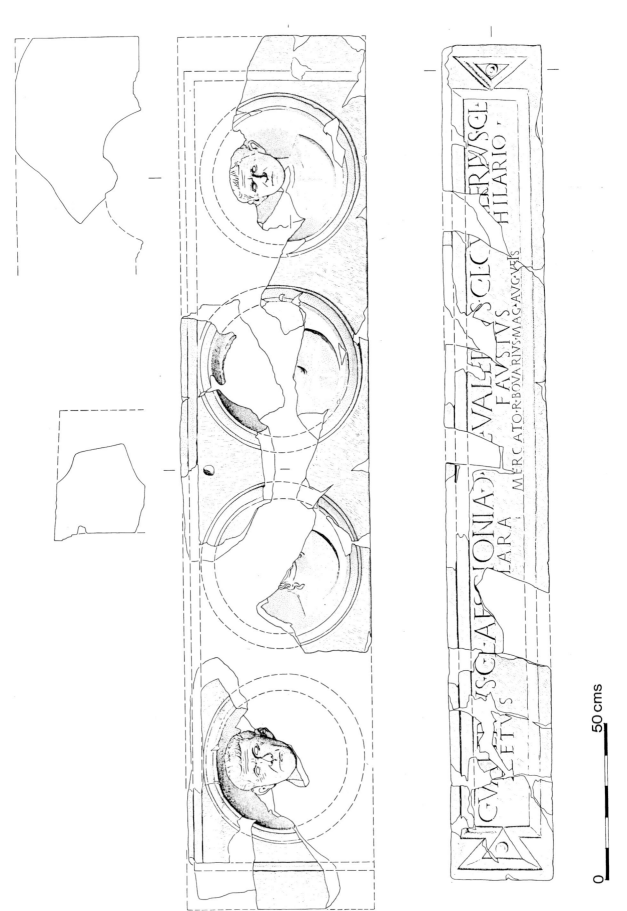

Fig. 135. The freed people tomb monument (inscription no. 3). (SA)

Fig. 137. Inscription no. 4. *(KW)*

bus) type, and the use of the word *Dis*, rather than its more usual abbreviation, *D*, suggests that the tombstone may be a fairly early example of this type. The letterforms and workmanship are also comparable to that of cat. 2 above, dated by Purcell (1988a: 286) to the early Imperial period.

The letters of the third line might be VIDI, possibly an Avidius or Helvidius, identifying the builder of the monument, perhaps the husband or son of the Herennia who is remembered. There would probably be room for a *praenomen* at the beginning of line 3, and a *cognomen* on line 4.

The workmanship is of low quality, shown by the poor letterforms, particularly the E and N in the middle of the name, and the letter spacing. This, together with the roughness of the block, suggests that the builder may have been of fairly low status.

The name Herennia is very common in both Rome and other towns in Italy, though particularly so around Tibur (for example, *CIL* XIV 3660, 3777, 4239). The tombstone of a Herennia Ianuaria was found at Casale Spezzamazze, between the Cassia and the Flaminia, but this probably

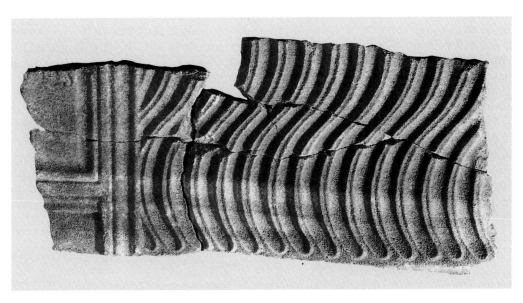

Fig. 138. Sarcophagus with inscription no. 5. *(KW)*

Fig. 139. The Herennia inscription (no. 6). *(KW)*

dates to the second century AD (Reynolds 1966: 56-67).[57] Reynolds noted that there may be a relationship between this woman and M. Herennius Picens, suffect consul of AD 1 and patron of the *municipium* of Veii (*CIL* XI 3797). In the light of the contents of cat. 3 above, a link between the Herennia of the Monte Gelato inscription and M. Herennius Picens seems quite possible. The dating of the inscription would certainly allow such a relationship with him or his family.

DISCUSSION

The original location of these inscriptions is by no means certain, and that of cat. 2 has been discussed elsewhere (Gilliver 1990: 195). Although it is conceivable that marble might have been brought into the site at Monte Gelato for reduction to lime, it seems unlikely that rough blocks of local stone such as cat. 1-2 and 6-7 would be brought in from a distance for building materials. A settlement is known to have existed at Monte Caio, a kilometre to the north of Monte Gelato, and it is possible that the inscriptions may have been set up there originally.[58] However, a road runs past the site at Monte Gelato and a mausoleum fronted on to it. This would certainly have been an appropriate place for the other funerary inscriptions, and this seems to be the most likely origin for them. Indeed, a Roman cemetery is now known some 200 m to the northwest (cf. Fig. 8).

The inscriptions dating to the early Imperial period, cat. 2, 3 and 7, are particularly interesting for a number of reasons. In the earlier publication of cat. 2 and 3, Purcell suggested (1988a: 291) that they might indicate a particular period of prosperity, and this is confirmed by the rich marble sculptures which are roughly contemporary.

Cat. 3 and 7 also suggest links between the settlement at Monte Gelato and the *municipium* of Veii, rather than the nearer *municipium* of Falerii. The cattle merchant, C. Valerius Faustus, was a member of the Imperial cult at Veii, whilst Aescionia, his wife (?), may well have been a freedwoman of the family of Aescionius Capella, a *duumvir* of the *municipium*. Cat. 7 also provides a possible link with the family of M. Herennius Picens, patron of Veii. The style of the large funerary monument, cat. 3, suggests links with the city of Rome, as does Faustus's involvement in the cattle trade. Veii is known to have had close links with the city, illustrated by the record of the *centumviri* of the *municipium* meeting in the Temple of Venus Genetrix in AD 26 (*CIL* XI 3805).

Unfortunately the inscriptions provide no clue as to the function of the site other than the possibility of local officials at work in cat. 2. The epigraphic record of the early Imperial period does, however, suggest the presence of persons of fairly low status, but probably linked with Veii and Rome through patronage and the cattle trade, and hints at the importance of the relationship between town and countryside at this time.

---

[57] A woman of the same name was joint dedicator of a tombstone to her husband Sulpicius Felix in Volsinii (*CIL* XI 2791), and a relationship between the two women is not impossible.

[58] For a tombstone of A. Petronius Urbanus from Monte Caio, see Tomassetti (1877: 263).

GRAFFITI (Fig. 140)[59]

Five buff-ware sherds with graffiti were recovered from the upper fill of the fish-pond. It is a context dating to the later second century AD and overlaid the deposit containing the 'stork-vase' with the long Greek inscription (below, Figs 239-42). The 'stork-vase' is an unusable waster, and must have been made on or near to the site. These graffiti are an additional pointer to the presence of Greek speakers at the Mola di Monte Gelato.

1. A small sherd with a deeply scored graffito.
   [...]ωκ[...]
   omega kappa
2. A sherd with a deeply scored graffito.
   ]A[
   alpha (or possibly LV[...])
3. Shoulder of a jar. The graffito may be read either as Greek or Latin.
   AL [...] or AI [...]
   In view of the context, R.S.O. Tomlin has suggested AI[ILIVS...], Ae[lius].
4. Small sherd from the shoulder of a small jar, apparently with one name written over another, possibly with some scratching out.
   [...] VFANI\[...]
5. Rim and shoulder of a jar.
   [...]ΕΙΑΣΥ[...]

MARBLE SCULPTURE, OBJECTS AND VENEER OF THE ROMAN PERIOD, by Amanda Claridge

1. **Statuette of Venus** (Fig. 141)
   Marble: medium-coarse crystalled translucent white.
   Dimensions: maximum preserved height, 0.404 m; width across shoulders 0.26 m; across nipples 0.14 m.
   Site ref.: MG89, L157, SF 529.
   Find-spot: from a rubble layer in the corridor south of the fish-pond, phase 3 (AD 350-550).

   The statuette was about two-thirds life-size. Only the upper torso as far as the navel survives. The head has broken away at the base of the neck, the left arm at the shoulder, the right arm just below the shoulder. The head originally turned slightly to the proper left. Two twisted locks of hair fell to the shoulders on either side. The right arm was bent at the elbow and crossed the chest just below the right breast, with the fingers of the hand extended to mask the lower half of the left breast. The stump of a strut of marble which once connected the forearm to the body, the tips of the third and fourth fingers and a trace of the thumb, are preserved. The left arm reached downwards over the left hip (where the scar of a connecting strut indicates its position). The weight of the body was apparently posed on the left leg.

   The basic elements are those of the well-known Capitoline Venus type (Rome, Musei Capitolini inv. no. 409; LIMC 11, 1-2: 52, no. 409). However, the nature of the fracture across the abdomen suggests that the lower half of the Monte Gelato statuette was draped, in one of the variations on the Capitoline Venus theme (Di Vita 1955: 17 and 23, no. 24, pl. 10,2). Completely nude Venuses have usually fractured at or near the knees rather than higher up the body.

   The workmanship is very good; all surfaces are carefully finished, the flesh smoothed with abrasives. The carving of the two twists of hair on the shoulders was pursued somewhat further on the left than on the right (an indication perhaps of the intended principal view): the channel between the locks on the left was deepened and the locks themselves set off from the flesh with the aid of a fine drill (diameter 2.5 mm) working a series of near vertical holes, subsequently trimmed and modified with a fine flat chisel. On the right, the detail remained as first drafted with the chisel.

2. **Statuette of a reclining nymph** (Fig. 142)
   Marble: fine crystalled, highly translucent, yellowish white, possibly Dokimeion.[60]
   Dimensions: maximum preserved length 0.705 m; height 0.195 m.
   Site ref.: MG 87, D76, SF 68.
   Find-spot: laid upside-down in a late Roman floor.

   The fragment comprises part of a two-thirds life-size reclining female figure, with a mantle draped over her hips and legs, arranged in elaborate folds around the bent left knee. With the exception of the tips of the first three toes of the right foot, both feet are intact. The carving is excellent, the use of the drill to deepen the folds and to emphasize surface detail on the folds being subsequently carefully pursued with fine flat chisel-work. All carved surfaces were smoothed to a light polish with rasps and abrasives.

   The figure type, presumably a nymph, is one much used for fountain figures in Rome and the West during the first three centuries AD (Kapossy 1969: 18), and compares particularly closely with an example in Copenhagen (Poulsen 1914: no. 400a, pl. VI), in the pose, in the arrangement of the drapery, and in dimensions.

   The underside of the figure presents an oblique, sawn surface with a dowel hole at the upper end (probably the cause of the fracture at this point). The area around the dowel hole has been lightly roughened with a pointed chisel. In other words, the surface seems to have been prepared for attachment to another block of marble, not simply the result of cutting up the sculpture for reuse in the floor in which it was found. If the figure was originally made in two (or more) pieces of marble, that would suggest a relatively early date, sometime before the end of the first century AD, when high-quality marble was apparently in short supply (Claridge 1988b). The style and workmanship are also indicative of the early Empire.

3. **Fragment of a small male head** (Fig. 143)
   Marble: medium crystalled white, degraded.
   Dimensions: maximum preserved height 0.145 m; width of eye 24 mm.
   Site ref.: MG90, M74, SF 683.

---

[59] I am most grateful to M.W.C. Hassall and R.S.O. Tomlin for their comments on photographs of these sherds (TWP).

[60] Analysis by Keith Matthews (British Museum Research Laboratory) indicated that it could be Proconnesian, Carrara or Dokimeion (see below).

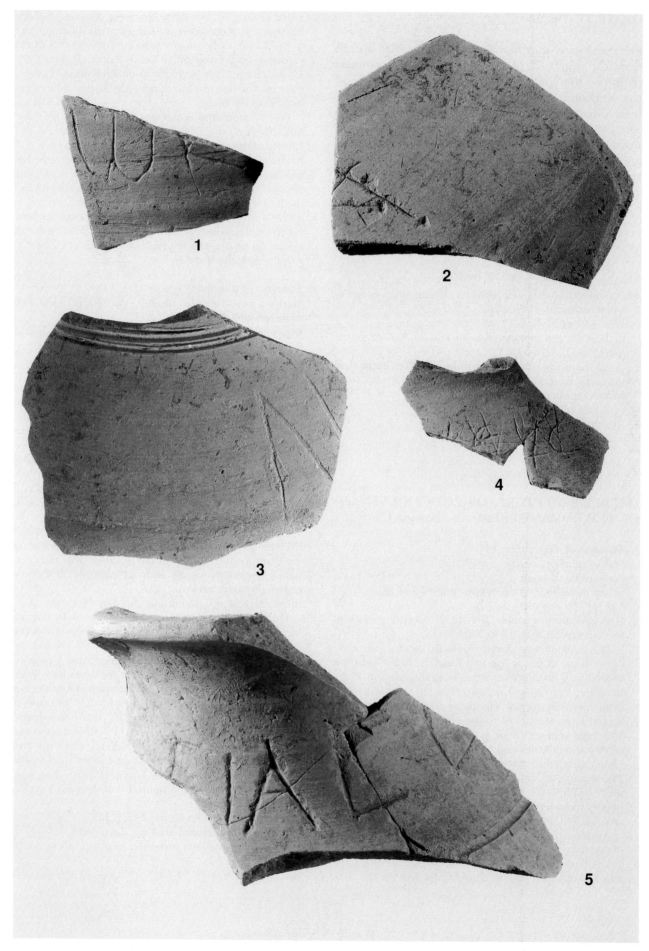

Fig. 140. Graffiti (1:1). *(KW)*

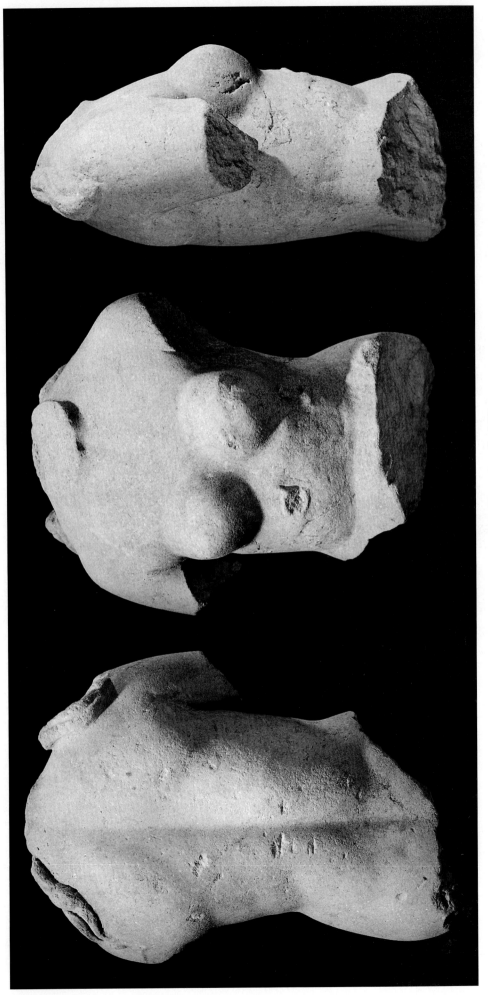

Fig. 141. Venus (cat. 1). *(KW)*

Fig. 142. Reclining nymph (cat. 2). *(KW)*

Find-spot: silty layer above Roman road, phase 5/6 (late ninth century +).

Battered and water-worn, the fragment consists of an oblique section of the upper left side of a head, including the left eye, about two-thirds lifesize. The hair is the only distinguishing feature, with long straggling curls over the brow and to the side, covering the ear. The curls extend only a short distance back from the face; behind, the narrower shape of the skull appears almost smooth. There is no sign of a fillet at the point where the curls end; it is possible that the smoothness indicates a Phrygian cap.

The head belongs to that indefinable category of idealized youth which sometimes denotes Apollo, Eros, the young Dionysos, or Narcissus, a Genius, Lar or an Ephebe. A Phrygian cap would suit Ganymede.

4. **Fragment of a large marble basin (*labrum*)** (Figs 144 and 145)

Marble: fine crystalled translucent white.

Dimensions: height 0.225 m; greatest preserved width 0.54 m.

Site ref.: MG89, L105, SF 533.

Find-spot: upper fill of fish-pond (later second century AD).

The original upper outer diameter of the basin was about 1.04 m. (3½ Roman feet). The edge of the rim was decorated with an egg-and-dart motif; the top of the rim bore a band of beads in high relief. The inside of the basin was plain and smoothly polished. The outside bore a whirling pattern of fluting, the flutes alternately convex (cabled) and concave in profile, terminating in hemispheres outlined with *tondini* and interspaced with darts. In the middle of the underside is a flat circular surface, dressed with a fine claw chisel, where the basin will have been mounted on a supporting pedestal.

Two fragmentary basins from the villa at Chiragan in southwest France had the same whirling pattern of fluting (but not cabled), and appear to have been the same size and shape (Joulin 1901: 85-6, pl. VII, nos. 81 and 82).[61] A basin in the Naples Museum, reputedly found at Pompeii (*Museo Borbonico*, III: pl. XLV), compares closely in size, shape and general type of decoration (its fluting is straight). It has two handles. A larger one, without handles and in *pavonazzetto* marble, was found near Rome in the 1790s (Amelung 1908: 30-1, no. 9, pl. 3). Such

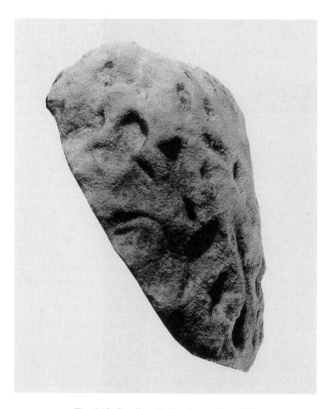

Fig. 143. Small male head (cat. 3). *(KW)*

---

[61] From the 1826-30 excavations Joulin gave their diameter as 1.0 m and described the marble as grey '*bleu turquin*' from Italy. The shapes are difficult to determine from the photographs.

Fig. 144. Marble *labrum* (cat. 4). *(KW)*

basins could serve various functions, but are especially associated with the *caldaria* of bath-houses (Daremberg and Saglio 1877-1919: *s.v. Labrum*).

5. **Neck of a small marble crater** (Fig. 146)
Marble: fine crystalled white with faint grey flecks.
Dimensions: diameter (outer edge of rim) 0.34 m; maximum preserved height 0.225 m.
Site ref.: MG 89, L105, SF 547.
Find-spot: upper fill of fish-pond (later second century AD).

Recomposed from fifteen fragments, the neck is almost complete. The profile and proportions are those of a crater, broken at the point where the swelling of the bowl commenced.[62] Since the hollowing of the interior was almost vertical, the walls became extraordinarily thin towards the bottom (less than 50 mm in places). The start of a change in profile is just visible on the inside. On the outside, the stump of a tiny strut of marble presupposes a small loop handle parallel with the wall of the vase, of which there would have been two, springing from the bowl below. The missing bowl may have been decorated, but otherwise the vase was plain, with a simple rim and a highly polished surface. Its size and weight would permit a relatively tall and slender pedestal, perhaps like that on the vase from the peristyle of the Villa of San Marco at Stabiae (Fig. 147) (Jashemski 1979: 331, fig. 530).

6. **The relief from the tomb of the Valerii** (Figs 135, 136, 148, 149)
Marble: fine crystalled translucent off-white with faint grey patches. Stable isotope analysis (Matthews, below) indicates either Carrara or Dokimeion; visual appearance favours Carrara.
Overall dimensions: height 0.62 m; width *c.* 2.8 m; depth front to back 0.42 m. Tondi: outer diameter 0.52 m; width of frame 0.4 m; distance between centres of tondi 0.62 m. Heads: chin to top of brow – (Zetus) 0.18 m; (Hilario) 0.15 m.

Site refs: MG 87, C59, SF 135, 147 (Zetus), 151, 163; MG 88, C62, SF 17 (Hilario).
Find-spot: limekiln, fourth century AD.

Four individuals were represented by their portrait busts in high relief, each set off against a plain concave background within a circular frame, which is ornamented with a shallow convex moulding between two fillets. The surrounding field is dressed with a fine claw-chisel (five teeth, 13 mm wide). The whole was enclosed by an outer rectangular frame of single cyma recta moulding. The back of the block was left rough, worked with a pick-hammer; the underside was dressed flat with a medium claw (five teeth, 24 mm) and subsequently roughened with a pick, presumably to provide a key for cement. There are no clamps or dowel holes on any surviving part of the block. It is thus unlikely to have been placed directly on top of another block, which means that if, as seems reasonable to suppose, it and the inscription block found with it (Gilliver, this volume, cat. 3) belong together, set into the façade of a tomb, then a brick or masonry cornice probably ran between them.

According to the inscription, the two portrait heads which survive are those of C. Valerius Zetus, at the far left, and C. Valerius Hilario, to the far right. Zetus's head (Fig. 148) shows a middle-aged man with a hooked nose and jutting chin. Heavy lines furrow his forehead and deeply scored crow's-feet radiate from the outer corners of his eyes. The eyes are rather roughly cut, with upper and lower lids of equal weight, the upper overlapping the lower at the outer corner. The eyeball is flattened in the area of the pupil and the tear duct is marked with a small drill hole (diameter 2 mm). That the left eye is distinctly higher than the right is presumably an error on the part of the sculptor. The hair is shaped as a cap of short locks hugging the temples and rendered with shallow slightly curving grooves, using the edge of a flat chisel. The flesh surfaces are smoothed with abrasives.

Hilario's head (Fig. 149) is smaller and more finely featured but very similar in other respects, sharing the wrinkles, crow's-feet and profile (the chin especially). The

---

[62] Compare the profile drawings in Grassinger (1991).

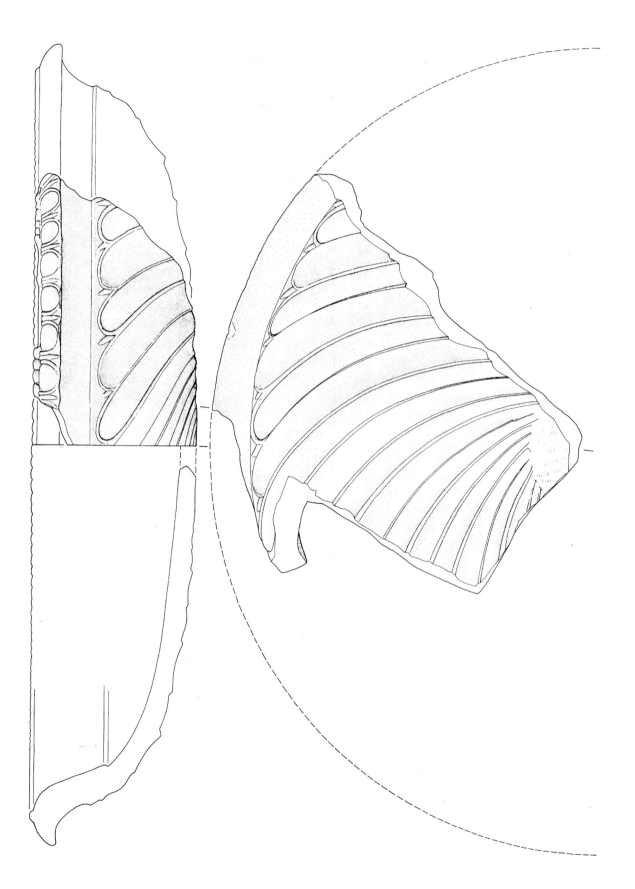

Fig. 145. Marble *labrum* (1:5). (SA)

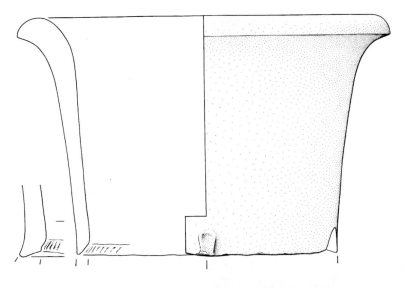

Fig. 146. Marble crater (cat. 5) (1:3). *(KW/SC)*

hair, worked with a fine flat chisel (4 mm wide), following a slightly bull-nosed chisel (8-9 mm wide), is only fully finished on the proper left side and over the brow, where it has a faint parting. Of the ears, the left is well worked, the right remains rough; the mouth and nostrils are chisel cut; the eyes have faint drill holes in their inner corners, the left one more strongly marked. There are possible traces of a rasp on the right cheek; for the rest the flesh is smoothed with abrasive.

The technique and the moderately 'Republican' portrait style, with its serious, rather down-at-mouth expression, close-cropped hair and sharply lined features, find numerous parallels among the freedmen grave reliefs of Rome, dating variously from the early Augustan to the Claudian period.[63] The size and shape of the male busts

and what little remains of Aescionia [Hi]lara's bust (centre left) are characteristically Tiberian or early Claudian. The loose corkscrew curls beside [Hi]lara's neck most closely resemble those found on portraits of Agrippina Major and Minor and some private individuals, probably dating from around AD 20-40 (for examples, see Zanker and Fittschen (1983: 5-6, no. 4, pls 4-5, Beilage 1-2, 3c-d) and Poulsen (1962: no. 35, pl. LV; no. 74, pl. CXXIX; no. 75, pl. CXXXI).[64]

The particular design of the relief as a whole has no precise equivalent among the reliefs from Rome but, like its sole companion from South Etruria (the monument of the Gessi found on the Via Cassia near Viterbo (Comstock and Vermeule 1976: 201, no. 319; Frenz 1985: 86, no. 14; Kockel 1993; J 1, pl. 68)), it was probably pro-

---

[63] Compare Kockel (1993), examples in Group I 4-6, I 12 (pls 63-5) and J 4 (pl. 71) early Augustan; L 5 (pl. 91a) mid-Augustan; L 8 (pl. 95a) mid-late Augustan; L 18 (pl. 102 c-d), L 23 (pl. 108) Tiberian?; M 5 (pl. 116 c-d, 117) Tiberian-Claudian.

[64] The comparison with portraits of Poppaea and consequently later dating which I allowed for in the preliminary report (Claridge 1988b: 294) was, on further reflection, not justified.

Fig. 147. Marble vase from Villa San Marco, Stabiae. *(AC)*

shell and the outer frame shaped as a wreath of laurel or oak, with rosettes or more extensive floral ornament in the spandrels; some are further embellished by being set within an architectural framework or held by erotes. The comparative simplicity of the Mola di Monte Gelato design could have been merely a measure of economy (less decoration naturally costing less to carve), but, even if only by default, it also gives a stronger impression of a series of portraits on shields hanging on a wall – the genuine *clipeatae imagines* of contemporary honorary, votive and aristocratic Roman funerary practice.[66]

7. The marble veneer

Four hundred and seventy-one loose fragments of marble revetment were retrieved from the excavations, scattered in 80 contexts, ranging in date from the late second century AD to the medieval period.

The largest single group (124 pieces) came from the upper fill of the fish-pond, L105, deposited in the later second century, and very possibly deriving from the nearby bath-house. The group consisted mainly of variegated grey/white marble mottled and veined with dark grey and black (*bardiglio fiorito*) from Carrara (ancient Luna), sawn into relatively thin slabs (6-13 mm), probably from floors or low vertical surfaces (such as dados or risers on steps); a smaller quantity of a paler *bardiglio* in rather thicker slabs (12-23 mm), some with rounded edges, which suggests the veneer of steps or ledges (for example, of pools); and seven fragments of plain greyish white Carrara of a thickness (50-3 mm) suitable for thresholds. There was also a piece of flat moulding which could come from a door-frame; six pieces of dark red limestone (*rosso antico*) quarter-round strip moulding; and three recognizable elements of an *opus sectile* panel or floor, their measurements compatible with each other: a rectangle (0.13 × >0.2 m) and an isosceles triangle (0.125 × 0.18 m) in the variegated grey/pink/flesh-red marble '*portasanta*' (from the island of Chios), and an isosceles triangle (0.09 × 0.125 m) in the black/white/red breccia *africano* (from Teos, western Turkey).

A predominance of monochrome greys and whites and a dearth of coloured marbles also characterize the rest of the finds, many of which could be further residue from the same source(s) as those represented in the fill of the fish-pond. In addition to quantities of thin *bardiglio* veneer and other Carrara veined and plain monochromes, and some thicker fragments in medium crystalled greyish white and white banded-with-grey of Proconnesian (Marmara) type and perhaps other eastern mediterranean marbles, the north cistern (also filled by *c.* AD 200), and the large room (A) and adjoining corridor, yielded several sizeable pieces of the green-and-white variegated *cipollino* (from Euboea) and fragments of a flesh-pink and white limestone breccia, apparently *breccia corallina* (from Bilecik, Turkey).

duced by a workshop in the city. As a type, not many Roman freedmen chose to have their portraits set in tondi and no two designs are alike. Kockel has catalogued eight, which he has dated from the early Augustan (20s BC) to the early Claudian period.[65] All are far more richly decorated – and more overtly funerary in character – than the Mola di Monte Gelato one, most having the field within the tondo fluted like a scallop

---

[65] (a) Boston, Museum of Fine Arts 1972.918. Comstock and Vermeule 1976: 205, no. 325; Kockel 1993: K4, 169, pl. 18b. Mid-late Augustan. (b) London, British Museum, Sc. 2275. Relief of the Antistii. Kockel 1993: 178, L 4, pl. 90B, 93d-e; Kleiner 1977: 207, no. 20; Frenz 1977: 178-9, no. J 5. (c) London, British Museum, acc. no. 1914.6-24.4. Kockel 1993: 203, M 9, pl. 118d; Walker 1985: 53-4, fig. 44. (d) Rome, Museo Nuovo, Palazzo dei Conservatori no. 2306. Kockel 1993: 164, J 16, pl. 78a. (e) Rome, Museo Nuovo, Palazzo dei Conservatori no. 2230. Relief of the Bennii. Three tondi in architectural frame. Kockel 1993: 191, L 21, pl. 106a-c, 107a-b. (f) Rome, Museo delle Terme, no inventory number (*MNR* I/7 part 2, 288-9, ix.49). Kockel 1993: 224, O 39, pl. 133e. (g) Formerly Lowther Castle. Kockel 1993: 216, O 5, pl. 128d. Tiberian or later. (h) Rome, Art market (in 1978). Kockel 1993: 231, O 72, pl. 138d.

The type occasionally recurs (for example, Dresden, Albertinum Hn 379 (Kockel 1993: 202, M 7, pl. 118c), Flavian or Trajanic). One other example, in the garden of the Palazzo Colonna in Rome (Kockel 1993: 170, K 5, pl. 85a), is a half-figure in a tondo, like the later medallion portraits on grave altars and sarcophagi. For further discussion, see Kockel (1993: 14 and 55).

[66] Winkes (1969) remains the standard work, but see also Vermeule (1965), Neumann (1988) and Smith (1990: 131).

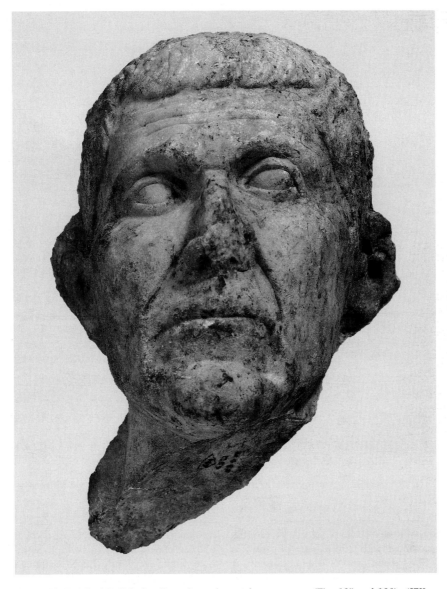

Fig. 148. Head of C. Valerius Zetus from the tomb monument (Figs 135 and 136). *(KW)*

STABLE ISOTOPE ANALYSIS OF THE MARBLE, by Keith Matthews[67]

Samples were submitted in 1987 from the heads of C. Valerius Zetus and Aescionia [Hi]lara from the tomb monument (cat. 6, above; it was not realized at the time that they belonged to a single monument). A sample from the nymph (cat. 2) was also provided. The marble of the tomb monument was described as being fine crystals, translucent and of a creamy white colour; this led to the suggestion that it may have been Pentelic. The marble used for the nymph was described as being fine crystalline, highly translucent, and of a yellowish white colour: it was suggested that the source may have been the Dokimeion quarries in Asia Minor.

EXPERIMENTAL PROCEDURE

The experimental procedure is based on the work of McCrea (1950), although it was not applied to the provenancing of classical white marble until the early 1970s (see for example, Craig and Craig (1972); Coleman and Walker (1979)).

The samples were supplied in the form of powder that had been obtained by drilling the sculptures. The sampling was undertaken by Amanda Claridge, then of the British School at Rome, following sampling instructions provided

[67] I am indebted to Professor Norman Herz of the University of Georgia, USA, for making his database of marble quarry analyses available. Also, thanks are due to Dr T.W. Potter for providing much detailed information about the history attached to these pieces, and to Amanda Claridge for the physical descriptions of the sculptures themselves and for taking the samples. Dr Susan Walker of the Department of Greek and Roman Antiquities of the British Museum has also provided much useful advice and information.

Fig. 149. Head of C. Valerius Hilario from the tomb monument (Figs 135 and 136). *(KW)*

by the British Museum Research Laboratory. From this powder, 10 mg was reacted with 100% orthophosphoric acid under vacuum. The carbon dioxide thus obtained was isotopically analysed using a VG micromass 602D mass-spectrometer. The isotopic ratio (δ) obtained is given in parts per mil (‰, that is, per thousand) relative to the PDB standard (Craig 1957), where

$$\delta = \frac{(Rsample - Rpdb) \times 1000\ ‰}{Rpdb}$$

and R= 13C/12C pr 180/160. The standard error on these measurements is typically $\pm$ 0.05 ‰.

RESULTS

The results are given in Table 51 and are also plotted graphically (Fig. 150) as the carbon isotope ratio δ 13C versus the oxygen isotope ratio δ 180. Also on the plot are the 90% ellipses (Leese 1988) of isotopic signatures obtained from quarry data very kindly made available by Professor Norman Herz of the University of Georgia, and supplemented by Carrara data from quarry samples measured by the British Museum Research Laboratory. The ellipses selected include those for some of the more important marble quarrying areas in antiquity, and for which data, albeit limited, are available.

The results (1 and 2) of the tomb monument can be seen to fall within the ellipses of Dokimeion and Carrara. It was suggested from the visual appearance of the marble that the Pentelic quarries were a possible source, but clearly this is not the case. However, it would seem to be difficult to resolve the origins further at this stage, and perhaps use of an alternative analytical technique such as NAA (see, for example, Mello, Monna and Oddone (1988)) might resolve the issue. On balance, the marble is more likely to be from Carrara, but this cannot be said to be certain.

Table 51. Isotopic analysis of the marble.

no.	description	reference no.	BMRL no.	δ 13 C ‰	δ 180 ‰
1	Head of Zetus	C59, SF 147	30786T	1.84	-2.62
2	Head of Aescionia	C59, SF 151	30787R	1.92	-2.53
3	Nymph	D76, SF 68	30785V	2.27	-2.27

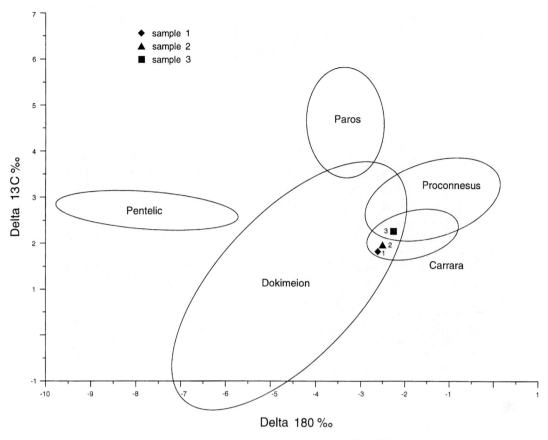

Fig. 150. Stable isotope analysis of the marble. *(KM)*

From the analysis of the sample from the nymph (3) it can be seen from the result that three different sources for the marble are indicated: Proconnesus, Carrara, and Dokimeion. It was suggested from the physical appearance that Dokimeion was the likely source: however, in view of the inconclusive nature of the isotopic result, further study is indicated, as suggested above.

THE EARLY MEDIEVAL SCULPTURE, by John Osborne

In early medieval Italy there were considerably fewer contexts in which sculpture could be employed than there had been in classical Antiquity. Virtually all the patronage of work in the medium of stone was commissioned either by or for the Christian Church, and in the pre-Romanesque period the possibilities for such activity were limited almost exclusively to the categories of church fixtures and furnishings: capitals and bases, choir and chancel screens, ciboria, altars, pulpits, tomb slabs and sarcophagi. This development had already taken place in late Antiquity, and from the first half of the sixth century there are splendid examples of the carver's art which survive in churches in Rome, Ravenna, Constantinople and elsewhere.

Another significant outburst of activity took place in the Italian peninsula and on the Dalmatian littoral during the period from roughly the mid-eighth to the mid-ninth centuries. Although initiated under the Lombard monarchy, the phenomenon reached a peak during the reigns of Charlemagne and his immediate successors, and its comparative longevity is without question a direct consequence of the substantially increased wealth enjoyed by ecclesiastical institutions during the so-called Carolingian 'renaissance'. The sculpture which has survived from this period reveals its own very particular repertory of designs and motifs, very different from those of the age of the emperor Justinian. Patterns are primarily abstract and based on either geometric or vegetal forms, with the substantial use of interlaced and plaited designs, coupled with circles, spirals, rosettes, lilies, vines, crosses, and a wide variety of other ornamental devices, all of which may be found in abundance throughout the northern and central regions of the Italian peninsula as well as on the eastern shore of the Adriatic. While some of these motifs have their origins in earlier ecclesiastical sculpture, many reveal the substantial influence of a more general decorative vocabulary which has its roots in the arts of late Antiquity, for example in the designs of mosaic floor pavements, while others suggest links with the ornament to be found in contemporary manuscript illumination. The repertory of designs clearly transcended the specific medium employed. Animal figures are rare, and for the most part limited to creatures with a long tradition of symbolic significance in Christian art, for example peacocks or lambs; and human figures are rarer still. Although the quantity of sculpture that survives from the Carolingian period is vast, very little can be dated precisely, and the mechanics of the transmission of designs have yet to be understood. For example, no convincing answer has yet been found to explain how the same repertory of patterns could be used with such regularity at sites as widely separated as Aquileia and Rome, or Pavia and Split. Indeed, the question of the origins of the apparently widespread revival of sculpture in the Carolingian period, the sources of the individual designs, and the possible influences of Lombard art or that of contemporary Byzantium, are issues that continue to generate considerable debate (see for example the studies of Haseloff (1930), Kautzsch (1939), Verzone (1945), van Essen (1957), and Romanini (1971; 1991)).

Most of the decorated early medieval pieces uncovered during the Mola di Monte Gelato excavation can be loosely assigned to a date *circa* AD 800, based on the specific designs employed for the relief decoration: plaited ribbons, interlocking rings, circles interlinked with lozenges, and so on. These all have good parallels in Rome and other parts of Italy from the time of the Carolingian revival. The technique used in the carving is also characteristic of the period: triangular or 'V'-shaped cuts, usually described by the German term *Kerbschnitt*. Both a point and a chisel were employed, thus revealing, as elsewhere, a remarkable degree of continuity with the tools and practices employed in late Antiquity (cf. discussions of Ward-Perkins (1971) and Macchiarella (1976)).

Almost all the pieces were found divorced from their original context, many having been later re-

Fig. 151. The altar (?) screen (1:3). *(SA)*

Fig. 152. The altar (?) screen. *(KW)*

deployed in the construction of new floors or walls, and consequently the exact purposes for which they were originally produced can only be guessed at. Many, however, display pegs or grooves which reveal that they had been intended to be fitted together with others, as part of larger constructions. It seems evident that the small church on the site could, in the first half of the ninth century, boast of a substantial chancel screen in addition to other items of church furnishings, many of them made of reused marble. Nor were these poor cousins to their counterparts in the more important and no doubt wealthier basilicas of Rome itself. The quality of the carving is easily the equal of that found elsewhere, and in one instance perhaps even grander. The fragment with the lamb and cross, which possibly served as an altar frontal (cat. 1), may be regarded as a true masterpiece of the age. It has few equals, and its discovery here says much about the economic power and status of the *domus-cultae*.

CATALOGUE

1. **Fragment of an altar frontal (?) with the 'Agnus Dei'** (Figs 151 and 152)

Site ref.: B13, SF 175; found built into burial 2 (cf. Fig. 96). Marble. 0.47 × 0.32 × 0.08 m.

The fragment constitutes the lower left corner of a large and probably square panel with an elaborate decoration in carved relief. In a central medallion are the hindquarters, feet and tail of a lamb, shown standing in front of a large Latin cross. There is a small socket at its centre. It is not clear whether the cross stands on an elevated base, or, as seems more likely, it is held in the lamb's raised foreleg. Inscribed as if hanging from the left transverse arm of the cross is the Greek letter *alpha*, presumably once balanced by an *omega* on the right, now lost. The central medallion is itself framed by a concentric outer ring decorated with a plaited ribbon design. In the lower corner of the panel, outside the ring, there is a rosette with seven petals.

The piece is of particular interest for its iconography. The image of the cross with pendant letters *alpha* and *omega* has its origins in early Christian art, and is ultimately derived from passages in the Book of Revelation which refer to Christ in this cryptic fashion (Book of Revelation 1.8, 21.6, 22.13). Its use carried on into the Middle Ages in a variety of media, including sculpture: for example the seventh- or eighth-century panels in the church of San Leonardo at Aquilea, near Lucca (*CSA* I: no. 1), and the cathedral at Amelia (*CSA* XII: no. 1). The concept of Christ as the sacrificial lamb of God ('Agnus Dei') may similarly be found throughout the New Testament and subsequent patristic literature, based on the words spoken by John the Baptist upon first seeing Jesus (John 1.29 '*Ecce agnus Dei, ecce qui tollit peccatum mundi*') and the subsequent vision of the apocalyptic lamb in the Book of Revelation. Lambs representing Christ, the apostles, and indeed Christians in general, were again a popular image in the visual arts from the earliest centuries of the faith, and one or more lambs holding crosses in their foreleg are not uncommon in early medieval Italian sculpture: for example, a seventh-century tombstone from San Vincenzo at Galliano (Cassanelli 1987: fig. 284), an eighth-century sarcophagus in Sant'Apollinare in Classe at Ravenna (*Corpus Ravenna* II: no. 59), and other eighth-century panels in Santa Maria Assunta at Gussago (*CSA* III: no. 201) and at Cividale (*CSA* X: nos. 340 and 353). In Rome itself, lambs bearing crosses appear on a plaque now in the Palazzo Senatorio on the Capitoline (*CSA* VII: no. 32) and the problematic reliquary altar in the church of Santa Maria del Priorato on the Aventine (*CSA* VII: 4 no. 33).

However, the combination of the two elements – the upright cross with apocalyptic letters, and the single lamb, or 'Agnus Dei', standing in front – is highly unusual, and seemingly without parallel in Italian sculpture of the Carolingian era. There are, however, related images which have survived in other media, for example a group of triumphal arch mosaics in Roman churches, in which the lamb and the cross are placed on a throne set between seven large candlesticks, following the text of the Book of Revelation. This occurs in the sixth-century church of Santi Cosma e Damiano and again, perhaps more significantly, on the triumphal arch of Santa Prassede, a project of Pope Paschal I (817-24). The issue is complicated by the fact that the depiction of Christ in the form of a lamb had been specifically prohibited in the years just prior to the onset of iconoclasm: by the 82nd canon of the Quinisext Council, held in Constantinople in 692 (for the text see Mango (1972: 139-40)). Although there had initially been strong Roman reaction against this decision, prompting Pope Sergius I to incorporate John the Baptist's words into the text of the mass (*Liber Pontificalis* I, 376), the image does disappear from Roman art throughout the course of the eighth century (see discussions of Nordhagen (1976: 165-6) and Davis-Weyer and Emerick (1984: 27-8)). If Nordhagen and Davis-Weyer and Emerick are correct in linking the revival of Agnus Dei imagery in Rome with the pontificate of Paschal I, then this may provide an important chronological indication for the production of the Mola di Monte Gelato relief. It seems likely that such an image would have occupied a position of importance in the decorations of the church, perhaps as an embellishment for the front of the altar, for which it would be both theologically and liturgically appropriate.

Also worthy of note is the small hole terminating the spiral form made by the lamb's tail. This rather unusual

occurrence has a precise parallel in another piece from the site (cat. 7), presumably a product of the same sculptor or workshop.

2. **Fragment of a pilaster supporting an octagonal colonnette (probably from a chancel screen or iconostasis)** (Figs 153 and 154)
Site ref.: D29, SF 53; found built into the wall dividing the church from the baptistery (cf. Fig. 74). Marble (in two pieces). Pilaster: $0.36 \times 0.26 \times 0.14$ m. Colonnette: 0.2×0.13 m (diameter).

The principal face or front of the pilaster is decorated with one of the most characteristic and widely diffused designs from the period of the eighth and ninth centuries: two ribbons, each with two furrows or grooves, are arranged in a pattern of interlocking circles and diamond-shaped lozenges. (For the pattern, see discussions by Verzone (1945: 176-8 ('*cerchi intrecciati a rombi*'); and in *CSA* II: 17 ('*nastri bisolcati che formano cerchi annodati e intrecciati a losanghe*').) Excellent parallels may be found throughout the Italian peninsula: for example at Ventimiglia, Pavia, Venice, and Aquileia in the north (Verzone 1945: pl. lxii no. 105; Peroni 1975: no. 125; Kutzli 1974: pl. 2; *CSA* X: nos. 194, 275, 294), and closer at hand in pieces from Santa Maria Maggiore at Tuscania (*CSA* VIII: no. 366), San Saba in Rome (*CSA* VII: 4, no. 144c), and the abbey of San Pietro in Valle at Ferentillo (*CSA* II: nos. 29, 32-9).

The narrower side face bears the simple design of a single plaited ribbon set within a recessed field. Of the two carved faces, this is the less worn, with the result that the sharp triangular cuts (*Kerbschnitt*) of the two grooves in the ribbon are well-preserved. Once again, the design itself was widely popular, with good parallels in all regions, including Rome, where it appears for example on the portal of the San Zeno chapel in the church of Santa Prassede (*CSA* VII: 1, no. 90). A rather useful comparison may also be made to the ninth-century pilaster from San Pietro in Valle at Ferentillo, which similarly has the design of circles and lozenges on its main face (*CSA* II: no. 29).

In the smoothed but undecorated back face of the pilaster there is a vertical groove (width 50 mm, depth 20 mm) for the attachment of the adjoining section of the screen. A slightly larger groove in the left side (width 60 mm, depth 25 mm) similarly reveals where the adjoining section was inserted, and confirms that the pilaster was positioned at a corner. A small hole and shallow groove in the top suggest that something once was inserted in this face as well.

Screens of this type appear to have been widely popular in Rome in the early Middle Ages. An excellent and well-preserved example, probably still in its original configuration, survives to the north of the city, not far from Monte Gelato, in the church of San Leone at Capena (Matthiae 1952; *CSA* VIII: no. 180). Although the specific designs of the Capena iconostasis are different from those in question here, it is worth noting that the arch over the central opening is similarly supported by octagonal colonnettes of approximately the same size (*CSA* VII: nos. 192-3).

3. **Fragment of an octagonal colonnette** (not illustrated)
Site ref.: Sforzini 1983, Frag. 'A'; from deposits overlying the bath-house. Marble. 0.22×0.13 m (diameter).

The colonnette presumably belongs to the same screen as in cat. 2.

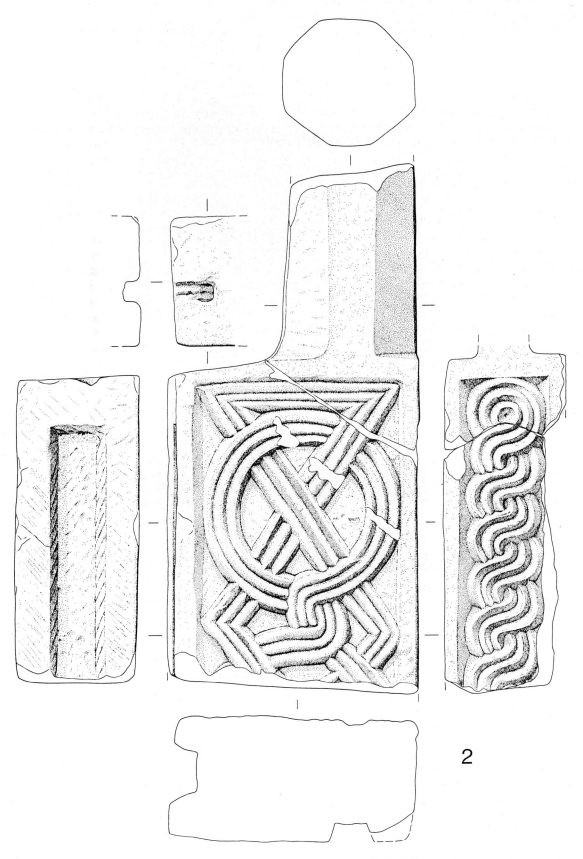

2

Fig. 153. The chancel screen or iconostasis (1:4). *(SA)*

Fig. 154. The chancel screen or iconostasis. *(KW)*

4. **Fragment of a pilaster or architrave** (Fig. 155)
   Site ref.: B1, SF 11; unstratified, over church. Marble.
   0.26 × 0.155 × 0.065 m.
      Although all four faces of the piece have been cut
   and smoothed, only one bears carved ornament: a
   design of two intertwined ribbons creating a pattern of
   interlocking circles. (For the design, see Verzone (1945:
   178-9: '*doppio intreccio di cerchi alternati*').) The same pattern may also be found in cat. 5 and 6, which are presumably other fragments of the same piece. Good parallels may be found throughout the region north of

Rome, for example in the cathedral of Civita Castellana,
the church of Sant'Andrea at Ronciglione, and the
church of San Pietro at Tuscania, all assigned to the
ninth century (*CSA* VIII: nos. 59, 270, 390).

5. **Fragment of a pilaster or architrave** (Fig. 155)
   Site ref. D374, SF 351; built into the base of the second
   font (cf. Fig. 86). Marble. 0.2 × 0.155 × 0.065 m.
      See above, cat. 4. This section was clearly at one end, as
   is suggested both by the termination of the relief pattern
   and by the fact that the end is notched for attachment.

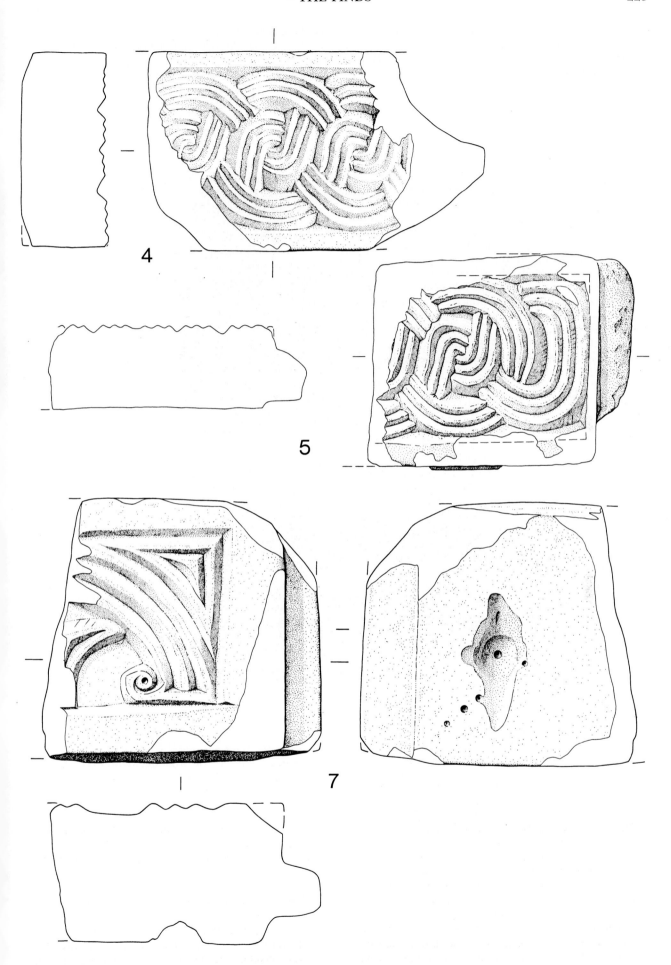

Fig. 155. Medieval sculpture (1:3). *(SA)*

6. **Fragment of a pilaster or architrave** (not illustrated)
Site ref.: D301, SF 323; from a pit associated with a reconstruction of the font drainage system. Marble. 0.2 × 0.15 × 0.065 m.

   See above, cat. no. 4.

7. **Fragment from the end of an architrave or cornice (?)** (Fig. 155)
Site ref.: D38, SF 94; found in the make-up for the latest baptistery floor. Marble. 0.215 × 0.19 × 0.105 m.

   The design on the one decorated face consists of a series of semicircles enclosing trilobate lilies. The semicircles have two grooves, and terminate with a curlicue spiral containing a pointed hole. While such holes are not entirely unprecedented in early medieval Italian sculpture (cf. *CSA* I: no. 35; VII: 2, no. 312), the practice is quite rare, and can perhaps here be regarded as a peculiarity or 'signature' of the sculptor or workshop concerned (cf. cat. 1). The fragment clearly comes from the end of the original piece, as it is notched for insertion. There is also a hole in the back face, perhaps for a metal clamp.

8. **Fragment from the end of an architrave or cornice (?)** (Fig. 156)
Site ref.: D3, SF 41; found in the destruction deposit over the latest baptistery. Marble (in two pieces). 0.49 × 0.26 × 0.09 m.

   The design on the decorated face consists of a series of overlapping semicircles, each with a curlicue termination containing a pointed hole. In the triangular spaces created by the semicircles there are trilobate lilies. The pattern is thus rather similar to that of the preceding piece (cat. 7), although not identical, and the dimensions are clearly different. The holes in the spirals do, however, mark it as a product of the same sculptor or workshop. Patterns created by semicircles were popular in the Carolingian period for the decoration of horizontal elements such as architraves or cornices (for the design cf. Verzone (1945: 172-4: '*archetti intrecciati*')). A good parallel in Rome is provided by a late eighth-century cornice in the church of Santa Maria in Cosmedin (*CSA* VII: 3, no. 106), although this lacks the spiral terminations and floral additions. For the latter, compare the pattern of overlapping circles on a plaque from the Roman church of San Saba (*CSA* VII: 4, nos. 93-4).

9. **Fragment with design of concentric circles** (Fig. 156)
Site ref.: A5, SF 1; from the fill over the bath-house, by the church. Marble. 0.23 × 0.16 × 0.12 m.

   A central pointed hole is enclosed in four outer concentric rings. This design is rare in the early Middle Ages, which generally preferred spirals to rings, but not without some parallels (cf. *CSA* I: nos. 32-3; VII: 3, no. 42; VIII: no. 389; *Seminario*: fig. 245). One end of the piece has a large groove (diameter 50 mm) for attachment.

10. **Fragment with design of plaited ribbon** (Fig. 156)
Site ref.: Sforzini 1983, SF 387; from the fill over the bath-house. Marble. 0.19 × 0.085 × 0.095 m.

    All four sides of the piece are finished, but only one is decorated with a rather worn design of a single plaited ribbon, with holes at the centre of each section. There are good parallels throughout Italy, including an architrave from Trajan's Market in Rome (*CSA* VII: 2, no. 189).

11. **Fragment** (Fig. 157)
Site ref.: D1, SF 158; from the plough-soil over the baptistery. Marble. 90 × 60 × 35 mm.

    The one worked side displays an outer border, and, in the recessed field, a circular line with two prominent holes on raised bases. It is possible that these form part of the decoration of the outer ring of a halo, comparable to those on depictions of the evangelist symbols at Cividale (*CSA* X: no. 332).

12. **Fragment with ribbon design** (not illustrated)
Site ref.: D 319, SF 350; from the fill of the recut drain for the second font. Marble. 0.15 × 0.13 × 0.045 m.

    The one decorated face displays part of an outer border and an angular fragment of a ribbon design, perhaps from a lozenge. The pattern may have been similar to that on the main face of the pilaster (cat. 2), but the border widths are different, and thus this is not a fragment of the same piece.

13. **Decorated fragment** (Fig. 157)
Site ref.: A12, SF 2; from the fill over the bath-house. Marble. 0.165 × 0.14 × 0.075 m.

    The one decorated face displays part of an outer border and what may be the curlicue termination of a ribbon design.

14. **Decorated fragment** (not illustrated)
Site ref. B1; in the plough-soil over the church. Marble. 110 × 70 × 60 mm.

    One face has two strands of a ribbon design.

15. **Decorated fragment** (Fig. 157)
Site ref.: B1, SF 877; from the plough-soil over the church. Marble. 130 × 50 × 50 mm.

    One face is decorated with two forms terminating in spirals, a design widely used for borders throughout Italy and Dalmatia, and ultimately deriving from late classical mosaic pavements. There are many parallels in Rome (cf. *CSA* VII: 1, no. 18; VII: 2, nos. 5, 46-8; VII: 3 nos. 122, 224, 231, 263; VII: 4, nos. 16-17, 45a, 235-7).

16. **Decorated fragment** (Fig. 157)
Site ref.: C51, Special find no. 1; from the top fill over the limekiln. Marble. 120 × 65 × 50 mm.
    One face has part of a ribbon design.

17. **Decorated fragment** (Fig. 157)
Site ref.: D219, SF 300; from the fill over the baptistery. Marble. 0.13 × 0.1 × 0.04 m.
    One face has part of a ribbon design.

18. **Decorated fragment** (Fig. 157)
Site ref.: J4, SF 334; from the fill at the side of the paved road, and stratigraphically in a later position. Tufo block. 0.245 × 0.19 × 0.18 m.
    One face has remnants of an interlaced ribbon design.

19. **Decorated fragment** (Fig. 158)
Site ref.: Sforzini C, SF 388; from the fill over the bath-house. Tufo block. 0.26 × 0.22 × 0.105 m.
    Interlace design.

Fig. 156. Medieval sculpture (1:3). *(SA)*

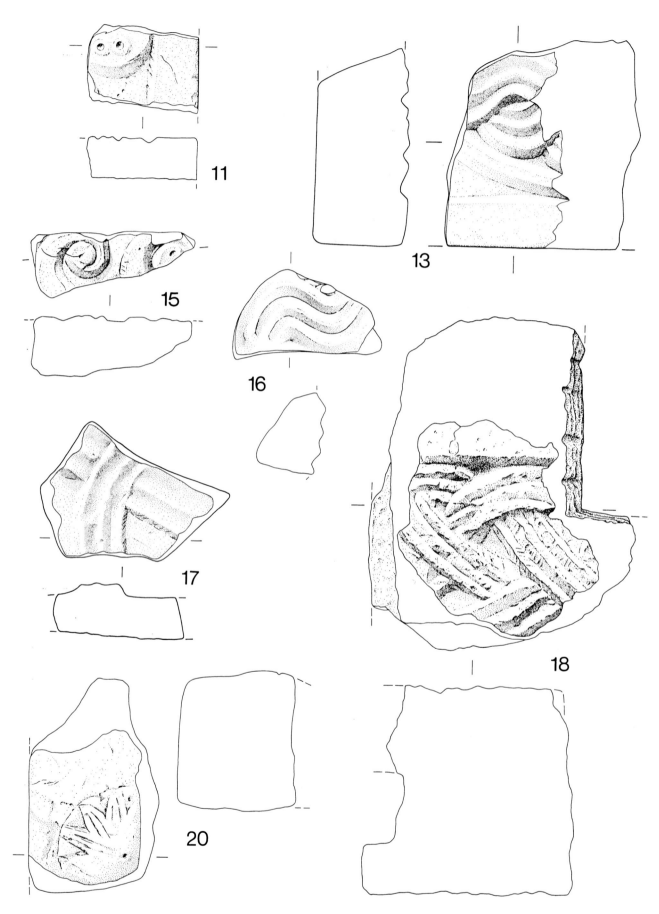

Fig. 157. Medieval sculpture (1:3). *(SA)*

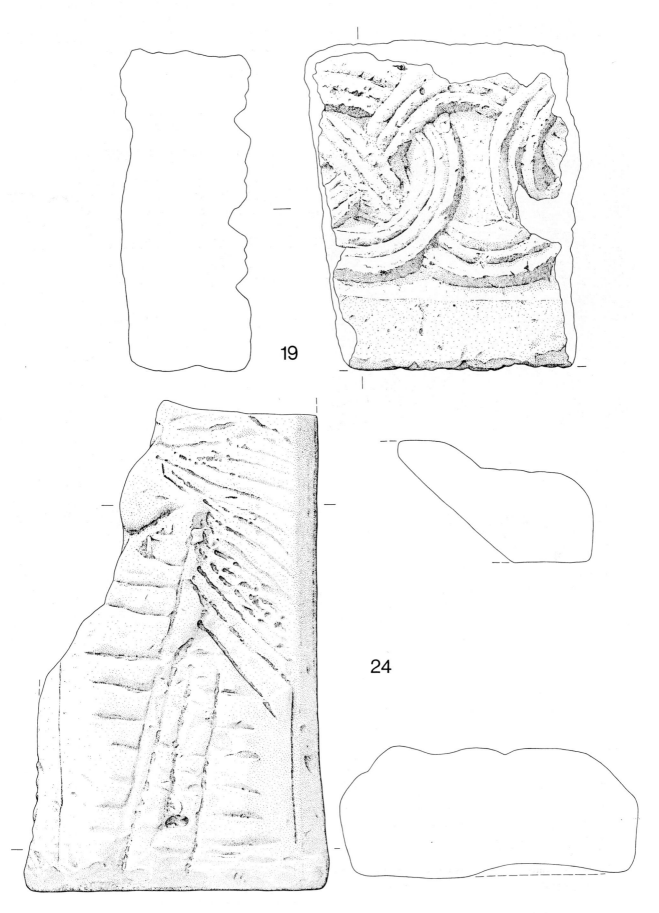

19

24

Fig. 158. Sculpture of certain (cat. 19) and possible (cat. 24) early medieval date (1:3). *(SA)*

Fig. 159. Architrave and frieze block (cat. 1), set into a medieval tomb (Fig. 94, no. 71). Note the late Roman post-holes in the floor (Fig. 39, D360). For the section of the block, cf. Fig. 164, no. 1. *(KW)*

20. **Decorated fragment** (Fig. 157)
    Site ref.: B4/5, SF 17; from a disturbed burial close to the church. Limestone. 0.16 × 0.1 × 0.11 m.

    One face has five petals of a floral design. An interesting comparison is provided by the pattern on the volute of an Ionic capital from Trajan's Market at Rome (*CSA* VII: 2, no. 234).

21. **Column fragment** (not illustrated)
    Site ref.: A20, SF 5; from the fill over the church. Marble. 0.17 × 0.18 × 0.06 m.

    The evidence of a curved moulding suggests that this triangular fragment comes from the bottom of a small column.

22. **Fragment** (not illustrated)
    Site ref.: D29, SF 53; built into the wall dividing the church and baptistery. Marble. 0.15 × 0.11 × 0.08 m.

    Undecorated, but with grooves at both ends and a small hole in the top, suggesting that it once formed part of a larger assemblage.

23. **Nine undecorated marble fragments from the church (three) and the baptistery (six)** (not illustrated).

24. **Fragment** (Fig. 158)
    Site ref.: D38, SF 90; found in the make-up for the latest baptistery floor. Marble. 0.39 × 0.25 × 0.11 m.

A large piece, with extensive evidence of chisel cuts, but no apparent decoration.
    Editor's note: Prof. Osborne does not regard this piece as either figural or of medieval date.

25. **Column base** (cf. Fig. 160, no. 5).
    From the plough-soil over the church. Marble.

ARCHITECTURAL ELEMENTS, by Janet DeLaine

1. **Architrave and frieze block** (Figs 159 and 160).
    Built into tomb 71. Grey volcanic tufo. Total height 0.38 m, minimum length 1.0 m, depth not visible. Architrave with two fascia, lower with vertical face 58 mm high, upper with sloping face 92 mm high. Lower architrave moulding of cavetto, with tall vertical band above where remaining mouldings have been cut back; total height 42 mm. Frieze with simple convex profile 78 mm high, crowned by remains of a series of mouldings 78 mm high beginning with a narrow fillet, followed by a ?cavetto, rest cut back.

    The removal of the cornice mouldings during the reworking of this block makes it difficult to date. The two-stepped architrave was relatively common on small entablatures of the late Republic and early Empire, with either the upper or the lower fascia taller, but does not appear again until the Hadrianic period where it is associated with the Asiatic style of architectural ornament and the upper fascia is always the taller (Strong 1953). While the convex frieze and the remains of tall and presumably complex architrave and frieze cornices would be in keeping with a date in the mid to late second century AD, the absence of the usual moulding between the architrave fascia means that a date in the Augustan period cannot be excluded.

2. **Cornice fragment** (Figs 160 and 161)
    From top fill of north cistern. (A second fragment was found on the surface in 1970.) Grey volcanic tufo. Maximum preserved height 0.34 m, length 0.82 m, depth 0.395 m. Cyma reversa 66 mm high with Type B decoration (Strong 1953: 120 n. 14 and fig. 1), fillet, ovolo 55 mm high with egg-and-tongue, fillet, corona with plain backward sloping face 68 mm high and slightly hollowed underside, fillet, shallow cavetto with fluting, sima mouldings damaged.

    Several factors combine to suggest a late Republican-early Imperial date for this cornice. The strongly sloping, plain corona has Italic precedents and still appears towards the end of the first century BC (Strong 1963: 75), while in most post-Augustan cornices the corona is vertical or carved as a shallow cavetto, and is frequently decorated. The ovolo and cyma reversa decorations have close parallels in the *peperino* cornice once attributed to the central of the three Forum Holitorium temples and generally given an early first century AD date (Crozzoli Aite 1981: figs 10 and 59).

3. **Fragment of block with moulding on long edge** (Fig. 162)
    In a medieval context in site M. Grey volcanic tufo. Maximum preserved dimensions 1.0 × 0.4 m. Cyma reversa with Type B decoration, Y-shaped 'tulips' between ringed arches with pendant flowers.

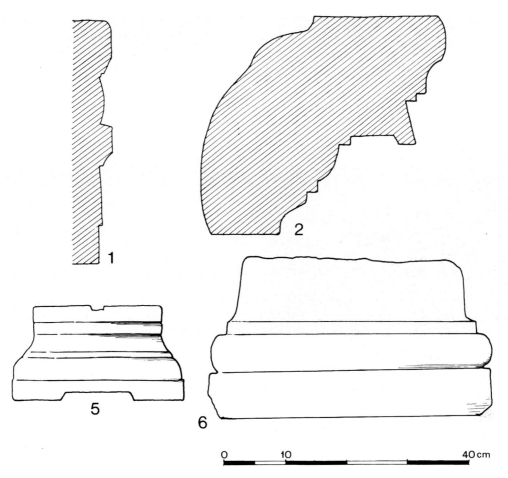

Fig. 160. Architectural fragments. *(TWP)*

Fig. 161. Cornice fragment (cat. 2). For the section cf. Figure 160, no. 2. *(KW)*

Fig. 162. Block with moulding (cat. 3). *(KW)*

This type of decoration has a long life, and appears in many variant forms. The relatively small, close arch-rings and the small leaf point appearing in the Y of the 'tulip' suggest an earlier rather than a later date, probably in the first half of the first century AD.

4. **Corner of architectural block** (Figs 163 and 164).
In a medieval context in site M (subsequently stolen). Grey volcanic tufo. Maximum preserved dimensions 0.88 × 0.66 × 0.5 m high. Two adjacent decorated vertical faces meet at right angles. The finished edge of each face is treated as a flat band 0.13 m high, as is the vertical edge at the angle, 70 mm wide. Each face is decorated with the same design of a broad vertical volute of concave cross-section rising from the surviving edge of the block and scrolling away from the angle to end in a four-petal rosette in the eye of the volute. The space between the vertical edge and the volute is filled with a leafy stem rising from behind the volute and curling in the same direction to end in a bell-shaped flower. Total width of the design *c.* 600 mm.

This unusual fragment may form part of a pilaster capital of some non-standard volute type, but has its closest parallel in a marble acroterion in the *Terme* museum of late Republican-early Augustan date (Pettinau 1984). The most likely context for this piece would be a small temple or a funerary monument, the latter being the source of several marble acroteria of similar size but with more complex acanthus scroll decoration also in the *Terme* museum, such as those from a temple-tomb found at Torrenova (Pensabene 1985). The columns of this structure have been reconstructed as approximately 4.7 m in height, which may suggest the scale of the building to which our piece may have belonged.

5. **Column base** (Fig. 160)
Unstratified in fill over the church. In white marble, with worn powdery surfaces. Maximum diameter 280 mm.

6. **Column base** (Fig. 160)
In late Roman fill over rooms on the lowest terrace (cf. Fig. 60). In dark grey volcanic tufo. Maximum diameter 460 mm.

THE BRICK AND TILE, by C.M. Gilliver with O.J. Gilkes

About 2,000 kg of brick and tile were found, of which 922 kg was quantified as a representative sample. As a collection it was relatively fragmentary, and not suited to the quite elaborate analysis attempted for the nearby site at Ponte Nepesino (Stone 1984). The range of fabrics was, however, classified by eye and each fabric was named with a letter (A to I). Subsequently samples of each were submitted for petrological analysis (Freestone, below). This showed that nearly 90 per cent of the sample comprised brick and tile in 'petrofabric 1', which Freestone regards as almost certainly of local origin. Indeed, some greenish, overfired tiles are close to being wasters (fabric F). The manufacture of tiles is attested lower down the valley at Narce, in the fourth and third centuries BC; here the clays beneath the volcanics were exploited (Potter 1976: 79). 'Petrofabric 2' accounts for about ten per cent of the sample, but a local origin is less certain. The other fabrics are very rare (amounting together to *c.* one per cent of the sample) and of unknown origin. The precise figures are as follows: Petrofabric Group 1: Fabric A – 312 kg, Fabrics B/C – 363 kg, Fabric D – 140 kg, Fabric F – 4 kg; Petrofabric Group 2: Fabric E – 93 kg; Other Petrofabrics: Fabrics G, H and I – 10 kg.

Fig. 163. Architectural block (cat. 4). *(KW)*

Fig. 164. Architectural block (cat. 4). *(KW)*

It should be noted that on the main site all the tiles would appear to be of Roman date, although some were reused in early medieval contexts (including *a cappuccina* burials). Medieval tile production does not seem to have started in this area until the twelfth century, a matter discussed further under the section on Castellaccio below. No stamped names were identified on any of the tiles; indeed, they were generally very rare in the sample from the Ager Faliscus field survey.

TYPES

Bricks and tiles

1. One *bessalis*, 0.2 × 0.21 m (L157, late Roman rubble).
2. Two *pedales*?, neither of which was complete: (a) 0.27+ × 0.27+ m (M23, late Roman wall collapse); (b) 0.28+ × 0.28+ m (K101, unstratified).
3. *Sesquipedales*: (a) 0.43 × 0.44 m (B48, from burial 11, *a cappuccina*) (Fig. 165,6); (b) 0.45 × 0.45 m, with a hobnailed boot print (C2, burial 2); (c) 0.44 × 0.43 m, with a paw print of a large dog (C2, burial 2).
4. *Bipedales*: (a) 0.585 × 0.577 m (D229, from burial 37); (b) *c.* 0.58 × 0.57 m (D229, from burial 37).

Several of these bricks and tiles were reused in later burials, as is the case with the two *bipedales*. Vitruvius described the use of three types in the construction of heated floors: *sesquipedales* below, and *bessales* to form the *pilae* which supported the floors of *bipedales* (*De Architectura* v. 10.2). *Sesquipedales* also made up the floor of the 'lobby' room in the northern part of the site (E63: Fig. 51).

Roof tiles

Large quantities of both tegulae and imbrices (cf. Fig. 165,7) were found in all areas and all phases of the site, but except for the tegulae reused in the *a cappuccina* burials, most were in a very fragmentary state. Two types of tegula were found: rectangular, *c.* 0.4 × 0.6 m with flanges *c.* 30-40 mm wide, cut away at the bottom (Fig. 165,1,5); and rhombus-shaped, *c.* 0.335 m wide at bottom, 0.48 m at top, 0.25 m high, with flanges *c.* 30-40 mm wide, cut away at the bottom as above (Fig. 165,2-4).

Gutter tile?

A section of channelled tile was found (M61, hillwash), possibly a fragment of guttering, 0.275 × 0.16 m, with flanges 60 mm high and widths of 37 mm along one edge, 20 mm along the other (Fig. 166,8).

Box flue-tiles

Fragments of box flue-tiles were found in all areas of the site, particularly from the upper layer of the fish-pond (L105), but only one complete flue-tile was found. It is 0.165 × 0.11 m, and 0.37 m long, with rounded exterior and interior angles.

Backing for mosaic emblemata?

A broken piece of tile, 0.3 × 0.23+ × 0.04 m, possibly originally of *sesquipedalis* size, with a small ridge around the edge on the top side, was found unstratified in deposits over the church. Rough parallel scoring on this face was probably applied after firing. Amanda Claridge has suggested that

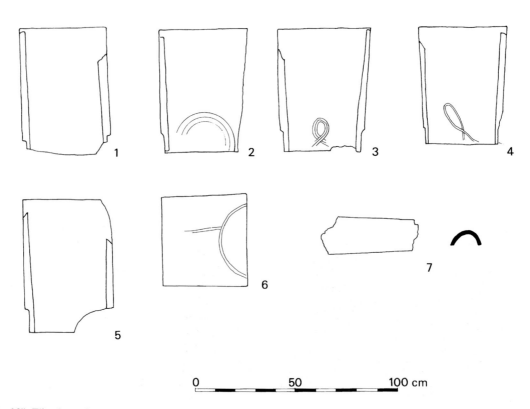

Fig. 165. Tiles from the *a cappuccina* burials in the early medieval church. Burial no. 11: 104,7; burial no. 10: 5-6. *(TWP)*

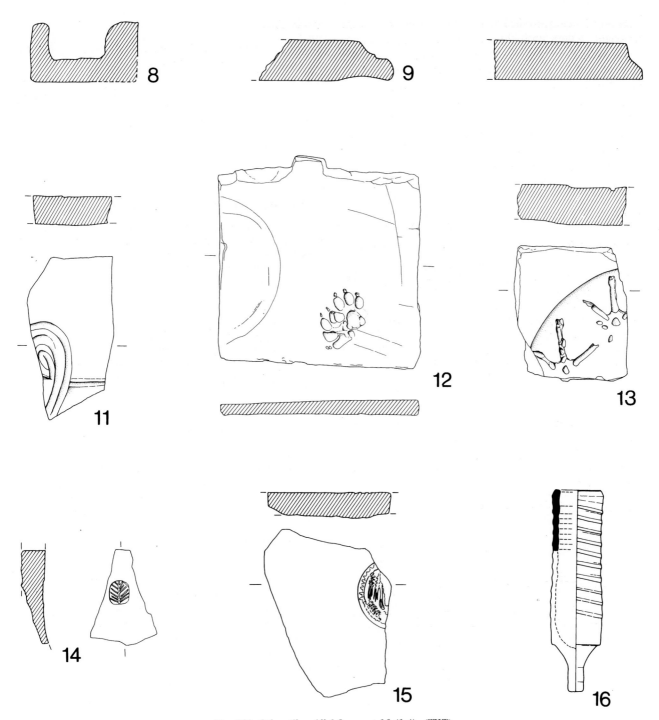

Fig. 166. Other tiles. All 1:2 except 16 (1:4). *(TWP)*

the tile may have been the backing for a mosaic emblemata, though these rarely have the small ridge noted. If this were the case, it could suggest local mosaic manufacture in addition to the tiles, though there are no traces of concrete on the tile to determine whether it was made for this purpose.

Architectural elements

1. Eight sections of tile column drum (seven from the lime-kiln and one from Trench H, unstratified). It is suggested that all had a radius of *c.* 0.2 m, though all sections were badly damaged at the edges and towards the centre, so it is impossible to be accurate, or to determine

how the centre of the column was constructed. The height of the sections varied from 33 to 50 mm. The percentage of the column diameter each tile made up are as follows: 10.7 per cent, 11.0 per cent, 11.0 per cent, 12.4 per cent, 12.7 per cent, 14.7 per cent, 15.0 per cent, 16.0 per cent.

2. Two sections of tile column capital/base, both broken, both with radius of *c.* 0.2 m, and probably from the same columns as the sections of drum above (C1, unstratified over church) (Fig. 166,9).

3. Fragment of engaged tile column capital/base, radius of *c.* 0.2 m, with traces of red paint on exposed surface (E17, rubble over large Roman room, phase 4) (Fig. 166,10).

4. Section of engaged tile column drum, radius *c.* 0.275 m, height 55 mm (unstratified).
5. *Pedalis*, 0.285 × 0.285 m, with remains of mortar on both faces of one half, and red paint on the other half of one face (E69, late Roman fill).

Brick columns of the type suggested by the remains listed above were common in the second century AD, and there are many comparable examples from, for example, Trajan's Market, Rome, from Ostia (Horrea III xvi 1, on the Cardo degli Aurighi), and from tombs on the Via Appia.

MARKS

A number of marks on the tiles, probably for tallying, were recorded: concentric circles (four examples: Fig. 165,2); loops with crossed ends (twelve examples: Fig. 165,3,4; Fig. 166,11); S-shaped motif (one example, not illustrated).

The first three were made with the fingers, whilst the last was produced with a tool of some kind. All such marks on tegulae were made at the bottom end of the tile. A 'pie crust' design also produced by the fingers was noted on one floor tile, though the complexity of the motif suggests that this may not be a simple tally mark.

Prints noted on tegulae and floor tiles were of: (a) dogs, large and small – four examples (Fig. 166,12); (b) sheep – two examples; (c) goat – three examples; (d) hobnailed boot – two examples; (e) foot of bird, possibly a dove or a pigeon (possibly made with a bird's foot being used as a stamp rather than the bird alighting on the tile (C/D1, unstratified over baptistery) (Fig. 166,13).

The number of prints shows that the tiles were laid out to dry on the ground, and the rough underside of the tiles suggests that this was a sandy surface.

STAMPS

Two stamps were noted: (a) a small stylized palm leaf stamp, found on a fragment of a tegula (C1, unstratified over church) (Fig. 166,14); (b) half a circular stamp with a corn sheaf design (M79, late-Roman silt) (Fig. 166,15).

CASTELLACCIO

Very small amounts of tile were found in all the trenches on the Castellaccio site. The fabric types were generally comparable with those from the main site and again probably represent local production. The tiles were of poor quality, tending to be rather friable, and this suggests new production rather than reuse of earlier tiles, but probably using the same clay sources as in the earlier periods. Most of the tiles were fairly small fragments of tegulae and imbrices which were much thinner than earlier examples from the main site. No stamps or marking of any kind were noted on the tiles.

The nearby site at Ponte Nepesino affords an interesting parallel (Stone 1984). Although first occupied in the ninth century (but with some earlier, Roman, material), medieval tiles did not reach the site before the twelfth century, and also used forms and fabrics that are quite distinct from Roman types. This closely mirrors the situation at Monte Gelato, where medieval tiles do not occur on the main site (abandoned *c.* AD 1100), but do at Castellaccio, first occupied in the eleventh-twelfth centuries. The principal difference between the two sites is in the range of fabrics, which are much more diverse at Ponte Nepesino – fourteen Roman and nine medieval. Even though these were identified by hand inspection rather than by analysis, and thus are likely to be in reality fewer, the contrast is striking, and may reflect Ponte Nepesino's much more prominent location on the Via Amerina.

VAULTING TUBE (FIG. 166,16), by R.J.A. Wilson

A single vaulting tube was found, in late Roman fill (D345) over flooring close to the later baptistery. It is in petrofabric 1, and thus likely to be of local origin. It conforms to the standard form of these artefacts, known from examples in many places in the Roman world (Wilson 1992; Storz 1994). The tube is cylindrical, but with one end narrowing to form a nozzle-like projection, to enable each tube to interlock neatly with its neighbour. It is open at both ends and has lightly corrugated surfaces inside and out, made by the potter's fingers while the tube was being fashioned on the wheel. Rows of such tubes, fixed together during construction with plaster, created a rapidly built, strong centering for the pouring of a mortared rubble aggregate vault (or dome) above; there was no need for the timber centring which is required for a conventional concrete vault. The underside of the tubes was concealed beneath a layer of plaster. The corrugation on the tube served to improve its adherence both to this plaster and to the mortar above; normally there are traces of the latter still adhering to the tubes, although apparently not in this case.

The Monte Gelato tube is 51 mm in diameter and 0.214 m in length. The tubes in north Africa, where the most plentiful instances of the use of vaulting tubes occur, vary between 0.07 and 0.32 m long, although most are between 0.12 and 0.2 m long and between 50 and 110 mm in diameter. The Monte Gelato tube is more elongated than most African tubes, in having a length more than four times its diameter; but this has no particular significance, and recorded instances of vaulting tubes from Italy show a wide variety of sizes.

The earliest known use of vaulting tubes occurs in the dome in a bath building at Morgantina (Sicily) in the third century BC (Allen 1974: 376-9), but they only came into widespread use in the second half of the second century AD, especially in barrel vaults and semi-domes. In public buildings they are found most frequently in bath-houses and, later, in the semi-domes of Christian chapels and churches: but they occur in domestic architecture as well, in both town houses and villas, especially in bath suites and corridors. Which of the structures excavated at Monte Gelato actually used vaulting tubes is uncertain; indeed it is possible that the tube represents building debris derived from some other nearby structure and tipped here at a later stage. But if the vaulting tube does belong to one of the excavated structures at Monte Gelato, the most likely candidates are the bath suite, constructed *c.* AD 100, and the semi-dome of the church, erected *c.* AD 400. If the former, the vaulting tube would be of exceptional interest, because there are currently very few structures anywhere in the Roman world known to have used vaulting tubes between the third century BC and the second century AD (Wilson (1992: 110-12) reviews the evidence). But the tiny size of the known rooms of the bath building make it unlikely, in fact, that vaulted rooms were ever built there. Much more probable is the use of tubes in the semi-dome of the church's apse, for it is indeed in early Christian churches that the vast majority of Italian examples of vaulting tubes occurs – most notably in Ravenna, in a series of churches from the late fourth century to the middle of the sixth (Bovini 1960), but also in Milan, Perugia, Pavia, Rome and elsewhere. Apart from Rome, where tubes were employed in three fifth-century churches – Santo Stefano Rotondo, Sant'Agata dei Goti and Sant'Anastasia – as well as in the now destroyed oratory of Santa Croce al Laterano, the nearest place to Monte Gelato to have yielded vaulting tubes is Santa Rufina, from a fourth-century mausoleum there (Cotton, Wheeler and Whitehouse 1991: 239, 263-4).

ANALYSIS OF THE BRICK AND TILE FABRICS, by I.C. Freestone

INTRODUCTION

The bricks and tiles from the excavation at Monte Gelato were divided into eight fabrics on the basis of hand specimen examination. The present report is concerned with the thin-section examination of a reference series of the tile fabrics, to determine their interrelationships.

RESULTS

To distinguish them from the hand specimen fabric groups A-I, the thin-section groups are referred to as 'petrofabrics'.

Petrofabric 1

Fabric A (BMRL 40948P). A fine grained, very calcareous clay matrix with sparse quartz silt, contains common coarse sub-angular translucent red-brown particles, up to several millimetres across. The majority of these particles appears to consist predominantly of sideromelanitic material, an alteration product of volcanic glass. They show small round vesicles, and include fine polygonal leucites and occasionally fine clinopyroxene. Rare brownish grains of sedimentary origin are also present. Also included are sparse green to colourless pyroxene grains of sand grade, and occasional rounded grains of micritic calcite.
Fabric B/C (BMRL 40950Q). This fabric is similar to fabric A, with more abundant clinopyroxene and, in addition, the presence of occasional coarse leucite and also olivine.
Fabric D (BMRL 40954T). Possibly an oxidized version of the same fabric, with fewer altered volcanic rock inclusions.
Fabric F (BMRL 40955R). This appears to be an overfired version of the same fabric.

Petrofabric 2

Fabric E (BMRL 40953V). A distinctive fabric consisting of a brown birefringent non-calcareous clay matrix with common coarse silt. This contains an abundant poorly sorted sand, consisting of sub-angular to sub-rounded quartz grains typically of medium grade but up to several millimetres in diameter.

Petrofabric 3

Fabric G (BMRL 40952X). A brown birefringent clay matrix with common fine laths of mica. There is no apparent calcite in the matrix. Set in the matrix are common poorly sorted medium grade sub-angular sand grains composed predominantly of grains of sanidine feldspar, green to colourless pyroxene and fine-grained volcanic rock.

Petrofabric 4

Fabric I (BMRL 40951Z). An isotropic clay matrix containing abundant medium to coarse silt and common fine mica. There are few diagnostic mineral inclusions, just a few grains of clinopyroxene and altered volcanic rock approximately 0.3 mm in diameter. Common voids with carbonized halos, elongate in form from around one millimetre to several millimetres long, appear to represent burnt out vegetal matter, possibly chaff.

Petrofabric 5

Fabric H (BMRL 40949Y). An isotropic clay matrix with common quartz silt contains common poorly sorted sand grains of fine to coarse grade. The sand is composed of volcanic rock fragments, sanidine and plagioclase feldspar and clinopyroxene, with occasional biotite and sphene.

DISCUSSION

As commonly occurs, the petrological examination has significantly reduced the number of fabrics recognized in the field (from eight to five). This is not surprising; field classification often depends heavily upon colour (a reflection of firing conditions) and the apparent size and abundance of inclusions, while the thin-section classification depends on the identification of the inclusions.

Of particular interest is the grouping of the predominant hand specimen fabrics A-D, along with Fabric F, into a single petrofabric. These fabrics were grouped together on the basis of their calcareous matrices and the similar volcanic minerals that they contain, especially the dominance of the clinopyroxene-leucite association and the low concentration of feldspar. Fabric D is the least firm member of this group – its calcite concentration appears a little lower and its feldspar a little higher. The variations observed within petrofabric 1 are those which might be expected within a single deposit. Thus it is possible that this petrofabric represents a single manufactory. However, it would be necessary to examine a range of tiles in fabrics A-D to demonstrate beyond reasonable doubt that they were identical. In view of their abundance and the fact that the local geology is almost entirely volcanic in origin, the fabrics grouped as petrofabric 1 are likely to represent a relatively local production.

Petrofabrics 3, 4 and 5 also contain inclusions of volcanic origin, but differ from petrofabric 1 in

some significant respects. Petrofabric 3 has no
matrix calcite, implying a different clay source, and
sanidine feldspar is the dominant inclusion, implying that the volcanic rocks of the source area were
different. Petrofabric 4 also represents a different
clay source, as its matrix is very silty and contains
common mica. Volcanic inclusions are rare in this
sample. Petrofabric 5 is characterized by the common occurrence of both sanidine and plagioclase
feldspar.

Finally, Petrofabric 2 (hand specimen fabric E) is
distinctive in its lack of volcanic inclusions and
abundance of quartz. This fabric clearly originated
in sedimentary deposits. Such deposits are rare in
the region, and outcrop only where the rivers cut
through the thick blanket of volcanic deposits to
the underlying Pleistocene sediments. The nearest
outcrop occurs at the modern tilery some 2.0 km
down the river Treia, and a further outcrop occurs
at Narce. The origin of this fabric could well be
more distant, however.

WALL-PLASTER, by C.M. Gilliver

Painted wall-plaster was found in a large number of
contexts in the main area of the site, but for the
most part these pieces were very small, and in a
very fragmentary condition. Two larger deposits
were excavated, but these were also very fragmentary.

1. Panels of purple, yellow and red separated by narrow
   white borders *c.* 5-7 mm wide. From the late second-century fill of the cistern at the northern end of the site
   (L104, L143).

   The surviving decorative elements comprised green
   vegetation and flowers of yellow and white with green
   stems.
2. Quantities of wall-plaster in poor condition from the
   rubble of the late wall collapse east of the plunge bath
   (M23, Justinianic wall collapse).

   These panels had rather faded red, green and some
   darker colours, possibly black or purple, with some surviving fragments of green vegetation.

THE COINS, by Richard Hobbs

In total, 58 coins were recovered from the excavations. All except one were of bronze, and approximately half (31) were too worn to attribute to individual issuers. At least 46 coins were of the Roman
period (from Trajan to Marcian), at least four were
early Byzantine, one was Ostrogothic (cat. 57), and
the latest coin was a ninth-century silver denarius
of Pope Hadrian III. This coin, issued alongside
those of Charles the Fat, is perhaps the rarest, with
only around a thousand genuine papal coins
known in total (Grierson and Blackburn 1986).

INTERPRETATION

Deliberate burial

Two coins were found in burial contexts, and
hence were almost certainly deliberately placed.
The first was a coin of Honorius (cat. 46), found in
the mouth of a skeleton in an *a cappuccina* burial
(no. 26). The second coin was a denarius of Pope
Hadrian III (cat. 58), found in a child inhumation
in the baptistery (no. 43). There was also a coin of
Gratian (cat. 22) in the fill of burial no. 60, but this
has been treated as a casual loss.

Casual losses

The contexts of the majority of the coins from the
site are very likely to represent casual losses, as
there is no evidence to suggest that any were part
of a scattered hoard. The rates of coin loss varied
over the history of the site, as shown in Table 52
(columns 2 and 3). By far the largest number of
coins (over 60 per cent of the total) date to the
late fourth and early fifth centuries AD. This fact
has to be interpreted with caution, for a number
of reasons.

Firstly, the coins of this date are generally smaller,
lower value coins, and therefore more likely to be
lost and not recovered. This contrasts with the
second-century material, composed of larger module bronze asses and dupondii. The early Imperial
material is therefore more significant in terms of
intensity of occupation than mere numbers might
suggest: taking into account their greater weight
and value and their lower likelihood of being lost,
even a few coins can be regarded as a significant
group. In numismatic terms, the site may therefore
have been occupied as intensively in the early
Empire as in the later period.

Secondly, and more importantly, comparisons
with data collected from Rome (Reece 1982), represented in Table 52 and Figure 167, show that a
loss pattern of this nature is not unusual. In Rome
too, the majority of coins found (over 80 per cent)
dates to the late fourth and early fifth centuries AD.
Loss in the second and third centuries AD, like
Monte Gelato, is comparably low, with a sharp
increase in period 6 (AD 350-400), a slight fall in
period 7 (AD 400-50), and a significant fall in the
subsequent periods (8 and 9) to levels comparable
with the early Empire.

Therefore, despite Monte Gelato's firmly rural
location, it does not appear to have been isolated
from Rome and wider changes in coin circulation
during the Empire, although with such a small
sample observations can only be very general. At the
very least, the coin evidence certainly supports the
stratigraphic evidence which indicates a continuous
occupation of the site during much of the Roman
and into the Byzantine periods.

Table 52. Distribution of coins per period, comparing Monte Gelato and Rome.

Note: the periods were chosen because the bulk of the material was unable to be dated to more specific historical or numismatic phases. The methods used for comparing material from sites is fully explained by Reece (1987). Reece's data from Rome were a mixture of scattered hoards and stray losses from the Palatine area in the centre of Rome. Although a rather crude sample, the data are sufficient to establish a good comparative cross-section of coins lost throughout the Roman period and beyond.

period of issue	Monte Gelato – coins per period	Monte Gelato – coins per thousand	Rome – coins per period	Rome – coins per thousand
AD 100-150 (1)	1	17.86	73	12.28
AD 150-200 (2)	2	35.71	68	11.44
AD 200-250 (3)	1	17.86	45	7.57
AD 250-300 (4)	5	89.29	129	21.71
AD 300-350 (5)	3	53.57	417	70.18
AD 350-400 (6)	21	374.99	2,774	466.85
AD 400-450 (7)	12	214.29	2,224	374.28
AD 450-500 (8)	5	89.29	201	33.83
AD 500-550 (9)	6	107.14	11	1.85
total	56		5,942	

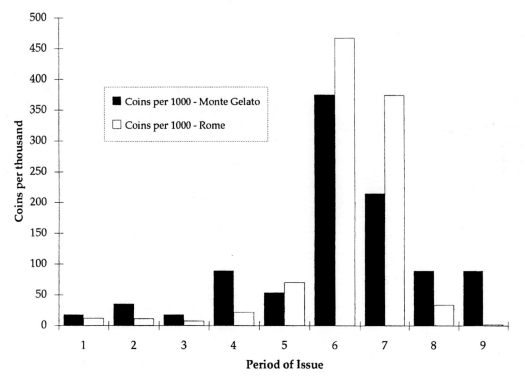

Fig. 167. A comparison of coin-loss between Rome and Monte Gelato. *(RH)*

CHRONOLOGICAL LIST OF SITE FINDS

1. Trajan (AD 98-117). Rome. AE as.
   obv. IMP CAES NERVA TRAIAN AVG GERM PM
   rev. TR POT COS III PP S C
   Weight: unknown.
   Cat. ref.: *BMC* 740.

Site ref. : MG86, B1, SF 7.
Find-spot: unstratified.

2. Marcus Aurelius (AD 159-60). Rome. AE dupondius.
   obv. AVRELIVS CAESAR AVG P II F
   rev. TR POT XIIII COS II SC
   Weight: 9.35 g.
   Cat. ref.: *RIC* 1355.

Site ref.: MG89, L101, SF 416.
Find-spot : hillwash.

3. Empress (Crispina?) (late second century AD). Mint uncertain. AE as.
   obv. female bust r.
   rev. Venus (?) seated l.
   Weight: 18.06 g.
   Cat. ref.: –.
   Site ref.: MG90, S10, SF 705.
   Find-spot: fill of rock-cut road, phase 2/3.

4. Trajan Decius (AD 249-50). Rome. AE sestertius.
   obv. IMP C M TRAIANVS DECIVS AVG
   rev. [DACIA FELIX] SC
   Weight: 16.96 g.
   Cat. ref.: RIC 114a.
   Site ref.: MG89, M47, SF 563.
   Find-spot: robbed north wall of bath-house, phase 3.

5. Claudius II (Divus) (AD 268-70). Rome. AE radiate.
   obv. radiate bust r.
   rev. CONSECRATIO eagle
   Weight: 1.18 g.
   Cat. ref.: – (barbarous).
   Site ref.: MG89, M, SF 395.
   Find-spot: unstratified.

6. Claudius II (Divus) (AD 268-70). Rome. AE radiate.
   obv. radiate bust r.
   rev. CONSECRATIO altar
   Weight: 0.96 g.
   Cat. ref.: – (barbarous).
   Site ref.: MG89, L124, SF 415.
   Find-spot: layer beneath paved road.

7. Diocletian (c. AD 298). Rome. AE radiate fraction.
   obv. IMP DIOCLETIANVS AVG
   rev. VOT XX in wreath
   Weight: unknown.
   Cat. ref.: RIC 86 (Δ).
   Site ref.: MG86, B1, SF 15.
   Find-spot: unstratified.

8. Uncertain (late third century AD). Mint uncertain. AE radiate.
   obv. radiate bust r.
   rev. illegible
   Weight: 1.32 g.
   Cat. ref.: –.
   Site ref.: MG88, H01, SF 190.
   Find-spot: unstratified.

9. Uncertain (late third century AD). Mint uncertain. AE radiate.
   obv. radiate bust r.
   rev. illegible
   Weight : 0.39 g (fragment).
   Cat. ref.: –.
   Site ref.: MG88, D52, SF 319.
   Find-spot: collapsed roof, end of phase 3.

10. Uncertain (?third-fourth centuries AD). Mint uncertain. AE.
    obv. illegible
    rev. illegible
    Weight : unknown.
    Cat. ref.: –.
    Site ref.: MG86, A36, SF 35.
    Find-spot: from the fill of the bath-house hypocaust, phase 3.

11. Constantine I (AD 326-37). Trier. AE folles.
    obv. CONSTANTINVS AVG
    rev. BEATA TRANQVILLITAS in ex., .PTR.
    Weight: 3.22 g.

Cat. ref.: RIC 369.
Site ref.: MG90, M1, SF 666.
Find-spot: unstratifed.

12. House of Constantine (AD 330-5). Mint uncertain. AE folles.
    obv. illegible
    rev. GLORIA EXERCITVS (2 standards)
    Weight: unknown.
    Cat. ref.: –.
    Site ref.: MG86, A35, SF 27.
    Find-spot: from the fill marking the abandonment of the bath-house hypocaust, phase 3.

13. Constantius II (AD 353-8). Mint uncertain. AE 3.
    obv. DN CONSTANTIVS PF AVG
    rev. FEL TEMP REPARATIO (fallen horseman type)
    Weight: unknown.
    Cat. ref.: –.
    Site ref.: MG86, A35, SF 26.
    Find-spot: from the fill marking the abandonment of the bath-house hypocaust, phase 3.

14. Constantius II (AD 353-8). Mint uncertain. AE 3.
    obv. DN CONSTANTIUS PF AVG
    rev. FEL TEMP REPARATIO (fallen horseman type)
    Weight: 1.67 g.
    Cat. ref.: –.
    Site ref.: MG88, E44, SF 265.
    Find-spot: in the fill in the lobby, phase 3/4.

15. Constantius Gallus (AD 353-8). Mint uncertain. AE 3.
    obv. bust r.
    rev. FEL TEMP REPARATIO (fallen horseman type)
    Weight: 1.95 g.
    Cat. ref.: –.
    Site ref.: MG88, E44, SF 277.
    Find-spot: in the fill in the lobby, phase 3/4.

16. Julian II (AD 355-63). Mint uncertain. AE 3.
    obv. DN FL CL IVLIANVS NOB CAES
    rev. VOT X MVLT XX in wreath
    Weight: 2.73 g.
    Cat. ref.: –.
    Site ref.: MG90, M119, SF 772.
    Find-spot: in the fill of a slot cut into a late Roman floor, phase 3.

17. Constantius II (AD 358-61). Mint uncertain. AE 3.
    obv. illegible
    rev. SPES [REIPVBLICAE]
    Weight: 1.37 g.
    Cat. ref.: –.
    Site ref.: MG89, M26, SF 452.
    Find-spot: layer of silt, by the paved road, phase 3.

18. Valens (AD 364-78). Mint uncertain. AE 3.
    obv. [DN V]ALEN-[S PF AVG]
    rev. SECURITAS REIPVBLICAE
    Weight: 1.84 g.
    Cat. ref.: –.
    Site ref.: MG90, M144, SF 837.
    Find-spot: layer of silt, on a late Roman floor, phase 3.

19. House of Valentinian (AD 364-78). Mint uncertain. AE 3.
    obv. bust r., pearl diadem
    rev. [SECURITAS REIPVBLICAE]
    Weight: 1.02 g (fragment).
    Cat. ref.: –.
    Site ref.: MG89, M26, SF 439.
    Find-spot: layer of silt, by the paved road, phase 3.

20. House of Valentinian (AD 364-78). Mint uncertain. AE 3.
    obv. bust r.

rev. ? [SECURITAS REIPVBLICAE]
Weight: 1.32 g.
Cat. ref.: –.
Site ref.: MG89, M38, SF 580.
Find-spot: rubble layer, with *opus reticulatum*, tile and silt, phase 3.

21. House of Valentinian (AD 364-78). Aquileia. AE 3.
obv. bust r.
rev. GLORIA ROMANORVM in ex., SMAQS
Weight: 2.11 g.
Cat. ref.: *RIC* 7 ff.
Site ref.: MG90, M97, SF 770.
Find-spot: layer of silt over a late Roman floor, phase 3.

22. Gratian (AD 367-83). Rome. AE 3.
obv. DN GRATIANVS PF AVG
rev. SECVRITAS REIPVBLICAE in ex., SM•RB
Weight: 1.92 g.
Cat. ref.: *RIC* 28b.
Site ref.: MG86, A34, SF 21.
Find-spot: from the fill of burial 60, phases 5-6.

23. Valentinian II (AD 375-8). Rome. AE 3.
obv. DN VALENTINIA-NVS IVN PF AVG
rev. SECVRITAS REIPVBLICAE
Weight: unknown.
Cat. ref.: *LRBC* II, 738 (T).
Site ref.: MG86, B32, SF 22.
Find-spot: level of the second church, phase 6.

24. Uncertain (late fourth century AD). Mint uncertain. AE 3.
obv. illegible
rev. Salus
Weight: 0.69 g.
Cat. ref.: –.
Site ref.: MG87, A41, SF 43.
Find-spot: unstratified.

25. Uncertain (?fourth century AD). Mint uncertain. AE.
obv. illegible
rev. illegible
Weight: 0.70 g.
Cat. ref.: –.
Site ref.: MG87, A42, SF 46.
Find-spot: unstratified.

26. Uncertain (?fourth century AD). Mint uncertain. AE.
obv. illegible
rev. illegible
Weight: 0.93 g.
Cat. ref.: –.
Site ref.: MG87, A42, SF 47.
Find-spot: unstratified.

27. Uncertain (?fourth century AD). Mint uncertain. AE.
obv. illegible
rev. illegible
Weight: 0.20 g (fragment).
Cat. ref.: –.
Site ref.: MG87, A42, SF 50.
Find-spot: unstratified.

28. Uncertain (?fourth century AD). Mint uncertain. AE.
obv. illegible
rev. ?Securitas
Weight: 0.69 g.
Cat. ref.: –.
Site ref.: MG87, D166, SF 157.
Find-spot: in possible beam slot, phase 3.

29. Uncertain (late Roman, ?fourth century AD). Mint uncertain. AE.
obv. illegible
rev. illegible
Weight: 0.79 g.
Cat. ref.: –.
Site ref.: MG88, D3, SF 205.
Find-spot: destruction level in baptistery, phase 7.

30. Uncertain (late Roman, ?fourth century AD). Mint uncertain. AE.
obv. illegible
rev. illegible
Weight: 0.47 g.
Cat. ref.: –.
Site ref.: MG88, D220, SF 246.
Find-spot: destruction level in baptistery, phase 7.

31. Uncertain (?fourth century AD). Mint uncertain. AE.
obv. illegible
rev. illegible
Weight: 0.80 g.
Cat. ref.: –.
Site ref.: MG89, L147, SF 462.
Find-spot: top fill of north cistern, phase 3.

32. Uncertain (?fourth century AD). Mint uncertain. AE.
obv. illegible
rev. illegible
Weight: 0.17 g (fragment).
Cat. ref.: –.
Site ref.: MG89, M38, SF 571.
Find-spot: rubble layer, phase 3.

33. Uncertain (?fourth century AD). Mint uncertain. AE.
obv. illegible
rev. illegible
Weight: 1.01 g.
Cat. ref.: –.
Site ref.: MG90, M97/37, SF 757.
Find-spot: silt over late Roman floor, phase 3.

34. Uncertain (?fourth-fifth centuries AD). Mint uncertain. AE.
obv. illegible
rev. illegible
Weight: 0.51 g (fragment).
Cat. ref.: –.
Site ref.: MG88, E42, SF 266.
Find-spot: on floor in the large room, phase 3.

35. Uncertain (?fourth-fifth centuries AD). Mint uncertain. AE.
obv. illegible
rev. illegible
Weight: 0.29 g (fragment).
Cat. ref.: –.
Site ref.: MG88, E106, SF 364.
Find-spot: on floor in the large room, phase 3.

36. Uncertain (?fourth-fifth centuries AD). Mint uncertain. AE.
obv. illegible
rev. illegible
Weight: 0.78 g.
Cat. ref.: –.
Site ref.: MG90, M94, SF 736.
Find-spot: rubble fill, phase 3.

37. Uncertain (?fourth-fifth centuries AD). Mint uncertain. AE.
obv. illegible
rev. illegible
Weight: 0.18 g (fragment).
Cat. ref.: –.
Site ref.: MG90, M103, SF 756.
Find-spot: debris from early medieval kiln, phase 5.

38. Uncertain (?fourth-fifth centuries AD). Mint uncertain. AE.

obv. illegible
rev. illegible
Weight: 0.95 g.
Cat. ref.: –.
Site ref.: MG90, M97, SF 766.
Find-spot: silt over late Roman floor, phase 3.

39. Uncertain (?fourth-fifth centuries AD). Mint uncertain. AE.
obv. illegible
rev. illegible
Weight: 0.75 g.
Cat. ref.: –.
Site ref.: MG90, M143, SF 800.
Find-spot: cut into drain, phase 3.

40. Uncertain (?fourth-fifth centuries AD). Mint uncertain. AE.
obv. illegible
rev. illegible
Weight: 1.05 g.
Cat. ref.: –.
Site ref.: MG90, M145, SF 814.
Find-spot: worn rubble cobbling over demolished wall and part of tessellated floor of the plunge bath, phase 3.

41. Uncertain (?fourth-fifth centuries AD). Mint uncertain. AE.
obv. illegible
rev. illegible
Weight: 0.91 g.
Cat. ref.: –.
Site ref.: MG90, M136, SF 821.
Find-spot: occupation layer over bath-house, phase 3.

42. Uncertain (?fourth-fifth centuries AD). Mint uncertain. AE.
obv. illegible
rev. illegible
Weight: 0.81 g.
Cat. ref.: –.
Site ref.: MG90, M159, SF 824.
Find-spot: fill of tank cut into late Roman floor, phase 3.

43. Uncertain (?fourth-fifth centuries AD). Mint uncertain. AE.
obv. illegible
rev. illegible
Weight: 0.33 g (fragment).
Cat. ref.: –.
Site ref.: MG90, M97, SF 836.
Find-spot: silt over late Roman floor, phase 3.

44. Uncertain (?late fourth-early fifth centuries AD). Mint uncertain. AE.
obv. illegible
rev. ?VICTORIA AVGGG
Weight: 0.96 g.
Cat. ref.: –.
Site ref.: MG90, M135, SF 784.
Find-spot: medieval dump, phase 5/6.

45. Uncertain (late fourth-early fifth centuries AD). Mint uncertain. AE.
obv. illegible
rev. illegible
Weight: 0.52 g.
Cat. ref.: –.
Site ref.: MG87, A42, SF 49.
Find-spot: unstratified.

46. Honorius (AD 410-23). Rome. AE 4.
obv. DN HONORI-VS PF AVG

rev. VICTORIA AVGG
Weight: unknown.
Cat. ref.: *LRBC* II, 828.
Site ref.: MG86, A23, SF 6.
Find-spot: from the mouth of a skeleton, in burial 26, phase 5/6?

47. Uncertain (?fourth-sixth centuries AD). Mint uncertain. AE.
obv. illegible
rev. illegible
Weight: 0.10 g (fragment).
Cat. ref.: –.
Site ref.: MG87, A41, SF 43.
Find-spot: unstratified.

48. Uncertain (?fourth-sixth centuries AD). Mint uncertain. AE.
obv. illegible
rev. illegible
Weight: 1.03 g.
Cat. ref.: –.
Site ref.: MG88, H2, SF 184.
Find-spot: hillwash.

49. Uncertain (?fourth-sixth centuries AD). Mint uncertain. AE.
obv. illegible
rev. illegible
Weight: 0.61 g.
Cat. ref.: –.
Site ref.: MG88, D48, SF 258.
Find-spot: ashy layer in baptistery, phase 3+.

50. Uncertain (?late fourth-sixth centuries AD). Mint uncertain. AE.
obv. illegible
rev. illegible
Weight: 0.61 g.
Cat. ref.: –.
Site ref.: MG88, D301, SF 320.
Find-spot: pit in baptistery, phase 6.

51. ?Marcian (AD 456-7) (fifth-sixth centuries AD). Mint uncertain. AE.
obv. illegible
rev. ?monogram
Weight: 1.02 g.
Cat. ref.: –.
Site ref.: MG90, M109, SF 769.
Find-spot: disturbed grave, phase 6.

52. Uncertain (?fifth-sixth centuries AD). Mint uncertain. AE.
obv. illegible
rev. ?monogram
Weight: 0.29 g.
Cat. ref.: –.
Site ref.: MG89, L122, SF 416.
Find-spot: fill of roadside drain, phase 3+.

53. Uncertain. (?fifth-sixth centuries AD). Mint uncertain. AE.
obv. illegible
rev. ?monogram
Weight: 0.52 g.
Cat. ref.: –.
Site ref.: MG90, M115, SF 780.
Find-spot: silt layer, over late Roman floors, phase 3.

54. Justinian I (AD 527-65). Carthage. AE 20 nummi. Fig. 168
obv. DNJVST[INIANVS PP]

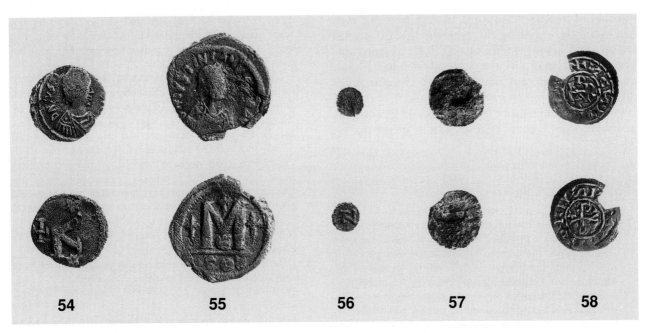

Fig. 168. Coins of Justinian (cat. 54-6), Totila (cat. 57) and Pope Hadrian III (cat. 58). *(KW)*

rev. ⊕̸Ҝ̌

Weight: 6.19 g total.

Cat. ref.: *MIB* 187.

Site ref.: MG88, D52, SF 302.

Find-spot: collapsed roof, end of phase 3.

55. Justinian I (AD 527-65). Constantinople. AE 40 nummi. Fig. 168.

obv. DNJVSTINIANVS PP AVG

rev. +M+

Weight: 16.75 g total.

Cat. ref.: *MIB* 87.

Site ref.: MG88, D52, SF 323.

Find-spot: collapsed roof, end of phase 3.

56. Justinian I (AD 527-65). ?Constantinople. AE nummus. Fig. 168.

obv. bust r.

rev. ᚱ√

Weight: 0.57 g.

Cat. ref.: *MIB* 94.

Site ref.: MG88, D52, SF 332.

Find-spot: make-up layer in baptistery, ?phase 5.

57. Baduila (Totila) (Ostrogoth) (AD 541-52). ?Constantinople. AE 10 nummi. Fig. 168.

obv. DN BADV [ELA REX]

rev. FLOREA [SEMPER]

Weight: 3.06 g.

Cat. ref.: *MIB* 90b.

Site ref.: MG88, D, SF 335.

Find-spot: unstratified.

58. Pope Hadrian III (AD 884-5). Rome. AR denarius. Fig. 168.

obv. SCSPETRVS, in centre

rev. CAROLVSIMP, in centre

Weight: 0.87 g.

Cat. ref.: *CNI* XV, p. 76 no. 1.

Site ref.: MG88, D135, SF 381.

Find-spot: found in infant burial, no. 43, in the baptistery, phase 5.

THE SMALL FINDS (FIGS 169–76), by Lindsay Allason-Jones

The small finds cover a wide date-range, from prehistoric to medieval times, although the majority belongs to the Roman period. The materials represented are silver, copper alloy, lead, bone, glass, fired clay, jet and stone. There is also some ironwork, discussed separately (Jackson, below).

The largest group comprises the lead. Much of this is in the form of strips and plugs and was found in burials, the baptistery or the bath-house. While the pieces from the last two contexts can be identified or postulated as waterproofing – strips pushed into cracks to stop leaks – the fragments from the burials are less obvious. It is possible that they performed a similar function in lead coffins. The two lead ingots and the amount of waste found in the fill of the graves suggests that either coffins were being sealed *in situ* or that leadworking was being carried out in close proximity. Two of the lead items can be identified as tackle for river fishing.

The bulk of the copper-alloy objects is pieces of jewellery or domestic artefacts, with only two pieces offering a possible military origin: a piece of binding (cat. 24) and an openwork harness mount (cat. 25). As with the lead, there were several signs of metalworking in the form of copper-alloy casting waste, offcuts and a clay mould (cat. 144).

One small group of objects which can be found in the lead, iron and copper-alloy sections, is the hooked rods which have been tentatively identified as clips for securing thin slabs of marble veneer. Only one of the more common T-shaped clips was found.

The bone material was represented largely by needles and pins cut from ungulate long bones. A number of needles was found, of varying sizes, with two methods of making the eyes: the first group has an unusual arrangement of one long rectangular hole with a small circular hole above and below; the second group has had two small circular holes drilled close together so that they link.

There are remarkably few glass beads in comparison with the quantity of jewellery in other materials.

OBJECT OF SILVER

1. Fig. 169. Very large finger-ring (modern ring size W). The hoop has a D-shaped cross-section which expands slightly at the shoulder to enclose a flat oval panel on which a motif has been incised. Too little survives of the motif for an accurate identification to be attempted although a peacock's head has been suggested. The shoulders each have three very lightly incised transverse lines and a single line marks the edge of the central panel. Cf. Pompeii: Siviero 1954: pl. 230a, no. 425; first century BC-first century AD.
   Internal diameter 20.5 mm; W. 1.5 mm; T. across panel 5.5 mm. M86, SF 727. Phase 5/6.

OBJECTS OF COPPER ALLOY

2. (Not illustrated.) Humped bow of oval section from a simple bow brooch. The head, pin and most of the catch-plate are missing. First century BC-first century AD. Cf. Famà 1985b: tav. 60, no. 6.
   L. 25 mm; W. 3 mm; T. 3.5 mm. SF 390. Plough-soil

3. Fig. 169. Brooch of the Aucissa type with a vestigial bar head. The strip bow has a marked curve and is decorated on the face with a wide central rib with flanking grooves. The raised edges have been notched to give a beaded effect. The lower bow has two shallow transverse grooves before tapering to the moulded foot with its conical terminal. The catch-plate is short and has a limited turnover. The pin is missing.
   This type of brooch originated in Gaul in the Augustan period and spread widely throughout the Empire during the first and second centuries AD. Cf. Waldbaum 1983: nos. 681-2; Fisch and Toll 1949: pl. X, nos. 8 and 10.
   Total L. 41.5 mm; W. of head 9 mm; L. of catch-plate turnover 9 mm; T. of bow 2 mm. L165, SF 602. Fish-pond, early second century.

4. (Not illustrated.) Head-plate of a square-headed brooch showing traces of white metalling on one face. The surviving fragment indicates a flat border with a central transverse rib below which is a countersunk area leading to the missing bow. Cf. Crummy 1983: no. 90. Second century AD.
   W. 10 mm; H. 7 mm; total T. 4 mm. M9, SF 762. Phase 5/6.

5. (Not illustrated.) Fragment of a circular-sectioned rod. Brooch-pin?
   L. 22 mm; T. 2 mm. M104, SF 739. Phase 2.

6. Fig. 169. Annular strip ring with a shallow convex face. The hoop expands to a central panel which is not delineated but has a stamped motif consisting of a circle divided into four segments by an internal cross. Each segment contains a small stamped circle. The ring has been made by overlapping the pointed ends of a strip and soldering the two together with tin. The join has then been polished smooth.
   Objects decorated with similar motifs have been found in a number of sixth-century contexts in Britain and Frisia: Ritchie 1971: 105, no. 34; Roes 1963: 40, pl. XXXIX, no. 9.
   Int. D. 19 mm (modern ring size S); W. 1.25 mm; T. 3.75-7 mm. A28, SF 8. Phase 5/6 (burial no. 26).

7. (Not illustrated.) Annular bracelet of oval section with blunt terminals. The condition is poor but traces survive of worn transverse ribs arranged in well-spaced groups. This is a common form throughout the Roman Empire from the first century AD onwards.
   Int. D. 69 × 52 mm; W. 1.5 mm; T. 2 mm. M67, SF 676. Phase 5.

8. (Not illustrated.) Distorted length of D-sectioned wire with one rounded end surviving. Bracelet?
   W. 3 mm; T. 1 mm. L105, SF 595. Fish-pond, later second century.

9. Fig. 169. Solid, rectangular-sectioned arm of a folding rule with a rounded end. Close to the upper end a rectangular block with a circular boss projects from one side. The end itself is cut obliquely, leaving a circular hinge loop with a rectangular stop panel below it. The length of the rule is equal to a Roman foot, and three faces of the shank have incised dots variously spaced to indicate smaller fractions of a foot: on one face a single central dot indicates quarters, on the second face dots are placed every 18 mm, dividing the rule into sixteenths, while on the third face the dots are every 25 mm, indicating twelfths.
   The rounded end of this rule suggests that it was a dual-purpose instrument, doubling as a pair of dividers or compasses (circinus). See Adams (1984: fig. 84); cf. Ward-Perkins and Claridge 1976: no. 266. For a parallel from Bonn, cf. Büsing in *Rheinische Landesmuseum Bonn* 2/93.
   L. 148 mm; W. 3 mm; T. 3.5 mm. D1, SF 45. Plough-soil.

10. Fig. 169. Incomplete buckle of lentoid section. There is a crossbar with a depressed seating for the pin but the iron hinge-pin has been held proud by two projections each pierced by a circular hole.
    W. 27 mm; L. 25 mm; T. of hoop 4 mm. M9, SF 423. Phase 5/6.

11. Fig. 169. Annular ring buckle of circular section. The oval-sectioned pin is made from a different copper alloy and is wrapped loosely round the ring, suggesting either a replacement or that the buckle was fabricated from a plain ring and a length of wire by an amateur hand.
    Int. D. of ring 14.5 mm; T. 2.75 mm; L. of pin 23 mm; T. of pin 2 mm. M38, SF 673. Phase 5.

12. Fig. 169. Small triangle cut from a larger sheet. The surviving edge is rounded and decorated by transverse nicks and an incised marginal line. The face has been heavily silvered or tinned while the back shows traces of adhesive or solder.
    This has been cut from a rectangular mirror of Lloyd-Morgan's (1981) Type Ad, a mainly first-century AD form. Dr Lloyd-Morgan has suggested (pers. comm. 1991) that Type A decorated mirrors 'may well have been Italian in inspiration. The distribution of these mirrors probably reflects trade in these luxury items from one or more workshops in Italy itself'.

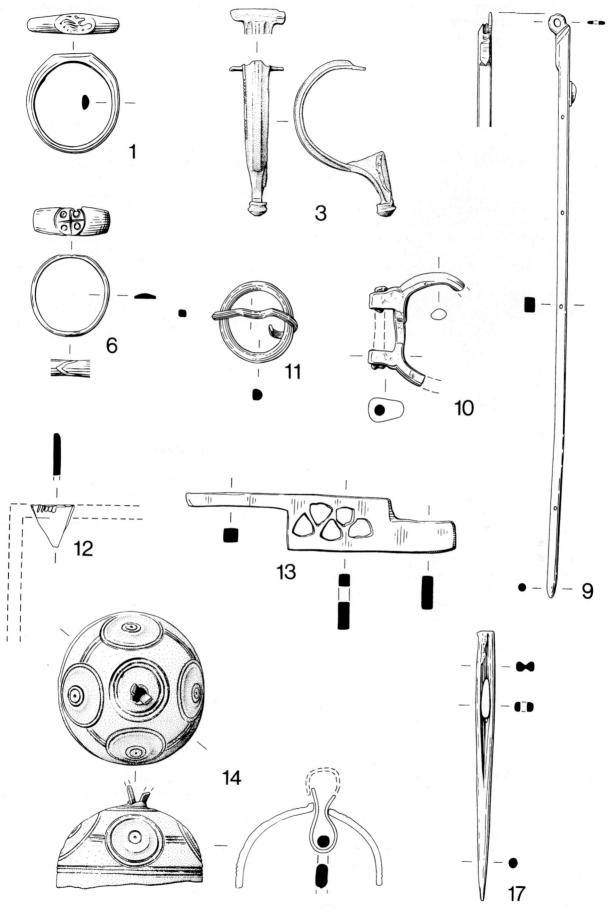

Fig. 169. Objects of copper alloy (1:1). *(SC/SA)*

Fig. 170. Copper-alloy jug (cat. 15). *(KW)*

Similar decoration can be seen on a bronze vase from Istanbul, which has been dated to AD 400 or later (Comstock and Vermeule 1971: no. 484), and on a bottle from Syria (Richter 1915: 196, no. 517).
D. 38 mm; T. of walls 2 mm. D338, SF 386. Phase ?5.

15. Figs 170 and 171. Jug with a splayed flanged base decorated with incised lines on the slope. The body of the vessel rises from a bulge at the top of the base. Around the neck there is a series of shallow ribs and incised lines. The flared rim is indented on the inner edge, suggesting a seating for a lid. There is a roughly circular hole with a washer or solder scar around it impinging on the lowest register of the neck decoration: this may have held a safety chain for the lid. The missing handle was attached to the rim and to the body – traces of lead/tin solder survive both on the rim and to the left of an area of damage on the body.

This tall elegant form of jug is well known from fourth- and fifth-century AD contexts in silver and copper alloy, although examples are usually highly decorated: for example, Petrossa: Strong 1966: 188-9, fig. 37a; Esquiline Treasure: Shelton 1981: cat. no. 61; Tăuteni-Bihor: Dumitraşcu 1973: tav. XLV-LXVI. The closest parallels are two silver vessels from Tomb 2 at Qustul in Nubia: Emery and Kirwan 1938: pl. 64B. See also Arnason (1936: fig. 1). From this list of parallels it may be seen that the distribution is wide although the production centre may well have been in Italy.
H. 261 mm; D. of base 75 mm; max. D. of body *c.* 90 mm; int. D. of rim 41 mm. A36, SF 29. Phase 3, fill of bath-house hypocaust.

16. (Not illustrated.) Curved rod of rectangular section with rounded edges. Possibly part of a bucket handle.
L. 62 mm; T. 6 mm; W. 7.5 mm. D6, SF 60. Phase 7.

17. Fig. 169. Short thick needle of oval section with a long oval eye set in a groove which runs from the blunt head and tapers well down the shank on both faces.
L. 66 mm; max. W. 5 mm; max. T. 3 mm; eye 10 × 2 mm. D6, SF 55. Phase 7.

18. (Not illustrated.) Incomplete needle of oval section which flattens at the head. The long rectangular eye is not countersunk. The point is bent to a right angle.
L. 126 mm; max. W. 4.5 mm; T. 3.5 mm. L105, SF 499. Fish-pond, later second century.

19. (Not illustrated.) Needle of oval section lacking both head and tip. The rectangular eye is not countersunk.
L. 71 mm; T. 2 mm; W. 1.5 mm. L105, SF 540a. Fish-pond, later second century.

20. Fig. 171. Thick elliptical plate, broken at one end and hooked at the other with shallow ribbing across the curve. Similar pieces have been found in lead and iron (iron cat. 3) and may have been used to secure marble veneer.
L. 28 mm; max. W. 8 mm; T. 4 mm. H22, SF 326. Phase 3.

21. Fig. 171. Thick strip with a hooked end. Marble veneer revetment clip, similar to above.
L. 33 mm; max. W. 6 mm; T. 2.5 mm. M47, SF 573. Phase 3.

22. Fig. 171. Stud with an oval-sectioned tapering shank which is pierced at its mid-point by a circular hole. The conical head emerges from a facetted disc neck. Variant on the 'bell-shaped stud' form? See Allason-Jones (1985) and Davidson (1952: pl. 63, nos. 852-7).
L. 36 mm; W. of head 7 mm; T. of shank 3 × 5 mm. C1, SF 77. Plough-soil.

Other examples from Italy include those from the Castello Sforzesco, Milan; Soprintendenza alla Antichità, Salerno, no. 1621; Museo Archeologico Mecanate, Arezzo; Museo Civico, Bologna, no. 321; and Museo Etrusco Guarnacci, Volterra, no. 946. (I am grateful to Dr Lloyd-Morgan for these references.)
L. 11 mm; W. 12 mm; T. 2 mm. M132, SF 786. Phase 3.

13. Fig. 169. Latch-lifter with a rectangular centre-plate through which five interlocking triangles, arranged in two rows, have been cut. The tang is square in section, the tip is rectangular in section. Cf. Settefinestre: Famà 1985a: tav. 7, nos. 3-11.
L. 70 mm; W. 14 mm; T. 2.5-5 mm. A29, SF 10. Phase 5/6.

14. Fig. 169. Incomplete bell, now hemispherical, but possibly part of a globular rumbler bell. Three incised lines run around the surviving edge. The body is decorated with four groups of incised circular motifs, each consisting of double ribs around a double dot-and-ring motif. Each roundel is joined to its neighbour by a band of three incised horizontal lines which were incised before the roundels. A circle of three incised concentric lines surrounds a roughly cut hole at the top. The clapper is incomplete – all that survives is an iron loop held in place by a length of folded copper-alloy wire, which protrudes from the hole. One of the ends of the wire is complete, indicating that the loop was penannular or hooked.

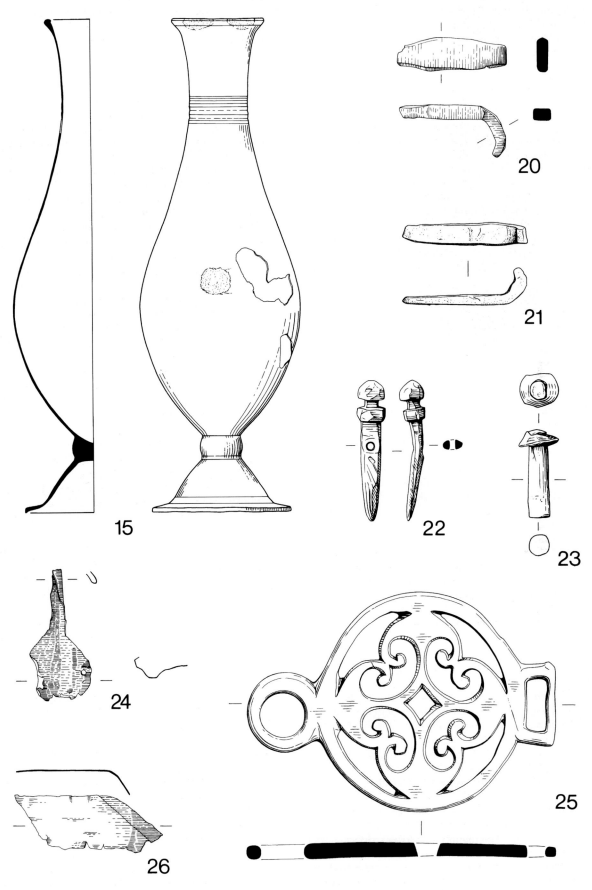

Fig. 171. Objects of copper alloy. All 1:1, except 15, 24, 26 (1:2). *(SC/SA)*

23. Fig. 171. Oval-sectioned rod with one end pushed carelessly through a small circular washer.
    L. 22 mm; T. 5 mm; D. of washer 10.5 mm; T. of washer 0.5 mm. M23, SF 484. Phase 3.

24. Fig. 171. Curved length of U-sectioned binding, the edges of which splay out into two wings, each pierced by a small hole. The wings have been pulled apart, suggesting that the binding was deliberately removed.
    L. 65 mm; W. across binding 7 mm. D168, SF 160. Phase 6, burial 59.

25. Fig. 171. Large openwork harness mount. The centre is circular with a plain border surrounding four conjoining peltae arranged with inward pointing terminals around an open lozenge. A rectangular loop projects from one side opposite a circular loop on the other side. Both loops show signs of wear.
    Openwork harness mounts are widespread in military contexts in the second to fourth centuries AD, although exact parallels are rare. A comparable piece from Dura Europos has the peltae arranged with their terminals pointing out from a solid centre (Fisch and Toll 1949: pl. II, 15).
    D. of circle 57 mm; rectangular loop int. 14 × 5.5 mm; circular loop int. 12 mm; T. 3 mm. D52, SF 316. Roof collapse, c. mid-sixth century.

26. Fig. 171. Trapezoidal sheet with three deep nicks cut from one edge. There are traces of lead/tin solder on the back.
    L. 90 mm; W. 26 mm; T. 1 mm. L149, SF 545. North cistern, late second century.

27. Fig. 172. Two pieces of a T-shaped sheet pierced by three lozenge-shaped holes, one in the centre of the crossbar, the other on the midline at the lower end of the shank. There are traces of lead/tin solder on the back. Similar pieces, which probably came from boxes, are known from Settefinestre (Famà 1985a: tav. 10, no. 4) and Olynthus (Robinson 1941).
    L. 50 mm; W. across arms 31 mm; W. across shank 9.5-12 mm; T. 0.75 mm. L147, SF 463. North cistern, late second century.

28. Fig. 172. T-shaped sheet similar to above, but with a longer crossbar which has three holes drilled through, one in the centre and one at each end. A fourth hole is drilled through the end of the shank.
    L. 57 mm; W. across arms 70 mm; W. across shank 20 mm; T. 0.5 mm. L105, SF 583. Fish-pond, late second century.

29. (Not illustrated.) Fragment of a disc washer.
    D. 23 mm; T. 2 mm; W. of hole 5 mm. M97, SF 760. Phase 3.

30. (Not illustrated.) Roughly rectangular sheet with a central rectangular hole which has been punched through and left untrimmed, suggesting that the sheet was riveted to leather or wood.
    L. 11 mm; W. 9 mm; T. 0.33 mm. M139, SF 797. Phase 5.

31. (Not illustrated.) Distorted rectangular plate pierced by three headed rivets.
    L. 20 mm; W. 7 mm; T. 0.75 mm; L. of rivets 5 mm. Q10, SF 702. Phase 6/7.

32. (Not illustrated.) Fragments of a narrow strip with silver metalling on one face and traces of lead/tin solder on the reverse. One piece is pierced by a circular hole.
    W. 13.5 mm; T. 1 mm; W. of hole 2.5 mm. L104, SF 430. Phase 2+.

33. (Not illustrated.) Length of oval-sectioned wire coiled into a ring with overlapping terminals.
    Int. D. 11.5-13 mm; W. 1.5 mm; T. 1 mm. B1, SF 9. Phase 7.

34. (Not illustrated.) Short length of oval-sectioned wire bent to a shallow S-shape.
    L. 17 mm; W. 1.5 mm; T. 1 mm. J2, SF 398. Phase 3.

35. (Not illustrated.) Annular oval ring of semi-oval section.
    Int. D. 29 × 23 mm; W. 2 mm; T. 3.5 mm. D110, SF 152. Phase 6.

36. (Not illustrated.) Penannular ring with butted ends. The shank is of semi-oval section but the ends are oval in section.
    Int. D. 15 mm; W. 3 mm; T. 3.5 mm. E106, SF 363. Phase 3.

37. (Not illustrated.) Penannular loop of circular section with nipped ends. Chain link?
    L. 16 mm; T. 1.25 mm. L102, SF 425. Phase 3.

38. (Not illustrated.) Curved rod of circular section narrowing to semi-oval section towards one end.
    L. 33 mm; W. 4.5-5.5 mm; T. 4.5-5 mm. A12, SF 25. Phase 6.

39. (Not illustrated.) Length of circular-sectioned wire bent to a shallow S-shape.
    L. 54 mm; T. 2.75 mm. M126, SF 779. Phase 3.

40. (Not illustrated.) Rectangular-sectioned rod with a splayed rounded end. From metalworking?
    L. 37 mm; W. 1.5 mm; T. 1.5 mm. J1, SF 342. Phase 7.

41. (Not illustrated.) Triangular sheet with roughly cut edges. One corner is folded and another is partly folded and then folded back on itself. A small hole cuts through the latter corner.
    L. 137 mm; total W. c. 212 mm; T. 1 mm. D6, SF 659. Phase 7.

42. (Not illustrated.) Several fragments of narrow strip.
    W. 12.5 mm; T. 0.33 mm. L105, SF 406. Fish-pond, late second century.

43. (Not illustrated.) Crumpled trapezoidal sheet.
    W. 11.5-13 mm; L. 8 mm; T. 0.5 mm. M38, SF 569. Phase 5/6.

44. (Not illustrated.) Distorted strip with tapering edges. Offcut?
    L. 47 mm; W. 3-7.5 mm; T. 1 mm. L105, SF 540b. Fish-pond, late second century.

45. (Not illustrated.) Fragment of metalworking waste.
    L. 10 mm. E1, SF 264. Phase 7.

OBJECTS OF LEAD

46. Fig. 172. Length of water pipe made by soldering the long edges of a lead sheet together and then applying a separate strip along the join. A sliver of lead of a different alloy has at one time been applied between the pipe and the strip, presumably to correct a leak. This suggests that the pipe was either above ground or easily accessible. An old pick (?) hole has distorted the pipe near one end.
    This falls within Vassy's (1934) Type 1B. See also Cochet and Hansen (1986: 29, fig. 5), Adams (1984: 275, pls 582-4); and Kraus and von Matt (1975: pl. 65), who show a length of similar piping at Pompeii used as a downcomer stapled to a wall.
    L. 511 mm; int. D. 61 × 90 mm; T. 6 mm; W. of strip 20 mm; T. of strip 6-10 mm. C1. Plough-soil.

47. Fig. 172. Pipe of tapering circular section with an expanded lip at the narrower end. There is a gash

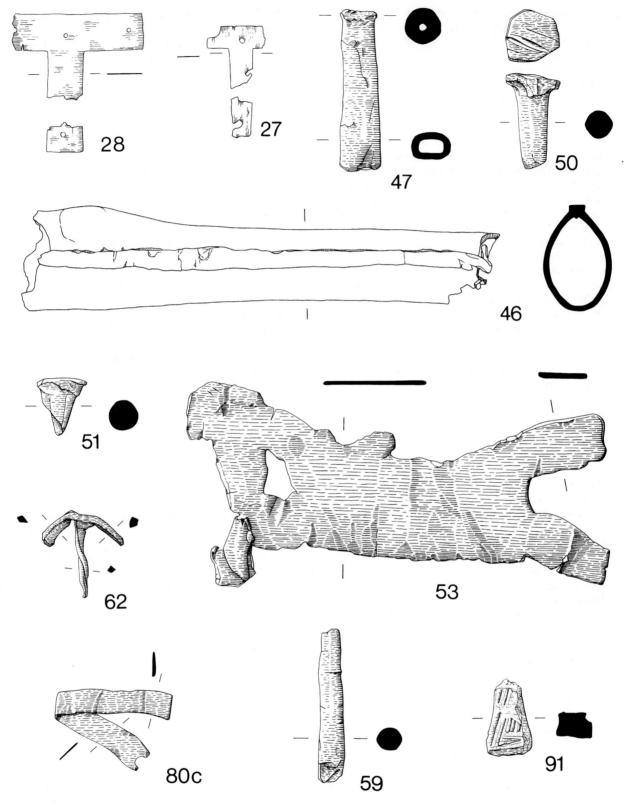

Fig. 172. Objects of copper alloy (28, 29), and lead. All 1:2, except 50, 51, 59 (1:1), and 46 (1:4). *(SC)*

across the face where a rivet or a pick has gone through.

L. 82 mm; W. 17-21 mm. H1, SF 196. Phase 7.

48. (Not illustrated.) Rough crescent of lead of lozenge section. See Bass and von Doorninck (1982: 308-9, fig. 13.3, LW20), who have identified similar pieces from

Yassi Ada and Herculaneum as fishing lures. See also Oppian, *Halieutica* iii. 144.

L. 42 mm; W. 14 mm; T. 8 mm. M104, SF 738. Phase 2.

49. (Not illustrated.) Rectangular strip folded in half lengthwise. Although this is a simple piece and could have had a multitude of uses, Bass and von Doorninck

have identified similar pieces from Yassi Ada as seventh-century weights for fishing nets (1982: 306-9).

L. 42 mm; W. (folded) 10 mm. L105, SF 550. Fish-pond, late second century.

50. (Not illustrated.) Plug with a disc head and a thick circular-sectioned shank. The head is deeply scratched.

D. 16 mm; H. 24 mm; T. of shank 8 mm. B8, SF 23. Phases 6-7, burial no. 18.

51. Fig. 172. Disc-headed stud or plug with a wrapped conical shank. This was found with a quantity of scrap lead and may have been destined for recycling.

D. 13 mm; H. 14 mm. B80, SF 33a. Phases 5-6, burial no. 12.

52. Fig. 172. Plug with circular-sectioned shank and roughly expanded ends.

L. 24 mm; T. of shank 7.5 mm. D212, SF 208. Phase 6, burial no. 47.

53. Fig. 172. Large dolium tie with a flange at the waist. Cf. Frova 1973: taf. 138, no. 42; Cotton 1979: 82, fig. 18, no. 7.

L. 103 mm; W. 36 mm; T. 24 mm. C/D1. Plough-soil.

54. Fig. 173. Large dolium tie with one end still attached to the pot. The outer face is scored with a series of oblique lines. See above.

L. 96 mm; max. W. 34 mm; max. T. 15 mm. C51, SF 203. Fill of limekiln, early-mid fifth century.

55. (Not illustrated.) Small dolium tie with only one end surviving.

L. 66 mm; T. 6-16.5 mm. E32, SF 356. Phase 3.

56. (Not illustrated.) 'Butterfly'-shaped dolium tie. Cf. Annechino 1982: fig. 3B.

L. 94 mm; W. 19-28 mm; T. 21 mm. K101, SF 393. Plough-soil.

57. (Not illustrated.) Circular-sectioned rod with one undercut bent end.

L. 57 mm; T. 7.25 mm. E32, SF 355. Phase 3.

58. (Not illustrated.) Triangular-sectioned rod with one rounded end and one twisted end. Waste.

L. 43 mm; W. 5 mm; T. 5.5 mm. H3, SF 360. Phase 7.

59. Fig. 172. Curved, circular-sectioned, tapering rod. The wider end is cleft, the narrow end is hollowed.

L. 40 mm; W. 5.5-7 mm. M27, SF 523. Phase 5.

60. (Not illustrated.) Curved, triangular-sectioned strip.

L. 43 mm; T. 7 mm; W. 10 mm. M105, SF 867. Phase 3.

61. (Not illustrated.) Blunt hook of tapered circular section. Marble clip?

L. 86 mm; T. 7.5-13.5 mm. M95, SF 729. Phases 5-6.

62. Fig. 172. T-shaped cladding clamp with a twisted shank.

L. 43 mm; W. across arms 44 mm; T. of arms 5 mm. D80, SF 80. Robbing trench of bath-house, phase 7.

63. (Not illustrated.) Large wide strip with a bifurcated end. The other end is also indented and has an irregular hole cut through it. Strapping?

L. 248 mm; max. W. 89 mm; T. 2 mm. C/D1. Plough-soil.

64. (Not illustrated.) Carefully cut strip with one thick rounded end and parallel sides, folded in three.

L. 151 mm; W. 10 mm; T. 1-4 mm. A19, SF 4. Phase 3.

65. (Not illustrated.) Strip with parallel sides, folded in half.

Total L. 91 mm; W. 11.5 mm; T. 1 mm. B22, SF 14. Phases 6-7, burial no. 18.

66. (Not illustrated.) Rough strip pierced by a hole and broken across a second hole.

L. 106 mm; W. 12.5 mm; T. 2 mm. B29, SF 16. Phase 5, burial no. 13.

67. (Not illustrated.) Distorted strip tapering to a point.

L. 62 mm; W. 1.5-4.5 mm; T. 1.25 mm. B32, SF 18. Phases 5-6, burial no. 11.

68. (Not illustrated.) Quantities of scraps, strips and casting waste, presumably destined for recycling. It includes: (a) a rectangular strip folded in half lengthwise, L. 37

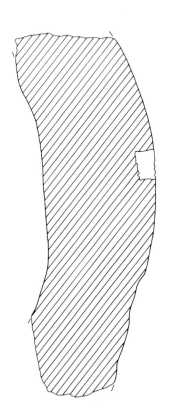
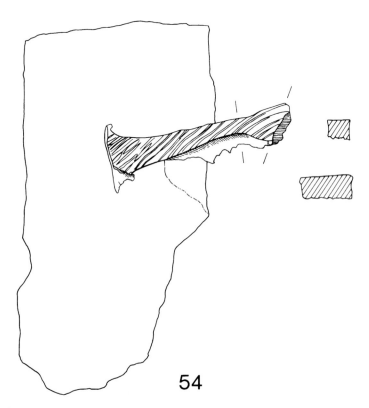

54

Fig. 173. Lead dolium tie (1:2). (SC)

mm; W. 22 mm; (b) strip with tapering sides, torn across a rivet hole, L. 45 mm; W. 12-16 mm. B64, SF 31. Phase 6/7.

69. (Not illustrated.) Four strips of waste. One piece is folded in half and has been cut obliquely across one end.
L. 97 mm; W. 13.5 mm; T. 1-2.5 mm. B80, SF 33. Phase 6.

70. (Not illustrated.) Waste apparently left after strips have been cut from a sheet and folded into three, possibly for recycling.
L. 60 mm, max. T. 3 mm. D5, SF 44. Phase 6, burial no. 93.

71. (Not illustrated.) Four strips: (a) distorted with parallel sides, curled at one end, L. 52 mm; W. 10 mm; T. 1 mm; (b) thickened rounded end of a strip, L. 19 mm; W. 7.5 mm; T. 0.5-2 mm; (c) rectangular, L. 32 mm; W. 9-11.5 mm; T. 1 mm; (d) rectangular with three cut sides, L. 35 mm; W. 13-15 mm; T. 1 mm. C2, SF 69. Phase 6, burial no. 2.

72. (Not illustrated.) Incomplete rectangular strip with bevelled edges.
L. 32 mm; W. 10 mm; T. 2 mm. C43, SF 85. Phase 6, burial 2.

73. (Not illustrated.) Rough strip folded in half.
L. 38 mm. D107. Phase 5, burial no. 24.

74. (Not illustrated.) Narrow wedged strip now folded in three. Coffin fitting?
Total L. 103 mm; W. 8-19 mm; T. 1-3 mm. C56, SF 110. Phase 6, burial no. 2.

75. (Not illustrated.) Incomplete strip with parallel sides. One edge has a neat triangle cut from it, possibly part of a rivet hole.
L. 44 mm; W. 12 mm; T. 1 mm. D107, SF 126. Phase 5, burial no. 24.

76. (Not illustrated.) Strip with parallel sides and a thick rounded base. The top is curled and incomplete. Roof tie?
L. 38 mm; W. 10 mm; T. 2-3 mm. D107, SF 131. Phase 5, burial no. 24.

77. (Not illustrated.) Carefully cut strip with parallel edges and tapered end, folded obliquely.
Total L. 146 mm; W. 11.5 mm; T. 2 mm. E16, SF 232. Phase 3.

78. (Not illustrated.) Two strips, one folded in half, the other tapered: (a) L. 110 mm; W. 5-12 mm; T. 1 mm; (b) L. 48 mm; W. 4.5-9 mm; T. 0.5 mm. E16, SF 249. Phase 3.

79. (Not illustrated.) Two strips with tapering edges: (a) L. 35 mm; W. 10 mm; T. 1 mm; (b) L. 44 mm; W. 10 mm; T. 1 mm. D244, SF 261. Phase 6.

80. Fig. 172. Three strips: (a) irregular distorted shape, L. 23 mm; (b) narrow with expanded end, L. 91 mm; W. 5-13 mm; T. 1.5 mm; (c) parallel sides which expand to enclose a rivet hole, broken across a second hole, folded in two, total L. 111.5 mm; W. 13-15 mm; T. 1-2 mm. D299, SF 318. Phase 6.

81. (Not illustrated.) Distorted strip.
L. 110 mm. D301, SF 338. Phase 6.

82. (Not illustrated.) Flat strip which expands to a ragged end which is pierced by a small, off-centre, circular hole.
L. 56 mm; W. 9.5-13.5 mm. D317, SF 348. Phase 3.

83. (Not illustrated.) S-shaped, rectangular-sectioned rod.
L. 97 mm; W. 10.5 mm; T. 10 mm. L162, SF 584. Phase 3.

84. (Not illustrated.) Distorted strip with parallel sides and blunt ends. A small hole is pierced near the edge at one end.
L. 113 mm; W. 11 mm; T. 1.5 mm. M75, SF 680. Phase 6.

85. (Not illustrated.) Two distorted strips: (a) L. 71 mm; W. 7-12 mm; T. 1 mm; (b) L. 108 mm; W. 7-12 mm; T. 1 mm. M64, SF 696. Phase 6.

86. (Not illustrated.) Rough trapezoidal sheet.
L. 58 mm; W. 112 mm; T. 2.5-14 mm. L101, SF 465. Phase 7.

87. (Not illustrated.) Sheet of irregular shape but with a smooth concave face.
L. 56 mm; W. 50 mm; T. 4 mm. L143, SF 470. Phase 2.

88. (Not illustrated.) Rectangular sheet with oblique ends.
L. 44 mm; W. 31 mm; T. 5 mm. M143, SF 802. Phase 3.

89. (Not illustrated.) Incomplete circular cake of lead with chamfered edges. Crucible residue? Cf. Meates 1987: 91, no. 225.
D. 90 mm; D. of base of crucible 75 mm?; max. T. 11 mm. D01, SF 234. Plough-soil.

90. (Not illustrated.) Bun-shaped ingot. Cf. Healy 1978: 160, pl. 47 (copper); Penhallurick 1986: 234 (tin).
D. 84 mm; T. 15 mm; weight: 625 g. E1, SF 217. Plough-soil.

91. Fig. 172. Incomplete triangular block with incised lines running parallel with the base and one sloping side. Keying for plaster?
H. 38 mm; W. 14-22 mm; T. 13 mm. E1, SF 254. Unstratified.

92. (Not illustrated.) Incomplete triangular block with two chamfered edges.
L. 26.5 mm; W. 21 mm; T. 3.5 mm. D284, SF 383. Phase 6, burial 68.

93. (Not illustrated.) Large rectangular block with oblique ends. A copper-alloy nail has left a scar in one edge. Ingot?
L. 132 mm; W. 57 mm; T. 9-19 mm; weight: 1.125 kg. D345, SF 378. Phase 5?

94. (Not illustrated.) Irregular block which appears to have been forced into a corner whilst still malleable. Waterproofing?
H. 26 mm; L. 32 mm; W. 28 mm. P17, SF 447. Phases 5-6.

95. (Not illustrated.) Rough block of triangular section with a deep groove down the apex.
L. 77 mm; W. 20 mm; T. 15 mm. M143, SF 804. Phase 3, bath-house robbing.

96. (Not illustrated.) Large irregular block with a wide groove along one face. Waterproofing which has been applied over a curved bar?
Total L. 160 mm; L. of bar 116 mm; W. of bar 15 mm; T. of bar c. 14 mm. M126, SF 782. Phase 2, bath-house.

97. (Not illustrated.) Distorted strip.
L. c. 180 mm; W. 5.5-11.5 mm; T. 1 mm. M126, SF 782. Phase 2, bath-house.

98. (Not illustrated.) Small incomplete hollow disc. Nail cover?
D. 10 mm; T. 0.33 mm. B64, SF 31. Phases 5-6, burial no. 12.

99. (Not illustrated.) Lead disc.
D. 12 mm; T. 1 mm. E1, SF 214. Phase 7.

Unidentifiable lead was also found in the following contexts. Most appears to have been casting waste or strips: C46, SF 86. Phases 6-7, burial no. 8; D94, SF 95. Phase 6; D173, SF 154. Phase 6, burial no. 25; D168, SF 156. Phase 6, burial no. 59; A42. Not phased; H10, SF 189. Phases 5-6; D219, SF 303. Phase 7?; D279, SF 315. Phase 6; E182, SF 374. Phase 1; M26. Phase 3; M26, SF 453. Phase 3; S4, SF 716. Phase 2; U/S, SF 730. Plough-soil; M103, SF 734. Phases 5-6; M97, SF 765. Phase 3; M97, SF 767. Phase 3.

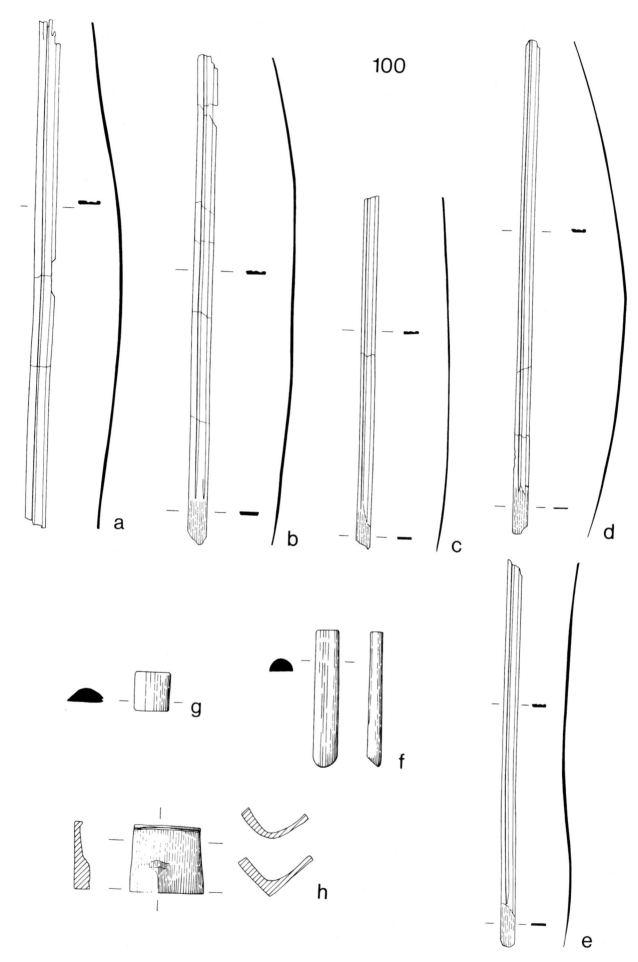

Fig. 174. Elements of the bone fan (1:2). *(SC)*

THE BONE OBJECTS

100. (a-e) Fig. 174. Fourteen fragments of flat narrow strips cut from (ungulate?) long bones, each decorated with two deep grooves, probably parts of a fan (see below). One edge is rounded and raised above the face, the other edge is flat. The groove nearest the ribbed edge is narrower than that nearest the flat edge. The decoration peters out at the terminals to a flat rough area with a rounded end. Unfortunately none of the strips survives with both ends complete.

The fragments vary in length (see below), but the longest reconstructed length of a strip is 268 mm. All the pieces are 8 mm wide and 1.25 mm thick. Lengths of individual fragments are: 175 mm; 36 mm; 51 mm; 203 mm; 83 mm; 101 mm; 27 mm; 57 mm; 20 mm; 37 mm; 55 mm; 67 mm; 134 mm; 43 mm. These join to give five strips measuring 268 mm; 256 mm; 180 mm; 203 mm; 260 mm (100 a-e). L105, SF 546/557/590.

100. (f) Fig. 174. One element of a two-piece handle cut from an (ungulate?) long bone. The piece is undecorated and semi-oval in section. One end is rounded, the other undercut obliquely. The back shows file marks. There is no rivet or indication of the method of attachment.

L. 70.5 mm; W. 12.5 mm; T. 6.5 mm. L105, SF 590.

100. (g) Fig. 174. Rectangular block of semi-oval section, cut from an (ungulate?) long bone with a deep narrow groove running down one edge. The surface is undecorated.

L. 20 mm; W. 19 mm; T. 6.5 mm. L105, SF 531e.

100. (h) Fig. 174. Section cut from an (ungulate?) long bone. The inner surface has been roughly smoothed but not polished. The walls are of uneven thickness and the outer face has been pared to form a rim at one end and a stepped corner at the other. The sides have been cut straight by a saw and trimmed by a file. The area between the stepped corner and the plain edge is slightly roughened with transverse striations as if not intended to be seen. The rest of the outer face has been polished.

H. 34 mm; L. 29.5 mm; W. 24 mm; T. 3-8 mm. L105, SF 564.

The pieces described above all come from the same context (the upper layer of the fish-pond, of the late second century AD), and appear to come from the same object. While the last artefact (100h) could be identified as the corner of a furniture fitting (cf. Richter 1926: fig. 313; Henig 1983: pl. 136), taken in association with the other elements it is more convincing as part of a fan, elements 100a-e being the fan spokes, element 100f being part of the handle, element 100g being part of the catch and element 100h being one half of the case cup.

There are a number of references to the fan (*flabellum*) in Roman literature. Martial described one made of peacocks' feathers (xiv. 67) and also suggested that there was another form which was painted or dyed green (iii. 82). Fans which were not intended to open and shut were leaf-shaped with a rigid handle (Smith 1865: 539). Another type (the *muscarum*) was used to keep flies off rather than to keep its owner cool (Martial xiv. 67). Strato (*Epigrammata* 22) referred to a linen fan stretched on a light frame, and it may be this type which is depicted on a tombstone from Carlisle (Coulston and Phillips 1988: no. 498), a tombstone from Autun (Eydoux 1962: fig. 362) and possibly on a fourth-century mosaic from Piazza Armerina (Balsdon 1962: pl. XII).

Details can be observed from the examples of fan cases found at York (Liversidge 1968: 148) and Argentomagus (Saint-Marcel, Indre: Coulon and Fauduet 1991). As the York example was found in a coffin and no spokes were recovered, it has been suggested that the fan was a strip of pleated leather or fabric which folded into the cases at each end and was opened by turning one handle through 360° to make a circular fan (see Coulon and Fauduet (1991) for a reconstruction drawing).

The Monte Gelato pieces seem to suggest that there was another form, although there is a marked similarity in the appearance of element 100h to the section linking the case and handle on both the York and the Argentomagus fans. The Monte Gelato fan has at least five, probably more, spokes. The roughened end of each spoke suggests that they were shaved in order to fit snugly together when the fan was shut whilst the single raised edge of each spoke may have been designed to stop the spokes 'overshooting' during closing. It is this raised edge, the shaved ends and the length of the strips which argues against these pieces being furniture or box inlay.

There are no fragments from the context or from the site which can be identified as fan cases. The suggested reconstruction, therefore, is of a two-piece handle held in place together with the ends of the spokes by elements 100g and 100h and secured by a separate band, possibly of metal, which fitted over the striated area on element 100h. It is possible that the fan did not open to the full circle shown on the Carlisle and Autun tombstones. There is no indication as to the material, which was presumably glued to the spokes: linen, chicken skin or fine leather would all have been suitable.

101. Fig. 175. One element of a two-piece handle of semi-oval section, cut to a curve from an (ungulate?) long bone. The piece is undecorated and semi-oval in section. One end is rounded and the other blunt. Cancellous material has been left untrimmed on the back. This is not the second piece of the fan handle, discussed above, but probably came from a knife.

L. 72 mm; W. 12-16 mm; T. 7 mm. L101. Plough-soil.

102. Fig. 175. One element of a two-piece handle with a semi-oval section, curved in both planes with a slight taper. One end is blunt, the other shows iron staining.

L. 60 mm; W. 14-15 mm; T. 5 mm. L105. Fish-pond, later second century.

103. Fig. 175. Fragment of bone or ivory inlay, originally a triangular piece with an arc cut from the apex. The face is decorated with a series of deep wide grooves, mostly following the edge of the piece.

L. 55 mm; W. 29 mm; T. 1 mm. L105, SF 587. Fish-pond, later second century.

104. Fig. 175. Centre-plate from a composite comb, cut from a long bone. The sides have been sawn straight, while the two edges have notches indicating that the teeth of the comb were cut after the pieces had been assembled. The notches on one edge are finer and closer together than those on the other edge.

Composite combs were manufactured from the third to the thirteenth centuries. Examples from Italy include Luni (Frova (1973: tav. 139, nos. 28, 29) has given further parallels from Brescia, Testona, and Ibligo-Invillino, all of post-Roman date).

L. 20.5 mm; W. 21.5 mm; T. 3.5 mm. M93, SF 741. Phase 3.

105. Fig. 175. Incomplete spindle with a bulging circular-sectioned shank. Both ends are broken but one had a

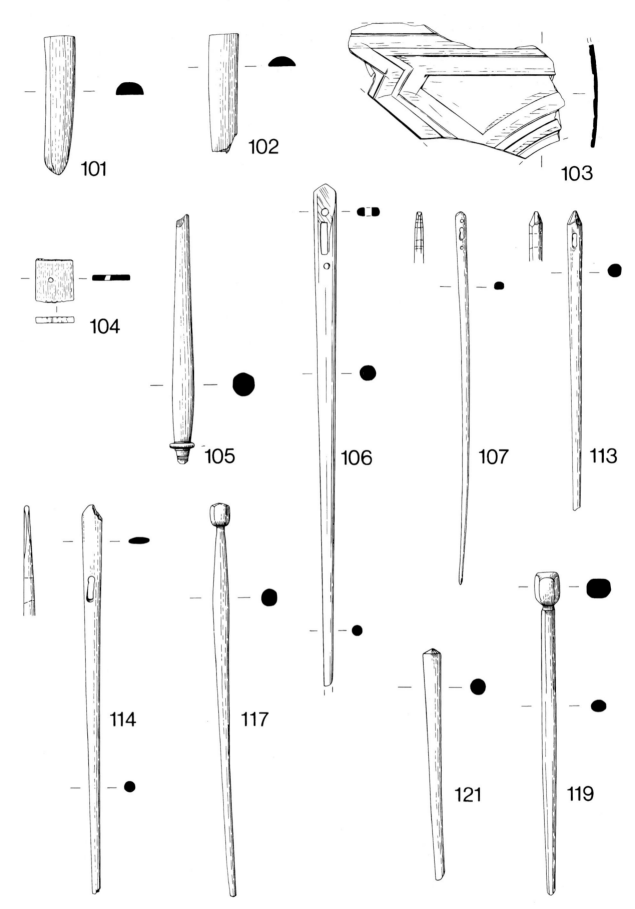

Fig. 175. Objects of bone. All 1:1 except 101 and 102 (1:2). *(SC/SA)*

pronounced ridge with two incised lines below it; cf. Wild 1970: pl. IIIb; MacGregor 1985: fig. 101, no. 3.
L. 63 mm; max. T. 7 mm. C/D1. Plough-soil.

106. Fig. 175. Large needle of circular section. The shank tapers from the flat pointed head which is pierced by three holes: a long rectangular hole with a small circular hole above and below. This arrangement of the eye is seen at Settefinestre: Famà 1985c: tav. 18, no. 6.
L. 131 mm; max. W. 6.5 mm; max. T. 4 mm; eyes: 8 × 2.5 mm; 2.5 mm; 2 mm. L105, SF 585. Fish-pond, later second century.

107. Fig. 175. Very fine needle with a slightly curved, oval-sectioned shank which narrows towards the pointed flat head. The point is well-shaped but flat. The head is pierced by two linked circular holes with a smaller circular hole above and below.
L. 96 mm; max. W. 3 mm; T. 2.5 mm; eyes: 3 × 1.5 mm; 1 mm; 1 mm. L165, SF 630. Fish-pond, early second century.

108. (Not illustrated.) Incomplete, oval-sectioned needle which tapers from the broken head. The arrangement of the eyes appears to have been similar to that described above: two linked circular holes and two separate holes.
L. 44 mm; max. W. 3 mm; max. T. 2.5 mm, eyes: 3 × 1.5 mm; 1mm. L165, SF 605. Fish-pond, early second century .

109. (Not illustrated.) Head of a needle which flattens to the rounded head. The elongated eye has been made by drilling a series of linked holes.
L. 20 mm; W. 5 mm; T. 2.5 mm; eye: 7 × 2 mm. L105, SF 506. Fish-pond, later second century.

110. (Not illustrated.) Incomplete needle of oval section with a pointed head. The eye has been formed by drilling two linked circular holes.
L. 48 mm; W. 3.5 mm; T. 3 mm; eye: 3 × 1.5 mm. L105, SF 520. Fish-pond, later second century.

111. (Not illustrated.) Needle with tapering, circular-sectioned shank and a conical head. The eye has been formed by drilling two linked circular holes.
L. 78.5 mm; T. 4 mm; eye: 3.5 × 2 mm. L165, SF 608. Fish-pond, early second century.

112. (Not illustrated.) Incomplete needle of tapering circular section. The pointed conical head has cancellous material left down one side which would have snagged on fine material, thus limiting its use. The eye has been formed by drilling two linked circular holes.
L. 39 mm; max. T. 3.5 mm; eye 3.5 × 2 mm. S10, SF 720. Phase 2/3, rock-cut road.

113. Fig. 175. Incomplete needle with a circular, slightly facetted shank, which tapers from the conical head. The eye has been made by drilling two linked circular holes.
L. 76.5 mm; max. T. 4 mm; eye: 3.5 × 1.5 mm. M104, SF 737. Phase 2.

114. Fig. 175. Incomplete needle of circular section which flattens and expands to a flat rounded head. The eye has been made by drilling a series of linked circular holes.
L. 101 mm; max. W. 5.5 mm; max. T. 3.5 mm; eye: 6.5 × 1.5 mm. L105, SF 539b. Fish-pond, later second century.

115. (Not illustrated.) Incomplete, large needle of circular section flattening at the head. The eye appears to have been rectangular.
L. 52 mm; W. 5 mm; T. 4 mm. SO4, SF 706a. Phases 2-3, rock-cut road.

116. (Not illustrated.) Incomplete pin with a globular, undercut head and a bulging, circular-sectioned shank. Cf. Francolise: Cotton and Métraux 1985: fig. 26, no. 2: c. 30 BC-AD 200.
L. 49 mm; max. T. 3.5 mm; D. of head 4.5 mm. L105, SF 531c. Fish-pond, later second century.

117. Fig. 175. Incomplete pin with a globular head, narrow neck and bulging, circular-sectioned shank.
L. 102 mm; T. 4 mm; D. of head 5 mm. L105, SF 405. Fish-pond, later second century.

118. (Not illustrated.) Incomplete pin with a roughly shaped, undercut, cylindrical head and a bulging, circular-sectioned shank.
L. 64 mm; T. of shank 3.25 mm; T. of head 4 mm. L105, SF 539a. Fish-pond, later second century.

119. Fig. 175. Pin of oval section with a narrow neck and a cylindrical head.
L. 83 mm; T. of shank 4 mm; W. of head 7 mm. SO3, SF 719. Phases 2-3, rock-cut road.

120. (Not illustrated.) Small pin with a circular-sectioned shank, conical head and flattened point.
L. 51 mm; T. 2 mm. L105, SF 531d. Fish-pond, later second century.

121. Fig. 175. Incomplete pin with a tapering, circular-sectioned shank and a shallow conical head.
L. 60 mm; T. 4.75 mm. L105, SF 653. Fish-pond, later second century.

122. (Not illustrated.) Small pin with a circular-sectioned shank and a rounded head.
L. 52 mm; T. 2 mm. L105, SF 506a. Fish-pond, later second century.

123. (Not illustrated.) Incomplete pin of circular section with a blunt head which has untrimmed cancellous material.
L. 70 mm; T. 4 mm. SO4, SF 752. Phases 2-3, rock-cut road.

124. (Not illustrated.) Circular-sectioned rod with a trimmed point. The shaping suggests that this has broken off a large pin and been reworked.
L. 49 mm; T. 2.5 mm. L105, SF 593. Fish-pond, later second century.

125. (Not illustrated.) Three fragments from a circular-sectioned pin.
Total L. 110 mm; T. 4.5 mm. L105, SF 579. Fish-pond, later second century.

126. (Not illustrated.) Oval-sectioned pin shank. Both ends are broken but one has snapped across a groove, making it unclear whether the piece was finished or had a grooved neck.
L. 47 mm; T. 4.5 mm. M172, SF 849. Phase 3.

127. (Not illustrated.) Circular-sectioned pin shank.
L. 20 mm; T. 4 mm. D3, SF 56. Phase 7.

128. (Not illustrated.) Bulging, circular-sectioned pin shank.
L. 52 mm; T. 3.5 mm. L105, SF 506b. Fish-pond, later second century.

129. (Not illustrated.) Tapered fragment of a circular-sectioned pin shank.
L. 24 mm; T. 2.5 mm. L105, SF 506d. Fish-pond, later second century.

130. (Not illustrated.) Fragment of a circular-sectioned pin shank. The tip is expanded to a rounded point.
L. 41 mm; T. 2.5 mm. L105, SF 531a. Fish-pond, later second century.

131. (Not illustrated.) Fragment of a tapered, circular-sectioned pin shank.
L. 78.5 mm; T. 3.5 mm. L105, SF 531b. Fish-pond, later second century.

132. (Not illustrated.) Fragment of a circular-sectioned pin shank.
    L. 29 mm; T. 3 mm. L105, SF 531f. Fish-pond, later second century.
133. (Not illustrated.) Fragment of a bulging, circular-sectioned pin shank.
    L. 79 mm; T. 4 mm. L105, SF 586. Fish-pond, later second century.
134. (Not illustrated.) Fragment of a bulging, circular-sectioned pin shank.
    L. 30 mm; T. 3.5 mm. M172, SF 861. Phase 3.
135. (Not illustrated.) Thin, rectangular-sectioned strip, slightly curved with a polished surface. The back is rough. Inlay?
    L. 78 mm; W. 3 mm; T. 1.5 mm. L165. Fish-pond, later second century.

OBJECTS OF GLASS

136. Fig. 176. Annular ring of 'natural' pale blue glass, made by fusing the ends of an oval-sectioned strip so that the join projects outwards. The face has a median rib with flanking grooves, emphasized by a painted matt-brown stripe which peters out at the join. There is a small transverse nick on the inner face opposite the join, which has been made by a file.
    Int. D. 15 mm; W. 3 mm; T. 5 mm. E77, SF 284. Phase 3.
137. (Not illustrated.) Acid yellow, translucent, oval drum bead. The glass is very bubbled and striated.
    D. 6.5 × 7.5 mm; H. 3.5 mm; hole 2 mm. D1, SF 183. Phase 7.
138. (Not illustrated.) Small melon bead of very pale blue, almost cream-coloured, opaque glass. According to Hencken (1950), melon beads have a wide geographical and chronological spread within western and northern Europe, beginning in the Iron Age and continuing in use in the Germanic areas until the Viking Age. In the military zones melon beads appear to have been used singly and may have had a talismanic significance (Allason-Jones 1989: 1); but the complete necklace of melon beads found in the House of the Cervi at Herculaneum suggests that in Italy they were considered decorative (Tran Tam Tinh 1988: fig. 195, inv. no. 532). See also Famà (1985d: 233 and fig. 144).
    D. 10 mm; H. 7 mm; hole 5.5 mm. L165, SF 577. Fish-pond, early second century.
139. Fig. 176. Melon bead of weathered dark blue translucent glass with a marvered swirl of white.
    D. 18 mm; H. 10.5 mm; hole 6 mm. SO4, SF 750. Phases 2-3, rock-cut road.
140. (Not illustrated.) Strip of dark brown glass with parallel sides. Both ends are cut to an off-centre point. Traces of a fixing deposit on the back suggest a piece of inlay.
    L. 35 mm; W. 6 mm; T. 0.5 mm. M97, SF 763. Phase 3.
141. (Not illustrated.) Bun-shaped inset of opaque white glass.
    D. 11 × 12 mm; T. 5.5 mm. E11, SF 233. Phase 2.
142. (Not illustrated.) Bun-shaped inset or counter of opaque white glass.
    D. 20 mm; T. 6.5 mm. L105, SF 597. Fish-pond, later second century.
143. (Not illustrated.) Incomplete bun-shaped counter, now cream in colour and opaque and powdery.
    D. 18 mm; D. 6 mm. L105, SF 598. Fish-pond, later second century.

OBJECTS OF FIRED CLAY

144. Fig. 176. Part of a mould. The channel is rectangular with a step in the base.
    Max. H. 23 mm; L. 54 mm; max. W. 48 mm; Depth of channel 12 mm; W. of channel 15 mm. C51, SF 145. Limekiln, early-mid fifth century.
145. Fig. 176. Conical toggle or spindle-whorl of fine buff fabric with a circular central hole. The narrow top is flat and plain, the wider base is rounded and is decorated with a series of incised oblique lines. The walls are decorated with a series of vertical comb impressions just above the base.
    H. 32 mm; D. 21-39 mm; hole 9-12 mm. B26, SF 13. Phase 5/6.
146. (Not illustrated.) Incomplete spindle-whorl of fine cream tile fabric with stone, glass and tile inclusions. The hole has been drilled from both ends.
    D. 70 mm; T. 20 mm; hole 13 mm. H3, SF 186. Phase 7.

JET BRACELET

147. Fig. 176. Fragment of a hinged bracelet of semi-oval section. One end has a groove cut across the tip, which impinges on a series of lines incised around the shank. The other end has broken across a hole which has been bored from the end and from the outer face.
    The material has been identified as jet by Dr J.M. Jones of the Organic Geochemistry Unit of the University of Newcastle upon Tyne. Using a high resolution microscope, and adapting techniques used by oil companies in geological exploration, Dr Jones has indicated that this sample has a high ranking equal to the quality jet found in the neighbourhood of Whitby, Yorkshire, England. Although other sources of jet were used by craftsmen in the Roman period, British jet was recognized by Solinus as being of better quality and was exported to the Continent in the late third and fourth centuries AD (*Collectanea rerum memorabilium* xxii). Unfortunately, the jet deposits in Lycia and Pamphylia, described by Pliny (*Naturalis Historia* xxxvi), have not yet been subjected to comparable analytical techniques, so the exact source of the jet used for the Monte Gelato bracelet must remain uncertain.
    Hinged, segmented bracelets of copper alloy are common in the Celtic provinces, particularly in Hallstatt and La Tène contexts (Cunliffe 1988: 61), but examples in jet or shale have not yet been recognized. A possible parallel might be seen in RGZM Mainz (Hagen 1937: Taf. 22, no. B15.1).
    Int. D. 45 mm; W. 8 mm; T. 13-15 mm. SO3, SF 715. Phases 2-3, rock-cut road.

OBJECTS OF STONE

148. Fig. 176. Large drum-shaped weight of white limestone with a flat top, concave base and convex sides. The two ends of a now damaged iron loop are set into the top and fixed with lead caulking. Between the arms of the loop two serifed saltire crosses have been incised.
    The basic unit of weight was the *libra*, which divided into twelve *unciae*. Taking wear and the loss of part of the iron loop into account, the surviving weight of this

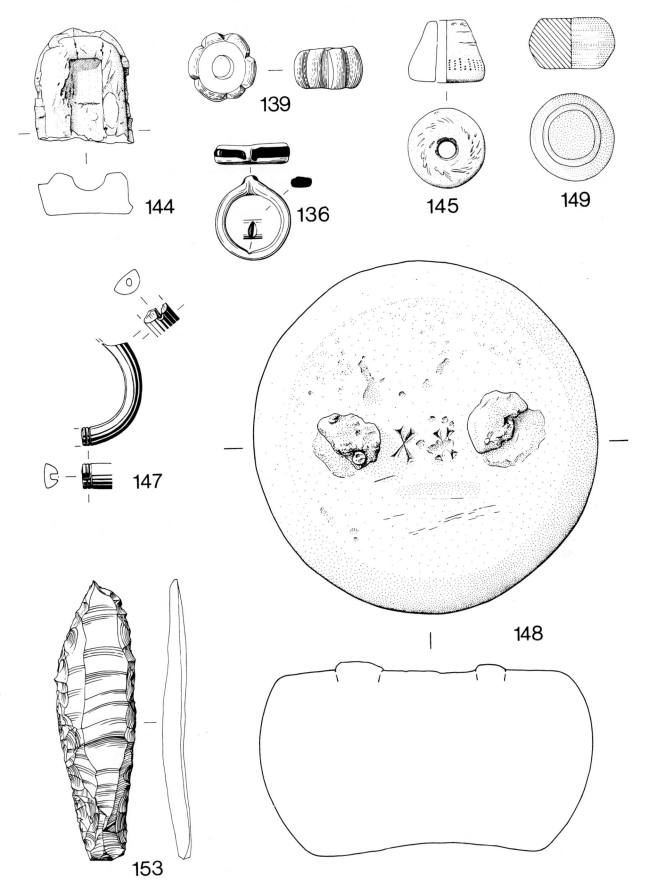

Fig. 176. Objects of glass (136, 139), fired clay (144, 146), jet (147), stone (148, 149) and flint (153). All 1:2, except for 136, 139, 153 (1:1). *(SC/SA)*

example suggests that it originally represented 20 *unciae* or two *dextantes*, with each saltire cross indicating one *dextans*. See Kraus and von Matt (1975: pl. 246) for a pile of similar weights found in the stone depository of the Forum at Pompeii, each of which had an indication of its weight inscribed on the top.

H. 103 mm; D. 180 mm; D. of top 163 mm; D. of base 125 mm; weight 6 kg. L101, SF 446. Plough-soil.

149. Fig. 176. Small drum-shaped weight with flat top and base and convex sides. There is no indication of the weight represented, nor of a loop, but it is possible that it equalled four *unciae* (one *triens*).

D. 45 mm; D. of top 27 mm; D. of base 30 mm; weight 102 g. L105, SF 576. Fish-pond, later second century.

150. (Not illustrated.) Whetstone of rectangular section, tapering to both ends. Well-used.

L. 103 mm; W. 24 mm; T. 15 mm. C32, SF 93. Phases 5-6, burial no. 9.

151. (Not illustrated.) Fragment of a whetstone of rectangular section. Micaceous siltstone.

L. 69 mm; W. 26 mm; T. 25 mm. D244, SF 260. Phase 6.

152. (Not illustrated.) Fragment of a whetstone of rectangular section with convex faces. The surviving end is chamfered. Ian Freestone reports: 'The whetstone was examined in thin-section in the polarizing microscope. In thin-section it was seen to consist of abundant spherules or peloids of microcrystalline silica (chert), typically 0.03-0.1 mm diameter, set in a matrix of micritic calcite. In some areas of the section the spherules are calcareous (microsparrite) indicating that the silica represents a replacement texture. Elongate calcareous spicules, typically 0.1-0.2 mm are common. The stone is classified as a cherty limestone or, more technically, a silicified biopelmicrite.

L. 39 mm; W. 33.5 mm; T. 15 mm. L162, SF 640. Phase 3.

AN UPPER PALAEOLITHIC FLINT BLADE, by Jill Cook

153. Fig. 176. Although an unstratified find, this 75 mm long, retouched blade has fresh, sharp edges and is unpatinated. It is made from good-quality flint and the blank was struck from a single platform core. The piece exhibits bilateral, convergent retouch on the dorsal surface. On the left edge the retouch scars vary from semi-invasive at the proximal end to more abrupt and marginal at the distal end. On the right edge the retouch is abrupt and marginal. Both edges are convex. The distal end is not damaged and has not been shaped to a true point. Its general tip form may therefore be referred to as rounded.

Overall, the character of the retouch and edge shape, as well as the cross-sectional and longitudinal form, indicates that this is a late Upper Palaeolithic retouched blade of type L2 in the typology of Laplace (1964). Upper Palaeolithic finds are relatively uncommon from this region and the discovery of this well-made tool in good condition is noteworthy.

THE IRONWORK, by Ralph Jackson

INTRODUCTION

The assemblage is modest in size but includes some interesting pieces, most notably the bridle-bit (cat. 18), auger (cat. 19), and pruning knife (cat. 23), as well as the hoard (cat. 12-19). Table 53 provides a breakdown of the surviving recognizable objects other than nails. While it would be incautious to extrapolate too much from such a small sample, a number of comments are perhaps justifiable. The explanation for the marked preponderance of fixed (structural) objects over portable objects in phase 2 may simply be that few rubbish deposits of that phase were excavated. Alternatively, it is possible that it reflects a careful control of materials: debris was not allowed to accumulate and metals would not have been casually discarded. Almost all that remained were the structural fixtures and fittings which were not easily removed or retrieved for recycling at or after the end of that period of occupation. Notable in phase 3 is the tool and implement component, which is high even without the contents of the hoard. That this implies intens-

Table 53. Identifiable iron objects, excluding nails.

category of object	all phases		phase 2		phase 3		phases 5-6		phase 7	
	no.	%	no.	%	no.	%	no.	%	no.	%
weapons	0	0	0	0	0	0	0	0	0	0
transport items	1	2.4	0	0	1	5.6	0	0	0	0
craftsmen's tools	7	16.7	0	0	7	38.9	0	0	0	0
agricultural implements	2	4.8	0	0	1	5.6	1	14.3	0	0
knives and household utensils	5	11.9	0	0	1	5.6	2	28.6	2	33.3
personalia	2	4.8	0	0	0	0	0	0	2	33.3
keys, locks and door furniture	2	4.8	2	18.0	0	0	0	0	0	0
structural ironwork and fittings	23	54.8	9	82.0	8	44.0	4	57.1	2	33.3

ity of agricultural and craft activity may be a valid deduction, as it accords with other evidence, for example, the conversion of the courtyard building to agricultural/'industrial' usage. In phases 5/6 and 7 tools are virtually absent and the few pieces of ironwork have a strong sepulchral emphasis. Two knives and a fitting (cat. 31-3) were probably grave-goods, and knife cat. 38 could also be from a disturbed grave.

CATALOGUE

(Weight measurements have been supplied for those objects which are complete, or virtually so, and in a relatively uncorroded state.)

Phase 2

1. Fig. 177. Key. A small slide key with an extremely short shank. The suspension loop is partially broken and the

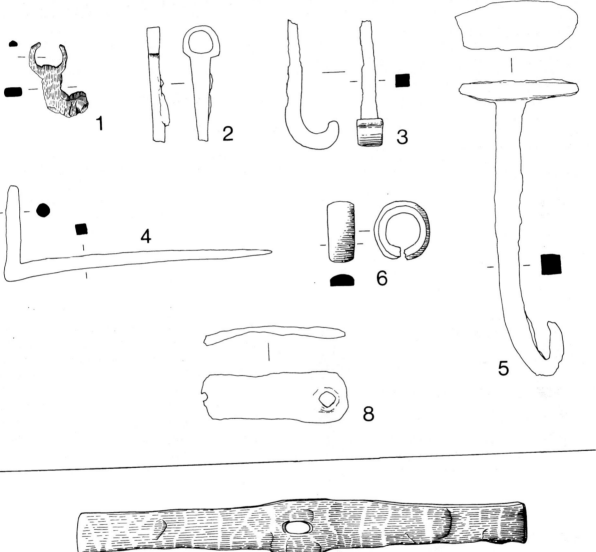

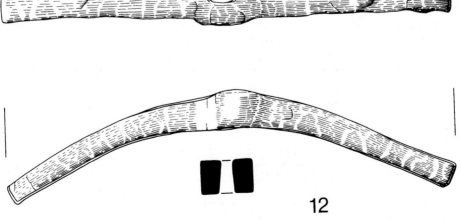

Fig. 177. Objects of iron. 1-8, phase 2; 12, sixth-century group (1:2). *(SC/RJ)*

bit is too corroded to determine the arrangement of the teeth.

L. 40 mm. L165, SF 632. Fish-pond, early second century.

2. Fig. 177. Key handle? A tapered, rectangular-sectioned rod with a D-shaped collar-like suspension loop. Broken at the narrow end. Probably the shank of a slide key.

L. 61 mm. L105, SF 507. Fish-pond, later second century.

3. Fig. 177. Hook. A J-shaped hook with a tapered, rectangular-sectioned stem broken at its narrow end. The broad end terminates in a smoothly-curved and lipped open blunt hook. The form is reminiscent of the hooked terminal of some cauldron chains (cf. Manning 1983).

L. 70 mm+. E11, SF 361. North cistern, second century.

4. Fig. 177. Hook/hinge staple. A long, slender L-shaped wall-hook or staple for a drop-hinge. The rectangular-sectioned spike is lightly curved with a sharp tip. The upright is of rounded rectangular cross-section with a rounded head.

L. 148 mm. L105, SF 449. Fish-pond, later second century.

5. Fig. 177. T-clamp. A medium-sized clamp of normal form, with short, flat, spatulate arms, one broken at the end, and a square-sectioned stem tapered to a point. Mineral-replaced wood grain in the corrosion products shows that the central part of the stem was embedded in a wooden post/joist, with the tip hammered back and the head standing proud to secure, for example, a box flue tile, a flat tile, or a stone slab.

L. 157 mm. L105, SF 538. Fish-pond, later second century.

6. Fig. 177. Ring. A small, heavy, neatly-made circular ring. The inner face is flat, the outer convex with bevelled sides. The split is a product of corrosion. The size and form do not preclude identification as a finger-ring, but other possible uses include that of a handle collar from a tanged tool or implement.

D. internal 20 mm, external 32 mm. L147, SF 468. North cistern, second century.

7. (Not illustrated.) Ring. A sub-circular ring made of rounded square-sectioned rod.

50 × 46 mm. L143, SF 461. North cistern, second century.

8. Fig. 177. Nailed strip/binding. A flat rectangular-sectioned strip, slightly curved. One end is complete, with a nail hole near the rounded terminal. The other end is broken across a second nail hole. Its function is uncertain – possibly a broken binding/hinge strap/bucket staple.

L. 79 mm+. L105, SF 407. Fish-pond, later second century.

9. (Not illustrated.) Binding. A small fragment of parallel-sided binding, both ends broken. One nail hole remains. Width cf. cat. 8.

L. 37 mm+. L105, SF 509. Fish-pond, later second century.

10. (Not illustrated.) Binding. Many fragments of thin sheet: some 'box-like' pieces, some with a neatly finished 'rim'; all with organic fragments fused to the corrosion products on both faces; no nail holes. Possibly box/chest reinforcing or parts of a lock.

Fig. 178. Group of ironwork and a horse trapping, found in sixth-century roof collapse. *(KW)*

T. 0.3-0.5 mm. L105, SF 519, 542. Fish-pond, later second century.

11. (Not illustrated.) Stud. The perimeter of the thin discoidal head is badly chipped. The spike is bent and broken.

D. 28 mm+. L105, SF 559. Fish-pond, later second century.

– Nails. Forty-seven examples, mainly broken, most of the commonest Roman form, Manning's Type 1b (Manning 1985: 133ff., fig. 32), a square-sectioned, tapered spike with a flat head, but also including disc-headed and domed-headed varieties.

– Unidentifiable fragments of rods, bar and strip: SF 464, 565, 624, 633, 636, 747, 819.

Phase 3 (Phases 3,3+ and 3/4 contexts)

Hoard, from context D52 (collapse of roof tiles), dated to the sixth century AD (Fig. 177)

12. Figs 177 and 178. Hammer. A well-made, slender, medium-weight, elliptical hammerhead with equal arms of crisp rectangular cross-section. The straight faces are lightly-domed and one is a little burred through use. The thick walls expand around the small slender rectangular eye, which has a slight vertical taper (slip eye). It is probably a metalworker's tool, though it differs from the normal cross-peen hammer of Roman blacksmiths in the form of the eye, in its marked curvature, and in the combination of working faces.

L. 248 mm; face (a) 21 × 12 mm; face (b) 21 × 10 mm; weight *c.* 525 g. D52, SF 306.

13. Figs 178 and 179. Axe-adze or mattock. A heavy, well-made tool, more probably for woodworking than agriculture, for the blades are comparatively thin and still quite sharp, with no major damage. Both blades have convex cutting edges, the adze blade being slightly asymmetric and long in comparison. The eye is almost circular and has no vertical taper. Its side walls have very low lugs. There is no sign of mineral-replaced wood in the corrosion products within the shaft-hole, so the tool may have been without its handle on deposition.

L. 305 mm; W. adze 67 mm; W. axe 64 mm; weight *c.* 1.35 kg. D52, SF 305.

14. Figs 178 and 179. Axe-adze or mattock. A medium-weight, well-made tool more probably for woodworking than agriculture, for reasons as cat. 13. There is an even greater disparity than cat. 13 in the relative size of the axe and adze components. The sub-circular shaft-hole has thin walls – now distorted and broken – with prominent lugs top and bottom. Breakage probably occurred before deposition. No mineral-replaced wood remains could be seen in the corrosion products within the shaft-hole.

L. 312 mm; W. adze 72 mm; W. axe 50 mm (orig. *c.* 55 mm); weight *c.* 800 g. D52, SF 313.

15. Figs 178 and 180. L-clamp. A large, heavy L-shaped staple, with a tapered, rectangular-sectioned, spiked shank and a slightly irregular, tongue-shaped arm. There is no trace of mortar or mineral-replaced wood-grain in the corrosion products on the shank.

L. 277 mm; weight *c.* 500 g. D52, SF 304A.

16. Figs 178 and 180. L-clamp. Another example, virtually identical to cat. 15.

L. 270 mm; weight *c.* 480 g. D52, SF 304B.

These are very large examples of a common structural fitting more usually encountered in its T-shaped form (see cat. 5). Driven into heavy timber or embedded in masonry, they probably secured wall cladding or suspended ceiling components.

17. Figs 178 and 180. U-clamp. A heavy, slightly sinuous, rectangular-sectioned bar, turned over and broken at each end. If the turned-over ends are, as they appear to be, the broken stubs of spiked arms, then this was probably a very large, broad U-shaped clamp used to secure together two masonry blocks.

L. 295 mm; weight *c.* 420 g. D52, SF 308.

This is a small and rather enigmatic hoard which owes its preservation to the fact that it was sealed by debris from a structural collapse, thus hiding it from, for example, later scavengers and disturbance. It is likely that prior to the demise of the building the objects were contained in a leather or cloth bag suspended from a wall-peg or rafter. Individually none of the pieces is especially diagnostic or closely datable, nor, collectively, do they provide evidence of any single coherent use – they comprise three tools and three pieces of structural ironwork. There is, however, a unifying factor – that of weight. For all are large, heavy objects which together amount to more than four kilogrammes of what was potentially readily reusable metal. In Antiquity most materials, but especially metals, would have been assiduously collected for recycling, and scrap was doubtless an important source of iron. The fact that two of the pieces were broken (12 and 17) and that the tools were probably lacking their handles, tends to support the hypothesis that the objects, either damaged or out of use items, had indeed been assembled for reuse.

18. Fig. 181. Bridle bit. A complete two-link snaffle bit with the cheek-pieces in place. The links are simple, of rounded rectangular cross-section. The cheek-pieces comprise a neatly-made gently-tapered bar with one everted and one plain terminal and a lightly-keeled outer face. Within the eyed centre-plate of one are retained two small looped plates, each with a central rivet, which secured the end of the leather bridle strap and the reins.

L. links, 75 mm, 77 mm; cheek-pieces, 125 mm, 126 mm. D50, SF 72.

19. Fig. 181. Spoon auger. A large, robust example lacking only its wooden crossbar handle. The stout, elongated trapezoidal head is slightly flanged at the top, where it projected a little through the handle socket. There is a marked angular shoulder at the junction with the long, octagonal-sectioned stem. The spoon bit is long and broad, of crescent-shaped cross-section, and is set back at a slight angle to the stem. Augers have a long history, and an essentially similar spoon auger was found in the first-century AD Pit XVI at the Roman fort of Newstead in Scotland (Curle 1911: 280-1, pl. LIX,14). Its bit width is the same – *c.* 30 mm – and it has an octagonal-sectioned stem, but it is slightly shorter – *c.* 300 mm – and the head is lanceolate.

Closer still in size – L. 375 mm, but also with a lanceolate head, is an example from a hoard of ironwork buried near the Roman fort at Brampton, Cumbria, England, in *c.* AD 125 (Manning 1966: 15-16, no. 11). See also Jacobi (1897: 209, fig. 28,17 and pl. 34,7), for an example from the Saalburg fort, Germany. Closer geographically and chronologically is an example of similar form and weight from Villa Clelia (Imola)

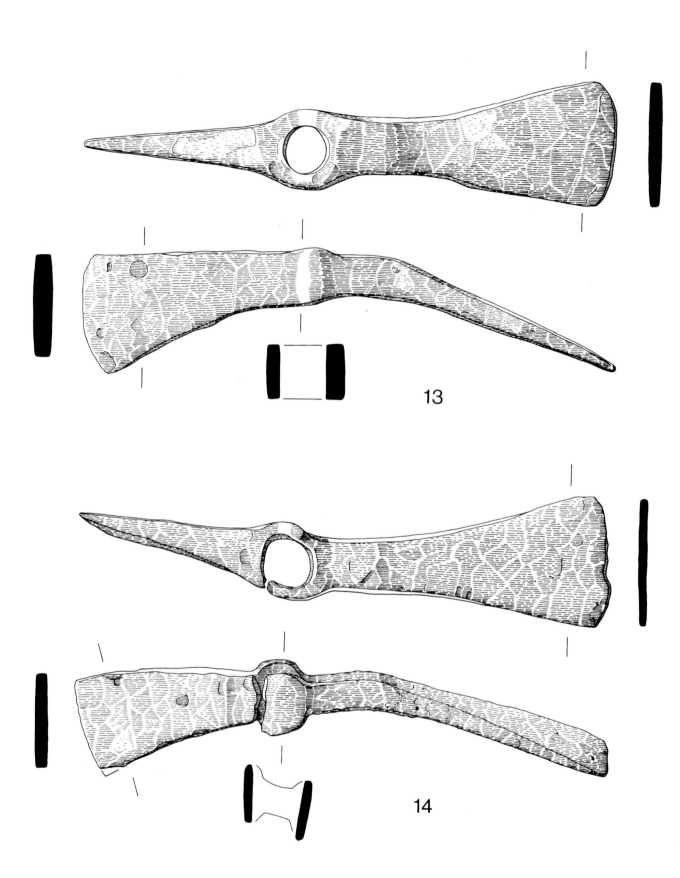

Fig. 179. Iron axe-adzes (or mattocks) from the sixth-century group (1:2). *(SC)*

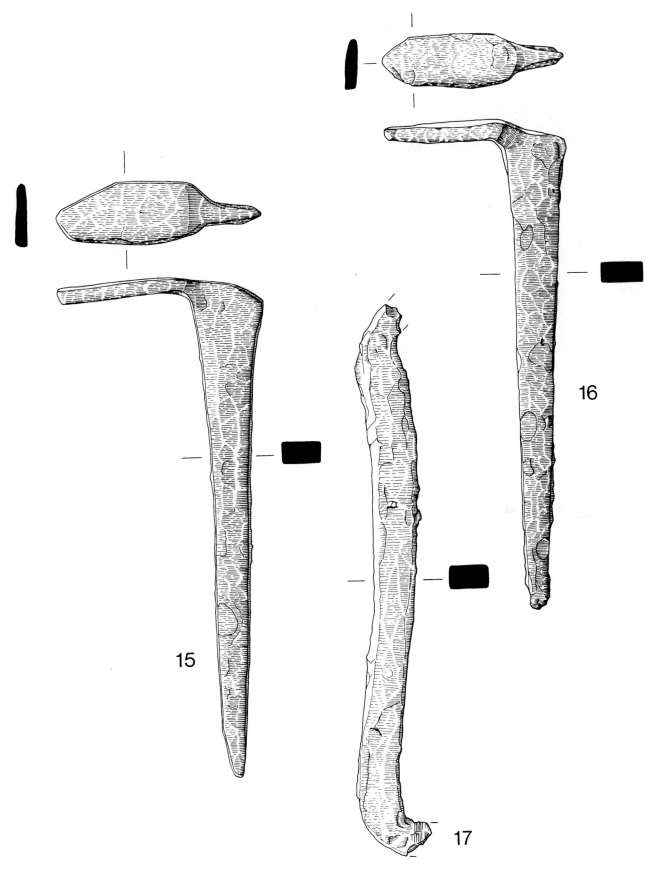

Fig. 180. Iron objects from the sixth-century group (1:2). *(SC)*

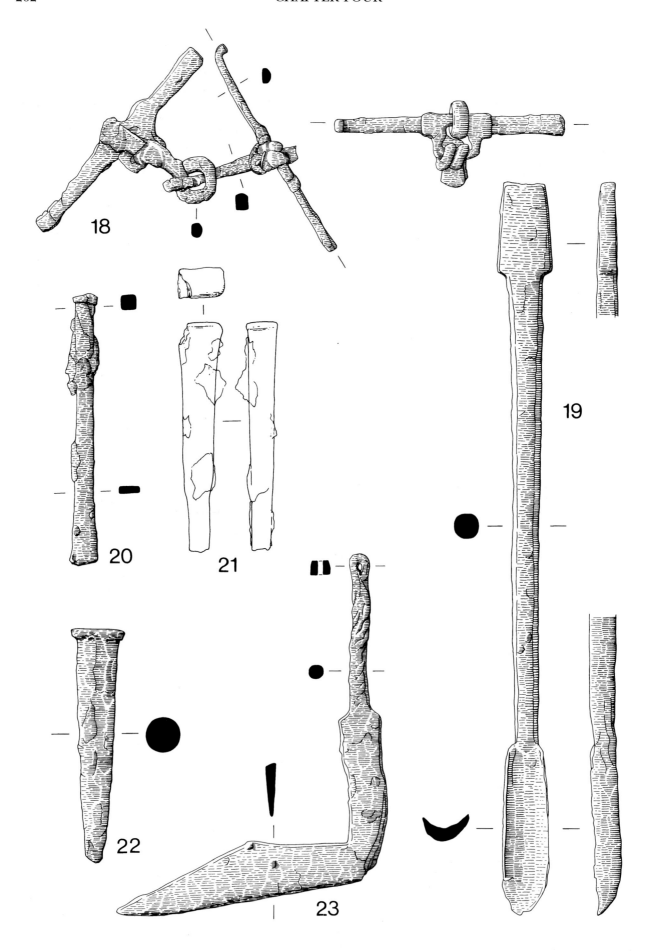

Fig. 181. Iron objects from contexts of phase 3 (late Roman) (1:2). *(SC/RJ)*

(Baruzzi 1987: fig. 1,f). It weighs 450 g and is dated to the sixth century AD. For a medieval Turkish example (c. AD 1300+) from Sardis, see Waldbaum (1983: 53, pl. 13,165).

L. 390 mm; L. bit 89 mm; W. bit 28 mm; weight c. 500 g. M23, SF 444. From the wall collapse onto the lower terrace. Sixth century.

20. Fig. 181. Chisel. A small, well-made, light, slender chisel with rectangular cap-like head, solid, rounded rectangular-sectioned handle and elongated triangular, flat rectangular-sectioned blade. The cutting edge is formed by a gentle bevel on one face only. It was probably a carpenter's paring chisel.
L. 142 mm. M161, SF 827.

21. Fig. 181. Chisel? A rectangular-sectioned rod, broad at the top, with an expanded, lightly-domed, slightly burred head, tapering to a square-sectioned stem, broken at the lower end. Probably a tool handle, perhaps a solid-handled chisel: cf. Manning 1985: 23, pl. 10,B38 and pl. 11,B39, two solid-handled mortise chisels of the mid-first century AD from Hod Hill.
L. 122 mm. M38, SF 551. From an intrusion into the bath-house drain.

22. Fig. 181. Punch/point. A stout, heavy, strongly-tapered tool with round, cap-like head and circular-sectioned stem. The point is blunt. This was a blacksmith's or mason's tool.
L. 126 mm; weight c. 250 g. A17, SF 3.

23. Fig. 181. Pruning knife? A finely-made J-shaped knife, with three distinct sections: (1) the handle – a candy-twisted, rounded square-sectioned rod with a small looped terminal; (2) the rear part of the blade – a flat, rectangular-sectioned bar, parallel-sided and lightly-curved, blunt on both edges, and with a marked flange on the lower part of the outer edge, presumably a provision for, or a product of, hammering; (3) the sharp part of the blade – a medium heavy blade of compressed triangular shape, and triangular cross-section set at a right angle to the blunt rear part. The blade back is thick and strongly ridged. The cutting edge is almost straight but is very lightly hollowed near the angle (probably a product of use and whetting) and is gently convex as it rises to the tip. The careful design and characteristic shape of this tool indicate that it was made for a very specific use, though it would doubtless have served several functions. The flanged platform attests use as a hammer which, with the blade, would have made a convenient combination tool well-suited to the needs of viticulture – pruning and the setting of stakes.
L. handle 85 mm; L. handle and rear blade 173 mm; L. blade 135 mm; weight c. 140 g. M144, SF 838. From silt over the late Roman floor on the lower terrace.

24. Fig. 182. Knife. A large tanged blade of triangular cross-section. The end of the tapered, flat rectangular-sectioned tang is broken, but there is probably little missing. It is set centrally to the blade which it meets with a step top and bottom. The blade's cutting edge is straight and runs parallel with the lightly-ridged back, except in the region of the tip, where it rises in a lightly convex curve to form a blunt point.
L. 184 mm; weight 55 g. M23, SF 443. From the wall collapse onto the lower terrace. Sixth century.

25. Fig. 182. Linch pin? An L-shaped tapered rod of circular cross-section. The additional labour involved in making a circular rather than a square-sectioned rod renders it unlikely that the long stem was to be embedded in a wall. Thus it was probably not a wall hook or nail. More likely it was a securing pin or bolt used either vertically or horizontally.
L. 148 mm. E70, SF 283. From silt on the Roman floor of the large room, upper terrace.

26. Fig. 182. Revetment clip. A tapered, flat, rectangular-sectioned rod, broken at one end. The complete terminal has the turned-back pointed tip characteristic of these small clamps, which were used for securing costly wall-claddings. The missing end, which would have terminated in two small ear-like hammered flanges, was embedded in a mortar joint, while the angled, pointed tip was engaged in a small drilled socket in the edge of, for example, stone panels. Although seldom identified, the type is known both in iron and copper alloy – see Waldbaum (1983: 66-7, pl. 19, 266-77) for an example from Sardis, and Jackson (forthcoming) for examples from Via Gabina villas G10 and G11; and, wrongly identified as surgical instruments, examples in the Museo Nazionale, Naples, inv. no. 78083 and s.n. 18-20.
L. 61 mm. J2, SF 324. [Another probable fragment was found in a phase 2 context – L105, SF 578.]

27. Fig. 182. Joiner's dog. A small woodworking clamp, of broad U-shape, with a flat rectangular-sectioned bar and two small short spikes, one bent back, the other broken.
L. 47 mm. M26, SF 454. From silt on a late Roman floor, lower terrace.

28. Fig. 182. Collar. An elliptical strip, carefully forged, of rounded concavo-convex cross-section, broken at both ends. Its form is reminiscent of the collared rings of some shackles (see, for example, Neville (1856: 9, pl. 2, figs 21-2) for an example from Great Chesterford, Essex, of the fourth century AD), but too little survives for certainty, and many other uses are possible.
L. 61 mm; D. c. 60-70 mm. E32, SF 353. Pit cut into the floor of the large room, upper terrace.

29. Fig. 182. Staple and link. A long, slender, rectangular ring or link, probably the end of a chain, held in the eye of a small securing split spiked-loop.
L. loop 38 mm; link 62 × 16 mm. M164, SF 847. From a cut into the bath-house drain.

– Nails. Thirty-six examples, as phase 2 nails.

– Unidentifiable fragments of rods, bar and strip: SF 267, 445, 526, 754, 764, 816.

Phases 5-6 (Phase 5, 5/6 and 6 contexts)

30. Fig. 182. Reap hook/pruning hook? A broad curved blade fragment made from very thin sheet, with a very slight curved thickening and a cutting edge on both the concave and convex sides. Breakage prevents certainty, but this is probably the tip of a hooked blade of a type used very widely in agriculture. For a discussion of the type, see, Manning (1985: 53-8). The very thin blade of this example would limit the potential uses, but a variety of light agricultural and, perhaps, viticultural tasks may be envisaged.
L. 89 mm. E36, SF 263. From the area of the early medieval pottery kiln.

31. Fig. 182. Knife. Blade fragment only, bent and broken. A slender, flat, triangular-sectioned blade with a straight back and an almost parallel straight cutting edge which rises gently at the tip.
L. 77 mm. D2, SF 876. From a disturbed burial in plough-soil.

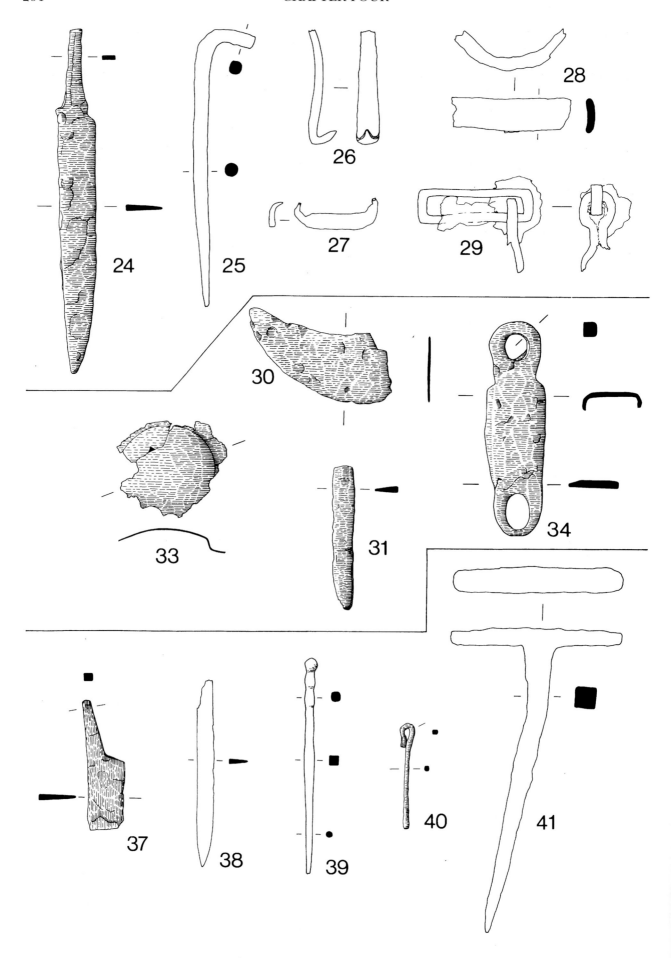

Fig. 182. Objects of iron. 24-9, phase 3; 30-4, phases 5-6; 37-41, phase 7 (1:2). *(SC/RJ)*

32. (Not illustrated.) Knife. The handle plate from a small knife broken at, or short of, the junction with the blade. The plate is of flat rectangular cross-section, with near-parallel sides, and is pierced by two small rivets. The mineral-replaced remains of the wooden handle plates that they secured are preserved in the corrosion products on both faces.
L. 53 mm; W. 16 mm. D68. Perhaps associated with burial no. 101.

33. Fig. 182. Coffin fitting? A fragmentary, large, low-domed, circular boss made from very thin iron sheet. Only a small section of the shallow channelled rim survives and no nails or nail holes are visible. It is perhaps a coffin or box fitting or a personal adornment.
D. at least 74 mm. D135, SF 382. Burial no. 43 (with a coin of AD 884-5 (cat. 58)).

34. Fig. 182. Looped plate/staple. A sub-rectangular plate with flanged sides and a loop at each end. Function uncertain.
L. 116 mm. M80, SF 699.

35. (Not illustrated.) Corner bracket/window grille? A flat rectangular-sectioned, parallel-sided strap with a discoidal terminal perforated by a central nail hole. The other end is broken just beyond a right-angled corner. Mineral-replaced wood grain adheres to the corrosion products on the inner face of the disc terminal.
L. 58 mm; W. 16 mm. S4, SF 744.

36. (Not illustrated.) Door stud? A heavy domed-headed stud, the spike/shank almost completely broken away. This is probably a strengthening/decorative stud from a door or chest.
D. 33 mm. M38, SF 555.

– Nails. Sixty-five examples, mainly broken, most of the commonest Roman form, Manning's Type 1b (Manning 1985: 133ff., fig. 32), but also including T-headed and domed-headed varieties. For nails from the burials, see Table 54.

– Unidentifiable rod fragments: SF 375, 516.

Phase 7 (Phase 6/7 and 7 contexts)

37. Fig. 182. Knife. A small tanged knife. The broken tang is in line with the lightly concave blade back. The cutting edge is gently convex and may have been toothed, but too much of the end of the blade is missing to be sure of the form.
L. 72 mm. D321, SF 343.

38. Fig. 182. Knife. Only the broken blade remains. It is very thin, of triangular cross-section, with a straight back and near-parallel straight cutting edge, which rises in a gentle convex curve to form the tip.
L. 99 mm. B1.

39. Fig. 182. Pin. A finely-made decorative pin with a spherical head. The upper stem was ornamented with a series of mouldings, now partially obscured by surface depletion and corrosion. There is an expansion at the centre of the stem, at which point the cross-section is square. Beneath this the stem tapers and becomes more rounded to the point of breakage, which is probably not far short of the original end.
L. 114 mm. E1, SF 241.

40. Fig. 182. Pin. A slender pin, with rounded square-sectioned shank and neatly-formed, closed crook-shaped terminal loop. The shank expands towards its point of breakage. Its function is uncertain, though clearly decorative, and possibly modern.
L. 56 mm. M, unstratified, SF 678.

41. Fig. 182. T-clamp. A well-made medium-sized example of normal form, with narrow, thick arms and a square-sectioned, spiked stem, now bent. Probably residual from Phase 2 or 3.
L. 166 mm. E1, SF 242.

42. (Not illustrated.) Door stud? A very large, heavy, domed-headed stud or bolt, its square-sectioned stem broken.
D. 53 mm. H1, SF 193.

– Nails. Thirty-nine examples, mainly broken, most of the commonest Roman form, Manning's Type 1b (Manning 1985: 133ff., fig. 32), but also including T-headed, disc-headed and stud-headed varieties. For nails from the burials, see Table 54.

– Horseshoe, probably modern. SF 67.

– Wire, modern. SF 496.

– Unidentifiable rod fragments: SF 65, 330.

THE GLASS, by Jennifer Price

All the glass from Monte Gelato is blown free-hand unless otherwise stated. Virtually all the glass fragments found at Monte Gelato were affected by weathering to some extent. Details of their condition have not been included in the catalogue entries.

CATALOGUE

First century AD

1. Figs 183 and 184. Fragment of the body of a cylindrical cup with chariot-racing scenes. Yellow-brown; mould-blown; few small bubbles visible; vertical side. There are two decorative zones separated by a horizontal cordon. In the upper zone are parts of two circus features; in the lower zone, parts of two racing teams – a horse's head, a charioteer leaning back with a bent raised left arm and the right arm bent in to the waist, a wheel of a chariot and part of one horse's hind leg and tail.
Present H. 36 mm; Dim. 36 × 34 mm; T. 2.0-2.5 mm. L101, SF 437. Hillwash, phase 7.

2. Fig. 184. Fragment of the rim of a hemispherical cup. Dark blue vertical rim, edge cracked off. There is a ground horizontal abraded band on the upper body.
Present H. 30 mm; rim D. 80 mm; T. 2-3 mm. S10. Rock-cut road, phases 2-3.

Other early Roman fragments

(a) Fragment of body of a (?) wide convex bowl. Dark blue. Dim. 22 × 25.5 mm; T. 2.5-3.5 mm. L147, SF 493. North cistern, late second century.

(b) Fragment of the body of a (?) convex bowl. Opaque light blue. Dim. 21.5 × 22.5 mm; T. 1.5 mm. M126, SF 778. Phase 3.

(c) Fragment of the body of a convex lower body of a 'Hofheim cup'. Yellow-brown. Dim. 14.5 × 20.5 mm; T. 2.5-4 mm. B54. Phase 6.

Table 54. Iron nails from burial contexts.

burial context no.	small find no.	phase	no. of nails	length if complete (in millimetres) and additional comments
2 (C2)	103, 104	6	2	48
2 (C56)	109, 118-20	6	4	72, 66 The upper and lower shank of one nail have two different wood grain directions. From coffin corner?
2 (C58)	137-43, 148	6	8	56, 68 One T-headed
7 (C23)	66, 76, 83	6/7	3	38
8 (C46)	83, 87, 98, 101, 106, 108, 111, 115-17, 130, 161-70	6/7	16	69, 68, 70, 72
12 (B64)	32	5/6	1	
12 (B80)	34	5/6	15	97 The upper and lower shank of one nail have two different wood grain directions. From coffin corner?
17 (B73)	30	5/6	1	
37 (D229)	238	6	1	60
40 (D214)	212	6	1	
55 (D92)	102	6/7	1	
59 (D168)	-	6	2	
67 (D276)	275	5/6	1	
85 (L173)	642	6/7	1	206 Stud-headed
87 (E99)	321	3+	1	

Fig. 183. Fragment of glass chariot beaker (cat. 1). *(KW)*

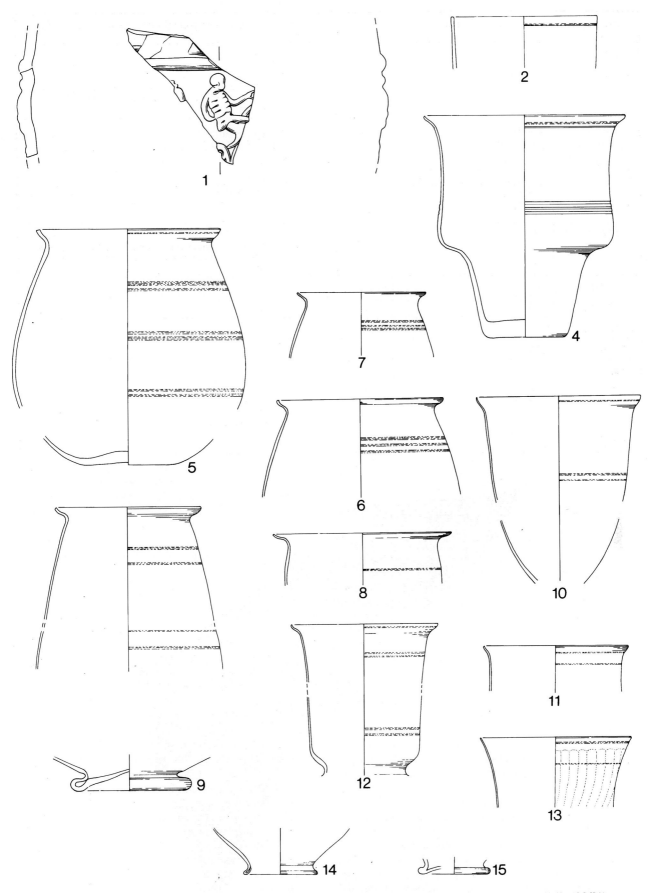

Fig. 184. Glass vessels. 1-2, first century AD; 4-15, late first to mid second centuries AD. All 1:2 except no.1 (1:1). *(SC/SA)*

Late first-mid second centuries AD

Colourless

Beakers and cups

Coloured trail decoration

3. (Not illustrated.) Seven fragments, three joining, from the body of an indented vessel. Colourless ground, opaque yellow trails; very little weathering; very small bubbles. The fragments are parts of the body, including the lower body above the base. The trails are not marvered flush with the surface.
Dim. (largest fragment) 28 × 20 mm; T. 0.75 mm. L165 and L184. Fish-pond, early second century.
Also:

(a) Two joining fragments. Dim. 17 × 9 mm; T. 0.65 mm. M172. Drain, phase 3.

Wheel-cut and abraded decoration

4. Fig. 184. Thirty-three fragments, many joining, of a carinated beaker. Greenish-colourless; small bubbles; outsplayed curved rim, edge cracked off and ground; straight, slightly concave upper body expanding out to curved carination; truncated conical lower body; slightly concave thick base. There are two horizontal wheel-cut lines at the junction of the rim and body, and three horizontal wheel-cut lines above the carination.
H. 118 mm; rim D. 110 mm; D. base 44 mm; T. 1.5-4+ mm. L184. Fish-pond, early second century.
Also:

(a) Fragment of the straight upper body of a biconical cup. There are single wheel-cut lines on the upper body and above the carination. Present H. 67 mm; T. 1 mm. L104. Phase 2.

(b) Two fragments of a form comparable to (a). There is a single abraded band above the carination. Present H. 61 mm; T. 0.7-1.5 mm. M172. Drain, phase 3.

(c) A fragment of a form comparable to (a). There is a single wheel-cut line on the upper body. Present H. 31 mm; T. 1.5 mm. D243. Phase 3.

(d) A fragment of a form comparable to (a). Pale greenish colourless. There is a single wheel-cut line on the upper body. Present H. 24.5 mm; T 1.5 mm. L146. Phase 2.

5. Fig. 184. One hundred and twenty-five fragments, many joining, of an ovoid beaker. Curved rim, edge cracked off and ground, convex body expanding out, lower body tapering in to concave base. There is an abraded band on the rim, two bands on the upper body, two bands above the maximum girth, and two bands on the lower body.
Present H. (rim fragment) 97 mm; rim D. 100 mm; T. 1-6 mm. L165 and L184. Fish-pond, early second century.
Also:

(a) Thirty-three fragments of the body and base of an ovoid (?) beaker/bowl. Small bubbles; outsplayed rim, edge missing; upper body convex expanding out; wide convex lower body tapering in to tubular pushed in base ring. There is a band of three abraded lines on the upper body. Dim. (largest fragment) 50 × 50 mm; T. 1-2.5 mm. L165.

6. Fig. 184. Eighteen fragments, some joining, of the rim and body of a convex beaker. Curved rim, edge cracked off and ground; convex body expanding out. There is a faint abraded band on the rim, three close-set abraded bands on the upper body, and two on the lower body.
Present H. (rim fragment) 54 mm; rim D. 90 mm; T. 1+ mm. L165. Fish-pond, early second century.

7. Fig. 184. Fragment of the rim of a beaker. Outsplayed slightly curved rim, edge cracked off and ground; convex upper body expanding out. A band of abraded lines was noted on the rim, and three bands on the upper body.
Present H. 34 mm; rim D. *c.* 90 mm; T. 1 mm. L105. Fish-pond, later second century.

8. Fig. 184. Fragment of the rim of a convex cup or beaker. Dull; small bubbles visible; outsplayed curved rim, edge cracked off and ground; convex upper body expanding out. There is a horizontal abraded band on the upper body.
Present H. 29 mm; rim D. 96 mm; T. 1 mm. S10. Rock-cut road, phases 2-3.

9. Fig. 184. Fifteen fragments of the rim, body and base of a carinated beaker. Greenish colourless; outsplayed curved rim, edge cracked off; slightly convex upper body expanding out to curved carination (mostly missing); wide convex lower body tapering in to tubular base ring and concave base with pointed central kick. There are two horizontal abraded lines on the upper body and two above the carination.
Present H. (rim) 86 mm, (base) 19 mm; rim D. 80 mm; D. of base 60 mm; T. 0.5-1.5+ mm. E179. Pit, phase 3.
Also:

(a) Fragment of the rim of a beaker. Outsplayed curved rim, edge cracked off, slightly convex body expanding out. Present H. 24 mm; rim D. 90 mm; T. 1 mm. E179. Pit, phase 3.

10. Fig. 184. Twelve fragments of the rim and body of a beaker. Thin glass; curved rim, edge cracked off and ground; straight upper body; convex lower body, curving in towards base (missing). An abraded line was noted on the rim and two on the body.
Present H. (rim fragment) 50 mm, (base fragment) *c.* 40 mm; rim D. 90 mm; T. 1.5 mm. E179. Pit, phase 3.

11. Fig. 184. Five fragments of the rim and body of a cylindrical beaker or cup. Small curved rim, edge cracked off and ground; straight side. There is a narrow horizontal abraded band at the base of the rim and also on the upper body.
Present H. 25 mm; rim D. 80 mm; T. 0.7+ mm. M172. Drain, phase 3.
Also:

(a) Two fragments of the body, concave side and carination of a beaker or cup. There is an abraded line above the carination. M172. Drain, phase 3.

(b) Fragment of the straight body of a beaker or cup. It has two abraded lines. L105. Fish-pond, later second century.

(c-o) Thirteen body fragments. Abraded bands were noted. L165. Fish-pond, early second century.

(p) Fifty-nine body and base fragments of (?) beakers or cups. These fragments had no abraded decoration. L165. Fish-pond, early second century.

12. Fig. 184. Thirteen fragments, some joining, from the rim, body and base of a conical carinated beaker. Pale greenish colourless; small bubbles; grey/black inclusions; outsplayed curved rim, edge cracked off and ground; thin-walled, straight upper body tapering in; angular carination above small tubular pushed in base ring (missing). There are bands of abraded lines on the rim, the upper body, and above the carination.
Present H. at least 85 mm (reconstructed by overlapping three fragments); rim D. *c.* 80 mm; T. 0.7-1.2 mm. L165. Fish-pond, early second century.

13. Fig. 184. Three fragments of the rim and body of a cylindrical beaker or cup. Very thin glass; slightly everted straight rim, edge cracked off and ground; straight side; faint vertical ribbing on body. There is an abraded band below the rim, and another on the upper body.
Present H. 39 mm; rim D. 84 mm; T 0.1+ mm. L165. Fish-pond, early second century.

14. Fig. 184. Three joining fragments of the lower body and base of a (?) beaker. Some small bubbles; lower edge of curved carination, straight lower body tapering in to small tubular base ring and thin domed base (mostly missing).
Present H. 25 mm; D. of base c. 40 mm; T. 0.5-1.5 mm. L165. Fish-pond, early second century.

15. Fig. 184. Fragment of the lower body and base of a (?) cup. Small bubbles; lower body tapering in to low outsplayed tubular base ring; domed base (centre missing).
Present H. 7 mm; D. of base 40 mm; T. 1 mm. S04. Rock-cut road, phases 2-3.

Abraded lines and indented decoration

16. Fig. 185. Twenty-five fragments of the rim, body and base of an indented beaker. Slight pale greenish tinge; some small bubbles; outsplayed curved rim, edge cracked off and ground. The tall straight side has four long oval indents extending from the upper body to above the concave base. There are abraded lines on the rim.
H. (reconstructed) c. 160 mm; rim D. 80 mm; D. of base 40 mm; T. 0.3-3.5 mm. L165. Fish-pond, early second century.

17. Fig. 185. Seventeen fragments of the rim, body and base of an indented beaker. Pale greenish tinge; outsplayed curved rim, edge cracked off and ground. The tall straight side has four long deep oval indents, extending from the upper body to above the concave base. There is an abraded band on the rim, and two bands on the upper body.
Present H. (rim) 46 mm, (base) 54 mm, (as reconstructed) 178 mm; rim D. 100 mm; D. of base 46 mm; T. 0.5-2.5+ mm. L165. Fish-pond, early second century.

18. (Not illustrated.) Body fragment of a beaker. Some small bubbles. The tall straight body has one narrow oval indent.
Present H. 50 mm; T. 0.5 mm. L184. Fish-pond, early second century.

Also:
– Two body fragments of indented vessels.
– Two body fragments.

Bowls and plates

19. Fig. 185. Rim fragment of a cylindrical bowl. Slightly incurved tubular rim, formed by folding edge up, out and down; vertical upper body.
Present H. 14 mm; rim D. c. 170 mm; T. 0.7 mm. L165. Fish-pond, early second century.

20. Fig. 185. Ten fragments of the rim, body and base of a shallow bowl or plate. Very pale greenish; small bubbles, aligned parallel to rim; very thin glass; small tubular rim, edge bent up, out and down; straight side tapering in to tubular base ring with figure-of-eight fold, flat base (centre missing).
H. 84 mm; rim D. 180 mm; D. of base c. 160 mm; T. 0.3-0.7 mm. L165. Fish-pond, early second century.

Jugs

21. Fig. 185. Seven fragments, some joining, of the rim, neck and handle of a jug with a pouring spout. Greenish colourless; small elongated bubbles; trefoil mouth, edge fire-rounded, elongated and raised pouring spout, end folded in, neck tapering in; upper handle attachment opposite pouring spout, vertical thumb rest with one pinched projection above rim; curved ribbon handle.
Present H. (excluding handle) c. 30 mm; present length (handle fragment) c. 38 mm; T. 1.5 mm. L165. Fish-pond, early second century.

22. Fig. 185. Fragment of the handle of a jug or bottle. Pale greenish colourless; lower attachment of thick broad ribbon handle; thin-walled body, broken edges of handle.
Present length 79 mm; T. (body) 0.5 mm. L165. Fish-pond, early second century.

Also (all fish-pond, early second century):
(a) Neck fragment of a jug or flask. Greenish colourless; very streaky weathering. L165.
(b) Neck fragment of a jug or flask. L165.
(c) Three ribbed body fragments. L165.

Blue-Green
Bowls

23. Fig. 185. Fragment of a tubular rim. Vertical rim, edge bent out and down, side tapering in.
Present H. 22 mm; rim D. 160 mm; T. 0.5 mm. P01. Temple-mausoleum, unstratified.

24. Fig. 185. Fragment of a high base ring, probably from a bowl or plate. Small bubbles; tall vertical tubular base ring.
Present H. 25 mm; T. 0.5 mm. L165. Fish-pond, early second century.

Also:
(a) Fragment of a high base ring, as cat. 24. Present H. 44 mm; T. 0.7 mm. L173. Burial no. 85, phase 6/7.
(b) Small fragment of a high base ring, as cat. 24. Present H. 10 mm; T. 0.5 mm. S03. Rock-cut road, phases 2-3.

25. Fig. 185. Fragment of the lower body and base of a (?) bowl. Wide lower body, tapering in to outsplayed tubular base ring, concave base (centre missing).
Present H. 11 mm; D. of base 54 mm; T. 1 mm. S10. Rock-cut road, phases 2-3.

Jugs

26. Fig. 185. Twenty-four fragments of the rim, handle, neck, body and base of a jug with a trefoil mouth. Flaring rim, edge rolled in and pinched to form pouring spout; cylindrical neck expanding out to wide convex shoulder and upper body; convex lower body tapering in to open base ring and concave base; rod handle applied to upper body and attached to rim edge opposite to spout; folded angular 'thumb rest' above rim.
Present H. (rim and handle) c. 105 mm, (base) 30 mm; D. of base 64 mm; T. 0.75-1.25 mm. E179. Pit, phase 3.

27. Fig. 185. Fragment of the handle of a small thin-walled jug. Small round bubbles in body, black streaks and elongated bubbles in handle; convex body, lower attachment of ribbon handle with two ribs; body broken to edges of handle.
Present H. 26.5 mm; T. (body) 0.2 mm. C/D 1. Unstratified.

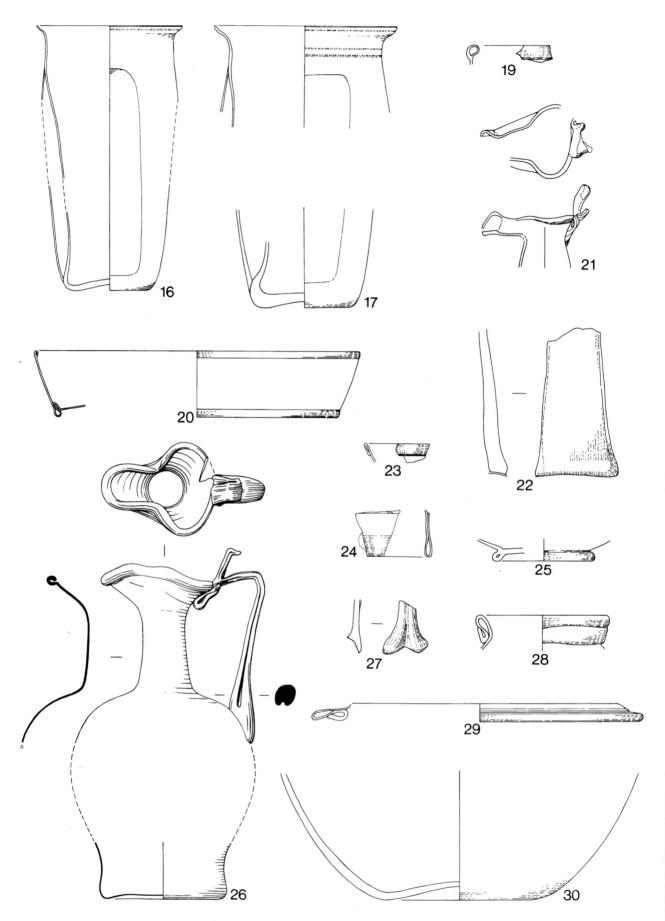

Fig. 185. Glass vessels, late-first to mid-second centuries AD (1:2). *(SC)*

Jars

28. Fig. 185. Fragment of the rim of a jar. Vertical collar rim, edge rolled inwards, then bent out and down to form figure-of-eight fold, upper body expanding out.
Present H. 18 mm; rim D. 74 mm; T. 1.5 mm. N. Medieval cave.

29. Fig. 185. Five joining fragments of the rim of a large jar. Broad horizontal folded rim, edge rolled inwards then bent out, down and in to form double loop.
Present H. 7.5 mm; rim D. 180 mm; T. 1 mm. L138. North cistern drain, second century.

30. Fig. 185. One hundred and sixty-one fragments, twelve of which join, from the lower body and base of a large thick-walled jar. Wide convex body, tapering in to convex base. There is a ring of wear on the base edge.
Present H. c. 98 mm; D. of base 84 mm; T. 1.5-5 mm. L165 and L184. Fish-pond, early second century.
Also:

(a) Three body fragments of a similar jar. L165. Fish-pond, early second century.

(b) Two very thick body fragments. Melted. M138. Phase 6.

Flasks and unguent bottles

31. Fig. 186. Fragment of the rim and neck of a flask or jug. Vertical rim, edge fire rounded; cylindrical neck.
Present H. 16 mm; rim D. 40 mm; T. 0.4 mm. L165. Fish-pond, early second century.

32. Fig. 186. Fragment of the neck and body of an unguent bottle. Small elongated bubbles; lower part of cylindrical neck, tooling marks at junction with low conical body, expanding out to junction with base (missing).
Present H. 32 mm; neck D. 22 mm; T. 1.5 mm. L165. Fish-pond, early second century.
Also (both fish-pond, early second century):

(a) Fragment of a neck. L165.

(b) Fragment of a neck with a constriction at the base. L165.

33. Fig. 186. Fragment of the lower body of a small ovoid unguent bottle. Small bubbles; convex body tapering in to small flattened base (centre missing).
Present H. 22 mm; T. 1-2.25 mm. S13. Rock-cut road, phases 2-3.

34. Fig. 186. Fragment of the body and base of a small conical unguent bottle. Low conical body, with slightly concave profile expanding out, concave base.
Present H. 16 mm; D. of base c. 22 mm; T. 2-2.5 mm. L165. Fish-pond, early second century.

35. Fig. 186. Fragment of the body and base of an ovoid unguent bottle or flask. Small round bubbles; convex lower body; concave base.
Present H. 16 mm; D. of base c. 40 mm; T. 1.5-3 mm. L165. Fish-pond, early second century.

36. Fig. 186. Fragment of the body and base of a (?) flask or jug. Bubbles, some in bands; convex body, concave base with pontil mark.
Present H. 8 mm; D. of base 32 mm; T. 0.8-3+ mm. L165. Fish-pond, early second century.

37. Fig. 186. Fragment of the lower body and base of a (?) globular flask. Few small bubbles; wide convex body tapering in; small thick-walled concave base with pontil mark.
Present H. 16 mm; D. of base 42 mm; T. 1.5-4+ mm. S04. Rock-cut road, phases 2-3.

Bottles

38. Fig. 186. Fragment of the rim and neck of a bottle, flask or jug. Some wear on rim edge; small diagonal folded rim, edge bent out, up and in, junction smoothed inside cylindrical neck.
Present H. 21 mm; rim D. 38 mm; T. 2.5 mm. C/D1. Unstratified.

39. Fig. 186. Fragment of the rim of a bottle. Horizontal folded rim, edge bent out, up, in and flattened on top.
Present H. 8 mm; rim D. 46 mm. B1. Unstratified.

40. Fig. 186. Three joining fragments of the handle and body of a square bottle. Curved shoulder and flat vertical side; angular ribbon handle with multiple reeding, pulled down to slight points on body.
Present H. c. 40 mm; T. (body) 1 mm. L165. Fish-pond, early second century.

41. Fig. 186. Fragment of the shoulder and handle of a (?) bottle. Curved shoulder; lower attachment of thick, square-sectioned rod handle.
Present H. 46 mm; Dim. 31 × 13 mm; T. (shoulder) 1 mm. S12. Rock-cut road, phases 2-3.

42. (Not illustrated.) Fragments of the body and base of a square bottle. Straight side; small part of base with raised linear (?) moulding parallel to base edge. The base edge and angle are worn, with vertical scratches on body.
Present H. 41 mm; T. 2-5 mm. L165. Fish-pond, early second century.

43. Fig. 186. Fragment of the base of a square bottle. Small bubbles; small part of vertical side, edge of concave base; raised circular pellet at corner of base, edge of another raised motif (? circular ring).
Present H. 6 mm; Dim. 19 × 20 mm; T. 2.5-3 mm. S04. Rock-cut road, early second century.
Also:

(a) Fragment of the neck of a bottle and twelve small body fragments of square bottles. L165. Fish-pond, early second century.

(b) Three body fragments of square bottles. L105. Fish-pond, later second century.

(c) One body fragment of a square bottle. L147. North cistern, late second century.

(d) One body fragment of a square bottle. M123. Phase 3.

(e) One body fragment of a square bottle. M87. Phase 3.

(f) One body fragment of a square bottle. M108. Phase 3.

Late second-early third centuries AD

Colourless
Cups and bowls
Wheel-cut decoration

44. Fig. 186. Four joining fragments of the body of a globular bowl or flask. Wide convex middle and lower body. There are parts of four horizontal bands of abraded and wheel-cut lines.
Present H. c. 58 mm; max. body D. c. 130 mm; T. 1-3.5 mm. L105. Fish-pond, later second century.

45. Fig. 186. Three fragments, two of which join, from the body of a globular bowl or flask. Small oval bubbles; wide convex body. There were parts of two circular bands of wheel-cut and abraded lines arranged round the middle of the body.
Dim. 46 × 42.5 mm; T. 1.5 mm. M38/M32. Mid-sixth century +.

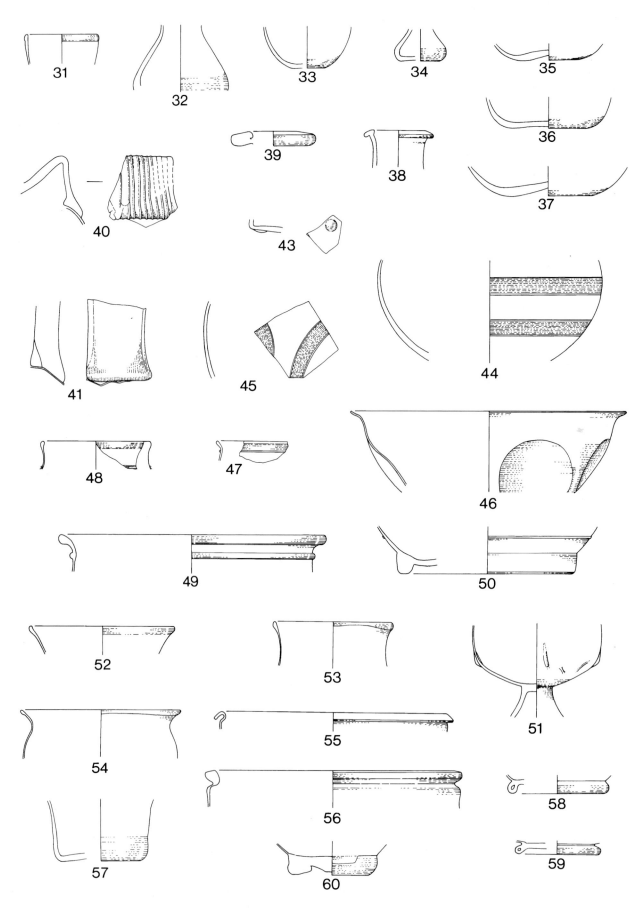

Fig. 186. Glass vessels. 31-43, late first to mid second centuries AD; 44-61, late second to early third centuries AD (1:2). (SC)

Also:

(a) Three body fragments, as cat. 44 and 45. There is a single horizontal abraded or wheel-cut line. S04. Rock-cut road, phases 2-3.

Wheel-cut and indented decoration

46. Fig. 186. Nineteen fragments, some joining, of the rim and body of a thin-walled, shallow indented bowl. Curved rim, edge cracked off and ground; convex body with at least seven indents. There is an abraded line on the rim.
Present H. 47 mm; rim D. 150 mm; T. 0.5 mm. M172/M38. Drain, phase 3; deposits of mid-sixth century.
Also:

(a) Nine body fragments with indents. L105. Fish-pond, later second century.

Trailed decoration

47. Fig. 186. Fragment of the rim of a cup or small bowl. Slightly out-bent rim, edge fire-rounded and thickened; convex upper body expanding out. There is an unmarvered horizontal trail below the rim.
Present H. 11 mm; rim D. c. 100 mm; T. 0.6+ mm. L105. Fish-pond, later second century.

48. Fig. 186. Fragment of the rim of a cup or beaker. Vertical rim, edge fire-rounded and thickened; upper body expanding out. There is a horizontal unmarvered trail on the upper body.
Present H. 15 mm; rim D. 60 mm; T. 0.5 mm. C/D1. Unstratified.

49. Fig. 186. Fragment of the rim and body of a bowl. Greenish colourless; small elongated bubbles aligned parallel to rim; outsplayed rim, edge fire-rounded and thickened; convex upper body. There is a horizontal unmarvered trail below the rim.
Present H. 20 mm; rim D. 146 mm; T. 1+ mm. (No reference.)
Also:

(a) Fragment of the rim and body of a bowl, as cat. 49. It has a horizontal unmarvered trail. M172. Drain, phase 3.

50. Fig. 186. Fragment of the body and base of a bowl. Greenish colourless; small circular bubbles; wide, slightly convex body tapering in, concave base (centre missing); thick trailed base ring. There is a horizontal unmarvered trail on the lower body.
Present H. 25 mm; D. of base 96 mm; T. 1.5 mm. L163. Phase 3.
Also:

(a) Small fragment of a concave base, with a thin trailed base ring. E11. North cistern.

Punched decoration

51. Fig. 186. Three joining fragments of the body and stemmed foot of a cup. Upper body almost cylindrical, carination, lower body slightly convex and tapering in; separately blown cylindrical stem and foot (edges missing); horizontal ring of small vertical pinched projections at carination.
Present H. c. 48 mm; T. (body) 0.5-1.5 mm. M38/S04. Deposits, mid-sixth century; rock-cut road, phases 2-3.
Also:

(a) Two fragments of a convex lower body, similar to cat. 51. M172. Drain, phase 3.

Undecorated

52. Fig. 186. Two fragments of the rim of a cylindrical cup. Slightly outsplayed rim, edge fire-rounded; straight upper body.
Present H. 17 mm; rim D. 80 mm; T. 1 mm. L105. Fish-pond, later second century.

53. Fig. 186. Three joining fragments of the rim of a cylindrical beaker. Very thin; rim edge fire-rounded and thickened; upper body tapering in slightly.
Present H. 25 mm; rim D. 66 mm; T. 0.1+ mm. M172. Drain, phase 3.
Also:

(a) Four fragments of the rim and body, as cat. 53. M172. Drain, phase 3.

(b) Fragment of a rim, as cat. 53. M125. Burial 79, phase 6.

(c) Four fragments of a rim, as cat. 53. S04. Rock-cut road, phases 2-3.

54. Fig. 186. Two joining fragments of the rim of a cup or bowl. Everted rim, edge fire-rounded and thickened; convex upper body expanding out.
Present H. 27 mm; rim D. 88 mm; T. 0.7+ mm. E179. Pit, phase 3.
Also:

(a) Fragment of a rim, as cat. 54. L138. Drain, phase 2.

55. Fig. 186. Fragment of the rim of a bowl or jar. Horizontal outsplayed rim, edge fire-rounded and thickened; convex body expanding out.
Present H. 8 mm; rim D. c. 130 mm; T. 1 mm. S04. Rock-cut road, phases 2-3.

56. Fig. 186. Two joining fragments of the rim of a cylindrical bowl. Pale greenish colourless; little visible weathering; small elongated bubbles aligned horizontally with rim; horizontal outsplayed rim, edge fire-rounded and very thick; small convex shoulder; vertical upper body.
Present H. 20 mm; rim D. 140 mm; T. 1 mm. S04. Rock-cut road, phases 2-3.

57. Fig. 186. Fragment of the lower body and base of a (?) beaker. Straight side, expanding out slightly above thick flat base.
Present H. 33 mm; D. of base 50 mm; T 1.7-3.5 mm. L105. Fish-pond, later second century.
Also:

(a) Fragment of a base, as cat. 57. A17. Phase 3.

(b) Fragment of a base, as cat. 57. S04. Rock-cut road, phases 2-3.

58. Fig. 186. Fragment of the base of a (?) small bowl. Convex lower body, tubular pushed in base ring.
Present H. 10 mm; D. of base 54 mm; T. 1-1.5 mm. L105. Fish-pond, later second century.

59. Fig. 186. Fragment of the base of a (?) small bowl. Wide lower body; outsplayed tubular base ring; slightly convex base (centre missing).
Present H. 7 mm; D. of base 46 mm; T. 1 mm. L147. North cistern, later second century.
Also:

(a) Fragment of a base, as cat. 59. Greenish colourless. S04. Rock-cut road, phases 2-3.

60. Fig. 186. Fragment of the base of a bowl. Convex side and base; trailed and flattened base ring.
Present H. 7 mm; D. of base c. 60 mm; T. 1.5+ mm. L105. Fish-pond, later second century.

61. (Not illustrated.) Fragment of the lower body and base of a (?) beaker. Very thin glass in body; slightly convex lower body; convex base with added disc and prominent pontil mark; thick trailed base ring, flattened on bottom surface.

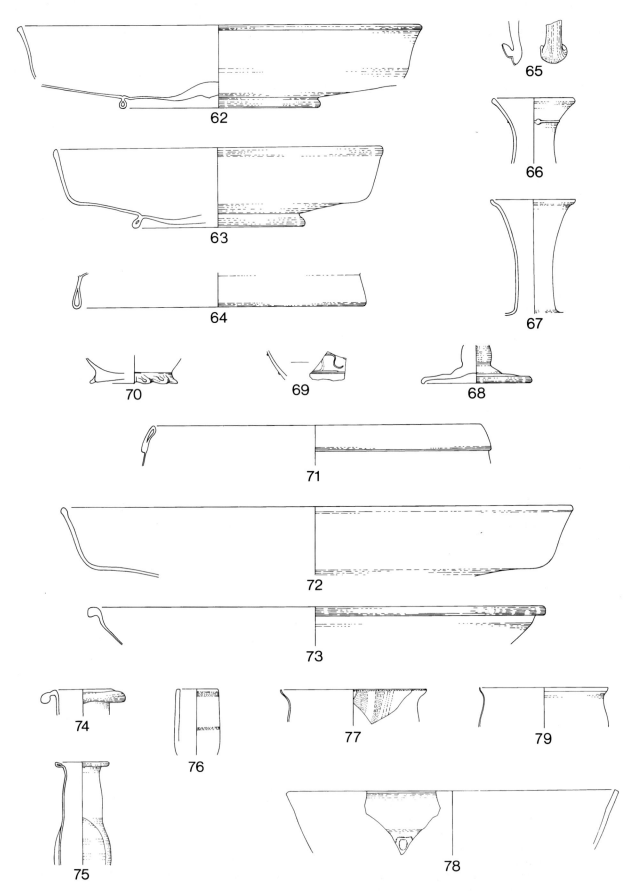

Fig. 187. Glass vessels. 62-75, late second to early third centuries; 76-9, fourth century AD (1:2). *(SC)*

Present H. 16 mm; D. of base *c.* 38 mm; T. 0.1+ mm. M172. Drain, phase 3.
Also:

(a) Fragment as cat. 60 and 61. Greenish colourless. M172. Drain, phase 3.

(b) Fragment as cat. 60 and 61. Greenish colourless. C/D1. Unstratified.

(c) Fragment as cat. 60 and 61. E11. North cistern, later second century.

(d) Fragment as cat. 60 and 61. Greenish colourless. S01. Rock-cut road, phases 2-3.

(e) Fragment as cat. 60 and 61. Greenish colourless. S12. Rock-cut road, phases 2-3.

62. Fig. 187. More than twenty fragments, many joining, of a shallow cylindrical bowl. Rim edge fire-rounded and thickened; upper body slightly concave, tapering inwards; rounded carination, wide flat lower body and base; tubular base ring; convex base; centre of base high and domed with pontil mark.
Present H. (rim fragment) 29 mm, (base fragment) 13 mm; rim D. 230 mm; D. of base 108 mm; T. 0.5-1 mm. L105. Fish-pond, later second century.

63. Fig. 187. More than thirty fragments, many joining, of a shallow cylindrical bowl. Rim edge fire rounded and thickened; straight upper body tapering inwards; rounded carination; wide slightly concave lower body; tubular base ring; convex base (centre missing).
Present H. (rim fragment) 33 mm, (base fragment) 12 mm; rim D. 180 mm; D. of base *c.* 96 mm; T 0.5-2.5 mm. L105. Fish-pond, later second century.
Also:

(a) Rim fragment, as cat. 62 and 63. Rim D. 170 mm. L105. Fish-pond, later second century.

(b) Rim fragment, as cat. 62 and 63. Rim D. 160 mm. L105. Fish-pond, later second century.

(c) Two rim fragments, as cat. 62 and 63. L146. Phase 2.

64. Fig. 187. Ten fragments of the high base ring of a bowl. Vertical folded base ring with tubular edge; small part of concave base.
Present H. 20 mm; D. of base *c.* 160 mm; T. 0.7-1 mm. L105. Fish-pond, later second century.
Also (fish-pond, later second century):

(a) Fragment of a base ring, as cat. 62-4. L105.

(b) Two fragments of a base, as cat. 62-4. L105.

Jugs

65. Fig. 187. Fragment of the handle and body of a (?) small jug. Thin-walled convex body; lower attachment of curved rod handle; broken edges of body neatly worked to edge of handle.
Present H. 23 mm. C/D1. Unstratified.

Flasks

66. Fig. 187. Fifteen fragments of the rim and neck of a flask. Outsplayed rim, edge fire-rounded and thickened; funnel mouth; narrow cylindrical neck. Horizontal unmarvered trail at junction of mouth and neck.
Present H. 35 mm; rim D. 46 mm; T. 1.25+ mm. L105. Fish-pond, later second century.

67. Fig. 187. Twenty-seven fragments, many joining, of the rim, neck and shoulder of a flask. Outsplayed curving rim, edge cracked off and ground; funnel mouth; cylindrical neck; shoulder expanding out.
Present H. *c.* 58 mm; rim D. *c.* 46 mm; T. 1.5 mm. L105. Fish-pond, later second century.

68. Fig. 187. Four fragments, two joining, of the stem and foot of a flask or cup. Solid globular stem; applied disc foot with fire-rounded edge.
Present H. *c.* 24 mm; D. of base *c.* 60 mm; T. foot 1.5+ mm. L105. Fish-pond, later second century.
Also:

(a) Three fragments of a stem and foot, as cat. 68. L105. Fish-pond, later second century.

(b) Fragment of a foot, as cat. 68. L173. Burial 85, phase 6/7.

(c) Fragment of a solid globular stem, as cat. 68. Reworked edges. E16. Phase 3.

Miscellaneous body and base fragments

69. Fig. 187. Fragment of body. Convex side. There is a horizontal unmarvered trail, and also curved meandering trail, which partially overlies the horizontal trail.
Dim. 18 × 19 mm; T. 1.25 mm. L105. Fish-pond, later second century.
Also:

(a) Twelve body fragments with horizontal trails. L105. Fish-pond, later second century.

(b) Three body fragments with horizontal trails. L147. North cistern, late second century.

70. Fig. 187. Fragment of a lower body and base. Convex side tapering in; thick concave base (pad added); six pinched points in ring at base edge.
Present H. 14 mm; D. of base *c.* 40 mm; T. 1.5 mm. PO1. Temple-mausoleum, unstratified.
Also:

(a) Fragment of a body and base, as cat. 70. It has two pinched points. M75. Phase 6.

Blue-green, greenish colourless and yellow-green
Bowls

71. Fig. 187. Fragment of the tubular rim of a bowl. Pale blue-green; little visible weathering; elongated bubbles aligned parallel to rim; slightly inturned rim, edge bent out and down to form narrow curved tube; straight upper body.
Present H. 24 mm; rim D. *c.* 190 mm; T. 1 mm. S04. Rock-cut road, phases 2-3.

72. Fig. 187. Two joining fragments of the rim and body of a large shallow bowl. Pale greenish; rim edge fire-rounded and thickened; straight upper body tapering in to rounded carination; flat lower body, tapering in to base ring (missing).
Present H. 33 mm; rim D. 280 mm; T. 1.5-2.5 mm. M172. Drain, phase 3.

73. Fig. 187. Fragment of the rim of a bowl. Pale yellow-green: outsplayed rim, edge fire-rounded and thickened; convex upper body tapering in.
Present H. 26 mm; rim D. *c.* 250 mm; T. 0.4-2 mm. L105. Fish-pond, later second century.
Also:

(a) Fragment of a wide concave base, with pontil mark, from a (?) bowl. Greenish colourless. S10. Rock-cut road, phases 2-3.

Jugs, flasks, unguent bottles

74. Fig. 187. Fragment of the rim and neck of a jug, flask or unguent bottle. Pale blue-green; horizontal folded rim, edge bent out, down and up; cylindrical neck.
Present H. 16 mm; rim D. 46 mm; T. 1 mm. L105. Fish-pond, later second century.

Also (both fish-pond, later second century):
(a) Two fragments of a large discoid unguent bottle. Greenish colourless. L105.
(b) Fragment of a small curved ribbon handle with edge ribs. Blue-green. L105.
75. Fig. 187. Two joining fragments of the rim, neck and body of an indented unguent bottle. Blue-green; small horizontal rim, edge rolled in and flattened; short neck; upper part of one (of four) indented sides.
    Present H. 56 mm; rim D. *c.* 30 mm; max. W. body 30 mm; T. 1+ mm. C/D1. Unstratified.

Fourth century

Strongly coloured
76. Fig. 187. Fragment of the rim and neck of a flask. Dark blue; small elongated bubbles aligned vertically; vertical rim, edge cracked off and ground; cylindrical neck, tapering in. There are horizontal bands of abraded lines at rim and on neck.
    Present H. 34 mm; rim D. 24 mm; T. 2-2.5 mm. S03. Rock-cut road, phases 2-3.

Colourless/greenish colourless
Beakers, bowls, cups
Coloured trail and abraded decoration
77. Fig. 187. Fragment of the rim of a cylindrical beaker or cup. Colourless ground, with opaque white marvered streaks; small bubbles; curved rim, edge cracked off and ground, almost straight upper body. There are slightly diagonal opaque white streaks marvered flush with the surface. A horizontal abraded band occurred on the rim.
    Present H. 19 mm; rim D. 80 mm; T. 0.6 mm. D5. Burial no. 93, phase 6.

Wheel-cut and abraded decoration
78. Fig. 187. Fragment of the rim of a cup or bowl. Greenish colourless; no bubbles visible; vertical, slightly curved rim, edge cracked off and ground; slightly convex side. Below the rim, there is a horizontal wheel-cut line and also a broad band of abraded lines; on the upper body, there is a horizontal band of abraded lines above a finely abraded circle (possibly the head of letter, such as B or P or R) and a small part of a horizontal motif, perhaps the serif from a second letter.
    Present H. 18 mm; rim D. 90 mm; T. 1 mm. C/D1. Unstratified.
79. Fig. 187. Fragment of the rim of a beaker or cup. Colourless; very thin; small bubbles; curved rim, edge cracked off and ground; slightly convex side expanding out. There is a narrow wheel-cut line on the rim.
    Present H. 21 mm; rim D. 70 mm; T. 0.3+ mm. A42. Unstratified.
80. Fig. 188. Two fragments of the rim and base of a conical beaker. Greenish colourless; very thin; many small bubbles; curved rim, edge cracked off and smoothed; upper body slightly convex; lower body straight, tapering to thick concave base. There is a broad horizontal band of abraded lines on the rim, and three bands on the upper and lower body.
    Present H. (rim) 34 mm, (base) 50 mm; rim D. 86 mm; D. of base 36 mm; T. 0.5-3.5 mm. A17. Phase 3.
    Also:
(a) Fragment with a similar base. D. of base 36 mm. L149.

81. Fig. 188. Fragment of the rim of a beaker or bowl. Greenish colourless; small bubbles visible; curving rim, edge cracked off and smoothed; slightly convex upper body. There is a broad band of abraded lines on the rim.
    Present H. 21 mm; rim D. 72 mm; T. 0.5-1 mm. C46. Burial no. 8, phase 6/7?
    Also:
(a) Fragment with a similar rim. Rim D. *c.* 100 mm. M38.

Abraded and indented decoration
82. (Not illustrated.) Fragment of the rim of a hemispherical or shallow indented bowl. Greenish colourless; small bubbles; small curved rim, edge cracked off and smoothed; convex side tapering in. There is a faint band of abraded lines on the rim, and slight evidence for an oval indent on the body.
    Present H. *c.* 25 mm; rim D. *c.* 120 mm; T. 0.6+ mm. D301. Pit, phase 6.

Undecorated
83. Fig. 188. Fragment of the rim of a bowl. Colourless; elongated bubbles aligned parallel to the rim; vertical wedge-shaped stepped rim, rounded top edge; straight side tapering in.
    Present H. 13 mm; rim D. *c.* 240 mm; T. 1-1.5 mm. L104. North cistern, top fill, phases 2-3.
    Also:
(a) Fragment with a similar rim. S04. Rock-cut road, phases 2-3.

Flask or jug
Colourless trail decoration
84. Fig. 188. Fragment of a rim. Greenish colourless ground, translucent blue trail; very thin; bubbly; everted rim, edge fire-rounded, funnel mouth. There is a thick horizontal unmarvered trail below the rim.
    Present H. *c.* 12 mm; rim D. *c.* 70 mm; T. 1+ mm. C/D1. Unstratified.

Yellow-green
Bowls
Coloured blob and abraded decoration
85. Fig. 188. Fragment of the body of a (?) hemispherical bowl. Yellow-green ground, dark blue blob; bubbly; convex side. There are horizontal bands of abraded lines above and below the large circular unmarvered blob.
    Present H. *c.* 53 mm; T. 0.75-1.75 mm. L104. North cistern, top fill, phases 2-3.

Abraded decoration
86. Fig. 188. Fragment of the rim of a (?) hemispherical bowl. Many small bubbles; outsplayed curving rim, edge cracked off and left rough; slightly convex upper body. There is a horizontal band of abraded lines on the upper body.
    Present H. 33 mm; rim D. 100 mm; T. 1-1.5 mm. M104. Phases 5-6.
87. Fig. 188. Two joining fragments of the lower body and base of a bowl or beaker. Convex lower body tapering in; concave base.
    Present H. 12 mm; D. of base 30 mm; T. 1-1.5 mm. D52. Roof collapse, *c.* mid-sixth century.

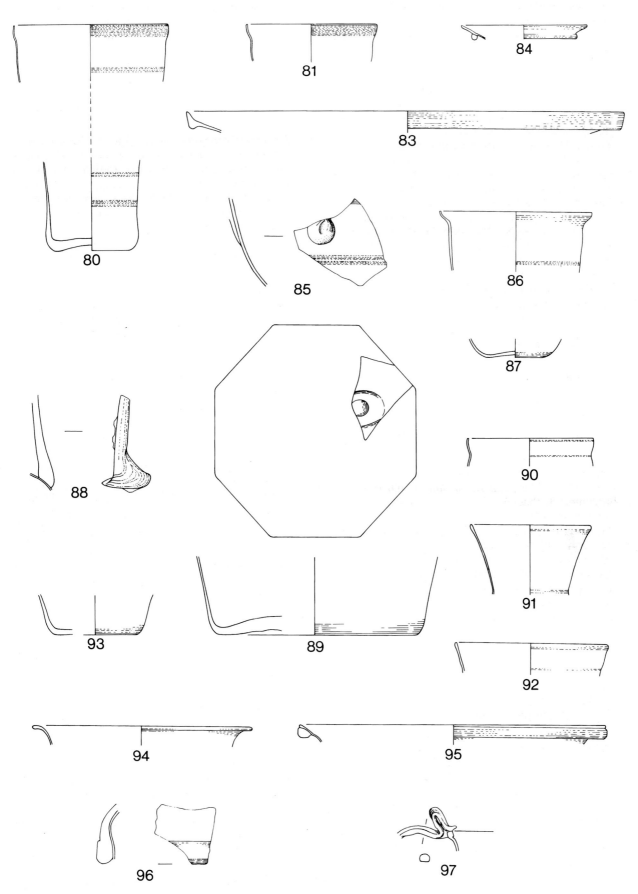

Fig. 188. Glass vessels, fourth century (1:2). *(SC)*

Also:

(a) Fragment of a base, as cat. 87. D. of base 38 mm. M145. Phase 3.

(b) Fragment of a base, as cat. 87. D. of base 38 mm. M38. Deposits, mid-sixth century.

Jugs and bottles

88. Fig. 188. Fragment of the handle and body of a jug. Convex body with lower attachment of straight ribbon handle (one edge rib surviving).
Present H. 53 mm; T. (body) 1 mm. M164. Phase 3.

89. Fig. 188. Twelve fragments, two joining, of the body and base of a mould blown hexagonal (?) bottle or jug. Sharp body and base angles; concave base with raised boss near centre. There are parts of at least three vertical slightly convex sides with very pock-marked and uneven surfaces, either from the mould or because they have been affected by heat. There is wear on the base edge, and vertical scratches on some of the body fragments.
Present H. 41 mm; width of sides 45 mm; T. 1-2.5 mm (body), to 8 mm (base). M38/M172. Deposits, mid-sixth century; drain, phase 3.

Also:

(a) Two fragments of body and base edge probably from cat. 89. Present H. 56 mm. M32. Phase 6.

(b) Fragment of body, probably from cat. 89. M79. Phase 3.

Blue-green

Beakers and cups

Abraded decoration

90. Fig. 188. Fragment of the rim of a beaker or small bowl. Curved rim, edge cracked off and smoothed; convex upper side. There is an abraded band at the junction of the rim and body.
Present H. 14 mm; rim D. *c.* 70 mm; T. 1 mm. S03. Rock-cut road, phases 2-3.

Also:

(a) Fragment of body with abraded lines. S10. Rock-cut road, phases 2-3.

Undecorated

91. Fig. 188. Fragment of the rim of a (?) beaker. Small bubbles; fire rounded rim; slightly concave side tapering in.
Present H. 40 mm; rim D. 68 mm; T. 0.7-1.5 mm. S04. Rock-cut road, phases 2-3.

92. Fig. 188. Fragment of a rim, as cat. 91.
Present H. 17 mm; rim D. 86 mm; T. 1 mm. L146. North cistern, phase 2.

93. Fig. 188. Fragment of the base of a (?) beaker. Few small bubbles; straight side tapering in to small thick concave base.
Present H. 20 mm; D. of base *c.* 46 mm; T. 1.5-2.5 mm. S12. Rock-cut road, phases 2-3.

94. Fig. 188. Fragment of the rim of a bowl or cup. Small bubbles aligned parallel to rim; horizontal outsplayed rim, edge fire-rounded, upper body tapering in.
Present H. 10 mm; rim D. *c.* 120 mm; T. 1-1.5 mm. S04. Rock-cut road, phases 2-3.

Also:

(a) Fragment of a rim, as cat. 94. Rim D. 98 mm. S04. Rock-cut road, phases 2-3.

Bowls

Trailed decoration

95. Fig. 188. Fragment of the rim of a bowl. Very thin; outsplayed rim, fire-rounded; upper body tapering in. There is a thick unmarvered trail on the outside of the rim.
Present H. 10 mm; rim D. 170 mm; T. 0.5+ mm. M79. Phase 3.

Undecorated

96. Fig. 188. Fragment of the rim of a (?) large bowl or jar. Part of curved folded rim, edge probably rolled in and then bent out and down to touch inside layer of glass, top missing.
Dim. 30 × 32 mm; T. (inside layer) 1 mm. E01. Unstratified.

Jug

97. Fig. 188. Fragment of the rim and handle of a jug. Small bubbles; folded rim, edge rolled in and flattened; funnel mouth; upper attachment of rod handle on rim, folded and pinched into vertical thumb rest.
Present H. *c.* 28 mm; T 1.5 mm. C1. Unstratified.

Fifth century and later

Pale green, greenish colourless and blue-green

Cups and beakers

Coloured trail decoration

98. Fig. 189. Fragment of the rim of a (?) cup or beaker. Greenish colourless ground, fine opaque white spiral trail; everted rim, edge thickened and fire-rounded. There are eight closely set, narrow, partly marvered trails on the body below the rim.
Present H. 10 mm; rim D. *c.* 100 mm; T. 0.7 mm. D50. Phase 3.

99. Fig. 189. Fragment of the rim of a (?) conical cup. Pale green ground, narrow opaque white trails; small bubbles; fire-rounded and thickened rim edge; upper body tapering inwards. There are four trails on the rim and upper body, now weathered but probably marvered flush with the surface.
Present H. 11 mm; rim D. 70 mm; T. 0.8 mm. D316. Phase 3.

100. Fig. 189. Fragment of the rim of a small conical cup or beaker. Pale green ground, opaque white trails; small bubbles; rim edge fire-rounded and thickened, side tapering inwards; faint diagonal ribbing on upper body. There are four marvered trails, closely set on the rim.
Present H. 17 mm; rim D. 60 mm; T. 0.5-1.2-5 mm. D218. Phase 7.

101. Fig. 189. Fragment of the rim of a conical cup or beaker. Pale greenish ground, opaque white trails; very thin; fire-rounded and thickened rim; straight upper body tapering in. Marvered trails are present in two close-set bands of four trails below the rim, and on the upper body.
Present H. 17 mm; rim D. 70 mm; T. 0.4-1 mm. M36. Phase 3.

102. Fig. 189. Fragment of the rim of a conical cup or beaker. Dark blue-green ground, opaque white trails; bubbly; fire-rounded and thickened rim, upper body tapering in. Marvered trails, closely set in two bands, are present on the body.
Present H. 19 mm; rim D. 70 mm; T. 0.5-1.5 mm. D219. Phase 6.

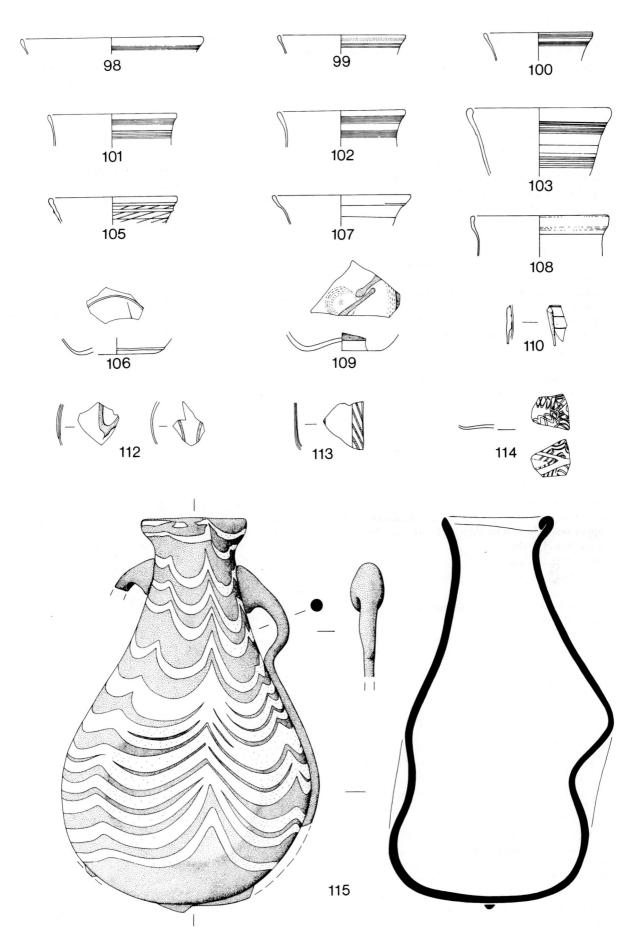

Fig. 189. Glass vessels, fifth century AD and later. All 1:2, except 115 (1:1). *(SC/SA)*

103. Fig. 189. Fragment of the rim of a conical cup or beaker. Pale green ground, opaque white trails; bubbly glass; slightly inturned rim, edge fire-rounded and thickened; straight upper body tapering in. There is a band of six close-set trails not marvered flush with the surface below the rim, a single trail on the upper body, and eight close-set trails on the middle of the body.
Present H. 37 mm; rim D. 80 mm; T. 0.7-1 mm. D94. Phase 6.

104. (Not illustrated.) Fragment of the rim of a (?) cup or beaker. Colourless ground, opaque white trail; dull, no weathering visible; slightly inturned rim, edge fire-rounded, thick. There is a trail on the rim which is not marvered flush.
Dim. 7 × 10.2 mm; T. 1 mm. D220. Phase 6.

105. Fig. 189. Fragment of the rim of a conical cup or beaker. Pale green ground, opaque white trails; optic-blown; fire-rounded and thickened rim; upper body tapering inwards. There is faint diagonal ribbing on the body. The band of four trails below the rim is not marvered flush.
Present H. 16 mm; rim D. c. 70 mm; T. 0.7-1 mm. M64. Phase 6.

106. Fig. 189. Fragment of the body and base of a cup. Pale green ground, opaque white trail; bubbly; convex side; concave base. The trail at the junction of the body and the base is not marvered flush.
Present H. 6 mm; T. 1-1.5 mm. B1. Unstratified.
Also:
(a) Colourless fragment of a straight body. The opaque white trail is not marvered flush. Dim. 18.5 × 9 mm; T. 0.25 mm. D57. Burial no. 39, phase 6/7.
(b) Fragment of a convex body. Blue-green. There are four widely spaced opaque white unmarvered trails. Dim. 20 × 22 mm; T. 0.8-1.5 mm. D 301. Pit, phase 7.

107. Fig. 189. Fragment of the rim of a (?) conical cup or beaker. Pale green ground, opaque yellow trails; everted rim, edge fire-rounded; straight upper body tapering in. Three widely spaced trails, now weathered, were probably not marvered flush.
Present H. 17 mm; rim D. 76 mm; T. 0.5-1 mm. M72. Burial no. 77, phase 6/7.

108. Fig. 189. Fragment of the rim of a (?) conical drinking cup. Blue-green ground, opaque yellow spiral trail; small oval bubbles aligned parallel to rim; fire-rounded and thickened rim, slightly inturned edge; straight side. The narrow horizontal trail on the upper body is not marvered flush.
Present H. 23 mm; rim D. 76 mm; T. 0.7-1.5 mm. A5. Unstratified.

109. Fig. 189. Fragment of the base of a (?) cup. Dark blue-green ground, opaque yellow trails; very bubbly; convex lower body; concave base; pontil mark. There is a broad horizontal marvered trail on the lower body, and two trail terminals on the base.
Present H. 8 mm; D. of base c. 35 mm at concavity; T. 1.5-2.5 mm. B36. Burial no. 10, phase 5/6.

110. Fig. 189. Three fragments of the convex body of a (?) cup. Dark blue-green ground, opaque yellow trails; parts of the side with widely spaced narrow unmarvered trails. One fragment has a vertical strip (perhaps an ornamental handle) applied to the trails.
Dim. (fragment with vertical strip) 18.5 × 11 mm; T. 1 mm. D107. Burial 24, phase 5.
Also:
(a) Fragment of a convex body. Dark blue-green; two

opaque yellow trails. Dim. 12 × 9.5 mm; T. 0.4 mm. C/D1. Unstratified.

111. (Not illustrated.) Fragment of body. Greenish colourless ground; translucent dark red streaks marvered flush with surface; convex side above base.
Dim. 17.4 × 12.4 mm; T. 0.5-1.25 mm. B1. Unstratified.

112. Fig. 189. Six fragments, four joining, of body. Pale greenish colourless ground; translucent blue trails; convex side. There is a zig-zag unmarvered trail and a horizontal unmarvered trail.
Dim. (largest fragment) 22.5 × 16 mm; T. 0.3-0.7 mm. D273. Font sump, phase 6.

113. Fig. 189. Fragment of body. Colourless ground and colourless strips with diagonal opaque yellow marvered trails; straight side expanding out to curved carination; parts of two vertical strips applied to side.
Dim. 25.3 × 21.5 mm; T. 0.2-0.6 mm. B1. Unstratified.

114. Fig. 189. Fragment of a base. Greenish colourless ground; greenish colourless and opaque white twisted canes; small concave base; four canes applied to outside surface and marvered flush with surface, meeting at centre of base.
Dim. 20.3 × 19.0 mm; T. 1-1.5 mm. B36. Burial no. 10, phase 5/6.
Also (same burial):
(a) Small fragment of body. Dim. 10 × 7 mm; T. 0.25 mm. B36.

Flask
Coloured trail decoration
115. Figs 189 and 190. Indented flask with two handles, complete. Pale greenish colourless ground; opaque white feathered trails; rim slightly flared, edge rolled up, in and flattened; cylindrical neck expanding to globular body, with two uneven circular indents, producing flattened profile; very small concave base; spiral trail wound from lower body to rim, marvered flush with surface and manipulated into festoons; two thin vertical rod handles, applied below rim and attached to upper body, each with trail extending to base (much of trails now missing); pontil mark applied over the handle trails.
H. 100 mm; rim D. 31 mm; max. body D. 67 mm. D107. Burial no. 24, phase 5.

116. Fig. 191. Fragment of body. Greenish colourless ground; dark blue and greenish colourless trails; straight side; two thick v-shaped greenish colourless unmarvered trails above two similar dark blue trails.
Dim. 28 × 24 mm; T. 0.5+ mm. Z7. Castellaccio, twelfth-century deposit.

Yellowish colourless
Beakers and cups
Trailed decoration
117. Fig. 191. Fragment of the rim and upper body of a conical beaker. Yellowish colourless; rim edge fire-rounded and thickened; straight upper body tapering in. There are four unmarvered trails on the upper body.
Present H. 26 mm; rim D. c. 100 mm; T. 0.3-1 mm. B26. Burial no. 106, probably fifth century.

Undecorated
118. Fig. 191. Five fragments, two joining, of the rim and upper body of a (?) conical beaker or lamp. Yellowish

colourless; small elongated bubbles aligned parallel to rim; fire-rounded and thickened rim; straight side tapering in.

Present H. *c.* 40 mm; rim D. 88 mm; T. 0.5-1 mm. S03. Rock-cut road, phases 2-3.

119. Fig. 191. Fragment of the rim and upper body of a (?) conical beaker or lamp. Yellowish colourless. As cat. 118.

Present H. 15 mm; rim D. 86 mm; T. 0.3-0.7 mm. N30. Medieval cave, phases 5-6.

120. Fig. 191. Fragment of the rim and upper body of a (?) conical beaker or lamp. Yellowish colourless. As cat. 118.

Present H. 15 mm; rim D. 68 mm; T. 0.5-1 mm. D6. Phases 6-7.

Also:

(a) Fragment of a rim, as cat. 118-20. M64. Phase 6.
(b) Fragment of a rim, as cat. 118-20. B1. Unstratified.
(c) Fragment of a rim, as cat. 118-20. D218. Unstratified.
(d) Fragment of a rim, as cat. 118-20. A19. Phase 3+.
(e) Fragment of a rim, as cat. 118-20. B29. Phase 7.
(f) Fragment of a rim, as cat. 118-20. D266. Phase 3.
(g) Fragment of a rim, as cat. 118-20. A34. Burial no. 60, phase 6?
(h Fragment of a rim, as cat. 118-20. L101. Unstratified.

Yellow-green
Beakers, cups and lamps

121. Fig. 191. Fragment of the rim and body of a (?) cup. Everted rim, edge fire-rounded and thickened; convex side expanding out.

Present H. 18 mm; rim D. *c.* 80 mm; T. 0.5-1 mm. M106. Phase 6.

122. Fig. 191. Two fragments, rim and base, of a (?) conical beaker or lamp. Thin glass; rim slightly inturned, edge fire-rounded and thickened; upper body tapering in; straight lower body tapering to very small concave base; pontil mark.

Present H. (rim) 18 mm, (base) 27 mm; rim D. 74 mm; D. of base 10 mm; T. 0.3-2 mm. B80. Burial no. 12, phase 5/6.

123. Fig. 191. Fragment of the rim of a (?) conical beaker or lamp. Slightly everted rim, edge and upper body as cat. 122; distorted by heat.

Present H. 13 mm; rim D. *c.* 66 mm; T. 1 mm. A35. Phase 6.

124. Fig. 191. Fragment of the rim of a (?) conical beaker. Rim as cat. 122; upper body nearly vertical.

Present H. 25 mm; rim D. 76 mm; T. 0.2-1.2 mm. A5. Unstratified.

125. Fig. 191. Fragment of the rim of a (?) conical beaker. Slightly everted rim, edge fire-rounded and thickened; upper body nearly vertical.

Present H. 15 mm; rim D. 56 mm; T. 0.2-0.6 mm. A34. Burial no. 60, phase 6?

126. Fig. 191. Fragment of the rim of a (?) conical beaker. As cat. 125.

Present H. 12 mm; rim D. 70 mm; T. 0.5 mm. M38. Deposits, mid-sixth century.

Also:

(a) Fragment of a rim. A29. Phase 6.
(b) Fragment of a rim. M32. Phase 6.
(c) Fragment of a rim. M139. Phase 6.
(d) Fragment of a rim. B4. Burial 99, phase 6.
(e) Fragment of a rim. D6. Phase 6.
(f) Two fragments of rim. A21. Phase 6.

Fig. 190. Early medieval glass flask (cat.115). *(KW)*

(g) Two fragments of rim. A21. Phase 6.
(h) Fragment of a rim. M143. Phase 3.
(i) Fragment of a rim. A23. Burial no. 26, phase 5/6?
(j) Fragment of a rim. C/D1. Unstratified.

Blue-green and green-blue (peacock blue)
Beakers, cups and lamps

127. Fig. 191. Fragment of the rim of a (?) conical beaker or lamp. Pale blue-green; thin glass; rim edge fire rounded; upper body tapering in.

Present H. 16 mm; rim D. 90 mm; T. 0.7-1.5 mm. M64. Phase 6.

Also:

(a) Fragment of a rim. D218. Unstratified.
(b) Fragment of a rim. B8. Burial no. 18, phase 6/7.
(c) Fragment of a rim. M64. Phase 6.
(d) Fragment of a rim. B64. Burial no. 12, phase 5/6.
(e) Fragment of a rim. A35. Phase 6.

128. Fig. 191. Fragment of the rim of a (?) conical beaker or lamp. Deep green-blue (peacock blue); rim edge fire-rounded; upper body tapering in.

Present H. 15 mm; rim D. 76 mm; T. 1 mm. D244. Phase 6.

129. Fig. 191. Fragment of the rim of a (?) conical beaker or lamp. Deep green-blue (peacock blue); rim edge fire-rounded; upper body tapering in.

Present H. 25 mm; rim D. 70 mm; T. 0.5-1 mm. B26. Burial no. 106, probably fifth century.

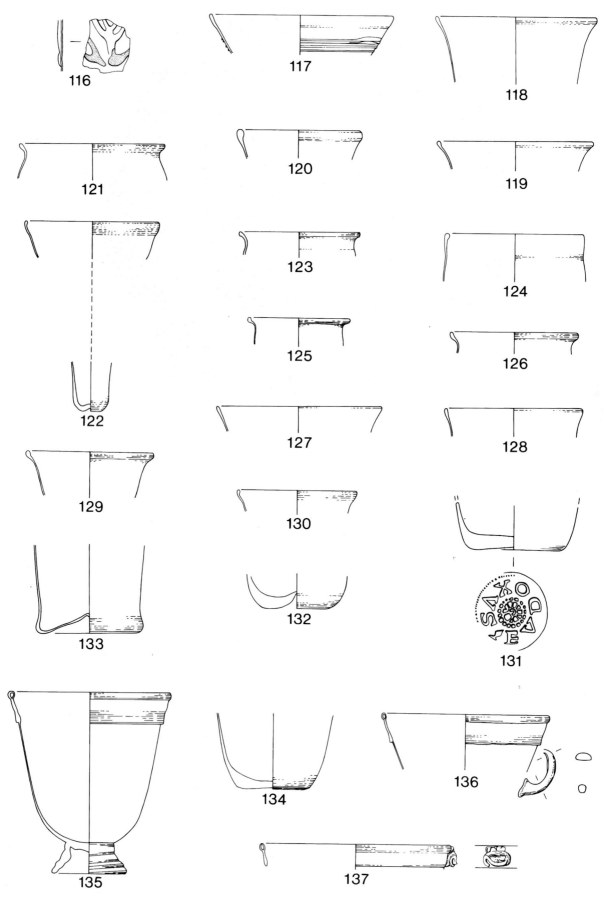

Fig. 191. Glass vessels, fifth century AD and later (1:2). *(SC)*

Fig. 192. Base stamped EUDOXUS (cat. 131). *(KW)*

Also:

(a) Fragment of a rim. B1. Unstratified.

(b) Fragment of a rim. J1. Unstratified.

(c) Fragment of a rim. E69. Phase 3.

(d) Fragment of body, with trail. M14. Phase 6.

(e) Fragment of body, with trail. M10. Phase 5.

(f) Fragment of body. D316. Phase 3.

Various colours

Beakers, bowls, cups and lamps

130. Fig. 191. Fragment of the rim of a (?) conical beaker or lamp. Greenish colourless; rim slightly inturned, edge fire-rounded; upper body tapering in.
Present H. 12 mm; rim D. 66 mm; T. 0.5+ mm. C46. Burial no. 8, phase 6/7?
Also:

(a) Fragment of a rim. C46. Burial no. 8, phase 6/7?

(b) Fragment of a rim. S03. Rock-cut road, phases 2-3.

(c) Fragment of a rim. M26. Phase 3.

(d) Fragment of a rim. M92. Phase 3.

131. Figs 191 and 192. Fragment of the lower body and base of a (?) conical beaker. Pale green; some small bubbles; straight lower body tapering in to thick concave base with impressed stamp. There is a rouletted ring enclosing E V D O X V S anticlockwise in a ring, with a leaf stop between S and E, and a rosette and ring of dots at the centre.
Present H. 25 mm; D. of base 48 mm; T. 2-9 mm. S04. Rock-cut road, phases 2-3.

132. Fig. 191. Fragment of the lower body and base of a (?) conical beaker. Pale green; some bubbles; straight lower body; concave base with central pointed kick.
Present H. 17 mm; D. of base 36 mm; T. 2.5-5.5 mm. H29. Unstratified.

133. Fig. 191. Fragment of the lower body and base of a (?) conical beaker. Greenish colourless; straight lower body expanding out above concave base with central pointed kick; pontil mark.
Present H. 45 mm; D. of base 54 mm; T. 1.5 mm. M23. Phase 3.
Also:

(a) Fragment of a similar base, also with a pontil mark. D. of base 32 mm. M136. Phase 3.

134. Fig. 191. Two joining fragments of the lower body and base of a (?) conical beaker. Colourless; straight side tapering in; thick slightly concave base; pontil mark.
Present H. 41 mm; D. of base 40 mm; T. 1-4.5+ mm. C/D1. Unstratified.

135. Fig. 191. Eighteen fragments, most joining, of a small footed bowl. Greenish colourless; vertical collar rim, tubular at top, formed by bending edge out and down; long convex body; applied conical base formed by twisting a trail four times round the bottom of the body; pontil mark.
H. 95 mm; rim D. 90 mm; D. of base 40 mm; T. 0.5-1.5+ mm. C51. Limekiln, early-mid fifth century.
Also:

(a) Fragment of a rim, as cat. 135. D317. Phase 6.

(b) Two fragments of rim. C46. Burial no. 8, phase 6/7?

(c) Fragment of a rim. B36. Burial no. 10, phase 5/6.

(d) Fragment of a rim, as cat. 135. D301. Phase 6.

136. Fig. 191. Three fragments of the rim, body and handle of a (?) small bowl or lamp. Pale yellowish colourless; very thin glass; vertical collar rim, tubular at top, formed by bending edge out and down; straight side tapering in; scar on outside of rim, probably from handle; one small vertical curved rod handle, not attached.
Present H. 33 mm; rim D. 92 mm; T. 0.24 mm. C51. Limekiln, early-mid fifth century.

137. Fig. 191. Fragment of the rim and handle of a (?) small bowl or lamp. Pale yellowish colourless; vertical collar rim, tubular at top, formed by bending edge out and down; handle attachment on outside of rim.
Present H. 13 mm; rim D. 104 mm. C1. Unstratified.

138. Fig. 193. Fragment of the rim of a (?) bowl or lamp. Yellowish colourless; vertical tubular rim, edge rolled out and down; straight side tapering in; handle scar on outside edge of rim.
Present H. 19 mm; rim D. 86 mm; T. 0.5+ mm. C46. Burial no. 8, phase 6/7?

139. Fig. 193. Fragment of the rim of a (?) bowl or lamp. Greenish colourless; tubular rim, edge rolled out and down; handle scar on outside edge of rim.
Present H. 6 mm; rim D. 82 mm; T. 0.5+ mm. C/D1. Unstratified.

140. Fig. 193. Fragment of the rim of a (?) bowl or lamp. Greenish colourless; tubular rim, edge rolled out and down; handle attachment on rim edge.
Present H. 8 mm; rim D. 106 mm; T. 0.5+ mm. B66. Phase 6.
Similar tubular rims:

(a) Fragment of a rim. Greenish colourless. D266. Phase 6.

(b) Fragment of a rim. Greenish colourless. D47. Phase 6.

(c) Fragment of a rim. Pale blue-green. D94. Phase 6.

(d) Fragment of a rim. Pale blue-green. B34. Phase 6.

(e) Fragment of a rim. Pale blue-green. D6. Phase 6.

(f) Fragment of a rim. Greenish colourless. B64. Burial no. 12, phase 5/6.

(g) Fragment of a rim. Greenish colourless. B80. Burial no. 12, phase 5/6.

(h) Fragment of a rim. Yellow-green. B34. Phase 6.

(i) Fragment of a rim. Deep green-blue (peacock blue). D4. Burial no. 95, phases 6-7.

141. Fig. 193. Fragment of the rim of a (?) small bowl or lamp. Yellowish colourless; fire rounded and thickened rim; side tapering in; handle scar on top of rim.
Present H. 14 mm; rim D. 80 mm; T. 0.5+ mm. A34. Burial no. 60, phase 6?

142. Fig. 193. Fragment of the handle and body of a (?) lamp. Yellowish colourless; conical body; lower attachment of vertical curved rod handle.
Present H. 50 mm; T. 0.5+ mm. C/D1. Unstratified.

143. Fig. 193. Fragment of the handle of a (?) lamp. Yellow-green; vertical rod handle, lower attachment flattened against body (missing).
Present H. 53.5 mm. M26. Phase 3.

144. Fig. 193. Fragment of the handle and body of a (?) lamp. Pale blue-green; little weathering; bubbly; convex side with horizontal unmarvered trails; lower attachment of small vertical angular rod handle.
Present H. 32 mm; T. 0.1+ mm. C/D1. Unstratified.

145. Fig. 193. Fragment of the handle and body of a (?) lamp. Pale blue-green; convex side; lower attachment of small vertical angular rod handle.

Present H. 27.5 mm; T. 0.1+ mm. C42. Phase 6.
Also:

(a) Fragment as cat. 144-5. Dark blue. C/D1. Unstratified.

(b) Fragment as cat. 144-5. Pale blue-green. C2. Burial no. 2, phases 5-6.

(c) Fragment as cat. 144-5. Pale blue-green. C47. Phase 6.

(d) Fragment, (?) as cat. 144-5. Pale blue-green. M86. Phase 6.

(e) Fragment, (?) as cat. 144-5. Pale blue-green. M132. Phase 3.

146. Fig. 193. Fragment of the lower body of a lamp. Pale green; narrow conical body terminating in convex base; pontil mark.
Present H. 37 mm; max. D. 21.5 mm; T. 0.5+ mm. B1. Unstratified.

147. Fig. 193. Fragment of the lower body of a lamp. Pale green. As cat. 146.
Present H. 33.5 mm; max. D. 22.5 mm; T. 0.7+ mm. B80. Burial no. 12, phase 5/6.

148. Fig. 193. Fragment of the lower body of a lamp. Pale green. As cat. 146.
Present H. 34.5 mm; max. D. 21 mm; T. 0.7 mm. C57. Burial no. 2, phases 5-6.

149. Fig. 193. Fragment of the lower body of a lamp. Pale blue-green. As cat. 146.
Present H. 40.5 mm; max. D. 17 mm; T. 0.7 mm. C42. Burial no. 2, phases 5-6.
Also:

(a) Fragment as cat. 146. Deep green-blue (peacock blue). C/D1. Unstratified.

(b) Fragment as cat. 146. Deep green-blue (peacock blue). B1. Unstratified.

(c) Fragment as cat. 146. Blue-green. M92. Phase 3.

150. Fig. 193. Two joining fragments of the lower body, stem and base, of a small cup. Pale greenish; thin glass; convex lower body tapering in, pinched into stem; folded into double layered base ring with tubular edge; base with high kick filling hollow stem.
Present H. 29 mm; D. of base 35 mm; T. 0.1+ mm. B49. Burial no. 11, phase 5/6.

151. Fig. 193. Fragment of the lower body, stem and base of a small cup. Yellowish colourless. As cat. 150.
Present H. 22 mm; D. of base 40 mm; T. 0.1+ mm. D6. Phase 6.

152. Fig. 193. Fragment of the lower body, stem and base of a small cup. Blue-green. As cat. 150.
Present H. 21 mm; D. of base 38 mm; T. 0.5+ mm. D6. Phase 6.
Also:

(a) Fragment as cat. 150-2. Yellowish colourless. M97. Phase 3.

(b) Fragment as cat. 150-2. Yellowish colourless. C/D1. Unstratified.

(c) Fragment as cat. 150-2. Yellowish colourless. D166. Phase 3.

(d) Fragment as cat. 150-2. Yellowish colourless. D92. Burial no. 55, phase 6-7.

(e) Fragment as cat. 150-2. Yellowish colourless. A34. Burial no. 60, phase 6?

(f) Fragment as cat. 150-2. Yellowish colourless. D48. Phase 3.

(g) Fragment as cat. 150-2. Yellowish colourless. D166. Phase 3.

(h) Fragment as cat. 150-2. Yellowish colourless. M74. Phase 6.

(i) Fragment as cat. 150-2. Yellowish colourless. B64. Burial no. 12, phase 5/6.

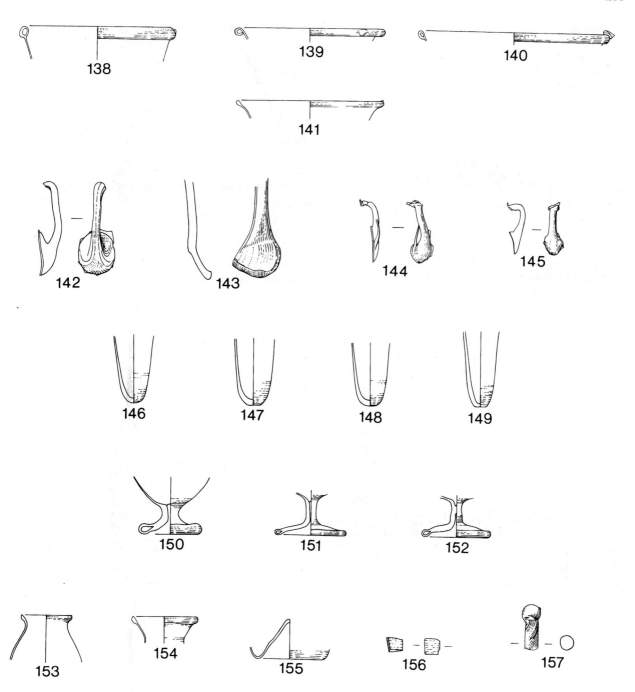

Fig. 193. Glass vessels, fifth century AD and later (1:2). *(SC)*

(j) Fragment as cat. 150-2. Yellowish colourless. M32. Phase 6.

(k) Fragment as cat. 150-2. Dark greenish. A34. Burial no. 60, phase 6?

153. Fig. 193. Fragment of the rim of a (?) flask or small jar. Greenish colourless; everted rim, edge fire-rounded; almost straight body expanding out.
Present H. 29 mm; rim D. 28 mm; T. 0.7+ mm. D273. Font sump, phase 6.

154. Fig. 193. Fragment of the rim of a (?) flask. Greenish colourless; thin glass; everted rim, edge fire-rounded; funnel mouth; top of narrow cylindrical neck; thick trail round outside edge of rim.
Present H. 13 mm; rim D. 36 mm; T. 0.1+ mm. B32. Burial no. 11, phase 5/6.

Also:

(a) Fragment of a rim, as cat. 154. Blue-green. B80. Burial no. 12, phase 5/6.

155. Fig. 193. Fragment of the high concave base of a (?) flask, bowl or lamp. Pale green; very bubbly; narrow straight lower body; small very high conical base with central kick; pontil mark.
Present H. 23 mm; D. of base *c.* 36 mm; T. 1 mm. C23. Burial no. 7, phase 6/7?

Also:

(a) Fragment of a base, as cat. 155. Greenish colourless. C/D1. Unstratified.

(b) Fragment of a base, as cat. 155. Deep green-blue (peacock blue). D273. Font sump, phase 6.

(c) Fragment of a base, as cat. 155. Pale green. D301.

Phase 6.

Also:

– Two fragments of body, with 'optic-blown' designs. Yellowish colourless.

– Two fragments of body, with horizontal unmarvered trails. Pale blue-green.

– Fragment of body, with meandering unmarvered trail. Pale blue-green.

Objects[68]

Tesserae

156. Fig. 193. Cube-shaped lump. No worn surfaces; semi-opaque dark blue.
8.7 × 8.9 × 7.8 mm. D33. Unstratified.

Also:

(a) Cube-shaped lump, as cat. 157. Semi-opaque dark blue. B64. Burial no. 12, phase 5/6.

(b) Cube-shaped lump, as cat. 157. Semi-opaque peacock blue. C/D1. Unstratified.

Pin-shaped rod

157. Fig. 193. Fragment of a rod with a globular terminal. Dark peacock blue; solid cylindrical shaft with slight anti-clockwise twist; globular end. There is a scar on the end, perhaps from a pontil.
Present length 23.5 mm; D. (rod) 8.5 mm. D81. Phase 6.

THE LAMPS, by D.M. Bailey

Some 127 lamps and fragments were found at this site and only two of them, cat. 62 and 63, were made outside Italy, apparently in Tunisia and Tripolitania respectively. All the others are central Italian products and most were probably made in Rome or its immediate vicinity; the very late Roman or early medieval lamp, cat. 60, may have been made at the site itself, and cat. 61, of early medieval date, is of uncertain provenance but is probably local. Very few of these lamps were manufactured before the end of the first century AD, the bulk of them being of the second century AD and the beginning of the third century. Most of these second- to third-century lamps came from a single source, the fish-pond, into which they were dumped in two main deposits: L105 and, below it, L165. Although L165 has, on the whole, earlier lamps than L105, there was a slight amount of mixing between the deposits, as there are joins of lamp fragments from both deposits – for example, cat. 4 and 5. The earliest lamp from the fish-pond is probably cat. 6, which could have been made as early as about AD 50, but more likely is as late as most of the lamps from the same deposit, Standard Italian Loeschcke 1919 type VIII lamps, produced between about AD 90 and 160 (cat. 12-24 include

many of these from L165). However, the upper deposit, L105, also included lamps of this type, together with a larger quantity of late Italian Loeschcke 1919 type VIII lamps (amongst cat. 29-50) of about AD 150 to 225+, some of which type were found in the lower deposit, L165. The quantity of the recovered lamps thereafter drops dramatically, with one lamp only of fourth-century date (cat. 54), three lamps of about AD 375-450 (cat. 55-7), three lamps of the fifth or sixth century (cat. 58-9, 63), and two lamps of early medieval date, the seventh- to eighth-century cat. 60, and cat. 61, probably of the tenth century AD.

Cat. 1, a small fragment of a volute lamp with an incomplete shoulder form, could be the earliest lamp from the site, made probably between AD 40 and 100, but as the date-range of its type shows, it need not be any earlier than the end of the first century. It was residual in its late Roman find-spot in area E (the 'large room'): see Figure 12 for the areas of the site. Equally, cat. 2 and 3, although possibly of a date well before AD 90 could well be later – cat. 2 came from the lower deposit in the fish-pond and cat. 3 from the early medieval pottery kiln, where it was residual.

Both the Loeschcke 1919 type V cat. lamps 4 and 5 are late forms of the type (Bailey 1980 type Civ) and are not earlier than AD 90 or later than AD 150; indeed, cat. 4, signed for the firm L. Munatius Adiectus, probably dates before AD 130. Each of the two lamps is made up from fragments that came from both major deposits in the fish-pond.

Central Italian Loeschcke 1919 type VIII lamps form the largest proportion of the lamps found (109 out of 127), and are divided almost equally between early forms, dating between about AD 50 and 160 (only two – cat. 6 and 7 – could be as early as AD 50; some 54 lamps are likely to be no earlier than AD 90), and the later forms, dating between about AD 150 and 225+ (53 examples).

The two lamps (cat. 6 and 7) of Bailey 1980 type Oii, with ovule decoration on their shoulders, are of a type made between AD 50 and 110; again neither may have been made or deposited before AD 90. Cat. 6 came from the lower deposit in the fish-pond; cat. 7 was residual in a late Roman context on the lower terrace.

Cat. 8-10 are of the narrow-shouldered Bailey 1980 type Piii of Loeschcke 1919 type VIII and are likely to date between AD 90 and 140. Two of them, cat. 8 and 9, came from the lower level of the fish-pond, and cat. 10 was residual in a post-Roman deposit. Cat. 11 is close to the shape of Standard Italian Loeschcke 1919 type VIII lamps, but has a decorated shoulder. It came from the lower level of the fish-pond and probably dates between AD 90 and 150.

---

[68] See also, for a glass ring, beads and counters, Allason-Jones, this volume, nos. 136-43.

There are some 50 examples of Standard Italian Loeschcke 1919 type VIII lamps (Bailey 1980 type Pi): cat. 12-27 and uncatalogued fragments. Of these, five are of the later, shallow, form, probably dating to AD 140-80, and the remainder of the earlier, deeper form, of about AD 90-160. Four of the earlier versions are signed – LMADIEC (cat. 12), MVNTREPT (cat. 14), BASSA (cat. 18), GABMERC (cat. 24) -, and one (cat. 23) has a plain footprint stamp. Of the later standard form, one fragment (cat. 27) bears a stamp, probably of L. Fabricius Masculus, but perhaps of one of the other lamp-makers with the same nomen (*CIL* XV 6429-35). These lamps came from various sources on the site, but mostly from the fish-pond: part of cat. 13 came from the very lowest level (L184), but joins another sherd from the lower level L165, in which were also found cat. 12, 14, 16-17, 20-1, part of 23, 26 and sixteen uncatalogued fragments. From the higher level, L105, came cat. 19, 22, part of 23 (joining a sherd from the lower level) and nine uncatalogued fragments. Cat. 24-5 and two uncatalogued sherds came from the fill of the north cistern, which was probably constructed in the second century AD. An uncatalogued fragment came from below the *selce* road, another from a floor in area E and one from a post-hole, apparently of early Imperial date, also in area E. Cat. 27 was residual in a post-Roman deposit. From a trench across the rock-cut road, west of the main site, came cat. 15 and 18, and four uncatalogued sherds.

The 53 late Italian Loeschcke 1919 type VIII lamps cat. 28-50 (and uncatalogued fragments) are divided into several sections, but none is likely to be from before AD 140 (cat. 28), the bulk being later than AD 160; in most cases the shape of the lamps of this type continued to be made up to at least AD 225 and perhaps rather later. The makers' names include Passerius Augurinus (cat. 38), L. Fabricius Masculus (cat. 45) and L. Caecilius Saecularis (cat. 49); Fabricius was on the whole an earlier lamp-maker than were the other two, working sometime between AD 150 and 180, the others perhaps flourishing between about AD 180 and 225. Most of these late versions of Loeschcke 1919 type VIII lamps came from the fish-pond: cat. 29-30, 34-7, 39-42, 44-7, 49-50 and 24 uncatalogued sherds came from the later deposit, and cat. 28 and four uncatalogued fragments came from the earlier deposit (one of the last goes with a lamp fragment from the later level). Cat. 31, 43 and 48 came from the north cistern, that was probably filled in the late second century AD. An uncatalogued fragment came from a pit in area E, and cat. 32 from the rock-cut road to the west of the main site. Cat. 38 was found in a late Roman deposit in a drain in area M and was no doubt residual, as was cat. 33 from a post-Roman hillwash at the north of the site, and an uncatalogued sherd from the topsoil of a post-Roman terrace to the east of the main site. The central Italian *Firmalampe*, cat. 52, of Bailey 1980 type Nvi, is of the same date as the late Italian Loeschcke 1919 type VIII lamps above, about AD 160-225+, and came from the earlier level in the fish-pond. Roughly of the same date is the pine cone lamp cat. 53, but the lamp-stand/thymiaterion cat. 51 is probably somewhat earlier, roughly contemporary with the Standard Italian Loeschcke 1919 type VIII lamps. The former comes from post-Roman hillwash to the north of the site, and the latter from the very lowest fill of the fish-pond.

Of the later lamps from the site (of which there is nothing earlier than the fourth century) there is part of a very late form of Bailey 1980 type M, a wall-lamp of the fourth century AD (cat. 54), and also three of the copies of imported African red slip ware lamps of Hayes 1972 type I that were made in Rome about AD 375-450 (cat. 55-7). Two lamps (cat. 58-9), based upon imported African lamps of Hayes 1972 type II, are of the fifth century or perhaps well into the sixth century AD; they are probably of Italian manufacture. The wall-lamp, cat. 54, came from contemporary occupation deposits on the lower terrace. The Hayes 1972 type I lamps (Bailey 1980 type Si) came from late Roman silt in area H (cat. 56), from a post-Roman ash layer on the lower terrace (cat. 57), and from post-Roman silt in area L (cat. 55). The lamps of Hayes 1972 type II (Bailey 1980 type Siii) were found in late Roman to post-Roman fill/rubble in area E (cat. 59) and post-Roman rubble in area M (cat. 58).

Only the rear, with a large applied handle, remains of lamp cat. 60, which has a wide filling hole at the rear top. Enough survives to show that it had been made in a mould: the internal joint is very evident. I am informed by Paul Roberts that the fabric indicates that it was most probably made in the vicinity of Monte Gelato, and it seems to be a local version of a late Roman or early medieval shape stemming ultimately from Sicily (see Bailey (1988: 208-9)), but also made in southern Italy and probably at Rome. In shape it perhaps resembles a large version of the Sicilian Bailey 1988 Q 1872. The comparable local pottery fabric is of the seventh or eighth century, and the shape of the lamp would not argue against this; the lamp came from an orange-coloured fill in area M, of post-Roman date (cf. Fig. 63).

The wheelmade lamp cat. 61 is of post-Roman manufacture, made at some time in the early medieval period. It is one of a long-lived shape found throughout the Mediterranean and beyond – examples of the same basic form (flared bowl with a domed cover) have been found at Corinth (the earlier lamps of Broneer 1930 type XXXV: before the tenth century AD), at Cnidus, Sacidava in Romania, in eastern Anatolia, at Benghazi, and, with flared necks, at Carthage (for all these see Bailey 1988 Q 3343; add to the references given there Fulford and Peacock (1984: 240)): dates between the fourth century (probably too early) and the eleventh century have been suggested for these. In many cases, the smaller the dome, the later the lamp, as in the case of some Mameluke-period examples from Egypt and Jordan, of the thirteenth to fifteenth centuries, where the dome is merely a small cone in the centre ('Amr 1984: 208, fig. 2,4). A form shallower than ours found in some numbers at Palermo is dated between the ninth and twelfth centuries (Bonanno 1979: 357). Cat. 61 was found in a tenth-century deposit in area D and is probably of that date.

One of the two lamps that may be imports, cat. 62, is a very small fragment of nozzle with long decorative tongues underneath. The fabric could be Italian, and go with Bailey 1980 type Q lamps of about AD 150-225, but the tongues are found more often on African lamps like Bailey 1988 Q 1710-12. The raised edge of the area of the wick hole is not normally found on these Loeschcke 1919 type VIII lamps, either from Italy or Tunisia. Possibly this is a late central Italian *Firmalampe* of Loeschcke 1919 type X, but even here the curve out to the body indicates an unusually short nozzle. The fragment came from the fill of the north cistern. The other imported lamp, cat. 63, was perhaps made in Tripolitania during the fifth century AD: the form of the shoulder is rather different from most of these Tripolitanian lamps (Brants 1913 type XXIV, the source of which was first identified by Hayes (1972: 314-15); see also the discussion by and references in Bailey (1988: 204). Cat. 63 was found in post-Roman rubble in area M.

The discus scenes include: a figure of Victoria with a palm branch (cat. 16); an unidentified seated or enthroned figure, part of a larger scene (cat. 49); human heads surviving from lost figures (cat. 8 and 39), the former uncertain, the latter probably a woman; a dramatic mask of a slave, one of three on the discus (cat. 10). Animals are also depicted: a lion on cat. 5; a hare on cat. 4; a dog on a couch, perhaps the Sothic Dog of Isis on the Sacred Couch of Serapis; on cat. 46; the rear leg of an animal on cat. 56; a cock or peacock on cat. 55; two wing-tips, on cat. 18 and 20, the former perhaps of an eagle (or perhaps of Victoria), the latter perhaps of a gryphon; and a scallop shell, on cat. 13. Part of a larger scene, apparently with a tree on the left, is shown on cat. 26, and palm branches decorate cat. 15 and 28; rosettes adorn cat. 7, 30, 38 and 58. A crescent is shown on cat. 19. Very slight indications show that the discuses of cat. 21, 22, 37, 40, 43, 44 and 47 were decorated, the scenes of which have not been identified, although cat. 47 may have the foot of a couch-leg.

Several makers' names are found on the Monte Gelato lamps, all Italian and all are likely to have worked in the vicinity of Rome, if not at Rome itself. They range in date from late Flavian until Severan times:

BASSA (cat. 18). Bassus (*CIL* VIII 22644 48; X 8053 33; XIII 10001 66; XV 6337) made lamps of various shapes at some time between late Flavian times and the early Antonine period (Bailey 1980: 91); Pavolini (1980b: tabella I) has dated Bassus's *Vogelkopf-lampen* between AD 130/40 and 160); there may have been more than one maker with this name.

LCAESAE (cat. 49). L. Caecilius Saecularis (*CIL* XX 4969 13; V 8114 17; VIII 22644 52; IX 6081 13; X 8053 41; XI 6699 39; XII 5682 17; XIII 10001 17; XV 6350) was a prolific and (as far as his figure-types were concerned) inventive lamp-maker, who worked during late Antonine and Severan times (Bailey 1980: 91-2; Pavolini 1980b: tabella I: AD 180/90 to the first decade of the third century).

LFABRICMAS (cat. 45). L. Fabricius Masculus (*CIL* II 6256; V 8114 46; VIII 22644 101; X 8053 74; XI 6699 78; XII 5682 40; XIII 10001 127; XV 6433): the dating given by me previously (Bailey 1980: 95) (late Flavian to early Antonine) may be too early, and Pavolini has suggested (1980b: tabella I) AD 150-80.

]FAB[(cat. 27). This may be from any one of the Fabricii, most probably Masculus as the last, but perhaps Aeuelpistus, Agat( ), Heraclides or Saturninus (*CIL* XV 6429-35; Bailey 1980: 94-5), all of whom worked during the Antonine period or a little earlier.

GABMERC (cat. 24). Gabinius Merc( ) (*CIL* VIII 22644 113; XI 6699 94; XIII 10001 142; XV 6460). Pavolini (1980b: tabella I) has dated his *Vogelkopf-lampen* to about AD 120/30-50.

LMADIEC (cat. 4 and 12). L. Munatius Adiectus (*CIL* V 8114 87; VIII 22644 219; X 8053 121; XI 6699 130; XII 5682 71; XIII 10001 216; XV 6560): a date in the late Flavian to Trajanic periods is probable (Bailey 1980: 98) or perhaps a little later (Pavolini 1980b: tabella I).

MVNTREPT (cat. 14). L. Munatius Threptus (*CIL* III 10184 33; V 8114 91; VIII 22644 10 and 226; X 8053 140; XI 6699 135; XII 5682 78; XIII 10001 218; XV 6565): late Flavian to early Antonine (Bailey 1980: 98).

PASAVGV (cat. 38). Passerius Augurinus (*CIL* III 12012 71; V 8114 105; IX 6081 54; X 8053 160; XI 6699 156; XIII 10001 247; XV 6610): late Antonine and probably well into the third century AD (Bailey 1980: 99).

The assemblage of lamps from Monte Gelato, a small rural site of no great importance, shows no surprises, except perhaps the early medieval lamp cat. 61, which I have not been able to parallel in Italy. There is nothing as early as the Augustan structures on the site, and the lamps indicate a main occupation and use between late Flavian times and the Severan period (or possibly the rubbish dumps of this period were found and others were not located). Very limited usage of pottery lamps occurred from the later fourth to the middle of the sixth century, glass lamps perhaps being employed to a greater extent; a locally made lamp of the seventh or eighth century was found, and a wheel-made lamp probably of the tenth century may also have been made in the vicinity of the site. Perhaps the most interesting aspect of these lamps is that the Roman Imperial examples, except for two possible African imports, were nearly all made at Rome or its immediate neighbourhood, and thus travelled by road the 34 km to the site. Several mechanisms for this travel can be envisaged: purchase at a local market or shop supplied from Rome; purchase at Rome by visiting locals; purchase at the site from travelling pedlars.

CATALOGUE

Central Italian volute lamps and early Loeschcke 1919 type VIII lamps

1. Fig. 194. Underbody and part of rim from a volute lamp. Shoulder form IIb, III or IV (for shoulder forms, see Loeschcke (1919: 25, fig. 2)). Buff clay; brown slip.
L. 24 mm. E138. *c.* AD 40-100.

2. Fig. 194. Right front part of a volute lamp, probably Broneer 1930 type XXI or perhaps Loeschcke 1919 type IV (Bailey 1980 type Diii or type Bii). Shoulder form IIIa. Buff clay; bright red slip.
L. 48 mm. L165. *c.* AD 70-100.

3. Fig. 194. Underbody from a volute lamp of Loeschcke 1919 type VIII. Orange clay; red slip.
L. 36 mm. E90. *c.* AD 40-120.

4. Figs 194 and 195. Fragmentary Loeschcke 1919 type V lamp (Bailey 1980 type Civ). Shoulder form VIIb. Air-hole. Discus: hare leaping to left. Raised circular base; LMADIE[C] incuse. Orange-buff clay; orange slip traces.
L. 91 mm; W. 68 mm. L105 and L165 (joined). *c.* AD 90-130.

5. Fig. 194. Right front part of a lamp similar to cat. 4. Shoulder form VIIa. Discus: lion to left. Orange-buff clay; orange slip traces.
L. 58 mm. L105 and L165 (joined). *c.* AD 90-150.

6. Fig. 194. Right front fragment with part of nozzle from Loeschcke 1919 type VIII lamp (Bailey 1980 type Oii). Shoulder form VIIIa, with impressed ovules. Air-hole. Plain discus. Buff clay; red slip.
L. 52 mm. L165, SF 655. *c.* AD 50-110.

7. Fig. 194. Shoulder and discus from Loeschcke 1919 Type VIII lamp (Bailey 1980 type Oii). Near shoulder-form VIIIb, with impressed ovules. Discus: rosette. Buff clay; red slip.
L. 24 mm. M144. *c.* AD 50-110.

8. Fig. 196. Rear right part of Loeschcke 1919 type VIII lamp (Bailey 1980 type Piii), with handle spring. Shoulder form VIIb. Discus: unclear – probably a human head. Buff clay; red slip.
L. 69 mm. L165. *c.* AD 90-140.

9. Fig. 196. Front right part of Loeschcke 1919 type VIII lamp (probably Bailey 1980 type Piii). Shoulder form VIIIb. Air-hole. Buff clay; red slip.
L. 54 mm. L165. *c.* AD 90-140.

10. Fig. 196. Discus from Loeschcke 1919 type VIII lamp (Bailey 1980 type Piii). Slave mask (one of three: cf. Bailey 1980 Q 1326); concentric circles round filling hole. Buff clay; red slip.
L. 24 mm. M167. *c.* AD 90-140.

11. Fig. 196. Shoulder from Loeschcke 1919 type VIII lamp (near standard form). Shoulder form VIIb, with impressed ovules. Buff clay; brown slip.
L. 32 mm. L165. *c.* AD 90-150.

Standard central Italian lamps of Loeschcke 1919 type VIII (Bailey 1980 type Pi)

12. Figs 195 and 196. Almost complete lamp. Shoulder form VIIa. Plain discus. Raised circular base; LMADIEC incuse. Buff clay; orange slip.
L. 95 mm; W. 66 mm. L165, SF 609. *c.* AD 90-130.

13. Fig. 196. Fragmentary, with non-joining sherd. Shoulder form VIIb. Discus: scallop shell. Air-hole. Raised circular base. Buff clay; purple-brown slip.
L. 87 mm. L165 and L184 (joined; + L184 non-joining). *c.* AD 90-160.

14. Figs 195 and 197. Fragmentary. Shoulder form VIIa. Plain discus. Raised circular base; MVNTREPT incuse. Buff clay; brown slip.
L. 96 mm. L165, SF 607 and SF 655 (joining). *c.* AD 90-160.

15. Fig. 197. Discus and shoulder sherd. Shoulder form VIIa. Discus: palm branch (one of two). Buff clay; red slip.
W. 27 mm. S10. *c.* AD 90-160.

16. Fig. 197. Rear right part with handle. Shoulder form VIIb. Discus: Victoria with palm branch. Raised circular base. Buff clay; red-brown slip.
L. 83 mm. L165, SF 631. *c.* AD 90-160.

17. Fig. 197. Rear part with handle. Shoulder form VIIIb. Plain discus. Orange-buff clay; orange slip traces.
W. 62 mm. L165, SF 622. *c.* AD 90-160.

18. Figs 195 and 197. Rear part with handle. Shoulder form VIIb. Discus: tip of wing. Raised circular base; BASSA incuse. Orange-buff clay; red to brown slip.
L. 81 mm, W. 70 mm. S4, SF 714. *c.* AD 100-60.

19. Fig. 198. Fragment of left side. Possibly Loeschcke 1919 type V. Shoulder form VIIb. Discus: crescent. Orange-buff clay; orange slip traces.
L. 56 mm. L105. *c.* AD 90-150.

20. Fig. 198. Rear part with handle. Shoulder form VIIb. Discus: wing of gryphon? Orange-buff clay; orange slip traces.
W. 38 mm. L165. *c.* AD 90-160.

21. Fig. 198. Rear left part with handle. Shoulder form VIIa. Discus: part of unidentified scene. Yellow-buff clay; purple-brown slip.
L. 52 mm. L165. *c.* AD 90-160.

22. Fig. 198. Handle sherd. Shoulder form VIIa. Discus: part of unidentified scene. Yellow-buff clay; purple-brown slip.
L. 44 mm. L105, SF 652. *c.* AD 90-160.

23. Fig. 198. Handle, underbody and base. Raised circular base; impressed plain footprint stamp. Buff clay; orange slip traces.
L. 98 mm. L105 and L165 (joining). *c.* AD 90-160.

24. Figs 195 and 198. Base sherd. Raised circular base; [GAB]MERC incuse. Buff clay; orange-brown slip.
W. 46 mm. L149. *c.* AD 100-60.

– Six nozzle and shoulder sherds. Shoulder forms VIIa (four examples) and VIIb (two examples). L105 (two examples, including SF 652), L149, L165 (two examples), S10.

– Five nozzle sherds. L105 (two examples), L143, L165, M104.

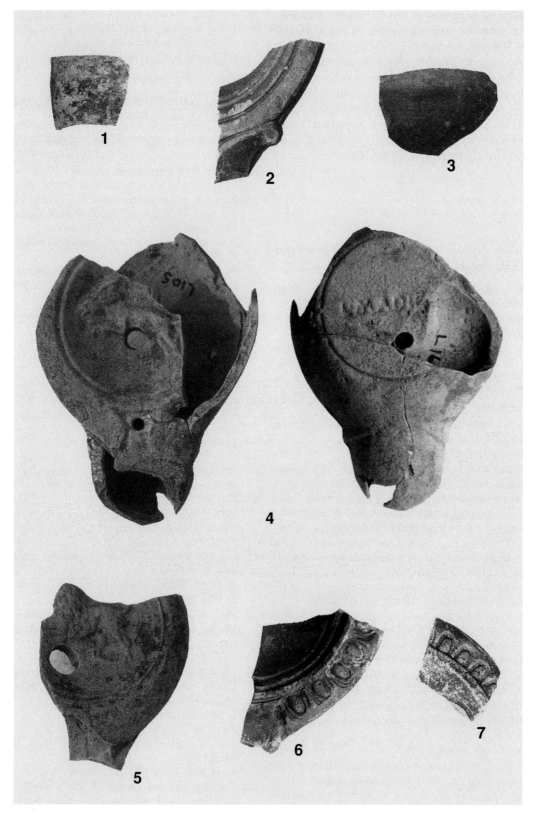

Fig. 194. Central Italian lamps. *(DB)*

– Eight shoulder and body sherds. Shoulder-forms VIIa
  (five examples) and VIIb (two examples). E42, E179,
  L105 (two examples), L165 (four examples).
– Four raised base sherds. L105 (two examples), L165
  (two examples).
– Nine handle sherds. L105, L165 (five examples), S3, S4,
  S10.

**Late standard central Italian lamps of Loeschcke
1919 type VIII (Bailey 1980 type Pi)**

25. Fig. 198. Rear part with handle. Shoulder form VIIb.
    Raised circular base. Buff clay; orange-red slip traces.
    W. 62 mm. L143. *c.* AD 140-80.
26. Fig. 198. Rear left part with handle. Shoulder form

VIIb. Discus: uncertain; tree or floral on left. Buff clay; orange slip traces.
W. 64 mm. L165. *c.* AD 140-80.

27. Figs 195 and 198. Base sherd; [L].FAB[R ... incuse. Yellow-buff clay; thin orange slip, brown in places.
W. 26 mm. M167. *c.* AD 140-80.

– Body sherd. L165.

– Base sherd. L165.

Late central Italian Loeschcke 1919 type VIII lamps (Bailey 1980 type Qiii)

28. Fig. 198. Two non-joining sherds. Shoulder form VIIIa. Discus: radiating palm branches. Orange-buff clay; orange slip.
W. 46 mm and 50 mm. L165. *c.* AD 140-80.

Late central Italian Loeschcke 1919 type VIII lamps (Bailey 1980 type Qi)

29. Fig. 199. Fragment of the rear and right side, including handle and part of heart-shaped nozzle. Shoulder form VIIIb, vine tendrils in relief. Buff clay; thin orange slip.
L. 121 mm. L105, including SF 596. *c.* AD 170-225.

30. Fig. 199. Discus and shoulder. Shoulder form VIIIb, vine tendrils in relief. Discus: rosette. Orange-buff clay; thin orange slip.
L. 38 mm. L105. *c.* AD 170-225.

31. Fig. 199. Discus and shoulder sherd. Shoulder form VIIIb, vine tendrils in relief. Plain discus. Deep buff clay; no slip.
L. 43 mm. E11. *c.* AD 170-225.

32. Fig. 199. Shoulder fragment. Shoulder form VIIIb, vine tendrils in relief. Dark buff clay; no slip.
L. 28 mm. S4, SF 712. *c.* AD 170-225.

33. Fig. 199. Shoulder fragment. Shoulder form VIIIb, vine tendrils in relief. Orange clay; red slip.
L. 25 mm. L101. *c.* AD 170-225.

34. Fig. 199. Shoulder and discus. Shoulder form VIIIb, tendrils in relief, probably vine. Plain discus. Yellow-buff clay; thin orange slip.
W. 41 mm. L105. *c.* AD 170-225.

35. Fig. 199. Fragment of shoulder near nozzle. Shoulder form VIIIb, tendrils in relief. Air-hole. Yellow-buff clay; thin orange slip.
W. 30 mm. L105. *c.* AD 170-225.

36. Fig. 199. Nozzle and shoulder fragment. Heart-shaped nozzle. Buff clay; thin orange slip.
L. 32 mm. L105. *c.* AD 170-225.

37. Fig. 199. Shoulder fragment. Shoulder form VIIIb, two rows of ivy-leaves in relief. Small part of decorated discus. Dark buff clay; thin orange slip traces.
W. 24 mm. L105. *c.* AD 170-225.

– Three shoulder sherds from similar lamps, all with tips of relief leaves, and one with part of heart-shaped nozzle. L105.

– Two base sherds probably from this type of lamp. L105 and L165.

Late central Italian Loeschcke 1919 type VIII lamps (Bailey 1980 type Qiv)

38. Figs 195 and 200. Complete. Shoulder form VIIb, shoulder plain. Discus: rosette. Heart-shaped nozzle. Air-

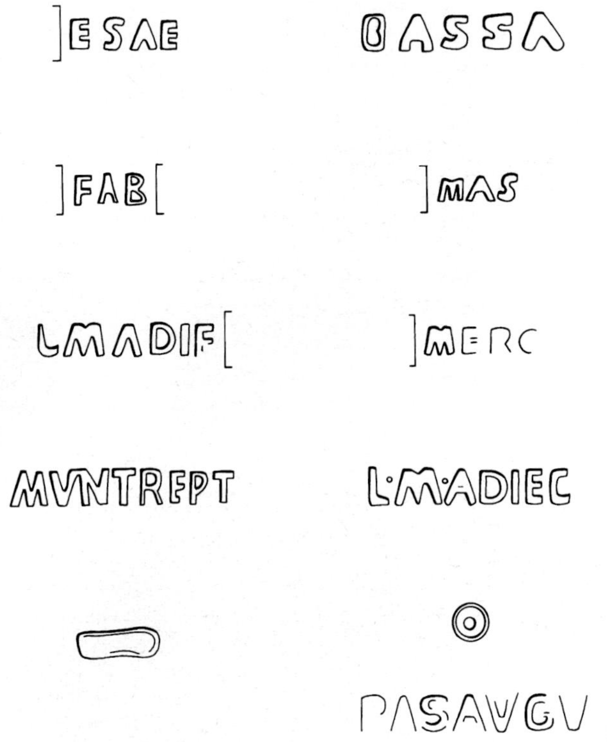

Fig. 195. Lamp stamps (1:1); the numbers refer to the catalogue entries. *(SC)*

hole. Base-ring: PASAVGV with ring-and-dot above and below, incuse. Buff clay; thin red slip.
L. 116 mm; W. 82 mm. M172, SF 862. *c.* AD 180-225.

39. Fig. 200. Handle and discus. Shoulder form VIIIb, shoulder apparently plain. Discus: head of woman to right. Dark buff clay; thin orange to dark brown slip.
L. 44 mm. L105. *c.* AD 160-225+.

40. Fig. 200. Discus sherd. Part of an uncertain scene, perhaps floral. Brown-buff clay; orange slip traces.
L. 32 mm. L105, SF 575. *c.* AD 160-225+.

Late central Italian Loeschcke 1919 type VIII lamps (Bailey 1980 type Qii)

41. Fig. 200. Rear right part, with handle. Near shoulder form VIIIb, impressed ovules. Discus apparently plain. Brown-buff clay; brown to dark brown slip.
L. 68 mm. L105. *c.* AD 160-225+.

42. Fig. 201. Two non-joining sherds: rear, with handle, and part of heart-shaped nozzle. Shoulder form VIIIb: wide shoulder with rows of raised points between ridges. Buff clay; thin orange slip traces.
L. 23 mm; W. 69 mm. L105. *c.* AD 160-225+.

43. Fig. 201. Discus sherd. Shoulder form VIIIb, rows of raised points? Discus: uncertain scene; two overlapping bow-shaped objects. Buff clay; thin red slip traces.
L. 28 mm. E11. *c.* AD 160-225+.

44. Fig. 201. Two non-joining sherds: rear left, with handle; part of underbody. Shoulder form VIIIb, band of incuse S-curves. Discus: uncertain pattern. Base-ring. Buff clay; red slip.
L. 45 mm; W. 54 mm. L105. *c.* AD 160-225+.

45. Figs 195 and 201. Part of base ring.]MAS. Buff-brown clay; thin red slip traces.
W. 24 mm. L105. *c.* AD 150-80.

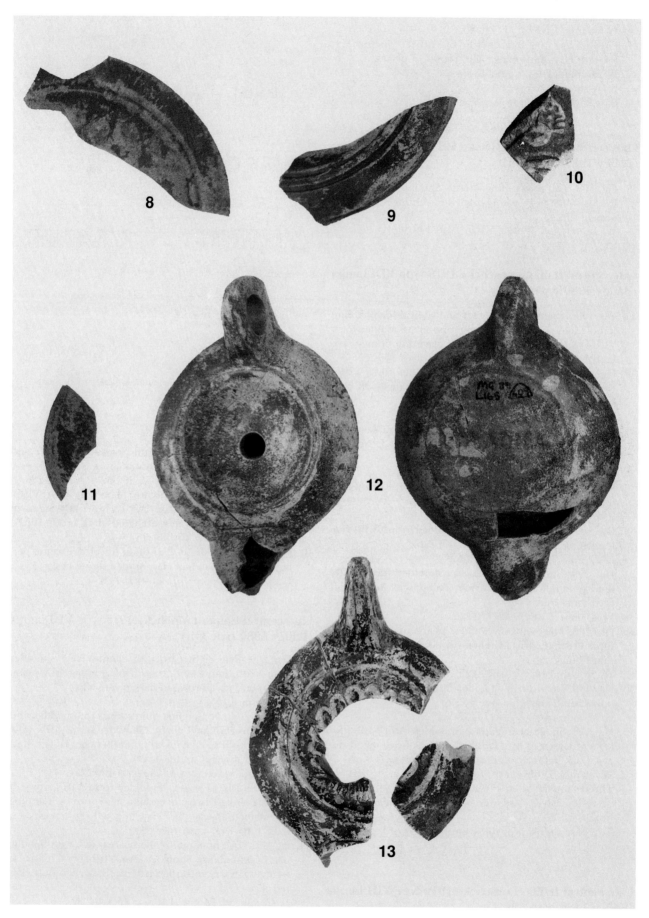

Fig. 196. Central Italian lamps. *(DB)*

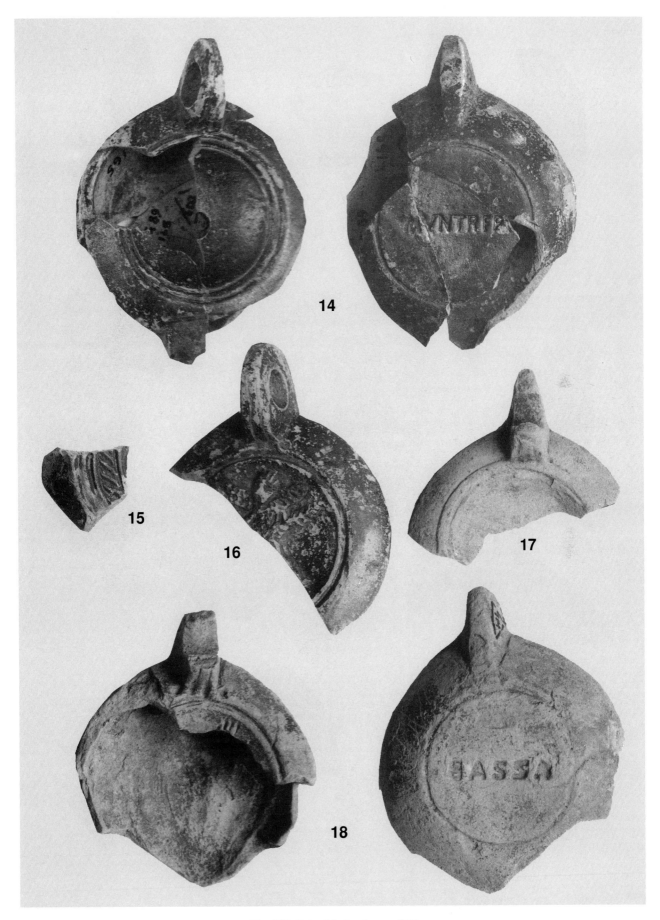

Fig. 197. Central Italian lamps. *(DB)*

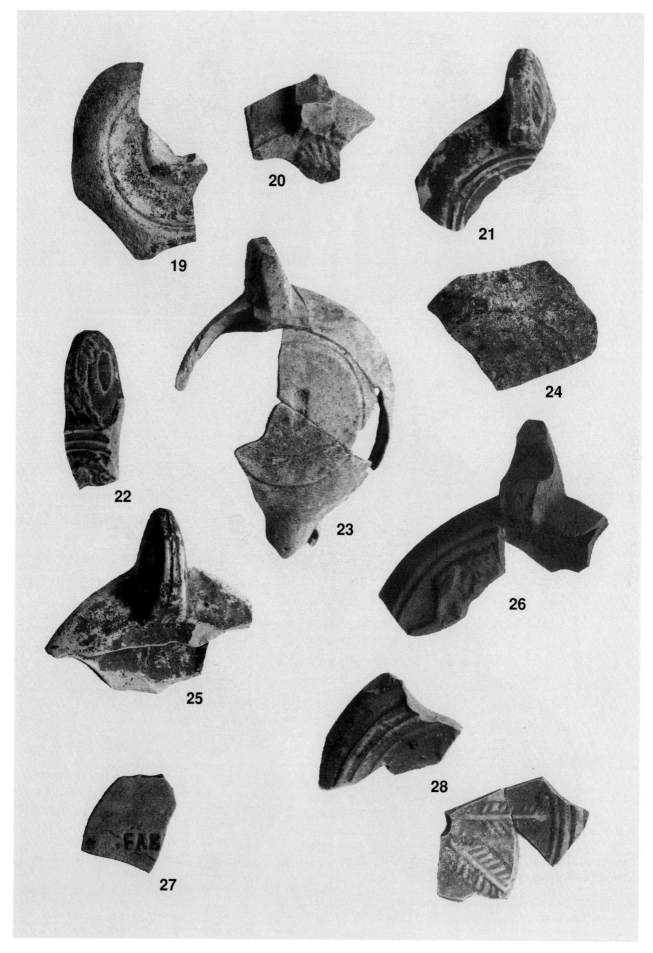

Fig. 198. Central Italian lamps. *(DB)*

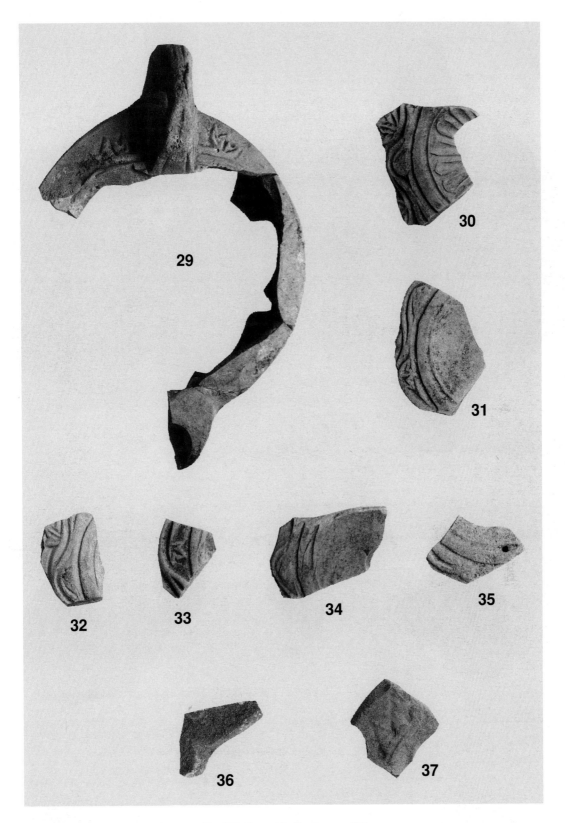

Fig. 199. Central Italian lamps. *(DB)*

Late central Italian Loeschcke 1919 type VIII lamps (Bailey 1980 type Qviii)

46. Fig. 201. Part of rear, with handle. Shoulder form VIIIb, impressed ovules. Discus: dog on couch (Sothic Dog?). Buff clay; thin red slip.
L. 58 mm. L105. *c.* AD 160-225+.

47. Fig. 201. Front right shoulder. Shoulder form VIIIb, impressed ovules. Discus: foot of couch? Yellow-buff clay; thin orange slip.
L. 41 mm. L105. *c.* AD 160-225+.

48. Fig. 202. Rear part, with handle. Shoulder form VIIIb?, myrtle-wreath in relief. Multiple base ring with row of raised points on inner ring and a pelta-shaped foot on outer ring. Buff clay; thin red slip.
W. 45 mm. L147. *c.* AD 160-225+.

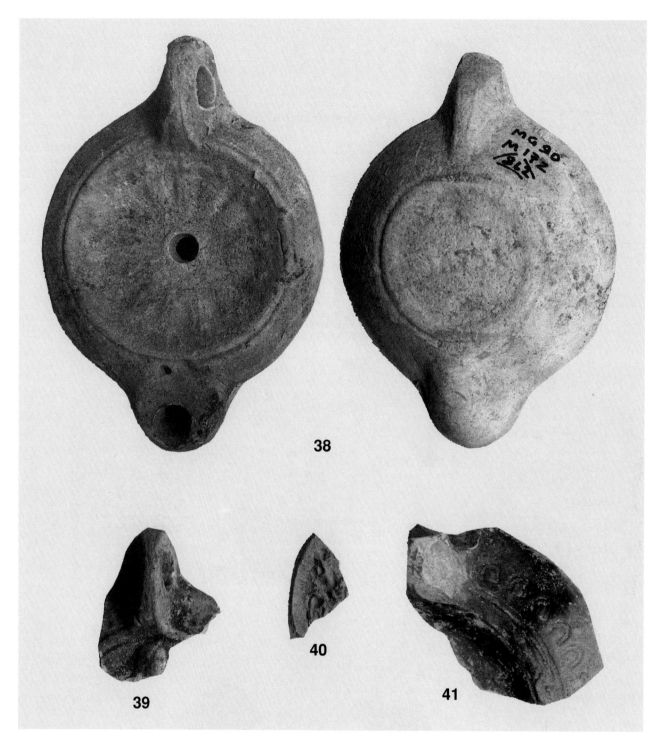

Fig. 200. Central Italian lamps. *(DB)*

Late central Italian Loeschcke 1919 type VIII lamps (Bailey 1980 type Qix)

49. Figs 195 and 202. Front left part. Shoulder form VIIIb, myrtle wreath in relief. Discus: uncertain scene – lower part of seated figure? to right at left, facing something on the right. Base ring: [LCA]ESAE incuse. Orange-buff clay; thin orange slip.
L. 54 mm. L105, including SF 592. *c.* AD 180-225+.

50. Fig. 202. Shoulder sherd. Shoulder form VIIIb, impressed ivy-leaves between grooves. Buff clay; thin red slip.

L. 30 mm. L105. *c.* AD 160-225+.

– Twenty-five sherds from late central Italian Loeschcke 1919 type VIII lamps (Bailey 1980 type Q):
Four nozzle sherds. L105 (three examples, including SF 652), L165.
Five body sherds. E182, L105 (three examples), L165.
One raised base sherd. L105.
Five base ring sherds. L105 (there is also a sherd from L165 from the same lamp as one from L105).
Ten handle sherds. K101, L105 (nine examples).

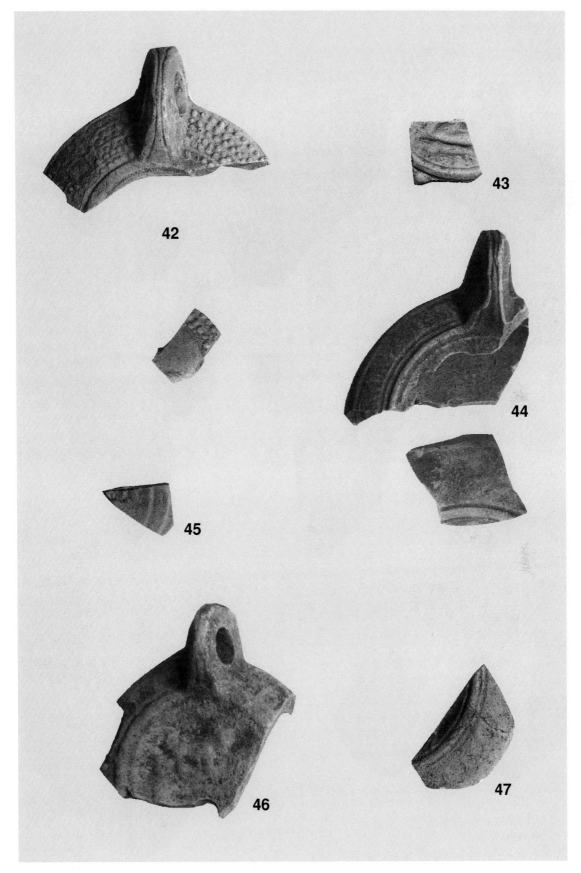

Fig. 201. Central Italian lamps. *(DB)*

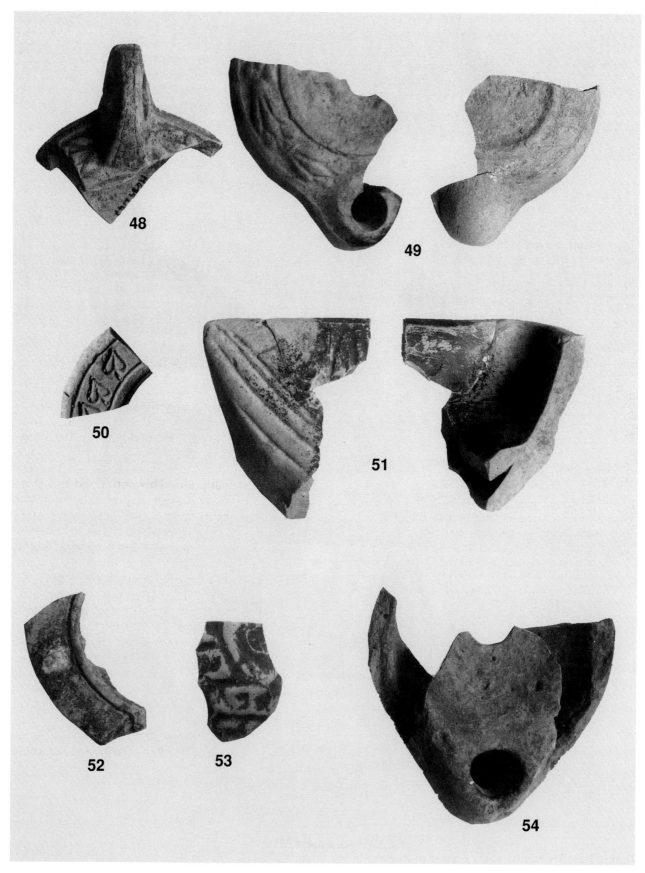

Fig. 202. Central Italian lamps. *(DB)*

Central Italian lamp-stand and thymiaterion

51. Fig. 202. Upper part of a combined incense-burner and lamp-stand. One face of the rectangular bowl decorated with impressed floral pattern. The base of the bowl is applied within the mould-made body. Indications of an applied lamp on plain side of bowl at right angles to the decorated face. Buff clay; orange slip traces.
H. 44 mm. L184. *c.* AD 100-60.

Central Italian *Firmalampe* of Loeschcke 1919 type X (Bailey 1980 type Nvi)

52. Fig. 202. Front left part. Shoulder form IX; lug broken away; incuse diagonal defining nozzle. Buff clay; orange slip.
L. 44 mm. L165. *c.* AD 160-225+.

Central Italian plastic lamp in form of a pine cone (early form of Bailey 1980 type T)

53. Fig. 202. Underbody and base ring. Buff clay; orange slip.
L. 36 mm. L101. *c.* AD 175-225.

Central Italian wall-lamp (very late form of Bailey 1980 type M)

54. Fig. 202. Front sherd with ill-defined nozzle, discus (plain) and base. Buff clay; no slip. Cf. Provoost 1976: 568, figure, type 3[B].
W. 65 mm. A17. Fourth century AD.

Central Italian lamps of Hayes 1972 type I (Bailey 1980 type Si)

55. Fig. 203. Rear part with unpierced handle. Devolved branch pattern on shoulder. Discus: head of cock or peacock. Deep orange clay; orange slip.
L. 42 mm. M32, SF 481. *c.* AD 375-450.
56. Fig. 203. Front left part. Series of impressed ring-and-dot patterns on shoulder. Discus: rear leg of animal (longitudinal on lamp). Orange-buff clay; orange slip.
L. 38 mm. H6. *c.* AD 375-450.
57. Fig. 203. Nozzle sherd. Deep orange clay; orange slip.
W. 34 mm. D104. *c.* AD 375-450.

Italian lamps of Hayes 1972 type II (Bailey 1980 type Siii)

58. Fig. 203. Top of lamp, with unpierced handle. Branch pattern within shoulder. Discus: rosette; rows of raised points on each side of nozzle-channel. Orange clay; orange slip.
L. 80 mm; W. 71 mm. M38, SF 548. *c.* AD 400-525.
59. Fig. 203. Left side. Curved and slanting relief lines within shoulder. Orange-pink to light brown clay; brown slip.
L. 92 mm. E16. *c.* AD 450-550.

Italian late Roman or early medieval lamp

60. Fig. 203. Rear of a mould-made, probably elongated, lamp with a substantial applied vertical band-handle. Low-placed carination. Buff clay; no slip.
W. 40 mm. M86. Seventh or eighth century AD?

Italian early medieval wheel-made lamp

61. Fig. 204. Fragmentary: most of rim lost. Wheel-made conical shape with inserted domed top and flaring rim. Large wick hole cut through top; central filling hole; applied bridge separating filling hole and wick hole. Unturned base. Coarse clay containing pieces of quartz, with brown surface and black core.
D. at rim 110 mm; H. 70 mm. D307, SF 656. *c.* tenth century AD.

Imported lamps

Tunisian? lamp of Loeschcke 1919 type VIII

62. Fig 205. Nozzle sherd. Raised rim round upper edge; elongated tongues on underside. Buff clay; red slip traces.
L. 24 mm. E11. *c.* AD 160-225+.

Tripolitanian? lamp, perhaps of Brants 1913 type XXIV

63. Fig. 205. Shoulder sherd with a plain sloping shoulder. Sunken top with joined spirals in relief. Deep orange clay; red slip.
L. 26 mm. M138. Fifth century AD.

THE ROMAN COMMERCIAL AMPHORAE, by Paul Arthur

Various fragments of commercial amphorae, all of Imperial date, were found during the excavations at Monte Gelato. Save for some scattered pieces, quantitatively insignificant and often not particularly well stratified, most came from the deposits found in the fish-pond. This contained two principal fills: L165, the lower deposit, dated to the early second century AD; and L105, the upper deposit, dated to the late second century AD. The whole fish-pond contained 1,495 amphora sherds, weighing a total of 144.100 kg. Some 798 fragments (61.850 kg) were recovered from the upper deposit and 697 (82.250 kg) from the lower deposit.

Of particular interest are the various amphorae that, on quantity and distribution, were, in the writer's view, of local origin. Some confirmation has come from thin-section analysis conducted by Dr David Williams (University of Southampton). The results of his work are included in this report both under the description of the sampled vessels, where his contribution is noted in double quote marks, and in an appendix at the end. The original recording reference number (P000) is given where applicable.

CATALOGUE OF TYPES

Italian

Dressel 2-4

1. Fig. 206. Hard, gritty orange fabric, with a self-coloured slip surface, occasional muscovite and small iron-oxide nodules. It looks Italian, though may not be from the Campano-Latian area. P106. L165.

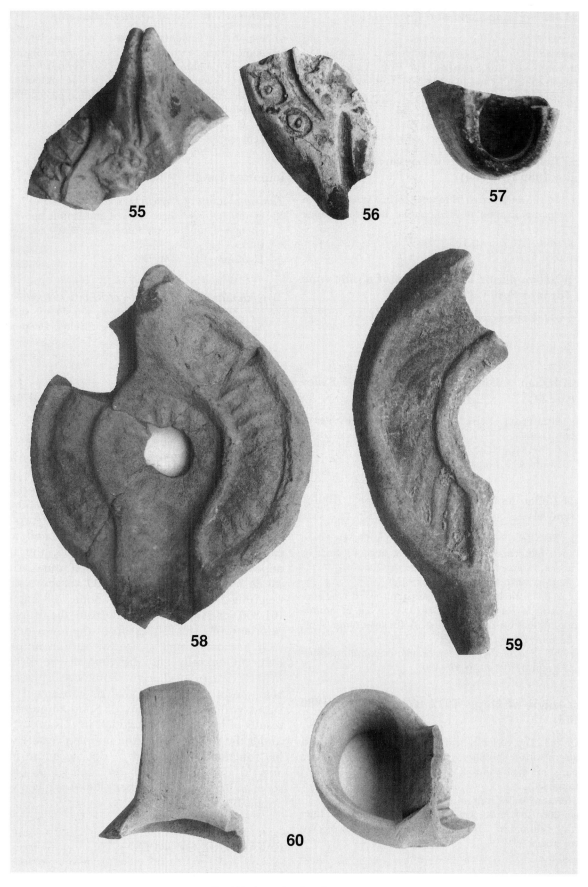

Fig. 203. Central Italian lamps. *(DB)*

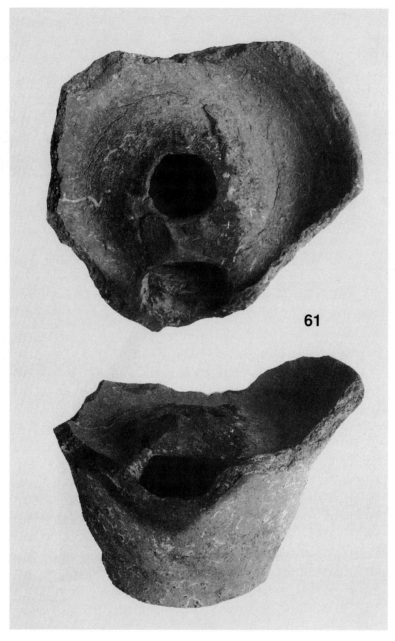

Fig. 204. Early medieval lamp. *(DB)*

2. (Not illustrated.) Hard, gritty orange-pink volcanic fabric with a cream exterior surface. Probably Campano-Latian. P104. L165.
3. Fig. 206. Light orange fabric with a pale brownish-cream exterior slip. Campano-Latian production. P111. L165.
4. Fig. 206. Medium hard cream-yellow (10YR 8/5) fabric with scattered dark specks, including volcanic glass. Probably a product of the area around Monte Gelato, as the fabric is similar to amphora type P105/169, discussed below. L105.
5. Fig. 206. As cat. 4 above. Soft (10YR 8/6) fabric with more inclusions than cat. 4. L105.

Type P105 (*Ostia* II, cat. no. 521/*Ostia* III, cat. nos. 369-70)

The amphorae here classed as type P105 would appear to be products of the general area in which Monte Gelato is sited. This is suggested by the quantity in which they have been found at the site and by their petrological characteristics. Furthermore, they are very similar to other amphorae found in great quantities in and around Rome. Though no intact examples have come to light during the excavations, the various fragments found suggest they are generally ovoid-bodied with ribbed handles, a small slightly everted rim and *omphalos* base. The fabric is generally quite fine and of a distinctive off-white/cream colour, though other, darker, hues exist. On morphology, the amphorae are not at all dissimilar to forms *Ostia* II, cat. no. 521/*Ostia* III, cat. nos. 369-70, or to Berenice mid-Roman amphora 13, to which they are clearly related. They are part of a tradition of central Italian amphorae now represented by a production site identified at Spello, in Umbria.

The identification of 'local' transport amphorae at Monte Gelato, probably both of Dressel's type 2-4 (above), and of the type illustrated here, is of great importance for an understanding of the somewhat problematic nature of the

Fig. 205. Imported lamps. *(DB)*

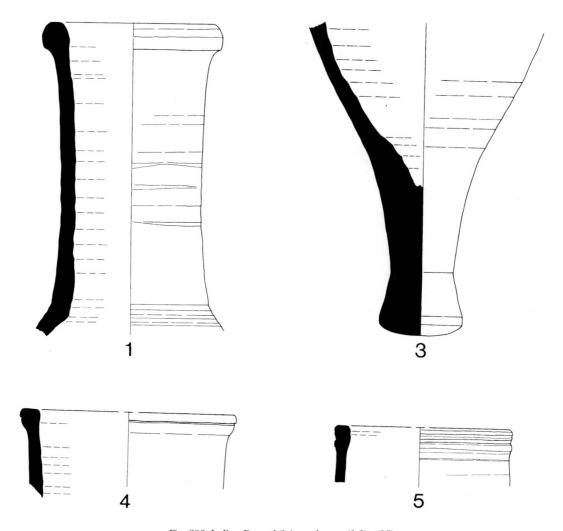

Fig. 206. Italian Dressel 2-4 amphorae (1:3). *(SC)*

Italian economy of the later first and second century AD. This will be discussed further below.

6.   Fig. 207. Hard yellow-beige fabric with abundant small calcareous and scattered red-brown inclusions (grog?: usually small but occasionally up to 7 mm), a little mica and an exterior beige slip. P105. L165.

7-11. Fig. 207. Local area production. L105.

12.   Fig. 207. Local amphora with traces of a Latin *titulus pictus* in red, on the shoulder, reading SEC.... Soft, cream-yellow fabric (10YR 8/3) with some scattered angular dark grey and reddish brown inclusions (<2 mm), a little biotite and perhaps occasional augite. Thin-section analysis indicates "a fairly fine-textured fabric containing a groundmass of silt-sized quartz grains, together with a few grains of sanidine, clino-

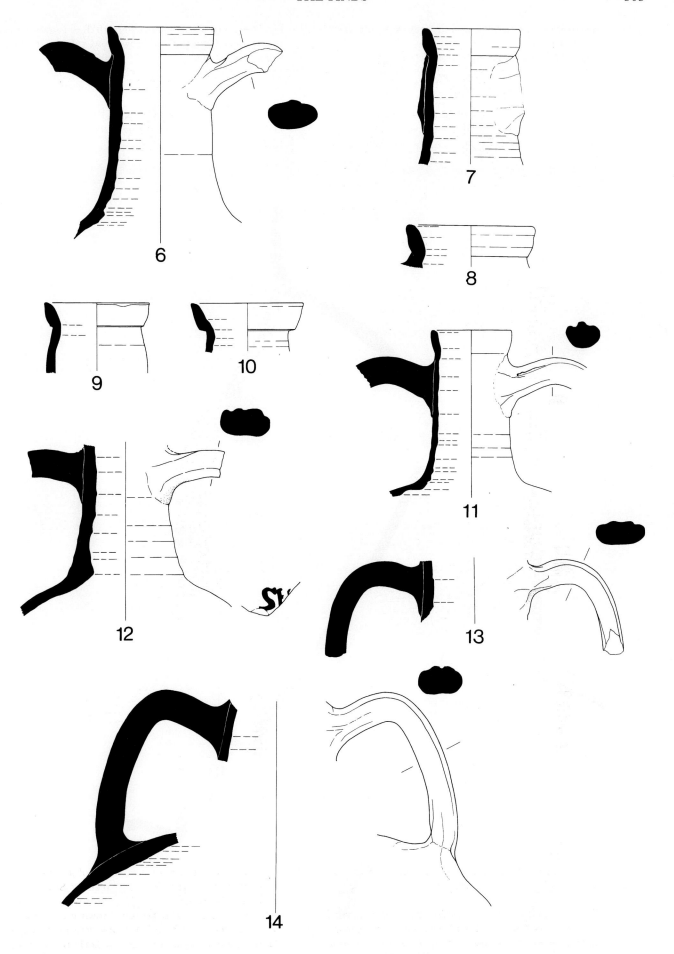

Fig. 207. Local P105 amphorae (1:3). *(SC)*

pyroxene, iron oxides and a little volcanic rock". P169. L105.

13. Fig. 207. Local area production. L105.
14. Fig. 207. Occasional large red (<3 mm) nodules in fabric. Local area production. L105.
15. Fig. 208. Local area production. L105.
16. Fig. 208. Local area production. L105.
17. Fig. 208. Thin-section analysis indicates a similar fabric to cat. 12, above. Local area production. L105.

18. Fig. 208. Fairly fine cream-yellow (10YR 8/5) fabric with few scattered minute red-brown and calcareous inclusions. P167. L105.
19. Fig. 208. Inner part of vessel section is pale to light orange (7.5YR 7.5/6 to 5YR 7/7) in colour. Local area production. L105.
20. Fig. 208. Local area production. L105.
21. Fig. 208. Few visible inclusions. Local area production. L105.

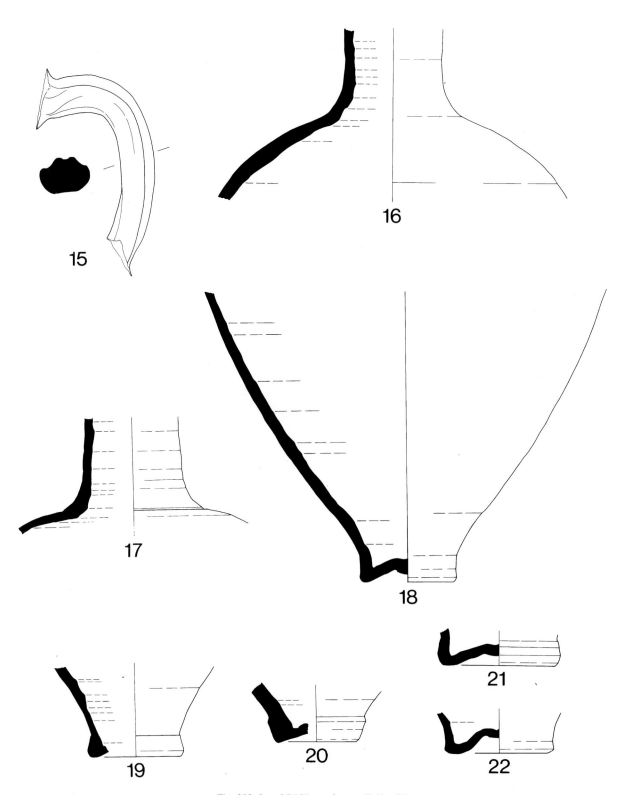

Fig. 208. Local P105 amphorae (1:3). *(SC)*

22. Fig. 208. Inner part of vessel section is pale to light orange (7.5YR 7.5/6 to 5YR 7/7) in colour. Local area production. L105.

Type P23
23. Fig. 209. Hard, orange-brown (2.5YR 5.5/7) fabric with abundant minute red-brown angular inclusions, white calcareous inclusions, occasional minute quartz and dark grits. Similar vessels in a similar fabric come from a third-century context at Porta Pia, Rome. Results of examination through thin-section showed "a much coarser fabric than cat. 12, 17, 24 and 26. It contained frequent quartz grains, mostly under 0.3 mm in size, together with flecks of mica, some sanidine, plagioclase feldspar and iron oxides". Regional type. P23. Area B, unstratified.

Type P166
24. Fig. 209. Soft pale orange-yellow fabric (7.5YR 7/6), with scattered rounded and occasionally angular small greyish and some rounded orange inclusions (?grog; <5 mm), and a self-coloured slip. Thin-section analysis shows that the piece is of "a finer-textured fabric than cat. 12, 17 and 26, with a clay matrix containing sparse grains of quartz, sanidine, clinopyroxene and volcanic rock". Again, probably a regional type, though it is different from the local series, both in fabric and in handle type. P166. L105.

Type P98
25. Fig. 209. Very hard, mottled, orange-brown fabric (around 2.5YR 6/7), with a purple-grey core, abundant angular black pyroxene crystals, other volcanic rock and occasional minute white grits and dark red-brown (iron?) nodules. This vessel is almost certainly local and has been misfired. It is not certain whether this vessel was intended to be used as a commercial amphora or not. The overall shape is right for such a purpose, though strap handles seem generally not to have been preferred for vessels that had to stand a fair amount of heavy handling; moreover, the base looks too weak for such a purpose. This almost complete vessel is made up of 59 sherds, with a total weight of 4.300 kg. P98. L165.

Type P216
26. Fig. 210. Evanescent pale brown exterior wash. Thin-section analysis revealed "a similar looking fabric to cat. 12 and 17 above, but with more grains of clinopyroxene and fragments of volcanic rock". This could be a local jar. P216. L105.

Type P235
27. Fig. 210. Hard, pink-orange fabric (2.5YR 6/6) with a darker slipped surface and abundant small sub-angular dark inclusions. The handle is similar to those of amphorae variously identified as Tripolitanian or Sicilian. For the type see Panella (1973: 632, nos. 44-5). P235. L105.

Type P28
28. Fig. 210. Unusual rim, possibly not of an amphora. Hard, fine orange-pink (5YR 7/7) fabric with beige (7.5YR 7/6) surfaces. Local area production. L105.

Spanish

Beltran IV
29. Fig. 211. Beltran IVB. Hard and coarse, pale orange (2.5YR 6/8) fabric with cream-yellow (10YR 7/5) surfaces and an orange-brown (2.5YR 6/7) exterior slip. Abundant sub-angular inclusions (<4 mm) of mudstone/chert, limestone, quartz, quartzite and reddish brown rock. Spanish. L165.
30. Fig. 211. Beltran IVB; similar to *Ostia* LXI and Dressel 14. Hard, brownish-red fabric with abundant rounded and sub-angular sedimentary inclusions, quartz, quartzite, some red grog (?). Smoothing marks on shoulders. Cf. Panella 1973: 519-21, type LXI. Spanish. P100. L165.
31. Fig. 211. Beltran IVB. Hard, pale orange (2.5YR 6/7) fabric with a dark reddish grey (2.5YR 5/2) exterior slip, abundant muscovite and minute sub-angular calcareous and dark inclusions (<1 mm, though occasionally larger). Spanish. L165.
32. Fig. 211. Beltran IVB. Hard, red (2.5YR 6/7) fabric with abundant minute dark grits, some occasional calcareous specks and reaction rims. Lusitanian, though superficially the fabric looks African. This vessel accounts for ten sherds and 1.780 kg in Table 58. For this and the previous three vessels see Parker (1977). P101. L165.

Beltran IIa similis
33. Fig. 212. Related to Beltran IIa, Pelichet 46, *Ostia* form LXIII, though with a distinctive rim and different fabric to the 'usual' type. Hard, orange (2.5YR 6/8) fabric with abundant large (<3 mm) sub-angular to rounded red-brown, calcareous, quartz and other inclusions. Form *Ostia* LXIII appears at Ostia well into the second half of the second century, though it appears to be residual by the third century (Panella 1973: 512). L105.

Dressel 20
34. Fig. 212. Baetican Dressel 20 rim, of first-century type. Hard, yellow-pink fabric (5YR 7/5) with abundant 'mudstone'-like inclusions (<6 mm), scattered calcareous grits, and a cream-yellow exterior slip. For this and the following two vessels see, in general, Peacock and Williams (1986: 136-8, class 25). P107. L165.
35. Fig. 212. Baetican Dressel 2. Typical very gritty Baetican buff fabric with a thick exterior cream slip. P113. L165.
36. Fig. 212. Dressel 20? Stub in a hard orange-brown fabric (2.5YR 5.5/8), with abundant minute calcareous inclusions, scattered biotite mica and other grits. Spanish? P114. L105.

Uncertain types
37. Fig. 212. Hard, pale orange-yellow (2.5YR 6/6) fabric with cream (10YR 7.5/4) surfaces, abundant small rounded iron-oxide, reddish-brown and calcareous inclusions. Spanish. L165.
38. Fig. 212. Hard, orange (2.5YR 6/8) fabric, with a dark reddish grey (2.5YR 5/3) exterior slip and abundant sub-angular quartz, quartzite, limestone, dark grey and reddish brown inclusions (<3 mm). Spanish. L165.

Gaulish
39. Fig. 212. Dressel 30/Gauloise 4 type. Hard, fine, light orange-beige fabric with abundant minute white lime-

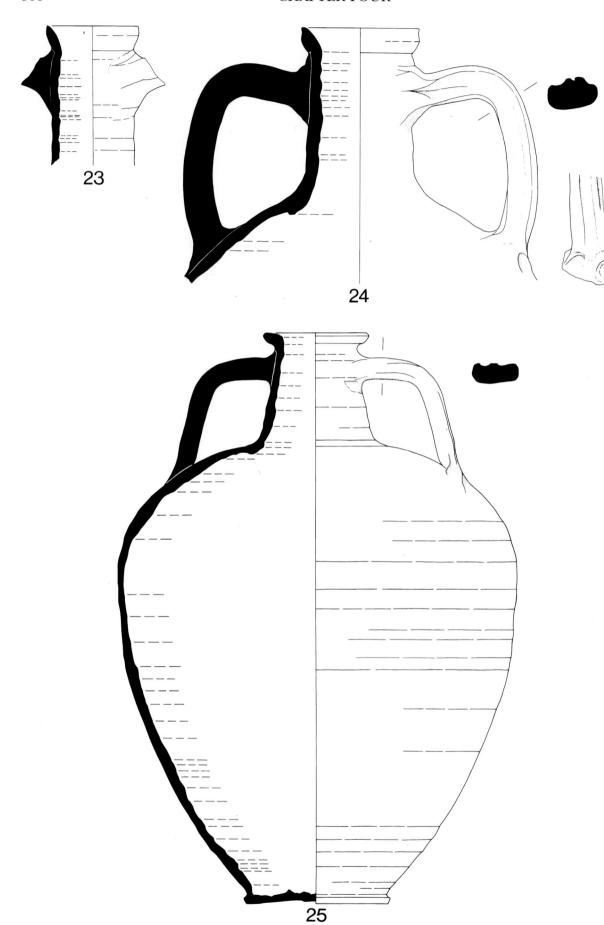

Fig. 209. Amphora types P23 (no. 23), P166 (no. 24) and P98 (no. 25) (1:3). *(SC)*

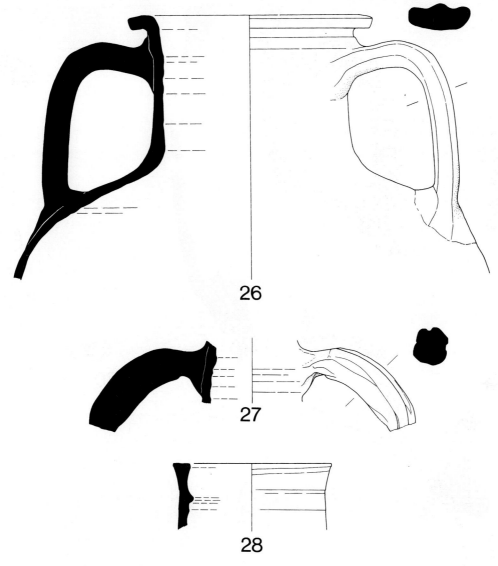

Fig. 210. Amphorae types P216 (no. 26), P235 (no. 27) and P28 (no. 28) (1:3). *(SC)*

stone inclusions and an overall cream-coloured exterior surface. See, in general, Laubenheimer (1985). P103. L165.

African (see also cat. 50, below)

40. Fig. 213. Small amphora or jug. Fine orange-pink fabric with abundant calcareous reaction rims and an off-white exterior slip which drips down the inside. The vessel appears to be from Tunisia, and the bulging neck is a feature common to that area: however, on fabric, it may possibly be from western Sicily, where ceramics of Imperial date are still little understood. P108. L165.
41. Fig. 213. Fabric is dark reddish grey towards the interior and orange towards the exterior, with a cream-coloured salt skin towards the top. North African. P110. L165.
42. Fig. 213. Orange-red fabric with abundant calcareous inclusions, minute quartz and occasional reaction rims. African. L165.

'Greek'

Koan

43. Fig. 214. Koan Dressel 2-4. Medium hard, fine, red-brown (2.5YR 6/6) fabric, with a thick greenish white (10YR 7.5/3) exterior skin, abundant minute mica and minute white calcareous inclusions. This virtually whole vessel accounts for 35 sherds and 4.300 kg in Table 55. The type has been discussed by Panella (1986: 617-19). P102. L165.
44. Fig. 214. Miniature Koan Dressel 2-4. Standard fabric, as above. P109. L165.

Agora G197

45. (Not illustrated.) An amphora type from the Meander valley of western Turkey. For the type see Panella (1986: 614, fig. 5 and note 7) and Peacock and Williams (1986: 188-90, class 45b). Only one body sherd was found. L105.

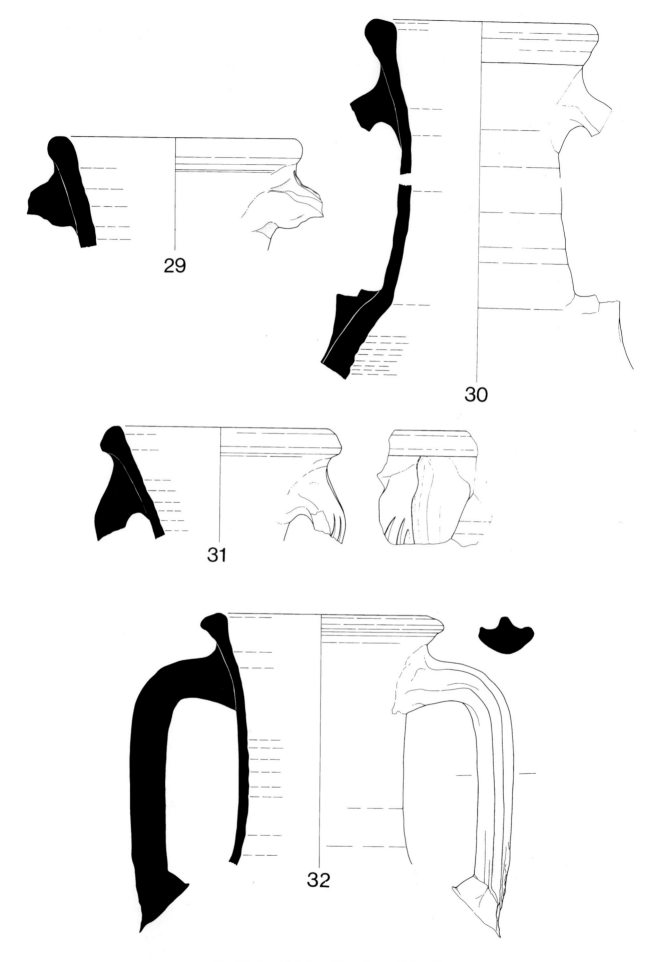

Fig. 211. Spanish Beltran IV amphorae (1:3). *(SC)*

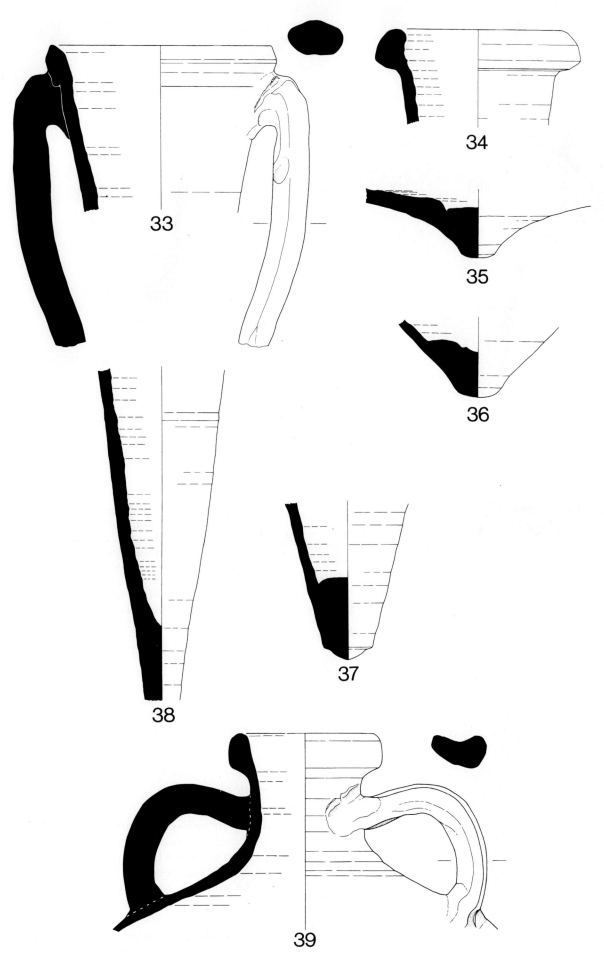

Fig. 212. Amphorae, various types. All 1:3, except 38 (1:6). *(SC)*

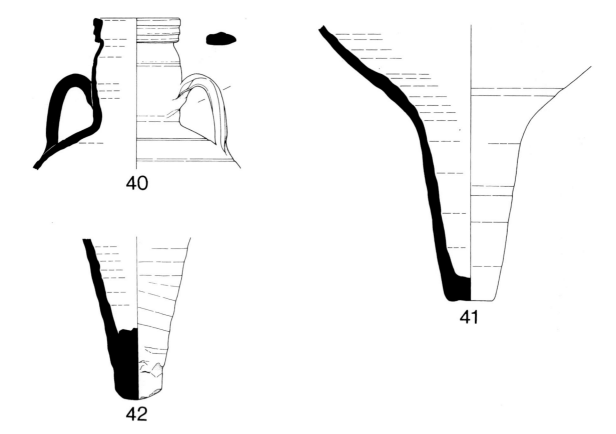

Fig. 213. African amphorae (1:3). *(SC)*

Uncertain eastern amphorae

46. Fig. 214. Unusual amphora. Highly micaceous (muscovite) dark reddish fabric (2.5YR 5.5/6), dirty grey-brown in handle section (5YR 5.5/3) and with a cream-brown exterior slip, with abundant small sub-angular calcareous inclusions (<1 mm). The general rim and neck type is represented by amphorae found in Aegean and Black Sea areas, though not associated with such a flattened handle; I have also seen similar fabrics in western Turkey. P239. L105.

47. Fig. 214. Ribbed shoulder from an amphora of probably eastern mediterranean origin. Hard pinkish red fabric (2.5YR 6/6) with abundant minute calcareous and brown inclusions, a little minute mica and a thick cream exterior slip. It probably dates no earlier than the fifth century, but is more likely to be sixth-century in date. P315. M144, fifth-sixth centuries AD.

Not identified

48. Fig. 214. Unusual amphora in a hard, orange-brown (2.5YR 6/5) fabric, yellow-brown (7.5YR 6.5/6) exterior slip, occasional minute calcareous inclusions, abundant minute dark inclusions and what appears to be volcanic glass. The vessel, in terms of its form, looks like a Levantine amphora, but apparent volcanic inclusions seemed to rule out such a possibility. For this reason the vessel was examined through thin-section, revealing "principal inclusions of grains of clinopyroxene, sanidine and quartz, together with flecks of mica and some fragments of volcanic rock". An Italian origin is suggested (cf. appendix). For a morphologically similar

vessel, perhaps of Eastern origin, see, for example, Panella (1968: 110, fig. XLI, no. 558, from Ostia). L165.

49. Fig. 214. Hard, reddish brown (2.5YR 5/6), slightly lighter self-coloured slip, scattered small white angular to rounded inclusions and very rare calcareous reaction rims. Uncertain provenance – possibly from the Aegean area, though the fabric does look somewhat similar to Tarraconensian examples. P112. L165.

Addendum (African)

50. Fig. 215. Spatheion. Upper part with knocked-off handles reused as a drainage pipe for the baptistery font. Produced in Tunisia, this piece is of a medium-sized vessel which is likely to be of later fourth- or fifth-century date. (I have not personally seen this piece.) P347. D317.

QUANTIFICATION

All the amphorae fragments from the two fish-pond deposits have been quantified under their respective types and principal fabric groups. This has been done both by number and by weight of sherds (Tables 55 and 56). In terms of cost-effectiveness with respect to the retrieval of information, this would seem to be the most efficient means of pottery quantification. The useful method of rim percentage quantification, or estimated vessel equivalents (EVES), was not adopted because of the relat-

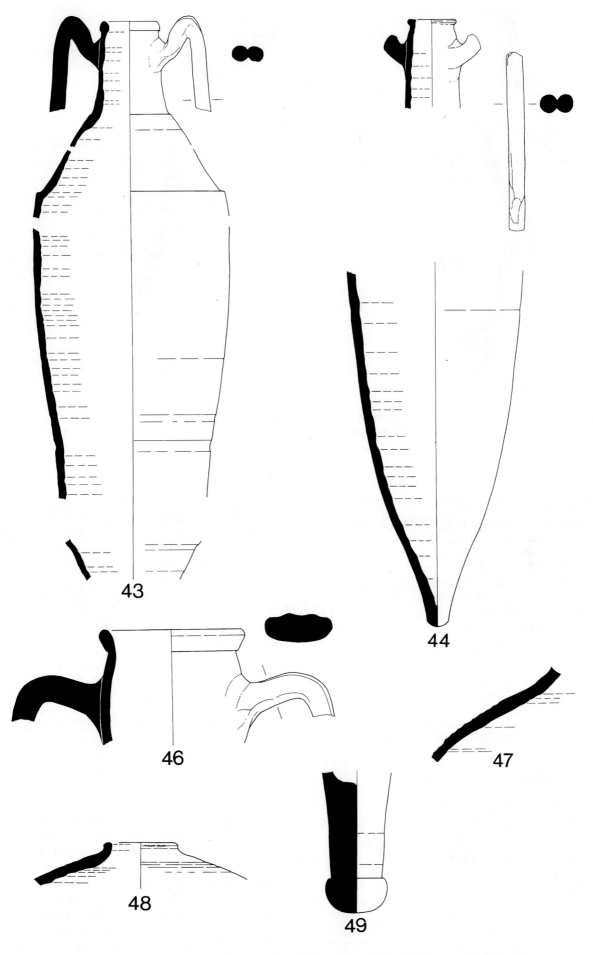

Fig. 214. Greek (43-4), Eastern (46-7) and unidentified amphora (48-9). All 1:3, except 43 (1:6). *(SC)*

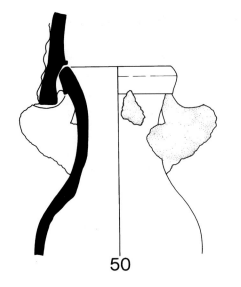

50

Fig. 215. Late Roman spatheion amphora (1:3). *(SC)*

ent mixed accumulations of ancient waste, but rapid accumulations with some virtually complete vessels that will, therefore, be abnormally well represented in the assemblage. This is certainly the case, for instance, with the Koan amphorae.

Some of the 1,495 sherds are likely to have been wrongly assigned, though the quantity of material studied will, for our purposes, swallow up a certain number of errors on the basis of 'safety in numbers'. The 'not identified' category is relatively high, ranging numerically from 28.7 per cent (context L165) to 46.9 per cent (context L105). When measured by weight, the proportion is, however, rather lower (11.8 per cent and 26.4 per cent respectively). Nevertheless, the more general trends should be clear enough with the present data.

ively low number of surviving rim sherds. Indeed, one of the drawbacks of the Monte Gelato assemblage is that the fish-pond deposits do not repres-

DISCUSSION

The Monte Gelato amphorae are particularly significant on two scores. Firstly, they have provided

Table 55. Quantification of all amphorae from context L165 (lower fish-pond deposit).

Note: the Dressel 2-4 category includes four fragments, presumed to be local, weighing 200 g (cf. cat. 4 and 5).

types	no.	%	weight (g)	%
ITALIAN				
Black sand Dr. 2-4 (Pompeian)	4	0.6	1,370	1.7
Campano-Latian Dr. 2-4	5	0.7	4,100	5.0
other Dressel 2-4	64	9.2	8,550	10.4
type P105	27	3.9	2,680	3.3
no. 25 (type P98)	59	8.5	4,300	5.2
NORTH AFRICAN				
Tunisian	65	9.3	5,770	7.0
no. 40	5	0.7	240	0.3
SPANISH				
Dressel 20	27	3.9	4,000	4.9
Beltran IVB	22	3.2	6,130	7.5
others	92	13.2	24,250	29.5
GREECE/ASIA MINOR				
Koan	35	5.0	4,300	5.2
Koan miniature	20	2.9	950	1.2
uncertain	43	6.2	2,600	3.2
GAULISH				
Dressel 30	29	4.2	3,280	4.0
NOT IDENTIFIED				
no. 48	1	0.1	100	0.1
no. 49	1	0.1	450	0.5
light fabrics	22	3.2	2,300	2.8
dark fabrics	176	25.3	6,880	8.4
TOTAL	697		82,250	

Table 56. Quantification of all amphorae from context L105 (upper fish-pond deposit).

types	no.	%	weight (g)	%
ITALIAN				
Dressel 2-4	9	1.1	1,550	2.5
miniature Dressel 2-4	1	0.1	150	0.2
type P105	280	35.0	22,120	35.8
no. 24 (type P166)	4	0.5	720	1.2
no. 26 (type P216)	5	0.6	1,550	2.5
NORTH AFRICAN				
Tunisian	10	1.2	1,170	1.9
Tripolitanian	6	0.8	550	0.9
SPANISH				
Beltran II	17	2.1	1,900	3.1
others	30	3.8	5,420	8.8
GREECE/ASIA MINOR				
Koan	50	6.3	9,000	14.6
Agora G197	1	0.1	20	0.03
no. 46 (type P239)	1	0.1	350	0.6
uncertain	1	0.1	50	0.1
GAULISH				
Dressel 30	9	1.1	1,000	1.6
NOT IDENTIFIED				
light fabrics	323	40.0	13,400	21.7
light fabrics (ribbed)	3	0.4	200	0.3
dark fabrics	48	6.0	2,700	4.4
TOTAL	798		61,850	

much needed archaeological evidence for the production of commercial amphorae, and thus for the production of surplus liquid agricultural products, from the hinterland of Rome. Secondly, they have further supplemented our knowledge of Roman exchange systems in both a crucial area and a crucial period. The second point will be examined first.

The continuity in use of wine amphorae from the island of Kos in the Dodecanese down to the end of the second century AD is interesting, though the various sherds from L105 may represent the remains of one long-lived vessel. Whether cat. 46 (type P239) could also be residual is difficult to say, though it does bear a superficial similarity to the early variant of the Eastern form Kapitan I, which appears in the second half of the second century (Panella 1986: 615-16). Alongside a minor quantity of Gaulish amphorae, the presence of Greek vessels suggests that inhabitants of Monte Gelato may have been discriminating enough to have required certain provincial wines from time to time. Alternatively, it may echo the evidence of graffiti from the same deposit, and the inscribed 'stork-vase', for the presence of Greek-speakers on the site; they may well have preferred Greek wines.

There is a far greater variety of Spanish amphorae in the earlier deposit, though Beltran IVB (Lusitanian?) garum amphorae predominate. Unsurprisingly, there are many fewer in the deposit of the late second century. It may be remarked that there is a low overall presence of Dressel 20 oil amphorae from Baetica, although these are exceedingly common in Rome; this perhaps implies that there were good local sources for oil for Monte Gelato and other areas of the Roman Campagna, which could not, however, satisfy the demands of the *urbs*. A little oil seems also to have come from north Africa.

As regards Italian vessels, the standard early Imperial west-coast wine container, form Dressel 2-4, is well represented in context L165 and diminishes greatly in the later context L105. This is now a well-established pattern. The examples from L105 may be the latest products of the series, as such types were produced up to the beginning of the third century, at least in the Rome area (see, for example, Freed (1989)). However, the type was gradually

Table 57. Quantification of wine amphorae from context L165 (lower fish-pond deposit).

types	no.	%	weight (g)	%
Italian imports	73	32.2	14,020	50.4
type P105	27	11.9	2,680	9.6
Greece/Asia Minor	98	43.2	7,850	28.2
Gaulish	29	12.8	3,280	11.8
TOTAL	227		27,830	

Table 58. Quantification of wine amphorae from context L105 (upper fish-pond deposit).

types	no.	%	weight (g)	%
Italian imports	10	2.8	1,700	4.9
type P105 (+ P166)	284	79.8	22,840	65.3
Greece/Asia Minor	53	14.9	9,420	26.9
Gaulish	9	2.5	1,000	2.9
TOTAL	356		34,960	

being supplanted by new vessels, generally of reduced capacity, throughout western Italy, from the end of the first century.[69] This process may be seen at Monte Gelato, where local Dressel 2-4 vessels account for 0.3 per cent numerically against 3.9 per cent of type P105 in context L165, and 0 per cent against 35.1 per cent in context L105 (Tables 55 and 56; see also Tables 57 and 58 for the general trend).

The production of mid-Imperial local amphorae in the area of Monte Gelato is especially interesting as evidence for local self-sufficiency in wine at times when, it has been argued, much of Italy was suffering a chronic shortage of wine produced within the peninsula. Indeed, not only is self-sufficiency attested, but exportation, at least to the capital, is implied by the very manufacture of transport containers. Panella has already suggested (1989: 144) the possibility of production centres along the Tiber valley and, to judge from the various fabrics now identified at Monte Gelato, Porta Pia (pers. comm. R. Schinke), Fosso della Crescenza (Arthur 1983: 80) (this last with its distinctive foraminifera), and elsewhere, they were probably fairly numerous. However, large-scale seaborne shipment of these vessels is probably to be excluded, not only because of their general absence on overseas consumption sites, but also because of their ring base which, it seems, was especially manufactured for the purposes of land or, at best, river transport.

An examination of probable Rome-area transport containers in and around Rome, taking the percentages of such vessels against all identified wine amphorae, is summarized in Table 59. The Via Nova, Crypta Balbi and Via Sacra figures are taken from Ciotola et al. (1989), whilst the Ostia figures come from Panella (1989). The earliest examples of the form date to the mid-first century AD, both at Luni and Rome, though at that time it appears to have been of secondary importance to wines contained in amphorae of Dressel 2-4 form. The later first-century contexts show growing proportions of Rome-area vessels. These supplement the declining proportions of wine amphorae, in particular of form Dressel 2-4, arriving from other areas along the Tyrrhenian coast. By the mid-second century, Rome-area vessels rapidly increase in proportion, becoming the commonest wine amphora in the Rome area and remaining so for the entire second century and perhaps the early years of the third.[70] According to the Terme del Nuotatore evidence, a drastic slump *may* finally appear by late Severan or post-Severan times, though more information is needed, especially from third-century contexts. This pattern may seem, in part, to support Carandini's revised views on the Italian economy (1989: 519), which envisage a new phase of suburban villas coming to the fore no later than the reign of Marcus Aurelius, perhaps partly specializing in viticulture for a specifically Rome-oriented

---

[69] I had already suspected this over ten years ago: cf. Arthur 1983: no. 8. See, especially, Panella (1989).

[70] Whilst I disagree with Purcell's Imperial boom in Italian viticulture (Purcell 1985), I agree that the new, early Imperial, vineyards of Spain and Gaul did destroy it. Archaeology seems, evermore, to be adding shades of grey to what, at times, seem to be historical arguments posed in black and white.

Table 59. Percentages of probable Rome-area transport containers against all other amphorae in published contexts in and around Rome.

site	%	date range
Via Nova, Rome	2.0	AD 64
Terme del Nuotatore, Ostia	4.7	c. AD 70-90
Crypta Balbi, Rome	3.6	c. AD 80-90
Monte Gelato	11.9	early second century AD
Via Sacra, Rome	15.2	c. AD 110
Terme del Nuotatore, Ostia	2.9	c. AD 120-40
Meta Sudans, Rome	26.1	mid-second century AD
Terme del Nuotatore, Ostia	13.5	c. AD 160-80
Monte Gelato	79.8	late second century AD
Terme del Nuotatore, Ostia	2.4	c. AD 190-210
Terme del Nuotatore, Ostia	0	c. AD 230-50

market. Furthermore, field-survey evidence from Rome's northern hinterland does not suggest any great slump in rural occupation and farming until the third century.[71]

Some vessels that are similar to P105 seem to have been marketed outside the Rome area and, perhaps, even abroad, albeit on a limited scale. A kiln site producing similar forms of amphora has been unearthed at Spello in Umbria: this has led Panella to see the type as essentially a container for *hirtiola* or *irtiola*, a typical Umbrian wine known to both Columella and Pliny (Panella 1989: 146). A clearly related type was also produced at Santarcangelo di Romagna in the late first and second centuries (Stoppioni Piccoli 1983: tav. III, no. 12). In Italy the form has been recognized at Ostia, Bolsena, Settefinestre, Cosa, Luni, Cures Sabini, Pisa and elsewhere (Panella 1989: 144 and n. 18; Pasquinucci and Storti 1989: 114 (for Pisa)). If the type is also to be recognized in Riley's mid-Roman amphora 13, which has yet to be proven, then a distribution of the type and its variants outside Italy covers parts of ex-Yugoslavia, Greece, Libya, Crete, Tunisia and Malta (Riley 1979: 197; Hayes 1983: 144-5, type 7 (for Crete)). This would certainly allow for some reassessment of Italy's supposedly ailing economy in the second century.

The evidence from Porta Pia and, to a lesser extent, from Fosso della Crescenza, suggests not only that the type was produced in the hinterland of Rome, but that it continued to supply wine to the capital during at least part of the third century.[72]

The negative evidence from Ostia (Table 59) might suggest that it was no longer exported, even along the Italian coast. The next step clearly is to identify the various centres of production, both by fabric and by nuances of form, so as to be able to recognize respective chronologies and market areas, as well as to attempt the reduction of the frustrating unidentified categories.

Evidence for circulation of amphorae in late Imperial or post-Imperial times is slight, though whether this represents a lack of commodities imported from overseas or their arrival at the site after having been transferred to other, less fragile or local, containers is difficult to say. The small proportion of late Roman amphorae on rural sites in Italy is, none the less, quite frequently documented. Monte Gelato has yielded a number of unidentified ribbed amphora sherds from contexts M144 (cat. 47) and M164, associated with fourth- to early fifth-century African red slip ware, as well as north African spatheion rims from contexts M87, K102 and D317, again all fourth- or fifth-century in date.[73]

APPENDIX: A NOTE ON THE PETROLOGY OF SOME AMPHORAE FROM MONTE GELATO, by David Williams

Thin-section analysis of some amphorae suspected to be of local production showed that, to a greater or lesser extent, volcanic sand was present in each sample: for example, the potassic feldspar sandine, clinopyroxene, plagioclase and

---

[71] See, Potter (1979: 140-1), as well as the overall discussion on the chronology of villas and wine by Tchernia (1986: 264-71).

[72] The type, in a distinctive medium to dark reddish brown fabric, was also present at Via Gabina site G11 (pers. obs. 1976-7). For Porta Pia, see, now, Bird (1993: 82-96) and Schinke (1994: 117-22).

[73] I am grateful to Tim Potter for entrusting to me the study of the amphorae from the Monte Gelato excavations. Kate Gilliver kindly discussed the Roman tile fabrics from the Monte Gelato excavations and Robyn Schinke showed me the amphorae from the British School at Rome's excavations at Porta Pia, Rome, and shared her views on local amphora production. I am once again grateful to David Williams for having very rapidly provided me with thin-section analyses of selected pieces.

small pieces of volcanic rock. There are some differences amongst the various P105 sherds sampled that suggest that they were not all made at the same production centre. However, it is clear that these vessels certainly do not share the same fabric normally associated with the Berenice mid-Roman amphora 13 type-sample, which was found to contain little else but limestone, quartz and mica (Riley 1979; Peacock and Williams 1986: class 42). Instead, the volcanic nature of the inclusions present in the Monte Gelato sherds points to a likely origin somewhere in the Italian comagmatic region. A source fairly local to Monte Gelato would fit in with the petrology, that is the Rome volcanic province, including southern Etruria and northern Latium (Desio 1973), although somewhere else along the Italian volcanic tract is also a possibility.

THE ROMAN POTTERY, by Paul Roberts

INTRODUCTION

The catalogue and discussion below are intended to present a full account of the Roman pottery in circulation in the area of Monte Gelato between the early second and mid-sixth centuries AD. Given the very large quantity of pottery found, it was decided to concentrate on key contexts which yielded the most useful evidence. This selected material

was divided into the eight groups presented below, representing either single contexts or a group of contexts which seemed essentially contemporary. All datable fine-wares, irrespective of their find-spots, are listed in Table 60.

Examination of the material quickly revealed that the quantities of material representative of different periods vary considerably. The second to early third centuries are particularly well represented (Groups 1-3), as are the later fourth to mid-sixth centuries (Groups 5-8). Very little material, however, could be attributed with certainty to the mid-third to mid-fourth centuries (Group 4). Possible reasons for these fluctuations are discussed below.

In the primary recording of the Roman pottery from Monte Gelato, form and fabric series were established using Kenrick's (unpublished) system, originally designed for use with Romano-British pottery from excavations at Colchester. The system, with its standard notations for fabric, form, dimensions and weight, proved ideal for medium to large assemblages of Roman Imperial date. Ideally, full quantification of as much material as possible is desirable and necessary for meaningful comparison with material from other sites. However, the scarcity of large sealed groups resulted in the full

Fig. 216. Group of pottery from the lower fill of the fish-pond, early second century AD. *(KW)*

Fig. 217. Group of pottery from the upper fill of the fish-pond. Later second century AD. *(KW)*

quantification of only Groups 1 and 2 from the fish-pond (Figs 216 and 217).

Throughout the text relating to these groups, and in Table 61, a minimum number of vessels is used, obtained either by rim count, or by significant sherd count (SSC). This method of quantification involves, in addition to the counting of rim sherds, the counting of base and body sherds which form, fabric or finish indicate as not belonging to any rims already counted. SSC is generally most effective in quantifying fine-ware and table-ware vessels which are usually smaller, more distinctive and more easily reconstructable. However, it can also be helpful for coarse-ware vessels, particularly in smaller deposits such as Group 2, where recognition of constituent parts of individual vessels is more feasible. Given that SSC represents the nearest approximation to the minimum number of vessels, it should, I believe, be used wherever possible, with quantification by rim count (or weight) alone a useful, though less satisfactory, system.

DISCUSSION

The homogeneity of Group 1 (120s-30s AD) implies that it accumulated in a relatively short time, perhaps little more than a decade, while the diversity of material, from lamps and table-ware to amphorae, fine-wares and kiln wasters, suggests that it is fairly representative of many aspects of on-site activity. The quantity of material is considerable, particularly given the presence of other large near-contemporary deposits (Group 3 below). Together these reveal a very large-scale generation of refuse, and imply a high degree of economic activity on the site in the Hadrianic period. This is contemporary with the apparent boom in rural site density (and presumably general levels of population, as suggested by the results of the South Etruria survey (Potter 1979: 133)).

The fine-ware in Group 1 is predominantly Italian in origin (Italian sigillata and glazed ware), though it is interesting to note the first indications

Table 60. Fine-ware found at Monte Gelato.

KEY: B – base; BS – body sherd; P – profile; R – rim; unid. – unidentifiable.

form	date	fragments found	context
BLACK GLAZE			
unid.		3R, 1B	cistern (2R, 1B), S10 (1R)
ITALIAN SIGILLATA (forms and dates as in *Conspectus*)			
Consp. 3	*c.* AD 40-150	8R	L101 (1R), L165 (1R), S4 (4R), S10 (2R)
Consp. 7	mid-late Augustan	1R, 1BS	cistern
Consp. 21.3	first century AD	1R	L101
Consp. 33.3	first-early second centuries AD	1R	S4
Consp. 34.2	mid to late first century (+)	1P, 3R, 1BS	L105 (1R, 1BS), L165 (1P, 2R)
Consp. 36.2	Tiberian-late first century AD (+)	1R	L165
unid.		3R, 3B, 19BS	L101 (6BS), L165 (4BS), L184 (1R, 4BS), cistern (2R, 2BS), S4 (2B), S10 (1B, 3BS)
LATE ITALIAN SIGILLATA			
unid.		2R, 1BS	S3 (1R), S4 (1BS), S10 (1R)
EASTERN SIGILLATA B (forms as in Hayes (1985))			
Hayes 53	late first to mid second centuries AD	1R	cistern
Hayes 60	*c.* AD 100-50	1P	L165
Hayes 62	*c.* AD 80-120	1R, 1B	S4
unid.		1R	S4
GREEN-GLAZED WARE			
Martin 1992b: fig. 3	early second century AD	1R	L165
Martin 1992b: fig. 10	early second century AD	1BS	L165
conical beaker	early second century AD	1R	L165
open vessel	early second century AD	1R	S10
AFRICAN RED SLIP WARE (forms and dates as given by Hayes (1972; 1980))			
Fabric t.s.c. 'A'			
3A	late first to mid second centuries AD	3R	cistern, S4, S10
6B	mid to late second century AD	1P	cistern
6	second century AD	1R	S3
7	early to mid second century AD	1R	S3
8A	*c.* 110/20s-80s AD (+?)	1R	L105
8B	*c.* 160s-210/20s AD	1R	L105
9A	*c.* 110/20s-80s AD (+?)	3R	L105 (2R), S10 (1R)
9B	*c.* 160s-210/20s AD	2R	L105
8/9	second-early third centuries AD	1B	C59
7-10	second-early third centuries AD	1BS	L165
14A	early to mid second century AD	1P, 3R	L105 (1P, 1R), S3 (2R)
14B	mid to late second century AD (+?)	3R	C59, L101, S10
16	mid to late second century AD	1P	L105
27	*c.* AD 160-220	2R	S3
closed forms		3BS	L105 (1BS), cistern (2BS)
unid.		1R, 7B, 26BS	L105 (6B, 8BS), cistern (4BS), S3 (5BS), S4 (4BS), S10 (1B, 5BS)
Fabric t.s.c. 'A' – cooking-ware			
22	early to mid second century AD (+)	1R	L105
23A	early to mid second century AD (+)	1P, 5R	L105 (2R), L165 (1P, 2R), S4 (1R)
23B	mid second to early third centuries AD (+)	1P, 2R, 1BS	L105 (1P, 1BS), cistern (1R), S3 (1R)
23	second to third centuries AD (+)	1R, 3BS	L101 (1BS), S3 (2BS), S10 (1R)
182	mid second to mid third centuries AD (+)	1P, 2R	L105 (1P, 1R), S3 (1R)

form	date	fragments found	context
183/184	second to third centuries AD (+)	1R	L105
196	mid second to mid third centuries AD (+)	14R, 2B	L101 (3R, 2B), L105 (4R), cistern (2R), S3 (3R), S10 (1B, 5BS)
197	late second to mid third centuries AD (+)	11R, 4BS	L101 (1R), L105 (3R, 1BS), S3 (3BS), S4 (4R), S10 (3R)
Fabric t.s.c. 'C'			
35	late second to mid third century AD	1R	L105
50A	c. AD 230/40-325	2R	S3, S10
52B	c. 280/300 to late fourth century AD	1P	M87
53A	c. AD 350-430 (+)	1B	C1/D1
unid.		2BS	C59, S4
Fabric t.s.c. 'D'			
58	c. AD 290/300-75	1R	S4
61A	c. AD 325-80 (+)	1R	M74
61B	c. AD 380-440	3R	K101, L101, M164
67	c. AD 360-440	4R	K101, M79, M82, S4
92	early to mid fifth century AD	1R	M164
93A	c. AD 470-540	1P	D48
99A	late fifth century-c. AD 540	1R	C1/D1
stamp: Hayes type 4h	mid fourth to fifth centuries		M79
stamp: Hayes type 69b	mid fourth to fifth centuries		H1, L157
unid.		6BS	D45 (3BS), K101 (2BS), L101 (1BS)

Table 61. Quantification of Groups 1 and 2 (fish-pond).

	Group 1		Group 2	
class	vessels (by SSC)	% of total	vessels (by SSC)	% of total
FINE-WARE				
terra sigillata italica	10	5	2	1.5
eastern sigillata B2	1	0.5	-	-
green-glazed ware	3	1.5	-	-
African red slip ware	3	1.5	26	22.5
imports	**17**	**8.5**	**28**	**24.0**
colour-coated ware	40	20.0	41	35.5
table-ware	**57**	**28.5**	**69**	**59.5**
COARSE-WARE				
Pompeian red ware	-	-	5	4.5
dishes, bowls, cups	8	4.0	6	5.0
jars	61	31.0	18	15.5
cooking pots	57	28.5	3	2.5
flagons/jugs	12	6.0	11	9.5
miscellaneous	4	2.0	4	3.5
(lids)	(57)		(2)	
(bases)	(68)		(20)	
coarse-ware	**142**	**71.5**	**47**	**40.5**
TOTAL	199 vessels		116 vessels	

of the presence of African red slip ware (ARS), which is the predominant fine-ware in the later Group 2. This presence of ARS at such a relatively early stage in its import, together with the presence of glazed ware, now believed to have a northern Campanian or, more likely, a Roman source (Martin 1992b: 329), the large number of lamps of specifically Roman origin (Bailey, this volume), and Italian, Greek and Spanish amphorae (Arthur, this volume), indicates close economic ties with Rome. They serve as tangible markers for the important exchange of goods (much of which presumably has left no archaeological trace) between the site and Rome, either by direct purchase or by intermediate marketing systems.

The presence of kiln wasters (misfired vessels) of colour-coated ware and coarse-ware pieces in Group 1 strongly suggests, in addition, that the site also served as a centre of pottery manufacture. Much of this local/on-site production is very similar to pottery found in Rome, Ostia and the South Etruria survey, which suggests a ceramic community or koine, showing the strength of the economic and social ties which existed in the area. However, the vitality and individuality of the site's production is shown in particular in the variety of the colour-coated table-ware, most noticeably the 'stork-vase' (see below).

Pottery production at Monte Gelato seems to fit into the fourth of Peña's categories (Peña 1987: 441-4), namely manufacture linked to villas or other rural settlements, producing a diversified range of products aimed at the needs of the local market. Indeed, the range of pottery found at Monte Gelato is very comparable with that found on South Etruria sites 6 and 9, which Peña (1987: 444) has cited as typical of this mode of production.

Clearly, Monte Gelato in this period was only one of a (large?) number of rural sites producing domestic and/or architectural ceramics for local or medium-distance markets, perhaps in some cases exclusively for the sites themselves. Future analysis of fabrics may help to shed light on the nature of the mechanisms by which products were distributed over short and medium distances, an area still almost as under-researched as it was when discussed some fifteen years ago by Peacock (1982: 156).

The fine-wares in Group 2 (170s-90s AD) form an equally large or larger part of the deposit than was the case in Group 1, though the possibly different nature of Group 2 (discussed below) should be considered. With the exception of a small continued presence of Italian sigillata, ARS now dominated the markets which supplied the site, reflecting the increasing import of African products to Rome and indeed to Italy as a whole.

Colour-coated ware was still plentiful, though in a less idiosyncratic and smaller range of forms, suggesting that colour-coated ware was no longer manufactured on site. However, local production of transport amphorae seems to have increased substantially in this period (Arthur, this volume), and a production of so-called Pompeian red ware, perhaps of fairly local origin, appeared on local markets.

The coarse-ware may reveal other clues as to changes in the circumstances of the site and its markets. The general quality of coarse-ware in Group 2 is lower than that of Group 1, and the range of forms considerably reduced, some common forms of Group 1 disappearing altogether. Production of coarse-ware is not attested in Group 2, and this, together with the cessation of production of colour-coated ware, might indicate a decrease in the general level of economic activity on the site. The proportion of coarse-ware in Group 2 (40.5 per cent) is far lower than that of Group 1 (71.5 per cent), and this may indicate an alternative dumping site for food-preparation refuse; this in turn might suggest a restructuring of the site's main function areas.

In short, Group 2 seems to show considerable changes, both in the types of vessels used on the site and therefore, presumably, in the markets which supplied them. There might well have been a decrease in the number of manufacturing centres, as in the case of Monte Gelato itself, and this may reflect a decrease in demand. Peña (1987: 161) has suggested that the drop in the number of sites yielding ARS as opposed to Italian sigillata around some of his sites (for example, site 6) indicates a contraction of settlement, presumably the first signs of the much sharper contraction seen in the third century (below).

The period between the deposition of Group 2 (late second century) and that of Group 4 (mid-fourth century) is the least well represented in the ceramic record. Only two sherds of fine-ware representative of this period (ARS 50A – early version) were found (see Table 60), signalling a very sharp drop in imports to the site in comparison with the plentiful imports of the later second century. This paucity of evidence for the early third to mid-fourth centuries is also found in the lamps (Bailey, this volume), suggesting a period of sharply diminished economic activity on the site, very possibly its total abandonment, at some stage in the early third century. Such a situation seems to have persisted for at least a century, the only evidence of any activity being the presence of several coins (Hobbs, this volume); however, given the proven continuity in use of fourth-century coinage well into the fifth century, the evidence of the pottery and lamps may in this case be more reliable indicators.

A period of near or total abandonment of the site in the third and early fourth centuries finds parallels at other rural sites throughout the area of South Etruria (Peña 1987: 160 site 6; 211 site 9), while Potter (1979: 141-2) has spoken of 'massive' depopulation of the area. Elsewhere in Italy, at sites such as Settefinestre (Carandini 1985: 183-5), San Rocco (Cotton and Métraux 1985: 83) and Posto (Cotton 1979: 56) in Campania, Matrice in Molise (Roberts forthcoming) and San Giovanni di Ruoti in Basilicata (Freed 1982: 2) the same phenomenon seems to occur.

Altogether, the evidence suggests a period of decline or disruption in many areas of the Italian countryside, and/or a fundamental change in the methods of exploiting the land. Such major changes would clearly have had serious consequences for most elements of the settlement pattern, and this seems to have included marked changes at, and ultimately the abandonment of, the site of Monte Gelato itself.

Group 4, dating to the mid-fourth century, marks the reoccupation of the site and/or the resumption of detectable activity. The small sample, however, and the lack of contemporary deposits, strongly suggests that whatever the nature of the activity in this phase, it was on a very small scale (despite other indications, for example from the coins, to the contrary).

The group, though small, reveals considerable information on developments on the site and in the surrounding area. The reappearance of imported fine-ware (ARS) on the site, after an absence of a century or more, signals the site's return to participation in marketing networks. In the coarse-ware, forms and fabrics, some radically different from those of earlier deposits, suggest profound changes in the local ceramic tradition and/or in the sources of pottery for the site. This in turn suggests a period of considerable change, of which the abandonment of the site in the third century may have been a symptom.

Among the pottery in Group 5 (early to mid sixth century), the presence of ARS shows that the site's economic links with the markets around Rome were maintained, although the generally limited quantities of ARS reaching the site after the mid-fifth century should be noted (Table 60). The fabrics of the coarse-ware are consistent with those noted in Group 4 of well over a century earlier, suggesting a broad continuity of supply. The forms, however, are noticeably different, indicating the adoption of new types and not simply the development of those already existing. The new forms seen in Group 5 may represent the simplification not only of the forms themselves, but also, very importantly, the general range of forms available, a phenomenon seen elsewhere in Italy in the later Roman period (Roberts 1992: 421-2).

Group 6 (mid-sixth century+) contains no imported fine-ware, even as a fragmentary, residual element, thereby suggesting the continuing decline of imports seen from the mid-fifth century. It is significant that even a site so close to Rome as Monte Gelato could not always gain ready access to the fruits of international trade, assuming that the inhabitants of the site still wished to obtain them. The coarse-ware of Group 6 is quite different from the other late Roman assemblages, with forms, especially the cooking pots, unparalleled elsewhere. Given the large number of generally late Roman contexts (later fourth to mid-sixth centuries) on the site, the unusual forms support the idea of a slightly later date for the assemblage, while the absence of parallels suggests a period of low levels of refuse generation. As with Group 4, this may be indicative of a relatively low level of economic activity on the site.

In the period covered by Group 7 contexts (late fourth to mid-sixth centuries (+?)) ARS represents the only international fine-ware import to the site. No trace was found of Phocaean red slip ware (unsurprising, perhaps, given its scarcity in Rome itself), or of 'Tiber red slip' recently isolated in late Roman levels at Rome (T. Peña, pers. comm.). ARS, whilst not as plentiful as in second-century contexts, is none the less present in some quantities, implying a healthy level of economic activity on the site and sustained contacts with local markets. Rome was clearly predominant amongst these, as can be seen by the similarity of coarse-ware types and regional fine-ware forms.

Coarse-wares from Group 7 contexts, despite their broad chronological range, present several important groupings of forms which seem to have a chronological significance. At this point it is interesting to note the absence of forms that are recognizably sub-Roman or post-Roman, until the appearance of identifiable late eighth-century forms (Patterson, this volume). This contrasts with the evidence from sites such as Casale San Donato (H. Patterson, pers. comm.) and Madonna del Passo near Rieti (pers. obs.) which have revealed sub-Roman wares and forms.

The vessels in Group 8 attest the late Antique phenomenon of on-site burials, common to many rural sites from the later Imperial period. The earlier piece cat. 186 (mid-later fifth century) finds parallels in its fabric and diagnostic features with elements of Groups 5 and 7, while the later vessel cat. 187 (mid-later sixth century), though lacking definite parallels in material found on the site, is none the less still recognizably in the Roman period ceramic tradition.

Work currently in progress in and around Rome, such as the analysis of coarse-wares from sixth- to eighth-century deposits at the Crypta Balbi, Rome (L. Saguì, pers. comm.), may eventually permit some of the Group 7 material to begin to bridge the gap between the mid-late sixth and late eighth centuries on the site. On present evidence, however, there seems to be a complete absence of such material. Given that Monte Gelato's proximity to Rome makes it unlikely that the site would at any stage have been completely aceramic, the evidence seems to suggest the complete cessation of occupation, or its reduction to a level undetectable in the archaeological record, at some point in the mid-later sixth century.

FABRICS

A fabric series was constructed by eye, with the aid of a magnifier. While petrological and/or chemical analysis would have been desirable (and is planned), sufficient inclusions were visible to enable a satisfactory division into major fabric groups. This procedure was also adopted for fine-wares with the exception of the ARS, where Lamboglia's categories, terra sigillata chiara (t.s.c.) 'A', 'C' and 'D' are used (Lamboglia 1950; 1958; 1963; see Hayes (1972: 288)).

1. Soft clay with smooth/powdery feel and finely irregular fracture. Colour: orange (5YR 6/6; Munsell reddish yellow) to buff (10YR 8/4; Munsell very pale brown). Inclusions: very fine quartz, iron and silver mica (all infrequent).

2. Medium-hard clay with smooth/powdery feel and smooth fracture. Colour: orange (7.5YR 7/6; Munsell reddish yellow) to buff (10YR 8/3; Munsell very pale brown). Inclusions: medium to coarse iron (infrequent), fine silver mica, quartz and shiny black platelets (all very infrequent).

3. Soft clay with smooth/powdery feel and finely irregular fracture. Colour: off-white (2.5Y 8/3; Munsell not given) to buff (10YR 8/4; Munsell very pale brown). Inclusions: fine silver mica and lime (infrequent).

4. Medium-hard clay with smooth feel and smooth fracture. Colour: off-white (2.5Y 8/3; Munsell not given) to greenish buff (10Y 8/2; Munsell not given). Inclusions: fine gold mica, lime, iron and shiny black platelets (all infrequent).

5. Medium-hard clay with smooth feel and smooth fracture. Colour: orange (5YR 7/6; Munsell reddish yellow) to buff (10YR 8/4; Munsell very pale brown). Inclusions: fine-medium lime and fine iron (infrequent).

6. Soft clay with soapy feel and finely irregular fracture. Colour: light brown (7.5YR 7/6; Munsell reddish yellow). Inclusions: fine lime, silver mica and red particles (all infrequent).

7. Hard clay with smooth feel and finely irregular fracture. Colour: buff (10YR 7/4; Munsell very pale brown). Inclusions: coarse iron, medium lime, fine silver mica and quartz (all infrequent).

8. Very hard clay with smooth feel and hackly fracture. Colour: off-white (2.5Y 8/2; Munsell white). Inclusions: medium-coarse black particles (abundant) and medium red particles (frequent).

9. Hard clay with smooth feel and smooth fracture. Colour: buff (10YR 7/4; Munsell very pale brown). Inclusions: medium-coarse rounded brown and black particles (abundant), fine silver mica (frequent) and coarse lime (infrequent).

10. Medium-hard clay with smooth/powdery feel and smooth fracture. Colour: off-white (2.5Y 8/2; Munsell not given – 2.5Y 8/4; Munsell pale yellow). Inclusions: coarse quartz, medium-coarse shiny black platelets and silver mica (all infrequent).

11. Medium-hard clay with smooth feel and smooth fracture. Colour: orange (5YR 7/8; Munsell reddish yellow) to buff (10YR 8/4; Munsell very pale brown). Inclusions: fine to coarse quartz and iron, fine lime and black particles (all frequent), fine silver mica (infrequent).

12. Soft clay with soapy feel and smooth/finely irregular fracture. Colour: buff (10YR 8/4; Munsell very pale brown). Inclusions: fine quartz (infrequent).

13. Hard clay with smooth, occasionally pimply feel and finely irregular fracture. Colour: orange (5YR 7/8; Munsell reddish yellow) to brown (7.5YR 5/3; Munsell not given). Inclusions: coarse lime, medium-coarse iron, fine-medium quartz, fine silver mica and angular green particles (all frequent).

14. Hard clay with pimply feel and hackly fracture. Colour: orange (7.5YR 8/6; Munsell reddish yellow) to buff (10YR 8/4; Munsell very pale brown). Inclusions: fine to coarse black platelets and fine-medium quartz (frequent), coarse iron, fine silver mica and lime (infrequent).

15. Hard clay with slightly rough feel and hackly fracture. Colour: orange (5YR 6/6; Munsell reddish yellow) to brown (7.5YR 5/4; Munsell reddish brown). Inclusions: medium-coarse quartz, iron, shiny black platelets and gold mica (all abundant), angular green particles (infrequent).

16. Hard clay with smooth feel and finely irregular fracture. Colour: orange-red (2.5YR 6/6; Munsell light red). Inclusions: medium-coarse quartz, iron and silver mica (all abundant).

17. Hard clay with smooth feel and finely irregular fracture. Colour: light brown (7.5YR 7/4; Munsell pink) to orange (7.5YR 7/6; Munsell reddish yellow). Inclusions: medium-coarse rounded red particles (abundant).

18. Hard clay with smooth/pimply feel and hackly fracture. Colour: orange (2.5YR 5/6; Munsell red) to brown (7.5YR 6/4; Munsell light brown). Inclusions: medium-coarse quartz, fine to coarse gold mica and fine-medium iron (all abundant), coarse brown particles and fine silver mica (infrequent).

19. Very hard clay with pimply feel and finely irregular/hackly fracture. Colour: orange (5YR 6/8; Munsell reddish yellow) to brown (5YR 6/4; Munsell light reddish brown). Inclusions: fine-medium black particles (abundant), fine to coarse quartz, fine silver and gold mica (frequent).

20. Very hard clay with smooth feel and finely irregular fracture. Colour: red (2.5YR 7/4; Munsell not given) to brown (5YR 6/4; Munsell light reddish brown). Inclusions: medium quartz, iron and lime (infrequent), shiny black platelets and silver mica (very infrequent).

21. Hard clay with smooth feel and finely irregular/hackly fracture. Colour: brown (5YR 5/6; Munsell yellowish red). Inclusions: medium iron and fine to coarse white, red and black particles (all frequent).

22. Hard clay with smooth feel and finely irregular fracture. Colour: light brown (5YR 6/6; Munsell reddish yellow). Inclusions: fine quartz (abundant).

23. Hard clay with pimply feel and hackly fracture. Colour: red (5YR 6/6; Munsell reddish yellow) to purplish red (5YR 6/3; Munsell light reddish brown). Inclusions: fine to coarse quartz, gold mica and iron (all abundant), medium lime (infrequent).

24. Hard clay with pimply feel and hackly fracture. Colour: red (5YR 6/6; Munsell reddish yellow) to brown (7.5YR 4/4; Munsell dark brown). Inclusions: fine to coarse quartz and fine silver mica (abundant), medium-coarse iron (frequent).

25. Medium hard clay with rough feel and finely irregular fracture. Colour: brown (7.5YR 6/6; Munsell reddish yellow). Inclusions: fine silver mica and fine-medium quartz (abundant).

26. Hard clay with rough feel and finely irregular/hackly fracture. Colour: orange (5YR 7/8; Munsell reddish yellow) to brown (7.5YR 5/2; Munsell brown). Inclusions: fine to coarse quartz (abundant), fine gold mica and red and black particles (frequent).

27. Hard clay with smooth feel and hackly fracture. Colour: orange-brown (5YR 6/4; Munsell light reddish brown) to purplish brown (5YR 5/3; Munsell reddish brown). Inclusions: fine to coarse quartz, gold mica and iron (abundant), medium lime and shiny black platelets (frequent).

28. Very hard clay with smooth feel and hackly fracture. Colour: dark brown (7.5YR 5/4; Munsell brown). Inclusions: coarse quartz, fine to coarse gold mica, medium shiny black platelets, and medium-coarse iron (all abundant), medium lime (infrequent). An extremely dense fabric, with rough matrix.

Fine-wares

29. Hard clay with smooth feel and finely irregular fracture. Colour: buff (10YR 8/2; Munsell white). Inclusions: fine-medium black particles (frequent). Colour of glaze: interior = yellowish green (5Y 6/6; Munsell olive-yellow); exterior = bluish green (Munsell not given).

30. Hard clay with smooth, waxy feel and finely irregular fracture. Colour: orange (2.5YR 6/8; Munsell light red). Inclusions: fine-medium mica (frequent) and black particles (sparse). Reddish brown slip (2.5YR 6/6; Munsell light red).

31. Hard clay with smooth feel and finely irregular fracture. Colour: pink (2.5YR 7/6; Munsell not given). Inclusions: fine silver mica and lime (infrequent). Reddish brown slip (2.5YR 5/8; Munsell red), overall, semi-lustrous.

32. Very hard clay with smooth feel and smooth fracture. Colour: light red-brown (2.5YR 6/4; Munsell light reddish brown). Inclusions: fine silver mica and fine-medium red particles (infrequent). Reddish brown slip (2.5YR 5/8; Munsell red), overall, lustrous.

33. Hard clay with smooth feel and finely irregular fracture. Colour: pink (2.5YR 7/4; Munsell not given). Inclusions: fine silver mica (abundant). Dark reddish brown slip (2.5YR 4/6; Munsell red), overall, almost matt.

CATALOGUE

Throughout the catalogue the following structure has been used. After the general discussion of each group, the material from that group is divided up by ware and/or class, for example ARS, jars. Individual catalogue entries give, first, the catalogue number used for the identification of pieces in the catalogue and discussions, then a description of the form, with acknowledged nomenclature and dates (if known). Below this are the original recording reference number (P000), and details of dimensions and finish. In cases of multiple context groups (for example, Group 7) provenance is given. Below this, information is supplied on similar vessels from the same deposit and comparanda from other sites. All dates are AD unless specified otherwise.

Group 1 – L165 (lower fill of fish-pond) (Fig. 216)

Group 1, as well as being the largest single homogeneous deposit from the site, is also the earliest. Very small quantities of earlier fine-wares have been found on the site (Table 60), though all were from redeposited groups.

Group 1 comprises material from the lower fill of the fishpond. Excluding amphorae, lamps and glass (see Arthur, Bailey and Price, this volume), remains of at least 199 vessels were found by SSC, ranging from table-ware to vessels for cooking and storage. A wide range of imported fine-wares is present, including Italian sigillata, glazed ware, Eastern sigillata B2 and ARS; these suggest a date for the deposit in the later first quarter of the second century (c.120s-30s), a dating broadly supported by the evidence of the amphorae, lamps and glass vessels.

Italian sigillata comprises the largest group of imported fine-ware in the deposit (form numbers used below are those of Ettlinger in the *Conspectus* (1990) (hereafter *Consp.* plus form number)). All the identifiable forms (*Consp.* 3.2 (cat. 3), 34.2 (cat. 4), 36.2 (cat. 1)) form a homogeneous group, with no necessarily residual forms, though *Consp.* 36.2 (cat. 1), might be a little earlier. *Consp.* 3.2 (cat. 3) and 34.2 (cat. 4), are among the commonest forms of the later phases of Italian sigillata production, throughout all production areas (*Consp.* 56 and 112). The stamps on cat. 4a-b indicate origins for these vessels in the area of Arezzo.

Glazed ware began arriving in Italy in the later first century BC, from workshops in the Near East and Asia Minor (Maccabruni 1987: 167-8). The area of Tarsus in northern Syria seems to have exported a range of drinking vessels, especially ring-handled skyphoi, which have been found on several Italian sites, including Rome, Pompeii, and, on the Adriatic coast, at Adria (Hochuli Guysel 1977: Abb. 35).

Production in Italy seems to have begun in the mid-first century AD, certainly in northern Italy around Aquileia (Maioli 1983: 113), and there is evidence for production beginning at around this time in Lazio and Campania (Celuzza 1985: 163-5). Soricelli (1988: 253) has gone further, suggesting Puteoli as a possible origin for the 'honey-coloured' jugs and beakers found in Pompeii and Herculaneum. It seems likely, however, that the majority of vessels found in Rome, Ostia (see parallels below) and at Santa Rufina (Cotton, Wheeler and Whitehouse 1991: fig. 91, nos. 9-11), to which the Monte Gelato pieces bear most resemblance in terms of form, fabric and glaze colour, had a different origin, very probably in or near Rome.

The quantities of glazed ware found on Italian sites are generally small, as for example at the extensive villa at Settefinestre, where fewer than a hundred sherds were found, as opposed to thousands of sherds of Italian sigillata. Although it is very possible that the most prized table-wares (for those with the ability to afford them) were of metal, glazed ware, with its unusual finish, clearly reminiscent of metal, in particular bronze, may well have been relatively highly prized. If so, then the presence of three examples in the deposit gives an impression of relative affluence, this being confirmed by other prestige items from the site. It also shows clearly the access that the owners of the site enjoyed to the marketing systems operating in and around Rome and neighbouring centres.

Eastern sigillata B originated in the area of the Meander valley, probably in or near Tralles (Hayes 1972: 9), and was produced from the later Augustan period. Earlier products (Eastern sigillata B1) were distributed mostly around the Aegean, while the later wares (B2), though of lesser quality, were distributed throughout the central and eastern Mediterranean. The most recent and comprehensive discussions of the ware have been by Hayes (1985: 49- 70) and Kenrick (1985: 245-56).

ARS began to arrive in Italy from north Africa during the last quarter of the first century AD. The earliest pieces of ARS are found in Pompeii (Hayes 1972: 190, 205 and 207), though the ware would presumably also have begun to penetrate the markets of Ostia and Rome at an early date. By the turn of the century ARS comprised a sizeable minority of fine-ware assemblages at Ostia (Martin 1992b: fig. 3).The forms present in Group 1 do not represent the earliest forms of ARS import, but rather the late Flavian/Hadrianic types, in particular the small version of 23A (cat. 9), that characterize the first major period of the ware's penetration of Italy.

Taking the imported fine-ware as a whole, the scale of its presence at Monte Gelato demonstrates the ease of access enjoyed by the inhabitants to a whole range of imported goods from local and regional markets.

Colour-coated or slipped ware, locally made vessels decorated by total or partial immersion in a slip or suspension of clay slurry, was the most common type of table-ware used in many regions of Italy throughout the early-mid Imperial period. Peña (1987: 210) has assembled the evidence for a gradual development in the use of colour-coating, from its original use on smaller thin-walled pieces, such as beakers, to its application on a much wider range of forms such as bowls and jugs. Large quantities of the ware have been found on sites such as Cratere Senga (Garcea, Miraglia and Soricelli 1985: 262-3), Posto (Cotton 1979: 136-9) and San Rocco (Cotton and Métraux 1985: 203-17) in Campania; Santa Rufina (Cotton, Wheeler and Whitehouse 1991: fig. 74) in South Etruria; Settefinestre (Camaiora 1985: 172 and tav. 45) in central Etruria; Torre Rebibbia (Staffa 1984: 116-19) north of Rome; and, further afield, Matrice (Roberts 1988: 96-101) in Molise.

The numerous colour-coated vessels found in Group 1 form the majority of table-wares in the deposit, far outnumbering imported sigillata and glazed ware. The wide variety of forms ranges from broad shallow dishes (cat. 11) to tall narrow beakers (cat. 28).

Shallow dishes (cat. 11-17) show considerable variety, with one (cat. 11) revealing the influence of sigillata, probably late sigillata Italica (*Consp.* 48) or Eastern sigillata (Hayes 1985: form 62A). Much more obvious is the influence of sigillata on one of the most common colour-coated vessels, the flanged cup/bowl cat. 18, identical to the Italian sigillata form *Consp.* 34. The presence in the deposit of genuine sigillata examples of the form suggests that the colour-coated imitations reflect the enterprise of the local potters and their ability to respond to the demands of their local markets, rather than any difficulty in acquiring the original products.

Small, carinated cup/bowls (cat. 19-20) form a small but significant subgroup, including cat. 19 with its flaring, well-formed rim. Cat. 20 appears to be a local version of the thin-walled ware form Mayet XLIII (Mayet 1975), widespread throughout the western Mediterranean in the first and early second centuries (see Lopez Mullor (1989: 409-11)). The broad, shallow carinated bowl, cat. 23, is a common form and was to become the predominant colour-coated form in later deposits on the site and elsewhere (Staffa 1984: tav. II-III). Cat. 25-7 also have parallels around Rome. Cat. 29 differs from other bowls in the deposit, with its unusually deep, broad body.

Drinking vessels or pocula are well-represented, in particular ovoid vessels such as cat. 26 and 27. Of particular inter-

est is a tall, conical beaker cat. 28, a small version of the stork-vase (*pelargos?*), discussed below.

Of the forms of decoration applied to vessels before colour-coating, rouletting is the most common (for example on cat. 21-4 and 27-9), and with the exception of cat. 29 was fairly well and evenly applied. Applied 'petals' or 'scales' appear on two pieces (cat. 25 and 26), reflecting the frequent use of this motif on early Imperial table-wares, including thin-walled wares (Ricci 1985a: tav. CVII, nos. 14-17) and green glazed ware (as above cat. 6 and 7).

Almost without exception, the colour-coat of the vessels in Group 1 is thin (which explains its often poor state of preservation), dull and poorly applied, with frequent smears, dribbles and finger-marks. On all pieces the slip was applied overall, though its colour varies considerably between vessels and between different areas of the same vessel. This is presumably a result of chemical changes in the slip during firing, as is the occasionally metallic appearance of some pieces.

The bowls/dishes/cups comprise a limited range of bowls for preparation (cat. 32) and dishes for cooking and serving (cat. 33-5), all of a good standard of potting. Cat. 32, though of local fabric, seems to belong to a tradition of large, handled bowls found throughout the eastern and central Mediterranean during the first centuries BC and AD. Traces of direct contact with fire are present on cat. 33-5, indicating their probable use in on-hearth cooking.

Cat. 34 and 35 are in a fabric which, with its abundant volcanic inclusions, was probably an import from the volcanic areas of coastal Etruria or Campania. Cat. 34 seems part of the range of unslipped wares exported from these areas during the early Imperial period, while cat. 35, though of slightly unusual form, appears to be from the same workshops. Although these Tyrrhenian coast imports are present in the deposit, not a single sherd of Pompeian red ware, with its distinctive red finish, was found. This may indicate a decline in the output of the Pompeian red ware workshops, in which case the continuity of the unslipped wares is interesting.

The jars in the deposit divide into two main types; those with coarse fabrics and traces of burning, such as cat. 36 and 38, used for the preparation of food and liquids, and those with finer, levigated fabrics such as cat. 37 and 39, used presumably for storage and serving. Nearly all pieces are of a high potting standard, with even large, bulky vessels such as cat. 36a being evenly and (for coarse-ware) thinly walled.

Cat. 36a and 38a appear to have been used in on-hearth cooking or heating, the concentration of burning on the side opposite the handle indicating that the vessels were pushed directly into the flames or embers. Vessels from second-century deposits at Matrice (Roberts 1988: 112-13) and San Giacomo degli Schiavoni, Molise (Roberts 1993: 193) bear identical patterns of burning, suggesting their use in similar contexts. This method of slow, on-hearth cooking, using a terracotta pot (often the two-handled *pignatta*) can still be seen today in parts of Italy.

Cat. 37a, in a levigated fabric, with its wide mouth and double handles, was probably used for storage of foodstuffs, while cat. 39a, with its distinctive single round handle, may have been used for the short-term storage and serving of liquids.

In contrast to the general scarcity of parallels for the colour-coated vessels from the deposit, numerous comparanda have been found for the coarse-ware jars, in particular among the pottery found at Sutri (Duncan 1964). The robust cooking jar cat. 36 is very similar to Duncan's form

27, though with slightly heavier rim. Other close parallels include cat. 37 (Duncan's form 28), cat. 38 (Duncan's form 30), and cat. 39 (Duncan's form 31). As well as the local comparanda from Sutri, other parallels come from Ostia, and in particular from material found during the South Etruria field survey (Peña 1987). This implies either a broadly shared ceramic tradition in the manufacturing of pottery throughout South Etruria or a very extensive system of distribution, capable of bringing the products of a limited number of production centres to a very wide market. The latter model cannot be discounted, given the large numbers of imports which were in circulation; however, it seems likely that the bulk of the coarse-ware was produced by a number of centres broadly united by a ceramic koine. The idea of more diffuse production seems supported by evidence for manufacture at Monte Gelato. Three badly blistered and warped wasters of jars were found, similar to cat. 36a, 38a and 39a. Several other jars in the group, including cat. 36a, were heavily overfired. In view of this, and of the large numbers of very similar vessels present, it seems reasonable to propose a pottery workshop(s) at or near the site itself.

Nearly all the cooking pots found in the deposit are carinated, with broad overhanging rim and flat base (as cat. 43a). This type is commonly found in early to mid Imperial deposits throughout central and southern Italy, from Etruria (Dyson 1976: figs 42-3 and 56-7) to Campania (Cotton and Métraux 1985: figs 55-6) and Molise (Roberts 1992: figs 66 and 68). Burning on the exterior of rim and/or wall, as on cat. 43a-c, 45 and 48, indicates that they were used by being placed either directly on the hearth, or on a grille or tripod, as at the House of the Vettii, Pompeii. All of the cooking pots, even bulky pieces such as cat. 46-8, were well and evenly potted. With the exception of rims decorated with grooves (cat. 43 and 46) or cogged rouletting (cat. 43f), there were no examples of decoration. The cogging of cat. 43f suggests the piece belongs to the early-mid Imperial 'cogged ware' production, first noted by Threipland (1968) in the Ager Veientanus and Ager Faliscus, and noted elsewhere in Italy in first- and second-century contexts (Peña 1987: 211).

Cat. 43 is the most common type, extremely similar to Duncan's (1964) forms 20 and 23 from Sutri. The inclined rims of cat. 44 and 45 are quite unusual, as is the vertical handle under the rim of cat. 44, a feature unparalleled on other vessels from the site. The presence of large vessels such as cat. 46-8 implies the preparation and consumption of foodstuffs in some quantity, and may have implications for the size of the site's population. Cat. 46a-c, with their broad, rounded rims and distinctive deep grooves, are characteristic of the deposit, mirroring the situation on the South Etruria survey, where, on site 6, vessels similar to cat. 46 were the most common cooking pot form (Peña 1987: 166). Cat. 47 is unique, with its very deep, broad body. Cat. 48, with its distinctive triangular projection under the rim, and thickened inner edge, is fairly common in the deposit, this reflecting its popularity throughout much of central and northern Tyrrhenian Italy, from Ostia to Luni.

Cat. 49a-b, with their broad, shallow bodies, thickened rim and rounded base, are very different from the carinated pieces. The form may be related to pieces from Republican contexts near Sutri (Duncan 1965: form 24), where the carinated form seems to be absent until the early Imperial period, as at Cosa (Dyson 1976), where carinated pieces are absent from the 'Pottery Dump' (mid-late first century BC) but appear in '22 II' (mid-first century AD).

As with the jars, there is some evidence, in the form of kiln wasters, for local production; a near complete vessel similar to cat. 43a was found, very hard-fired and buckled into an elliptical form, while a sherd similar to cat. 46c was badly blistered and buckled, and cat. 47 was misshapen and hard-fired to the point of vitrification. Several other body sherds were found from unidentifiable cooking pots with similar firing defects.

The flagons/jugs of the deposit form a very homogeneous group, both in form and fabric. Cat. 50 may have had a broad flat base or a carinated base, leading to a ring foot as cat. 51 and 54. The two-handled flagon cat. 51 is the most common form in the group with the tall, broad neck and heavily-ribbed body also seen in cat. 52 and 54. Cat. 52 has a very unusual hollow rim and rounded handles in contrast to other handles in the group which have flattened, rectangular sections (cat. 50-2). Cat. 53 is the only jug in the group with a true pouring lip, though a drip groove was also seen on cat. 51. Several examples of cat. 54 are present, all with a thick ring foot and heavily ridged wall.

The similarity of the vessels in size and in shared diagnostic features suggests that all the flagons/jugs present in the deposit are the products of a small number of workshops, very probably only one. An example of cat. 51 was found in an underfired, crumbly fabric, implying a possibly local production centre, possibly on-site. Such production would have formed part of a shared tradition extending as far as Ostia.

Cat. 55 is widely known by the almost certainly erroneous term of 'amphora stopper'. Pavolini (1980a: 1009-12) has discussed the various interpretations of the vessel and its function, which are briefly as follows. Its use as an amphora stopper seems unlikely, given that plentiful amphorae retrieved intact from shipwrecks have as yet failed to yield a single example of the vessel used in connection with any closure device. They may conceivably have been used after the opening of the amphora, but again there is no archaeological evidence for this. Some, citing the frequent presence of the vessel in tombs, suggest that it was an unguentarium, or possibly a lamp. However, the crudeness of the vessel (and its porosity) seem to tell against these possibilities, especially given the presence of numerous colour-coated vessels and lamps of normal type in the deposit. Further suggestions include dice-cups (*frittili*), or drinking cups (*pocula*). Games involving dice were popular in the Roman world, but in surviving representations, for example from Pompeii (Ward-Perkins and Claridge 1976: no. 227), vessels such as cat. 55 are not represented. Its use as a drinking vessel would perhaps be difficult given its pointed base (damaged on cat. 55).

Cat. 56 is the only representative at Monte Gelato of a form often described as an '*incensario*' or incense-burner. Traces of burning restricted to the interior of the vessel could support such an identification, suggesting that it was used for the combustion of a commodity inside the vessel, rather than the heating of the commodity from outside. The form and decoration of the piece, and its uniformity on numerous sites of early Imperial date, suggest a specific function, but it is uncertain whether this was ritual or secular.

The large quantity of lids found, and the wide range of sizes, suggests that many of the vessels in the deposit would have been lidded. Only a small minority of the lids are in levigated fabrics, implying that the majority was used in cooking processes, on vessels such as jars and cooking pots. Cat. 57, with its triangular-sectioned rim, is by far the most common form of lid, and, as with certain jar (cat. 36)

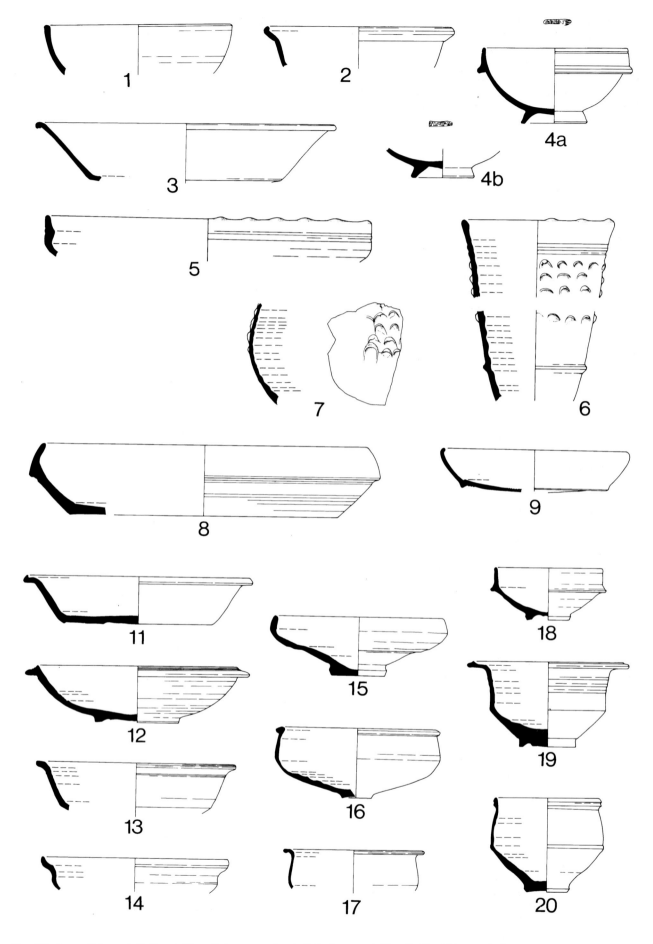

Fig. 218. Lower fish-pond: Italian sigillata (1-4), green glazed (5-7), Eastern sigillata B (8), African red slip ware (9-10), colour-coated (11-20) (1:3). *(SC)*

and cooking pot (cat. 48) types, seems to have enjoyed a very wide diffusion throughout South Etruria and Rome/Ostia. Cat. 60, illustrated here as a lid, but possibly also used as a dish, seems the only definite import. Its fabric is similar to, though a little more coarse and dark than, that of the imported cooking dishes cat. 34 and 35, and it may therefore share the same Tyrrhenian provenance. Hayes (1983: 108 and n. 31) has published examples of 'Italian baking lids' from Antonine levels at Knossos, and cited numerous parallels from the eastern Mediterranean. He has suggested an Etrurian or Campanian origin, with a possible concentration of exports in the earlier first century. The presence of examples in Group 1 (cat. 60) and Group 2 (cat. 95), however, both in a good state of preservation, suggest that export may have continued throughout, or re-started in, the early second century.

Italian sigillata

By SSC, the remains of ten vessels were found.

1. Fig. 218. Hemispherical cup. *Consp.* 36.2. Tiberian to late first century AD+.
   P4; rim D. 15 cm; fabric 32.
2. Fig. 218. Cup with straight wall and bevelled rim. *Consp.* not found.
   P2; rim D. 15 cm; fabric 31.
3. Fig. 218. Dish with sloping wall and bead rim. *Consp.* 3.2. Early/mid first to early second centuries AD.
   P3; rim D. 24 cm; fabric 31.
4. Figs 218 and 219. Hemispherical cup with short vertical rim and pronounced flange on wall. *Consp.* 34.2. Mid-first to early second centuries AD+.
   (a) P1; rim D. 11.5 cm; base D. 5 cm; H. 6 cm; fabric 32; CPRO *in planta pedis*
   C(LODIUS) PRO(CULUS) – Oxé and Comfort 1968: 158, nos. 452-4.
   (b) P5; base D. 5 cm; fabric 33;
   P.AV.PO. *in planta pedis*
   P.AV(ILLIUS) PO(?) – Oxé and Comfort 1968: 97, no. 219.
   Similar: one rim, rim D. 8 cm.

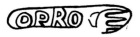 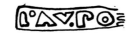

Fig. 219. Stamps on vessels 4a and 4b (x2). *(SC)*

Glazed ware

By SSC, the remains of three vessels were found.

5. Fig. 218. Dish with straight vertical upper wall and knobbed rim.
   P10; rim D. 26 cm; fabric 29.
   Cf. Ostia: Martin 1992b: fig. 3; Zevi and Carta 1987: fig. 109, nos. 82-3. Roselle: Michellucci 1985: tav. XIX, no. 27. Paphos (Cyprus): Hayes 1991: fig. XXII, no. 9.
6. Fig. 218. Beaker with tall conical body and knobbed rim. Four rows (surviving) of applied scale decoration. Above these, under rim, two rounded ridges; near base of vessel, a single, larger ridge.
   P8; rim D. 12 cm; fabric 29.
   Cf. Castelporziano: pers. obs. Rome: Carbonara and Messineo 1993: fig. 246, no. 1b (thin-walled ware).

7. Fig. 218. Closed vessel with rounded body. Three rows (surviving) of unevenly applied scale decoration.
   P11; fabric 29.
   Cf. Ostia: Martin 1992b: fig. 10.

Eastern sigillata B2

The remains of one vessel were found.

8. Fig. 218. Dish with broad, shallow body, straight wall and tall, inward curving rim. Hayes 60, second quarter of first to mid-second centuries.
   P6; rim D. 28 cm; base D. 22 cm; H. 5.5 cm; fabric 30.

African red slip ware (ARS)

By SSC, the remains of three vessels were found.

9. Fig. 218. Casserole with outward sloping wall and slightly rounded bottom, separated by a more or less pronounced ridge. Hayes 23A, early to mid second century.
   P7; rim D. 15 cm: base D. 12 cm; H. 3 cm; fabric t.s.c. 'A'.
   Similar: one rim, rim D. 16 cm.
10. (Not illustrated.) Sherd from wall of open vessel (cup/bowl) with traces of rouletting on exterior. Hayes 7-10, from *c.* 110s-80s.

Colour-coated ware

The remains of 48 vessels were found by SSC, including the unusual 'stork-vase', discussed in detail below (Murray, Parsons and Roberts, this volume).

Broadly, three main colour bands of slip were noted.

(a) Slip 1. Orange-red-brownish red (2.5YR 5/6-5/8; Munsell red, to 5YR 5/8-7/8; Munsell reddish yellow, to 7.5YR 7/8; Munsell yellow-orange).
(b) Slip 2. Brown (2.5YR 4/2; Munsell weak red, to 5YR 5/3; Munsell reddish brown, to 7.5YR 5/6; Munsell strong brown).
(c) Slip 3. Greenish brown (10YR 5/3; Munsell brown).

11. Fig. 218. Dish with broad, hooked rim, shallow body with straight wall and slightly raised foot.
    P13; rim D. 18.5 cm; base D. 12 cm; H. 3.5 cm; fabric 1; slip 1.
12. Fig. 218. Dish/bowl with flanged rim, rounded wall and ring foot.
    P19; rim D. 18 cm; base D. 6.5 cm; H. 4.5 cm; fabric 1; slip 1.
13. Fig. 218. Dish/bowl with narrow horizontal rim and carinated body.
    P27; rim D. 16 cm; fabric 1; slip 1.
14. Fig. 218. Dish/bowl with rounded, cupped rim and rounded body.
    P24; rim D. 15 cm; fabric 1; slip 2.
    Similar: two rim fragments, diameter not measurable.
15. Fig. 218. Dish with short, inturned rim, irregular rounded wall and solid bevelled foot.
    P22; rim D. 14 cm; base D. 4.5 cm; H. 4.5 cm; fabric 1; slip 1.
16. Fig. 218. Bowl with thickened, rounded rim, broad body with rounded wall and small ring foot.
    P26; rim D. 13 cm; base D. 2.5 cm; H. 5.5 cm; fabric 1; slip 1.
    Similar: four rim fragments, rim D. 10-12 cm.
    Cf. Rome: Carbonara and Messineo 1993: fig. 245, nos. 8a-d.
17. Fig. 218. Bowl with horizontal rim and broad body with rounded wall.
    P28; rim D. 11 cm; fabric 1; slip 1.

18. Fig. 218. Hemispherical cup with vertical rim, narrow flange and bevelled ring foot. Almost certainly a conscious imitation of Italian sigillata form *Consp.* 34.2.
P12; rim D. 8.5 cm; base D. 3.5 cm; H. 4 cm; fabric 1; slip 1.
Similar: four rim fragments, rim D. 8.5-12.5 cm.

19. Fig. 218. Cup/bowl with broad rim, ridged on upper surface, deep carinated body and false ring foot.
P17; rim D. 13 cm; base D. 4.5 cm; H. 6.5 cm; fabric 1; slip 2.
Cf. South Etruria survey: Peña 1987: site 6, 608, no. 3.

20. Fig. 218. Cup/bowl with double beaded rim, deep carinated body and bevelled ring foot.
P18; rim D. 8.5 cm; base D. 3.5 cm; H. 7.5 cm; fabric 1; slip 1.
Cf. Cosa: Marabini Moevs 1973: form LXIII, nos. 459-69.

21. Fig. 220. Cup/bowl with everted, ridged rim and deep, carinated body with straight upper wall. Single handle. Twelve rows of diamond rouletting on upper wall.
P36; rim D. 13 cm; fabric 1; slip 1.
Similar: one rim fragment, rim D. 13 cm.

22. Fig. 220. Cup/bowl with thickened, angular rim and straight inward sloping wall. Three rows of double oval rouletting on upper wall.
P29; fabric 1; slip 1.

23. Fig. 220. Bowl with tall, upright thickened rim and carinated body with rounded wall. Six rows of rouletting on exterior.
P32; rim D. 22 cm; fabric 1; slip 1.
Similar: three rim fragments, rim D. 18-27 cm; four base fragments, base D. 5-5.5 cm.
Cf. San Rocco: Cotton and Métraux 1985: fig. 47, no. 4. South Etruria survey: Peña 1987: site 6, 608, no. 1.

24. Fig. 220. Bowl with thickened, rounded rim and slightly rounded wall. Seven rows of rouletting on exterior.
P31; rim D. 19 cm; fabric 1; slip 2.

25. Fig. 220. Bowl with thickened rim, hooked on exterior, and rounded wall. Applied scale decoration on exterior.
P30; rim D. 24 cm; fabric 1; slip 2.
Cf. Ostia: *Ostia* III: tav. XX, no. 90; Zevi and Pohl 1970: fig. 31, no. 1, fig. 115, no. 46. Rome: Carbonara and Messineo 1993: fig. 244, no. 8a. Santa Rufina: Cotton, Wheeler and Whitehouse 1991: fig. 74, no. 17.

26. Fig. 220. Cup/beaker with everted rim, ovoid body and bevelled foot. Two rows of applied scale decoration on exterior.
P21; rim D. 7.5 cm; base D. 3 cm; H. 9 cm; fabric 1; slip 2.
Cf. Rome: Carbonara and Messineo 1993: fig. 246, no. 2a. Santa Rufina: Cotton, Wheeler and Whitehouse 1991: fig. 74, no. 24.

27. Fig. 220. Cup/beaker with everted rim, ovoid body and bevelled foot. Seven rows of closely packed rouletting on exterior.
P14; rim D. 8 cm; base D. 4.5 cm; H. 9.5 cm; fabric 1; slip 1.
Similar: four rim fragments, rim D. 7-8 cm; eight base fragments, base D. 3.5-5 cm.
Cf. Rome: Carbonara and Messineo 1993: fig. 243, no. 4.

28. Fig. 220. Beaker with tall, conical body, double beaded rim and bevelled foot.
(a) The 'stork-vase' (see below, pp. 356-66 and Figs 239-42).
(b) Eight rows of rouletting on exterior.
P16; rim D. 9 cm; base D. 4.5 cm; H. 12 cm; fabric 1; slip 3.

29. Fig. 220. Base of large bowl with bevelled ring foot and carinated body with straight lower wall. Five rows (surviving) of irregularly applied rouletting.
P33; base D. 9.5 cm; fabric 1; slip 2.

30. Fig. 220. Base of bowl with flat base and rounded, carinated body.
P23; base D. 5 cm; fabric 1; slip 2.

31. Fig. 220. Base of open form with bevelled ring foot.
P20; base D. 6.5 cm; fabric 1.
Similar: one base fragment, base D. 5 cm.

Bowls/dishes/cups
By rim count, the remains of eight vessels were found.

32. Fig. 220. Large bowl with broad rim angled downwards and carinated body with rounded shoulder and straight lower wall.
P97; rim D. 41 cm; fabric 14.
Similar: two rim fragments, rim D. 38 and 39 cm.
Cf. Rome: Staffa 1984: tav. IV, no. 61. Benghazi: Riley 1979: fig. 120, no. 801.

33. Fig. 221. Dish with tall, inturned rim, overhanging on exterior, and broad, shallow body with rounded wall and gently rounded base.
P42; rim D. 36 cm; base D. 27 cm; H. 7.5 cm; fabric 13. Burnt on exterior of rim.
Cf. Cosa: Dyson 1976: fig. 59, LS52. South Etruria survey: Peña 1987: site 6, 602, no. 10; site 13, 622, no. 18.

34. Fig. 221. Dish with inturned rim with groove on upper surface, slightly rounded wall and flat base. Ridge at edge of floor.
P37; rim D. 24 cm; base D. 18.5 cm; H. 6 cm; fabric 15. Burnt on exterior of base, wall and rim.
Similar: two rim fragments, rim D. 19 and 26 cm.
Cf. Cosa: Dyson 1976: fig. 45, 22 II 24-5. Luni: *Luni* I: tav. 73, 31 CM 2834/3; *Luni* II: tav. 131, 1 CM 4312.

35. Fig. 221. Tripod dish with flat rim and shallow body with rounded wall.
P60; rim D. 14 cm; fabric 15. Burnt on exterior of base.

Jars
Jars comprise the largest class of coarse-ware from the deposit, with the remains of 61 vessels being found by rim count.

36. Fig. 221. Jar with thickened, angular rim, tall narrow neck, ridged at base, broad ovoid body and flat base. Single handle with sub-oval section.
(a) P73; rim D. 20 cm; base D. 9.5 cm; H. 30.5 cm; fabric 13. Burnt on exterior of wall and rim opposite handle. Overfired.
Similar: six rim fragments, rim D. 15-18 cm (including waster); three base fragments, base D. 7-8.5 cm.
Cf. South Etruria survey: Peña 1987: site 1, 592, no. 7; site 6, 602, no. 8.
(b) P64; rim D. 6.5 cm; base D. 3.5 cm; H. 9.5 cm; fabric 13.
Similar: four rim fragments, rim D. 7-9 cm; two base fragments, base D. 5 and 6 cm.
Cf. Ostia: Zevi and Carta 1987: fig. 96, no. 98.
(c) P74; rim D. 13 cm; fabric 17.
Similar: three rim fragments, rim D. 14-16 cm.
Cf. Ostia: *Ostia* III: tav. LXVIII, no. 630; Zevi and Pohl 1970: fig. 87, no. 258. Rome: Carbonara and Messineo 1993: fig. 248, no. 11. South Etruria survey: Peña 1987: site 6, 600, no. 7.
Cf. (a-c) Sutri: Duncan 1964: fig. 12, nos. 103-6 (Duncan's form 27).

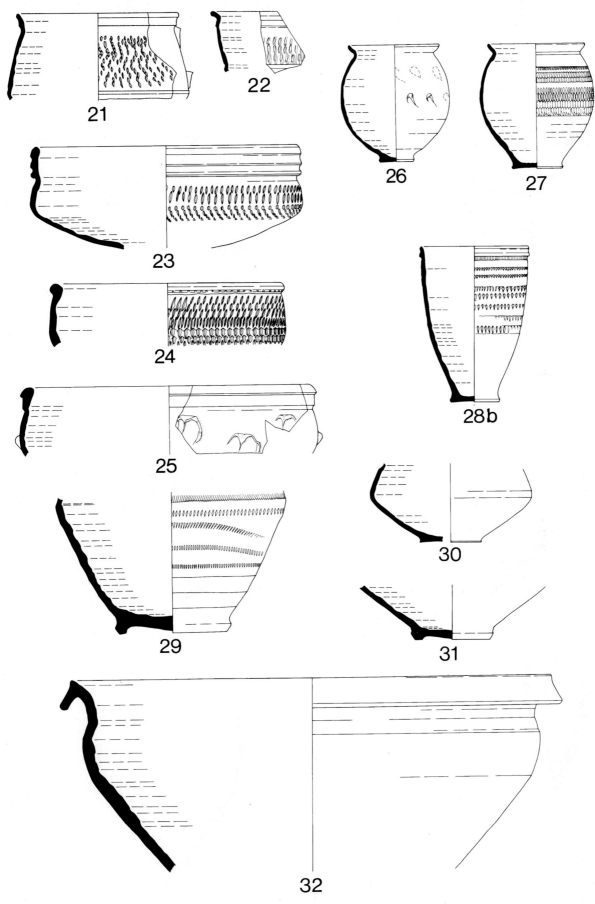

Fig. 220. Lower fish-pond fill: colour-coated (21-31), coarse-ware (32) (1:3). *(SC)*

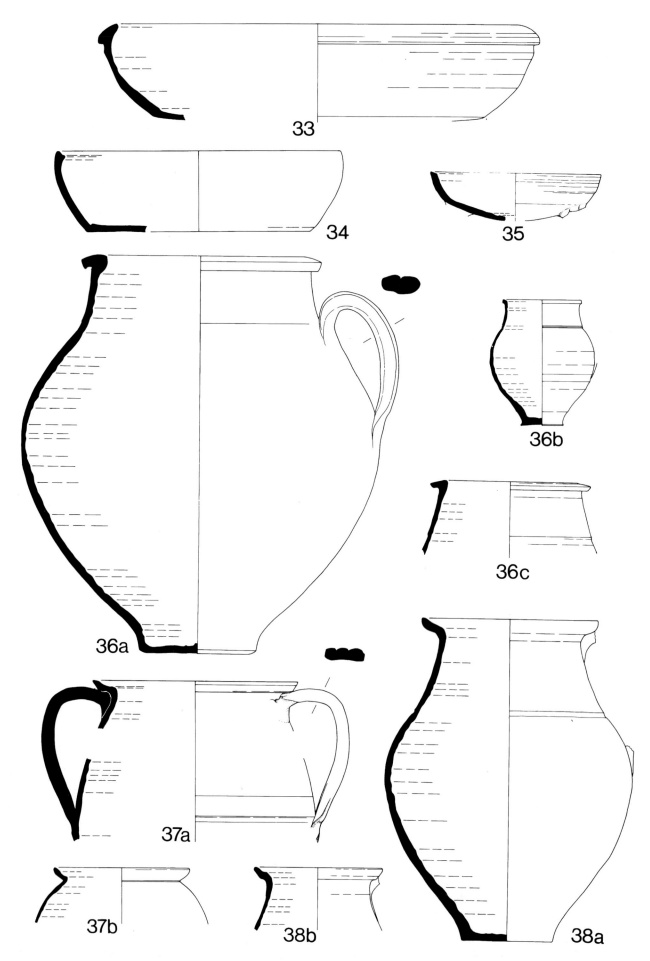

Fig. 221. Lower fish-pond fill: coarse-ware (1:3). *(SC)*

37. Fig. 221. Jar with everted rim, cupped on interior and rounded body. Two handles with broad rectangular section.
(a) P81; rim D. 17 cm; fabric 2.
Similar: three rim fragments, rim D. 17-21 cm.
Cf. Ostia: Zevi and Carta 1987: fig. 131, no. 274. South Etruria survey: Peña 1987: site 11, 618, no. 5.
(b) P70; rim D. 11 cm; fabric 13. Burnt on exterior of rim.
Cf. (a-b) Sutri: Duncan 1964: fig. 12, nos. 107-8 (Duncan's form 28).
38. Fig. 221. Jar with everted rim, ovoid body and flat base. Single handle.
(a) P67; rim D. 14 cm; base D. 7.5 cm; H. 25 cm; fabric 13. Burnt on exterior of wall and rim opposite handle.
Similar: fifteen rim fragments, rim D. 12-18 cm, including one waster; thirteen base fragments, base D. 5-7 cm.
Cf. South Etruria survey: Peña 1987: site 6, 600, no. 6.
(b) P68; rim D. 10.5 cm; fabric 13.
Similar: four rim fragments, rim D. 12-21 cm.
Cf. South Etruria survey: Peña 1987: site 9, 610, no. 2.
Cf. (a-b) Sutri: Duncan 1964: fig. 13, no. 112 (Duncan's form 30).
39. Fig. 222. Jar with horizontal rim, ovoid body and flat base. Single handle with round or rectangular section.
(a) Four grooves on exterior at shoulder.
P77; rim D. 10 cm; base D. 6 cm; H. 19.5 cm; fabric 2.
Similar: four rim fragments, rim D. 12-14 cm, including one waster; two base fragments, base D. 5 cm.
Cf. Sutri: Duncan 1964: fig. 13, no. 112 (Duncan's form 30).
(b) P79; rim D. 7 cm; fabric 2.
Similar: two rim fragments, rim D. 7 and 8 cm.
(c) (Not illustrated.) P65; rim D. 12 cm; base D. 7.5 cm; H. 25.5 cm; fabric 13. Warped, badly blistered on exterior.
40. Fig. 222. Jar with broad rim angled downwards, short neck and slightly rounded body.
P72; rim D. 18 cm; fabric 13. Burnt on exterior of rim and wall.
Cf. South Etruria survey: Peña 1987: site 1, 592, no. 9. Santa Rufina: Cotton, Wheeler and Whitehouse 1991: fig. 85, no. 13.
41. Fig. 222. Jar with everted, rounded rim and rounded body.
P71; rim D. 12 cm; fabric 13.
42. Fig. 222. Jar with everted rim and broad body.
P80; rim D. 15 cm; fabric 2.

Cooking pots

By rim count, 57 vessels were represented.
43. Fig. 222. Cooking pot with straight, broad rim, carinated body and flat base. Groove at outer edge of rim.
(a) P45; rim D. 20 cm; base D. 4.5 cm; H. 10 cm; fabric 13. Burnt on underside of base.
Similar: three rim fragments, rim D. 21-2 cm, including waster; 27 base fragments, base D. 4-7 cm.
Cf. Ostia: Zevi and Pohl 1970: fig. 86, no. 238.
(b) P44; rim D. 21 cm; fabric 13. Burnt on exterior of rim and upper and lower walls.
Similar: seventeen rim fragments, rim D. 20-8 cm.
(c) P56; rim D. 20 cm; fabric 13. Burnt on exterior of rim.
Cf. Ostia: Ostia III: tav. LIII, no. 435.
(d) P55; rim D. 19 cm; fabric 13.
Cf. Cosa: Dyson 1976: fig. 56, LS 17-19.
Cf. (a-d) Sutri: Duncan 1964: fig. 10, nos. 67-9 (Duncan's form 20).

(e) P53; rim D. 20 cm; fabric 13.
Similar: two rim fragments, diameter not measurable.
(f) (Not illustrated.) Two rows of rouletting on upper surface of rim.
P57; rim D. 26 cm; fabric 13.
Cf. Veientanus survey: Threipland 1968: 199, fig. 26, no. 2.
44. Fig. 222. Cooking pot with broad, thickened rim angled upwards. Vertical handle.
P54; rim D. 26 cm; fabric 14.
Similar: one rim fragment, rim D. 19 cm.
Cf. Ostia: Ostia I: tav. XIX, no. 391; Ostia II: tav. VIII, no. 14; Zevi and Pohl 1970: fig. 86, no. 471a.
45. Fig. 222. Cooking pot with thickened, flattened rim and shallow, carinated body with straight wall.
P40; rim D. 18 cm; fabric 13. Burnt on exterior of lower wall.
46. Figs 222-3. Cooking pot with broad, curved rim and deep carinated body with straight wall. Grooves/ridges on upper surface of rim.
(a) P43; rim D. 28.5 cm; fabric 13.
Similar: three rim fragments, rim D. 24-9 cm.
Cf. South Etruria survey: Peña 1987: site 1, 592, no. 1.
(b) P47; rim D. 26 cm; fabric 14.
Similar: seven rim fragments, rim D. 17-28 cm.
Cf. Cosa: Dyson 1976: fig. 54, LS4. Ostia: Ostia II: tav. XXVII, no. 478; Ostia III: tav. XXV, no. 138. Rome: Carbonara and Messineo 1993: fig. 248, no. 6. South Etruria survey: Peña 1987: site 13, 622, no. 4.
(c) P51; rim D. 25 cm; fabric 13.
Similar: four rim fragments, rim D. 23-6 cm, including waster.
Cf. Lugnano in Teverina: Monacchi 1990: fig. 13, no. 12. South Etruria survey: Peña 1987: site 6, 598, no. 10.
47. Fig. 223. Cooking pot with curved rim and deep body, widening towards base, with straight wall.
P48; rim D. 26.5 cm; fabric 13, almost vitrified. Waster.
Cf. South Etruria survey: Peña 1987: site 6, 598, no. 3.
48. Fig. 223. Cooking pot with broad rim, thickened and squared at junction with wall, triangular projection on underside of outer edge. Straight wall.
P46; rim D. 30 cm; fabric 13. Burnt on exterior of rim.
Similar: four rim fragments, rim D. 26-8 cm.
Cf. Gabii: Almagro-Gorbea 1982: fig. 2, no. 27. Lugnano in Teverina: Monacchi 1990: fig. 14, no. 18. Luni: Luni I: tav. 74, 12 CM2622/1; Luni II: tav. 196, 6 CS1740/1. Ostia: Pohl 1978: fig. 158, no. 223; fig. 110, no. 1601; Zevi and Carta 1987: fig. 131, no. 270b; Zevi and Pohl 1970: fig. 23, no. 8; fig. 30, no. 2; fig. 86, no. 232; fig. 117, no. 92. Rome: Cianfriglia et al. 1990: fig. 38, no. 306. South Etruria survey: Peña 1987: site 9, 610, no. 6.
49. Fig. 223. Cooking pot with heavy, rounded rim and broad shallow body with rounded base. Groove/ridge on upper part of rim.
(a) P39; rim D. 15 cm; H. 5 cm; fabric 13.
Cf. Rome: Carbonara and Messineo 1993: fig. 248, no. 6. Santa Rufina: Cotton, Wheeler and Whitehouse 1991: fig. 83, nos. 4 and 5.
(b) P38; rim D. 21 cm; fabric 13.
Cf. Cosa: Dyson 1976: fig. 55, LS12.

Flagons/jugs

By SSC, the remains of twelve vessels were found.
50. Fig. 223. Flagon with thickened, rounded rim, narrow neck and cylindrical body, widening towards base.

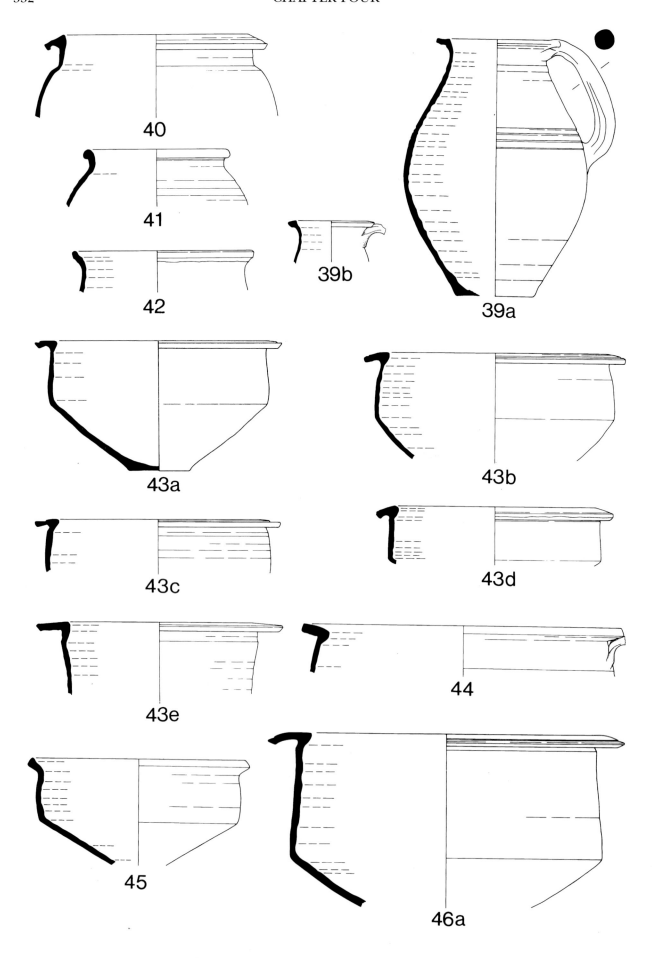

Fig. 222. Lower fish-pond fill: coarse-ware (1:3). *(SC)*

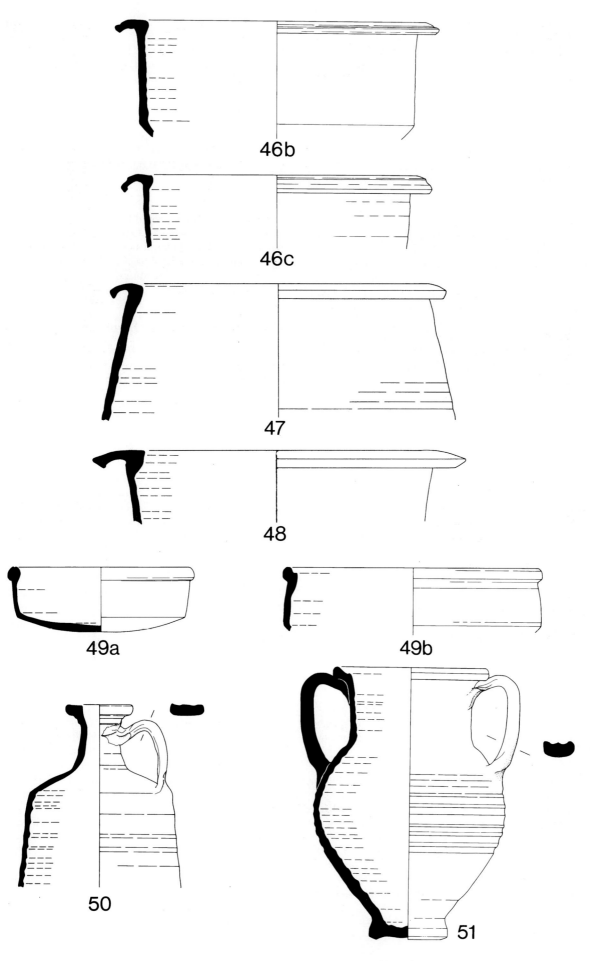

Fig. 223. Lower fish-pond fill: coarse-ware (1:3). *(SC)*

Single handle with rectangular section.
P88; rim D. 5.5 cm; fabric 2.

51. Fig. 223. Flagon with everted rim with broad groove on upper surface. Tall, broad neck and ovoid body with bevelled ring foot. Two handles with sub-oval section, bearing two deep broad grooves on upper surface. Series of ridges and grooves on body.
   P82; rim D. 12.5 cm; base D. 6.5 cm; H. 21 cm; fabric 3.
   Similar: two rim fragments, rim D. 15 and 16 cm, including one underfired; three base fragments, base D. 6.5 cm.

52. Fig. 224. Flagon with rounded, hollowed rim, tall narrow neck and rounded body. Two handles with rounded section.
   P85; rim D. 6.5 cm; fabric 3.
   Cf. Gabii: Almagro-Gorbea 1982: fig. 9, no. 141. Ostia: *Ostia* II: tav. XXI, no. 378; *Ostia* III: tav. XVII, no. 52.

53. Fig. 224. Jug with broad everted rim with pouring lip and broad groove on upper surface, tall narrow neck and broad body. Single handle with broad rectangular section and two shallow grooves on upper surface.
   P86; rim D. 7.5 cm; fabric 3.
   Similar: one rim fragment, rim D. 7 cm.
   Cf. Gabii: Almagro-Gorbea 1982: fig. 8, no. 113. Ostia: Zevi and Pohl 1970: fig. 84, nos. 168-9, fig. 109, no. 622. Rome: Carbonara and Messineo 1993: fig. 249, no. 16.

54. Fig. 224. Flagon/jug with bevelled ring foot, rounded body and tall, narrow neck. Possibly the lower part of a vessel as cat. 52.
   (a) P84; base D. 6.5 cm; fabric 3.
       Similar: three base fragments, base D. 6-8 cm.
   (b) P89; base D. 5 cm; fabric 2.

Miscellaneous

Remains of three vessels were found by SSC.

55. Fig. 224. 'Amphora stopper'. Vessel with broad, angular rim, tall narrow neck and rounded body.
   P84; rim D. 6.5 cm; fabric 3.
   Similar: one rim fragment, rim D. 5.5 cm; one base fragment.

56. Fig. 224. '*Incensario*'. Bowl with everted tripartite rim and carinated body.
   P41; rim D. 24 cm; fabric 13.
   Indented decoration on exterior of rim and carination.

Lids

By rim count, the remains of 57 lids were found.

57. Fig. 224. Lid with central knob, gently rounded body with ridged wall and everted rim with triangular-sectioned extremity.
   (a) P92; rim D. 22 cm; H. 5 cm; fabric 13.
       Similar: 32 rim fragments, rim D. 11-25 cm; fourteen knobs.
       Cf. Ostia: *Ostia* II: tav. XXVIII, no. 516. *Ostia* III: tav. XXXIV, no. 244; tav. LIX, no. 521; Pohl 1978: fig. 147, no. 84; Zevi and Carta 1987: fig. 131, no. 254; Zevi and Pohl 1970: fig. 87, no. 274. Rome: Cianfriglia *et al.* 1990: fig 33, nos. 164 and 166; fig. 46, no. 606. Santa Rufina: Cotton, Wheeler and Whitehouse 1991: fig. 87, no. 2. South Etruria survey: Peña 1987: site 6, 604, nos. 2 and 6.
   (b) P96; rim D. 20 cm; fabric 13.

58. Fig. 224. Lid with pinched knob, conical body and bevelled rim.
   P93; rim D. 12 cm; H. 3.5 cm; fabric 13.

Similar: fourteen rim fragments, rim D. 10-19 cm; four knobs.
Cf. South Etruria survey: Peña 1987: site 6, 604, no. 1.

59. Fig. 224. Lid with raised, rounded knob and flat body with thickened, rounded rim.
   P94; rim D. 13 cm; H. 1.5 cm; fabric 2.
   Similar: six rim fragments, rim D. 15-26 cm.

60. Fig. 224. Lid/dish with flattened top, rounded wall and thickened, rounded rim.
   P95; rim D. 23 cm; H. 2 cm; fabric 19.
   Cf. Cosa: Dyson 1976: fig. 60, LS57.

Bases

Excluding bases which could be attributed to vessels similar to those above, remains of four bases were found.

61. Fig. 224. Base of closed storage vessel (for liquids?) with ring foot with central *omphalos* and straight wall.
   P91; base D. 7.5 cm; fabric 2.
   Similar: three base fragments, base D. 6-7 cm.

Group 2 – L105 (upper fill of fish-pond) (Fig. 217)

Group 2 comprises material from the upper fill of the fish-pond. Although some joins were found between Groups 1 and 2, the numbers involved are very small – two lamps (Bailey, this volume) and one colour-coated piece – and may indicate post-deposition processes. Excluding amphorae, lamps and glass, the remains of at least 116 vessels were found by SSC. Imported fine-wares, almost exclusively ARS suggest a date for the assemblage of the 170s-90s AD, a date substantiated by the lamps, amphorae and glass.

In contrast to Group 1, the fine-ware in Group 2 consists almost entirely of ARS: the only exception is a small group of Italian sigillata. It is noteworthy that Italian sigillata still constitutes approximately ten per cent of assemblages in Ostia in the later second century (Martin 1992b: fig. 5).

The probability that cat. 62 is residual seems lessened by its good state of preservation (over 80 per cent of the rim is preserved). In addition, the form *Consp.* 34 is one of the latest forms in Italian sigillata production and it is quite possible that examples would still have been in circulation in South Etruria in this period. The form, with its thick heavy wall and flanged rim, bears a close resemblance to Hayes form 3 in Candarli ware (Hayes 1972: 320-1), though close examination of the fabric of the piece failed to reveal any large flakes of golden mica, one of the main distinguishing features of the ware (Hayes 1972: 316).

The assemblage of ARS from Group 2 seems homogeneous, with no piece necessarily residual or intrusive, and suggests a date for the deposit in the 170s-90s AD. Hayes 35 (cat. 69), though in fabric t.s.c. 'A'/'C' and dated by Hayes (1972) to the first half of the third century, is found in later second-century levels at Lambaesis (J.W. Hayes, pers. comm.), and does not therefore pose problems for the later second-century date proposed for Group 2.

The ARS is evenly divided between table-ware and cooking-ware. The table-ware includes Hayes 8A (cat. 63), 8B (cat. 64), 9A (cat. 65), 9B (cat. 66), 14A (cat. 67) and 16 (cat. 68), among the commonest ARS forms of this period. Less common are the closed form (cat. 70) and the deep bowl/dish Hayes 35 (cat. 69).

The ARS cooking-ware presents a range of casseroles, Hayes 23A (cat. 72), 23B (cat. 73), 183/4 (cat. 71) and 197 (cat. 74), and lids/dishes, Hayes 22 (cat. 75), 182 (cat. 76) and 196A (cat. 77). Hayes 23 is present in both the smaller version, also seen in Group 1 (cat. 9), and the larger vessel

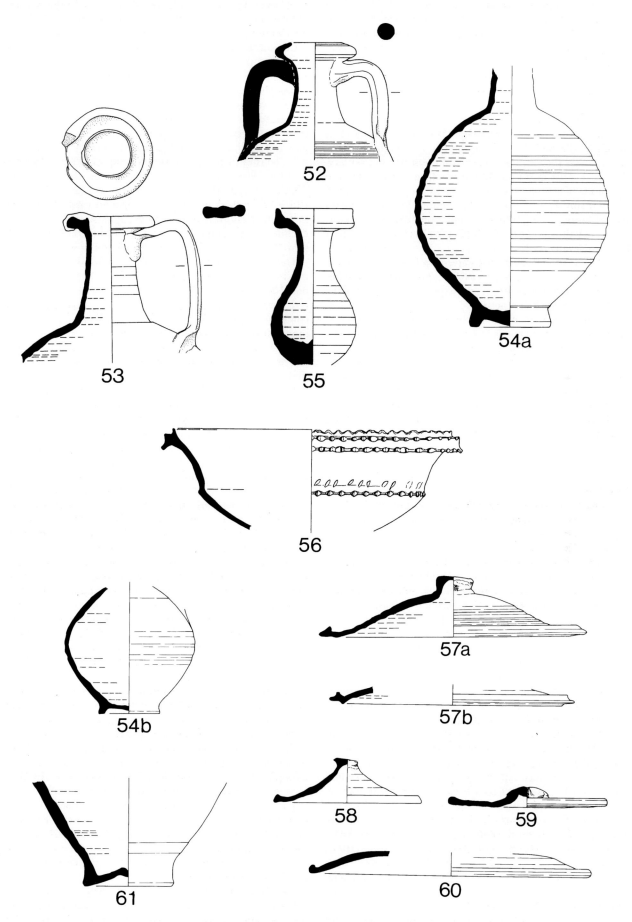

Fig. 224. Lower fish-pond fill: coarse-ware (1:3). *(SC)*

23B (cat. 72). I have suggested elsewhere (Cubberley, Lloyd and Roberts 1988: 114) that ARS form 23 may be an example of a baking cover or *clibanus/testum*: whilst this theory is as yet unproven, the absence of coarse-ware *clibani/testa* at Monte Gelato is noteworthy.

In Group 1, ARS forms only eighteen per cent of imported fine-ware, a figure somewhat lower than that found in contemporary deposits at Ostia (Martin 1992b: figs 3 and 4); yet the overwhelming predominance of ARS in the fine-ware assemblage in Group 2 (93 per cent) reveals the extent to which ARS had flooded the market. Although it is difficult to assess the relative values of different types of pottery, the size and variety of the ARS assemblage suggests that the site's inhabitants had the ability to gain access to and could afford quantities of the ware. This implies close contact with the marketing systems which brought pottery from the ports, almost certainly via Ostia, Rome and the Via Cassia/Amerina or Via Flaminia.

The total absence of glazed ware from Group 2 supports, perhaps, Martin's suggestion (1992b: 326) that the main floruit of the ware's production and export was in the Hadrianic and early Antonine periods.

The total number of colour-coated vessels in Group 2 is almost exactly the same as in Group 1, though in a slightly smaller range of forms. The standard of potting is noticeably lower than that of Group 1 pieces, with forms heavier, less evenly walled and poorly finished. It is interesting to note that the colour-coated ware from Group 2, whilst not yielding any evidence for on-site production, none the less attests a still vibrant local production, both of thin-walled finer table vessels, and larger, heavier forms.

Cat. 78 seems likely to have been used, along with the larger bowls cat. 90a-c and 91, as serving vessels for quantities of foodstuffs or liquids, whereas the other vessels seem to have been for individual consumption. Cat. 79 bears a close resemblance to the Italian sigillata form *Consp.* 34.2, a form also imitated in Group 1 (cat. 18). This strengthens the case for continuing popularity of the form, already suggested by the presence of cat. 62.

The carinated cups/bowls cat. 81-2 may be distantly related to cat. 19 in Group 1, though cat. 81-2 are less finely potted. Closer parallels are perhaps to be found between cat. 83 and 16, and cat. 84 and 20, indicating a degree of continuity in the ceramic tradition. Further continuity is shown by the group of large rouletted bowls cat. 90-1, a form which first appeared in Group 1 (cat. 23). The examples from Group 2, however, are generally larger, and were less well executed, with thick walls and crude rouletting and finishing. It is this less refined tradition that seems most evident on other sites throughout South Etruria and Rome/Ostia.

Some new forms were noted, such as the shallow dish cat. 85a, with its clumsy thick base and thick wall, and the ovoid jar/beaker cat. 87. This is one of the commonest colour-coated forms, but, with its uneven wall and poor colour-coat, compares very unfavourably with the well executed and finished beakers of Group 1 (for example, cat. 27).

Another new form is cat. 88, the ridged neck beaker, *boccalino/urnetta a collarino*, a common find in contexts of the later first to mid-third centuries (Marabini Moevs 1973: form LXVIII, pl. 46, 85, nos. 431-3 and pp. 237-8; Hayes 1983: 109; Garcea, Miraglia and Soricelli 1985: 262-3; *Ostia* I: tav. LXI, nos. 792-840 and pp. 65-7, nos. 143-9; Roberts 1992: 179). Many more bases (thirteen) than rims (two) similar to cat. 88 were found, suggesting that differing rims (cat. 87 perhaps) had the same base form. This would strengthen the argument for a limited number of workshops and/or potters. Cat. 89 was probably used either as a baby/invalid feeder, or as a lamp-filler, though the porosity of the vessel makes the latter suggestion less likely (D. Bailey, pers. comm.).

Certain forms which are common in Group 1 are absent from Group 2, in particular the range of broad dishes (cat. 11-14), the fine decorated ovoid beakers (cat. 26-7) and the *pelargos* beaker (cat. 28). In terms of decoration, rouletting was still widely used, especially on the larger bowls (cat. 90-3), but in general was more crude and less well impressed than on the earlier pieces. The slip, too, is generally thin, dull and patchily applied. Less care had been taken to hide the effects of firing, with several examples of cat. 88 and 90 showing clear ring-like stacking marks on the lower wall. Combined with the generally lower standard of potting (thick bases, thick and uneven walls and rims) in comparison with Group 1 vessels, this might suggest a general decline in the standards of ceramic production in the workshop(s) supplying colour-coated ware to the site.

The presence of the Pompeian red ware dishes is one of the more striking features of Group 2. First discussed in detail by Goudineau (1970) and Peacock (1977), Pompeian red ware, or internal red slipped cook-ware (Peña 1990), comprises a range of broad, shallow dishes and, less commonly, lids. It is characterized by the volcanic inclusions of its coarse fabric, and the application to the interior of the vessels of a thick red slip, which probably served as a non-stick cooking surface.

Mineralogical analysis of the ware indicates an origin in the areas of volcanic geology on the Tyrrhenian coast, in particular the bay of Naples, northern Campania and South Etruria (Peacock 1977: 179). Peña (1990), on the basis of his work on material from Cetamura in northern Etruria, has suggested a further point of origin in that area, characterized by a dense, coarse fabric but with non-volcanic inclusions.

Pompeian red ware, in production seemingly from the second century BC, was exported from the first century BC and enjoyed widespread distribution throughout the Mediterranean and beyond (Peacock 1977). The absence of the ware from Group 1, despite the wealth and variety of imported pottery in the deposit, may be useful in establishing a *terminus ante quem* for the end of this first, major period of the ware's popularity.

The presence in Group 2 of five vessels, whose condition and degree of preservation strongly suggest that they are unlikely to be residual, is therefore very interesting. It implies that in some areas there was a continuity or, rather, a resurgence in the manufacture and popularity of the ware in the mid to late second century. Such a resurgence has, in fact, been proposed by Hayes (1983: 108), who has noted quantities of this ware, with its less coarse fabric and slightly darker slip, in Antonine and later contexts on several sites including Knossos, Paphos (Cyprus) and Luni. The quantity of the ware in Group 2, contrasting with its total absence in Group 1, implies the return of the ware onto the markets serving Monte Gelato from the mid-second century.

The bowls/dishes are evenly divided between those in coarse fabrics, for use in cooking, and those in levigated fabrics, for serving. The standard of potting, in particular of cat. 97, is good.

Cat. 95 is in the same gritty fabric as cat. 60 in Group 1 and both pieces seem to belong to a class of (Tyrrhenian) Italian baking lids/dishes dating to the early Imperial period (Hayes 1983: 108). The good state of preservation of both pieces implies that manufacture and export of the ware could have continued well into the second century, and may be linked to the presence of Pompeian red ware in Group 2.

The baking dish cat. 96, with its thin flat base and thickened, inturned rim, may mark the first appearance of a form which, with some modifications, remained common into the late Imperial period (cat. 127 and 165). Cat. 97 continued the form and presumably the function of cat. 32 and shows a similar range of parallels throughout the eastern/central Mediterranean in the early Empire. Its very close parallel with the form of the glazed ware vessel from Ostia emphasizes the koine of ceramic tradition that existed in the area in the early to mid Imperial period.

Comparatively few jars were found in Group 2, less than one third of the total in the earlier group. Jars in coarse fabrics, bearing evidence of use in cooking are particularly scarce; only two were found, compared with over 30 (more than half the jar group) in Group 1.

The cooking pots of Group 2 show very considerable change, both in quantity and quality, from those in Group 1, and pose some interesting problems. From being the second largest class of coarse-ware in Group 1, with 57 vessels representing some 29 per cent of the total assemblage, only three were definitely identified in Group 2 (less than three per cent of the total). There may have been a wholesale rejection of terracotta cooking vessels in favour of metal, but the precedent set by earlier and later deposits shows little support for this hypothesis. Cooking vessels in ARS may have made up some of the shortfall, but the addition of six or seven ARS casseroles still fails to bring the representation of cooking pots up to anything near its former level.

The few cooking pots found are fairly similar in form. All share a broad flange with a sharp (cat. 101) or less accentuated (cat. 102) underhang on the rim, and appear to have a fairly broad carinated body. Cat. 101 seems to be derived from cat. 48 and enjoyed a similarly widespread diffusion (above) from Rome/Ostia, through South Etruria and as far as Luni. Cat. 102, though seemingly less common, is still part of the tradition of broad rimmed flanged cooking pots, though its distinctive sharp bead on the inner edge of the rim seems to mark it out from earlier pieces.

Other differences are apparent. The bodies of the vessels, though carinated, are much more rounded, and the lines less clear than on earlier examples. The grooved decoration of cat. 101 is absent from vessels in Group 1, as is the ridged and grooved carination of cat. 102. No trace was found of very large vessels similar to those present in Group 1 (cat. 46-8).

Cat. 98a-b, given their pair of vertical handles, the lack of traces of burning on cat. 98a and the small size of cat. 98b, have been classified here as jars. However, given their similarity to an unusual cooking pot from Group 1 (cat. 44), they may conceivably have been cooking pots, thereby lessening still further the representation of jars in the deposit. Cat. 99, though similar in form to cat. 98, was in a fine, levigated fabric and was probably used at table (though its essentially unstable rounded base is noteworthy). As with some of the colour-coated pieces in Group 2, such as cat. 88 and 90, cat. 99 bears a circular firing stack mark around its base. Cat. 100, though thin-walled, appears to have been used in cooking, as does a small, coarse-ware *boccalino a collarino* (not illustrated) similar to cat. 88.

No examples were found in the deposit of the coarse-ware jars cat. 36 and 38, which, seemingly current from the early Empire, so characterize the Group 1 assemblage. Even given that, Group 2 does not seem to present the wide range of coarse vessels seen in Group 1, and the complete absence of any trace of these previously very common forms suggests a change, possibly a substantial change, in the local ceramic tradition.

Not usually one of the larger classes of pottery in deposits of any given period, the flagons/jugs of Group 2 form the second largest class of coarse-ware. Nearly all the vessels in this class are in levigated fabrics, the only exception being cat. 103, the only trefoil jug in the group. Cat. 103 was also notable for its graceful shape, quite unusual among coarse-ware pieces in the deposit. The two-handled flagon cat. 104 continues an idea seen in Group 1 (cat. 52), though with differing rim and handles, while cat. 107 (though preserving no trace of a handle) was very similar to cat. 51 from Group 1. The most common form of the class, cat. 106, however, has no parallel in Group 1. Cat. 105 was striking, with its unusual cylindrical body and slashed cordon decoration. The ribbed decoration on cat. 104 and 107 recalls similar decoration on pieces in Group 1 (cat. 51 and 54a), and there is some similarity in the handle forms (though the round handle of cat. 52 has disappeared).

The mortarium, cat. 108, with its distinctive fabric, may not, unlike the majority of coarse vessels in the group, have been produced locally. Given its pocked and weathered underside it may also be residual. Cat. 109 seems part of a tradition, widespread throughout the Mediterranean, of large cylindrical or conical vessels, usually in levigated fabrics. I have suggested elsewhere (Roberts 1992: 82-3) that these were containers for human waste; Hayes (1983: 109), on the basis of earlier finds at Knossos and elsewhere, had earlier suggested '... a portable container for urine, vomit and the like – a necessary appendage to dinner parties such as one envisages at the villa'. Such vessels would no doubt have been equally useful in this period at Monte Gelato, where, even if the *symposia* suggested by the 'stork-vase' of Group 1 were a thing of the past, the consumption of wine, as evidenced by the quantity of drinking vessels and amphorae found, was still a popular activity.

The very small size of the lid sample (two examples) makes any conclusions extremely tentative, especially in view of the fact that both pieces were very poorly preserved, and therefore possibly residual. In this case the complete lack of identifiable, non-residual lids is very striking and adds weight to the idea of a separate dumping area for kitchen waste, including vessels such as cooking pots and jars which were likely to have been lidded.

Cat. 111, with its broadly flaring wall, might belong to a cooking pot similar to cat. 101-2 or the wide-mouthed vessel cat. 98. Cat. 112 seems similar to cat. 100 or other round-bodied jars. The ribbing on cat. 113 suggests that it may belong to a vessel similar to cat. 107, though the disappearance of the ring foot base which had been common in Group 1 is noteworthy.

One hypothesis to explain the sharply diminished quantities of coarse-ware in Group 2 compared with Group 1 involves a decrease in the scale of food preparation and consumption on the site, and, by implication, a decrease in population. The quantities of fine-ware and amphorae, however, which are broadly consistent with quantities found in Group 1, seem to argue against this, and instead lend weight to the idea of a separate dumping area for kitchen refuse. A likely candidate for this area is the fill of the rock-cut road (below), which contains much material contemporary with Groups 1 and 2.

Italian sigillata

By SSC, the remains of two vessels were found.

62. (Not illustrated.) Hemispherical cup with pronounced flange. *Consp.* 34.2. Mid-late first century+.
P135; rim D. 10 cm; fabric 31.
Similar: one body sherd.

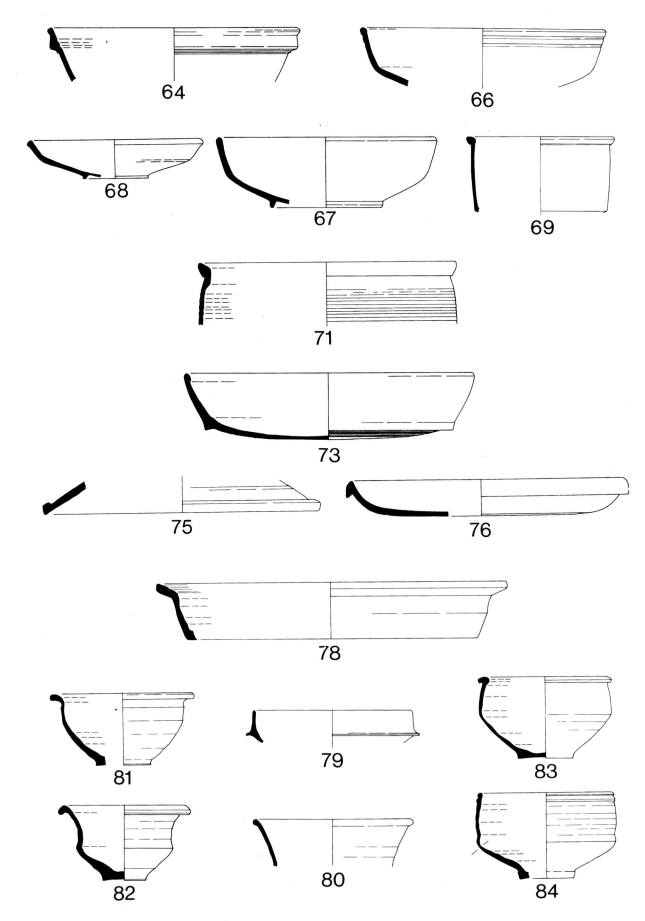

Fig. 225. Upper fish-pond fill: African red slip (64-76), colour-coated (78-84) (1:3). *(SC)*

African red slip ware

By SSC, the remains of 26 vessels were found.

63. (Not illustrated.) Carinated bowl with straight, flaring wall, sloping floor and small ring foot. Large convex moulding below rim, two grooves on outside. Rouletted decoration on moulding and above and below decoration. Hayes 8A, *c*.110-80s.
    P126; rim D. 19 cm; fabric t.s.c. 'A'.

64. Fig. 225. Bowl with heavy convex moulding below rim, with small ridge below. Two grooves on interior. Moulding undecorated. Hayes 8B, *c*. 160s-210/20.
    P127; rim D. 21 cm; fabric t.s.c. 'A'.

65. (Not illustrated.) Carinated bowl with curved body, rounded rim and small ring foot. Two grooves on outside below rim. Hayes 9A, *c*. 110-80s.
    P128; rim D. 20 cm; fabric t.s.c. 'A'.
    Similar: one rim fragment, rim D. 18 cm.

66. Fig. 225. Bowl with curved body and plain rim. Two grooves on outside below rim. Undecorated. Hayes 9B, *c*.160s-210/20.
    P129; rim D. 20 cm; fabric t.s.c. 'A'.

67. Fig. 225. Bowl with straight, sloping wall, sloping floor and small, low ring foot. Hayes 14A, mid-second century.
    P125; rim D. 18 cm; base D. 9 cm; H. 6 cm; fabric t.s.c. 'A'.
    Similar: one rim fragment, diameter 16 cm.

68. Fig. 225. Dish with low, flaring wall, sloping floor and small low ring foot. Hayes 16, 150-200+.
    P124; rim D. 15 cm; base D. 5.5 cm; H. 3 cm; fabric t.s.c. 'A'.

69. Fig. 225. Bowl with high vertical wall and thickened horizontal rim. Hayes 35, later second to first half of third century.
    P130; rim D. 12 cm; fabric t.s.c. 'A'/'C'.

70. (Not illustrated.) Handle from medium-sized closed vessel.
    P132; fabric t.s.c. 'A'.

71. Fig. 225. Casserole with everted rounded rim, squared and thickened on inner edge. Slightly rounded wall, ridged on interior. Hayes 183/184 variant?, second or third century.
    P120; rim D. 21 cm; fabric t.s.c. 'A'.

72. (Not illustrated.) Casserole with outward sloping wall and slightly rounded bottom separated by a flange. Hayes 23A, early-mid second century.
    P118; rim D. 18 cm; fabric t.s.c. 'A'.
    Similar: one rim fragment, rim D. 20 cm.

73. Fig. 225. Casserole with outward sloping wall and slightly rounded bottom, separated by a pronounced flange. The bottom is covered with fine grooves. Internally thickened rim. Hayes 23B, mid second-early third centuries.
    P117; rim D. 24 cm; base D. 20 cm; H. 5 cm; fabric t.s.c. 'A'.
    Similar: one body sherd, max. D. 19 cm.

74. (Not illustrated.) Casserole with heavy convex rim moulding with small hollowing to receive lid, vertical wall and rounded bottom. Series of small grooves and ridges on underside and interior of wall. Hayes 197, late second to mid-third centuries.
    P122; rim D. 23 cm; fabric t.s.c. 'A'.
    Similar: two rim fragments, rim D. 17 and 26 cm: one body sherd, max. D. 26 cm.

75. Fig. 225. Lid with thickened, rounded rim and domed body. Hayes 22, early-mid second century.
    P146; rim D. 23 cm; fabric t.s.c. 'A'.

76. Fig. 225. Lid/dish with thickened, hooked rim, curved on outer surface, curved wall and flat base. Hayes 182, second half of second to first half of third century.
    P121; rim D. 22.5 cm; base D. 13.5 cm; H. 3 cm; fabric t.s.c. 'A'.
    Similar: one rim fragment, rim D. 26 cm.

77. (Not illustrated.) Lid with thickened rim, convex on outside and fairly high conical domed body. Hayes 196A, mid-second to mid-third centuries.
    P119; rim D. 26 cm; fabric t.s.c. 'A'.
    Similar: three rim fragments, rim D. 16-26 cm.

Colour-coated ware

By rim count, the remains of 46 vessels were found.

As in Group 1, the slip on the colour-coated vessels in Group 2 is generally dull, thin and patchily applied. Variations in slip colour are equally common in Group 2, and four main bands of colour were noted.

(a) Slip 1. Orange/orange-red/brownish red (2.5YR 6/8; Munsell light red to 5YR 6/8; Munsell reddish yellow to 7.5YR 7/6; Munsell reddish yellow).

(b) Slip 2. Brown (5YR 5/6; Munsell yellowish red to 7.5YR 5/4; Munsell brown).

(c) Slip 3. Grey/green-brown (10YR 4/1; Munsell dark grey to 10YR 6/2; Munsell light brownish grey).

(d) Slip 4. Purple/reddish grey/reddish brown (2.5YR 5/1; Munsell not given to 2.5YR 6/4; Munsell light reddish brown).

78. Fig. 225. Dish with thickened rectangular rim angled upwards, straight wall and flat base.
    P139; rim D. 28.5 cm; base D. 24 cm; H. 4.5 cm; fabric 5; slip 3.

79. Fig. 225. Dish/bowl with upright rim and small flange.
    P145; rim D. 13 cm; fabric 5; slip 1.

80. Fig. 225. Dish/bowl with thickened rounded rim and curved wall.
    P146; rim D. 13 cm; fabric 5; slip 2.
    Similar: one rim fragment, rim D. 12 cm.

81. Fig. 225. Cup/bowl with everted thickened rim, hemispherical body and thick, flat foot.
    P138; rim D. 12 cm; base D. 4.5 cm; H. 6 cm; fabric 5; slip 2.
    Cf. Rome: Carbonara and Messineo 1993: fig. 248, no. 7.

82. Fig. 225. Cup/bowl with thickened overhanging rim, carinated body with concave upper wall and slightly hollowed flat base.
    P136; rim D. 11 cm; base D. 3.5 cm; H. 6 cm; fabric 5; slip 1.
    Similar: one profile, D. 11.5 cm.

83. Fig. 225. Cup/bowl with thickened rounded rectangular rim, carinated body and slightly hollowed flat base.
    P143; rim D. 11 cm; base D. 4.5 cm; H. 6 cm; fabric 5; slip 1.

84. Fig. 225. Cup/bowl with double beaded rim and carinated body with vertical upper wall and bevelled flat base.
    P142; rim D. 11 cm; base D. 4.5 cm; H. 7 cm; fabric 4; slip 3.
    Similar: one base fragment, base D. 3 cm.

85. Fig. 226. Dish/bowl with overhanging broad rim, conical body with straight wall and thick bevelled false ring foot.
(a) Seven rows of rouletting on exterior.
    P156; rim D. 21 cm; base D. 6 cm; H. 6 cm; fabric 7; slip 2.
(b) P140; rim D. 17 cm; fabric 5; slip 4.

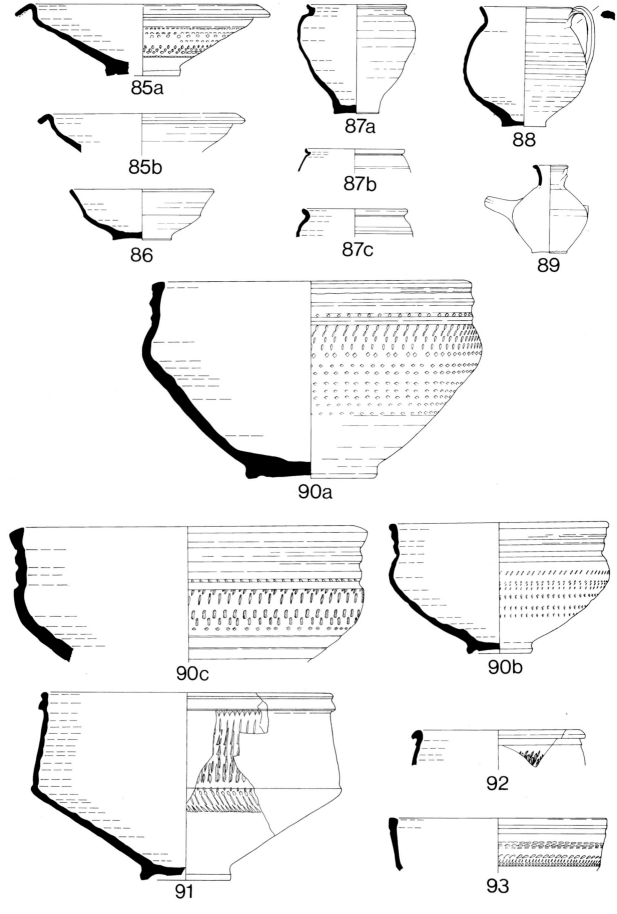

Fig. 226. Upper fish-pond fill: colour-coated (1:3). *(SC)*

86. Fig. 226. Cup/bowl with flaring carinated body and slightly hollowed flat base.
    P137; rim D. 12 cm; base D. 4.5 cm; H. 4 cm; fabric 5; slip 1.
87. Fig. 226. Cup/beaker with small, cupped rim, irregular ovoid body tapering towards simple flat base.
(a) P153; rim D. 8 cm; base D. 3.5 cm; H. 8.5 cm; fabric 6; slip 4.
(b) P152; rim D. 8 cm; fabric 4; slip 1.
    Similar: four rim fragments, rim D. 9-10 cm.
(c) P149; rim D. 9 cm; fabric 5; slip 4.
    Similar: one rim fragment, rim D. 9 cm.
88. Fig. 226. 'Boccalino/urnetta a collarino'. Cup/beaker with tall, everted rim underlined by rounded ridge or 'collar', spherical body and slightly hollowed flat base. Single handle with irregular section.
    P144; rim D. 7.5 cm; base D. 3.5 cm; H. 9.5 cm; fabric 6; slip 1.
    Similar: two rim fragments, rim D. 6 and 7 cm; thirteen base fragments, base D. 3-4 cm.
89. Fig. 226. Baby feeder? Closed vessel with narrow, beaded rim, tall narrow neck and spherical body with flat base. Long, narrow spout and single handle (missing).
    P151; rim D. 3 cm; base D. 3 cm; H. 7 cm; fabric 4; slip 2.
90. Fig. 226. Large bowl with vertical/slightly everted thickened rim bearing two or three ridges and grooves on exterior, carinated body rounded at carination, with ring foot. Rouletted decoration on exterior.
(a) Thirteen bands of rouletting on exterior.
    P158; rim D. 26.5 cm; base D. 11 cm; H. 16 cm; fabric 6; slip 1.
    Similar: three rim fragments, rim D. 23-8 cm; one base fragment, base D. 11 cm.
(b) Six bands of rouletting on exterior.
    P157; rim D. 18 cm; base D. 5.5 cm; H. 10 cm; fabric 4; slip 3.
    Similar: six rim fragments, rim D. 16-19 cm.
(c) Five bands of rouletting on exterior.
    P159; rim D. 29.5 cm; fabric 4; slip 1.
    Similar: two rim fragments, rim D. 27 and 31 cm.
Cf. (a-c) Ostia: Ostia I: tav. XIII, nos. 281-3. Rome: Staffa 1984: 116, tav. II, nos. 46-50; tav. III, nos. 51-8; tav. IV, nos. 59-60. San Rocco: Cotton and Métraux 1985: fig. 47, no. 4. South Etruria survey: Peña 1987: site 6, 608, nos. 1 and 2; site 9, 614, no. 4; 616, nos. 8 and 9.
91. Fig. 226. Bowl with thickened, double beaded rim, carinated body with straight wall and bevelled ring foot. Numerous bands of rouletting on exterior.
    P154; rim D. 24 cm; base D. 7.5 cm; H. 15 cm; slip 4.
    Similar: one base fragment, base D. 8 cm.
92. Fig. 226. Bowl with thickened, rounded overhanging rim, underlined by ridges on exterior and rounded wall. Four bands (surviving) of rouletting on exterior.
    P162; rim D. 14 cm; fabric 7; slip 2.
    Similar: one rim fragment, rim D. 26 cm.
93. Fig. 226. Bowl with thickened, squared rim and carinated body with straight upper wall. Two bands (surviving) of multiple rouletting on exterior.
    P161; rim D. 18 cm; fabric 6.

Pompeian red ware
By rim count, the remains of five vessels were found.
94. Fig. 227. Dish with curved wall and flat base. Ridge at base of wall.

(a) P223; rim D. 38 cm; base D. 32.5 cm; H. 5.5 cm; fabric 21.
    Similar: three profiles, D. 33-4 cm.
(b) P202; rim D. 19 cm; base D.16 cm; H. 3 cm; fabric 22.

Bowls/dishes/cups
By SSC, the remains of six vessels were found.
95. Fig. 227. Dish/lid with thickened rounded rim, thick rounded wall and flat base.
    P206; rim D. 36 cm; base D. 24 cm; H. 3 cm; fabric 19.
96. Fig. 227. Dish with thickened, rounded inturned rim, straight flaring wall and flat base.
    P226; rim D. 36.5 cm; base D. 28.5 cm; H. 7 cm; fabric 18.
    Very burnt on interior of base, exterior of wall and base.
    Similar: one base fragment, base D. 24 cm.
    Cf. Lugnano in Teverina: Monacchi 1990: fig. 15, nos. 29-30. Luni: Luni I: tav. 75, 19 CM1407; Luni II: tav. 269, nos. 17, 18 and 21.
97. Fig. 227. Bowl/basin with everted, thickened rim and carinated body, rounded at carination, with slightly rounded lower wall and bevelled ring foot.
    P205; rim D. 26 cm; base D. 12 cm; H. 17 cm; fabric 4.
    Similar: two base fragments, base D. 10 and 11 cm.
    Cf. Ostia: Martin 1992b: fig. 2 (in glazed ware).

Jars
By SSC, the remains of eighteen vessels were found.
98. Fig. 227. Wide-mouthed jar with broad rim angled upwards and slightly rounded wall. Vertical handle(s) with sub-rectangular section, joining immediately below rim.
(a) P233; rim D. 24 cm; fabric 19.
(b) P234; rim D. 11 cm; fabric 20. Burnt on exterior of rim and wall.
    Cf. (a-b) Rome: Quilici 1990: fig. 94, nos. 81 and 86.
99. Fig. 227. Jar with everted rim and carinated body with ridged wall and rounded base. Two vertical handles with rectangular section.
    P150; rim D. 13 cm; H. c. 15 cm; fabric 5.
    Cf. Ostia: Ostia III: tav. XIX, no. 80. Rome: Carbonara and Messineo 1993: fig. 247, no. 5.; Cianfriglia et al. 1990: fig. 46, no. 612.
100. Fig. 228. Jar with thickened, flattened rim, short broad neck and ovoid body with flat base.
(a) P229; rim D. 11 cm; base D. 4 cm; H. c. 13.5 cm; fabric 20. Burnt on exterior of wall.
    Similar: one base fragment, base D. 4 cm.
(b) (Not illustrated.) P200; rim D. 13 cm; fabric 5.
    Similar: nine rim fragments, rim D. 10-14 cm.
    Cf. Rome: Carbonara and Messineo 1993: fig. 248, no. 12a.

Cooking pots
By SSC, remains of three vessels were found.
101. Fig. 228. Cooking pot with broad horizontal rim with hooked triangular projection on underside of rim.
    P228; rim D. 26 cm; fabric 19.
    Two grooves on exterior of wall.
    Cf. Luni: Luni I: tav. 74, 12 CM2622/1. Ostia: Ostia I: tav. XIX, no. 399; Ostia III: tav. XVI, no. 49. Rome: Cianfriglia et al. 1990: fig. 45, no. 565; Quilici 1990: fig. 94, no. 84. South Etruria survey: Peña 1987: site 6, 598, no. 5.

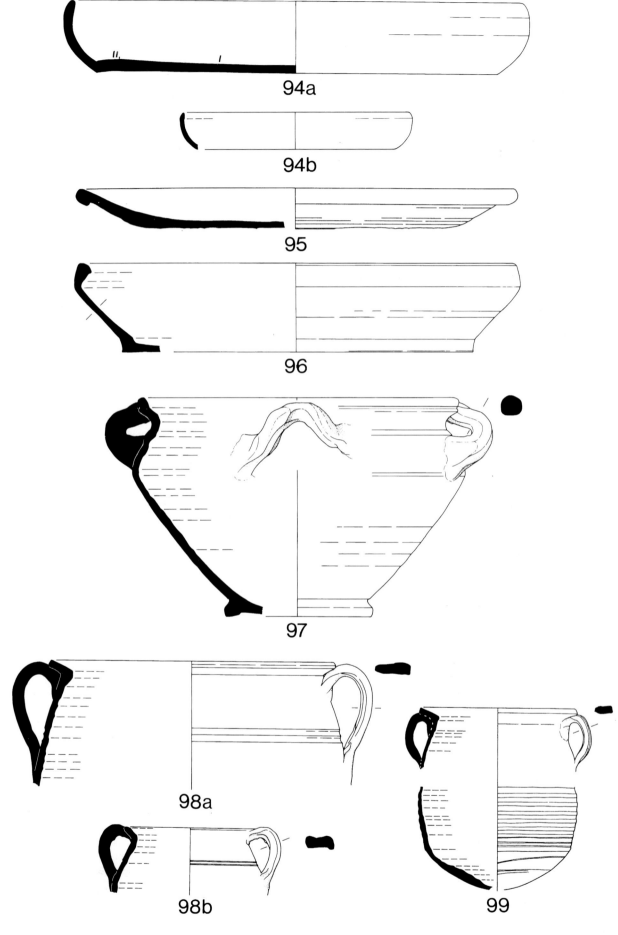

Fig. 227. Upper fish-pond fill: Pompeian red ware (94), coarse-ware (1:3). *(SC)*

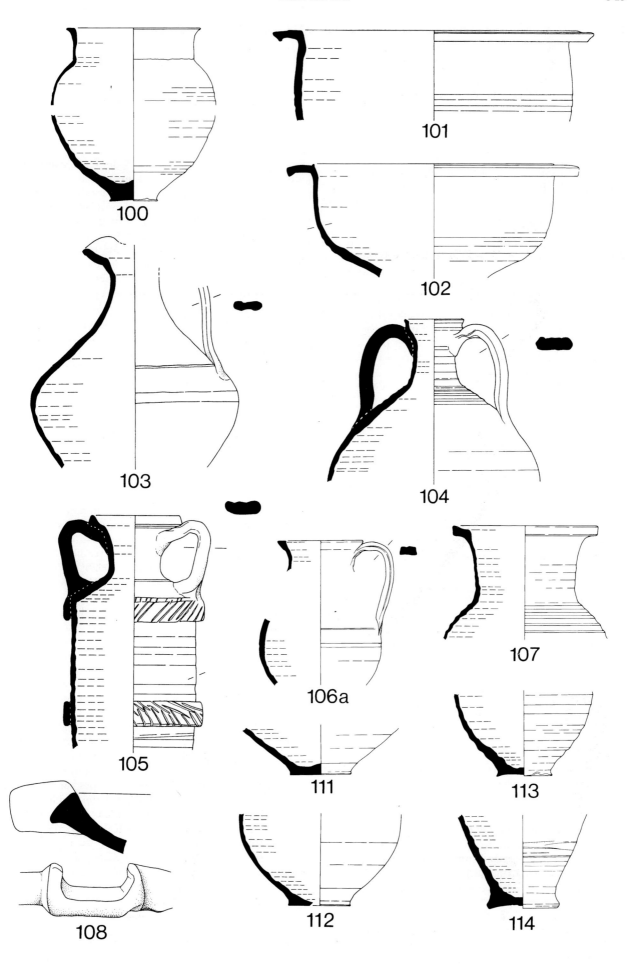

Fig. 228. Upper fish-pond fill: coarse-ware (1:3). *(SC)*

102. Fig. 228. Cooking pot with broad, gently curved rim, with small ridge at inner edge, and carinated body with rounded wall. Series of ridges at carination.
P227; rim D. 24 cm; fabric 18.
Similar: one body sherd, max. D. 20 cm.
Cf. Luni: *Luni* I: tav. 74, 11 CM1008. Santa Rufina: Cotton, Wheeler and Whitehouse 1991: fig. 84, no. 1.

Flagons/jugs

Remains of eleven vessels were found by rim count.
103. Fig. 228. Jug with trefoil rim, tall narrow neck and squat body with rounded wall. Single handle with irregular section.
P163; max. D. 17 cm; fabric 18.
104. Fig. 228. Flagon with everted, cupped rim, short narrow neck and spherical body. Two handles with rectangular section. Series of grooves at base of neck.
P215; rim D. 5 cm; fabric 5.
105. Fig. 228. Flagon with everted thickened rim, short narrow neck, angular shoulder and cylindrical body. Two handles with sub-oval section. Applied horizontal bands of clay at shoulder and on lower part of exterior, decorated with series of diagonal slashes.
P164; rim D. 8 cm; fabric 4.
106. Fig. 228. Flagon/jug with thickened bevelled rim, short wide neck and spherical body. Single handle with rectangular or barley sugar section.
(a) P211; rim D. 7 cm; fabric 7.
Similar: five rim fragments, rim D. 7-9 cm.
(b) (Not illustrated.) P235; rim D. 8 cm; fabric 5.
107. Fig. 228. Flagon with thickened rectangular rim, tall broad neck and rounded body.
P209; rim D. 12 cm; fabric 5.

Miscellaneous

By SSC, the remains of four vessels were found.
108. Fig. 228. Mortarium with thickened triangular rim, rounded wall and broad pouring spout.
P168; rim D. *c.* 40 cm; fabric 8. Extremely weathered.
109. (Not illustrated.) Bucket with broad rim and straight wall, tapering to flat base. From above, mouth of vessel has oval section.
P224; max. D. 35 cm; fabric 5.
110. (Not illustrated.) 'Amphora stopper'. Vessel with broad angular rim, tall narrow neck and rounded body.
P208; rim D. 6 cm; fabric 5.
Similar: one base fragment.

Lids

By rim count, the remains of two lids were found similar to cat. 57 in Group 1. (Not illustrated.)

Bases

Excluding bases which could be attributed to vessels similar to those above, the remains of twenty bases were found.
111. Fig. 228. Flat base and straight, flaring wall.
P231; base D. 5 cm; fabric 19.
Similar: four base fragments, base D. 4-7 cm.
112. Fig. 228. Flat base and rounded wall.
P232; base D. 5 cm; fabric 18.
Similar: three base fragments, base D. 5-6 cm.
113. Fig. 228. Flat base and rounded, ridged wall.
P214; base D. 4.5 cm; fabric 5.
Similar: seven base fragments, base D. 5-6 cm.

114. Fig. 228. Bevelled ring foot, slightly concave, with steep, straight wall.
P213; base D. 6 cm; fabric 5.
Similar: two base fragments, base D. 6 and 7 cm.

Group 3 – mid to late second-/early third-century comparanda

Unlike previous groups, Group 3 does not constitute an individual deposit, but rather it amalgamates two contexts which seem to be broadly contemporary with Groups 1 or 2. One of these, S10, is from the lowest fill of the rock-cut road. The overwhelming majority of the fine-ware in S10 indicates a second- to early third-century date (Italian sigillata *Consp.* 3; late Italian sigillata; ARS Hayes 3A, 9A, 14B, 23, 196, 197 and 50A (thin early version)). It should be noted that very small quantities of earlier (first century) and later (fourth century) material are also present.

The other context comprises the fill of the north cistern, and contains fine-ware dating to the second or early third century (Eastern sigillata B Hayes 53; ARS 3A, 6B, 9B, 23B, 196, and an unidentified closed form) with some residual material (first centuries BC and AD), a piece of fourth-century glass and a fourth-century coin. The large majority of fine and coarse pottery found in these two contexts, however, mirrors those types found in Groups 1 and 2. Some pieces supplement these forms and are discussed below. (The provenance is given after the fabric notation.)

In addition to the fine-wares listed above, a new form of glazed ware, cat. 115, was noted in S10. Like the examples in Group 1, it seems to be of Italian, and specifically Roman, origin. Colour-coated ware is very common in the contexts which make up Group 3. In addition to numerous examples of types cat. 87 and 90, a large colour-coated cup/beaker, possibly a variant of the *boccalino a collarino*, was noted (cat. 118). Its distinctive, pinched handle is paralleled in Roman productions of glazed ware (Martin 1992b: figs 6, 7 and 9), and thin-walled ware (Carbonara and Messineo 1993: fig. 243, no. 4 and fig. 244, no. 1)

In the coarse-ware, many of the bowl/dish forms found in Groups 1 and 2 are repeated in Group 3, including the Campanian? forms cat. 34 and 95. The large bowl (cat. 119) reflects a tradition seen in Group 2 (cat. 97) which encompassed much of the central Mediterranean. The heavily knobbed rim of cat. 120 is unusual, as is the straight-walled body of cat. 121. The jars from Group 3 contexts add no recognizably new forms to those found in Groups 1 and 2: the majority is variants of the tall-necked, ovoid bodied jars (cat. 36 and 38).

All cooking pots from Group 3 contexts are carinated with a broad rim, the standard type found in Groups 1 and 2. Especially common are variants of types cat. 43, 46 and 48. Cat. 122, with its very thick flanged rim and heavy body, may well be contemporary with the later examples seen in Group 2 (cat. 101 and 102), though the body still retains a sharp carination. Cat. 123, with its finer, hooked rim, seems to be closer to the feel of pieces in Group 1.

Few flagons/jugs in Group 3 differ substantially from examples in Groups 1 and 2. Especially common are ribbed vessels (as cat. 51, 54 and 107). Cat. 124, however, was conspicuous, with its angular carination and unribbed body. Apart from several examples of the so-called amphora stopper (cat. 55), few unclassified forms were found. The large storage jar cat. 125 is noteworthy for its decoration, which recalls that of pre-Roman pottery.

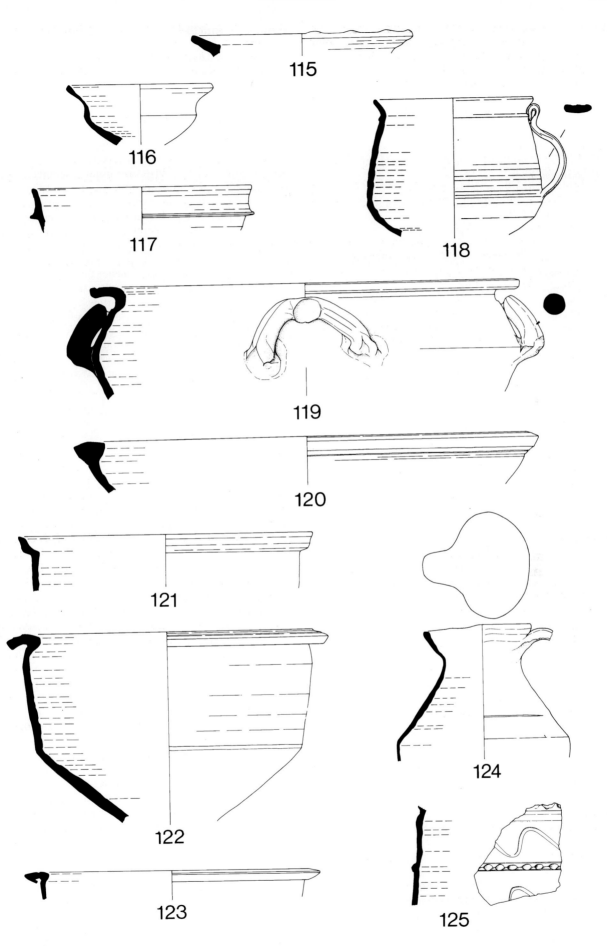

Fig. 229. Comparanda from groups of the mid to late second century: green glazed (115), colour-coated (116-18), coarse-ware (119-25) (1:3). *(SC)*

Green glazed ware

115. Fig. 229. Rim of an open vessel with broad knobbed rim angled upwards.
P256; rim D. 18 cm; fabric 29. S10.
Cf. Santa Rufina: Cotton, Wheeler and Whitehouse 1991: fig. 91, no. 10.

Colour-coated ware

116. Fig. 229. Cup/bowl with flaring, thickened rim and carinated body.
P261; rim D. 12 cm; fabric 7. Cistern.

117. Fig. 229. Bowl with straight rim and small, stubby flange.
P262; rim D. 18 cm; fabric 6. Cistern.

118. Fig. 229. Cup/beaker with everted rim underlined by ridge or 'collar', deep carinated body with rounded wall. Single 'pinched' handle with narrow sub-rectangular section. Series of shallow ridges/grooves above carination.
P368; rim D.13 cm; fabric 4. Cistern.

Bowls/dishes/cups

119. Fig. 229. Bowl with broad horizontal rim and rounded wall. Single horizontal handle with round section pressed onto wall. Groove at outer edge of rim.
P253; rim D. 35 cm; fabric 19. S10.

120. Fig. 229. Bowl with thickened, bevelled rim and rounded wall.
P264; rim D. 38 cm; fabric 4. Cistern.

121. Fig. 229. Bowl with everted, angular rim cupped on interior, and straight, vertical wall.
P265; rim D. 24 cm; fabric 8. Cistern.
Cf. Santa Rufina: Cotton, Wheeler and Whitehouse 1991: fig. 83, no. 8.

Cooking pots

122. Fig. 229. Cooking pot with broad, curved rim, ridged on upper surface and carinated body with straight, thick walls.
P266; rim D. 26 cm; fabric 18. Cistern.
Cf. Santa Rufina: Cotton, Wheeler and Whitehouse 1991: fig. 84, no. 1.

123. Fig. 229. Cooking pot with horizontal rim, sharply hooked on underside and straight wall.
P267; rim D. 24 cm; fabric 19. Cistern.
Cf. Ostia: *Ostia* III: tav. XIX, no. 85. South Etruria survey: Peña 1987: site 6, 598, no. 9; site 9, 610, no. 7.

Flagons/jugs

124. Fig. 229. Trefoil jug with tall flaring rim and tall conical upper body. Single handle.
P268; max. D. 9 cm; fabric 4. Cistern.

Miscellaneous

125. Fig. 229. Sherd from base of large closed vessel (storage jar?). Decoration consists of applied cordons bearing finger indentations, separating broad bands containing single incised wavy lines.
P255; fabric 20. S10.
Cf. South Etruria survey: Peña 1987: site 13, 624, no. 3.

Group 4 – fourth-century context (M87)

This small but significant group comprises the only recognizable sealed body of fourth-century material from the site. The ARS piece cat. 126 suggests a date for the group in the middle of the fourth century, an idea strengthened by the dissimilarity of the associated coarse-wares to earlier or later assemblages. The good state of preservation of the ARS bowl cat. 126 argues against its being residual. This seems reinforced by the absence of characteristic ARS forms such as Hayes 61B and 67, which are found in contexts of the third quarter of the fourth century and later (Table 60).

In the coarse-ware the forms seem to have developed from types found in earlier groups, though the degree of evolution has been considerable, as may be seen, for example, in the rims of jars and cooking pots. Many rim variants which were common in earlier periods disappear, and generally the impression is one of a smaller range of forms, often displaying a markedly reduced potting skill. The fabrics of the Group 4 pieces, which are uniformly heavier and coarser than those in earlier groups, contain volcanic inclusions which seem to rule out a very local manufacture, suggesting, instead, fairly distant centres of production.

The only diagnostic dish/bowl cat. 127 was similar in form to a piece from Group 2 (cat. 97) of over a century earlier. However, the grooves around the rim seem a late Roman feature (see also cat. 165 in Group 7). Jar forms seem to have simplified considerably in the later Empire, with plain, everted rims and oval bodies replacing the much broader range of types seen in Groups 1 and 2 (above).

All cooking pots found in Group 4 are still of the carinated casserole type, giving a useful *terminus post quem* for the appearance of the tub-shaped variety seen in Groups 5 (cat. 137-8) and 7 (cat. 170-4). However, the flanges of the Group 4 casseroles are much heavier than in previous periods, with thickened and ridged profiles, possibly the forerunners of later forms (Group 7, cat. 177-80).

African red slip ware

126. Fig. 230. Bowl with straight, steep wall, broad rim with flattened extremity and small, low ring foot. Hayes 52B (large variety), *c.* 280/300 to late fourth century. Appliqué on rim; seated animal (boar? lion?).
P299; rim D. 21 cm; base D. 5.5 cm; H. 5.5 cm; fabric t.s.c. 'C'.

Dishes/bowls/cups

127. Fig. 230. Dish/bowl with upright, thickened rim and tapering body with straight wall. Three deep grooves on exterior of rim.
P295; rim D. 30 cm; fabric 23.
Cf. Ostia: *Ostia* IV: tav. LII, no. 419.

Jars

128. Fig. 230. Jar with tall everted rim and broad rounded body.
P292; rim D. 12 cm; fabric 25.

129. Fig. 230. Jar with thickened everted rim and tall, narrow neck. One or more handles.
P297; rim D. 10.5 cm; fabric 27.

Cooking pots

130. Fig. 230. Cooking pot with broad rim, thickened heavily on underside, and grooved upper surface.

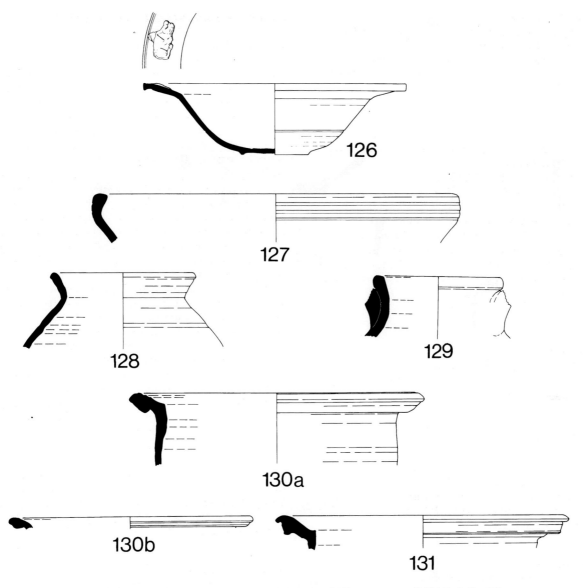

Fig. 230. Fourth-century group: African red slip ware (126), coarse-ware (127-31) (1:3). *(SC)*

(a) P293; rim D. 24 cm; fabric 23.
(b) P296; rim D. 20 cm; fabric 23.
131. Fig. 230. Cooking pot with broad rim, thickened and flattened with small hooked protrusion at extremity. P294; rim D. 24 cm; fabric 26.

Group 5 – 'Justinianic' contexts

Group 5 comprises material from two contexts (D48 and D52) associated with destruction levels, in particular roof collapse. Numerous joins between sherds from the two levels suggest that they were contemporary. Two coins of Justinian and one of Totila were found in D52, giving a *terminus post quem* of the mid-sixth century for the contexts. It seems likely, however, that the pottery is a little earlier – certainly the ARS piece cat. 132 should not long post-date the 520s. Indeed, the ARS bowl cat. 132 is one of the latest recognizable imports to the site.

With regard to the coarse-ware, it should be stressed that the typological developments of late Roman coarse pottery

in and around Rome are far from well-documented; future research will, it is hoped, sharpen the chronology of this and following groups (6, 7 and 8).

The coarse-ware shows uniformity of fabric with material from earlier contexts, but considerable differences in form. In the bowls the irregular body of cat. 133, and its apparent use in cooking, set it apart from vessels of similar size from earlier groups, as does the straight wall and heavily knobbed rim of cat. 134. Of the jars/flagons, cat. 135 is perhaps the 'local amphora' type more completely represented in Group 6 (cat. 146). Cat. 136 is distinctive for its minimal neck and rim.

Cooking pots are one of the more significant classes in Group 5, with the appearance of the tub-shaped cooking pot cat. 137a-b. This provides a useful *terminus ante quem* of the early sixth century for the introduction of tub-shaped form, a date that would fit with the presence of variants of the form in the Forum Cistern group at Cosa (Dyson 1976: FC20-21). Similarly, the complete absence from Group 5 of the carinated variety of cooking pot, standard in all earlier deposits, and one of the most characteristic forms of coarse-

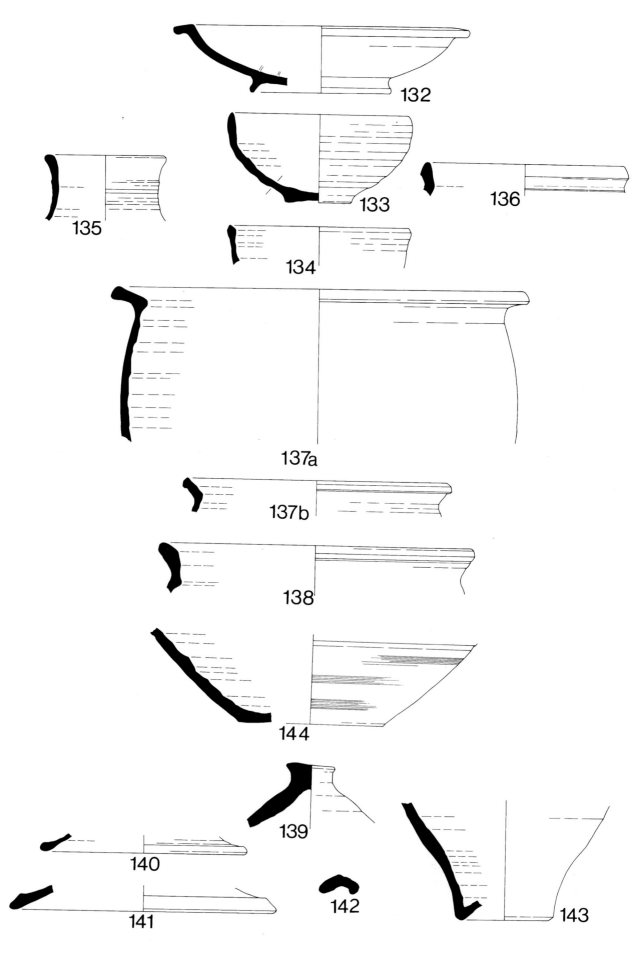

Fig. 231. Sixth-century contexts: African red slip ware (132), coarse-ware (133-43) (1:3). *(SC)*

ware in the Roman period in Italy, suggests wide-scale changes in the ceramic tradition.

The sharply folded handle cat. 142, quite unlike handles from earlier groups, seems to be a late Roman feature. A very similar piece (cat. 184) was found in another late Roman context (Group 7, below). The rilling (groups of fine grooves/striations) seen on cat. 144 also seems to be a standard late Roman technique.

African red slip ware

132. Fig. 231. Bowl with flat rim rounded on underside, broad shallow body with rounded wall and flaring ring foot. Hayes 93, late fifth to first quarter of sixth centuries AD.
P324; rim D. 24 cm; base D. 12 cm; H. 5 cm; fabric t.s.c. 'D'. D48.

Bowls/dishes/cups

133. Fig. 231. Bowl with vertical rim, irregular rounded wall and thick, flat base, slightly hollowed on underside. Numerous irregular ridges/grooves on exterior.
P317; rim D. 15 cm; base D. 5.5 cm; H. 6.5 cm; fabric 23. D52.
134. Fig. 231. Bowl with thickened, bevelled rim and vertical wall.
P329; rim D. 15 cm; fabric 23. D48.

Jars

135. Fig. 231. Jar/flagon with thickened, rounded rim and tall, broad neck.
P322; rim D. 10 cm; fabric 24. D52.
136. Fig. 231. Jar with small vertical rim and bevelled outer edge.
P319; rim D. 17 cm; fabric 24. D52.

Cooking pots

137. Fig. 231. Cooking pot with rectangular-sectioned rim, angled upwards, broad deep body with rounded wall and flat base.
(a) Bands of fine rilling on exterior.
P316; rim D. 34 cm; fabric 24. D52.
(b) P318; rim D. 22 cm; fabric 23. D52.
138. Fig. 231. Cooking pot with everted thickened rim, small rounded spur at base of rim on interior.
P328; rim D. 26 cm; fabric 26. D48.

Lids

139. Fig. 231. Knob of lid with conical body.
P327; knob D. 4 cm; fabric 27. D52.
140. Fig. 231. Lid with thickened, rounded rim and conical body.
P320; rim D. 17 cm; fabric 23. D52.
141. Fig. 231. Lid with thickened, triangular-sectioned rim.
P321; rim D. 22 cm; fabric 25. D52.

Miscellaneous

142. Fig. 231. Handle of closed form with rounded right-angled section.
P326; fabric 24. D52.

Bases

143. Fig. 231. Base of closed form (flagon/jug?) with rounded ring foot, central *omphalos* and rounded wall.
P323; base D. 8 cm; fabric 9. D52.
144. Fig. 231. Base with slightly rounded underside and straight wall.
P325; base D. 12 cm; fabric 27. D52.

Group 6 – context D86 (baptistery pit)

Group 6 comprises the material from a pit which, in terms of its stratigraphy, must post-date the contexts which make up Group 5. Given the dating of that group (early sixth century, probably pre-dating the 530s AD) and the slightly unusual nature of the material in Group 6, a date for the pottery (if not necessarily the date of its final deposition) in the mid-sixth century seems appropriate.

Cat. 145 with its heavy triangular rim, unique on the site, is the only dish/bowl found in the deposit. The jar/flagon cat. 146 may have been intended for short-distance transport as well as storage, in effect one of the last Roman amphora types seen on site. Ribbing as on cat. 146, when used on non-levigated pottery, seems almost exclusively a late Roman feature.

The jar(/cooking pot?) cat. 147 is unparalleled, and shows the advent of forms which blurred traditional distinctions. The body, with its wide mouth, is very unusual, while the base, burnished and noticeably convex, is solidly in the very late Antique tradition. Both cat. 146 and 147, however, are in the same heavy, volcanic fabric that was predominant on the site from the mid-fourth century, indicating some continuity of supply.

The cooking pots cat. 148 and 149 show some affinities with the tub-shaped form, though with considerable differences in the rim. I would suggest that they mark a development of the form into a hybrid jar/cooking pot such as cat. 147. The lids cat. 152a-b seem to share the same broad tradition.

Bowls/dishes/cups

145. Fig. 232. Bowl with squared rim, angled inwards and straight wall.
P340; rim D. 27 cm; fabric 27.

Jars

146. Fig. 232. Jar/flagon with thickened rounded rim, tall broad neck and ovoid body. Single handle. Deep, broad grooves on most of body.
P331; rim D. 12 cm; fabric 23.
147. Fig. 232. Jar/cooking pot with thickened, rounded rim, wide mouth, broad deep ovoid body and uneven, slightly rounded base.
P332; rim D. 27 cm; base D. 10.5 cm; H. 24 cm; fabric 23.

Cooking pots

148. Fig. 233. Cooking pot with thickened overhanging triangular rim and rounded carinated body, tapering towards flat base.
P335; rim D. 25 cm; base D. 10 cm; H. 19 cm; fabric 28. Two uneven grooves below rim on exterior.
Cf. Santa Rufina: Cotton, Wheeler and Whitehouse 1991: fig. 86, no. 28.

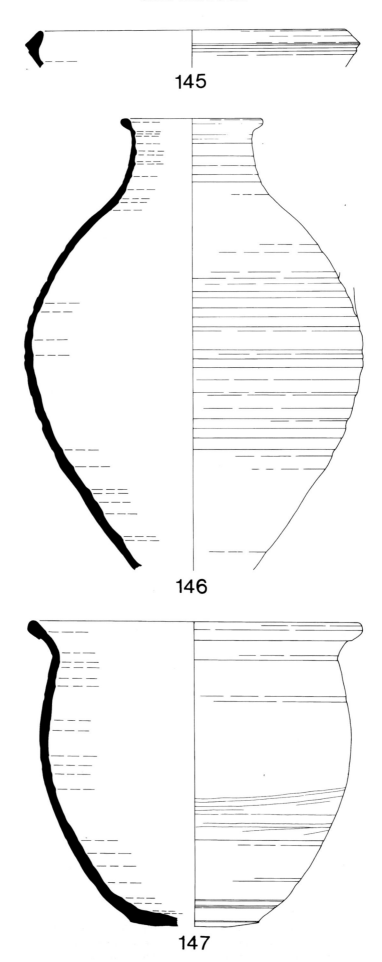

145

146

147

Fig. 232. Pit D86 (sixth century): coarse-ware (1:3). *(SC)*

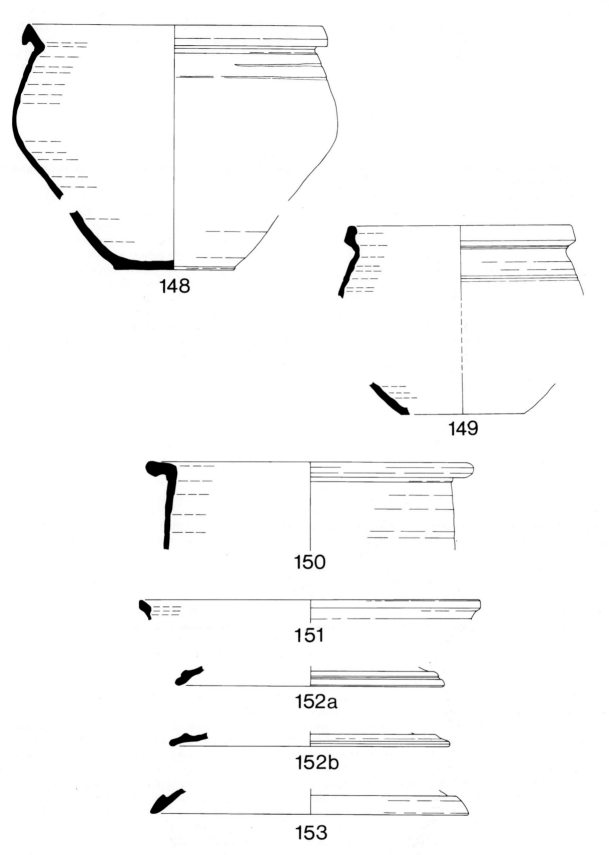

Fig. 233. Pit D86 (sixth century): coarse-ware (1:3). *(SC)*

149. Fig. 233. Cooking pot with offset right-angled-sectioned rim with cupped interior, squat rounded body and flat base. Two grooves below rim on exterior. P336; rim D. 19 cm; base D. 10.5 cm; H. 15 cm; fabric 23.

150. Fig. 233. Cooking pot with thickened horizontal rim, heavily rounded on underside and straight wall. Ridge on exterior below rim. P333; rim D. 27 cm; fabric 23.

151. Fig. 233. Cooking pot(?) with thickened rectangular-sectioned rim angled upwards.
P342; rim D. 28 cm; fabric 27.

Lids
152. Fig. 233. Lid with thickened rim. Rounded projection above rim.
(a) P339; rim D. 22 cm; fabric 27.
(b) P338; rim D. 23 cm; fabric 25.
Cf. (a-b) Santa Rufina: Cotton, Wheeler and Whitehouse 1991: fig. 87, no. 14.
153. Fig. 233. Lid with thickened, elongated triangular rim. P341; rim D. 26 cm; fabric 27.

Group 7 – late Roman comparanda

Group 7 comprises material from numerous contexts on the site, and is the most heterogeneous of all the eight groups presented here. Group 7 contexts are characterized either by the presence of late Roman imported fine-ware (exclusively ARS in this area), local fine-ware such as colour-coated ware or burnished ware, or coarse-ware types and fabrics such as those seen in Groups 4-6. The date-range for Group 7 is approximately 150 years, from the late fourth to the mid-sixth centuries AD. Whilst such a broad time-span is not ideal for obtaining maximum information from pottery, in particular from coarse-wares, the general lack of published material from the late Roman period in the area justifies presentation of the group.

The only imported fine-ware found on the site in this period is ARS, mostly t.s.c. 'D' forms such as Hayes 58, 61A, 61B, 67, 92 and 99A. Although there is a considerable group of these forms, it is numerically far inferior to the t.s.a. 'A' group, which covers a roughly equal time-span. Even allowing for some of the ARS cooking-ware forms from the site to be of late Imperial date (Tortorella 1981: 211), it is apparent that the levels of fine-ware import in the late Empire did not reach those seen in contexts of the second century (Groups 1-3).

Colour-coated wares or slipped wares are as much a feature of late Imperial contexts as they are of Groups 1-3. These later wares, however, are distinct from the earlier types in their forms (almost exclusively large and closed) and their decorative techniques (the use of wave combing). The slip is usually dull and thickly applied, ranging in colour from mid-brown (7.5YR 5/2; Munsell brown) to dull orange (7.5YR 6/6; Munsell reddish yellow). It is important to note that this slipped/totally immersed ware is quite different from the red painted tradition, with its consciously applied painted decoration, found in northern Etruria and over southern Italy during the late Roman period (for example, Freed (1982)). The absence of red painted ware from the site mirrors the ware's scarcity or absence from sites in and around Rome (Roberts 1992: 350), and underlines the extent to which Monte Gelato was part of Roman marketing systems.

Cat. 154 is the only open form in late colour-coated ware, the usual forms being jugs/flagons with one or two handles (cat. 155-9). Combed decoration is the only decoration identified on these vessels, either continuous (cat. 157) or in separate strokes (cat. 158).

Burnished ware (that is, pottery which was intentionally burnished to achieve a decorative effect, as opposed to pottery smoothed through the process of throwing), such as cat. 185 and a vessel in Group 6 (cat. 147), is very rare on the site. This contrasts with the frequent occurrence of the ware in south-central Italy (Roberts 1992: 364-6) and in northern Etruria, for example, at Fiesole (Fiesole: 195-9). It is interesting that the only form of burnished ware found is very similar to an imported sigillata form (ARS 61B), perhaps indicating a deliberate imitation of (though not necessarily the scarcity or lack of) imported originals (Roberts 1992: 134). As with red painted ware, the scarcity of burnished ware on the site is paralleled at Rome, and emphasizes the site's belonging securely to the Roman economic orbit.

The coarse-ware from Group 7 contexts is characterized by a relatively small range of forms, in fabrics similar to, or coarser than, those first seen in Group 4.

Cat. 161 and 162 are part of the tradition of flanged bowls seen in fine and coarse pottery and metalwork during the late Roman period. Cat. 162 is slightly unusual, with its inturned rim and thick heavy flange, possibly dating it a little later than cat. 161. Cat. 163 is similar in form to the cooking pot cat. 173, though its small size and the absence of burning suggest rather its use as a bowl. Cat. 165 shows the continuity of the form seen already in Group 2 (cat. 96) and repeats the grooves first seen on a fourth-century example (cat. 127).

Cat. 166, with its broad, shallow form, heavy walls and indistinct rim has entered into common archaeological usage as the 'dog-dish', though a more correct definition of the form might be as a baking dish used in on-hearth cooking. As such, it seems a likely forerunner of a common medieval form, the 'testello' or bread-baking dish. It is difficult to date the appearance of these Roman forerunners accurately, though some date in the early to mid sixth century seems likely, with some supporting evidence possibly appearing at sites such as San Giovanni di Ruoti and Madonna del Passo (Rieti). The late Roman examples may be distinguished from the medieval pieces by their dense, crumbly fabrics and their subsequently thick, rough bases and walls. This is perhaps one of the latest forms from the Roman period on the site, post-dating many of the other forms in Group 7.

The jars cat. 167-9 show a radical simplification of general forms in comparison with the early-mid Imperial period (Groups 1-3). Cat. 167a exhibits some of the most notable features of late Roman jars from the site, namely the dumpy body, flat base and simple everted rim. The simple handle section, and its joining directly at the top of the rim, is a very typical feature of late pieces throughout Italy (Roberts 1992: 335).

Cooking pots comprise by far the majority of vessels from Group 7 contexts, suggesting perhaps the predominance of the most basic of cooking vessels at this time, in contrast to the much wider range of forms seen in earlier deposits. This could in turn imply a decreasing sophistication of the market, a general simplification and impoverishment of culinary and other processes, and/or the inability of local suppliers to meet the market's demands. There is certainly a decrease in the quality of much late coarse-ware, both in the increased thickness and unevenness of the wall and the simple and heavy finishing of diagnostic features.

Cat. 170-4 show the range of variants of the tub-shaped cooking pot first noted in Group 5 (cat. 137 and 138). The popularity of the form in the Forum Cistern at Cosa suggests that the peak of the form's usage lies in the later fifth/early sixth centuries. Cat. 170a-d are recognizably similar in general form and diagnostic features (the thick rectangular rim underlined by a distinct ridge), whereas cat.

171 and 172 seem to share the same basic tub shape, though with different rims. Cat. 173 has a distinctive hollowed rim, though the body shape and ridge suggest it forms part of the group. Cat. 174, with the internal ridge, is very similar to a piece from Group 5 (cat. 138).

The remaining cooking pots, cat. 175-80, seem to represent the casserole type, with broad or thickened rim and carinated body. Similarities to pieces from earlier contexts, both in rim type and general body form, suggest that this casserole group may date to the mid/later fourth to fifth centuries, thereby pre-dating the tub-shaped variety of cooking pot (cat. 170-4).

Cat. 175-8a represent large vessels on a scale similar to some pieces from Group 1 (cat. 46-8), and may contribute to discussions on population size in the later phases of the site, for example whether there was a rise in population as has been suggested for other rural sites such as San Giovanni di Ruoti and San Vincenzo (Hodges 1988: 218-19). Cat. 176 and 177 could both be developments of mid fourth-century pieces from Group 4 (cat. 130), while cat. 178-80 may owe part of their inspiration to other fourth-century models (cat. 131). Forms cat. 178-80 are found in various late fourth-/early fifth-century contexts in and around Rome. These forms may represent the last phase in the development of the casserole type cooking pot, which characterized Roman deposits on the site and far beyond for over four centuries.

The lid cat. 181 has a ridged projection similar to pieces from Group 6 (cat. 152), while 182 is unparalleled. The flagon (funnel?) cat. 183 seems to represent one of the few examples of the use of cogging in the late Roman period, as opposed to the earlier tradition noted by Threipland (1968).

The handle cat. 184, with its sharply right-angled section, has a parallel dating to the late fifth/early sixth centuries (cat. 142), while the semi-rounded and burnished base of cat. 185 is paralleled in Group 6 (cat. 147), suggesting that cat. 185 and the dish cat. 166, together with the pieces from Group 6, may be among the latest forms from the Roman period on the site.

Colour-coated ware

154. Fig. 234. Bowl with thickened rounded overhanging rim.
P306; rim D. 23 cm; fabric 12. K101.
Cf. Santa Rufina: Cotton, Wheeler and Whitehouse 1991: fig. 87, no. 9.

155. Fig. 234. Flagon/jug with everted thickened rim and broad body. Two handles with round section.
P343; rim D. 10 cm; fabric 12. C59.

156. Fig. 234. Flagon/jug with offset thickened rim, tall broad neck and narrow squared body. Single groove on upper surface of handle.
P351; rim D. 10 cm; fabric 11. A19.

157. Fig. 234. Flagon/jug with everted rim.
P275; rim D. 6 cm; fabric 11. L157.

158. Fig. 234. Sherd from wall of closed vessel (flagon/jug?). Straight wall with ridge at neck. Two bands (surviving) of combed pendant arcs, separated by single groove.
P344; fabric 12. C51.

159. Fig. 234. Sherd from wall of closed vessel (flagon/jug). Curved wall with broad grooves and ridges near neck. Two bands (surviving) of continuous wave combing.
P309; fabric 12. M35.
Cf. Cosa: Fentress *et al.* 1991: fig. 17, no. 8.

Burnished ware

160. Fig. 234. Bowl with vertical rim, thickened and overhanging on exterior and straight wall. Irregular narrow strokes of burnishing overall. Single band of carefully incised diagonal strokes on lower part of wall.
P284; rim D. 27 cm; fabric 27. M145.

Bowls/dishes/cups

161. Fig. 234. Bowl with vertical rim, horizontal bevelled flange and tapering body with straight wall and flat base.
P280; rim D. 27 cm; base D. 10.5 cm; H. 11 cm; fabric 11. M111.
Cf. Luni: *Luni* I: tav. 73, 40 CM129; tav. 74, 2 CM131.

162. Fig. 234. Bowl with curved inturned rim and heavy, thickened triangular-sectioned flange, slightly rounded wall and flat base.
P361; rim D. 26 cm: base D. 10 cm; H. 11 cm; fabric 24. A12.

163. Fig. 234. Bowl with offset, thickened rim and vertical, rounded wall.
P269; rim D. 17.5 cm; fabric 27. E16.
Cf. Cosa: Dyson 1976: fig. 65, FC11.

164. Fig. 234. Bowl with thickened, round inturned rim and rounded wall.
P302; rim D. 36 cm; fabric 12. K103.

165. Fig. 234. Bowl with vertical thickened rim, slightly inturned and tapering body with straight wall. Four grooves on exterior of rim, two more on wall.
P303; rim D. 30 cm; fabric 27. K102.

166. Fig. 234. '*Testello*'. Dish with straight thick wall with flattened extremity.
P349; rim D. 36 cm; fabric 28. E160.

Jars

167. Fig. 235. Jar with everted rim, dumpy ovoid body with rounded wall and flat base. Single handle with sub-rectangular section, joining at rim.
(a) P310; rim D. 11.5 cm; base D. 8.5 cm; H. 14 cm; fabric 26. C59.
(b) P289; rim D.10 cm; fabric 24. M86.

168. Fig. 235. Jar with thin, everted rim and ovoid, ridged body.
P290; rim D. 8 cm; fabric 25. M79.

169. Fig. 235. Jar with rounded overhanging triangular-sectioned rim.
P314; rim D. 14 cm; fabric 24. E160.

Cooking pots

170. Fig. 235. Cooking pot with thickened rectangular-sectioned rim angled upwards and broad body with rounded wall and flat base. Distinct ridge at base of rim.
(a) P311; rim D. 25 cm; base D. 15 cm; H. 19.5 cm; fabric 23. C59.
Cf. Cosa: Dyson 1976: fig. 66, FC20-21.
(b) P312; rim D. 22 cm; fabric 23. D337.
Cf. Santa Rufina: Cotton, Wheeler and Whitehouse 1991: fig. 86, no. 33.
(c) P276; rim D. 21 cm; fabric 24. L157.
Cf. Cosa: Fentress *et al.* 1991: fig. 19, nos. 18a-b.
(d) P347; rim D. 24 cm; fabric 24. D247.

171. Fig. 235. Cooking pot with broad rectangular-sectioned rim.
P272; rim D. 23 cm; fabric 24. E16.

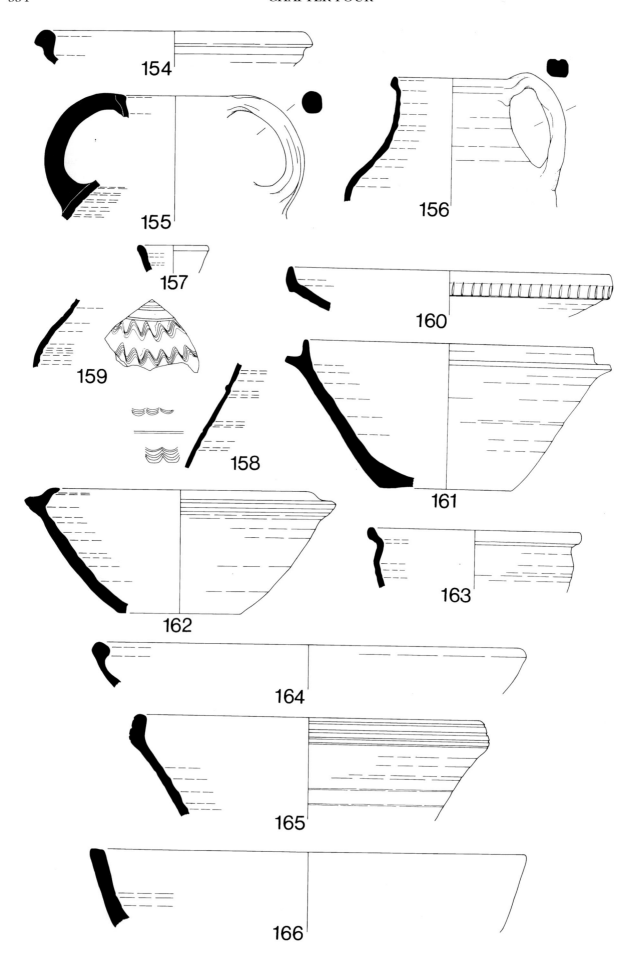

Fig. 234. Late Roman comparanda, various contexts: colour-coated (154-9), burnished (160), coarse-ware (161-6) (1:3). *(SC)*

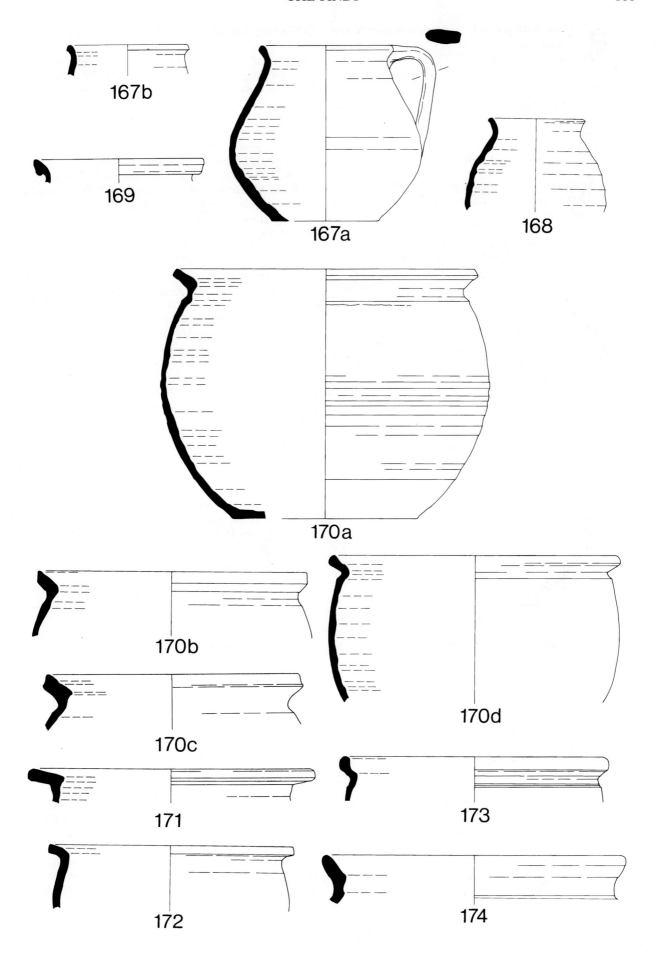

Fig. 235. Late Roman comparanda, various contexts: coarse-ware (1:3). *(SC)*

172. Fig. 235. Cooking pot with rectangular-sectioned rim and rounded wall.
    P274; rim D. 20 cm; fabric 24. E69.

173. Fig. 235. Cooking pot with offset, rounded, thickened rim, cupped on interior and sharp ridge at base.
    P278; rim D. 22 cm; fabric 24. L157.

174. Fig. 235. Cooking pot with tall, everted, rounded rim, ridge at base of rim on interior.
    P305; rim D. 25 cm; fabric 24. K101.

175. Fig. 236. Cooking pot with broad curved rim and straight wall.
    P307; rim D. 34.5 cm; fabric 26. M74.

176. Fig. 236. Cooking pot with everted rim, thickened on underside.
    P286; rim D. 33 cm; fabric 26. M144.

177. Fig. 236. Cooking pot with everted thickened rim, rounded and overhanging on underside.
    P283; rim D. 26 cm; fabric 27. M138.

178. Fig. 236. Cooking pot with everted thickened rim with ridge on underside.
    (a) P362; rim D. 26 cm; fabric 27. A12.
        Cf. Rieti field survey: pers. obs.
    (b) P301; rim D. 24 cm; fabric 24. K103.

179. Fig. 236. Cooking pot with tall everted rim, hooked at extremity and cupped on interior. Outward flaring wall.
    P281; rim D. 20 cm; fabric 23. M143.

180. Fig. 236. Cooking pot with thickened everted triangular rim with curved/cupped upper surface and sharp ridge at base of exterior. Straight vertical wall.
    (a) P400; rim D. 24 cm; fabric 27. M166.
        Cf. Rome: Staffa 1986: fig. 398, no. 194; fig. 399, nos. 201-2.
    (b) P287; rim D. 27 cm; fabric 28. M144.
        Cf. Rome: Gianicolo, pers. obs.

Lids

181. Fig. 236. Lid with rounded, upturned rim. Rounded projection on upper surface.
    P304; rim D. 22 cm; fabric 25. K101.
    Cf. Santa Rufina: Cotton, Wheeler and Whitehouse 1991: fig. 87, no. 14.

182. Fig. 236. Lid with thickened round rim and conical body with thick rounded wall.
    P330; rim D. 24 cm; fabric 23. K102.

Miscellaneous

183. Fig. 236. Neck/spout of vessel with tall, thin neck and broad body.
    P300; rim D. 4 cm; fabric 23. M105.
    Single continuous spiral of cogged decoration around neck.

184. Fig. 236. Handle of closed vessel (jar/flagon) with right-angled section.
    P346; fabric 23. D247.

185. Fig. 236. Base of vessel (jar/cooking pot?) with slightly rounded underside and steep wall. Uneven burnishing on underside only.
    P348; base D. 11 cm; fabric 23. E160.

Group 8 – burials

Though the smallest of the eight groups presented here, Group 8 none the less is of considerable importance in the light that it sheds on developments in and around the site. Cat. 186 has been dated by Arthur (pers. comm.) to the mid-later fifth century, a date span with which I broadly agree, perhaps extending it into the early sixth century, given the similarities in fabric and form with pieces from Groups 5 and 6. On the basis of its profile alone the vessel would probably be seen as a drinking vessel. However, the presence of burning, if not caused by a ritual associated with the burial, seems to indicate that it was used in cooking. If so, it represents a form and size unparalleled in other cooking vessels from the site, and may be indicative of increasing changes in traditional vessel forms.

The context of cat. 187 has produced a calibrated radiocarbon date of AD 565-635, making it one of the latest identifiable pieces from the Roman period on the site. As a whole, the vessel, with regard to its diagnostic features, is still recognizably Roman, though it is interesting to note that its fabric, to the naked eye, has more in common with the levigated fabrics seen in the late eighth-century kiln deposit from the site (Patterson, this volume). However, as stated above, the piece appears to be a singleton, and there is no ceramic evidence for any occupation of the site on any noticeable scale between the late sixth and late eighth centuries.

The pottery vessels were retrieved intact from burial contexts. (The provenance is given after the fabric notation.)

186. Fig. 237. Jar with thickened, rounded rim, slightly concave on interior, tall narrow neck and dumpy body with flat base. Single handle with sub-rectangular section. Single groove at base of neck.
    P360; rim D. 5 cm; base D. 4.5 cm; H. 10.5 cm; fabric 23. B26; burial no. 106. Slightly burnt on underside of base and on wall near handle.

187. Figs 237 and 238. Jar with short, straight everted rim, short neck and broad rounded body. Single handle with oval section.
    P402; rim D. 8.5 cm; base D. 6 cm; H. 7.5 cm; fabric: light yellowish brown clay with black (volcanic?) inclusions. D168, burial no. 59.

THE STORK-VASE, by Oswyn Murray, Paul Roberts and Peter Parsons[74]

THE VESSEL (FIGS 239 AND 240), by Paul Roberts

Form

When reconstructed, the vessel proved to be a tall, narrow beaker with a low base and shallow ring foot. The tapering lower wall broadens at the approximate mid-point of the vessel to become almost cylindrical. The rim is thickened and folded-over with two protrusions of rounded section on the exterior. Two holes had been drilled or punched di-

---

[74] This is substantially the same text as printed in *Papers of the British School at Rome* 59 (1991); 177-95.

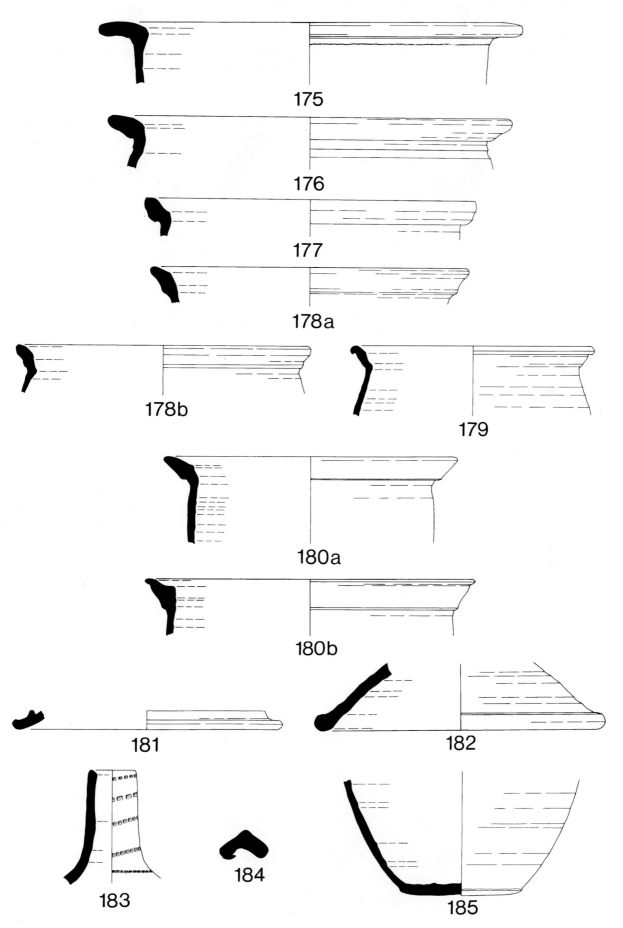

Fig. 236. Late Roman comparanda, various contexts: coarse-ware (1:3). *(SC)*

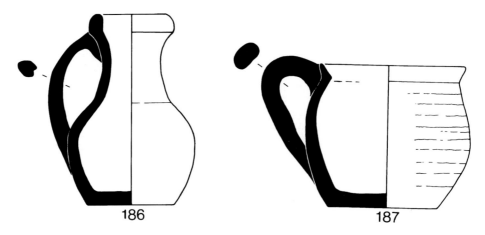

Fig. 237. Vessels from burials nos. 106 (left) and 59 (1:2). *(PR)*

agonally through the rim. The surfaces of these holes are coated with the same slip that covers the rest of the body, indicating that the holes were made before firing.

The measurements are as follows: rim diameter (max.) 13.5 cm; base diameter (max.) 7 cm; height 27 cm.

Severe warping of the vessel is evident. This seems to be associated with a large crack running vertically from the rim, through one of the holes, down the length of the body and then turning to run parallel to the base. Another crack or pair of cracks can be observed running across the base and into the foot ring.

Decoration and other marks

The exterior surface is covered with bands of rouletting, heavily applied. In some instances ridges have been left by the edge of the cog wheel, especially on the central part of the vessel. A Greek inscription is incised approximately two-thirds of the way down the vessel. Between the end and the beginning of the inscription appears the figure of a bird resting on a form of structure.

On the underside of the base, just inside the ring foot and in a somewhat uneven hand, is a second inscription in Greek (Fig. 241):

'Αβασκάντου καὶ 'Επινίκου.

Although the hand is almost certainly that of the main inscription, the base inscription is quite cursorily executed, with the end of the second name awkwardly close to the beginning of the first.

The central area of the underside of the base is occupied by the remains of two lines of letters. These have been badly damaged, firstly by two fissures which run through the ring

Fig. 238. Vessel of the later sixth century AD from burial no. 59. *(KW)*

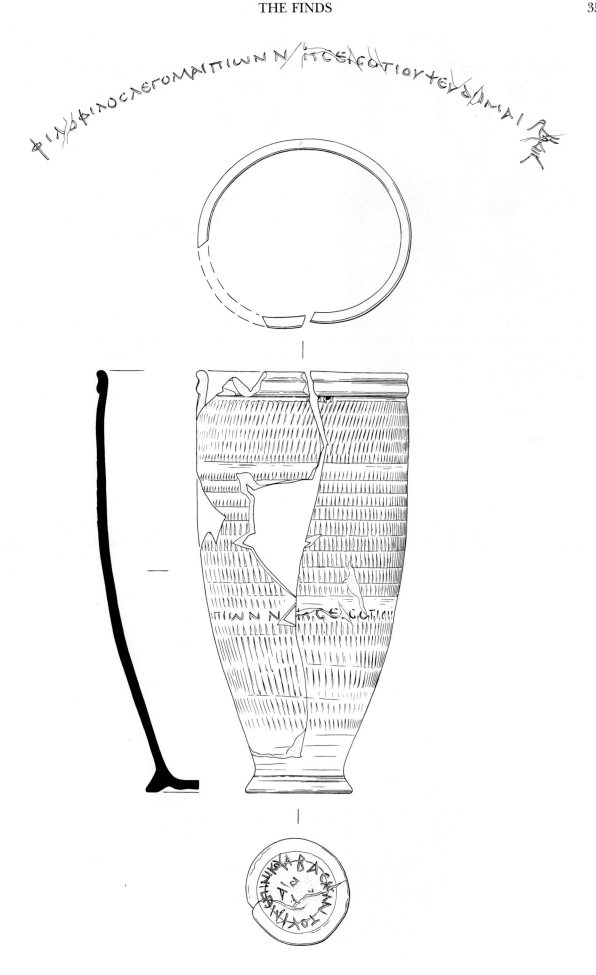

Fig. 239. The 'stork-vase' from the lower fish-pond deposit. Height: 0.27 m. *(SA)*

Fig. 240. The 'stork-vase'. *(KW)*

foot into the centre of the base and secondly by lamination and flaking of the surface. As a result, the only letters still legible with certainty are the initial letter of the first line, alpha, and the iota that follows it. The last letter of the first line is probably alpha or lambda. Those of the lower line are indecipherable. This inscription is too fragmentary to be interpreted with any confidence, although the possibilities include some form of tally or batch number, or a mark of ownership.

Slip

A dull, brownish red slip or colour-coat 2.5YR 5/8 (Munsell bright brown) is present on all surfaces of the vessel, including the underside of the base. Though generally thin, the slip was quite evenly applied, except for the area near the base where it is mottled and patchy. The slip is fairly well-preserved on the upper and lower parts of the vessel but very worn in the central area where the rouletting is most pronounced.

Fabric

The vessel is made of hard, pale reddish orange clay 2.5YR 7/4 (Munsell not given) to 5YR 8/4 (Munsell pink). The clay has a regular fracture and is smooth to the touch, becoming powdery where worn. To the unaided eye the fabric appears to contain very sparse inclusions of fine to coarse lime and fine mica and infrequent black particles. Microscopic analysis has yet to be undertaken.

Date

The vessel comes from the lower fill of the fish-pond (L165), a context of the early second century AD.

The bird

The bird depicted has a long, straight bill, oval head and a semicircular body, with slightly concave back and well-rounded chest (Fig. 242). A single stroke on the body indicates a wing, while two long strokes project to the rear, indicating the tail. The two angled strokes directly below the body are probably to be seen as the bird's legs. Close inspection of the series of lines below the bird suggests strongly that its upper element, consisting of three parallel, horizontal strokes, is intended to represent a nest, and that the nest rests on a pair of inclined strokes, very probably a stylized representation of a roof. From the vessel's first identification, this led to suggestions that the bird was a stork, since its close association with structures built by man is an image which has persisted till modern times. Dr Antero Tammisto (Finnish Institute, Rome) has made a detailed study of the representation of birds in Roman art, especially in wall-painting and mosaic, and believes that the bird as depicted could permit four possible identifications: stork, ibis, crane or heron.

According to Tammisto (pers. comm.) the ibis should be ruled out on the basis that in art its major distinguishing feature is its curved bill. On the vase the bird's bill is very straight. The crane can be discounted because its rather negative reputation in classical literature would seem to be at odds with the general spirit of the vase. The heron is a more serious possibility, but the generally large proportions of the bird and the fact that it is associated with a structure (which is not normally the case with herons in art or literature), seem to argue against this. Storks, on the other hand, are more than once shown in connection with buildings.[75]

The potters' marks

The two names Abaskantos and Epinikos, in the genitive case, which appear on the base of the vase, probably indicate either the makers or the owners of the vessel. Although graffito marks, presumably of ownership, are often found on the surface of pottery vessels in the ancient world, this was nearly always done after firing. It seems reasonable to assume that any marks of ownership on such an unusual piece as the 'stork-vase' would have been conspicuous and in the same style as the main inscription. Since neither of these considerations seem to apply to the concealed and

---

[75] A stork is depicted on the roof of a cottage or farm-building on a marble slab from the Columbarium of the Villa Pamphili, Rome (Peters 1963: 57 and fig. 48). According to Tammisto (pers. comm.), storks are shown on a tower in the Nilotic scene from the Casa dello Scultore in Pompeii.

Fig. 241. The inscription on the base of the 'stork-vase'. *(KW)*

rather carelessly executed inscription on the base, it seems more likely that the names denote the makers of the vessel. Analogy with signed Greek pottery of earlier periods (for example, the François vase) might suggest that one was the potter and the other the decorator and/or inscriber of the vase (assuming this division of labour).[76] But the uniqueness (at present) of this early Imperial vessel may allow for other possibilities.

Abaskantos was not an uncommon name throughout the Greek-speaking world.[77] However, it appears to belong exclusively to the Imperial period and first appears in Italy in the late Augustan/Tiberian era. Solin (1982: 844-7) has listed 221 examples from Rome, of which only five are written in Greek characters. The name appears to be particularly common amongst the lower social orders, since of 96 examples where status is given 93 are almost certainly slaves or freedmen. The name was fairly common among artisans, being found on bricks (for example, *CIL* XV 877, XV 1115), lead pipes (for example, *CIL* XV 7350, XV 7626) and on a lamp (*CIL* XV 6869). The appearance on a non-urban site of the name in Greek, at a period not far from the beginning of its popularity, is noteworthy.

Epinikos, although a more popular name than Abaskantos in the Greek-speaking world, was much less common in Italy. There are only fifteen known examples from Rome, of which three are written in Greek characters (Solin 1982: 50-1). Again, the name seems to belong to the lower social orders – in Solin's examples, where status is given, all are slaves or freedmen.

Discussion

With the exception of two very small versions of the vessel form in thin-walled ware found in the same deposit (Roberts, this volume, cat. 28), I know of no exact parallels. It should be noted, however, that the vase bears some similarity to Aco beakers (*Consp.* R12)

The colour-coated tradition to which the vessel belongs was well-established throughout mainland Italy during the Imperial period (though a comprehensive study has yet to be undertaken). These table-wares appeared in a multitude of forms, especially small- to medium-sized cups, bowls, dishes, beakers, jugs and jars, and were nearly always in a well-levigated clay, suggesting that their use was primarily for the consumption of liquids and food.

---

[76] For discussion of signatures on Greek vases and their possible meanings, see Boardman (1974: 11-3) and Cook (1972: 254-5).

[77] For onomastic evidence in the Aegean, on Cyprus and in Cyrenaica, see Fraser and Matthews (1987: 1 (Abaskantos), 159 (Epinikos)). I am grateful to Mrs E. Matthews for information from vol. III (forthcoming) on the occurrence of the names on the Greek mainland (excluding Attica), Dalmatia, Sicily and southern Italy.

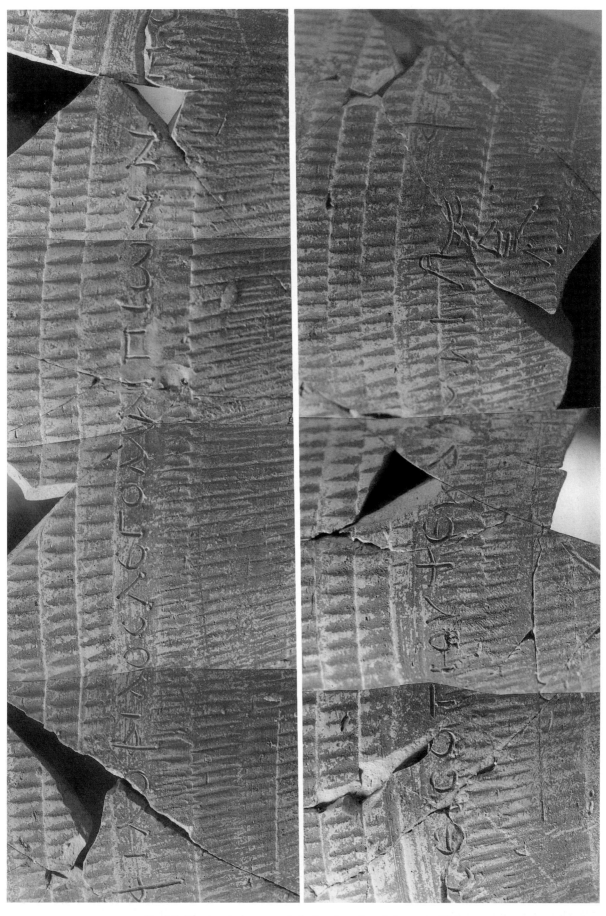

Fig. 242. The inscription around the 'stork-vase', and the stork. *(KW)*

The fabric, colour-coated finish, decoration and inscription of the 'stork-vase' imply strongly that it was a piece of table-ware, designed to be used for the consumption of a liquid. However, the size of the vessel raises some problems. With an estimated capacity of *c.* 1.25 litres, it held, when full, a far greater volume of liquid than the average cup or bowl. There is the possibility, therefore, that it was used either in the stage before drinking, for example in the mixing of wine and water, (though its tall, narrow form makes this less likely), or that it was intended to be used from one filling by more than one person.

The pair of holes below the rim suggest that the vase could have been suspended, either for display or storage. Vessels bearing suspension holes are not uncommon in pre-Roman and early Roman Italy.[78] Suspended vessels are also depicted in the stucco decoration of at least one Etruscan tomb.[79] If our vessel had ever been suspended for display, it would have been quite striking, and one of its presumably more significant features, the stork, could have faced outwards.

There must be some doubt, however, as to whether the vase was ever used in any capacity, since it is badly misfired. It was, in effect, a waster. The warping and fissures would have rendered the vase quite unusable for the consumption of liquids, and would have made it, at best, an ornamental piece. Indeed, the vessel's unusable state is very important, since it opens up the possibility of local manufacture (cf. further, Roberts, this volume).

THE INSCRIPTION, by Oswyn Murray

The most remarkable feature of the vessel is the inscription (Fig. 242), which runs around the body about two-thirds of the way down on a band apparently smoothed with the thumb after the decorative striations had been made. The inscription was incised before firing, and was carefully planned to fit the space available; beginning with the first word, it runs around the vase with a slight downward fall, ending up one decorative band (approximately 10 mm) lower than the starting point. The representation of the 'stork' is on this lower level, and does not quite fill the remaining space. The bird was therefore drawn after the inscription, but not apparently as an infill or afterthought, since it is not centrally placed, but slightly nearer to the end of the line than to its beginning. Thus the writer seems to have planned both inscription and drawing together, after the decoration had been applied, and to have inscribed them in that order.

Φιλόφιλος λέγομαι · πιὼν ν[ο]ήσεις ὅτι
οὐ ψεύδομαι

I am called a friend of friends; when you drink you will understand that I do not deceive.

The script is not documentary, but an elegant literary or semi-literary hand. The inscription might loosely be described as rhythmic, though not metrical. It is divided into two equal cola of nine syllables; at the central point after πιών there is a small gap, and the initial N of the next word appears slightly larger, as if the writer wished to mark something – clearly not a pause in the sense, but perhaps the rhythmic centre of the line. The inscription as a whole gives the impression of a carefully designed and executed sentiment, created for its position and for the function of the vase by an author of some literary skill and sophistication.

Φιλόφιλος is in literary texts an unusual word, found primarily in philosophical discussions of Φιλία: for instance, Aristotle, *Ethica Nicomachea* viii. 1155a29-30: 'τοὺς γὰρ φιλοφί-λους ἐπαινοῦμεν, ἥ τε πολυφιλία δοκεῖ τῶν καλῶν ἕν τι εἶναι' ('for we praise those who love their friends, and it is thought to be a fine thing to have many friends').[80] But it is not a specialized philosophical word: it is found in Polybius (i. 14.4) and Philodemus (*peri Parrhesias* ed. Olivieri F 50, 85); and its formation is discussed by Eustathius (*ad Iliadem* i. 690). A number of funerary stelai from Egypt, mainly of Roman Imperial date, show that it was in common use along with other φίλος compounds as a laudatory epithet of the dead, being presumably especially appropriate to those who lacked close ties of kinship.[81] It is also found in astrological texts of the Imperial age, in contexts where φίλος compounds and virtues are listed.[82] In general these uses suggest a non-literary word especially appropriate to contexts involving a series of φίλος compounds, but rarer in isolation.

Otherwise the language is unexceptional, and the form of the sentiment shows a number of characteristics found in inscriptions on drinking vessels from a wide range of periods in the Graeco-Roman world. We may note the following.

---

[78] For example, chalices, dishes and bowls from Etruscan tombs at Cerveteri; see Bosio and Pugnetti (1984: 52, 58-9). For drinking vessels from Samnite tombs near Gildone in Molise, see Macchiarola (1989: 62, 66).

[79] The end wall of the 'Tomba dei Rilievi', Cerveteri, features, amongst other objects moulded in stucco, a kylix suspended by its handle and a large dish suspended seemingly by a cord or thong. A pilaster in the same tomb features another kylix and a large jug-like vessel (Moretti 1978: 24-5).

[80] See also Aristotle, *Ethica Nicomachea* viii. 1159a33-4; *Rhetorica* ii. 1381b27; 1389a35; *De virtutibus et vitiis* 1250b32; 35; 1251b35.

[81] Dain 1933: 174 (Ptolemaic); *SEG* 30 (1980) nos. 1764 and 1769 (= *Arch. Pap.* 5 (1913), 167 no. 20); 35 (1985), nos. 1657 and 1668; the popular nature of the context is shown by the occasional substitution of π for φ These examples show that Michael was certainly correct to emend φιλόσοφος to φιλόφιλος in Plutarch, *Consolatio ad Apollonium* 120a. φιλοφίλου also appears on a stele from Thera (? third-fourth centuries AD), where it is probably the usual funerary epithet of the deceased rather than a patronymic (registered among the *dubia* by Fraser and. Matthews (1987: *s.v.*); Mrs Matthews informs me that the archive holds a possible fragmentary example of the name: Φι]λοφίλου, *Inschriften von Ephesos* no. 20 B 22 (54-9 AD)).

[82] Vettius Valens, *Anthologiae* (ed. D. Pingree, 1986) i. 2.56; i. 19.19; i. 20.27; cf. appendix I pp. 387.4; 411.8; see also *Catalogus Codicum Astrologorum* vii.205.

(1) The first person statement by the vase, 'I am ...'. This is a common form of statement among ownership graffiti in the archaic period, in the form 'I am the cup of ...'.[83] Some of these inscriptions compare with our vase in their complexity and wit (see (3) below); but the practice of first person ownership inscriptions seems much rarer in later periods, and I know of no example where the first person introduces a descriptive adjective without noun.

(2) The address to the user of the vase, which often takes the form of an encouragement to drink. Painted drinking inscriptions or toasts are found on Attic black and red figure cups; they are simple ones of the type, χαῖρε καὶ πίει εὖ (Immerwahr 1990: nos. 227, 228, 242, 251, 253-5). Scattered later examples can be found.[84] Again these simple messages can occasionally achieve greater heights; a painted inscription of the mid-third century AD reads, 'δίψαι σύ, καλὴ γὰρ εἶ' ('be thirsty for you are pretty') (Robinson 1959: K 19; cf. M 147, 149).

(3) The antithetical division of the sentiment into two contrasting parts. This seems almost a rule for the formulation of more complex messages written on cups. The earliest example is, of course, the famous 'Nestor's cup' from Ischia, which has been convincingly interpreted by Hansen in a manner which makes it perhaps the closest parallel yet available to our text, as a complex play on words and images which themselves evoke expectations in the drinker (Hansen 1976). Other convivial inscriptions, among those cited above, offer the same antithetical division, and involve simpler jokes or threats: 'I am the flask of Tataie; whoever steals me will go blind' (Jeffery 1990: pl. 47 no. 3). The formal division is, of course, also common in sympotic poetry like the Theognidean corpus, and is indeed a universal characteristic of those proverbial or gnomic utterances, in prose or verse, which tend to collect around the practices of conviviality in many cultures – such as the Biblical saying, 'Let us eat and drink: for tomorrow we die' (Isaiah 22.13; 1 Corinthians 15.32; cf. Ecclesiastes 8.15; cf. Luke 12.19).

(4) The reminiscence of a famous motif of drinking songs, in the collocation of drinking with truth. Alcaeus is the first to mention (but he surely did not invent) the proverb 'in vino veritas', which recurs in western literature in many different forms.[85]

All these characteristics place the inscription on our stork-vase in a typically convivial context. But there remains a number of problems. The first is the sporadic nature of the evidence for such inscriptions, and their apparent absence from any material comparable in date or circumstance of manufacture. The painted exhortations on Attic black and red figure pottery are some 600 years older; most of the inscribed first person statements are even earlier. Hellenistic pottery seldom offers more than a name, and certainly provides no such carefully constructed apophthegms. Similarly there seems to be nothing as elaborate in the occasional toasts and exhortations to drink found on samian ware.

The existence of a category known as *grammatikon ekpoma* ('inscribed drinking-cup') is attested in Athenaeus's exhaustive list of types of cup (xi. 465d-466e). But it has long been recognized that these are in fact special cups used for libations to the gods: they are represented in the surviving evidence by a large group of cups from both Greek and Roman periods inscribed with the name of a single deity in the genitive (Picard 1910; 1913; also, Wolters 1913: 198; Thompson 1934: 339). From the references in Athenaeus, it would appear that such cups could be old and valuable, and inscribed in gold lettering; most of our examples attest the practice at lower and less formal levels: the deities invoked from one collection of graffiti on Hellenistic cups, found in wells in the Corinthian tavern district, are more suggestive of pleasure than of serious religious observance (Broneer 1947: 240). The fact that cups with this particular very simple message were characterized as 'inscribed cups' suggests indeed that vessels inscribed for other purposes and with more complex messages were not common in the Graeco-Roman world.[86]

The closest parallels seem indeed to be in Roman glassware. A series of mould-blown beakers of the first-second centuries AD from Roman Syria have drinking inscriptions in Greek which run in a band around the sides; there are some half dozen messages involved, mostly invitations to drink of the type, 'be merry and rejoice', 'rejoice that you are here'.[87] Similarly the inscriptions found on late Antique glass are often elaborate literate toasts in Greek and Latin, in careful lettering running round the beaker or in tondos.[88] There is perhaps something reminiscent of Roman glassware in the shape of the Monte Gelato vase. But are such examples enough to allow us to suppose that it is an imitation in clay of a lost type of inscribed cup in a more expensive material, glass or metal?[89]

A second problem concerns the relationship between the inscription and the use of the vessel. The shape is somewhat unusual for a drinking cup, though (as Roberts has noted above) it has analogues in the Aco beakers. When filled, as he says, it would have contained about 1.25 litres, and have been of considerable weight. But it is scarcely large enough for the mixing of wine and water, and must surely in fact have been used as some form of loving cup, by more than one person.

That in turn raises the question, who are the speaker and the person addressed? The latter is surely the drinker, who (as he drinks) reads and understands that the former is not lying; if there is more than one drinker, then each drinker

---

[83] Examples have been given by Jeffery (1990: plate 1 no. 4; 47 no. 1; 47 no. 3; 66 no. 69; 67 no. 1; 68 nos. 17, 23; 72 no. 63). Most of these have been discussed by Burzachechi (1962: 28-36).

[84] The most interesting known to me is third-century BC (Lang 1976: G 15): 'πίη κακοδαίμων', 'a threat against the drinker'!

[85] Alcaeus F 366 Lobel-Page: οἶνος, ὦ φίλε παῖ, καὶ ἀλάθεα. For something of the literary history and significance of this famous phrase, cf. Rösler (1995).

[86] One cup described by Athenaeus (466e, 489c) had a long inscription, but was clearly exceptional: the alleged 'cup of Nestor' on display at Capua, made in silver on the model of Homer's description, with the relevant Homeric verses inscribed on it in gold – a show-piece of the metalworker's art.

[87] Harden 1935; for additions, see, Harden (1944-5); for illustrations, see, Oliver (1980: nos. 63-4) and Auth (1976: nos. 56-7).

[88] For instance, the 'Vita bona' jar – VITA BONA FRVAMVR FELICES (engraved, third-fourth centuries AD) (Harden *et al.* 1987: no. 115); or, BIBE VIVAS MVLTIS ANNIS (applied letters in cagework, fourth century AD) (Harden 1987; no. 134); cf. nos. 160 and 161 (gold letters, Christian, fourth century AD) in Harden (1987); Matheson 1980: no. 257 (gold lettering, third- fourth centuries AD).

[89] Are the Egyptian glass *toreumata* which Martial contrasts with traditional clay *pocula* perhaps engraved with letters rather than scenes (Martial, *Epigrammata* xi. 11)?

in turn experiences the same sensation with the same message. By analogy with other first person statements on vases, the speaker may well be the vase itself, which then demonstrates its friendly nature to each drinker in turn, as they partake of a rite of friendship (Burzachechi 1962: n. 21; Svenbro 1988: ch. 2). The sentiment is performative, the activity is mirrored in the text. But why the bird?

As Roberts has argued, from an artistic point of view the bird is ornithologically not a crane or an ibis, but a stork depicted as nesting on a rooftop. That analysis can be reinforced from the literary texts, if we assume that bird and sentiment have something to do with each other. Cranes are not friendly birds: they have a poor reputation in Antiquity. They are disliked by man, who accuses them of stealing the farmers' corn.[90] The ibis was famous, like the stork, for its alleged habit of eating serpents and other dangerous pests, and was known as an Egyptian sacred bird; but it had no clear place in classical thought (Thompson 1936: 106-14). By contrast, the stork is the bird of friendship. It is the symbol of filial piety, since it was believed in Antiquity actually to feed its aged parents (Thompson 1936: 221-5). It is also the symbol of friendship between man and the animal kingdom; in contrast to the crane it should not be harmed.[91] Pliny (*Naturalis Historia* x. 62) claimed it was an offence equivalent to homicide in Thessaly to kill a stork; and the bird is connected with the temple of Concordia in Juvenal (*Satura* i. 116).[92] Plutarch offered a contemporary Greek view: unlike swallows, 'the stork, who receives neither shelter nor warmth nor any security or help from us, pays a rent for his roof-top perch, by making the rounds and killing toads and snakes, which are treacherous and hostile to man' (*Moralia* 727F).

It makes sense, therefore, to suppose that it is not just the vase which speaks, but that the bird is also imagined as delivering the message. But is there not some closer connection between vase and stork?

Phaedrus, contemporary of our vase, and from the same social milieu as its creators, the educated servile and freedman class, told the famous fable of the fox and the stork. The fox invited the stork to dine and gave him liquid food on a flat dish, which the stork could not eat; when the stork returned the invitation, he presented the fox with pate in a tall vessel, and the fox in turn went hungry (Phaedrus I. 26).[93]

Hesychius, whose chief source, Diogenianus, belongs to the second century AD, in fact records *pelargos* as the name for an unknown pottery vessel shape: πελαργός ἄγγος τι κεράμεον (*s.v.* ed. M. Schmidt, π 1289). This meaning is otherwise unattested; but the name will surely have referred to a tall vessel. Perhaps in this beaker from Monte Gelato we have the first identifiable example of the ancient pottery shape of the *pelargos*. In that case stork and vase are identical; it is indeed a stork-vase, decorated with a stork, who delivers both as bird of concord and as loving cup a message for the participants in some social ritual of conviviality, whose exact character remains obscure.[94] Let us at least hope that the unfortunate misfiring of their cup, which has preserved it for us, did not deter the two craftsmen from creating a second vase more successfully for themselves.

The speaking vase plays upon the name of its shape, and elegantly invokes the literary characteristics of its bird-name to establish its specific function as a drinking vessel; it is not surprising to find so sophisticated a word-game inscribed in a script closer to literary than to documentary models. It is easy to be misled by the impressive luxury of the great villas of the Imperial aristocracy, perhaps like that at Monte Gelato, into believing that the owners were the men of culture in their age. In fact, of course, the true bearers of literary taste were their servants, the sophisticated class of freedmen and slaves who inhabited the back-quarters of the same urban and suburban villas as their masters. The stork-vase from Monte Gelato is a sudden and unexpected shaft of light into the lifestyle of men like Phaedrus, Epictetus and the heroes of Petronius's *Satyricon*.

THE SCRIPT (FIG. 242), by Peter Parsons

The inscription was inscribed on soft clay. Therefore, in assessing the script, we look for parallels not in the hard medium of stone inscriptions, but in pen-writing (on papyrus) and stylus-writing (on waxed tablets): that means parallels from the other side of the Mediterranean, since it is only in Egypt that climatic conditions have preserved thousands of examples of Greek writing.

Scripts are conventionally classified as 'book-hands', used for copying literary works, and 'cursive hands', used for writing documents. Cursive hands aim for speed, by adapting letter shapes, and ligaturing them together, in accordance with the law of least effort. In book-hands the letters stand separate from one another, and the forms aim at clarity and beauty; you can analyse the modulus (the shape of the letters individually and in relation), the ductus (the number and order of strokes of a letter), the shading (relative thickness and thinness of strokes), and the ornament (serifs and the like).

The Monte Gelato inscription comes close to book-hand: the letters distinct, no ligatures, no really cursive letterforms (except perhaps delta). The script is approximately bilinear: the letters, apart from phi, fit between two notional parallels – an effect emphasized here by the specially smoothed band in which the writing is confined. There is no consistent ornament (a sort of serif on the lambda of λέγομαι); but substantial shading, produced by the turning of the flat-bladed stylus (which also gives some strokes a tapering or wedge-shaped end).

Among letter shapes the following should be noted.

- A in a pointed shape (not the capital, or the looped form).
- Δ apparently in two movements, a curve which combines the left side and the base, and a long projecting backstroke. There is a certain likeness to the Latin uncial d; but that may be accidental, since similar forms do occur in Greek cursive.
- E and C with the cap added separately.
- M with the two central strokes in a single movement.
- O as usual, two touching arcs.

[90] Babrius 26; cf. Virgil, *Georgics* I. 120 with Mynors's note; see, in general, Thompson (1936: 68-75).

[91] Aesop, *Corpus Fabularum Aesopicarum*, 208 Hausrath, and Babrius 13: 'I am not a crane but a stork'.

[92] Cf. Publilius ap. Petronius, *Satyricon* 55: '*ciconia etiam, grata peregrina hospita / pietaticultrix gracilipes crotalistria*'.

[93] But Plutarch, *Moralia* 614e-f, told the same story about the crane.

[94] The rituals of Roman Imperial conviviality are a subject in need of investigation; see D'Arms (1990: 308-20) and Dunbabin (1991; 1995).

– Π with the top projecting either side.
– Υ in the V-shape.

Most of the forms could be paralleled in such calligraphic scripts as the 'Roman Uncial' (exemplified in the Hawara Homer – Turner 1971: no. 13; 1987: no. 13). But here, of course, the execution is much less formal and consistent, and parallels for the overall effect lie within Turner's category of 'informal round hands' (Turner 1987: 21). It is especially interesting to compare two examples of script incised on wax, which palaeographers have dated to the same general period as the Monte Gelato vessel. Firstly, there is a tablet in Berlin which copies an epigram of Posidippus (Schubart 1911: no. 17): the beginning is in a script rather like ours, with literary pretensions though not fully controlled, the end degenerates rapidly into cursive. Secondly, a tablet in the British Library (Turner 1987: no. 4) gives a moral maxim in an elegant bilinear script, and two attempts to copy it, no doubt by a schoolboy. The Monte Gelato scribe comes much closer to the copperplate of the master than to the gawky, tottering efforts of the pupil.

Whoever inscribed the vessel, then, had a good model in mind, and did the work carefully. That has its interest in assessing the character of the estate and its employees. It has also a wider interest for the question, how far the Greek diaspora of the Empire maintained a cultural unity. Palaeographers debate whether different areas practised different sorts of script. For documentary hands there is indeed some evidence of local peculiarities (Turner 1987: 17). For literary hands, the evidence itself (apart from the Herculaneum Library) is minimal. The Monte Gelato text adds interestingly to that evidence, and speaks for uniformity: I can see nothing in the script that would be surprising in Graeco-Egyptian manuscripts of the same period.

THE EARLY MEDIEVAL AND MEDIEVAL POTTERY, by Helen Patterson

INTRODUCTION

The early medieval and medieval ceramic sequence from the main site at Monte Gelato dates from the late eighth century, with the rebuilding of the church of the *domusculta*, until the abandonment of the site around the late eleventh to early twelfth centuries. Although there is slight evidence to suggest that some frequentation of the site could have occurred in the transition phase between the late Roman and early medieval periods, there appears to be a virtual gap in the ceramic sequence between the latest identifiable deposits of the mid-sixth century and the late eighth century. The seventh-century ceramic types recently identified at the Crypta Balbi, Rome, for example, do not appear to be represented in the Monte Gelato

deposits. The only exception is one vessel of probable sixth- to mid-seventh-century date, recovered from a tomb (Roberts, cat. 187). Similar vessels have been found in cemeteries in central-southern Italy, and are generally dated on the basis of associated metalwork and coins to this period (Peduto 1984; Salvatore 1982; 1983): a later sixth- to seventh-century date for the Monte Gelato vessel is further supported by radiocarbon dating.

In general, the evidence from Monte Gelato in fact conforms with the picture emerging elsewhere in the Roman Campagna, where there is a hiatus in the ceramic sequence, and in many cases the settlement evidence, from sometime in the early sixth century until the late eighth century. From the late eighth century, contemporary with the ecclesiastical reorganization of the Campagna, we witness an economic revival, a characteristic element of which is the emergence of a distinctive local ceramic tradition whose wares are common to both the urban centre and rural sites.

The material from Monte Gelato is of particular interest, however, because of the discovery of a small pottery kiln and related kiln dumps. In operation from the first phase of the early medieval settlement, in the late eighth century, until the mid to late ninth century, the kiln produced a range of domestic pottery, probably including some with painted decoration, in a refined fabric. Despite the presence of sporadic wasters recorded from both Rome and sites such as Pianabella (Ostia Antica),[95] this is the first pottery kiln of early medieval date to be identified in the area of Rome. The vessel forms are identical or very similar to those in use in Rome and the Roman Campagna during this period: however, the analysis of the material from the Monte Gelato dumps offers us a valuable opportunity to study the ceramic evidence, the range of forms and their relative proportions, from a production site and therefore in terms of production rather than as a reflection of consumption patterns.

The ceramic sequence and the nature of the assemblage

The sample derives from a series of often mixed deposits. There are few independent dating elements and the pottery is largely dated on the basis of parallels with material from other excavations, in particular with that of the Crypta Balbi, Rome (Bonifay, Paroli and Picon 1986; Manacorda *et al.* 1986; Saguì and Paroli 1990; Cipriano *et al.* 1991; Ceci 1992; Paroli 1992a; Romei 1992), which has established a datable typological sequence for the early medieval and medieval wares which is supported and confirmed by other

---

[95] For example, in Rome wasters of forum ware have been recorded from excavations in the Roman forum and at the Crypta Balbi (Whitehouse 1980: 186; Romei 1992: 382-3), while a waster of a ninth-century amphora was recovered from the vaults of Santa Maria in Cosmedin (Giovenale 1927: pl. Xla; Mazzucato 1977: fig. 70; Whitehouse 1980: 139). Outside Rome, a waster of ninth-century forum ware was recovered from excavations at Pianabella (Ostia Antica) (Patterson 1992).

Table 62. Late eighth- to early ninth-century kiln dumps: percentages of ceramic classes based on the number of fragments (A) and on sherd weight (B).

TRENCH	domestic pottery		(of which wasters)		painted pottery		kitchen-ware		Roman residual	
	A	B	A	B	A	B	A	B	A	B
E	99.5	99.6	0.2	0.2	0	0	0.1	0.1	0.4	0.3
M	96.7	94.5	0.9	0.5	0.4	1.0	2.3	3.1	0.6	1.4
D	98.6	99.0	0.1	0.1	0.7	0.4	0.6	0.4	0.1	0.2

Table 63. Quantification of vessel forms by typological group from the kiln dumps.

form	group	rim count		EVEs (trenches D and M only)
		no. of rims	% of no. of rims	
closed	1a	155	66.8	621%
	1b	15	6.5	-
	2	20	8.6	63%
	3	6	2.6	12%
	4	30	13.0	13%
	5	1	0.4	3%
	TOTAL	227	97.9	734%
open	TOTAL	4	1.7	10%

excavations in Rome itself, its ports, and the Roman Campagna.

The stratigraphy relating to the early medieval and medieval occupation of the site appears to have been heavily disturbed. Few late eighth- and ninth-century deposits had remained *in situ*, because of later activity on the site, and the large ceramic deposits recovered from the tenth- to eleventh-century phases (in particular from areas D and M) include a significant and often overwhelming amount of residual domestic pottery, including some wasters. In fact, in most deposits domestic pottery represents over 70 per cent of the assemblage. Presumably the kiln dumps originally deposited during the late eighth and ninth centuries were, at a later stage, removed in order to clear certain areas; certainly in some cases they appear to have been used for levelling surfaces prior to laying down floors. This frequent redeposition of the dumps from the kiln also accounts for the fragmentary state of the pottery and the lack of reconstructable pieces.

Quantification

As noted above, one of the most interesting aspects of the pottery from Monte Gelato is that it permits us to examine the material from a production site. However, the fragmentary nature of the sample and the fact that the majority was not found *in situ*, but was redeposited at a later date, is problematic. In order to achieve a valid assessment of the range of wares produced, it was decided to include in the type series material from the redeposited kiln dumps which, on the basis of parallels elsewhere, can be securely dated to the late eighth to early ninth centuries. In terms of quantification and in particular an estimate of the relative proportions of the vessel types produced at the kiln site, three large deposits were selected. The first, contexts E9 and E36, are two of the few kiln deposits to be found *in situ*, comprising the fill of the kiln itself and a dump from the kiln (1,041 sherds: 15.975 kg). The two other sets of kiln dumps examined were both redeposited at a later date. The first comprises a series of tips from Trench M (contexts 2, 4, 7, 11, 12, 14, 17, 19, 20, 21) which contains solely diagnostic material of the late eighth and ninth centuries (2,992 sherds: 37.382 kg); and the second is a large deposit from Trench D (D219) which, although it includes sporadic material of the later tenth and eleventh centuries, is worthy of note simply for the quantity of material, the overwhelming majority of which is of late eighth- to ninth-century date (3,381 sherds: 65.154 kg).

Table 62 gives the relative proportions of the ceramic classes represented in the selected kiln dumps, based on both sherd count and weight. Table 63 gives the relative proportions of the domestic pottery types (according to typological group) on the basis of rim count and, for the larger deposits from Trenches M and D, using the estimated vessel equivalent or EVEs method, as developed by Orton

Table 64. Percentage of ceramic classes by period.

	domestic pottery	(of which wasters)	painted pottery	kitchen-wares	forum ware/ sparse glazed ware	Roman residual
late eighth/ninth centuries	98.3	(0.4)	0.4	1.0	0	0.3
late ninth/tenth centuries	73.2	(0)	0	19.6	1.2	6.0
late tenth/eleventh centuries	80.7	(o)	0	13.0	4.3	2.0
late eleventh/twelfth centuries	81.9	(0)	0	9.5	2.0	6.6

(1975; 1982).[96] The relative proportions of the ceramic classes by occupation phase are given in Table 64. The percentages given in Table 64 and in the next are based on sherd counts.

Fabric

The fabrics of the pottery have been defined on the basis of their macroscopic characteristics with the help of a hand lens. Petrological analysis has only been completed on the forum/sparse glazed ware of late tenth-/eleventh-century date (Patterson 1992), but both thin-section analysis and neutron activation analysis are planned.

CLASSES OF POTTERY

The early medieval to medieval assemblage consists of the following ceramic classes: domestic pottery, domestic pottery with painted decoration, kitchen-wares and glazed wares, comprising forum ware and sparse glazed ware (see Table 64 for the percentages of the ceramic classes phase by phase). At Monte Gelato the overwhelming predominance of domestic pottery in contexts of the *domusculta* period (phase 5) clearly reflects its role as a production site: this is especially marked when compared with contemporary deposits from other excavations in Rome and the Roman Campagna. In the kiln dumps domestic pottery comprises an average of 98.3 per cent of the material, whereas in the large late eighth-century deposit from the Crypta Balbi, Rome, domestic pottery comprised 54.9 per cent (Saguì 1991) and at Santa Cornelia, in contexts of the late eighth-early ninth centuries, 68.6 per cent (Patterson 1991). Although the percentage of domestic pottery drops in later phases, the

quantification figures for these must be treated with some caution, given the high proportion of residual pottery. Forum ware and sparse glazed ware is not common; only one fragment of forum ware of ninth-century date was recovered and, although these products become more common from the tenth century, it is not until the late tenth/early eleventh centuries, with the appearance of the earliest examples of sparse glazed ware, that they are present in consistent, although small, quantities.

THE KILN PRODUCTS

The kiln site produced domestic pottery, frequently with incised decoration, but also very probably a small amount of pottery decorated with bands of red or brownish slip. The forms of the vessels indicate, on the basis of dated parallels from other sites, that the kiln was in operation during the late eighth and the first half of the ninth centuries. Production may have continued into the second half of the ninth century but does not appear to have persisted beyond this date.

The vessels were thrown on a wheel and the relatively standardized forms, the wire-cut bases, the use of decoration and the refined fabric indicate a certain degree of specialization. The range of forms and decoration are directly comparable to contemporary domestic ware assemblages from Rome and sites in the Roman Campagna: however, the Monte Gelato production lacks some of the finishing touches which are often characteristic of these productions, such as the lighter surface colour, often giving the appearance of a slip, and

---

[96] The EVE method, or estimated vessel equivalent, uses a measurement of the proportion of each individual rim's surviving circumference as a measure of the proportion of the whole pot represented in the assemblage. EVEs has been shown to be the most statistically reliable method of pottery quantification. It overcomes the main problems suffered by other quantification methods: such as sherd counts, affected by variable fragmentation patterns, and sherd weights affected by the variations in weight of different vessel forms. EVEs was applied to the material from the kiln dumps to estimate the relative proportions of vessel types produced at the kiln site: an estimate of the number of vessels represented would have been extremely difficult, if not impossible, in the case of a highly fragmented assemblage such as that of Monte Gelato.

the knife-trimmed bases (see, for examples, the Crypta Balbi, Rome – Romei 1986: 526; Paroli 1992a: 365; Santa Cornelia – Patterson 1991: 125; Pianabella – Patterson 1993a: 225).

Fabric

The vessels were fired in a reducing atmosphere, producing a light-coloured fabric (fabric 1) ranging from buff (Munsell 10YR 8/3) to reddish yellow (Munsell 5YR 5/6): some, frequently overfired, examples have a greenish tinge. The colour variations probably reflect the position of the vessels in the kiln: it is probable that those with a buff-coloured fabric, which comprise the majority of the examples, had received the most even firing, whereas the greenish examples were those situated closest to the heat source, and the reddish examples, oxidized as a result of exposure to the air, were probably those stacked in the uppermost levels of the kiln. (For an ethnoarchaeological study of colour variations caused by firing, see Nicholson and Patterson (1989: fig. 8, and p. 80).)

The fabric is refined, with a smooth feel and clean fracture, containing occasional small inclusions of limestone, mica, augite and iron oxide, although some examples, in particular the fabric of the larger handles, are noticeably coarser.

Forms

Production was limited mainly to closed forms of small and medium dimensions, although some larger vessels are represented. Presumably these vessels served a domestic purpose and were mainly used for containing liquids, although the possibility that some of the larger amphorae type vessels were also used for the transport of foodstuffs cannot be ruled out. The forms comprise handled jars and jugs with tubular or lip spouts and very occasionally lids. The vessels have flat, thick-walled bases, which are usually wire-cut, or *omphalos* bases and oval-section, often ridged, handles. Open vessels are rare. Bowls comprise only 1.7 per cent on average of the production repertoire and, like the lids, do not appear to have been produced on a regular basis. The overwhelming predominance of closed vessels conforms with assemblages from consumption sites. At the Crypta Balbi, Rome, open forms are present, if extremely rare, whereas they are completely lacking from assemblages of this period at Santa Cornelia and Pianabella. There is a surprising diversity among the few examples recovered, comprising carinated vessels often with flange or thickened rims, a hemispherical bowl and bowls with flaring walls.

Given the fragmentary nature of the sample, the type series is defined almost entirely according to rim form and consequently it is often not possible to determine the whole profile of a vessel. In particular it is often difficult to distinguish between handled jar and jug forms as the same rim forms are often characteristic of both vessel types. This problem is fairly common in domestic ware assemblages of this period and is probably a result of the tall thin-walled necks which are typical of the domestic pottery of this period and which are a natural fracture point (see, for example, the domestic pottery from the Crypta Balbi, Rome (Paroli 1992a: tav. 5, nos. 25-35, 37-43) and from Santa Cornelia (Patterson 1991: fig. 26, nos. 48-59)).

The following main typological groups have been identified (for quantification of vessel types, see Table 63). These groupings must, however, be treated with caution, as the fragmentary nature of the sample has made the identification of vessel types difficult.

Closed forms, Groups 1-6 (Figs 243-6)

These comprise 98.3 per cent of the domestic pottery from the kiln dumps. Both the handles and bases of these vessels are typical of contemporary domestic ware assemblages from Rome and sites in the Roman Campagna. The handles are usually oval in section and often lightly ridged (cat. 60-8). These characteristics die out during the later ninth and tenth centuries as handle forms become increasingly simplified, evolving into the strap handles typical of the later tenth/eleventh centuries onwards (cat. 103). The vessels have either *omphalos* (cat. 69) or flat thick-walled bases, which are usually wire-cut (cat. 70-5). In the kiln dumps flat bases predominate, comprising *c.* 70 per cent of the bases recovered.

Group 1. Two handled jars (anforette) or jugs with tall thin-walled, vertical or lightly in-flaring necks and thickened rims, one or two handles attached at the neck (cat. 1-32)
This group is by far the most common in all the kiln dumps examined, comprising on average 73.3 per cent of the domestic ware forms. The examples with the collared rim (cat. 1-16) are particularly characteristic, comprising 66.8 per cent of the total domestic ware forms: the types shown as cat. 1-6 and cat. 11-13 are the most common. The complete profiles of these vessels are unknown, but the majority belongs to two-handled jars, mainly of small to medium dimensions, although some larger vessels are represented, with the handles attached from the neck to the widest point of the body. The presence of occasional lip spouts, however, indicates that the same rim form is also characteristic of jugs (see, for example, cat. 42 and 43). The rims range from 9 to 11 cm in diameter. The handles are mainly of medium dimensions, oval in section and often ridged (cat. 29-32). The vessels may have had flat or *omphalos* bases.

At Rome and in the Roman Campagna these rim forms are typical of early medieval domestic pottery assemblages. The distinctive collared rims, in particular, are common from the second half of the eighth century and throughout the ninth century. The late eighth-century examples are characterized by light concentric ridges on the neck of the vessels (see, for example, cat. 2, 4, 7, 10), a feature which has largely died out by the earlier part of the ninth century and by the later ninth century has disappeared completely (see, for example, cat. 11, 13). At Monte Gelato two main types of collared rim are represented: those with a pronounced collar rim (for example, cat. 1-9), and those which are simply a continuation of the neck (for example, cat. 11-16). Examples similar to the first type are documented in contexts of the second half of the eighth to the first half of the ninth centuries from the Crypta Balbi, Rome (Paroli 1992a: tav. 5, no. 40), Santa Cornelia (Patterson 1991: fig. 26, nos. 48, 51, 55) and Pianabella (Ostia Antica) (Patterson 1993a: fig. 2, nos. 9-20). Examples similar to the second type continue to be attested at the same sites throughout the ninth century (Romei 1986: tav. VII, no. 1; Patterson 1991: fig. 26, nos. 50 and 53; Patterson 1993a: fig. 2, no. 20, fig. 5, no. 40).

The remaining rim forms included in this group are also similar, and in some cases identical, to examples of the late eighth and early ninth centuries from Rome and the surrounding area.

*Group 2. Two handled jars (*anforette*) or jugs with tall flaring necks and plain rims, one or two handles attached from the neck (cat. 33-40)*

This group represents 8.6 per cent of the assemblage from the kiln dumps. The complete profile of these vessels is uncertain: however, some of the rims (in particular cat. 33-6, 40) are very similar to those of the two-handled biconical jars with flat bases from the Crypta Balbi, Rome (Romei 1986: tav. VII, nos. 2-4) and Santa Cornelia (Patterson 1991: fig. 26, nos. 44-5), where they are present in ninth-century contexts. The rim diameter of these vessels ranges from 9 to 11 cm. The handles, attached at the neck, are small and oval in section.

Group 3. Jugs (?) with handle attached at the rim (cat. 41-3)

This group is problematic as it is mainly defined by the presence of a small, oval-section handle attached at the rim, and in most cases the examples are so fragmentary that the rim form of the vessel is uncertain. It represents 2.6 per cent of the material from the kiln dumps.

Group 4. Wide-mouthed jugs or jars with thickened vertical or lightly everted rims, probably with one handle, generally attached at the rim, and in some cases a tubular spout (cat. 44-58)

This group comprises 13 per cent of the forms from the kiln dumps. Some of the vessels have a small oval-section handle, attached generally at the rim, and it is likely that the tubular spouts (cat. 57, 58) also belong to this group. The diameters of the rims range from 9 to 13 cm. These forms very probably belong to the wide-mouthed jug or jar characteristic of late eighth- to early ninth-century contexts from Rome and sites in the Roman Campagna. It has several variations, but is characterized by a biconical or globular body with a flat base, one oval-section handle attached at the rim and sometimes a tubular spout (see, for example, vessels from the Crypta Balbi, Rome, of the second half of the eighth century (Paroli 1992a: tav. 5, nos. 20-1, 24), and, with painted decoration (Paroli 1992a: tav. 4, no. 11) and from Santa Cornelia of the late eighth to early ninth centuries (Patterson 1991: fig. 26, nos. 36-43). Some of the Monte Gelato rim forms are strikingly similar to examples from Santa Cornelia.

Group 5. Jar (?) with everted thickened rim and impressed decoration (cat. 59)

Only one example was recovered. It is identical to vessels present at the Crypta Balbi, Rome, in a late eighth-century deposit (Paroli 1992a: 366-8, tav. 5, nos. 22-3). This is not a common form, no examples having been recorded so far from sites elsewhere in the Roman Campagna.

Group 6. Lids (cat. 84-5)

Lids were not a regular element of the production repertoire, only two examples being recovered (comprising 0.4 per cent of the kiln groups). One example (cat. 84) has the same impressed decoration as one of the jar forms (group 5, cat. 59). No lids are recorded from other domestic ware assemblages of this period in Rome or the Roman Campagna.

Open Forms, Groups 7-10 (Figs 246 and 247)

These represent only 1.7 per cent of the kiln material.

Group 7. Bowls with flange rim (cat. 86, 87)

Two bowls of large diameter with a flange rim were recovered. Their profiles are unknown and similar forms are not known from other assemblages of this date. The forms, however, recall those of the Roman period.

Group 8. Carinated bowls (cat. 88-90)

Three carinated bowls are represented, including one (cat. 88) which is identical to an example from the late eighth-century deposit at the Crypta Balbi (Paroli 1992a: tav. V, no. 19). A second has a band of incised zigzag decoration running beneath the rim (cat. 89).

Group 9. Hemispherical bowls (cat. 91)

Only one example was found – a small vessel with an inturned rim. Similar forms are not known from contemporary domestic ware assemblages.

Group 10. Bowls with flaring walls and plain rims (cat. 92, 93)

Two examples were recovered. Both have a series of concentric grooves on the exterior surface. Although similar forms have not been recorded from other assemblages of this period, the distinctive impressed decoration noted on one of the jar and lid forms (cat. 59 and 84), present also on late eighth-century vessels from the Crypta Balbi (Paroli 1992a: tav. 5, nos. 22-3), is repeated along the rim of one of the bowls (cat. 93).

Decoration (cat. 75-84; cat. 49, 59, 89, 93)

Incised combed decoration is a typical feature of the domestic pottery of Rome and the Roman Campagna during the late eighth and, especially, the early ninth centuries. For Monte Gelato 2.3 per cent (minimum) to 3.7 per cent (maximum) of fragments from the three kiln dumps examined are decorated. On closed vessels decoration was, with a few exceptions (see, for example, cat. 75), applied to the upper half of the vessel, mainly on the shoulder and, to a lesser extent, on the neck. The most common motifs are incised bands of straight lines and incised bands of wavy lines: however, these often would have been elements of a larger motif comprising a band of wavy incised lines, or occasionally criss-crossing lines, bordered by bands of straight lines (cat. 77-80). The latter was probably the predominant motif on the closed vessels. A variety of other motifs is represented. In order of frequency they are: groups of oblique/horizontal incised lines often bordered by straight/wavy incised lines (cat. 49, 75, 81, 82); stabbed chevrons (cat. 83); and, in small quantities, impressed decoration (cat. 59, 84). Of the eight bowls, three are decorated with incised lines (cat. 89) or grooves (cat. 92, 93): this includes one which also has impressed decoration (cat. 93).

Domestic pottery with painted decoration (cat. 94-100)

It is very likely that the small amount of domestic pottery with bands of painted decoration was also produced at the kiln site, although this can only be confirmed through scientific analysis of the fabrics. In Rome and the Roman Campagna, pottery with bands of painted decoration was in use during the eighth and early ninth centuries. It is probable that painted decoration represents the final evolution of the preceding tradition of slipped pottery in the area of Rome (Whitehouse 1982: 73-4; Ciarrocchi 1993; Patterson 1993b). Although the slipped wares of Roman date have still to be clearly defined in this area, recent studies now suggest that painted decoration appeared alongside the partially or completely slipped products during the sixth and seventh centuries and by the late seventh or eighth centuries had finally replaced the latter (Patterson 1993a). This tradition therefore has analogies with the pottery of central-southern Italy where slipped and later painted pottery are an important element of the ceramic repertoire between late Antiquity and the Middle Ages (Arthur and Whitehouse 1982; Freed 1982; Patterson and Whitehouse 1992). Painted pottery was, however, never produced on any scale in the area of Rome, and its production was short-lived, probably as a result of the increasing availability of the glazed forum ware which, from the mid-ninth century, certainly at Rome, became increasingly common. In the late eighth-century deposit from the Crypta Balbi, Rome, painted pottery comprises only 3.4 per cent of the assemblage (Saguì 1991); at Pianabella (Ostia Antica), in contexts of the late eighth to early ninth centuries, it represents only 0.9 per cent of the pottery (Patterson 1993a), whereas at Santa Cornelia a sole fragment was recovered (Patterson 1991).

At Monte Gelato painted pottery comprises on average 0.4 per cent of the material from the kiln deposits. The fabric appears identical to that of the domestic ware and the forms, comprising solely closed vessels, jugs or jars (usually with tall vertical necks and thickened rims), are very similar to those of the domestic pottery (see in particular cat. 21-4). The decoration consists of bands of red to pale brown slip, generally applied around the top, exterior and occasionally the interior of the rim and on the body of the vessel, in oblique, curving or straight bands over the exterior surface. Although the forms are very similar to those of the late eighth-century vessels from Rome (Paroli 1992a: tav. IV), the decoration of the Monte Gelato vessels seems to have been applied fairly casually, and no examples have been identified with the well-defined motifs recorded from Rome and Ostia (Paroli 1992a: tav. IV; 1993a).

DOMESTIC POTTERY OF THE LATE NINTH/TENTH TO EARLY TWELFTH CENTURIES

The domestic pottery of this period is characterized by the appearance of amphora-type vessels with tall plain rims, sometimes with a band of incised straight lines on the shoulder (cat. 101). Similar forms are characteristic at Rome and on other sites in the Roman Campagna in contexts of the later ninth to tenth centuries. Frequent examples of the thick strap handles typical of these vessels are also present. The latest examples of domestic pottery present at Monte Gelato, of the late eleventh/early twelfth centuries, are thinner walled vessels with tall, slightly inverted rims and distinctive narrow strap handles (cat. 102, 103), the so-called globular amphorae or water jars typical of the domestic ware assemblages of this period in the area of Rome.

The fabric of the domestic pottery of the tenth century onwards (fabric 2) is similar to that of the

kiln products, but is more refined and harder. Fired in reducing conditions, it is a pale brown to reddish colour, hard fired with a smooth feel and clean fracture. A very refined fabric, it has a few visible inclusions consisting of fine mica, very occasional limestone, and minute rounded matt red inclusions.

The domestic pottery of this period therefore appears to follow the same evolution as that from Rome and other sites in the Roman Campagna. In this area, from the later ninth/tenth centuries, the closed forms of small and medium dimensions, typical of the eighth and ninth centuries, gradually become less common. By the second half of the tenth century they have disappeared completely and only one main form remains, a two-handled vessel of medium dimensions (see, for example, Romei (1986: tav. VIII, no. 4), Patterson (1993b: fig. 3f)). By the eleventh century this has evolved into the thin-walled globular amphora or water jar, used for the conservation of liquids, which dominates the domestic pottery assemblage until the beginning of the thirteenth century (Romei 1986: tav. VIII, no. 6; Patterson 1993b: fig. 3g). Contemporary with these changes, from the later ninth century decoration becomes increasingly simplified and by the eleventh century has disappeared. It should also be noted that, with the gradual standardization of the closed domestic pottery forms from the later ninth century, the production of open vessels, which were a standard element of ceramic assemblages of the Roman period and which continued to be produced in minimal quantities during the eighth and early ninth centuries, seems finally to cease.

KITCHEN-WARES (CAT. 104-24)

Most of the vessels show signs of scorching and were clearly used for cooking. The forms of the kitchen-wares comprise jars (cat. 104-15) and *testi da pane* or baking covers (cat. 116-23), the latter appearing only from the later ninth or tenth centuries. There is also one *tegame* or shallow dish (cat. 124).

The jars of the late eighth to early ninth centuries have the greatest diversity of rim forms (cat. 104-12), and are similar to vessels of this date from the Crypta Balbi, Rome, and Pianabella (Ostia Antica) (Saguì 1991: fig. 3; Patterson 1993a: figs 1 and 2). At Monte Gelato examples of all the forms illustrated were present in contexts of the *domus-culta* period. Of probable late eighth-century date are the jar with the thickened angular everted rim (cat. 105), the most common kitchen-ware form of this period, and the jar with the everted collared rim (cat. 104), which is identical to one of the most common kitchen-ware forms from the late eighth century deposit at the Crypta Balbi (Saguì 1991: fig. 3, no. 5).

The kitchen-ware jars of the tenth century onwards are typical of those found in Rome and on sites in the Roman Campagna: they are limited to one main form, which undergoes a gradual evolution (see, for example, Ricci (1986: tavv. XI-XIII) and Patterson (1991: fig. 24, nos. 6-20)). This is a globular vessel with a flat base and two strap handles attached at the rim and extending to the widest point of the body. Unlike the domestic pottery, the bases of the kitchen-ware vessels are not wire-cut.

Testi or baking covers first appear in post-*domus- culta* contexts and comprise *c.* 50 per cent of the kitchen-ware assemblage. (For a description of the history and function of these vessels, see Cubberley, Lloyd and Roberts (1988) and Patterson (1991).) The fabric of the *testi* is noticeably coarser than that of the jars; this is a common phenomenon in both Roman and medieval assemblages (Ricci 1986: 537; Cubberley, Lloyd and Roberts 1988: 106; Patterson 1991: 122), and presumably was the result of a deliberate attempt by the potters to increase the refactory properties of the clay. They are generally wide-mouthed vessels with flaring walls; in terms of diameter, the *testi* fall into two main groups, the first, and by far the larger group, ranging from 30 to 35 cm, the second, from 19 to 25 cm. Of the *testi* present in these contexts, some chronological distinctions can be made on the basis of datable parallels elsewhere (see, for example, for the Crypta Balbi, Rome, Ricci (1986: tav. XI-XIII); for Santa Cornelia, Patterson (1991: fig. 25)). The examples with thick walls and thickened rims (cat. 116-19) are probably of the later ninth to tenth centuries, the fabric of these vessels being noticeably coarse. The *testi* with thinner walls and a more refined fabric (cat. 120-2) are probably of the late tenth to eleventh centuries, and have the beginnings of the downturned lip which characterizes the later examples of this form. The latest *testi* form has a prominent vertical lip (cat. 123): similar forms are dated both at Rome and at Santa Cornelia to the twelfth century.

One example of a *tegame* was recovered in phase 6 (cat. 124). At Rome this form is present in contexts of the tenth to early eleventh centuries (Ricci 1986: tav. XII, no. 4), but does not seem to have been common outside the urban centre; no examples were recorded from Santa Cornelia or Santa Rufina.

The majority of the kitchen-wares (93.5 per cent) throughout the early medieval and medieval periods are of one fabric (fabric 3), fired in oxidizing conditions. It ranges from red-brown to dark reddish grey in colour (Munsell 5YR 4/3 to 5YR 4/2), and is soft to medium fired, with a rough feel and hackly fracture; it contains numerous ill-sorted inclusions, characterized by large plates of biotite, visible on the surface of the vessels, some augite, large angular transparent inclusions, frequent small yellowish inclusions and flint. This fabric appears to correspond to Schuring's fabric 1

(Schuring 1987: fig. 1), which is typical of the kitchen-wares in Rome and in the Roman Campagna during the early medieval and medieval periods. From the later tenth or eleventh centuries, the fabric of both the jars and *testi* becomes more refined, and the walls of the vessels become correspondingly thinner. The second fabric (fabric 4), present in minimal quantities, was identified only in kitchen-wares of the late eighth and early ninth centuries. It is dark grey-brown (Munsell 5YR 3/1), hard fired, with a rough feel and sandy fracture, containing numerous small yellowish white inclusions and some muscovite.

FORUM WARE AND SPARSE GLAZED WARE

The pottery discussed here belongs to the early medieval and medieval production of glazed pottery characteristic of Rome and the surrounding area, known as *ceramica a vetrina pesante* (Mazzucato 1972) or forum ware (Whitehouse 1965) and sparse glazed ware. These are not two separate classes of pottery, but two successive phases of a tradition of glazed pottery production which underwent a gradual evolution. (For discussion of this class, see Bonifay, Paroli and Picon (1986), Paroli (1986; 1990; 1992a; 1992b) and Patterson (1991; 1993b).) The term forum ware is used here to refer specifically to the early medieval *ceramica a vetrina pesante* of Rome and the surrounding area, which forms a distinctive and homogenous group. Although its origin and chronology have been the subject of much debate, the sequence established by the Crypta Balbi excavations, and now supported by finds from other excavations, seem to have established an initial date for the production of forum ware in the late eighth century. Forum ware and later sparse glazed ware underwent a gradual evolution. One of the main characteristics of this production is the progressive diminution in the amount of glaze used and, by the late tenth to eleventh centuries, with the first examples of sparse glazed ware, the diminution of the surface area of the vessel to which the glaze was applied. Production of sparse glazed ware finally ceased during the early thirteenth century.

At Monte Gelato no diagnostic forms of forum ware and sparse glazed ware were recovered, and this class is poorly represented compared to other sites in the Roman Campagna. Forum ware of ninth-century date is extremely rare, consisting of only one fragment, which has the applied petal decoration characteristic of the forum ware of this date. From the late ninth to tenth centuries forum ware is more common, comprising 1.2 per cent of the material from the quantified deposits, and includes some examples with incised wavy line decoration. It is not until the late tenth to eleventh centuries, however, that glazed products are present in consistent, although small, quantities. These examples represent a transitional phase in the evolution from forum ware to sparse glazed ware, and are characterized by a thinnish glaze with occasional patches of the vessel left unglazed. By the late eleventh to early twelfth centuries the glazed pottery consists solely of sparse glazed ware, this comprising 2.0 per cent of the assemblage.

Two fabrics have been identified (fabrics 5 and 6). Fabric 5 is characteristic of the forum ware products of the ninth to tenth/early eleventh centuries. Fired in oxidizing conditions, the colour ranges from reddish yellow (Munsell 5YR 6/6) to reddish grey (5YR 5/2) to grey (5YR 5/1); it is hard fired with a rough feel and fairly hackly fracture, containing numerous small matt yellowish white inclusions, fine mica and some angular black inclusions. Petrological analysis of examples of forum ware/sparse glazed ware of the late tenth to early eleventh centuries placed the Monte Gelato fabric in the same petrological group (group 9g, containing volcanic and sedimentary inclusions) as that of examples from Rome and other sites in the Roman Campagna, such as Santa Cornelia, Scorano, and Lucus Feroniae. Fabric 6, characteristic of the sparse glazed ware of the later eleventh to twelfth centuries is more refined. It is reddish yellow in colour (Munsell 5YR 6/6 to 7.5YR 7/6), hard fired, with a smooth feel and smooth fracture containing occasional small white and large rounded red inclusions.

CONCLUSION

In recent years our understanding of the early medieval and medieval ceramics of Rome and the Roman Campagna has improved dramatically, giving some fundamental insights into social and economic developments during this period. The discovery of the kiln site at Monte Gelato is a further, important, contribution to this knowledge.

The pottery sequence at Monte Gelato in general follows the pattern emerging elsewhere in Rome and the Roman Campagna. The late eighth-/ninth-century production is characterized by the variety of forms and the richness of the decoration, although this is most strikingly reflected in the forum ware products of this period (see, for example, Romei (1992)). It is significant that it is also seen in an everyday product such as the domestic pottery and, to a certain extent, the kitchen-wares. At the same time, however, the modest level of standardization of the vessel forms and the fact that the same forms often occur in other ceramic classes is indicative of a fairly modest scale of production. Certainly in the case of the Monte Gelato kiln site, the evidence suggests that this was the case (see below).

Although the ceramic sequence of the later ninth to tenth centuries onwards at Monte Gelato is not particularly clear, because of the high proportion of residual material, one can nevertheless detect the same general trends noted from other sites in this area. From the later ninth to tenth centuries the ceramic products are characterized by the reduction in the range of forms. These are increasingly limited to a restricted number of standardized forms, specific to each ceramic class, coinciding with the increasing simplification and gradual disappearance of the decoration both on the domestic pottery and the forum ware products. There is also a notable decrease in the amount of glaze used; in addition, the fabrics become increasingly refined and the walls of the vessels thinner. After the richness of the late eighth/ninth centuries, these elements seem to reflect a streamlining of production, to a more industrial form in terms of a reduction of time, work and costs. This coincides with an increase in the amount of pottery in circulation, especially evident in the Roman Campagna (Patterson 1993b: 323-6).

At Monte Gelato, as elsewhere in the Roman Campagna, the renewed evidence for the circulation of pottery in the late eighth century coincides with the reorganization of the territory by the papacy, with the foundation of the domuscultae as a fundamental element. Monte Gelato, like Santa Cornelia, was almost certainly a domusculta centre, part of a programme of rational exploitation of the territory and of the provisioning of the people of Rome. From the time of their foundation they yield the same ceramic products as are found in Rome itself, clearly reflecting the renewed links between the urban capital and its territory. Furthermore, although these rural sites were very probably supplied in part by production centres in or near Rome, the discovery of the kiln site at Monte Gelato clearly shows that from the very beginning social and economic conditions existed which favoured and stimulated the development of local production centres in the Roman Campagna itself. The evidence also suggests that these centres were not only producing pottery for everyday use, as at Monte Gelato, but probably also a small amount of a luxury product such as forum ware.

Although no production centres of this ware have yet been identified, petrological analysis of forum ware indicates that, from the initial phase of production in the late eighth and ninth centuries, production centres existed in the Roman Campagna (Patterson 1992; 1993b: 322). The kiln site at Monte Gelato is, however, the only direct evidence we have so far of a rural production centre. It is impossible to say how typical the Monte Gelato kiln is of production sites of this period, although the products themselves are typical of the domestic pottery in use throughout this area during the late eighth and early ninth centuries. However, the small dimensions of the Monte Gelato production site, consisting of a single, small kiln, only 1.95 m in length, apparently without any associated working structures, and situated a few metres from the church itself, is striking and suggests a fairly modest scale of operation.

On what basis these rural production centres were operating is unclear. The foundation of the *domuscultae* during the eighth century may have created favourable conditions for the emergence of independent specialist potters, attracted by the new markets which the *domuscultae* offered; furthermore, given that the function of the *domuscultae* was to provide food for the urban population, the potters may have exploited an already existing transport and distribution system to distribute their wares. At Monte Gelato it is unlikely that the large quantity of domestic pottery produced in the late eighth and early ninth centuries supplied only the needs of the small rural community. On the other hand it is equally possible that the Church, at least at the beginning, played a role in the production and distribution of pottery, perhaps with the presence of 'attached specialists' whose products may have supplied a number of *domuscultae* centres (Patterson 1993b: 322-3). Although the scientific analysis of ceramic products from consumption sites, particularly on a regional scale, can tell us much about the distribution mechanisms in operation, such information obviously acquires greater potential if the wares can be tied down to known production sites. It is only by plotting the real distribution of products from single manufacturing sites that we may go some way towards resolving these problems. In this context the scientific characterization of the fabric of the domestic pottery produced at the kiln site at Monte Gelato is of particular importance.

A further point worth taking into consideration is the function of the vessels produced at the Monte Gelato kiln. Although the majority was clearly for domestic use, serving primarily as containers for liquids, the possibility that some of the larger two-handled amphora-type vessels were also used for the transport of foodstuffs cannot be totally ruled out. Although they differ from the transport amphorae which continued to circulate in small quantities along the central-south Tyrrhenian coast during the eighth and early ninth centuries, the latter seem to have been for maritime transport, their distribution being primarily limited to major centres such as Rome and its ports, Naples, Reggio Calabria and sites in Sicily (Paroli 1992a; 1993b; Arthur 1993; Patterson 1993a; 1993b). These transport amphorae rarely reached the Roman Campagna: so far small quantities have been identified only at Santa Cornelia, whilst at Monte Gelato and Santa Rufina they are totally lacking (Patterson 1993b). However, given that the function of the *domuscultae* was to supply the urban populace with foodstuffs, including liquid produce such as wine (Christie and Daniels 1991: 6), it is possible that some of the larger pottery containers were used for the transport of goods on a local level, either to the urban centre or to other *domusculta* centres.

There appears to be a long tradition of ceramic production in this area, which must, at least in part, be linked to the availability of good clay sources (Peña 1987). Excavation and survey in the Ager Faliscus identified two sites in the valley of the river Treia with evidence for tile and pottery manufacture during the fourth and third centuries BC (Potter 1976: 81 and 161). A small non-industrial tile and brick production centre is still in operation today in this area. Located about a kilometre southwest of Mazzano Romano, it uses a wood-fired kiln and clay quarried from a local source. Samples of clay from the quarry and other clay sources in the area are currently being analysed at the British Museum Research Laboratory with the aim of comparing these clays with the fabric of the pottery from the Monte Gelato kiln.

CATALOGUE

The catalogue entries have the following format: the figure number; the reference number or 'P' number of that particular piece of pottery, assigned during the study of the material and marked on the fragment itself (or, where a P number was not assigned to the illustrated piece, the P number of an equivalent piece); the dimensions; and the fabric. There are then details of the context and phase. General comments follow, including details of similar pieces found at Monte Gelato and comparable material from other sites.

Kiln products (cat. 1-100)

Domestic Pottery (cat. 1-93)
Closed forms (cat. 1-85)
Group 1. Handled jars (anforette) or jugs (rims) (cat. 1-26)

1. Fig. 243. P500; rim D. 10.5 cm; fabric 1. E36, kiln dump. Phase 5.
2. Fig. 243. P504; rim D. 9.5 cm; fabric 1. M10, kiln dump. Phase 6.
3. Fig. 243. Cf. P504; rim D. 11.5 cm; fabric 1. E36, kiln dump. Phase 5.
4. Fig. 243. P601; rim D. 10 cm; fabric 1. M14. Phase 5.
5. Fig. 243. P608; rim D. 8 cm; fabric 1. M135, kiln dump. Phase 5.
6. Fig. 243. P720; rim D. 9 cm; fabric 1. D219, kiln dump. Phase 7.
7. Fig. 243. Cf. P503; rim D. 9.5 cm; fabric 1. M16, kiln dump. Phase 6.
8. Fig. 243. P505; rim D. 10 cm; fabric 1. E9, kiln dump. Phase 5.
9. Fig. 243. P551; rim D. 9.5 cm; fabric 1. M2, kiln dump. Phase 6.
10. Fig. 243. P563; rim D. 10.5 cm; fabric 1. M16, kiln dump. Phase 6.
11. Fig. 243. Cf. P509; rim D. 10.5 cm; fabric 1. M2, kiln dump. Phase 6.
12. Fig. 243. P506; rim D. 9.5 cm; fabric 1. E36, kiln dump. Phase 5.
13. Fig. 243. P507; rim D. 11 cm; fabric 1. E36, kiln dump. Phase 5.
14. Fig. 243. P647; rim D. 10.5 cm; fabric 1. P17. Phase 6.

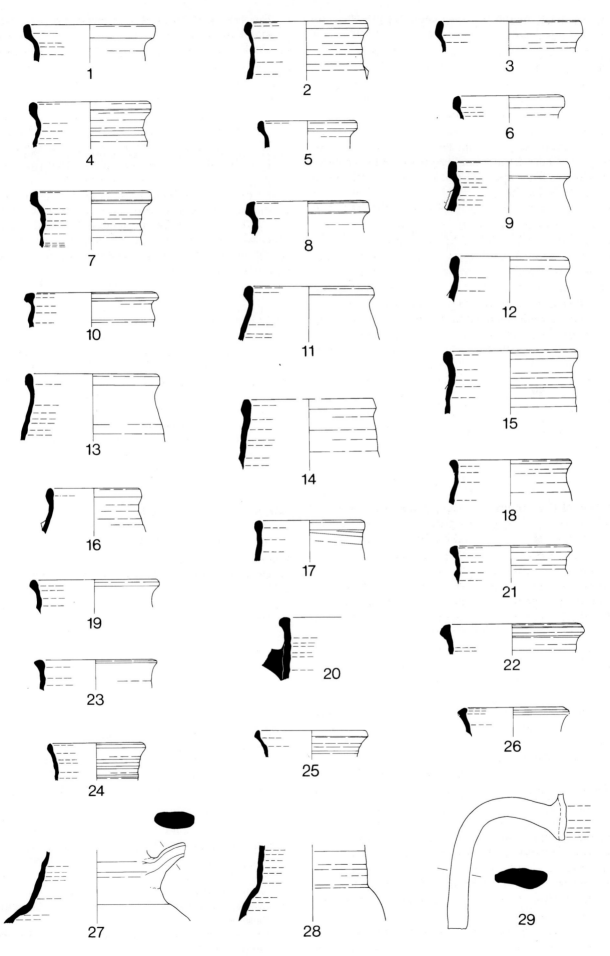

Fig. 243. Products of the early medieval kiln (1:3). *(SC)*

15. Fig. 243. P526; rim D. 11 cm; fabric 1. D215. Phase 6.
16. Fig. 243. P508; rim D. 7.5 cm; fabric 1. D219, kiln dump. Phase 7.
17. Fig. 243. P519; rim D. 9 cm; fabric 1. E9, kiln dump. Phase 5.
18. Fig. 243. P511; rim D. 10 cm; fabric 1. M112. Phase 5.
19. Fig. 243. P633; rim D. 10.5 cm; fabric 1. M106. Phase 5.
20. Fig. 243. Cf. P526. M19. Phase 5.
    Cf. Crypta Balbi, Rome: Paroli 1992a: tav. 5, no. 41; Pianabella (Ostia Antica): Patterson 1993a: fig. 2, no. 22. Both are of the second half of the eighth century.
21. Fig. 243. P561; rim D. 9.5 cm; fabric 1. M11, kiln dump. Phase 6.
22. Fig. 243. P510; rim D. 11 cm; fabric 1. E9, fill of kiln. Phase 5.
    Cf. Crypta Balbi, Rome: Paroli 1992a: tav. 3, no. 9 (of the second half of the eighth century).
23. Fig. 243. P518; rim D. 10 cm; fabric 1. E9, fill of kiln. Phase 5.
24. Fig. 243. P548; rim D. 8 cm; fabric 1. E36, kiln dump. Phase 5.
25. Fig. 243. P557; rim D. 8.5 cm; fabric 1. M11, kiln dump. Phase 6.
    Cf. Santa Cornelia: Patterson 1991: fig. 26, no. 55 (of the late eighth to early ninth centuries).
26. Fig. 243. Cf. P602; rim D. 9 cm; fabric 1. M72. Phase 6/7.
    Cf. Crypta Balbi, Rome: Paroli 1992a: tav. 5, no. 37 and (with painted decoration) tav. 4, no. 12 (both of the second half of the eighth century).

Neck and shoulder fragments (cat. 27, 28) and handles (cat. 29-32) probably belonging to above vessels

27. Fig. 243. P703; fabric 1. M61, kiln dump. Phase 6.
28. Fig. 243. P705; fabric 1. D219, kiln dump. Phase 7.
29. Fig. 243. P721; fabric 1. M61, kiln dump. Phase 6.
30. Fig. 244. Cf. P532; fabric 1. E9, kiln dump. Phase 5.
31. Fig. 244. Cf. P531; fabric 1. E9, kiln dump. Phase 5.
32. Fig. 244. Cf. P533; fabric 1. E9, kiln dump. Phase 5.

Group 2. Jugs or two handled jars (anforette) with tall flaring necks (cat. 33-40) (rims)

33. Fig. 244. Cf. P520; rim D. 12 cm; fabric 1. D219, kiln dump. Phase 7.
34. Fig. 244. Cf. P656; rim D. 8 cm; fabric 1. M72. Phase 6/7.
35. Fig. 244. P517; rim D. 10 cm; fabric 1. E9, fill of kiln. Phase 5.
36. Fig. 244. P525; rim D. 10 cm; fabric 1. E36, kiln dump. Fabric 5.
37. Fig. 244. P559; rim D. 8 cm; fabric 1. M18, kiln dump. Fabric 6.
    Cf. Pianabella (Ostia Antica): Patterson 1993a: fig. 5, no. 46 (of the late eighth century); Santa Cornelia: Patterson 1991; fig. 26, no. 60 (of the early ninth century).
38. Fig. 244. P552; fabric 1. M2, kiln dump. Phase 6.
39. Fig. 244. P558; rim D. 9 cm; fabric 1. M11, kiln dump. Phase 6.
40. Fig. 244. P549; rim D. 8 cm; fabric 1. D219, kiln dump. Phase 7.

Group 3. Jug (?) rims with handle attached at rim (cat. 41-3)

41. Fig. 244. P644; rim D. c. 6 cm; fabric 1. P9. Phase 6.

42. Fig. 244. Cf. P527; rim D. c. 8 cm; fabric 1. E9, fill of kiln. Phase 5.
43. Fig. 244. P527; rim D. 10 cm; fabric 1. E36, kiln dump. Phase 5.

Group 4. Wide-mouthed jug or jar rims, possibly with tubular spouts (cat. 44-58)

44. Fig. 244. Cf. P515; rim D. 11.5 cm; fabric 1. M19. Phase 5.
45. Fig. 244. P649; rim D. 10 cm; fabric 1. P17. Phase 5.
46. Fig. 244. P524; rim D. 10 cm; fabric 1. E36, kiln dump. Phase 5.
    Cf. Crypta Balbi, Rome; Paroli 1992a: tav. 5, no. 20 (of the second half of the eighth century).
47. Fig. 244. P512; rim D. 10 cm; fabric 1. E36, kiln dump. Phase 5.
48. Fig. 244. P514; rim D. 12 cm; fabric 1. D219, kiln dump. Phase 7.
49. Fig. 244. P560; rim D. 15 cm; fabric 1. M11, kiln dump. Phase 6.
    Cf. Santa Cornelia: Patterson 1991: fig. 26, no. 37, 39, 42 (of the late eighth/early ninth centuries).
50. Fig. 244. P523; fabric 1. D219, kiln dump. Phase 7.
    Cf. Santa Cornelia: as cat. 49.
51. Fig. 244. P528; fabric 1. M11, kiln dump. Phase 6.
52. Fig. 244. P515; rim D. 12 cm; fabric 1. M11, kiln dump. Phase 6.
    Cf. Santa Cornelia: Patterson 1991: fig. 26, no. 37 (of the late eighth century).
53. Fig. 244. P516; rim D. 11 cm; fabric 1. E9, fill of kiln. Phase 5.
    Cf. Santa Cornelia: Patterson 1991: fig. 26, nos. 36 and 38.
54. Fig. 244. P622; fabric 1. M64. Phase 6.
55. Fig. 244. P538; fabric 1. E36, kiln dump. Phase 5.
56. Fig. 244. Cf. P598; fabric 1. M19. Phase 5.

Tubular spouts probably belonging to above vessels

57. Fig. 245. P546; fabric 1. D219, kiln dump. Phase 7.
58. Fig. 245. P629; fabric 1. M61, kiln dump. Phase 6.

Group 5. Jar with impressed decoration (cat. 59)

59. Fig. 245. P638; rim D. 15 cm; fabric 1. P16. Phase 5/6. There is impressed decoration along the rim, as cat. 84 and 93.
    Cf. Crypta Balbi, Rome: Paroli 1992a: 366-8, tav. 5, nos. 22-3 (of the second half of the eighth century).

Handles (cat. 60-8)

60. Fig. 245. P530; fabric 1. D219, kiln dump. Phase 7.
61. Fig. 245. P535; fabric 1. M61, kiln dump. Phase 6.
62. Fig. 245. P723; fabric 1. M95, kiln dump. Phase 5/6.
63. Fig. 245. P725; fabric 1. E9, fill of kiln. Phase 5.
64. Fig. 245. P726; fabric 1. E9, fill of kiln. Phase 5.
65. Fig. 245. P727; fabric 1. E9, fill of kiln. Phase 5.
66. Fig. 245. P567; fabric 1. M18, kiln dump. Phase 5/6.
67. Fig. 245. P729; fabric 1. M61, kiln dump. Phase 6.
68. Fig. 245. P728; fabric 1. E36, kiln dump. Phase 5.

Bases of closed vessels (cat. 69-75)

69. Fig. 245. P731; base D. 10 cm; fabric 1. E9, fill of kiln. Phase 5.
70. Fig. 245. P542; base D. 10 cm; fabric 1. D219, kiln dump. Phase 7.
71. Fig. 245. P635; base D. 10 cm; fabric 1. P16. Phase 5/6.

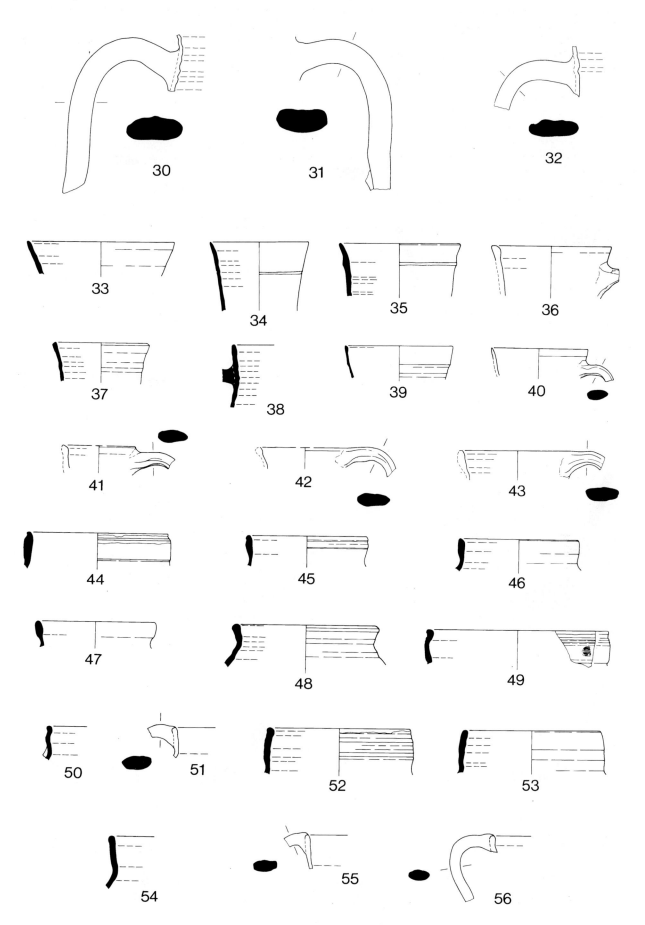

Fig. 244. Products of the early medieval kiln (1:3). *(SC)*

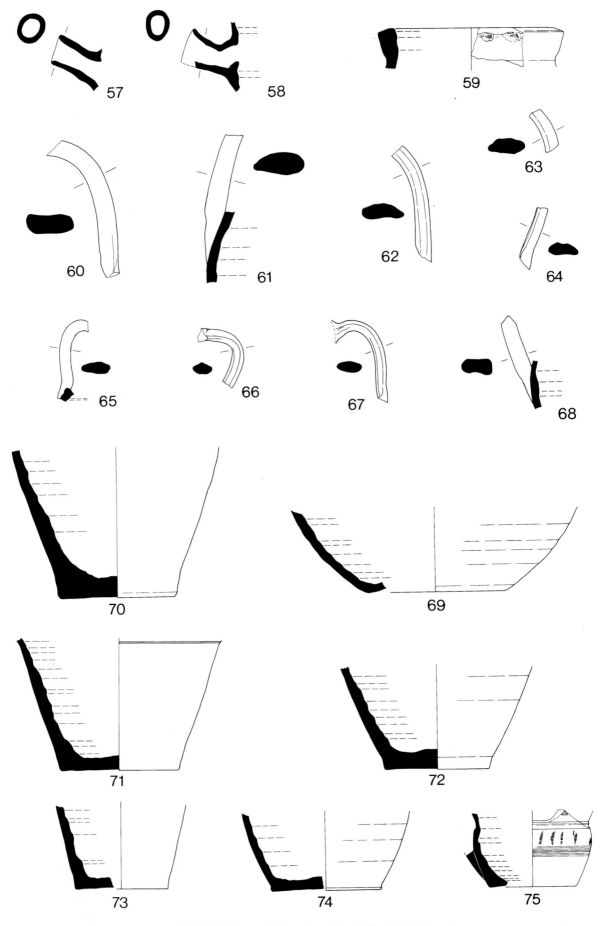

Fig. 245. Products of the early medieval kiln (1:3). *(SC)*

72. Fig. 245. P541; base D. 8.5 cm; fabric 1. M61, kiln dump. Phase 6.
73. Fig. 245. P627; base D. 8 cm; fabric 1. M2, kiln dump. Phase 6.
74. Fig. 245. P658; base D. 9 cm; fabric 1. B26. Phase 6.
75. Fig. 245. P555; base D. 7 cm; fabric 1. M145. Phase 5/6.

Incised decoration characteristic motifs (cat. 76-83)
76. Fig. 246. Fabric 1. M1, kiln dump. Phase 5/6.
77. Fig. 246. Fabric 1. P16. Phase 5.
78. Fig. 246. Fabric 1. M112. Phase 5.
79. Fig. 246. Fabric 1. M2, kiln dump. Phase 6.
80. Fig. 246. Fabric 1. D219, kiln dump. Phase 7.
81. Fig. 246. Fabric 1. D219, kiln dump. Phase 7.
82. Fig. 246. Fabric 1. M112. Phase 5.
83. Fig. 246. Fabric 1. B26. Phase 6.

Group 6. Lids (cat. 84-5)
84. Fig. 246. P642; rim D. 18 cm; fabric 1. P16. Phase 5. There is impressed decoration along the rim, as cat. 59 and 93.
85. Fig. 246. P547; rim D. 12 cm; fabric 1. M106. Phase 5.

Open forms – bowls (cat. 86-93)
Group 7. Bowls with flange rim (cat. 86, 87)
86. Fig. 246. P529; rim D. 30 cm; fabric 1. D219, kiln dump. Phase 7.
87. Fig. 246. P521; rim D. *c.* 35 cm; fabric 1. D219. Phase 7.

Group 8. Carinated bowls (cat. 88-90)
88. Fig. 246. P600; rim D. *c.* 35 cm; fabric 1. M19. Phase 5. Cf. Crypta Balbi, Rome: Paroli 1992a: tav. 5, no. 18 (of the second half of the eighth century).
89. Fig. 246. P631; rim D. *c.* 20 cm; fabric 1. M106. Phase 5. There is a concentric band of incised zigzag decoration beneath the rim.
90. Fig. 246. P621; rim D. 26 cm; fabric 1. M64. Phase 6.

Group 9. Hemispherical bowl (cat. 91)
91. Fig. 246. P648; rim D. 12 cm; fabric 1. P17. Phase 6.

Group 10. Bowls with flaring walls and plain rims (cat. 92, 93)
92. Fig. 247. P676; rim D. 22 cm; fabric 1. P16. Phase 5.
93. Fig. 247. P643; rim D. 33 cm; fabric 1. M102. Phase 5. There is impressed decoration along the rim, as cat. 59 and 84.

Domestic pottery with painted decoration (cat. 94-100)
Jugs or jars
94. Fig. 247. P626; rim D. 12 cm; fabric 1. M64. Phase 6.
95. Fig. 247. P734; rim D. 10 cm; fabric 1. M10, kiln dump. Phase 6.
    Cf. Crypta Balbi, Rome: Paroli 1992a: tav. 4, no. 12 (of the second half of the eighth century).
96. Fig. 247. P605; rim D.12 cm; fabric 1. M61. Phase 6.
97. Fig. 247. Cf. P169; rim D. 12 cm; fabric 1. M102, kiln dump. Phase 5.
98. Fig. 247. P625; rim D. 6 cm; fabric 1. M112. Phase 5. For a similar form, but without the painted decoration, see cat. 24.
99. Fig. 247. P700; fabric 1. M61. Phase 6.
100. Fig. 247. Body fragment. M61. Phase 6.

Domestic pottery of the late ninth/tenth to early twelfth centuries
Two handled jars (cat. 101-3)
101. Fig. 247. P637; rim D. 11 cm; fabric 1. P16. Phase 6.
     Cf. Crypta Balbi, Rome: Romei 1986: tav. VIIII (of the tenth century); Santa Cornelia: Patterson 1991: fig. 27, no. 67 (of the late ninth to tenth centuries).
102. Fig. 247. P611; rim D. 9 cm; fabric 1. M111. Phase 6.
103. Fig. 247. P556; fabric 1. D279. Phase 7.
     Cf. Crypta Balbi, Rome: Romei 1990: tav. XIX, no. 168 (from a globular amphora of eleventh-century date).

Kitchen-wares (cat. 104-24)
Jars (cat. 104-15)
104. Fig. 247. P717; rim D. 25 cm; fabric 3. M71. Phase 5. Heavily scorched on the interior and also partially on the exterior.
     Cf. Crypta Balbi, Rome: Cipriano, Paroli and Picon 1991: fig. 3, no. 5 (where it is the most common kitchen-ware jar form found in the large late eighth-century deposit).
105. Fig. 247. Cf. P610; rim D. 18 cm; fabric 3. M2. Phase 6.
     Heavily scorched on the exterior and around the interior of the rim.
     Cf. Crypta Balbi, Rome: Cipriano, Paroli and Picon 1991: fig. 3, no. 6 (of the second half of the eighth century).
106. Fig. 247. P607; rim D. 22 cm; fabric 3. M17. Fabric 5. Heavily scorched on the interior and on most of the exterior.
107. Fig. 247. P715; rim D. 11 cm; fabric 4. M21. Phase 5. Heavily scorched on the interior and partially on the exterior.
     Cf. Pianabella (Ostia Antica); Patterson 1993a: fig. 1, no. 10 (of the late eighth century).
108. Fig. 247. P618; rim D. 10 cm; fabric 3. M143. Phase 5. There are no signs of scorching.
     Cf. Pianabella (Ostia Antica), as cat. 107.
109. Fig. 247. P617; rim D. 11 cm; fabric 3. M143. Phase 5. There are no signs of scorching
     Cf. Crypta Balbi, Rome: Cipriano, Paroli and Picon 1991: fig. 3, nos. 12 and 13 (late eighth-century date).
110. Fig. 248. P716; rim D. 11 cm; fabric 3. M21. Phase 5. There is heavy scorching on the interior and also partially on the exterior.
111. Fig. 248. P646; rim D. 10 cm; fabric 3. P9. Phase 6. This is heavily scorched on the exterior and interior.
     Cf. Pianabella (Ostia Antica): Patterson 1993a: fig. 2, nos. 14 and 15 (of the early ninth century).
112. Fig. 248. P660; rim D. 9 cm; fabric 3. B26. Phase 6. It is heavily scorched on the exterior and interior.
     Cf. Pianabella (Ostia Antica) (of the early ninth century).
113. Fig. 248. Cf. P642; rim D. 22 cm; fabric 3. A35. Phase 6.
     This fragment is heavily scorched on the exterior and interior.
     Cf. Crypta Balbi, Rome: Ricci 1986: tav. XI, no. 12 (of the late tenth century); Santa Cornelia: Patterson 1991: fig. 24, no. 3 (of the eleventh century).
114. Fig. 248. P614; base D. 12 cm; fabric 6. M111. Phase 6. This is partially scorched on the exterior.
115. Fig. 248. P639; base D. 15 cm; fabric 3. P16. Phase 6. This sherd is partially scorched on the exterior.

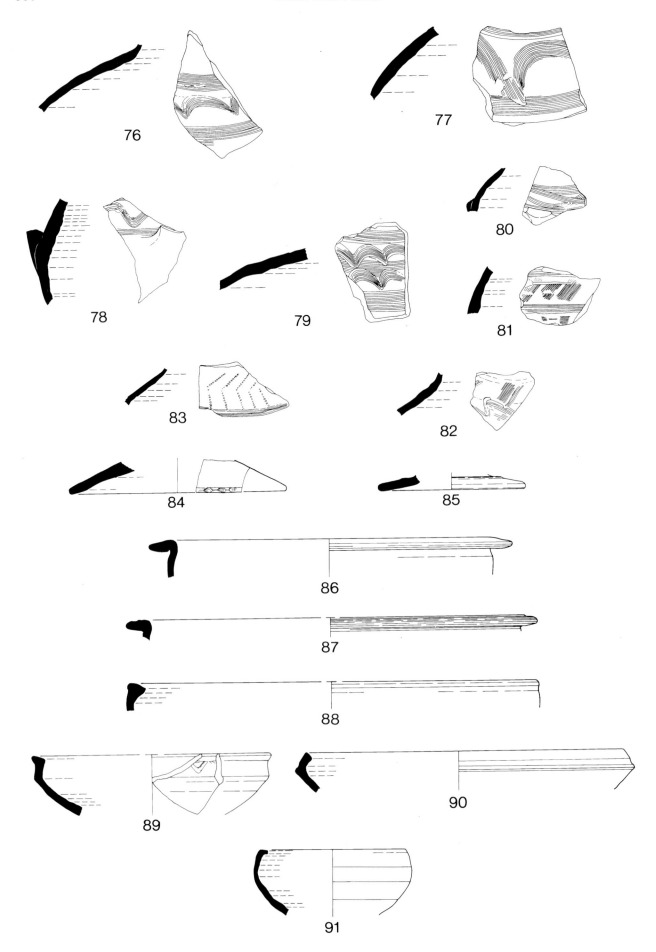

Fig. 246. Products of the early medieval kiln (1:3). *(SC)*

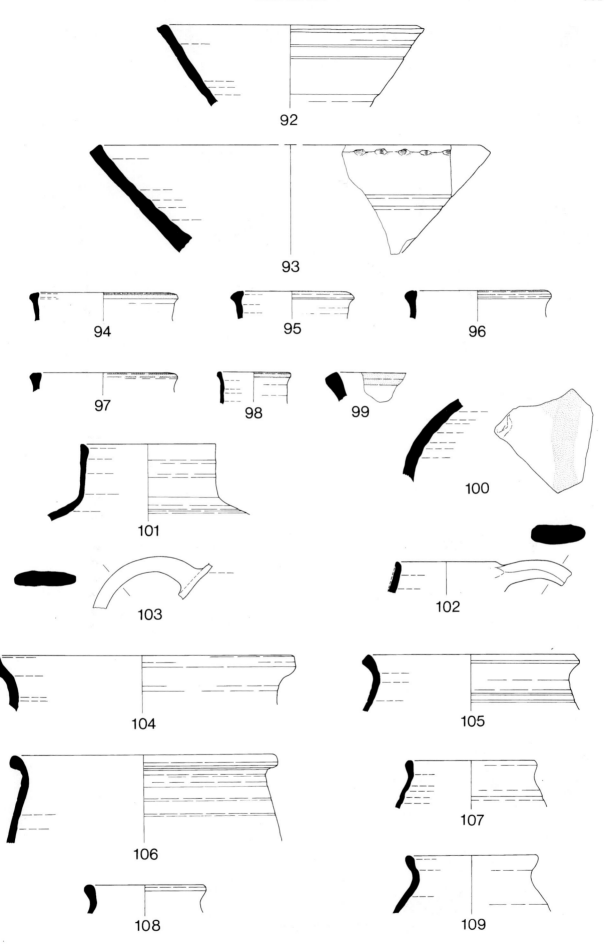

Fig. 247. Products (92-100) of the early medieval kiln, including domestic painted pottery (94-100), other domestic pottery (101-3), kitchen-wares (1:3). *(SC)*

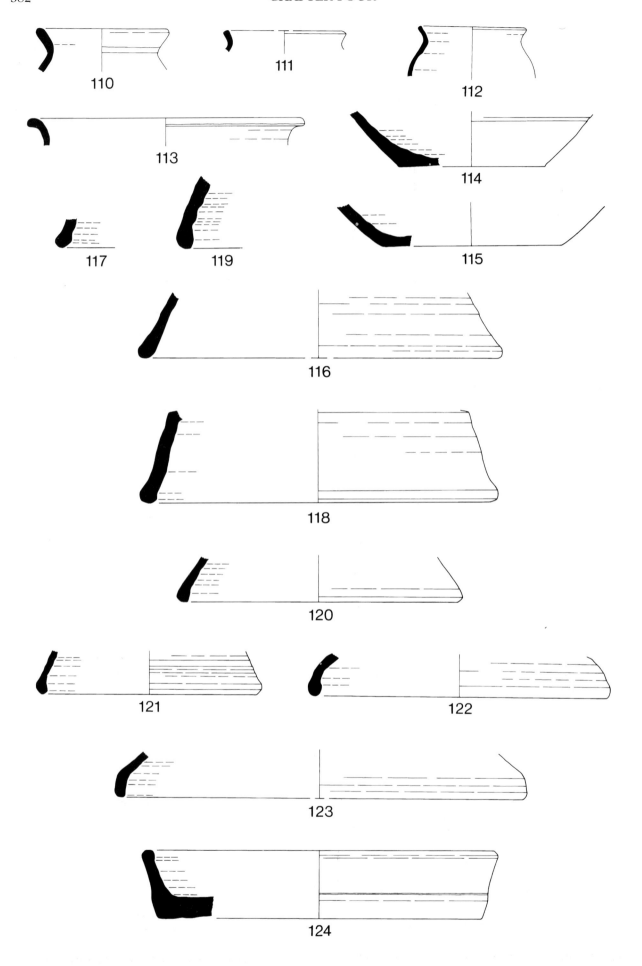

Fig. 248. Early medieval kitchen-wares (1:3). *(SC)*

Testi *(cat. 116-24)*

116. Fig. 248. Cf. P653; rim D. *c.* 30 cm; fabric 3. B60. Phase 3.

This is strongly scorched on the interior.

Cf. Crypta Balbi: Ricci 1986: tav. XI, no. 8; Santa Cornelia: Patterson 1991: fig. 25, no. 26 (of the late ninth to tenth centuries).

117. Fig. 248. P566; fabric 3. M16. Phase 6.

This is strongly scorched on the interior and partially scorched on the exterior.

Cf. Crypta Balbi and Santa Cornelia, as cat. 116.

118. Fig. 248. P659; rim D. 30 cm; fabric 3. B28. Phase 6.

This sherd is strongly scorched on the interior and partially scorched on the exterior.

Cf. Santa Cornelia: Patterson 1991: fig. 25, no. 28 (of the late ninth to tenth centuries).

119. Fig. 248. P654; fabric 3. A23. Phase 6.

There is strong scorching on the interior.

120. Fig. 248. P652; rim D. 24 cm; fabric 3. B38. Phase 6.

This is strongly scorched on the interior.

Cf. Santa Cornelia: Patterson 1991: fig. 25, nos. 28 and 29 (of the tenth to early eleventh centuries).

121. Fig. 248. P705. Rim D. 18 cm; fabric 3. M138. Phase 6.

This is strongly scorched on the interior.

Cf. Crypta Balbi, Rome: Ricci 1986: tav. XII, no. 9 (of the tenth to eleventh centuries).

122. Fig. 248. P570; rim D. 18 cm; fabric 3, more refined. M18. Phase 6.

There are no signs of scorching.

123. Fig. 248. P569; rim D. *c.* 35 cm; fabric 3, more refined. D279. Phase 7.

There are no signs of scorching.

Cf. Crypta Balbi, Rome: Ricci 1986: tav. XII, no. 11; Santa Cornelia: Patterson 1991: fig. 25, no. 34 (both of the late eleventh to twelfth centuries).

Shallow dish **(tegame)** *(cat. 124)*

124. Fig. 248. P613; rim D. 30 cm; fabric 3. M111. Phase 6.

This is partially scorched on the exterior.

Cf. Crypta Balbi, Rome: Ricci 1986: tav. XII, no. 4 (of tenth- to early eleventh-century date).

MAMMAL, REPTILE AND AMPHIBIAN BONES, by Anthony King

A total of 4,153 bones was examined, of which 2,002 (48.2 per cent) were identified to species. The remainder were allocated to size categories or parts of the skeleton (ribs, vertebrae, long bones) only (Table 65, Fig. 249). The identified assemblage, therefore, is of small/medium size, amenable to reasonably detailed analysis, but not capable of yielding statistics on aspects that require a large sample.

The bones are generally in a good state of preservation, especially from areas where the stratigraphy was deep, or from dumps (such as the well-preserved deposits in the fish-pond, L105/165). Approximately neutral soil conditions gave rise to little chemical attack on the buried bone, save where the stratigraphy was thin and bones were in direct contact with the tufo surface. In these circumstances, the bones were weakened, with evidence of friable surfaces, reflecting probable leaching of slightly acidic material over the bone.

A considerable degree of bone fragmentation had taken place before deposition, many small splints and spalls of bone being found. This is reflected in the relatively high proportion of the assemblage not identified to species. In addition, hand recovery by the excavators was of a generally high standard, resulting in many small bones and unidentifiable fragments consistently being recovered during the successive seasons of excavation. Bones were found in all phases of the site and in most zones within it. In general, however, the deeper stratigraphy at the north end of the main site, especially over the bath-house and in the north cistern and the fish-pond, contained the largest quantities and concentrations of animal bones. Those phases with most structural remains and stratigraphy were prolific of bones, especially phases 1/2 and 3. Phase 4 was elusive on site and exiguous in its bone assemblage. The medieval phases 5 and 6 had good bone assemblages, but redeposited Roman pottery in these phases warns of the possibility of redeposited bones having an effect on the numbers and statistics. Data for these phases should be examined with this in mind. Phase 7 includes the relatively uncontaminated Castellaccio site, and also the upper, often disturbed, medieval levels of the main site.

Three partially articulated animal skeletons were found during the excavation: a newborn pig from a phase 3 rubble infill (L157), and two dogs from the fish-pond of phase 2 (L105 and L165). Further details of the latter are given below. All the rest of the assemblage consisted of mixed dumps of more or less fragmented bones. It is likely that it represents waste from food and from bone-processing: however, in all probability, much of the bone recovered derives from secondary dumps in rubble fills or unused deep features, having been gathered from primary waste disposal sites around the site (for example, kitchen areas). A number of the bones from the later phases (6 and 7) show evidence of chewing by dogs or similar carnivores, and some (for example, from the emptied grave fill, burial no. 12) had been chewed by rats. This may indicate that some at least of the bone originally lay on the surface as fresh waste before being incorporated into stratified deposits.

THE MAIN DOMESTIC SPECIES (PIG, SHEEP, GOAT, OX)

Meat supply

The vast majority of the bones had been deposited as a result of food preparation or consumption, and it is clear that pig, sheep, goat and ox (together with domestic fowl: West, this volume) formed the basis of the meat supply, as might be expected. (Other mammal species that were defin-

Table 65. Mammal, amphibian and reptile bones: fragment count by phase.

phase	1-2	3	4	5	6	7	Sub-total
ox (*Bos taurus*)	20	27	3	17	40	7	114
sheep/goat (*Ovis aries/Capra hircus*)	64	176	7	93	174	70	584
pig (*Sus scrofa*)	210	*280	19	121	273	76	979
horse (*Equus caballus*)	1	1	1	-	3	1	7
dog (*Canis familiaris*)	**231	5	-	3	-	-	239
cat (*Felis catus*)	-	-	-	-	-	1	1
red deer (*Cervus elaphus*)	1	-	-	-	1	-	2
fallow deer (*Cervus dama*)	-	2	-	1	1	-	4
roe deer (*Capreolus capreolus*)	-	1	-	-	-	-	1
hare (*Lepus europaeus*)	-	-	-	-	2	-	2
black rat (*Rattus rattus*)	-	1	-	-	3	4	8
edible dormouse (*Glis glis*)	5	-	-	-	-	-	5
water vole (*Arvicola terrestris*)	-	-	-	-	5	-	5
bank vole (*Clethrionomys glareolus*)	-	-	-	-	13	11	24
wood mouse (*Apodemus sylvaticus*)	-	3	-	-	5	-	8
mustelid	-	-	-	1	-	-	1
ribs: large (ox, horse size)	10	8	-	10	19	-	47
ribs: small (pig, sheep size)	81	113	24	118	314	76	726
ribs: very small (cat size or smaller)	53	8	-	2	10	9	82
vertebrae: large	1	9	2	9	14	3	38
vertebrae: small	42	47	5	31	119	27	271
long bone fragments: large	6	11	5	3	9	2	36
long bone fragments: small	129	131	29	102	285	72	748
other fragments: large	-	1	-	1	1	1	4
other fragments: small	39	32	1	26	54	9	161
unidentified small mammal size	19	1	-	4	10	4	38
toad (*Bufo* sp.)	7	1	-	1	1	4	14
tortoise (*Testudo* sp.)	-	1	-	-	-	3	4
SUB-TOTAL	919	859	96	543	1,356	380	4,153

* of which 141 bones were from a neonate skeleton; ** of which 142 bones were from an adult skeleton and 81 bones were from a juvenile skeleton

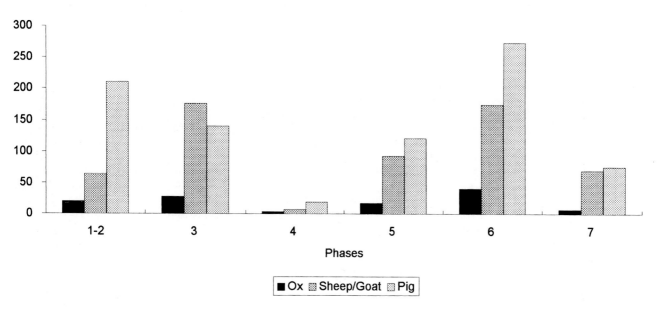

Fig. 249. Mammal bones: fragment count by phase. *(ACK)*

itely or probably eaten were deer (red, roe and fallow), hare and dormouse. The horse bones showed no evidence of having been butchered, so no positive conclusions can be drawn as to whether this species was exploited as a source of meat.)

As is readily apparent from Table 65 and Figure 249, pig bones were the most frequent in the fragment count in all phases (if the dog skeletons in phase 2 are excluded), and it therefore seems likely that cuts of pork were more frequently eaten than other meats. In phases 1-2, the proportion of pig to other bones was at its highest, forming *c.* 70 per cent of the total of the main meat sources (Table 66). This percentage declines sharply in phase 3 (late Roman) to *c.* 40 per cent (if the influence of the juvenile articulated

Table 66. Domestic species represented, (a) by fragment count (NISP) adjusted to count articulated skeletons as a nominal two bones each, (b) by percentage of the NISP for ox, sheep/goat and pig, (c) by minimum number of individuals (MNI), and (d) by NISP:MNI ratio.

phase	unit	ox	sheep/goat	pig	horse	dog	cat
1-2	NISP	20	64	210	1	12	-
	NISP%	6.8	21.8	71.4			
	MNI	1	3	5	1	3	-
	NISP:MNI	20:1	21:1	42:1			
3	NISP	27	176	141	1	5	-
	NISP%	7.8	51.2	41.0			
	MNI	1	11	5	1	1	-
	NISP:MNI	27:1	16:1	28:1			
5	NISP	17	93	121	-	3	-
	NISP%	7.3	40.2	52.3			
	MNI	1	5	3	-	1	-
	NISP:MNI	17:1	19:1	40:1			
6	NISP	40	174	273	3	-	-
	NISP%	8.2	35.7	56.0			
	MNI	1	9	8	1	-	-
	NISP:MNI	40:1	19:1	34:1			
7	NISP	7	70	76	1	-	1
	NISP%	4.6	45.8	49.7			
	MNI	1	4	3	1	-	1
	NISP:MNI	7:1	18:1	25:1			

skeleton on the numbers is discounted), but rises in subsequent phases to *c.* 50-8 per cent. Conversely, sheep/goat
has a modest level of representation in phases 1-2, *c.* twenty
per cent, but rises dramatically to *c.* 50 per cent in phase 3,
thereafter slipping back to 35-40 per cent. It was possible to
calculate the ratio of sheep to goats for two of the phases (3
and 6), using the criteria of Boessneck (1969). In phase 3
sheep predominated in a ratio of 10:1 over goats, and the
general impression for all the Roman phases is that sheep
were overwhelmingly the most common of the two species.
In contrast, the ratio in phase 6 is 1.75:1, in other words
approximately two sheep for every goat. It is not possible to
be certain whether this much more even mix of sheep and
goats is confined to phase 6, or is also a phenomenon of the
other medieval phases as well. Ox bones remain fairly constant throughout all phases at *c.* six-eight per cent.

Table 66 also gives the minimum number of individuals
(MNI) for the domestic species. This is a helpful calculation
in some ways, in that it demonstrates the small number of
animals necessary as an absolute minimum to provide this
assemblage. It is also, indirectly, an index of representation
of different parts of the body, since the NISP/MNI ratio
gives the number of bones (and teeth) that make up each
'minimum animal' in each phase. It can be seen that pigs
have a high NISP/MNI ratio and therefore are represented
by a wide variety of different parts of the body. Ox and
sheep/goat are lower in this respect, however. This is an
area of enquiry that will be explored further in the next section of the report.

Minimum numbers of individuals as a raw statistic, however, are rather misleading, since the actual number of animals slaughtered to make up the assemblage is very likely to
have been significantly higher. In fact the number of fragments themselves can be regarded as the maximum number
of individuals, if each bone is taken to come from a different individual. This, of course, is as unlikely as the minimum
number of individuals in reality, and the actual number
must lie between the two types of calculation. In terms of
the food supply to Monte Gelato, the bones themselves
represent, for example, cuts of meat and food waste, that
were discarded on site. It is unlikely, given the longevity of
site occupation and the nature of rubbish disposal on site,
that the bones came from a small number of animals originally, as implied by the MNI statistic. Therefore, the actual
number of individuals is more likely to have approached the
NISP figures. Each individual is probably represented by a
small number of bones, perhaps in the one to six range, to
allow for articulated joints, shattered bones, jaws, and other
factors. Dispersal during butchery, rubbish deposition and
after burial would all be factors that contributed to a low
number of surviving bones per animal (cf. King 1994).

Parts of the body, butchery and bone-working

The parts of the carcass for sheep/goat and pig (Table 67)
have been allocated to groups according to the scheme of
Barker (1982: fig. 190). The four groups, I (upper limb), II
(middle limb), III (crania), IV (lower limb and extremities),
are in rough order of quality of meat. Ribs and vertebrae
have not been included, despite being in zones of high-
quality meat, because of the uncertainties in allocating
them securely to species.

For pig, group I is fairly well represented in all phases, but
particularly in phases 6 and 7, where it forms about a third
of the total bones counted. This would favour the interpretation that the pig assemblage is largely food remains.
Group II is generally less common than I, and sees its best

representation in phase 5 at *c.* twenty per cent. Group III is
evenly represented at 21-5 per cent in all phases, contrasting with group IV, for which the Roman phases 1-2 and 3
present fairly high percentages, rising to 36 per cent in
phase 3, but generally lower in the medieval phases. Thus,
bone waste seems to have been more prevalent on the site
during the Roman phases.

In the case of sheep/goat, best-quality group I meat is
well-represented in phases 1-2, 6 and 7, at 37-40 per cent of
the total. Group II is also high in phases 6 and 7, at 32-3 per
cent. Groups III and IV are generally lower in percentage
representation, probably indicating that the sheep/goat
bones in all phases were largely food remains rather than
primary bone waste. Exceptions to the low presence of
groups III and IV occur in phases 1-2 (group III) and phase
3 (group IV), which seems to link with the pig bone pattern
in indicating a greater prevalence of bone waste on site in
the Roman period compared with the medieval phases. In
phase 5 the percentage of groups III and IV is slightly lower
than in earlier phases, and there is a further percentage
decline subsequently.

Direct evidence of butchery and dismemberment is not
very common, mainly due to the small percentage of ox
bones, which in most assemblages form the main body of
evidence for butchery marks. In phase 2, few bones display
clear marks, but it can be noted that many of the pig-/sheep-
sized vertebrae were split sagittally (that is, longitudinally),
implying the halving of the carcass and the production of
chops or a similar form of meat joint.

It is in phase 3 that cut and chop marks on the bones are
most common, and indeed give indications not only of
butchery for food, but of bone-, horn- and antler-working.
An ox horn-core has been sawn into sections, a sheep cranium has had its frontal/horn-core area sawn away and the
upper part of the core sawn off, a roe deer frontal/antler
has cut marks at the base of the antler on the cranium and
antler burr, and one of the bone fragments (probably from
a sheep-sized animal) has been neatly cut into a square.
Although this evidence is disparate in its nature, cumulat-
ively it differs from the other phases, and suggests that part
of the farm economy of the late Roman establishment included the working of bone, antler and horn products. In
addition, there is the possibility of hide production, suggested
by a fallow deer radius/ulna with cut and chop marks on
the shaft. The exploitation of deer carcasses in this way can
be paralleled at Settefinestre, where deer bones were most
prevalent in the mid/late Roman phases, and one of the
buildings was interpreted as an area for processing deer carcasses and hides (King 1985: 284-5).

Butchery marks normally associated with meat production
were also reasonably common in phase 3. For both pig and
sheep/goat, cuts to the scapula indicate separation of the
front limb from the ribcage, and further dismemberment of
the front limb clearly took place as well. The vertebrae were
chopped both sagittally and transversely, apparently indicating the breaking up of the carcasses into sections, but not
necessarily the splitting of the carcass longitudinally. This
hints at a less standardized, more ad hoc approach to butchery compared with phase 2, but much more evidence is
required from other assemblages to elevate this suggestion
to a working hypothesis of more widespread applicability.

In the medieval phases, there were fewer signs of butchery
or bone-working. Pig- and sheep/goat-sized vertebrae
continued to be chopped up in a variety of different direc-
tions during phases 5, 6 and 7. In phase 6, a horn-core cut
from an ox cranium indicates the removal of horn, presumably for working in some fashion.

Table 67. Parts of the carcass represented for pig and sheep/goat by phase, grouped according to the scheme of Barker (1982). The numbers of teeth and the tooth:bone ratio are also given.

| | | pig | | | | | sheep/goat | | | | |
		1-2	3	5	6	7	1-2	3	5	6	7
I	scapula	7	6	4	16	5	3	7	6	9	5
	humerus	7	6	6	7	5	7	8	2	17	6
	pelvis	5	5	3	8	-	5	7	9	13	4
	femur	9	5	4	16	6	3	10	4	13	5
II	radius	9	5	5	9	2	2	7	8	17	8
	ulna	3	3	4	3	1	1	3	1	9	-
	tibia	7	5	5	13	3	7	24	10	18	8
III	cranium	10	8	9	13	4	6	7	2	10	4
	maxilla	6	3	2	6	3	1	-	1	3	-
	mandible	10	7	6	14	4	5	11	4	5	3
	teeth	71	47	42	91	28	14	46	24	28	16
	core	-	-	-	-	-	-	1	-	-	-
IV	metacarpal	11	8	3	14	4	3	5	4	4	2
	metatarsal	13	8	8	17	4	4	6	5	5	2
	calcaneum	3	2	-	4	2	-	4	-	1	-
	astragalus	-	1	1	1	-	1	6	1	1	-
	carpal/tarsal	2	-	-	1	1	-	2	1	3	-
	phalanges	8	11	7	12	-	-	15	5	4	3
	others	31	9	8	28	3	5	5	6	12	1
%	I	28	22	17	47	16	18	32	21	52	20
	%	25.5	26.5	25.4	30.5	36.4	37.5	26.0	33.3	39.4	40.0
	II	19	13	14	25	6	10	34	19	44	16
	%	17.3	15.7	20.9	16.2	13.6	20.8	27.6	30.2	33.3	32.0
	III	26	18	17	33	11	12	19	7	18	7
	%	23.6	21.7	25.4	21.4	25.0	25.0	15.4	11.1	13.6	14.0
	IV	37	30	19	49	11	8	38	16	18	7
	%	33.6	36.1	28.4	31.8	25.0	16.7	30.9	25.4	13.6	14.0
%	T:B	71:141	47:92	42:75	91:182	28:47	14:53	46:128	24:69	28:144	16:51
	%	50.4	51.1	56.0	50.0	59.6	26.4	35.9	34.8	19.4	31.4

Age at death, pathology and animal husbandry

The general picture gained by analysing tooth wear and fusion of epiphyses for pig and sheep/goat is that the majority of pigs was slaughtered at a juvenile or subadult age, while sheep and goats mostly survived into adulthood (Tables 68 and 69).

Before looking at the age at death evidence in detail, an initial observation to make of the pig assemblage is the male:female ratio, as derived from the canine teeth. In the Roman and late Roman periods, the ratio is 1:2, but it rises in phases 5 and 6 to an overwhelming predominance of females at c. 1:10, before returning to an even 1:1 ratio in phase 7. The last figure may be anomalous, due to small sample size, but for earlier periods the general ratio is what might be expected from a husbandry regime where most of

the males are slaughtered young for surplus production and probable consumption elsewhere. This is especially the case in phases 5 and 6, when a definite pattern of possible export for slaughter of male pigs may have been part of the *domus-culta* economy (see below).

For pig, fusion of epiphyses indicates that in all phases 30-40 per cent of animals were older than c. one year at the time of slaughter. In addition 23-36 per cent were older than c. two years at the time of slaughter. Thus, 60-70 per cent were presumably killed as piglets or subadults, and up to 75 per cent had been killed by two years of age; this is a pattern of slaughter that is typical of many sites. Few male pigs survived into adulthood, and the majority of males must have been slaughtered for their meat value whilst still at a juvenile stage, since the flesh of adult boars tastes tainted. Castration is an option to avoid this problem, and

Table 68. Fusion of epiphyses for pig and sheep/goat. The number fused (F) and not fused (NF) is given for each group of bones, together with the group's percentage fused (i.e. surviving to be older than the approximate ages given for each group). Adapted from Bull and Payne (1982) for pig, and Silver (1969) and Bullock and Rackham (1982) for sheep/goat.

	phase months	1-2 F-NF	%F	3 F-NF	%F	5 F-NF	%F	6 F-NF	%F	7 F-NF	%F
PIG											
scapula	7-11	5-2		3-3		4-0		14-2		3-2	
pelvis	7-11	2-3		5-0		2-1		6-2		-	
radius p	11	0-1	59	3-1	68	0-3	71	1-2	69	1-0	63
humerus d	11+	1-1		1-3		2-0		0-3		1-1	
phal II	11+	2-0		3-0		2-0		1-1		-	
tibia d	19-23	1-0		0-2		0-4		0-3		0-1	
metacarpal d	19-23	2-3		0-2		-		0-6		0-3	
metatarsal d	19-23	2-8	30	0-2	31	1-3	36	1-7	23	0-2	0
phal I	19-23	1-3		4-3		3-0		5-4		-	
calcaneum	31-5	0-3		0-2		-		1-3		0-2	
femur p	31-5	1-4		0-2		0-1		0-8		1-3	
humerus p	31-5+	-		0-3		0-2		0-3		0-1	
radius d	31-5+	0.4	7	0-2	7	0-3	0	0-2	7	-	8
ulna	31-5+	0-2		1-2		0-1		0-1		0-1	
femur d	31-5+	0-1		0-1		0-1		0-3		0-2	
tibia p	31-5+	-		0-2		0-4		1-6		0-2	
SHEEP/GOAT											
humerus d	<12	0-1		3-2		0-1		3-3		0-3	
radius p	<12	1-0		3-0		1-0		7-2		2-0	
scapula	12	2-1	70	5-2	68	5-1	82	7-2	76	4-1	64
pelvis	12	4-1		4-3		8-1		11-2		3-1	
phal I	14-35	-		7-3		4-0		4-0		2-1	
phal II	14-35	-		3-0		-		-		-	
tibia d	35	1-0	100	4-3	65	0-2	63	3-1	80	0-2	50
femur p	36	1-0		1-2		1-1		1-1		1-0	
metacarpal d	47	0-1		3-0		3-0		-		0-1	
metatarsal d	47	-		2-1		3-0		0-2		-	
femur d	48	0-1	0	1-3	62	0-1	86	1-1	50	1-0	25
tibia p	48	-		2-1		-		2-0		0-2	
calcaneum	48-60	-		4-0		-		1-0		-	
radius d	48-60	1-0	100	-	71	1-0	100	5-3	60	-	0
humerus p	48-60	1-0		1-2		1-0		0-1		0-1	

it may be the case that some of the males were in fact castrates. There appears to have been another phase of slaughtering when animals were aged two-three years, since only up to eight per cent of bones were fused in the 31-5+ months bone group. This would support the suggestion that nearly all largely adult-sized animals had been slaughtered by three years, leaving a minority, probably breeding sows, to continue into middle and old age.

Although all phases are roughly the same in their bone fusion data, phase 5 is slightly different in having fewer an-imals over two years (only a single jaw aged at four or more years: see below and Table 69), and fewer juveniles at one year or less. This implies a condensed period of slaughter at one to two years of age for the majority of pigs in this phase. The *domusculta* is the dominant element in this phase, for which there is literary evidence indicating that *domuscultae* in general reared pigs for the Rome meat supply (see discussion). The pattern hinted at for Monte Gelato may be one of well-organized slaughter of young but almost mature animals. They would have been in their prime, and have

Table 69. Summary of age at death from mandible tooth wear. Approximate ages for pig are from Bull and Payne (1982).

PIG	age							
phase	2 m	6-10 m	1 y (-)	1.5-1.75	2	2+	3+	4+
2	-	-	3	1	-	2	-	-
3	2	1	-	2	1	-	-	1
5	1	-	-	-	2	-	-	1
6	2	2	-	3	-	4	1	-
7	1	-	2	-	-	-	-	-
TOTAL	6	3	5	6	3	6	1	2
% of total	43.8			28.1		28.1		
% still alive at end of stage	56.2			28.1		0		

SHEEP/GOAT		
phase	no. of mandibles	tooth wear
2	3	all adult
3	10	8 adult; 1 with M3 coming into wear; 1 with M2 coming into wear
5	3	all adult
6	2	2 with M3 coming into wear
7	2	both adult

represented the best return in meat value for the investment in terms, for example, of feed and herding.

The overall pattern for all phases for pig is supported by the tooth wear evidence, despite the relatively low number of mandibles available (Table 69). If all phases are taken as one group, 56 per cent are older than one year, and 28 per cent are older than two years. Thus, *c.* 72 per cent of the pigs had been killed by two years of age, a figure in close agreement with the fusion data. Twenty-eight per cent of the mandibles are of animals of two years or older, including three (nine per cent) of adults aged three or more, again a figure which appears to conform with the fusion evidence. Most other sites in the region have generally similar slaughter patterns, seen for instance at Settefinestre (King 1985: figs 192-3), Ponte Nepesino (Clark 1984: 129) and other medieval sites such as Farfa abbey (Clark 1987b: fig. 5).

As far as sheep/goat is concerned, the fusion of epiphyses indicates that in phase 3, about two-thirds of the animals were still alive at four years of age, and this dominantly adult pattern continues in the medieval period, and indeed is accentuated in phase 5. Only in phase 7 does a more typical fall-off in survival with age occur, but the data from this phase are not very numerous (as is also the case for phase 1/2). The small number of surviving mandibles supports the generally adult pattern. Nearly all have adult dentition, with the youngest having the second permanent molar coming into wear (that is, *c.* one year). This is a pattern also seen at nearby Ponte Nepesino (Clark 1984: 129) and at the later medieval site of Tuscania (Barker 1973: 161, 164) and elsewhere (Clark 1987a: 13). It can be contrasted with a pattern of more juvenile slaughter seen, for instance, at the wealthy urban site of Palazzo Vitelleschi, Tarquinia (Clark 1987a: 13; Clark 1989: 225-6) and Farfa abbey (Clark 1987a: 14; 1987b: 186).

In general, the adult pattern is one that would be associated with a wool pattern of husbandry, in which the animals (except non-breeding males) are allowed to survive into adulthood in order to obtain the maximum yield of wool and other renewable products such as milk and cheese. Slaughter would occur when wool quality and milk yield started to diminish amongst the older animals. This type of husbandry implies the existence of flocks of sheep (and to a lesser extent goats) that would have been composed of animals of a variety of ages. Their grazing needs would have been relatively great, and thus it is likely that extensive sheep pasture would have been required, either locally, or within the framework of a transhumance system. Unfortunately the bone evidence alone cannot indicate directly whether transhumant agriculture was practised at Monte Gelato.

Ageing data for oxen yielded few positive indicators. In all phases, fused epiphyses and adult teeth were dominant, giving the impression of a small number of cattle raised into adulthood, presumably for purposes such as use in ploughteams and traction. Milk, meat and hides may also have been (secondary) motives for keeping cattle.

A factor affecting and reflecting animal husbandry practices is that of the health of the animals. The Monte Gelato assemblages include very few specimens indicating poor health amongst the domestic stock. A phase 2 sheep/goat adult mandible with very worn teeth has so-called 'cauliflower' roots, indicating minor abcessing of the cheek teeth. A similar condition occurs in a phase 3 example, and a phase 6 sheep/goat mandible has very worn adult premolars. Dental pathologies also occur in pig: a very worn phase 3 third mandibular molar has clear indications of caries, a phase 6 female adult canine has been broken during the animal's lifetime (and was subsequently worn down on the broken surface), and a phase 7 upper jaw has a slightly impacted third adult molar in the process of eruption. Virtually all the dental conditions noted above occur in adult or elderly individuals, as might be expected. Non-dental abnormalities are rare: a sheep/goat acetabulum (phase 5) has slight lipping, perhaps due to an arthropathy, and a pig- or sheepsized rib has an exostosis joining it to its neighbour, perhaps in consequence of an injury. None of these conditions would have been life-threatening to the animals concerned, and they represent a very low proportion of the total bones for these species. It seems from the bones, therefore, that the general state of health of the stock was good.

Breeds and sizes

Calculations of withers heights are given in Table 70, based upon the measurements in the appendix to this section. The great majority of usable measurements for withers height calculations are for sheep/goat. These yield some significant size differences between late Roman (phase 3) and medieval (phases 5, 6 and 7) sheep and goats. Of the eleven phase 3 measurements, the range in withers heights is 0.6-0.78 m (mean 0.6745 m, standard deviation 54.8 mm). This compares with the eight phase 5, 6 and 7 measurements, which result in a range of 0.58-0.66 m (mean 0.62 m, standard deviation 36.3 mm). The phase 3 heights are in accord with other Roman data, such as from Settefinestre (range 0.67-0.75 m: King 1985: fig. 206) and Carminiello ai Mannesi, Naples (range 0.63-0.79 m, mean 0.7 m: King 1994: table 15), although they are a little on the small side. For the medieval phases, it is interesting to note the apparent diminution in average size, comparable to the range of 0.54-0.7 m obtained from the ninth- to tenth-century assemblage at nearby Ponte Nepesino (Clark 1984: 132). Indeed, the full set of measurements from Ponte Nepesino and those from Anguillara (Burnett, Clark and Sutherland forthcoming) indicate generally smaller-sized sheep and goats than at Monte Gelato. However, not all medieval assemblages have animals of this relatively small stature. The late medieval sites of Tuscania (Barker 1973: 173-6; cf. Clark 1984: 135) and Tarquinia (Clark 1989: 226, 306-7) have bones suggesting a rise in average size by that period, explained by Clark (1989: 226) as possibly being the result of better growth and development due to the greater use of transhumance after the agricultural revolution of the twelfth/thirteenth centuries. These variations could therefore indicate diachronic changes to sheep and goat breeds and sizes in South Etruria/North Lazio, or else they could be purely localized differences in breed selection resulting from the types of site excavated. More data are needed to draw further conclusions in this respect.

The general conformation of the sheep and goats is what might be expected of an unspecialized, unimproved stock. The limbs were not especially stocky or gracile, and none of the crania appear to be naturally hornless.

There are fewer measurements available for pig bones from Monte Gelato, and consequently fewer estimations of withers heights. The range of 0.64-0.78 m (Table 70) is on the small side compared with other Roman assemblages at Naples (Carminiello ai Mannesi; range 0.69-0.97 m, mean 0.75 m; King 1994: table 15) and Settefinestre (range 0.57-0.93 m; King 1985: fig. 206), but from the small number of available heights, it does appear that Roman pigs from phase 2 were on the whole larger (range 0.69-0.78 m) than those of the medieval phases 5 and 6 (range 0.64-0.72 m). This hints at changes in breeding conditions between the two periods, and may indicate that the pigs supplied for the Rome market in phase 5 (see below) were of a small-sized stock compared with their Roman period predecessors. Pig bones from Ponte Nepesino (Clark 1984: 140) and Anguillara (Burnett, Clark and Sutherland forthcoming) were of the same size range. Comparison with the later medieval assemblages at Tuscania (Barker 1973: 176-7) and Tarquinia (Clark 1989: 307-9) suggests that the smaller-sized animals continued to be the norm at that period.

In conformation, the pigs showed mainly 'primitive' characteristics, with long, straight-snouted crania, and no obvious signs of the early maturation associated with more recent selective breeding strategies.

Only one withers height calculation was available for ox, of 1.34 m from a phase 6 bone: this is within the expected range for both Roman and medieval cattle.

OTHER SPECIES

Dog

Dog bones are most common in phase 2, with a total of eight bones and teeth from scattered contexts and two skeletons, both from the fish-pond.

The more complete of the skeletons, 142 bones from two contexts, L105 and L165 (listed as skeleton II in Table 70 and the appendix to this section), is of an adult of medium/large stature, the shoulder height of which has been calculated at 0.595 m. This compares with a size range of 0.23-0.72 m for a sample of Romano-British dogs analysed by Harcourt (1974). The shape and general conformation of the bones suggest an undifferentiated breed without any marked characteristics. The animal was probably fairly elderly, since the teeth are worn, but no definite indication of age at death could be obtained. It had also suffered from a variety of pathological conditions that had affected the bones and teeth. One tooth (right first permanent mandibular premolar) had been lost ante mortem and the alveolus had healed over. One of the deciduous teeth (fourth mandibular molar on the right side) still exists anomalously as a pearly peg in position behind the third permanent molar. There are also signs of a healed injury to the side and back of the dog: three ribs had been broken c. 0.1 m from the dorsal articulation, one of them in two places, and rehealed. One of the lumbar vertebrae and the sacrum display a left lean or twist on their dorsal spines, possibly as a result of the animal's injury or from a limp arising from a limb pathology. Such a problem did in fact exist, since the left hind paw had suffered some sort of trauma which may have resulted in a limp. The left metatarsus IV was damaged on the ventral side of the distal end of the diaphysis, just above the epiphysis. Bony growth and a drainage hole were observed, probably from abcessing or osteomyelitis following a trauma (for example, tendon damage and infection). In addition, the bone element is shorter than its right-hand equivalent. Two of the proximal phalanges have bony exostoses on their plantar surfaces, which could also have been connected with the condition affecting the metatarsus. It is clear that the dog had suffered during its lifetime, but none of these pathologies need necessarily have caused the animal's death.

The other skeleton (I) consists of 81 bones from context L165 of a juvenile/subadult. Most of the long bones have unfused epiphyses, but the dentition is largely adult (that is, adult cheek teeth but deciduous incisors and canines). The animal was probably not quite fully grown, and the mandible measurements (for example, (1) total length) in the appendix show that the jaws were smaller than those of the other skeleton. The cause of death in this animal, approaching its prime, has left no trace on the bones themselves, and the only pathology visible is a non-life-threatening breakage of the left mandibular first molar.

Much less can be said about the other scattered dog bones. A mandible of a medium-sized animal came from the rock-cut road (S13), and a miscellaneous range of bones from other contexts and phases. Overall the representation

Table 70. Calculations of withers heights, using the ratios of von den Driesch and Boessneck (1974) (A) and Harcourt (1974) (B) (for dogs). The measurements are taken from the Appendix.

bone	measurement	value (mm)	ratio (A)	height (cm)	phase
OX					
metacarpal	GL	215	6.25	134	6
SHEEP/GOAT					
radius	GL	147	4.02	59 (sheep)	6
radius	GL	144	4.02	58	6
metacarpal	GL	131	4.89	64	3
metacarpal	GL	135	4.89	66	5
metacarpal	GL	121	4.89	59	5
calcaneum	GL	63	11.40	63 (sheep)	3
calcaneum	GL	56	11.40	64 (sheep)	3
calcaneum	GL	57	11.40	65	3
calcaneum	GL	63	11.40	72	3
calcaneum	GL	55	11.40	63 (goat)	5
astragalus	GLl	33	22.68	75	3
astragalus	GLl	29	22.68	66	3
astragalus	GLl	29	22.68	66	3
astragalus	GLl	34	22.68	78 (sheep)	3
astragalus	GLl	29	22.68	66	5
astragalus	GLl	29	22.68	66	6
metatarsal	GL	133	4.54	60	3
metatarsal	GL	153	4.54	69	3
metatarsal	GL	129	4.54	59	7
PIG					
calcaneum	GL	76	9.34	71	2
astragalus	GLl	36	17.90	64	5
astragalus	GLl	40	17.90	72	6
metacarpal IV	GL	66	10.53	69	2
metatarsal III	GL	84	9.34	78	2
metatarsal IV	GL	78	8.84	69	6

DOG skeleton II (phase 2)

bone	meas.	value (mm)	ratio (A)	height (cm)	ratio (B)	height (cm)
radius	GL	180	3.22	57.9	3.18+19.51	59.2
radius	GL	181	3.22	58.3	3.18+19.51	59.5
ulna	GL	212	2.67	56.6	2.78+6.21	59.6
ulna	GL	214	2.67	57.1	2.78+6.21	60.1
tibia	GL	199	2.92	58.1	2.92+9.41	59.0
fibula	GL	185	3.01	55.7		
average				57.3		59.5

of dog is low, especially in the medieval phases (Table 65). This could be a result of disposal practices on site, since most of the bone refuse had originated as dumps of food remains. Any dogs dying on site may have been disposed of away from the excavated area, with the notable exception of the two corpses dumped in the fish-pond infilling. The other scattered bones were probably the result of redeposited material being moved around on the site.

Cat

This species is remarkably rare, being represented by a single broken juvenile radius from a phase 7 destruction level (D6) over the rooms to the north of the second baptistery. Cats must have been rare or not present during the main occupation phases of the site, although the comments made above concerning the taphonomy of the bone assemblage in relation to the dog bones also applies in the case of cat. In other words, the species may be underrepresented in the bone record.

Horse

Horse bones were also surprisingly infrequent at Monte Gelato. There were a few bones from all phases except 5 (Table 65), apparently indicating small-scale use of this animal, presumably for transport purposes primarily. However, since none of the bones have butchery marks, it is unclear whether horse meat was part of the diet. If by custom it was not (as was likely to have been the case after the ban on its consumption by Pope Gregory III in AD 732), then it could be the case that horse is underrepresented in the bone assemblage, since it effectively falls into the same class as the dog and cat bones, discussed above. Only two of the bones could be measured (see the appendix), with results suggesting fairly small animals compared with the modern average. This is supported by the size of the other bones and teeth, which also tended to be on the small side. All the bones are of adults, and one incisor from the mausoleum infill (P6, phase 6) is from an elderly animal.

Hunted species

All three of the main species of deer are represented in the assemblage, but in very small numbers. A red deer (*Cervus elaphus*) distal radius, broken across 0.1 m from the distal end, came from the fish-pond (L165, phase 2), and a scapula head from a phase 6 dump (M4). Fallow deer (*Cervus dama*) is represented by a radius distal end and shaft from a phase 3 silt layer (M26), a radius/ulna shaft from the rock-cut road phase 3 upper fill (N30), a radius shaft from a phase 5 pit in the baptistery (D86) and a metacarpus proximal end and shaft from a phase 6 make-up layer (D244). One of the bones, that from N30, has chop and cut marks on the side of the shaft. It is likely that the bones are food remains, although it could be the case that the butchery marks result from hide removal (see butchery discussion above). A distinctive feature of this small assemblage is the lack of antlers of these two species, which are often the most common element found.

An antler was found, however, of a roe deer (*Capreolus capreolus*), from a phase 3 fill layer (M92). It is still attached to the frontal of the cranium and has a fore tine (the rear tine(s) having been broken away after deposition), as well as cut marks at the base of the antler on the skull and the burr. As with some of the other deer bones, the cut marks could have resulted from hide removal.

The presence of these three deer species is not unexpected, and indeed they are still found in very small numbers in central Italy in recent times (Corbet and Ovenden 1980).

The other hunted or trapped species present on the site is hare, most likely the brown hare (*Lepus europaeus*). Two articulated bones were found, a tibia distal end and a calcaneum, in a phase 6 occupation level in the second baptistery (D294). The bones both display unusual bony growth in the vicinity of the joint, probably following abcessing and infection after a trauma.

The low number of hunted species is probably an indication of the low importance accorded to this activity by the site's occupants. Certainly, deer and hare contributed little to the meat diet, but other products such as hides, antlers and fur may have been significant, especially in phase 3 when there are indications of bone-working and other 'industrial' uses of the bones (see butchery discussion above). Products resulting from these activities were probably exported from the site and were therefore not found in its rubbish deposits, a process that may also have applied to the venison as well, in view of its high value and status as a meat.

Small mammals

In phase 2, the only deposit with small mammal bones was the upper layer (L105) in the fish-pond. It contained two mandibles definitely identifiable as edible dormouse (*Glis glis*), together with eighteen postcranial bones of rat-/dormouse-size that could not be narrowed down to species. More than one species is, however, present. There is also a smaller, mouse-sized pelvis.

The presence of edible dormouse is very interesting, since the deposit was largely composed of food debris, and in view of Roman culinary practices relating to this species (Apicius viii. 397; Petronius, *Satyricon* 31), it is likely that the remains represent the consumption of this delicacy on the site. Archaeological finds of edible dormouse are known from two other sites, Pompeii (King n.d. a) and Settefinestre villa (King 1985: 283). All the finds so far date from the Imperial period, and indeed those from Settefinestre are roughly contemporary with, or a little later than, L105. Such finds seem to indicate that edible dormouse was not a rarity, and was part of both urban and rural diets, but probably still is a high-status item. It is to be hoped that other assemblages of small mammal bones will yield positive identifications of this species, to give further clarification of the extent of exploitation of the dormouse. Other species of dormouse have also been recorded archaeologically, from Pompeii (Jashemski 1979: 308), York (O'Connor 1986) and elsewhere, but it is much less likely that these were deliberately fattened and eaten by man.

The late Roman levels (phase 3) yielded a mandible of wood mouse (*Apodemus sylvaticus*) from rubble (L157) in the portico, a probable ship or black rat (*Rattus rattus*) pelvis from occupation layers above the bath-house (M136), and a rat-sized pelvis from wall collapse to the north of the (later) baptistery (D247). Wood mouse is often found in rural contexts where house mouse is uncommon, and will enter human habitation if house mouse is not present. As its name implies, its preferred habitat is woodland, and also scrub, gardens and hedgerows. The black rat spread to Italy from the Near East in the Republican period, and it is not surprising to find it in a rural context, given that it had already spread to the countryside in Etruria by the first century BC (King 1985: 288, 290).

In later phases most of the small mammal finds came from graves. Two graves (B8, B49) yielded crania and mandibles of bank vole (*Clethrionomys glareolus*), a species of some interest zoologically, since it is not currently found in Italy save for two pockets in Calabria and the Gargano (Corbet and Ovenden 1980: 50). This is probably a relict distribution, and the finds from Monte Gelato indicate that in the early medieval period, at least, the distribution was more extensive. Other species found in graves are water vole (*Arvicola terrestris*) (D31), wood mouse (D107) and black rat (B64, B80), all identified from mandibles or pelves, together with rat-, vole- and mouse-sized postcranial elements (also from D214 and D282). It is likely that these species burrowed into the graves, and into the vaults of the stone slab or *a cappuccina* burials. The presence of water vole may seem surprising and indicative of flooded conditions, but in fact this species can inhabit dry burrows and in warm climates often lives in grassland far from water.

There were a few other small mammal bones from rubble and destruction debris in phase 5 and later (from M38 and A35), of rodents of rat and vole size, and of a juvenile mustelid.

Amphibians and reptiles

All the twelve amphibian bones found are probably of common toad (*Bufo bufo*). Some of the smaller specimens may, however, have been of green toad (*Bufo viridis*), a species which can occupy similar habitats. Seven bones came from the fish-pond; one from the lowest silt layer (L184) and the others from the upper fill (L105). This was undoubtedly a good location for toads, and implies damp (but not noisome) conditions with plenty of insects to provide a food supply.

A single amphibian bone came from late Roman silt in the plunge bath (M146), and two others from grave fills of medieval date (B64, C29). Soft grave fills, possibly with large air spaces originally, would have provided good hiding places. Other amphibian bones were recovered from rubble and silt layers of early medieval date (A35, M32).

The only reptile remains found were four carapace fragments of tortoise. They could not be identified to species, but are similar to the present-day tortoise in the region, Hermann's Tortoise (*Testudo hermanni*). One piece came from the fill of the rock-cut road (S13) and three from Castellaccio (Z7). Tortoises can be eaten, and indeed still are in South Etruria, but there is no evidence from the excavated remains that this was the case at Monte Gelato.

DISCUSSION

Chronological changes

One of the first observations to make in this section of the report is that, when analysis began, there was concern that redeposition of Roman material in the medieval phases would obviate any results obtained about the latter. In the event, this has not proved to be a major cause of worry, since the results presented above have demonstrated that the medieval phases show individual characteristics in, for example, age at death patterns and average bone size, sufficient to demonstrate that the effect of redeposited Roman material is minimal and can be largely discounted.

In summary the main chronological characteristics and changes are as follows.

Phases 1-2

In these phases the fish-pond was by far the largest group of contexts yielding bones (Fig. 250), and was markedly dominated by pig. The other much smaller groups had similar characteristics, with the exception of the rock-cut road fill (which was effectively of phase 2/3 date, but has been included here) that had a relatively high proportion of ox bones, unusual for Monte Gelato. The pigs in phases 1-2 had generally been slaughtered while still juveniles, and the carcasses halved. The deposits yielded high numbers of waste elements of the skeleton, suggesting the slaughtering, preparation and disposal of primary waste on or near the site. In addition to the main food-providing species, the fish-pond yielded a wide range of other species: some being food sources (dormouse, chicken, thrushes: West, this volume), others being part of the general detritus dumped into the deposit (the dog skeletons, owl and jay bones), and others coming into the fish-pond because it formed a suitable habitat (toad). The range of food species is typical of early Imperial urban and villa assemblages (see below), and reflects the catholic tastes of the Roman (élite) population, as seen in the writings of Apicius and Pliny.

Phase 3

In the late Roman period, the pattern of deposition changed, with many areas of the site yielding bones (Fig. 251). The majority was found in the lower terrace area (over the early Roman bath-house), and over the adjacent road. The assemblage is predominantly one of sheep bones (and goat, to a lesser extent). The sheep were generally slaughtered as adults, suggesting a wool economy and the extensive grazing required to sustain it (see below). They were butchered in a less organized fashion than in phase 2, producing high proportions of waste elements, which also suggests a pattern of slaughter and carcass preparation/disposal on or near the site. The pig bones, although not so common in percentage terms as phase 2, continue to show a largely juvenile slaughter pattern with a high proportion of waste elements. A piglet skeleton was found in the portico area, probably an animal that had strayed into a semi-abandoned part of the site and found itself trapped.

Another characteristic of phase 3 is the presence of worked bone, and chopped and cut bones indicating on-site bone-working, including in one case the removal and possible working of antler. Some of the cut marks may also reflect the removal of hides. This activity fits in well with the other workshop activities in this period, and reflects the nature of the establishment as a working estate-centre with ancilliary activities attached to it.

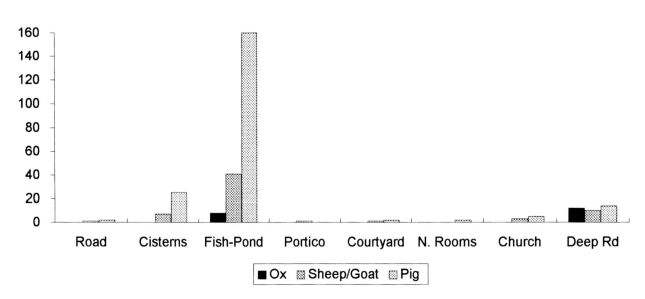

Fig. 250. Fragment count by zone, phases 1-2. *(ACK)*

Phase 4

Only 30 bones identifiable to species came from this phase, which in general was one of little activity on site. The bones (pig for the most part) appear to suggest a low level of food processing and consumption on the site at this time.

Phase 5

The establishment of the *domusculta* in the late eighth century saw a considerable revival at Monte Gelato, and the bone assemblage reflects this in a number of ways. The lower terrace and the road together form the largest source of bones (Fig. 252), and are dominated by pig overall (although the road has significant quantities of sheep/goat bones). Elsewhere there are very few bones, a feature that may be expected from the non-domestic and enlarged ecclesiastical area on the upper terrace.

The pig bones from this phase are of some interest, since they show an apparently organized pat-

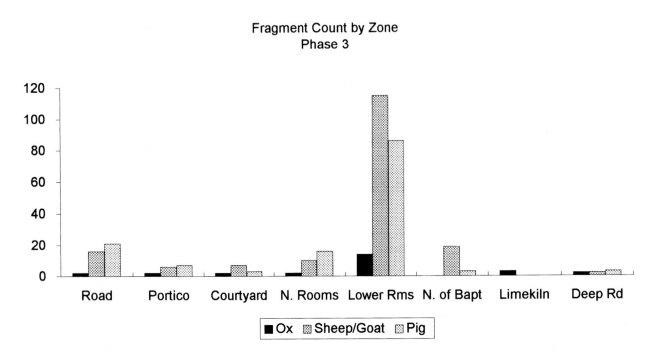

Fig. 251. Fragment count by zone, phase 3. *(ACK)*

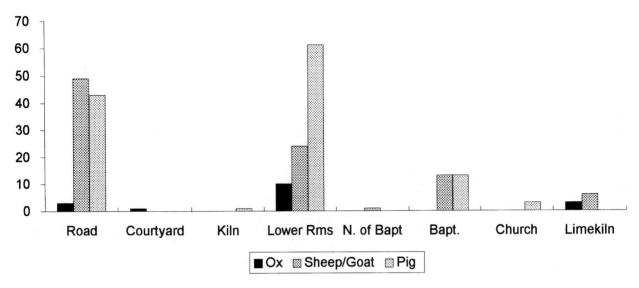

Fig. 252. Fragment count by zone, phase 5. *(ACK)*

tern of slaughter of animals at one or two years of age, when they had probably reached their prime in terms of size and meat/fat ratio. There was a high ratio of females to males, again indicating an organized system of husbandry, and in stature the pigs were slightly smaller than those of the Roman period, suggestive of a different breed, or a different pattern of rearing and maturing. It seems very likely that pigs were being raised at Monte Gelato for export to Rome, as one of the forms of produce referred to in the *Liber Pontificalis* in relation to the *domusculta* of *Capracorum* (Santa Cornelia, near Veii); '... and of the pigs which should each year be fattened in the *casales* in the said *domusculta*, one hundred head should be slaughtered and stored in the same storehouse' (*Liber Pontificalis* I, 501-2). This would form part of the food supply to Rome, for distribution to the poor at a period when conditions were difficult in the city, and when the popes were trying to reassert authority in the surrounding Campagna (cf. Potter 1979: 149-50; Llewellyn 1983: 243-4).

One of the features of the early medieval *domusculta* was the way in which the system reflected the Roman pattern of *fundi* (Wickham 1978; 1979). To a certain extent, the provisioning of pigs to Rome from Monte Gelato reflects this, but not in a straightforward way, since it is clear from the foregoing discussion that in phase 3 animal husbandry at Monte Gelato was focused on sheep and wool production, not pigs. However, the early Roman pattern was one in which pigs were probably reared as a saleable surplus production, seen at Monte Gelato itself and at other villas such as Settefinestre (King 1985). This early Roman pattern of high pig/pork production and consumption does con-

tinue into the late Roman period on exceptional sites, notably the fifth-century Schola Praeconum on the Palatine, Rome (Barker 1982). The age at death evidence at that site suggests provisioning from a well-organized slaughter at a relatively standardized age of two years or just after, and it has been pointed out by Whitehouse (1983) that the material from the excavations at San Giovanni di Ruoti in Lucania could indicate from its bone assemblage (Steele 1983) a well-organized culling of pigs that complements the Schola Praeconum pattern (cf. Barnish 1987: 159-60). Thus, there was apparently a late Roman system of pork supply to the capital, possibly going in part to sustain a pork-rich diet amongst certain sections of the population. Although in general there is a change to a greater emphasis on sheep and goat meat in the food supply in the late Roman period (see below), it could be the case that a pork-dominant meat diet continued in parts of Rome itself, and was in fact consciously revived by the encouragement of the popes within the context of the *domusculta* system. It is also the case, of course, that pigs are a good and efficient means of producing meat for supply to a large population, and their husbandry is well-suited to fit in with an agrarian system.

Phase 6

Once established, the pig-dominant pattern continues into the tenth/eleventh centuries. Again it can be seen that the lower terrace had a good number of bones (Fig. 253), but, interestingly, the same pattern of representation of species is very strongly shown in the baptistery and church areas. Most of the contexts yielding bones in these areas were

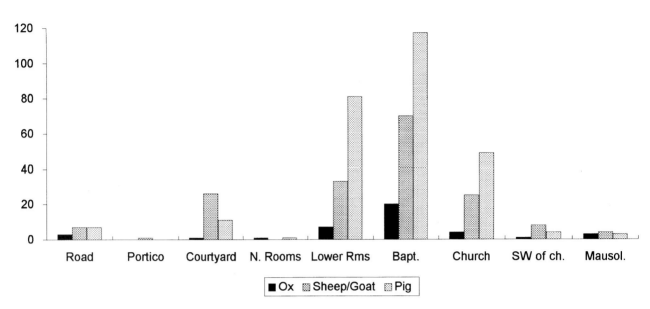

Fig. 253. Fragment count by zone, phase 6. *(ACK)*

make-up layers below floors and grave fills. It would appear that material was brought in, probably from contemporary dumps, to level up floors, and for other purposes. It seems less likely that the bones are redeposited disturbance from earlier phases, in view of the clear changes in species representation visible between phase 3 (the main potential source of earlier material) and the medieval phases. The grave fills were probably a secondary redeposition of this dumped material. Also present in the graves were small mammal bones, of rats and voles, either redeposited as well, or, more likely, of animals that had died in or close to a preferred habitat.

The general pattern established in phase 5 for pig continues in phase 6, but the age at death pattern is less controlled. Good cuts of pork are a feature of the assemblage, suggesting that a reasonable proportion of the bones was food debris from meals consumed on or near the site area. Another characteristic of this period is a change to an increased proportion of goats relative to sheep compared with earlier phases, which perhaps suggests a more domestic scale of sheep/goat husbandry compared with the larger-scale grazing necessary for the pattern visible in phase 3.

Phase 7
The assemblage from this phase is more mixed than those of previous phases and consequently less easy to explain (Fig. 254). The lower terrace rooms yielded the greatest number of bones, dominated by pig, as in phases 5 and 6, from which much of the material may be derived, since the stratigraphy indicates late medieval/modern interventions and disturbance of the site. In the court-

yard area, modern ploughing had disturbed all earlier phases and thus the material is probably hopelessly mixed. Only the twelfth-/thirteenth-century Castellaccio has a group from an undisturbed context, and it is notable that the small number of bones shows a predominance of sheep/goat. The phase 7 sheep/goat bones from the site as a whole show the slaughter of animals at a younger age than in previous phases. These factors may hint at a change in the dietary pattern and animal economy as the site goes into the later medieval period, one that is consonant with the sheep-dominant pattern established for Tuscania (Barker 1973). However, the small scale of the Castellaccio excavation and its short occupation leave this suggestion very much as a hypothesis waiting to be tested further against other late medieval sites in the locality. Nearby Mazzano Romano, which probably absorbed the population from Castellaccio, may be the best place for pursuing the question of the nature of animal production and consumption in the late medieval period.

Animal husbandry and the Monte Gelato hinterland

Although there are clear chronological changes at Monte Gelato, as outlined above, a constant element throughout is that the hinterland of the site retained the same essential characteristics. It is a plateau area sloping up towards the south into the eastern arm of the Monti Sabatini, and dissected, sometimes very deeply, by river valleys. The tufaceous soil is moderately fertile, but not especially so, and there are areas of heavier soils in which set-

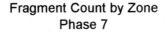

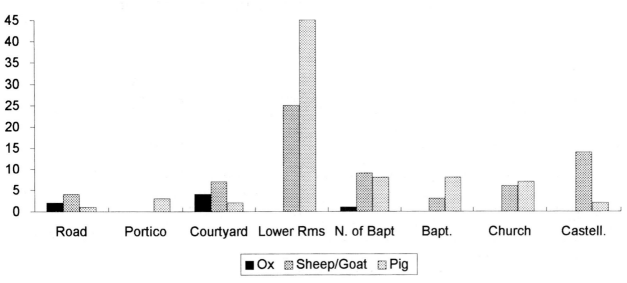

Fig. 254. Fragment count by zone, phase 7. *(ACK)*

tlement was sparse. One such area, the Morra, lies 2-3 km to the northwest of the site. It was identified as a largely blank area in Potter's field survey (Fig. 5), which may be due to the presence of woodland through much of the period of existence of the site. In addition, the zone to the south, towards Vallelunga, also contains few sites and potentially supported woodland habitats. These two areas could have been the focus for pig herding, particularly in the *domusculta* phase. Elsewhere, the land was probably cultivated for cereals and other crops, leaving limited territory set aside specifically for pasture in damper areas for cattle or in the hills for sheep. In the later Roman period, however, more extensive grazing for sheep is implied from the bone assemblage.

Into this topographical picture must be inserted any indicators of chronological change in the natural environment. Pollen analysis at Lago di Monterosi, *c.* 8 km from Monte Gelato (Bonatti 1970; Potter 1979: 23-4), has demonstrated a major period of clearance and growing of cereals in the late Republic and early Empire, that was followed by woodland advance in late Antiquity and the early medieval period. By the thirteenth century, however, this pattern had reversed again, and grass and cereal pollen indicate renewed clearance for agriculture. This picture is supported by other samples from Baccano and lake Vico, and is probably typical of the region as a whole, although it could be the case that localized clearance and agriculture may have existed around major late Roman/early medieval sites like Monte Gelato itself.

Sedimentation studies of the river valleys, such as at Narce (Cherkauer 1976; Potter 1979: 26-7), can be used to provide additional information. Dry climatic conditions seem to be indicated by low rates of deposition of sediment in the Treia valley, *c.* 250 BC-AD 150, after which rapid sedimentation occurred, due to flooding, probably as a result of a wetter climatic regime. These conditions lasted into the Middle Ages, with perhaps a brief return to stream downcutting at the end of the first millennium AD.

It seems, therefore, that phase 1/2 at Monte Gelato corresponds with a relatively dry climate and with considerable agricultural activity. This would favour the keeping of pigs, possibly in local woodland regions, but also in sties of the sort excavated at Settefinestre (Carandini 1985). Cattle would not be so compatible with these conditions, and sheep would need to be herded in a system that took them onto arable stubble after the harvest, but onto high pastures during the summer, so as not to compete directly for land used for the cultivation of crops.

Phase 3 appears to coincide with a climatic change to wetter conditions and the probably related downturn in the area cultivated. Political and economic conditions in Italy at this time also appear to have led to a reduction in the number of rural sites (Potter 1979: 138-46) and a de-intensification of agriculture. At Monte Gelato, the inhabitants of the late Roman site seem to have responded by herding sheep for wool. This would have taken up large areas of pasture, either on higher ground to the south or more distantly, or within the old arable fields. Obviously, arable cultivation must have continued, but probably on a lesser scale than in the early Roman period, and the indications are that woodland regenerated as sites (including Monte Gelato by the late seventh/eighth centuries) were abandoned or saw drastically reduced activity. That such regeneration can occur quite rapidly has been demonstrated at Castellaccio in the last 30 years: photographs taken in the 1960s (Fig. 118) show a relatively clear site with low scrub, now completely overgrown with rapidly established new woodland.

The *domusculta* regime was able to exploit the new woodland areas effectively by raising pigs intensively for surplus production. As mentioned above, suitable areas of woodland exist both to the north and south of the site, which were almost certainly more extensive then than they are now in the wake of modern agricultural improvements.

This pattern continued into phase 6, during which it seems most likely that pigs, sheep and goats were reared locally. It is unclear to what extent the *domusculta* system was perpetuated and surplus production continued. By phase 7, there are hints of a change to increased sheep husbandry, linked perhaps to the indications of woodland clearance and a return to more open conditions. At this point, *c*. AD 1300, the short-lived Castellaccio site was abandoned, and further changes to the settlement pattern and agricultural regime must be sought in the process of *incastellamento* that led locally to the creation of nucleated defended sites such as Mazzano (cf. Sereni 1982: 88-96).

Comparison with other sites

The early Imperial phases (1-2) at Monte Gelato offer many points of similarity with assemblages from contemporary urban and rural sites from Etruria, Latium and Campania (Table 71). The dominance of pig in the fragment count is a clearly observable feature at Settefinestre, Ostia, Pompeii and Naples. For all these assemblages, the pattern indicates pig meat supply drawn predominantly from juvenile or young adult animals. This applies both to producer sites (for example Settefinestre) and urban consumer centres. In the case of Settefinestre, it was argued that commercial production of pigs took place as an important part of the villa's economy during the second century, possibly supplanting or supplementing wine as a source of income (King 1985: 298). The archaeological and osteological evidence from Monte Gelato is less clear in this respect, but there is a strong probability that here, too, the nature of the pig husbandry practised would have produced a marketable surplus that presumably made its way to the fora in Rome or other cities, such as Veii.

Sheep and goat bones are consistently less well represented, and it is generally assumed that these animals were not so prominent in the agricultural economy as pigs. Interpretation of the classical agronomists suggests that arable agriculture, including vine and olive cultivation, dominated farming activity: pig herding could have been fitted into this, but little opportunity for extensive sheep farming would have been left, unless they were grazed away from the arable areas in summer while the crops were growing. This could have taken place within a system of localized movement of flocks rather than in a true transhumance system, and, for Monte Gelato, likely areas of summer pasture have been indicated in the previous section.

Cattle bones are always third in rank order of percentages in all the early Imperial assemblages, which reflects the low importance of beef in the meat diet. This may be due in part to religious factors (Prina Ricotti 1988; Dosi and Schnell 1984), but it is also the case that the usual agricultural regimes of the period were not such as could be easily compatible with large-scale cattle rearing. Establishment of low-level pasture would have competed directly with the arable land, effectively meaning that more cattle would have resulted in less cereals for humans. In addition, dry Mediterranean conditions during the summer produce few favourable areas for good pasture land (cf. White 1970: 276-84).

The remarkable consistency of the early Imperial assemblages from central-western Italy is a notable feature, reflecting in all probability a widespread consonance of diet and agriculture. This starts to break down by late Antique times (Table 71). Several urban sites, for example, Rome, Ostia and Naples, continue the early Imperial pattern, at least for the duration of the fourth century and into the fifth century. However, the later groups from Rome and Naples show a shift away from high pig percentages, so that, by the sixth century in Naples, sheep and goat bones were more common than those of pig. This trend is also seen in the rural sites, but there are hints of possibly crucial differences in the timing of the changes. Settefinestre, for instance, sees a gradual decline in pig numbers by the fourth century, that is earlier than comparable changes in the urban assemblages. At Monte Gelato, the phase 3 percentages are significantly shifted towards sheep and goats at a time when Roman and Ostian preferences were still orientated towards pig meat. For villas in southern Italy (San Giacomo and San Giovanni), the fourth and fifth centuries see sheep and goat dominant assemblages. It is possible that this demonstrates a shift in agricultural practice. At Monte Gelato, the shift is towards raising sheep for wool, and appears to coincide with regional pollen evidence for less cereal growing and perhaps wetter conditions. This may have been the case elsewhere as well: certainly Settefinestre saw a decline in general agricultural activity at the same time as the bone assemblage tended towards increasing sheep and goat numbers.

What this signified in general economic terms is not easy to determine. However, it is known from

Table 71. Comparison of the main domestic species representation (by NISP) with other assemblages, mainly from central western Italy.

site/phase	date	type	ox %	sheep/ goat %	pig %	total	reference
EARLY IMPERIAL							
Monte Gelato, 1-2	1-2	villa	6.8	21.8	71.4	294	this report
Settefinestre, II	1-2	villa	13.0	17.0	70.0	1,518	King 1985: fig. 188
Settefinestre, III	L2-E3	villa	6.1	15.5	78.5	710	"
Ostia, Terme Nuotatore	1-2	urban	12.8	31.8	55.4	1,381	IPU 1968; 1970; 1973; 1977
Ostia, Terme Nuotatore	L2-M3	urban	7.8	32.0	60.2	924	"
Pompeii, forum	1BC-E1	urban	14.0	20.0	66.0	1,478	King n..d. a
Pompeii, forum	E-M1	urban	10.6	27.1	62.4	502	"
Naples, Carminiello ai Mannesi (CM), III	L1	urban	5.8	23.4	70.8	137	King 1994
Naples, CM, IV	2-3	urban	1.9	34.0	64.1	103	"
LATE ANTIQUE							
Monte Gelato, 3	4-5	villa	7.8	51.2	41.0	344	this report
Settefinestre, IV	4	villa	16.6	30.6	52.8	757	King 1985: fig. 188
San Giacomo	E5	villa	15.1	54.1	30.7	205	Albarella 1993
San Giovanni di Ruoti	L4-M5	villa	13.5	53.4	33.1	148	Steele 1983
San Giovanni di Ruoti	M5-E6	villa	6.7	19.1	74.2	802	"
Ostia, Terme Nuotatore	L3-5	urban	12.2	20.4	67.3	147	IPU 1968; 1970; 1973; 1977
Rome, Palatine East	4	urban	0.6	22.1	77.3	655	Payne 1990
Rome, Schola Praeconum	5	urban	9.6	36.7	53.7	1,568	Barker 1982
Naples, Santa Patrizia	4	urban	1.6	19.6	78.8	547	Albarella & Frezza n.d. a
Naples, Girolomini	L4	urban	6.9	38.6	54.5	765	King n.d. b
Naples, via San Paolo	5-6	urban	18.3	32.9	48.8	164	Albarella & Frezza n.d. b
Naples, CM, VI	M5	urban	5.7	33.3	61.0	103	King 1994
Naples, CM, VII	L5-E6	urban	8.9	56.3	34.8	1,928	"
Naples, CM, VIII	L6-7	urban	8.5	49.8	41.7	1,646	"
MEDIEVAL							
Monte Gelato, 5	8-9	eccl.	7.3	40.2	52.3	231	this report
Monte Gelato, 6	10-11	eccl.	8.2	35.7	56.0	487	"
Monte Gelato, 7	11-12	eccl./cas.	4.6	45.8	49.7	153	"
Farfa, 1	to 9	eccl.	14.2	27.5	58.3	120	Clark 1987a: 23
Farfa, 2	10-12	eccl.	6.0	28.2	65.8	1,211	"
Farfa, 3	13-15	eccl.	8.1	28.5	63.4	6,226	"
Ponte Nepesino	9-10	cas.	35.7	24.9	39.5	474	Clark 1984
Anguillara	9-12	cas./eccl.	33.7	24.7	41.6	807	Burnett, Clark & Sutherland forthcoming
Scarlino	11-12	cas.	7.1	12.2	80.8	255	Tozzi 1981
Colle Castellano	9-10	cas./sett.	19.1	44.6	36.3	755	Clark forthcoming
Luni, 1	8	urban	9..8	46.2	44.0	987	Barker 1977
Luni, 3	8-11	urban	22.0	35.7	42.3	544	"
Naples, Santa Patrizia	8-9	urban	8.7	55.1	36.2	69	King n.d. c
Naples, via San Paolo	6-12	urban	40.9	17.1	42.1	252	Albarella & Frezza n.d. b
Tarquinia, 1	L12-14	urban	8.4	28.8	62.8	1,352	Clark 1989
Tarquinia, 2	L14	urban	8.1	52.2	39.7	6,852	"
Tarquinia, 3	L14-15	urban	11.5	52.1	36.4	217	"
Tuscania, pit 1	L13	urban	3.1	87.6	9.3	194	Barker 1973
Tuscania, pit 2	M14	urban	12.1	71.5	16.4	403	"

KEY:
Date: numbers refer to centuries; E – early; M – middle; L – late
Type: cas. – castle; eccl. – ecclesiastical; sett. – settlement

literary and archaeological sources that Italy and Rome in particular were supplied with basic foodstuffs from other parts of the Mediterranean, notably north Africa (cf. Carandini and Panella 1981). Local production declined after the second century, possibly because production costs were cheaper in the provinces. During much of the third century Monte Gelato itself was probably deserted, but revived in the mid-fourth century with an agricultural economy that included an emphasis on wool. It may be that this was an avenue for making a profit outside the realm of the food supply, since the urban food markets were still being supplied to a great extent from overseas. This may account for the perceived differences in the urban and rural assemblages. For the fourth century and part of the fifth, urban centres were able to sustain traditional dietary patterns, whilst rural sites had changed. Dislocation of the mediterranean supply routes in the mid-fifth century, however, would have upset this pattern, and it is probably after this time that urban and rural assemblages move into line again, on a pattern that has less pork and more mutton and goat meat, probably locally supplied.

This picture holds good with the exception of San Giovanni in the fifth/sixth century. Here, a midden with very high pig percentages appears to fly in the face of the model presented above. It is a special case, and has been presented by Whitehouse (1983) and Barnish (1987) as a site supplying the Roman market with pigs and pig meat. This is probably an example of specialist cash-cropping in order to satisfy the urban market demand, and also the *annona* distribution of pork that may have taken place in Rome at this time. However, this does seem to be exceptional, and the general trend in Italy, and indeed the western Mediterranean as a whole, in the late Antique period was towards a diet with less pork and more mutton and goat meat (cf. Jourdan 1976; King 1990; forthcoming b).

It is conceivable that Rome, due to its supplier sites like San Giovanni, was able to sustain a more traditional dietary pattern right through the late Antique period, but unfortunately there are no post-fifth-century or early medieval assemblages from the city to check this hypothesis. What is apparent from Monte Gelato, however, is that the establishment of the *domusculta*, designed by the papacy as a supply system for the city, saw a change back to a pattern with significant numbers of pigs. As discussed above, the pigs seem to have been deliberately reared as part of the supply system and are mentioned specifically in the surviving documents. This could have been because of the residual demand for pig meat by a Roman population that regarded pork as a traditional element of the diet.

Turning to the early medieval assemblages in general (Table 71), it can be seen that the site most similar to Monte Gelato in percentage terms is Farfa, although the latter has marginally lower levels of sheep and goat bones. This site, not far from Monte Gelato, in the Sabine hills, was an important abbey with extensive estates, from which its animal resources were almost certainly drawn. Both sites were ecclesiastical in nature, probably self-sufficient economically. The pattern, therefore, probably reflects a dietary preference for pork, followed by mutton. As in earlier periods, cattle were not a significant factor. In terms of agriculture, both sites seem to have exploited pigs in a similar manner, to judge from the age at death evidence (see above), but the sheep were treated differently at each site. At Monte Gelato, adults predominated and a wool pattern of husbandry is inferred that was probably a continuation of the economy of the late Roman establishment. At Farfa, sheep and goats were slaughtered young (Clark 1987a: 13-14; 1987b: fig. 5), presumably primarily as part of the meat supply. These differences are interesting, because they probably reflect the higher status of Farfa vis-à-vis Monte Gelato. The former assemblage demonstrates consumption of good-quality meat within a rich monastic context, while the latter, although still ecclesiastical, was a producer site for pork and wool being supplied to Rome and the papacy.

The differences concealed behind the apparent similarities of the two assemblages highlight an important aspect of medieval bone groups; their diversity. Table 71 is only a selection of sites, but it shows a wide range of percentages emphasizing different species. This contrasts with the early Imperial pattern, and is confirmed by the longer listings covering all of Italy in Clark (1987a) and Baker and Clark (1993). The main trend overall is towards higher sheep and goat percentages in the later medieval period (Clark 1987a: 12). This is most obvious in the case of Tuscania, where the local stock economy must have concentrated upon sheep husbandry, mainly for wool (Barker 1973: 167). Monte Gelato, as discussed earlier, has hints of a change to an increased emphasis upon sheep and goats in the small, mainly twelfth-century, assemblage, from Castellaccio.

An assemblage that contrasts with Monte Gelato is that from Ponte Nepesino, a contemporary site only 7 km distant. Here, an unusually high percentage of ox bones was found, which was interpreted as meat being imported to this garrison site (Clark 1984: 133-4). Certainly, the percentage is too high in relation to the other species to regard the cattle bones as originating solely from local resources, and it is likely that they represent tribute or provisions brought into the site. Other sites have unusual bone percentages as well, probably due to external provisioning (Clark 1987a: 12). Anguillara may be similar to Ponte Nepesino in its nature and has a similar bone assemblage, as noted by Burnett, Clark and Sutherland (forthcoming). Scarlino has an abnormally high percentage of pig bones from one part of the site, but continuing study of the material shows that within the castle were remains of a richer diet that included a higher percentage of beef (Clark 1987a: 12). Colle Castellano also has elements indicating provision of prime cuts of meat (Clark forthcoming). All these sites are linked by virtue of being high-status sites such as garrisons and castles, or at least having a significant presence of such elements that appears to have distorted the basic subsistence provisioning of the sites in favour of particular species.

The existence of bone assemblages such as these demonstrates the variability of medieval assemblages. The general picture seems to have been one of localized production and supply, at least for the poorer rural sites, conditioned by the regional topography and agricultural possibilities. High-status and urban sites could command more variety in their consumption, however, which led to unusual assemblages and noticeable differences in composition. Monte Gelato fits into this pattern by virtue of being a rural production centre for meat and wool, with aspects of similarity to other ecclesiastical sites. Many features of the medieval pattern of husbandry and diet remain obscure, however, and more assemblages are needed to test how far Monte Gelato was typical of its site type and period.

APPENDIX

Bone measurements are given in millimetres and the scheme and abbreviations of von den Driesch (1976) are used. * indicates that it is an estimated measurement. The context number and phase are given in brackets at the end of each entry.

Ox *(Bos taurus)*

scapula SLC 52, GLP 76, LG 60 (D229. Phase 6)
humerus SD 41, Bd 90, BT 85 (M38. Phase 5)
metacarpus DD 24, Bd 63 (M39. Phase 3)
   GL 215*, SD 41, DD 25 (M167. Phase 6)
proximal phalanx anterior GLpe 59, Bp 30, SD 25, Bd 28 (B26. Phase 6)
   GLpe 55, Bp 29, SD 25, Bd 27 (E16. Phase 3)
   GLpe 68, Bp 38, SD 33, Bd 35 (L165. Phase 2)
   GLpe 64, Bp 37, SD 31, Bd 34 (M17. Phase 5)
   GLpe 61, Bp 30, SD 25, Bd 29 (M20. Phase 5)
   GLpe 59, Bp 29, SD 25, Bd 29 (M33. Phase 6)
   GLpe 64 (M138. Phase 3)
pelvis LAR 87 (C51. Phase 5)
   LAR 68* (C59. Phase 3)
femur BD 78 (D301. Phase 6)
   DC 44 (L165. Phase 2)
naviculo-cuboid GB 51 (M145. Phase 3)
metatarsus Bd 55* (E76. Phase 3)
   Bp 45 (M145. Phase 3)
   Bp 39, SD 20, DD 19 (S10. Phase 3)
proximal phalanx posterior GLpe 62, Bp 33, SD 29, Bd 33 (M38. Phase 5)
medial phalanx GL 48, Bp 35, SD 30, Bd 32 (M27. Phase 5)
   GL 45, Bp 34, SD 27, Bd 29 (M146. Phase 3)
   GL 41, Bp 27, SD 22, Bd 21 (S10. Phase 3)

Sheep/goat *(Ovis/Capra)*

cranium (40) 119, (41) 41, (42) 35; definitely sheep (H30. Phase 3)
mandible (10) 23 (A10. Phase 2)
   (7) 76, (8) 54, (9) 23, (10) 22×8, (15b) 24, (15c) 21 (C51. Phase 5)
   (8) 48, (10) 24×9, (15a) 37, (15b) 25 (D6. Phase 7)
   (10) 17×7, (13) 53 (E94. Phase 5)
   (7) 68, (8) 47, (9) 22, (10) 17×7, (15a) 35, (15b) 22, (15c) 18 (E94. Phase 5)
   (9) 26, (15b) 27, (15c) 21 (E101. Phase 3)
   (9) 26, (15b) 21, (15c) 16 (L105. Phase 2)
   (10) 22×8 (L105. Phase 2)
   (10) 24×9 (L165. Phase 2)
   (10) 23×8 (M87. Phase 3)
   (10) 24×9 (M144. Phase 3)
   (7) 72, (8) 53, (9) 21, (10) 24×9, (15b) 22, (15c) 17 (M144. Phase 3)
   (7) 71, (8) 52, (9) 20, (10) 24×9, (15c) 18 (M144. Phase 3)
   (10) 21×9 (M146. Phase 3)
   (7) 72, (8) 51, (9) 22, (10) 23×9, (15b) 21, (15c) 18 (M161. Phase 3)
atlas GB 82*, GL 63, BFcr 53, BFcd 58*, GLF 53, H 44; probably male sheep (D247. Phase 3)
scapula LG 24, BG 19 (C51. Phase 5)
   GLP 34, LG 25, BG 22 (D80. Phase 7)
   SLC 18 (D81. Phase 6)
   GLP 31, LG 24, BG 22 (D279. Phase 6)
   GLP 36, LG 27 (D301. Phase 6)
   GLP 33, LG 24, BG 20 (M23. Phase 5)
   LG 26, BG 21 (M27. Phase 5)
   SLC 19*, GLP 36, LG 29, BG 22; definitely sheep (M146. Phase 3)
   GLP 30*, LG 24, BG 22 (Z7. Phase 7)
humerus Bd 30, BT 29 (A19. Phase 3)
   Bd 30, BT 29 (B26. Phase 6)
   Bd 30, BT 30; definitely sheep (D301. Phase 6)
   Bd 30, BT 29; definitely sheep (E32. Phase 3)
   SD 17, Bd 31, BT 30; probably goat (M21. Phase 5)
   SD 13, Bd 29, BT 27; proximal not fused (M164. Phase 3)
   Bd 30, BT 29; definitely goat (P16. Phase 6)
   Bd 29, HT 26; definitely sheep (Z7. Phase 7)
   Bp 41* (M38. Phase 5)
radius Bp 33, BFp 30 (A19. Phase 3)
   Bp 25, BFp 23 (D6. Phase 7)
   Bp 27, BFp 26 (D229. Phase 6)
   GL 147, Bp 32, BFp 29, SD 15, Bd 28, BFd 24; definitely sheep (D249. Phase 6)
   GL 144, Bp 28, BFp 26, SD 15, Bd 27, BFd 24 (D301. Phase 6)
   Bp 34, BFp 32, SD 17 (J10. Phase 6)
   Bd 35, BFd 31 (L105. Phase 2)
   Bd 31, BFd 29, SD 16; probably sheep (M26. Phase 3)
   Bp 30, BFp 28; definitely sheep (M38. Phase 5)
   SD 16, Bd 33, BFd 25 (M38. Phase 5)
   Bp 30, BFp 29; definitely goat (M106. Phase 5)
   Bp 35, BFp 32; probably sheep (M146. Phase 3)
radius + ulna GL 183 (D249. Phase 6)
ulna LO 39 (B26. Phase 6)
   DPA 26, SDO 22, BPC 18; proximal ephiphysis unfused; definitely of sheep (D133. Phase 6)
   LO 38, DPA 25, BPC 19 (D249. Phase 6)
   LO 40, DPA 24, SDO 21, BPC 17 (M38. Phase 5)
   LO 43, DPA 24, SDO 21, BPC 22 (M106. Phase 5)
metacarpus Bp 25 (D38. Phase 6)

Bp 26 (D345. Phase 4)
GL 135, Bp 25, SD 13, DD 10, Bd 28 (M38. Phase 5)
GL 121, Bp 23, SD 14, DD 10, Bd 25 (M38. Phase 5)
Bd 28 (M38. Phase 5)
DD 10, Bd 24 (M161. Phase 3)
GL 131, Bp 21, SD 13, DD 9, Bd 25 (M164. Phase 3)
DD 11, Bd 26 (M172. Phase 3)
proximal phalanx anterior GLpe 39, Bp 12, SD 10, Bd 12; definitely sheep (B24. Phase 6)
GLpe 35, Bd 11; definitely sheep (D80. Phase 7)
GLpe 34, Bp 12, Bd 12 (M38. Phase 5)
GLpe 36, Bp 13, SD 11, Bd 12 (M39. Phase 3)
GLpe 39, Bd 12, SD 10, Bd 12 (M109. Phase 6)
GLpe 33, Bd 13, SD 10, Bd 12 (M139. Phase 5)
GLpe 33, Bd 11, SD 8, Bd 10 (M144. Phase 3)
pelvis LAR 28 (D81. Phase 6)
LA 29, LAR 27 (D247. Phase 3)
LA 32, LAR 26 (M38. Phase 5)
LA 29, LAR 25 (Z7. Phase 7)
femur DC 20 (B29. Phase 7)
Bd 31*, SD 15 (C27. Phase 7)
DC 19 (L105. Phase 2)
DC 20 (M38. Phase 5)
Bd 40; just fused (M146. Phase 3)
Bp 44, DC 20 (M164. Phase 3)
tibia Bd 29 (D301. Phase 6)
Bp 37 (D319. Phase 6)
Bd 25 (D319. Phase 6)
Bd 25 (D323. Phase 6)
Bp 47, SD 15 (D344. Phase 6)
SD 16, Bd 27 (E28. Phase 3)
Bp 40 (M144. Phase 3)
SD 15, Bd 29 (M146. Phase 3)
Bd 28 (M146. Phase 3)
Bp 49 (M146. Phase 3)
Bd 29 (M164. Phase 3)
Bd 23 (N30. Phase 3)
calcaneum GL 63, GB 19; definitely sheep (D52. Phase 3)
GL 55, GB 20; definitely goat (D244. Phase 6)
GL 56, GB 18; definitely sheep (E28. Phase 3)
GL 57, GB 20 (M144. Phase 3)
GL 63, GB 22 (M146. Phase 3)
astragalus GLl 29, GLm 27, Dl 17, Bd 18; definitely sheep (A35. Phase 5)
GLl 29, GLm 27, Dl 16, Bd 19 (B80. Phase 6)
GLl 34, GLm 31, Dl 19, Bd 20; definitely sheep (M145. Phase 3)
GLl 33, GLm 32, Dl 19, Bd 21 (M146. Phase 3)
GLl 29, GLm 28, Dl 16, Bd 19 (M146. Phase 3)
GLl 29, GLm 28, Dl 16, Bd 18 (M172. Phase 3)
naviculo-cuboid GB 23 (B80. Phase 6)
GB 24 (M32. Phase 5)
GB 26 (M146. Phase 3)
metatarsus GL 129, Bp 18, SD 11, DD 10, Bd 23 (B1. Phase 7)
Bd 25* (D86. Phase 5)
SD 13, Bd 21 (L105. Phase 2)
SD 12, DD 10, Bd 25 (M38. Phase 5)
Bp 21 (M38. Phase 5)
GL 133*, SD 11, DD 9 (M39. Phase 3)
DD 8, Bd 21 (M74. Phase 5)
Bp 20, SD 10, DD 9 (M144. Phase 3)
GL 153, Bp 23, SD 12, DD 11, Bd 26 (M146. Phase 3)
proximal phalanx posterior GLpe 35, Bp 11, SD 9, Bd 9; probably posterior (H21. Phase 6)
GL 34, Bp 11, SD 8, Bd 10; probably sheep, probably posterior (M17. Phase 6)
GLpe 38, Bp 14, SD 10, Bd 12 (M39. Phase 3)

GLpe 34, Bp 12, SD 9, Bd 12 (M39. Phase 3)
GLpe 35, Bp 12, SD 10, Bd 12 (M79. Phase 3)
GLpe 40, Bp 14, SD 11, Bd 13 (M138. Phase 3)
GLpe 34, Bp 12, SD 9, Bd 12 (M139. Phase 5)
GLpe 40, Bp 13, SD 10, Bd 12 (M144. Phase 3)
GLpe 41, Bp 12, SD 10, Bd 12 (M144. Phase 3)
medial phalanx GL 26, Bp 12, SD 8, Bd 10 (M144. Phase 3)
GL 26, Bp 12, SD 9, Bd 10 (M144. Phase 3)
GL 23, Bp 10, SD 8, Bd 9 (M145. Phase 3)
distal phalanx Ld 29, DLS 35, MBS 6; definitely sheep (A35. Phase 5)
Ld 24, DLS 30, MBS 6; definitely sheep (M144. Phase 3)
Ld 24, DLS 30, MBS 7 (M164. Phase 3)

Pig (Sus scrofa)

cranium (28) 63, (30) 25, (31) 17 (D345. Phase 4)
mandible (6) 110, (7) 102, (7a) 87, (8) 55, (9) 47, (9a) 31, (10) 25×13, (11) 40*, (16a) 38, (16b) 38, (16c) 36; female (D301. Phase 6)
(4) 150, (6) 120, (7a) 99, (8) 66, (9a) 34, (10) 30×15, (11) 37*, (12) 57, (16a) 45, (16b) 38, (16c) 40, (21) 11; female (D301. Phase 6)
(9) 48, (9a) 35, (11) 36, (12) 61, (21) 9; female (D319. Phase 6)
(8) 66, (10) 30×17, (16a) 44 (D319. Phase 6)
(11) 40, (12) 57, (21) 13 (E186. Phase 3)
(10) 29×14 (L105. Phase 2)
(10) 32×15 (M74. Phase 5)
(10) 34×14 (M145. Phase 3)
atlas GLF 45 (L105. Phase 2)
GLF 45 (L105. Phase 2)
scapula GLP 34, BG 24, LG 28 (D321. Phase 7)
GLP 35, BG 24, LG 31 (M17. Phase 6)
SLC 20, GLP 31, BG 21, LG 25 (M38. Phase 5)
humerus BT 29 (A19. Phase 3)
Bd 37, BT 30 (M138. Phase 3)
radius Bp 27, SD 17 (D317. Phase 6)
Bp 27, SD 16; juvenile (E44. Phase 3)
Bp 28 (M79. Phase 3)
Bp 24, SD 14; proximal fusing, distal unfused (M145. Phase 3)
ulna BPC 15 (D86. Phase 5)
BPC 13 (D86. Phase 5)
DPA 40, BPC 23 (D227. Phase 6)
DPA 43, SDO 36, BPC 25 (E17. Phase 4)
DPA 37, SDO 28, BPC 20 (L105. Phase 2)
BPC 23 (M38. Phase 5)
metacarpus II GL 53, Bd 10 (L105. Phase 2)
metacarpus IV GL 66, Bp 14, B 11, Bd15 (L105. Phase 2)
pelvis LAR 26 (A19. Phase 3)
LA 29 (L165. Phase 2)
femur DC 24 (Z7. Phase 7)
tibia Bp 60 (D249. Phase 6)
Bd 31 (L165. Phase 2)
calcaneum GL 76, GB 22 including loose epiphysis (L105. Phase 2)
astragalus GLl 36, GLm 33, Dl 18, Bd 21 (A34. Phase 5)
GLl 40, GLm 37, Dl 21, Bd 22 (B21. Phase 6)
metatarsus II GL 51, Bd 10 (E11. Phase 2)
metatarsus III GL 84, LeP 84, Bp 18, B 14, Bd 17 (E11. Phase 2)
metatarsus IV GL 78, LeP 74, Bp 14, B 12, Bd 15 (D273. Phase 6)
metatarsus V GL 62, Bd 9 (M38. Phase 5)
proximal phalanx GLpe 31, Bp 17, SD 13, Bd 15 (D301. Phase 6)

GLpe 34, Bp 17, SD 14, Bd 16 (D316. Phase 3)
GLpe 37, Bp 15, SD 12, Bd 15 (L146. Phase 2)
GLpe 35, Bp 15, SD 12, Bd 14 (M87. Phase 3)
proximal phalanx for metapodial II/V GL 24 (D86. Phase 5)
medial phalanx GLpe 22 (A19. Phase 3)
GLpe 21, Bd 15 (D86. Phase 5)
GLpe 21, Bp 15, SD 13, Bd 13 (D301. Phase 6)
GLpe 31, Bp 19, SD 16, Bd 16 (E11. Phase 2)
GLpe 25, Bp 17, SD 14, Bd 14 (E74. Phase 3)
GLpe 20, Bp 13, SD 11, Bd 11 (L165. Phase 2)
GLpe 24, Bp 13, SD 9, Bd 10 (M38. Phase 5)
distal phalanx DLS 28, Ld 25, MBS 11 (A19. Phase 3)
DLS 29, Ld 26, MBS 12 (D86. Phase 5)
DLS 25, Ld 24, MBS 10 (D301. Phase 6)
DLS 27, Ld 27, MBS 11 (L105. Phase 2)
DLS 28, Ld 28, MBS 13 (L105. Phase 2)

Horse (Equus caballus)

proximal phalanx GL 84, Bp 52, BFp 49, Dp 33, SD 34, Bd 43, BFd 42 (E1. Phase 7)
GL 80, Bp 51*, BFp 49, Dp 35, SD 33, Bd 42, BFd 41 (E16. Phase 3)

Dog (Canis familiaris)

mandible(1) 137, (2) 134*, (3) 129, (4) 120, (5) 113, (6) 117*, (7) 76, (8) 68, (9) 62, (10) 32, (11) 37, (12) 32, (13) 20×8, (14) 18, (15) 8×6, (17) 12, (18) 53, (19) 24, (20) 18, (21) 36, (22) 162.14, (23) 163.4, (24) 164.98, (25) 163.84, (26) 153.2 (S13. Phase 2)
radius Bd 22 (D52. Phase 3)
metacarpus IV GL 55, Bd 8 (S10. Phase 3)
tibia Bd 20 (D50. Phase 5)
calcaneum GL 41, GB 10 (D52. Phase 3)

Dog skeleton I, juvenile/subadult (L165. Phase 2)

mandible (right) (1) 104, (3) 101, (4) 90, (5) 87, (7) 63, (8) 61, (9) 56, (10) 30, (11) 32, (12) 27, (13) 19×7, (14) 18, (15) 7×5, (17) 9, (19) 18, (20) 14, (21) 30, (23) 123.3, (24) 127.02, (26) 132.9
mandible (left) (8) 61, (9) 57, (10) 30, (11) 32, (12) 27, (13) 19×7, (14) 18, (17) 10, (19) 17, (20) 14, (26) 132.9

Dog skeleton II (L105 and L165. Phase 2)

mandible (right) (1) 150, (2) 149, (3) 143, (4) 130, (5) 124, (6) 130, (7) 84; to M4 87, (9) 7; to M4 74, (10) 36; to M4 39, (12) 36, (13) 22×9, (14) 20, (15) 9×6, (16) 5×5; M4 3×3, (17) 12, (18) 57, (19) 25, (20) 18, (21) 40, (22) 180.29, (23) 178.1, (24) 181.04, (25) 179.81
mandible (left) (21) 39
axis LCDe 51, LAPa 52, BFcr 32, BPacd 34, BPtr 44, SBV 25, BFcd 19, H 40
scapula HS 143, SLC 26, GLP 32, BG 20
SLC 26, GLP 32, LG 29, BG 20
humerus Dp 44, SD 13, Bd 34
Dp 44
radius GL 180, Bp 19, SD 13, Bd 25
GL 181, Bp 19, SD 13, Bd 25
ulna GL 212, DPA 26, SDO 22, BPC 20
GL 214, DPA 26, SDO 22, BPC 20
metacarpus (right) GL 24, Bd 6
metacarpus I (left) GL 24 Bd 6

metacarpus II (right) GL 62, Bd 9
metacarpus II (left) GL 62, Bd 9
metacarpus III (right) GL 72, Bd 9
metacarpus III (left) GL 72, Bd 9
metacarpus IV (right) GL 70, Bd 9
metacarpus V (right) GL 60, Bd 10
metacarpus V (left) GL 61, Bd 10
sacrum (three segments) GL 40, PL 39, GB 46, BFcr 26, HFcr 12
pelvis GL 156, LAR 24, SH 19, SB 10, SC 52
femur GLC 192, Bp 40, DC 19, SD 13 Bd 34
Bd 33
patella GL 20, GB 11
tibia GL 199, Bp 36, SD 13, Bd 24
Bp 36, Bd 24
fibula GL 185
astragalus GL 28
calcaneum GL 47, GB 20
metatarsus II (right) GL 70, Bd 9
metatarsus II (left) GL 69, Bd 9
metatarsus III (right) GL 78, Bd 9
metatarsus III (left) GL 77, Bd 9
metatarsus IV (right) GL 80, Bd 9
metatarsus IV (left) GL 76, Bd 10
metatarsus V (right) GL 72, Bd 9
(phalanges not measured)

Red deer (Cervus elaphus)

scapula LG 42, BG 30 (M4. Phase 6)
radius Bd 50, BFd 50 (L165. Phase 2)

Fallow deer (Cervus dama)

radius SD 17, Bd 32, BFd 27 (M26. Phase 3)
metacarpus Bp 28 (D244. Phase 6)

THE BIRD BONES, by Barbara West

A total of 249 bird bones was recovered. As can be seen from Table 72, most of the material came from phase 2 (second century), phase 3 (fourth-sixth centuries) and phase 6 (tenth-eleventh centuries). Domestic chickens comprise the majority of the identified bird bones, with only a few examples of other species.

Knife marks from butchery occur only on two chicken bones: one from context D91 (phase 6/7) and one from A23 (phase 6). Evidence of gnawing by dogs occurs on three chicken bones: two in phase 6 (D212 and D319) and one in phase 3 (M172). Extensive rodent gnawing was found on one chicken bone from phase 6 (A23).

Sex was determined using the presence or absence of the metatarsal spur, a late stage of spur development called the socket primordium (West 1982; 1985), and the mineralized deposit known as medullary bone, indicating egg-laying females (Driver 1982). Table 73 shows that males outnumbered females in phases 2 and 6. Medullary bone occurred only in phase 3.

The relative proportions of adult chickens to juveniles (Table 74) indicate that juvenile birds were well-represented in phases 2 and 6, but negligible in phase 3.

The measurements (Table 75) indicate that the Monte Gelato chickens at various periods were similar in size to those from contemporary European sites listed by Thesing (1977). No pathological specimens were found.

Table 72. Bird bones.

species ↓ phase →	2	3	3/4	5	5/6	6	6/7	7
chicken (*Gallus gallus*)	28	23	5	1	10	50	4	2
chicken/duck size	5	6	-	2	5	19	1	4
domestic duck (*Anas platyrhyncos*)	-	1	-	-	-	-	-	-
duck species	-	1	-	-	-	-	-	-
domestic goose (*Anser anser*)	-	-	-	-	-	-	1	-
goose species	-	1	-	-	-	-	1	-
goose size	-	-	-	-	-	-	1	-
dove species (*Columba* sp.)	-	1	-	-	-	-	-	-
tawny owl (*Strix aluco*)	1	-	-	-	-	-	-	-
jay (*Garrulus glandarius*)	2	-	-	-	-	-	-	-
song thrush (*Turdus philomelos*)	1	-	-	-	-	-	-	-
blackbird (*Turdus merula*)	6	-	-	-	-	-	-	-
thrush species (*Turdus* sp.)	11	-	-	-	-	-	-	-
chaffinch (*Fringilla coelebs*)	1	-	-	-	-	-	-	-
finch species (*Fringillidae*)	1	-	-	-	-	-	-	-
unidentified bird	37	6	2	-	1	6	2	-
subtotals (total = 249)	93	39	7	3	16	75	10	6
% of total sample in each phase	37	16	3	1	7	30	4	2

Table 73. Chicken sex ratios.

phase	2	3	6
males	2	1	3
females	-	1	1

Table 74. Chicken age ratios.

phase	2	3	6
adults	63% (15)	95% (18)	76% (31)
juveniles	37% (9)	5% (1)	24% (10)

DISCUSSION

An examination of the distribution of the bird bones across the site indicates that they represent scattered domestic refuse. All the wild species from phase 2 came from the fish-pond fills, the jay and female tawny owl, particularly, indicating nearby woodland. Jays need well-secluded woodland with dense foliage in which to nest, and are never far from trees, while tawny owls nest in hollow trees (Peterson, Mountfort and Hollom 1979). The other birds from this deposit, such as thrush, blackbird and chaffinch, are commonly found in woods and gardens. The suggestion that there may have been an aviary (cf. Chapter Three) should here be noted.

The patterns from both the age and sex data for chickens suggest a distinct change in activity in the late Roman period. Young, tender birds almost disappear from the diet in this period (phase 3), although they are well-represented in second-century and in medieval contexts. Furthermore, medullary bone occurs only in phase 3. Eating an egg-laying hen instead of her future eggs implies a disregard for subsistence levels, and a waste of dietary resources, suggesting a certain degree of affluence.

THE FISH BONES, by Caroline Cartwright

A total of 26 fish bones was recovered from Roman and medieval contexts. Standard techniques of optical microscopy were used to assist the identification of the fish bones, in conjunction with comparisons made to reference collections of mediterranean fish taxa.

THE IDENTIFICATIONS

Phase 2 (second century)

– One vertebral centra of *Anguilla anguilla* (eel); two unidentifiable spine fragments.
 L165. Fish-pond, early second century.
– Three fragments of spine and two fragments of dentary of *Alosa* sp. (shad); six unidentifiable spine fragments.
 L105. Fish-pond, late second century.
– Two scombrid neural spines.
 S10. Rock-cut road.
– One scombrid neural spine fragment.
 L143. North cistern, late second century.

Table 75. Chicken bone measurements.

phase	context	sex	measurements				
CORACOID			GL	Lm	Bb	Bf	
2	L165		61.0	58.0	17.0	14.3	
3	D316		53.4	-	14.8	12.6	
3	D316		53.8	-	14.9	11.9	
6	D107		52.0	49.6	12.7	10.9	
6	D273		53.0	50.8	14.0	12.2	
6	D301		48.4	46.0	13.2	10.8	
6	D301		48.7	45.7	-	10.5	
SCAPULA			Dic				
2	L105		12.2				
2	L165		13.3				
3	M143		10.0				
6	D266		11.4				
6	D273		11.9				
6	D301		11.4				
HUMERUS			GL	Bp	SC	Bd	
2	L165		-	-	7.0	14.3	
3	M121		69.8	18.4	6.6	14.8	
3	M50		-	-	6.7	14.2	
3	M136		-	-	6.3	13.2	
6	A23		-	-	7.2	16.3	
6	D319		-	16.2	5.8	-	
RADIUS			GL	SC	Bd		
2	E11		64.2	2.9	6.4		
2	L165		64.8	2.9	6.7		
ULNA			GL	Dip	Bp	SC	Did
3	L162		73.0	13.6	9.6	4.4	10.0
6	D301		-	13.3	9.2	4.2	-
METACARPAL			GL	Bp	Did		
3	M146		35.9	12.3	6.9		
6	D107		34.6	-	6.7		
TIBIA			La	Dip	SC	Bd	Dd
2	L105		22.5	-	-	-	-
2	L105		-	-	-	12.6	13.2
3	M114		-	-	-	10.0	10.7
3	M136	F	-	19.5	-	-	-
6	D168		-	-	-	10.5	-
6	D301		-	-	-	10.8	11.7
6	D301		-	-	6.2	10.0	9.9
FEMUR			Bp	Dp	SC	Bd	Dd
3	M121		-	-	6.3	15.8	12.7
3	D48		16.3	10.4	-	-	
6	D107		15.3	10.2	6.3	-	-
6	D319		-	-	6.5	14.4	12.0
6	D301		15.1	9.7	6.1	-	-
METATARSAL			GL	Bp	SC	Bd	
2	L105	M	-	-	-	15.6	
2	L105	M	98.8	14.9	7.5	15.4	
3	D316	M	100.3	15.6	8.7	17.3	
6	M64	F	74.9	-	6.2	13.7	
6	D168	M	91.9	14.1	7.8	16.1	

Phase 3 (late Roman)

– One fragment of dentary of *Pagrus pagrus* (sea bream).
E9. Occupation layer.

Phase 3/4 (late Roman)

– One fragment of dentary of *Diplodus* sp. (sea bream).
E16. Rubble/occupation.

Phase 5 (early medieval)

– One neural spine fragment, possibly of a scombrid; one
fragment of lateral scute of an *Acipenser sturio* (sturgeon).
M121. Mortar dump.

Phase 6 (medieval)

– One vertebra from the herring family, Clupeidae, possibly
from *Sardinia pilchardus* (sardine)
B80. Burial no. 12.
– One urohyal of *Pagrus pagrus* (sea bream).
D104. Ash layer.
– One fragmented haemal spine of *Pagrus pagrus* (sea
bream).
D282. Burial no. 46.
– One fragment of neural spine, possibly of a scombrid.
D15. Burial no. 28.
– One fragment of lateral scute of *Acipenser sturio* (stur-
geon).
A4. Burial no. 26.

DISCUSSION

The second-century fill of the fish-pond yielded
fourteen fragments of fish bone of which six pieces
could be identified to taxon. *Anguilla anguilla* (eel)
was present in the early second-century context of
L165. Eels are present today in freshwater habitats
and in surface marine waters around the atlantic
and mediterranean coasts (Whitehead *et al.* 1989).
Regular spawning migrations of eels take place
from mid-atlantic waters into freshwater rivers, estu-
aries and brackish lagoons in Europe (Wheeler and
Jones 1989; Whitehead *et al.* 1989). Elvers may
spend a variable amount of time in the freshwater
rivers (from five to twenty years); the maturing
adults then migrate back to marine waters (Wheeler and Jones 1989). Substantial quantities of eel
are often present as part of the fish-food refuse
from secular and monastic medieval (and later)
archaeological sites in Europe (Wheeler and Jones
1989; Van Neer 1994). It has been suggested that
eels could be fished from lagoons or rivers, possibly
using traps (Wheeler and Jones 1989). Although it
is somewhat problematic to postulate that the river
Treia (in whose valley Monte Gelato is situated)
may have contained eel populations during the second century, it is not impossible that eels caught
from freshwater locations could have been kept in
a fish-pond for short periods prior to being con-

sumed. However, it should be noted that, on other
archaeological grounds (cf. Chapter Three), there
is good reason to suppose that they may have been
kept as a decorative feature.

Alosa sp. (shad) was present in the late second-
century fill (L105) of the fish-pond. *Alosa* spp. are
anadromous (that is, they migrate from marine
waters to spawn in fresh water), semi-anadromous
or purely freshwater and range from pelagic
marine, estuarine to (freshwater) river and lake
environments (Wheeler and Jones 1989; White-
head *et al.* 1989). *Alosa alosa* (Allis shad) has a present-day distribution in marine pelagic waters
around the atlantic and western mediterranean
coasts; it has a migratory spawning far up rivers
(Whitehead *et al.* 1989). *Alosa fallax* (Twaite shad)
displays a marine pelagic present-day distribution
around the atlantic and mediterranean coasts; it
penetrates a short distance up rivers to spawn and
there are some entirely freshwater lacustrine (non-
migratory) populations (Whitehead *et al.* 1989). At
the present day, the Black Sea and Sea of Azov contain *Alosa caspia* and *A. pontica* anadromous and
semi-anadromous populations (Whitehead *et al.*
1989). Wheeler and Jones (1989), amongst others,
have noted the importance of migratory fish (particularly anadromous species) as a major (cyclic)
food source for coastal and riverine prehistoric and
early historic communities. LeGall's research
(1994) on freshwater fish in the south of France
has highlighted the importance of *Alosa* spp. (in
particular, *Alosa alosa*, which may attain a maximum
weight of 3 kg). Despite the fact that *Alosa alosa* is
considered to be primarily an atlantic fish at the
present day, during pre- and proto-historic periods
the distribution and adaptation of anadromous
migrators such as *Alosa alosa* is considered to be closely linked to thermotaxis which governs reproduct-
ive maturity; in consequence, distribution is not a
simple matter to reconstruct (LeGall 1994). Whilst
it may be suggested that prehistoric peoples tended
to utilize those taxa which lived within the immediate environs of their site (LeGall 1994), the same
suggestion cannot necessarily be made for the late
second-century occupancy of Monte Gelato, where
trade in exotic or foreign commodities (including
fish) is feasible. The distribution of marine and
freshwater *Alosa* spp. during the late second century in Italy can only be extrapolated from the present-day distribution described above, but it is clear
that freshwater *Alosa* spp. could have been stored
live on a temporary basis in a fish-pond prior to
consumption.

Other second-century contexts yielded three fragments of scombrid neural spines. The Scombridae
family comprises mainly epipelagic marine fish
such as mackerel and tuna which have a wide present-day distribution in temperate and tropical seas
(Collette and Nauen 1983; Wheeler and Jones
1989). In the Mediterranean, scombrid taxa such
as *Euthynnus* spp. (tunny), *Auxis* sp. (bullet tuna),

Katsuwonus pelamis (skipjack tuna), *Sarda sarda* (Atlantic bonito), *Scomber* spp. (mackerel), *Thunnus* spp. (tuna) represent important food sources at the present day and in the archaeological record (Collette and Nauen 1983; Wheeler and Jones 1989; Whitehead *et al.* 1989).

Late Roman contexts produced two dentary fragments of sea bream: *Pagrus pagrus* and *Diplodus* sp. Both belong to the Sparidae family which frequents temperate and tropical coastal waters (Whitehead *et al.* 1989). These, too, have been important sources of food in the past and are still commercially exploited today (Wheeler and Jones 1989; Whitehead *et al.* 1989). There were insufficient sparid bones present to utilize any osteometric techniques (such as those used by Desse and Desse-Berset (1994) on Sparidae, Serranidae and Scombridae) for the evaluation of size reconstruction of fish present on the archaeological site.

A phase 5 context (M121) of the early medieval period produced one possibly scombrid neural spine fragment, and one fragment of lateral scute of *Acipenser sturio* (sturgeon). Although very rare at the present day, *Acipenser sturio* has a distribution on atlantic coasts (including the coasts of the Baltic and North Seas) and the northern coasts of the Mediterranean and of the Black Sea (Whitehead *et al.* 1989). *Acipenser sturio* is an anadromous fish which inhabits saline nearshore waters and frequently undertakes extensive sea migrations; river spawning takes place over spring and summer (Whitehead *et al.* 1989). Desse-Berset's documentation (1994) of numerous sturgeon bones at Arles (France), dating from the sixth century BC through to the second century BC, has provided an ideal opportunity not only for evaluating the role of the sturgeon as a prized source of caviar, but also for evaluating the value set on sturgeon *meat* as a luxury food. It is possible that the presence of sturgeon in two medieval contexts at Monte Gelato similarly reflects the high status of the sturgeon during the Middle Ages.

Other medieval contexts (phase 6) yielded fragmented remains of *Pagrus pagrus* (sea bream) and a vertebra from the Clupeidae family, possibly *Sardina pilchardus* (sardine). The presence of sardines, either preserved in brine or salt within amphorae or as hallec (plain salted fish), and garum (fish sauce) from Roman contexts in Europe has been well documented (for example, Wheeler and Locker 1985; Van Neer 1994). The possible sardine vertebra from a medieval grave could, however, simply be food refuse from freshly caught sardines, widely available in coastal pelagic waters of the Mediterranean (Whitehead *et al.* 1989). Two other medieval contexts, both from graves, produced a fragment of scombrid neural spine and another lateral scute fragment of *Acipenser sturio* (sturgeon).

As the overall quantity of fish bones from Monte Gelato is small, no estimations of (minimum) numbers of individuals of fish can be put forward, using techniques such as those described by Nichol and Wild (1984), Wheeler and Jones (1989) and Van Neer (1994).

THE CHARRED PLANT REMAINS, by John Giorgi

INTRODUCTION

During the excavations soil samples were systematically collected for the recovery of plant remains, to gain information on the range of plants cultivated, gathered, utilized or imported onto the site; on crop husbandry and processing activities; on the use of different areas of the site over time; and on the character of the settlement.

Sampling and processing methods

Soil conditions at the site limited the preservation of plant remains to charred material. Samples were recovered from potentially well-stratified and datable contexts from a wide range of features across the site. The fills of drains (eight samples), burials (five samples) and burnt layers (six samples) were the most frequently sampled features.

A total of 679.5 litres of sediment was collected, equivalent to just over ten litres a sample, although individual sample size was variable. Thus, large quantities were taken from potentially 'rich' contexts, for example, 37 litres from a Roman cistern, while smaller features containing less than ten litres of sediment were 100 per cent sampled.

The samples were processed on a Siraf flotation tank with mesh sizes of 0.5 mm and 1.0 mm for the recovery of the flot and residue respectively. The residues were dried and sorted for environmental and artefactual evidence.

Identification

The flots were dried and sorted for charred plant remains using a binocular microscope and the material was identified with the aid of modern seed reference material, charred archaeobotanical material and seed reference manuals, housed in laboratory facilities at the British School at Rome.

RESULTS

Twenty-five of the 67 samples produced charred plant remains from thirteen of the sampled zones. However, the quantity of material was very low, with a total of just 162 plant items or almost one seed for every 4.2 litres of processed soil. A low seed density of just one seed for every two litres of sediment was also recorded at the Roman villa site of Settefinestre, Tuscany (Jones 1985).

However, there was great variability between the size of individual assemblages. Thus, one sample from context D86 produced 70 seeds, equivalent to seven seeds per litre of soil, or just over 43 per cent of all the plant remains recovered from the site, while 21 of the 25 productive samples contained fewer than ten plant items. Plant remains were, nevertheless, recovered from virtually all the sampled periods of the site, although phases 3 and 5/6 produced the best results. The results are tabulated in Tables 76 and 77.

Cereals

Cereals accounted for over 50 per cent of the total assemblage, represented virtually entirely by grains. Wheat (*Triticum* sp.) was the most common grain in the samples, while barley (*Hordeum* sp.), millet (*Panicum miliaceum*) and oat (*Avena* sp.) were also identified. However, almost 35 per cent of the cereal grains were too fragmented to be identified to either genus or species level and were simply classified as indeterminate cereal grain fragments.

Free-threshing wheats

The most common wheat was represented by a number of squat, rounded grains belonging to either hexaploid bread wheat (*Triticum aestivum* s.l.) or tetraploid macaroni wheat (*Triticum durum*). Both species are free-threshing (that is, the grains separate freely from the husks), although it is difficult to separate the two wheats on the basis of the grain morphology alone.

According to the documentary records, the primary use of naked wheats in both the Roman and medieval periods, would have been for human consumption (Spurr 1986; Cortonesi 1988). Bread wheats produce a soft flour with good bread-making qualities and would have probably been exclusively used for leavened bread. Macaroni wheat is not mentioned in the Roman documentary sources and the familiar forms of pasta are not recorded in Italy until the fourteenth century (Jones 1966).

The cultivation of naked wheats requires richer soils than glume wheats and Pliny (*Naturalis Historia* xviii. 46) recommended that they should be cultivated in dry, sunny, open fields. While bread wheat is less drought-resistant than hard wheat and the latter less tolerant of cold conditions, both species could have potentially been cultivated at Monte Gelato. Wheats may have been autumn- or spring-sown, although producing a better yield if autumn-sown.

Glume wheats

A poorly preserved wheat glume base from a late Roman sample may belong to any one of three glume wheats: emmer (*Triticum dicoccum*), einkorn (*Triticum monococcu*m), or spelt wheat (*Triticum spelta*). This suggests that glume wheats may have been cultivated during the Roman period at the site, although it may simply be a weed of the other cereals. The literary evidence suggests that emmer was used in the Roman period for making a sweet bread and may also

Table 76. The charred plant remains from the Roman period.

phase	2						3					
feature type	DR	WL	GY	RUB	RUB	DR	DR	SLT	FL	SLT	ASH	ASH
context	L138	L165	E154	L157	L162	E142	E76	M35	A36	H30	D48	D49
volume of soil (litres)	2	18	3	2	5	10	10	10	10	10	20	10
Triticum durum/aestivum (durum/bread wheat)	-	-	2	-	-	1	-	-	1	1	-	-
Triticum sp. (wheat)	-	-	-	-	-	-	-	1	-	-	-	-
Triticum sp. (wheat, glume base)	-	-	-	-	-	-	-	-	-	-	1	-
Hordeum sativum (barley)	-	-	-	-	-	-	1	-	-	-	-	-
Hordeum/Triticum sp. (barley or wheat)	-	-	-	-	-	-	-	1	-	-	-	-
Avena sp. (oat)	-	-	-	-	-	-	-	-	-	-	1	-
Panicum miliaceum L. (common, broom-corn millet)	-	-	-	-	-	-	-	-	1	-	-	-
Cerealia (indeterminate cereal)	-	-	5	-	-	1	-	1	-	2	-	-
Lens culinaris (lentil)	-	-	-	-	-	-	-	-	-	2	-	-
cf. *Lens culinaris* (cf. lentil)	-	-	-	-	-	1	-	-	-	-	-	-
Vicia faba (celtic bean/horsebean)	-	-	-	-	-	-	-	-	-	-	-	1
Vicia/Lathyrus sp. (vetch/tare/vetchling)	-	-	-	-	-	1	-	1	-	-	-	-
Pisum sativum L. (pea)	-	-	-	-	-	-	-	-	-	-	-	1
Pisum sp. (pea)	-	1	-	-	-	-	-	-	-	-	-	-
Leguminosae indet.	-	-	-	1	-	-	-	-	-	-	-	-
Rumex acetosella agg. (sheep's sorrel)	-	-	-	-	-	-	-	-	-	1	-	-
cf. *Olea europaea* (olive)	-	-	-	-	-	1	-	-	-	-	-	-
Galium sp. (bedstraw)	-	-	-	-	-	-	-	-	-	-	-	1
Lolium sp. (rye grass)	-	-	-	-	-	-	-	-	-	5	-	-
Gramineae indet.	-	-	-	-	-	-	-	-	-	2	-	-
indeterminate	1	2	-	-	1	-	-	-	-	-	-	4

Feature types: ASH – ash, burnt layer; DR – drain fill; FL – fill; GY – gully fill; RUB – rubble fill; SLT – silt; WL – wall fill

Table 77. The charred plant remains from the medieval period.

phase	5				5/6					6/7			
feature type	ASH	PIT	SLT	PIT	GR	GR	GR	FL	GR	SP	GR	RUB	RUB
context	D337	D86	M32	H15	B32	B49	B80	B28	B36	D272	B8	D3	D73
volume of soil (litres)	10	10	10	10	10	10	10	10	10	10	10	10	10
Triticum monococcum (einkorn)	-	-	-	-	-	-	-	-	-	1	-	-	-
Triticum durum/aestivum (durum/bread wheat)	-	10	-	-	1	-	-	-	1	-	-	2	-
Triticum spp. (wheat)	-	4	-	-	-	-	-	-	-	-	-	-	-
Hordeum sativum (barley)	-	6	-	-	3	-	-	-	-	-	-	-	-
Hordeum/Triticum sp. (barley or wheat)	-	-	-	-	-	-	-	-	-	-	-	2	-
Avena sp. (oat)	-	-	-	-	-	-	-	1	-	-	-	-	-
Avena sp. (oat, floret)	-	-	-	-	-	-	-	-	-	2	-	-	-
Panicum miliaceum L. (common or broom corn millet)	-	-	-	-	5	1	3	-	-	-	-	-	-
Cerealia (indeterminate cereals)	-	17	-	-	2	1	-	-	-	-	1	-	-
Lens culinaris (Lentil)	-	10	-	-	-	-	-	-	-	-	-	-	-
Vicia faba (celtic bean/horsebean)	-	1	-	-	-	-	-	-	-	-	-	-	-
Vicia/Lathyrus spp. (vetch/tare/vetchling)	3	-	-	-	-	-	-	-	-	-	-	3	-
Pisum sativum L. (pea)	-	-	-	-	-	-	-	-	-	-	-	-	1
Leguminosae indet.	-	21	1	1	-	-	-	-	1	-	-	-	-
Rubus sp.	-	-	1	-	-	-	-	-	-	-	-	-	-
Olea europaea (olive)	1	-	-	-	-	-	-	-	-	-	-	-	-
Lolium sp. (rye grass)	-	1	-	-	-	-	-	-	-	-	-	-	-
Bromus sp. (brome)	-	-	-	-	-	-	-	-	-	-	-	1	-
indeterminate	-	-	-	-	-	-	-	1	-	-	1	-	2
Feature types: ASH –ash, burnt layer; FL – fill; GR – grave fill; RUB – rubble fill; SLT – silt; SP – sump fill													

have been used as animal feed. Glume wheats require parching to free the grains from the husk but have a good storage potential, with their husks protecting the grain against insect and fungus infestation.

Einkorn is represented by one grain from the early medieval phase of the site. Again, this may simply be a weed of the other cereals, although its cultivation in parts of central Italy in this period is confirmed by its presence in large numbers at the medieval hilltop site of Montarrenti near Siena, Tuscany (Giorgi 1989a).

Einkorn may grow in a wide range of soils even in marginal environments and is still cultivated today in remoter areas of Italy for use as animal fodder along with emmer (Perrino and Hammer 1982). In the early medieval period it may have also been used together with other cereals for bread.

Barley

Barley was the second most common large-seeded cereal represented at the site. The diagnostic cross-section and ridges on the dorsal surface of the grain and the recovery of both straight and twisted grains suggests that most of the grains belong to six-row hulled barley (*Hordeum vulgare*), although one grain was identified as naked barley (*Hordeum vulgare* var. *nudum*).

Barley may have been used for both human and animal consumption in both the Roman and medieval periods. It was the main animal fodder in Roman Italy, used as cattle

(Pliny, *Naturalis Historia* xviii. 13-5) and horse feed (Columella, *De Re Rustica* ii. 9.14). Barley was also used to produce a flat bread or polenta, particularly by the rural and urban poor and mixed with wheat it made 'excellent food for the slaves' (Columella, *De Re Rustica* ii. 9.16). Indeed, it was considered too costly to use as normal livestock fodder in the regions around cities. The Romans also used it in the preparation of drinks and medicines (Pliny, *Naturalis Historia* xxi. 65-6).

Barley can grow in a wide range of soils and climatic conditions and in drier soils than wheat, although it is less tolerant than glume wheats of wet soils. The Roman agronomists recommended its cultivation on dry, aerated, highly fertile soils. Barley has a short growth cycle and may have been autumn or spring sown or both, although medieval documents suggest that it was sown more in autumn than in spring (Cortonesi 1988).

Oat

Two grains of oat (*Avena* sp.) and several oat floret bases were recovered, although the chaff was too fragmentary to establish whether the oats were wild or cultivated species. The Roman agronomists usually referred to oat in its wild form (*Avena fatua*) although Columella (*De Re Rustica* xi. 2.75) noted its use as a fodder crop. In the medieval period, literary evidence suggests that oat was not an important crop in this part of Italy (Cortonesi 1988).

Common or broom-corn millet

Ten grains of this small-seeded cereal (*Panicum miliaceum*) were identified, both by the triangular embryo which extends up to half the length of the caryopsis, and by the rounded morphology of the grains. Millet may have been used for both animal and human consumption in the Roman and medieval periods. It produces a heavy flat bread and may have been used for porridge. Pliny (*Naturalis Historia* xviii. 117) noted that it was used by the lower classes for bread together with other cereals and legumes. Although only one grain was found in the Roman deposits, its use as human food is illustrated by primary deposits of thousands of common millet grains fused together in a Republican period vessel from the Piazza Centro d'Italia, Rieti (Giorgi 1989b).

Millet survives better on poorer soils compared to other cereals and is tolerant of drought, but relatively intolerant of cold conditions. It was widely cultivated in central and southern Italy in the Roman period (Pliny, *Naturalis Historia* xviii. 24-5). It may be sown both in the spring and perhaps more commonly in the summer (Pliny, *Naturalis Historia* xviii. 49, 50, 54, 55, 60), and, with a short vegetative cycle of three to four months, it could be used as a famine crop in the event of crop failure (Strabo v. 1.2; Spurr 1986: 96).

Legumes

Legume seeds made up just over 33 per cent of all the charred material from the site, although these are often difficult to identify as charred remains as they tend to fragment and loose diagnostic features, such as their seed coats or hilum. Three cultivated species were identified; several seeds of horsebean (*Vicia faba*) and pea (*Pisum sativum*) plus thirteen seeds of lentil (*Lens culinaris*). However, a relatively large number could only be reduced to *Vicia/Lathyrus* species, while just over 50 per cent of the pulses could not even be identified to genus.

Pulses are an important source of protein, and the literary sources suggest that the legumes would have been used as human food, often together with cereals to make bread and soup (porridge), as well as for animal food in both periods. In the Roman and medieval periods, legumes would have been mainly grown in fields, although they were sometimes planted in gardens. Pulses may have been either autumn or spring sown, as they may produce a yield with a relatively short vegetative cycle (Hillman 1981). The role of the legumes in the agricultural cycle appears to have been appreciated by the Roman agronomists. For example, Columella stressed the need to use legumes in rotation with cereals to restore nitrogen levels to the soil. The two-field rotation system was common in early medieval Italy (Wickham 1981: 95), in which the legumes were grown in the fallow year and in the same field as the cereals.

Horsebeans and peas

Horsebeans were the most widely cultivated legume in the Roman period on both small and large farms. According to Columella (*De Re Rustica* ii. 10.9) they grow best on fertile, well-drained soils, although they can adapt to most soil types, producing less if sown in spring. In Roman Italy horsebeans were highly valued as human food. However, Roman literary references to the use of peas are scarce and, although they appear in the recipe books of Apicius, there are no records of its use as animal fodder. Pliny (*Naturalis Historia* xviii. 123) recommended that peas should 'be sown [in spring] in sunny places as they dislike the cold ... in light easily worked soils'.

Lentils

The fact that lentils can grow in a range of soils and climatic conditions with a short growth-cycle of just three to four months, sown in either autumn or spring (Columella, *De Re Rustica* ii. 10.15), made them attractive to both the small and large farmer in the Roman period. Columella (ii. 10.4) recommended that the lentil be sown in 'poor, loose soil or rich, but above all dry, as when it is in flower it is easy to damage through excessive growth or humidity'.

Vetches

Some of the vetches from the site may either be arable weeds or the residues from its cultivation as forage. On smaller farms, in particular, they may have served as both human and animal fodder in the Roman period (Spurr 1986).

Olive

Only two stones of olive (*Olea europaea*) were found. Olives would have been used as an edible food, for the extraction of oil (for cooking and lighting), and in the Roman period for ointments and medicines (Columella xii. 52). An advantage of olive cultivation over many other crops is that it can be grown on steep slopes and in a rocky environment, drawing on water through an extensive root system.

Blackberry/raspberry

A single blackberry/raspberry (*Rubus* sp.) seed was recovered from a medieval context, and may represent the residue from fruit collected for food or from brambles growing nearby.

Weeds

Twenty-three seeds, 14.1 per cent of the total assemblage, belong to other plants, the poor condition of which made identification to species level difficult. This limits the ecological information that may be extracted, as different species within the same genus may have significantly different habitats. The even distribution of the different seeds suggests that these probably represent the residues of weeds, either imported onto the site with the harvested cereals, or growing on waste ground within or in the close vicinity of the site: for example, bedstraw (*Galium* sp.) and sheep's sorrel (*Rumex acetosella* agg.), which grow on both wasteland and cultivated ground (Baroni 1980). Some of the smaller legume seeds may also have been weeds of cereal crops.

Grasses make up the largest group, with *Lolium* species representing virtually 50 per cent of all identified weed seeds, the majority of which probably belongs to darnel (*Lolium temulentum*). This grows as a weed of arable fields and on rubbish dumps. Darnel is frequently found in grain storage deposits as its similar seed size makes it difficult to separate from the grain. Indeed, the medieval agronomist Pietro De' Crescenzi (1310) described it as a particularly troublesome weed of grain stores, with harmful side effects. However, in the Roman period, darnel was also ground up and applied to sores (Spurr 1986: 62) and fed to African hens (Varro, *De Re Rustica* iii. 9.20).

DISCUSSION

The small quantity of plant remains at the site does not allow detailed comparisons to be made between the Roman and medieval periods on the basis of the frequency of individual species. However, the range of plants in each period and the number of samples in which a particular species occurs provide some indication of possible changes in the broad range of plants utilized.

The range of crops in the Roman period

The twelve productive samples from the Roman period contained small quantities of bread/macaroni wheat, barley, millet, oat, lentil, horsebean, pea and olive, the majority of which was recovered from nine late Roman samples.

Other archaeobotanical evidence for the Roman period in central Italy, albeit limited at present, shows that the range of crops at Monte Gelato has been found elsewhere. For example, the villa site of Settefinestre in the Ager Cosanus produced a small assemblage of possible free-threshing wheat, emmer/spelt wheat, barley, oat, lentil, pea, olive, grape and hazelnut (Jones 1985). Free-threshing wheats were the most common grain in first century BC deposits from the Regia Vesta, the Forum, Rome, along with single grains of emmer, barley and millet, and one horsebean (Giorgi 1991). However, it is rarely possible to establish the relative importance of the individual crops in the agricultural economy on the basis of the archaeobotanical record alone.

The plant remains from this period are mainly from fills, and are well distributed across the site in low quantities, providing little information on the possible use of different features or areas for agricultural activities. The only evidence from the site for the residues of farming activities associated with the harvesting and cleaning of cereal crops was one glume base and several possible arable weed seeds. Such activities may have taken place in an unexcavated area of the site or such material may simply not have survived.

The range of crops in the medieval period

Whilst only a very small assemblage is available for the purposes of comparison, there are few indications of any significant change in the range of crops from the Roman to the medieval period. There is a single grain of einkorn, which is not represented in Roman contexts; but it is otherwise a similar collection, with bread/macaroni wheat and barley as the predominant element.

Studies on charred plant remains from other early medieval sites in central Italy also show that naked wheats and barley are usually the most common grains in samples: millet, emmer, oat and rye are also often present, although usually in smaller quantities. For example, deposits of the ninth-eleventh centuries from the rural site of Le Mura di Santo Stefano, near Anguillara, produced rich charred assemblages of free-threshing wheats and six-row barley. Emmer, einkorn, millet and rye were found in sufficient quantities as to suggest their cultivation, while horsebean, lentil, grasspea/dwarf chickling and several grape seeds were also identified (Costantini et al. 1983).

However, perhaps the best evidence for the cultivation of a wide range of cereals in the early medieval period comes from the hilltop site of Montarrenti near Siena, with an extensive tenth-/eleventh-century deposit of grain, probably representing a storage deposit burnt in situ. Interestingly, einkorn was the best represented grain, although free-threshing wheat grains, hulled barley, foxtail and broom-corn millet, as well as sorghum, were all recovered in very large quantities, such as to suggest their cultivation. Other possible crops included horsebean, pea, grass pea/dwarf chickling, fig and grape (Giorgi 1989a).

Documentary evidence also suggests that a variety of small- and large-grained cereals were cultivated in the early medieval period in the Sabina region, north of Rome (Toubert 1973; Leggio et al. 1988), while eighth- to ninth-century agrarian contracts from Tuscany include wheat, rye, barley, emmer, spelt, common millet and foxtail millet (Andreolli 1981).

The small assemblages of plant remains from the thirteen samples were recovered from a range of fills, and were well distributed over eight areas of the site. The exception is the sample from an ash layer (D86), recovered from a pit in the baptistery, which contained a total of 70 plant items or almost 43 per cent of all plant remains from the site. This assemblage included cereal grains (bread/macaroni wheat and barley) and legumes (lentils, horsebean), which presumably represent foodstuffs which were discarded after being burnt, probably in the advanced stages of food processing and preparation. The remaining samples throw little light on the nature of the features from which they were retrieved. Just one potential arable weed, a Lolium species, possibly darnel, was identified. The low seed numbers may be simply due to the absence of agricultural activities in the excavated area.

However, documentary evidence shows that Monte Gelato formed part of the domusculta of Capracorum, established in the late eighth century. The Liber Pontificalis mentions the cultivation of wheat and barley at the estate, with the annual harvest being transported to the granaries of the Holy Church. Wine, together with various vegetables that grew in the fields and on separate plots of the estate, were taken to the chief cellarer of the Holy Church and stored apart. The vegetables mentioned may include some of the pulses found in the samples although no grape seeds were identified. Thus the plant remains do not greatly extend the literary evidence for the produce of the domusculta.

Chapter Five

IL *PATRIMONIUM TUSCIAE* DELLA CHIESA ROMANA
TRA VI E X SECOLO: NOTE SULLE SUE PERTINENZE FONDIARIE

by Federico Marazzi

INTRODUZIONE[97]

Gli scavi condotti presso la Mola di Monte Gelato tra il 1986 e il 1990 hanno offerto per la prima volta, forse, nell'Etruria Meridionale, l'opportunità di seguire nel dettaglio le vicende di un sito rurale quasi ininterrottamente occupato durante tutto il corso del primo millennio d.C. I risultati più importanti, e forse più attesi, che sono stati conseguiti riguardano principalmente i secoli tra il V e il X, e aiutano a scrivere con maggior precisione di quanto fosse stato sinora possibile, alcune pagine di una storia assai affascinante: quella della vita nel territorio romano dopo il collasso di quel grande sistema integrato che fu Roma con il suo Suburbio nell'antichità. Un sistema così complesso e vitale per la sopravvivenza economica della metropoli capitale dell'Impero, da far apparire ancora nella seconda metà del IV secolo, agli occhi di Ammiano Marcellino, Otricoli come 'porta' stessa del Suburbio (Cappelletto 1983: 32-6, 63-5). L'interpretazione dei risultati della ricerca archeologica degli anni '60 e '70 nel territorio circostante Roma (vedi bibliografia di riferimento in Marazzi (1988a)) tendeva invece ad accentuare in maniera forse eccessivamente drastica il regresso dell'insediamento nel periodo successivo alla prima metà del III secolo d.C., stabilendo una troppo rigida equazione tra crisi del sistema della villa classica e un declino economico-demografico *tout-court*. Una rilettura delle fonti scritte relative ai patrimoni fondiari dei *potentiores* degli ultimi due secoli dell'Impero in Occidente, ivi compreso lo stesso demanio imperiale, ha però posto in rilevo alcuni temi di forte suggestione per il lavoro dell'archeologo. Da un lato ha sottolineato la trasformazione strutturale della organizzazione della grande proprietà fondiaria nell'Italia centro-meridionale tardoantica, che meno sentiva il bisogno di una diffusa rete di *villae* e puntava piuttosto su un diffuso appoderamento ella forza-lavoro agraria, coordinata da un ridotto numero di centri padronali, talora di grandi dimensioni; dall'altro ha indicato l'esistenza di nuclei proprietari rilevanti nell'area prossima alla città all'interno dei patrimoni di alcuni dei più cospicui latifondisti romani (si vedano come riferimenti generali in proposito Mazza (1986: 119-93), Vera (1986) e Barnish (1987)).

Si è posto pertanto il problema di ridefinire, entro un quadro storico complessivo più coerente, come un grande centro di consumo, quale Roma fu almeno sino agli inizi del VI secolo (quantunque in un contesto di tendenziale declino), potesse esercitare il suo influsso sulla regione circostante.

Su diversi fronti, la ricerca archeologica ha prodotto risultati di rilievo negli ultimi anni, che dimostrano lo sforzo di attivare nuove piste di ricerca al fine di identificare una rete insediative che, sebbene in condizioni di generale regresso in termini di densità e di condizioni di vita materiale, dové mantenersi, tra IV e VI secolo, più complessa di quanto non si fosse creduto in passato. Si segnalano in questo senso le importanti considerazioni che sono state svolte dal Fiocchi Nicolai (per l'Etruria Meridionale) e dal Guyon (per il Suburbio ad est di Roma) in lavori che rivestono il raro pregio di rapportare l'analisi di complessi cimiteriali cristiani con – se così si può dire – il loro 'bacino di utenza' nel territorio (Guyon 1987; Fiocchi Nicolai 1988); contemporaneamente emergono nuove possibilità di analisi complesse su intere sub-regioni, quali quella condotta dal Leggio sulla Sabina (Leggio 1989), in grado di avanzare più che ipotesi sulla capacità del mercato romano di tenere in vita l'economia del versante tiberino di quest'area in epoca tardoantica; ed infine nuove analisi su specifici casi urbani, quali quelli di Porto e di Falerii Novi (Coccia 1993; Munzi e Crifani 1995), hanno offerto, da diverse prospettive, il quadro di un affievolimento graduale della densità insediativa e della vitalità economica dei due centri, che consente, fra l'altro, di sperare in future fruttuose possibilità di spiegare in maniera più comprensibile l'apparente discrasia tra una supposta crisi repentina dei siti urbani e rurali laziali in età tardoantica e la incredibile moltiplicazione, nello stesso periodo, delle circoscrizioni diocesane.

---

[97] Un grazie particolare ad Alfredo Carnassale, che sta conducendo un'indagine sulla struttura dei patrimoni fondiari nella regione romana nel corso del X secolo, per alcuni fruttuosi scambi di idee. È doveroso ricordare che quanto trattato in questo contributo è parte di un più ampio studio sui patrimoni laziali della Chiesa Romana tra IV e X secolo, di prossima pubblicazione (Marazzi in corso di stampa) e che il problema delle proprietà papali nella Tuscia è stato da me trattato già in occasione di un convegno su Bracciano e il suo territorio, edito nel 1994 (Marazzi 1994b).

I risultati degli scavi a Mola di Monte Gelato hanno acquisito grande importanza all'interno del dibattito cui si è qui accennato. E ne hanno rivestita ancor maggiore per l'analisi della fase successiva, che si apre con il traumatico ventennio della guerra greco-gotica, e che conosce quindi, con la successiva' invasione longobarda, la 'riduzione' di Roma a città di frontiera dell'Impero Romano d'Oriente. Uno dei tratti di collegamento fra queste due fasi storiche nell'Etruria Meridionale, è la presenza costante di dati, fra IV e X secolo, inerenti proprietà fondiarie della Chiesa Romana. Questo elemento assume particolare rilievo se si considera l'appartenenza dell'insediamento di Mola di Monte Gelato al complesso di beni fondiari componenti la *domusculta* pontificia di *Capracorum*, fondata da Papa Adriano I (772-95); appartenenza rafforzata dalle nuove indicazioni topografiche emerse dalle ricerche di Sforzini (comm. pers.). Rimandando ad altra sede l'esame dei problemi concernenti le fonti che trattano della *domusculta* di *Capracorum* (Marazzi 1988a; 1991a; 1991b; 1993; 1994a; in corso di stampa), ci soffermeremo qui a offrire una panoramica dei dati disponibili per la ricostruzione delle pertinenze fondiarie pontificie, che sono alla base di ogni possibilità di ricostruire, a partire dalle fonti scritte, le modalità di articolazione della proprietà fondiaria nella regione.

Come è ben noto, la Tuscia ospitò possessi e fondazioni cristiane romane sin dalla tarda antichità.[98] La *inlustris foemina* Vestina lasciò al *titulus* da lei stessa fondato al tempo di Papa Innocenzo (401-17) (*Liber Pontificalis* I, 221-2), delle *possessiones* nei territori di Veio e di *Forum Clodii*. Quest'ultima, la *possessio Antonianum*, è l'unica che afferisca direttamente al territorio che ci interessa più da vicino, di cui si abbia conoscenza dalle liste tardoantiche del *Liber Pontificalis*. In precedenza, Costantino aveva donato proprietà nei territori di Nepi e Veio alla cattedrale di Ostia e al *titulus Sylvestri* (*Liber Pontificalis* I, 170-87, *passim*); ma, a quanto ci risulta, fu la basilica di Santa Croce in Gerusalemme, per la quale si conoscono beni nei territori di Veio e di *Falerii Novi*, ad accumulare interessi più cospicui in quest'area (*Liber Pontificalis* I, 179-80). Non dobbiamo tuttavia dimenticare che, complessivamente, ci troviamo in presenza di concentrazioni fondiarie quantitativamente risibili, rispetto a quelle che ci sono note per le aree a sud di Roma, nelle quali si distribuiscono le pertinenze delle fondazioni costantiniane principali, come la basilica e il battistero lateranense.

Dopo questo insieme di dati, che non superano il primo quarto del V secolo, si stende un velo di silenzio che non si squarcerà sino al pontificato di Gregorio Magno (590-604). E, a quel momento, gli elementi a nostra disposizione saranno di natura assai diversa, rispetto a quelli visti per la tarda antichità. I possessi ecclesiastici romani appariranno, a quell'epoca, essenzialmente come beni inquadrati all'interno della struttura dei *Patrimonia Sanctae Romanae Ecclesiae*. Vale a dire di quel complesso di proprietà sottoposte direttamente al controllo del vescovo di Roma, e probabilmente inquadrate, sotto il profilo giuridico, come beni della cattedrale romana.[99]

Una situazione, quindi, diversa da quella dei beni elencati nelle biografie dei papi di IV e V secolo, anche se non bisogna dimenticare che fu proprio nel corso del venticinquennio finale del V secolo che i papi consolidarono forme di controllo più puntuali sulle dotazioni delle varie chiese romane. In particolare, per quanto riguarda chiese titolari e per quelle fondazioni di più incerta definizione – che potrebbero quasi definirsi dei *tituli* imperiali -, come la *ecclesia Hyerusalem*.[100]

Pertanto, in linea di principio, non potremmo escludere che le dotazioni fondiarie di queste due categorie di chiese abbiano subìto rimodellamenti e che parti di esse possano essere state 'fagocitate' dal *patrimonium* centrale della Chiesa Romana. Ma, all'atto pratico, non abbiamo alcuna indicazione concreta di ciò e, pertanto, per noi la storia dei possedimenti fondiari pontifici in Tuscia si apre al volgere del VI secolo.

IL *PATRIMONIUM TUSCIAE*

È probabile una sua attestazione già nel 599, con la lettera IX, 96 di Gregorio, che cita una *massa Gratiliana* presso Blera; tale toponimo ricompare in un documento di affitto di proprietà papali risalente al pontificato di Onorio (625-38) ma, ancora una volta, non ne è chiarito l'inquadramento patrimoniale;[101] per una menzione del *Patrimonium Tusciae* che si può ritenere quasi certa si deve attendere il pontificato di Sergio (687-701) quando, in una epigrafe, si ricordano almeno tre *fundi* siti nella Tuscia romana (De Rossi 1870).[102] Il De Rossi, che

---

[98] Sulle liste di beni fondiari annesse alle fondazioni di edifici di culto, per il periodo compreso fra il pontificato di Silvestro I (314-35) e Sisto III (432-40), riportate dal '*Liber Pontificalis*' e sulla loro dislocazione, si veda principalmente Pietri (1976: 77-96 e 558-73); il problema della localizzazione delle unità fondiarie distribuite nelle prossimità di Roma, che compaiono in questi elenchi è stato affrontato, proponendo nuove e interessanti soluzioni, da De Francesco (1990).

[99] Sul problema della nascita dei *Patrimonia Sanctae Romanae Ecclesiae*, ci permettiamo di rinviare a Marazzi (1991b), con bibliografia di riferimento. Restano comunque punti di riferimento insuperati i contributi di Pietri (1966; 1978; 1981) sulla fase storica compresa tra la seconda metà del V secolo e il primo quarto del VI, che vede al centro il decisivo quinquennio del pontificato di Gelasio I (492-6), durante il quale si plasmò, assai probabilmente, la struttura di una gestione più centralizzata e razionale dei patrimoni della Chiesa di Roma.

[100] Sui *tituli* e sullo *status* delle fondazioni imperiali, in qualche modo assimilabili ai primi, si veda ancora Pietri (1976: 4-14).

[101] Deusdedit, *Collectio Canonum*.

[102] Il testo di questa epigrafe, con alcune varianti rispetto alla lettura offerta dal De Rossi, fu riproposto dal Duchesne in una nota alla biografia di Papa Sergio (*Liber Pontificalis* I, 379-80, nota 38).

commentò l'epigrafe suddetta, per analogia con il *Patrimonium Appiae*, la cui menzione è chiaramente conservata nel testo mutilo dell'epigrafe, ritenne di completare la localizzazione dei suddetti tre *fundi* collocandoli, appunto, *in Patrimonio Tusciae*. Tuttavia, è solo con il pontificato di Gregorio II (715-31), che si ha una insindacabile attestazione di tale circoscrizione patrimoniale attraverso una serie di contratti di locazione regestati nella *Collectio Canonum* di Deusdedit. Il Patrimonio della Tuscia includeva allora tutto il territorio fra la riva destra del Tevere ed il mar Tirreno: infatti le attestazioni documentarie ci consentono di localizzare beni lungo gli assi delle vie Aurelia, Cornelia, Clodia e Flaminia. Molto probabilmente la attestazione di un *casalis* lungo la via Portuense, nel corso del pontificato di Onorio I, è da ascrivere al *Patrimonium Tusciae* anche se, come si è detto in precedenza, non lo si può affermare con certezza. Non tutte le pertinenze fondiarie di questo patrimonio sono localizzate in relazione agli assi viari: in molti casi il referente geografico è rappresentato da territori cittadini o, più semplicemente, distanze in miglia da Roma. Dalla documentazione dell'epoca di Gregorio II si evince l'esistenza di un nucleo di beni nel territorio di *Forum Clodii* ed un altro all'VIII miglio della via Clodia. Un unico *fundus* è noto al XIV miglio della via Flaminia: tuttavia, è da ritenere che in quest'area le pertinenze fondiarie della Chiesa Romana fossero di ben altro rilievo, se, come ha suggestivamente proposto la Bosman, la *domusculta* al XIV miglio *Patrimonio Tusciae* fondata da Papa Zaccaria (l'unica di cui si riporti la localizzazione all'interno di un *patrimonium*) è da collocare, appunto, al XIV miglio della Flaminia (Deusdedit, *Collectio Canonum* III: can. 118).[103] Il limite, verso l'esterno, del *patrimonium*, doveva necessariamente coincidere con il limite del ducato romano (Bavant 1979: 41-89; e, più recentemente, Sennis (1996: 36-9 e tav. XVII)). Successivamente, due documenti ci informano sulle pertinenze pontificie nell'area della Tuscia romana: un diploma dell'854 emesso da Leone IV in favore del monastero di San Martino presso San Pietro in Vaticano (Schiaparelli 1901: 432-7); un'altro del 906, emesso da Sergio III in favore del vescovo di *Selva Candida* (Marini 1805: papiro XXIV). Essi esorbitano dall'arco di tempo di cui ci occupiamo in questo paragrafo, ma ne esamineremo comunque il contenuto, poiché i beni in essi elencati rientrano nell'area dell'antico ducato bizantino di Roma, nel quale i pontefici detenevano possessi anche precedentemente alla metà dell'VIII secolo: pertanto i dati che da questi documenti si raccolgono possono essere indizi di concentrazioni proprietarie di data anteriore al IX secolo. Il diploma dell'854 presenta tuttavia vari problemi, che esamineremo rapidamente. La elencazione dei beni fondiari, innanzitutto, non concerne solo l'area della Tuscia romana, ma tocca anche alcune proprietà situate nel territorio di Velletri. Inoltre, l'ordine con cui queste proprietà appaiono nel documento sembra piuttosto casuale e non sistematicamente 'agganciato' alla geografia dei *patrimonia*. Dopo una serie di beni interni alla *nova civitas Leoniana*, appare un gruppo di *fundi ... omnes invicem quoerentes*, i quali sono localizzati fra il IV ed il V miglio della via Clodia, si registra una serie di quattro *fundi* e una *casa* la cui posizione è lungo la via Cornelia, a partire dalla *porta Sancti Petri Apostoli*, sino, almeno, a Boccea (Cecchelli Trinci 1980): è chiaro che queste entità fondiarie sono accomunate dal fatto di gravitare entro un'area prossima alla città. Ad esse segue la menzione di un gruppo consistente in una *massa*, un *fundus* e un monastero con altre proprietà annesse, situati a *Centumcellae*, ovvero Civitavecchia, e nei dintorni. Quindi entrano in scena le proprietà *in territorio Billiternensi* (= di Velletri), che avevamo preannunciato, composte da due *fundi*. Subito dopo si ritorna al V miglio della Clodia, con quattro *fundi* dei quali viene detto che sono *ex corpore suburbani patrimonii*: ma il testo è corrotto in questo punto e ci manca la parola decisiva, ossia il nome del *patrimonium*, così come non possiamo escludere che nel gruppo fosse compreso almeno un altro *fundus*. Si prosegue con un *fundus* sito nel *territorio Collinense*, quindi lungo la via Flaminia, all'altezza del XXV miglio,[104] e poi si conclude con sette *fundi ex corpore massae Vurianae*, allo stesso XXV miglio da Roma, che il documento sibillinamente dice *positos Urbe Vetere*. L'*Urbs Vetus* in questione non può certo essere Orvieto, che si trova ben più distante da Roma, e francamente non sapremmo proporre una soluzione definitiva e convincente al problema.[105] Quali conclusioni generali trarre da questo complesso documento? È chiaro che gran parte dei toponimi dovrebbe rientrare nel *Suburbanum Patrimonium Tusciae*, che analizzeremo qui di seguito: almeno tutti quelli al IV-V miglio della via Clodia, e quelli nel tratto iniziale della via Cornelia. Ma perché questa appartenenza è esplicitata solo nel caso del gruppo di quattro *fundi* siti al V miglio della Clodia e non per gli altri? E, perché, altrettanto, il riferimento al *patrimonium* manca per tutti gli altri beni fondiari elencati? Ci si potrebbe accontentare dell'idea che le lacune del testo abbiano proprio interessato quei

---

[103] È il *fundus Capanianus*, menzionato nel canone 119 del libro III della *Collectio Canonum* di Deusdedit (Bosman 1994).

[104] Il testo del documento è in realtà corrotto nel punto in cui viene espressa la distanza in miglia; l'integrazione con la indicazione del XXV miglio è ricavata dal fatto che a questa altezza della Flaminia si trovava, appunto, il *territorium Collinense*. Su di esso, nell'antichità classica, si veda Tomassetti ((1913 (1979): 355ss.); si tratta di una partizione territoriale che compare solo nei documenti medievali e che 'formava un triangolo irregolare con base sulla riva destra del Tevere, tra Santa Maria e Torrita, e il vertice presso Campagnano, incluso anche il Soratte; ... è da escludere che derivasse il suo nome dall'esistenza di un'antica città *Collina*' (Tomassetti 1913 (1979): 355-7).

[105] L'unico centro antico della zona è *Capena* (Potter 1985: 88-9; Cambi 1990).

passi che menzionavano i *patrimonia*: ma è chiaramente una soluzione che lascia più di qualche sospetto. Una risposta più articolata potrebbe essere cercata nel fatto che questo diploma contiene l'affiliazione al monastero di San Martino al Vaticano di altri quattro istituti religiosi dell'area prossima a San Pietro: i gruppi di possessi fondiari elencati (escluso quello stornato dal *patrimonium suburbanum*) sarebbero potuti originariamente appartenere proprio a quegli altri enti che venivano ora a ricadere sotto il controllo del monastero di San Martino. Questa ipotesi, tuttavia, si scontra con il fatto che la *pensio* annua richiesta al monastero di San Martino per il possesso perpetuo di questi beni doveva essere versata alle *rationes ecclesiasticae*, presupponendo quindi un passaggio, anche se momentaneo, all'interno della contabilità centrale della Chiesa Romana. La soluzione più credibile può forse contemplare ambedue le eventualità: e cioè che beni originariamente di alcuni enti siano stati 'travasati' nella contabilità centrale pontificia, senza essere aggregati ad alcun patrimonio, per poi essere distaccati in perpetuo in favore del monastero di San Martino, con l'aggiunta di *fundi* 'storicamente' propri del *Patrimonium Tusciae Suburbanum* (vedi oltre).

Il diploma del 906 è invece assai meno complicato, poiché tratta due grandi blocchi fondiari, due *massae*, la *Clodiana* e la *Cesana*, localizzate al XX miglio da Roma in territorio di Nepi e confinanti fra loro (cf. Radke 1981: 303-14). Nel territorio di Nepi erano posti anche i tre *fundi* superstiti dalla lapide di Sergio I in favore del *titulus* di Santa Susanna. La complessità del problema dell'identificazione dell'asse viario cui effettivamente alludono le fonti altomedievali quando si riferiscono alla via Clodia non consente conclusioni definitive, ma è da ritenere che la menzione del territorio di Nepi contempli piuttosto un riferimento alla via Cassia che non alla Clodia vera e propria, cosa che, del resto consentono di dedurre il toponimo stesso di *massa Cesana* e quello, ad essa interno, di *fundus Martinianus*.[106]

In conclusione, la documentazione di cui disponiamo ci consente di individuare con certezza i seguenti nuclei fondiari all'interno del *Patrimonium Tusciae*.

Sull'asse delle vie Cassia-Clodia:

(a) alcuni *fundi* sono attestati fra 715 e 731, all'VIII miglio della via Clodia: in assenza di un'indagine topografica più approfondita, non ce la sentiamo in alcun modo di andare al di là di una generica localizzazione fra La Giustiniana e La Storta;

(b) un gruppo di beni – il più cospicuo – intorno al lago di Bracciano, nel territorio di *Forum Clodii* (attestati fra 715 e 731) ed in quello che era allora considerato territorio di Nepi, vale a dire l'area compresa, all'incirca, fra Cesano e Monterosi; lo stesso territorio di Nepi è documentato per tre fondi, non localizzabili con maggiore precisione, al tempo di Sergio I;

(c) fra 599 e 638 è nominata due volte la *massa Gratiliana*, sita nel territorio di Blera: non viene esplicitamente attribuita al *Patrimonium Tusciae*, ma è chiaramente di proprietà della Chiesa Romana.

Lungo la fascia costiera:

(a) un *casalis* lungo la via Portuense, presso la chiesa dei Santi Abdon e Sennen, documentato fra 625 e 638, ma non esplicitamente attribuito al *Patrimonium Tusciae*;

(b) un *fundus* è noto al X miglio della via Aurelia fra 715 e 731;

(c) si giunge quindi nel territorio di Civitavecchia dove è attestata una *massa* nel periodo fra 625 e 638; si deve quindi attendere l'854 per vedere documentata un'altra *massa* nello stesso territorio, fra quelle attribuite al monastero di San Martino al Vaticano. Ambedue le *massae* non sono esplicitamente associate al patrimonio della Tuscia.

Lungo l'asse della via Flaminia:

(a) fra 625 e 638 vengono locati dalla Chiesa una serie di terreni fra la porta Flaminia e ponte Milvio: non sono esplicitamente associati al patrimonio;

(b) al XIV miglio della via si registra un *fundus* per il periodo 715-31, al quale potrebbero essere associati i beni che andarono a formare la elusiva *domusculta in XIV miliario patrimonio Tusciae*, costituita al tempo di Zaccaria;

(c) nell'854 appare un *fundus in territorio Collinense*: come tutti quelli del diploma in favore di San Martino al Vaticano, non è associabile con certezza al *Patrimonium Tusciae*;

(d) ancora all'854 e allo stesso documento, si riferiscono sette *fundi* da una *massa* sita a 25 miglia da Roma, nel territorio detto di *Urbs Vetus*, che corrisponde all'incirca all'area degli attuali Rignano Flaminio e Faleria.

Localizzazione incerta:

(a) una *massa Castelliana* locata al monastero di San Silvestro al Soratte fra 715 e 731 (Tomassetti 1884: 425-8).[107]

---

[106] Il *fundus Martinianus* richiama ovviamente il nome del lago di Martignano, che si trova ad est di quello di Bracciano; sulla *massa Cesana* e sui suoi dintorni, si veda Wickham (1978: 156-7). Tale *massa* sembra essersi conservata integra e caratterizzata essenzialmente da un'insediamento colonico sparso sino agli inizi del XII secolo, quando parte di essa fu distaccata dal patrimonio della diocesi di *Portus – Silva Candida*, in favore del monastero di San Paolo fuori le mura. Sulla connessione della *massa Cesana* con il territorio di Nepi in epoca altomedievale, si rinvengono utili informazioni in Penteriani e Penteriani Iacoangeli (1986: 35-76).

[107] Per la verità, il Tomassetti argomentava la sua ipotesi anche in funzione del fatto che il locatario della *massa Castelliana* era il monastero di San Silvestro al Soratte, in posizione contigua, quindi, a Civita Castellana.

IL *PATRIMONIUM TUSCIAE SUBURBANUM*

Il *Patrimonium Tusciae Suburbanum* appare per la prima volta nei contratti regestati dell'epoca di Gregorio II inclusi nella *Collectio Canonum* di Deusdedit (lib. III, can. 149), proponendo un gruppo di cinque *fundi* e due *casales*, dei quali due *fundi* sono detti *via Aurelia extra portam Sancti Pancratii* e i restanti si trovano invece al VII miglio della Clodia. Dei quattro *fundi* al V miglio della Clodia, che compaiono nel diploma di Leone IV dell'854 e che appartengono con certezza a questo stesso *patrimonium* abbiamo parlato poco sopra, così come di quell'altro gruppo, ancora sulla Clodia, fra IV e V miglio, di cui però non viene indicata la modalità di aggregazione all'amministrazione patrimoniale pontificia. L'impressione che si ricava dalla analisi degli scarsissimi dati a disposizione è che questa circoscrizione patrimoniale occupasse quell'area del Suburbio romano che si trova a ridosso della basilica vaticana.

Indubbiamente, si sarà notato come, a partire dalle osservazioni schematiche sulle proprietà pontificie note, sia da rimarcare la concentrazione di beni in quello che, ancora nell'VIII secolo viene identificato con molta chiarezza come *territorium Foroclaudiensis*. Il problema è, ovviamente, quello di capire quale fosse il valore di una circoscrizione territoriale basata su un centro urbano che doveva essere ormai sostanzialmente abbandonato.

Il Duchesne notava che la sede episcopale di *Forum Clodii*, certamente attestata sino agli inizi del secolo VI, risultava già rimpiazzata da quella di *Manturanum* (attuale Monterano?) nel 649 (Duchesne 1973; Marazzi 1994b). Lo studio della chiesa di San Liberato, posta all'estremità nordoccidentale della città romana, non ha potuto chiarire se tale edificio, nelle sue forme attuali, sia o meno l'erede di una fondazione di epoca tardoantica, come, ad esempio, si è stabilito con certezza per la cappella costruita nell'insediamento rurale a Mola di Monte Gelato (Marazzi 1988b; Marazzi, Potter and King 1989).

Del resto, ad oggi, è in generale il problema delle fasi tardoantiche ed eventualmente altomedievali dell'abitato di *Forum Clodii* a rimanere assolutamente irrisolto.

Per ciò che concerne più da vicino il tema del quale ci stiamo qui occupando, la particolare questione di 'come' sia finita la diocesi di *Forum Clodii* non è assolutamente di secondaria importanza. Come dimonstrano chiaramente diversi esempi dall'epistolario di Gregorio Magno, la circostanza della soppressione di una sede vescovile comportava la conseguenza di un trasferimento delle pertinenze fondiarie della stessa a vantaggio di un'altra sede, generalmente la più prossima.[108]

Nel nostro caso, la massiccia presenza di proprietà fondiarie pontificie nel territorio di *Forum Clodii* potrebbe avere origine tanto da un parziale rilevamento di beni della diocesi di colà, trasferita a *Manturanum* non sappiamo in quali circostanze e condizioni, tanto da un eventuale incameramento dei beni cittadini di *Forum Clodii* stessa, contestualmente a proprietà del fisco imperiale, che sappiamo occupavano la zona dell'attuale Vicarello.

In ogni caso, qualunque fosse l'origine di queste proprietà, esse, nel corso della prima metà dell'VIII secolo, sono, come si è visto, tutte inquadrate nell'ambito del *Patrimonium Tusciae*. A quest'epoca, ancora caratterizzata dalla dipendenza di Roma da Bisanzio, i *patrimonia* si qualificano per essere delle entità geograficamente ripartite che la Chiesa Romana crea per coordinare la gestione delle sue proprietà private. Successivamente, nel fluido quadro politico che caratterizza il distacco dei pontefici dall'Impero d'Oriente, i *patrimonia* restano sospesi fra la precedente funzione di carattere meramente amministrativo interna alla Chiesa in quanto privata proprietaria di beni fondiari, e una nuova, più estesa valenza di circoscrizioni entro le quali si articola la nascente signoria pontificia sul Lazio.

Proprio la Tuscia costituisce in questo senso un caso particolarmente significativo. Tutta la zona corrispondente, grosso modo, all'area dell'odierna provincia di Viterbo, con estensioni sino alla parte più meridionale dell'attuale Toscana, acquisite in seguito alle donazioni di Carlo Magno del 787, vengono riconosciute in seguito come *Patrimonia Sancti Petri in Tuscia*, senza che il papa vi abbia realmente delle proprietà, ma nella prospettiva di esercitarvi piuttosto diritti di signoria politica.[109]

Sarebbe comunque esercizio piuttosto fine a se stesso voler tracciare una linea retta e definita fra valenze 'pubbliche' e 'private' dei *patrimonia* pontifici fra tardo VIII e IX secolo, poiché l'enfasi sull'uno o sull'altro aspetto varia a seconda delle specifiche contingenze. Il dato di fondo è che, nel delicato momento della fuoriuscita dall'orbita bi-

---

[108] Per il Lazio, gli esempi disponibili sono quelli delle fusioni della sede di *Tres Tabernae* con Velletri (lettera II, 48 dell'agosto 592); di *Nomentum* con *Cures Sabini* (III, 20 del gennaio 593). Tuttavia, anche nei casi in cui un vescovo fosse nominato semplicemente *visitator* di un'altra sede, egli aveva mano libera sui patrimoni di quest'ultima (ancora per le zone prossime a Roma si vedano gli esempi del vescovo di Terracina fatto *visitator* della sede di Formia – lettera VII, 16 dell'aprile 597 – e di quello di Narni fatto *visitator* della sede di Terni – lettera IX, 60 del novembre 598). Per il *Registrum Epistolarum* di Gregorio Magno, si è fatto riferimento alla edizione a cura di Ewald e Hartmann (1887-99).

[109] *Codex Carolinus* (ed. Gundlach 1892), lettera no. 80 del 787ex.-788in.; la formulazione dell'atto di cessione della Tuscia ai pontefici si trova nella conferma che di essa fu emanato da Ludovico il Pio nell'817, nota sotto il nome di *Pactum Hludowicianum* (*Capitularia Regum Francorum*: 353-5).

zantina, i vari *patrimonia Sancti Petri* (nel Lazio ne esistevano ben otto)[110] erano l'unico tipo di partizione territoriale sulla quale i pontefici potessero contare per definire 'a loro misura' il territorio del quale andavano assumendo il controllo.

Il territorio del quale qui ci occupiamo, come si è visto nella elencazione delle pertinenze del *Patrimonium Tusciae*, ci offre un interessante punto di vista su alcuni risvolti di quella grande operazione politico-urbanistica, che fu la fondazione della *Civitas Leoniana*, da parte di Papa Leone IV (847-55):[111] vale a dire la prima recinzione del Vaticano per mezzo di un circuito murario. La gestione di questo baluardo fortificato, gravitante sui due poli della basilica petriana e del mausoleo di Adriano, fu affidata, nei fatti, ai monasteri *deservientes* la basilica stessa. In uno di questi – quello dedicato a San Martino – crebbe lo stesso pontefice. E il primo documento del cartario del Capitolo di San Pietro contiene appunto una vastissima concessione *in perpetuo* di beni al suddetto monastero, comprendenti tanto alcune delle principali istituzioni assistenziali e ricettive che si erano andate affollando intorno alla basilica vaticana, quanto cospicui blocchi fondiari nel Suburbio ad immediato ridosso, lungo le vie Clodia e Cornelia (Marini 1805: papiro XXIV). Un documento pervenutoci in una copia del tempo di Papa Leone IX (1049-54) ci informa del fatto che analoga operazione era stata compiuta contemporaneamente in favore dell'altro monastero vaticano di Santo Stefano Maggiore.[112] Nelle due carte si osserva come le pertinenze dei due monasteri fossero spesso confinanti fra loro, andando quindi a formare un retroterra di territori compattamente controllati dal clero vaticano.

Ancora gli inventari delle tenute della Campagna Romana, compilati agli inizi del nostro secolo, mostrano in quelle stesse aree una sorprendente perduranza di blocchi proprietari legati alle istituzioni religiose o assistenziali vaticane.

L'altro interlocutore di rilievo dei pontefici, all'interno delle grandi transazioni fondiarie, note dalla documentazione superstite, risulta essere la sede episcopale di *Silva Candida*. La più legata ai pontefici, tra le sedi suburbicarie, viene ampiamente beneficiata da Sergio III nel 906, in seguito, si dice, alle devastazioni che le sue proprietà avevano subìto a causa della *pagana infestatio* delle campagne di Roma (da parte dei Saraceni?). Come apprendiamo da documenti del tardo X e della prima metà dell'XI secolo, analoghi provvedimenti furo-

no presi, per beni siti nella stessa zona, in favore del vescovo di Porto (come è noto, le due sedi furono poi unificate da Callisto II fra il 1120 e il 1124).[113]

Il ruolo di queste due sedi episcopali, come ha recentemente notato il Llewellyn, è stato, con alterne vicende, nel corso dei secoli tra IX e XI, quello di puntellare gli sforzi dei pontefici nel controllare lo scacchiere nordoccidentale del territorio romano, e di coordinare al massimo livello il clero cittadino (Llewellyn 1991: 214-23). Nel 1026, Papa Giovanni XIX (1024-32) affidava al vescovo di *Silva Candida* il controllo della Città Leonina, ed in particolare dei quattro monasteri all'interno di essa.[114]

Si congiungono, a questo punto, due diversi percorsi, ambedue aventi come punto di partenza la vecchia struttura centralizzata dei *patrimonia* pontifici. La crisi di questi ultimi sembra evidenziarsi nel corso della seconda metà del IX secolo, a causa, probabilmente, del degenerare delle concessioni *ad longissimum tempus* con le quali erano gestiti. Ciò spinge i pontefici ad accrescere il ruolo di alcune istituzioni autonome, ma strettamente subordinate alla autorità pontificia, quali il clero della basilica vaticana (proveniente dai monasteri ad essa circostanti) ed alcune fra le sedi suburbicarie, quelle non legate a centri urbani che potessero in qualche modo porsi in competizione con Roma, quali appunto Porto, Ostia e *Silva Candida*.

Abbiamo già visto quale fosse il ruolo di due di essi nel controllo di vaste estensioni di terra in prossimità del Vaticano, nonché di una serie di varie funzioni all'interno dello stesso, e ciò, pertanto, rende estremamente evidente il valore dei provvedimenti di Giovanni XIX.

Dal nostro punto di vista, questo episodio può essere a buona ragione considerato il punto di arrivo di questo schematico tentativo di leggere alcune vicende della Roma altomedievale, attraverso il loro riflesso su quella parte del Suburbio che si estende da Roma verso nord, lungo le vie Flaminia, Cassia, Clodia e Aurelia.

BREVI CONSIDERAZIONI DI SINTESI SULLA STRUTTURA DELLA PROPRIETÀ PONTIFICIA E DELLA PROPRIETÀ FONDIARIA IN GENERALE NELL'AREA DELLA TUSCIA

Ci limiteremo alla considerazione dei dati emersi per il periodo compreso tra VI e IX secolo, poiché, per il periodo successivo, non si può parlare del-

---

[110] Trattasi dei *patrimonia Appiae* e *Appiae Suburbanum*, *Labicanum*, *Tiburtinum*, *Sabinense*, *Tusciae* e *Tusciae Suburbanum*, *Urbanum*. Non tutti questi *patrimonia* sono egualmente documentati, dal punto di vista della quantità di attestazioni, né da quello dell'arco cronologico entro cui esse sono distribuite. Questo elenco, pertanto, ritrae la situazione dei *patrimonia* pontifici laziali nel periodo immediatamente precedente alla fine del domino bizantino su Roma, vale a dire all'epoca del pontificato di Gregorio II (715-31).

[111] Sulla nascita della *Civitas Leoniana*, ci permettiamo di rinviare ad un nostro contributo, all'interno del quale si può trovare una bibliografia aggiornata sul problema delle fondazioni di 'città nuove' da parte dei pontefici nel corso del IX secolo (Marazzi 1994b; in corso di stampa).

[112] Edito in 'Sancti Leonis IX papae opuscula, epistolae et decreta pontifica', in *Patrologia Latina* vol. CXLIII, coll. 717-23.

[113] Sull'unificazione delle sedi di *Portus* e *Silva Candida* si veda Kehr (1907: 20, 27).

[114] La bolla di Giovanni XIX per il vescovo di *Silva Candida* è edita da Marini (1805: papiro XLVI).

l'esistenza di un *Patrimonium Tusciae* della Chiesa Romana come di un'unità organizzativa del patrimonio fondiario pontificio; questo termine appare allora definitivamente connotarsi come una embrionale circoscrizione amministrativa del dominio papale sul Lazio.

Brevemente, varrà sottolineare, nell'ordine, elementi comuni, per la Tuscia, rispetto agli altri quadranti del Suburbio ove la Chiesa Romana possedeva beni fondiari, e quindi peculiarità di quest'area. Queste considerazioni potranno ovviamente peccare di schematismo, tenendo presente la scarsità dei dati in relazione al lungo arco di tempo preso in considerazione.

Analogamente a tutte le altre zone del Suburbio romano, anche per la Tuscia il lessico adottato nei superstiti documenti che descrivono l'articolazione delle proprietà pontificie, subisce scarsissimi cambiamenti nell'alto medioevo rispetto alla tarda antichità: *massae* e soprattutto *fundi* ne costituiscono ancora l'ossatura portante. Ci si chiede a cosa si debba tanta stabilità nel lessico impiegato dalla documentazione. Sicuramente non si può sottovalutare il fatto che le testimonianze che qui prendiamo in esame devono essere valutate con cautela in quanto strumenti per una lettura globale della struttura della proprietà agraria nel territorio della Tuscia. I patrimoni pontifici hanno senza ombra di dubbio goduto – almeno sino alle soglie del IX secolo – di una stabilità e di una continuità di amministrazione e documentazione che non doveva avere paragoni in area romana. Questo fatto ha potuto contribuire in misura determinante alla conservazione di una rete di toponimi di origine antica e ad una più generale stabilità della struttura delle unità proprietarie. Parimenti, anche il relativamente ridotto numero di *massae* documentate per il territorio di cui qui ci occupiamo (nove menzioni su 70 per tutto il Suburbio romano nel periodo compreso fra metà VI e inizi X secolo), risponde all'idea che si ha per il periodo tardoantico di una minor presenza (ad esempio rispetto ai quadranti sud ed est del Suburbio) di grandi agglomerazioni fondiarie di questo tipo (Marazzi 1988a).

Tornando ai *fundi*, va detto che, anche nell'ambito del poco che ci conosce sulle proprietà non appartenenti alla Chiesa Romana, essi risultano comunque una categoria ben rappresentata. Basterebbe in questo senso citare l'iscrizione di Santa Maria in Cosmedin, databile intorno al sesto-settimo decennio dell'VIII secolo (Bertolini 1947: 142-5), che contiene l'elenco di un insieme di beni fondiari ceduti da due laici di alto rango alla suddetta diaconia. La presenza, in questa lista, di due toponimi 'Scrofanus' e 'Trea' (che ricordano il moderno centro di Sacrofano e il fiume Treia che scorre presso Monte Gelato), lascia pensare che la localizzazione di queste proprietà sia da porsi nell'area a nord di Roma. Lo spoglio della documentazione per i secoli X e XI (assai più abbondante e diversi-

ficata quanto alle origini), sembra indicare, stando alle sintesi dello Wickham (1978; 1979), ma anche alle più vecchie analisi a suo tempo svolte dal Tomassetti (1910), che il *fundus* continuò ancora a rappresentare la forma più tipica di unità ubicativa della proprietà agraria nel territorio a nord di Roma.

Il problema che si pone nell'esaminare l'insieme dei *fundi* noti per l'area della Tuscia è se sia esistito un atteggiamento meramente passivo rispetto all'eredità del reticolo fondiario stabilitosi nel corso dell'antichità, ovvero se i secoli dell'alto medioevo abbiano conosciuto un rinnovamento non solo della toponimia fondiaria, ma anche della struttura del reticolo stesso, con la nascita di nuove parcelle. Il quesito che qui poniamo per questo limitato settore del territorio romano vale ovviamente anche per l'insieme di esso. Indubbiamente il nostro giudizio, per le ragioni che abbiamo ricordato in precedenza, può essere convogliato verso l'enfatizzazione di una preminenza dell'eredità antica data la rilevanza, per i secoli VII-IX, delle nozioni sulle proprietà pontificie rispetto alla globalità dei dati conosciuti. Tuttavia, si possono notare alcuni elementi interessanti. È vero che, tranne che nei casi di prediali chiaramente riconducibili all'onomastica gentilizia romana, è assai arduo stabilire con sicurezza l'epoca di origine di un toponimo fondiario; ma si possono però evidenziare casi di mutamenti 'in corso' nella denominazione di alcuni *fundi*, nella documentazione dell'VIII secolo, che ci testimoniano dell'esistenza di un processo quanto meno di giustapposizione di nuovi nomi ai vecchi prediali romani: si vedano i *fundi* denominati *Lucretianus*, *Lampadiorum* e *Flavianus* (siti nel quadrante est del Suburbio), che, alla metà dell'VIII secolo venivano anche individuati, rispettivamente, come *Musta*, *Fornellus* e *Casa Monachorum* (Deusdedit, *Collectio Canonum* lib. III, can. 254). Non stupirebbe se potessimo venire a conoscenza del fatto che, col tempo, i nuovi toponimi hanno soppiantato i più antichi. A tale proposito va anche considerato che, mentre considerando nel loro insieme i toponimi dei *fundi* noti per tutto l'arco di tempo compreso tra il VI e gli inizi del X secolo, quelli riconducibili a prediali romani si aggirano intorno al 50 per cento, limitandoci solo ai dati relativi al IX e agli inizi del X secolo, questa percentuale scende drasticamente a poco più del 24 per cento. Tenendo presente che in questa fase più tarda la gran parte della documentazione non riguarda più i *patrimonia* della Chiesa Romana, ma quelli di altri enti ecclesiastici, si può avanzare l'ipotesi di una effettiva esistenza di un processo di rinnovamento della toponomastica fondiaria, e forse anche di creazione *ex-novo* di nuove parcelle proprietarie, per la cui identificazione si continuava ad usare l'ormai vetusto termine di *fundus*. Ulteriori chiarimenti su questo problema, anche attraverso una rinnovata lettura critica delle fonti disponibili per i secoli X e XI, sarà della massima importanza, poiché rappresenterà una interessante chiave interpretativa per comprendere, più in generale, la mentalità con cui, a Roma, si guardava all'ordinamento del territorio; una mentalità senza dubbio fortemente legata a costumanze vecchie di secoli, anche se nulla possiamo dire in merito, ad esempio, sulle procedure di delimitazione dei *fundi* in uso nell'alto medioevo e sulle modalità di registrazione e contabilizzazione degli stessi presso i loro proprietari, al di là del poco che si conosce sui *Patrimonia Sanctae Romanae Ecclesiae*, che corrispondono, dal punto di vista giuridico, a quelli della cattedrale di Roma.

I *fundi* non costituivano, comunque, l'unico tipo di unità ubicativa fondiaria presente nel territorio romano. Nel territorio della Tuscia è particolarmente ben rappresentato un'altro tipo di unità, la cui effettiva natura costituisce da tempo una *crux* interpretativa per gli studiosi (Castagnetti 1980; Montanari 1989; Migliario 1992): si tratta del *casalis*. Questo termine, usato per designare un tipo di unità fondiaria, appare in epoca assai tardiva all'interno del lessico tecnico-agrario latino, sicuramente non prima del V secolo. Esso è attestato, fra VII e IX secolo, in tutto il territorio romano, ma la Tuscia ospita ben dodici delle 21 attestazioni note. Conformemente alle conclusioni tratte dalla Migliario, si può senz'altro concordare sul fatto che, anche in area romana, esso definisca, in linea di massima, una partizione fondiaria in qualche misura subordinata e interna al *fundus*. Abbiamo infatti frequentemente la menzione di *fundi* che vengono locati *cum casalibus et appendicibus eius*, mentre mai accade il contrario. Tuttavia, ed anche questo in conformità alle indicazioni della Migliario, sin dalla loro prima attestazione in area romana, i *casales* costituiscono anche entità fondiarie autonome, che sono oggetto di specifiche transazioni, ovvero che, dotati di proprio toponimo, compaiono tra gli appezzamenti confinanti di altri *fundi* e/o *casales*. In taluni casi, come ad esempio i passi del *Liber Pontificalis* che descrivono la struttura della neonata *domusculta* di *Capracorum*, i *casales* sono nominati tra i terreni aggregati alla nuova fondazione, in un elenco di pertinenze che li vede secondi ai *fundi*, ma che non ne definisce alcun esplicito rapporto di subordinazione a questi ultimi. E ci si chiede, perciò, quale fosse la ragione che indiceva a designare un tipo di unità fondiaria come *fundus* e un'altra come *casalis*. Secondo la Migliario, tale termine passa 'dall'indicare un appezzamento agricolo collegato strettamente al *fundus*, ma da esso distinto perché non ancora organizzato, ... a designare un'estensione di terreno conquistata, o riconquistata, alla coltivazione, e godente di una propria autonomia catastale solo in assenza di strutture agrarie preesistenti' (Migliario 1992: 384). Ma non si può forse del tutto escludere che l'uso del termine stia anche ad enfatizzare l'idea di un'unità fondiaria caratterizzata da una presenza insediativa stabile al proprio interno.

In area romana, tra VIII e IX secolo, un'altro termine – *colonia* – sembra designare esplicitamente piccole unità fondiarie ritagliate per l'appoderamento di gruppi o forse nuclei familiari di rustici. Nel territorio della Tuscia si localizza il più cospicuo insieme noto di questo tipo di parcelle: si tratta di quindici *coloniae* interne alla *massa Cesana*, che Sergio III cede in blocco, nel 906, alla diocesi di *Silva Candida* (Marini 1805: papiro XXIV). Le quindici colonie costituiscono, insieme a tre *fundi* l'insieme del territorio della *massa*, insieme ad altri non specificati *vocabuli*. È da ritenere che le quindici *coloniae* costituissero delle entità fondiarie di istituzione relativamente recente, per l'ampliamento dell'area coltivata all'interno della *massa*, precedentemente forse limitata ai soli *fundi*. Il documento in questione offre alcune informazioni sul tipo di gestione cui era sottoposta la *massa Cesana*. Insieme alla proprietà vengono infatti trasferiti al diretto godimento della diocesi di *Silva Candida* anche i *rustici* che vi risiedono. Al loro interno si distinguono quattro categorie di persone: i *coloni* e tre gruppi di individui apparentemente di condizione non libera, vale a dire, per ordine, i *massaritti*, i *tributarii* e gli *angariales*. La compresenza di questi gruppi fa pensare ad una suddivisione del territorio della *massa* in settori caratterizzati da diverse prassi gestionali e da diversi rapporti con il proprietario. Susseguentemente alla citazione delle quattro categorie di *rustici*, si afferma che esse dovranno essere cedute al nuovo detentore della *massa, cum omni censu, atque dationibus, et functionibus nec non angariis*. Sembra di cogliere, nel testo del documento, una simmetria tra le varie suddivisioni della manodopera agricola e le corresponsioni dovute da ciascun gruppo alla proprietà. La figura del colono sembra pertanto collegata al pagamento di un censo e quindi all'esistenza di un qualche rapporto da locatario a locatore nei confronti della proprietà, definito da patti scritti. Più complesso è interpretare la posizione delle altre tre categorie. Un primo esame lascerebbe pensare che si tratti di persone di condizione personale non libera, ed il cui rapporto con la proprietà fosse regolato in base a consuetudini non scritte e prevedesse corresponsioni di natura non monetaria, tra le quali vengono qui esplicitamente menzionate le prestazioni d'opera. Tuttavia non si può dimenticare come sia rischioso inferire conclusioni troppo nette sulla condizione giuridica della manodopera agricola a partire dalle classificazioni terminologiche: se, ad esempio, è vero che il termine *massarius* identifica in linea di massima individui di *status* personale non libero, è anche vero che vi sono attestazioni del contrario (Modzelewski 1978; Montanari e Andreolli 1983: 115-18). Si può altresì pensare che questi individui lavorassero all'interno dei tre *fundi*, in opposizione ai *coloni*, insediati sulle altre parcelle di nuova formazione. Ma anche in questo caso si deve usare estrema prudenza. Del resto, questo documento è l'unico ad offrire un'indicazione sulla possibile esistenza di manodopera servile all'interno delle terre pontificie laziali e anche in aree assimilabili a quella romana per tradizioni gestionali della proprietà (come la Romagna, vedi Pasquali (1985)) le soluzioni ad analoghi quesiti restano ancora piuttosto vaghe.

Per concludere, possiamo dire che il *Patrimonium Tusciae* della Chiesa Romana (vale a dire, come sembra, quello della cattedrale di Roma), mostra di serbare al suo interno, almeno sino all'VIII secolo, una struttura fondiaria forse non troppo modificata rispetto ai secoli della tarda antichità. Più plastica doveva essere l'articolazione interna dei patrimoni fondiari di altri enti ecclesiastici ovvero di laici, ma va tenuto presente che la '*economic unit*' più comune della proprietà terriera nel territorio romano, durante il IX secolo, continua ad essere ancora il *fundus*, anche grazie alla creazione di nuove parcelle classificate in questo modo.[115] Un conservatorismo lessicale, se così si può dire, che non ha confronti in altre aree del Lazio (come la Tuscia già longobarda e la Sabina), ove il *fundus* appare nello stesso periodo come una realtà residuale, limitata entro un numero di casi sempre decrescente.

Non tutto il territorio, però, come si è visto, era suddiviso in *fundi*. E in alcuni casi (se vedano i *fundi invicem quoerentes* siti al IV-V miglio della via Clodia, menzionati nella concessione di Leone IV dell'854, in favore di San Martino al Vaticano) essi ci appaiono come delle vere e proprie 'isole' di terreni definiti in questo modo, circondati da entità fondiarie di altro tipo (dei *casales*), ovvero da porzioni di terreno non delimitate (come le due *valles* che confinano sul quarto lato con il suddetto gruppo di *fundi*).

Le lettura della documentazione sul Patrimonio della Tuscia ci consente di immaginare un ordinamento del territorio che non ha conosciuto variazioni strutturali di rilievo rispetto ai secoli dell'antichità tardiva, quanto piuttosto una semplificazione delle proprie componenti costitutive. I territori cittadini, ad una certa distanza da Roma, continuano ad essere i referenti basilari per la localizzazione delle proprietà. Le superfici coltivate sono generalmente raggruppate in unità fondiarie dotate di confini e nomi propri; l'insediamento rurale è sparso all'interno di tali unità, che talora si mostrano dotate di propri luoghi di culto. La presenza di edifici in rovina, che in vari casi vengono menzionati tra le caratteristiche interne di questo o quel fondo, ci lasciano intravvedere i vuoti lasciati dalla regressione demografica altomedievale, ma anche l'incapacità – e forse il disinteresse – di provvedere alla manutenzione dell'ingente patrimonio edilizio rurale, ereditato dall'antichità, riducendo al minimo indispensabile le strutture per l'abitazione e la produzione. Fenomeno che è stato del resto ben testimoniato dal caso stesso di Monte Gelato, ove la fattoria tardoromana fu solo in minima parte recuperata – e forse 'capita' – nella sua complessità planimetrica al momento delle ricostruzioni del tardo VIII secolo, che pure videro la profusione di notevoli risorse, ad esempio nella ricostruzione della chiesa.

---

[115] Analogo ragionamento vale per la *massa fundorum*, anch'essa prodotto della ristrutturazione fondiaria tardoantica. Ben testimoniata nel territorio della Tuscia, la *massa*, in questo come in altri settori del suburbio romano mostra chiaramente di essere un agglomerato di *fundi* cresciuto intorno a un *fundus* principale e eponimo, che forse era il cuore dei possedimenti di un *dominus* tardoantico (Vera 1995: 350-1).

Chapter Six

CONCLUSIONS

While necessarily repetitive of some of the arguments advanced in previous chapters, it will be as well to draw together the principal conclusions. It should be recognized that these are not cast in stone. Erroneous decipherment of the evidence in both the field and the study is a commonplace in archaeology, while mistakes and omissions in recording inevitably recur. Moreover, on a site as large as this, one can be certain that further investigation will bring modifications and additional perspectives. Although this is a 'final' report, its interim nature, as part of an ongoing programme of research by many archaeologists, requires emphasis. The perceived facts have been described as faithfully as possible; their interpretation is necessarily more provisional.

THE VILLA OF C. VALERIUS FAUSTUS (?)

Although the sherds found in field survey in the 1950s and 1960s indicated a Republican origin for the site, this was not supported by the results of the present excavations. The first buildings were laid out in the Augustan period, the choice of position no doubt influenced by the extraordinary beauty of the setting. The waterfalls, in particular, make this one of the most delightful places along the Treia valley, a point that will not have been lost upon an owner who was clearly conscious of the merits of ostentatious display. Moreover, the Mola di Monte Gelato has the additional advantage of easy accessibility via a good system of communications, not least by means of a country track (later to be paved), with the town of Veii, and with Rome itself. Thus, municipal obligations could be fulfilled easily, and the urban markets were likewise readily accessible, factors of enduring significance for much of the site's history.

The Augustan complex was indeed ornate. Although relatively little of its plan could be recovered, it was clearly provided with an imposing façade, embellished by some of the fine architectural elements found in the excavations. All was laid out in Roman feet, and within were gracious rooms, floored in mosaic and with painted wall-plaster; a courtyard with a pool and clumps of trees; and marble statuary (one from a nymphaeum) and other elements, such as a *labrum* from a fountain. There were probably ducks in the pool, to judge from the bones, as well as a small fish-pond, which provided a home for eels, very likely kept as pets (cf. Pliny, *Naturalis Historia* ix. 170-1) rather than for commercial purposes. Moreover, the bones also may indicate the existence of an aviary, with tawny owls, jays, chaffinches, thrushes and the like, perhaps penned in by nets in the trees in the courtyards. In short, the excavated evidence provides an extraordinary parallel for the features in the villa near Casinum, owned and described by Marcus Terentius Varro (116-27 BC); it is almost as though Monte Gelato was an 'off-the-peg' villa, based upon a reading of Varro (cf. Purcell 1988b: 196).

No *pars rustica* was discovered, although there would have been ample space for it; certainly, its existence cannot be ruled out without much more extensive investigation. The question of the identity of the owner may here be relevant. We earlier offered the very tentative suggestion that the tomb monument of the Valerii, which, from its size and preservation, was surely erected nearby, may record the name of the first owner, namely C. Valerius Faustus. As *magister* of the *Augustales* of Veii (a title likely to be of Augustan date), he would have been an important local official, and his profession, a cattle merchant, included some very rich people (Gilliver 1990; this volume). He is precisely the sort of *nouveau riche* who would have wished to construct for himself an elegant country residence – but conveniently close to Veii – and one can easily imagine him (or, more probably, one of his educated Greek slaves) consulting his edition of Varro's *Rerum rusticarum*. And certainly, as a *mercator bovarius*, we could expect him to have provided his villa with a *pars rustica*.

That much is, however, speculation. The links with Veii are nevertheless supported by the otherwise very rare *nomen* of his presumed wife, Aescionius, which is paralleled by that of a *duumvir* of Veii, Aescionius Capella, who was honoured by the *Augustales*; and by the tombstone of Herennia, who could have been connected with M. Herennius Picens, consul of AD 1 and patron of Veii. The pointers are, therefore, that in the main the early Imperial inhabitants of the Mola di Monte Gelato directed their attentions southward, towards Veii and Rome, rather than to local towns such as Nepi and Falerii Novi. Even so, the *Augustales* themselves were an important factor in promoting relations between Rome and the settlements in its hinterland, doubtless as a result of official encouragement. Colleges are known at Nepi (*CIL* XI 3200) and Falerii Novi (*CIL* XI 3083), and *seviri* are attested at Lucus Feroniae (Jones 1963: 286). They helped to foster the integration of the *urbs* and its *territorium*, a matter further highlighted by Purcell's study of other epigraphic evidence from the region: this reveals a Campagna that, in early to mid Imperial times, became populated not only by the 'great men of the City', but by 'a very large number of humbler merchants, shopkeepers, freedmen and *apparitores*', namely servants of magistrates (Purcell 1983: 161, 166). The picture gleaned from the present work would seem to provide a clear affirmation of this process.

CHANGES IN THE EARLY SECOND CENTURY

No refuse or occupation deposits of the first century AD were found, a situation that only began to change in the years after AD 100. Around the same time, the original entrance was blocked off by the construction of a simple, linear bath-house in front of it. Beside it ran the road, now paved with *selce* blocks, and two cisterns were built to provide the water. By about AD 130, the lower part of the fish-pond had been filled in, and had presumably gone out of use (although a thin skin of plaster over this dump might represent a new floor). In this deposit were pottery wasters, and a new type of wine amphora, of local production; although there were no significant plant remains in this deposit, we infer that the farming side of the villa was under development. Even so, the quality of the refuse requires emphasis, especially the glass, while the 'stork-vase' and graffiti attest the presence of literate Greeks, presumably slaves. Likewise, the bones of delicacies such as dormice attest a high standard of living. The elegant temple-tomb of perhaps *c.* AD 150, situated on the far side of the road, and in splendid and prominent isolation on a ridge, must surely have been the burial place of the villa's still-rich owners.

The potential Trajanic date (and the limited nature of the chronological evidence should be stressed) for the initiation of these changes is a matter of some interest. Whilst models of crisis and catastrophe in Italian agriculture towards the end of the first century AD no longer carry great conviction (Purcell 1985; Patterson 1987), it may prove to mark something of a watershed in the workings of the rural economy in parts of Italy. Trajan's reorganization of the *annona* (Rickman 1980: 90), and the implementation of the *alimenta* by Nerva and Trajan (cf., most recently, Woolf (1990)), must have played their part; indeed, alimentary schemes were set up at both Capena and Lucus Feroniae. Likewise, Domitian's edict discouraging the production of wine, enacted 'when there was a great glut of wine, but a shortage of corn' (Suetonius, *Domitian* vii. 2), may have been a factor, although modern scholarship tends to stress the increased production of Italian wine at the time (Purcell

1985; Tchernia 1986), a point borne out by the findings at Monte Gelato (where local amphorae account for 65 per cent of the total by the late second century) and probably Settefinestre (Carandini 1985). At the latter site, Trajanic additions included extra accommodation (presumably for slaves), a bath-house, and a building convincingly interpreted as a pigsty. Both an enhanced level of agricultural activity, and a greater diversity, must be envisaged.

As Patterson (1987: 119), *inter alii*, has stressed, Trajan's edict of AD 106-7, requiring candidates for election to the senate to invest one third of their wealth in land in Italy (Pliny, *Epistulae* vi. 19), may have been an additional catalyst for change. A desirable property like Monte Gelato, set in fertile land and within easy reach of Rome, might well have seemed an appropriate acquisition and one suitable for development. As field survey has shown (Fig. 5), there was certainly extensive, apparently unoccupied, terrain both to the west and the south, sufficient for an estate of some 150 hectares. This is a figure not incomparable with those inferred for rich villas like that of Settefinestre in the Cosa region, and would allow for pasturage and cereal cultivation, as well as the growing of vines. Without discovering the farm buildings, we cannot say that this *was* the economic emphasis; but it is easy to see how the profits reflected in the rich array of second-century finds from the site could have been created.

THE DEMISE OF THE VILLA

There can be no doubt that features such as the fish-pond and cisterns were obliterated with dumps of refuse in the late second-early third centuries. Moreover, these features contained a sufficiency of architectural and decorative elements, such as the broken *labrum*, to show that the surrounding buildings were largely demolished. In an earlier discussion (Chapter Three) – and one much influenced by the seemingly violent and comprehensive nature of the destruction – we were tempted to speculate that this might have resulted from the purging of one of Severus's opponents, and the consequent breaking up of his country residence. Certainly, we cannot argue for a process of gradual decay, and the finds show that the inhabitants were prosperous to the last.

To many, this picture will, however, seem colourful, especially in the light of the well-documented decline of Tyrrhenian villas in the second half of the second century, and of settlement generally in South Etruria, especially from the third century. A pattern for long linked with the collapse of the so-called 'slave mode of production', Monte Gelato will doubtless be seized upon as a further exemplar of the same process, not least since the epigraphic evidence unequivocally attests the presence of slaves. Without here wishing to be drawn into the broader debate (in which regional considerations may ultimately prove to be of particular importance: Rathbone 1983: 162), it is nevertheless pertinent to stress these signs of an abrupt demise: to invoke a more generalized model for the period as the explanation for the villa's abandonment is to ignore the archaeological indications that, for once, are relatively explicit. To be sure, it would be more satisfactory to be able to demonstrate that the villa had been burnt down, but on a site with so much subsequent occupation, it would perhaps be optimistic to hope that unambiguous traces had survived.

ABANDONMENT, EARLY THIRD CENTURY – c. MID-FOURTH CENTURY

No structures of this period were identified, with the possible exception of a tile floor in the small 'lobby' room. There was also a virtual absence of third-century pottery, even in residual contexts, and also of glass. There were six coins of the mid to late third century, and two of the earlier part of the fourth century, all either in late Roman deposits, or unstratified. Given the other indications of a lengthy period of abandonment, the likelihood is that they survived as small change when the site was refounded around the middle of the fourth century.

THE LATE ROMAN SETTLEMENT

The very different character of the community that reoccupied the site c. AD 350 is manifested both by the architecture and by the finds. Although many of the old wall lines were followed, sometimes incorporating still-upstanding opus reticulatum from the Augustan villa, the new work was relatively crude and variable in style. There was no detectable use of mosaic or wall-plaster, and timber was widely employed for partitions and other features. In short, these buildings would seem to have been essentially utilitarian in purpose, and of unostentatious design.

The courtyard was apparently retained as such in this period (although it would require more extensive excavation to establish this with certainty). The portico was, on the other hand, blocked in, creating one or more rooms. In the northwest corner were some curious wooden structures, tentatively interpreted as storage bins, for agricultural produce. Nearby, the former 'large room' of the villa was rebuilt, partly as a stable (or byre), with wooden stalls and drains, and partly as a workshop. Here, there was a hearth with bronze-casting waste, and two rock-cut squarish pits, against a wall. In one were substantial quantities of glass, from five second-century vessels; these could represent the fruits of scavenging in glass-rich deposits like those in the fish-pond, with the intention of recycling it.

There was another workshop, also with metalworking hearths, as well as features interpreted as a tank and a box, constructed on the site of the baths. In the next room was a second stable (or byre), again with timber stalls and drains. Iron tools from the area included a metalworking hammer, and instruments for carpentry; some of the iron may have been collected together for recycling. Other artisan activities included the carving of bone, characteristic offcuts of which survived, and in all probability the production of wool and hides; this is inferred from the prevalence of old sheep (now the dominant species, as opposed to pig in the early Imperial deposits) in the animal bone assemblages. There were also some spindle-whorls.

A further industrial activity was the production of lime in a kiln of substantially larger dimensions than normal. There will have been no shortage of marble in the vicinity, whether from tombs or ruinous villas, and we have shown earlier (Chapter Three) that there was a ready market for lime in Rome, for use in works of construction and maintenance. Agricultural produce may also have been transported to the city. While animal husbandry reverted to the traditional sheep/goat economy of the region (and Romans, by contrast, especially favoured pork: Barnish 1987), the plant remains point to the cultivation of bread/macaroni wheat and barley, as well as millet, oats, lentils, horse-beans, peas and olives. There is no way of determining how much of a surplus there was (if indeed any); but the recovery of 24 late Roman coins is an indication of some participation in wider markets (cf. Barnish 1995).

We can also suggest that the settlement was considerably enlarged in the late Roman period. Buildings of this date (possibly of the fifth-sixth centuries, rather than the fourth) were encountered on both the eastern and western margins of the site, but had no early Imperial predecessors. There was also a new structure over the former cisterns. The establishment of a more village-like community may be implied by this, with a not insubstantial population. Even so, the small quantities of African red slip ware and imported amphorae do not support the idea of any great affluence: rather, this was the home to relatively impoverished farmers and artisans, quite conceivably tenants or even slaves. As noted earlier, Melania owned 62 settlements/estates near Rome, each with some 400 slaves who farmed the estate (Jones 1973: 90): it is not impossible that Monte Gelato numbered amongst them.

The addition of a small church to the settlement, at a date that cannot be closely assigned, but could be c. AD 400 (cf. Chapter Three), suggests, however, other explanations. Given the site's later importance as an ecclesiastical centre, and the benefactions of land, made by Constantine to the Church, in the vicinity of Veii and Nepi, we have already offered the hypothesis that it may have become papal property in the late Roman period. Indeed, consideration should be given to the idea that it could have been a monastic foundation. This was a not infrequent phenomenon in the fifth century, and the picture of craftworking, so very fully documented at Monte Gelato, would be consistent with this. Furthermore, literary sources commonly record an association between monasteries and water-mills from an early date, and the likelihood is that the present mill at the Mola represents the successor to earlier ones, exploiting the advantageous configuration of the river at this point (cf. Barnish 1995: 135). Nor would the presence of females in the graves of this period (for example, burials 105 and 106) be an impediment to this interpretation, since wives and other female relatives could be included in monastic foundations (Barnish 1995: 134). The late Roman settlement at San Vincenzo (Hodges 1993; 1995) here affords many similarities, and it is indeed Barnish's fascinating discussion of it as a possible monastic estate-centre that allows much of this paragraph to be written.

We shall say something more of other, more local, parallels shortly; but first the subsequent history of the late Roman settlement must be summarized briefly. As many of the drawn sections graphically illustrate, the fifth and first half of the sixth centuries saw a gradual running down of many parts of the site. The wooden bins and the limekiln went out of use *c.* AD 400 (the latter perhaps because of the adjacent construction of the church), and in areas like the corridor and the workshop on the lower terrace, hearths began to build up over the mortar floors. There is an image of a gradual degeneration into a state of squalor. The latest imported fine-ware vessel to reach the site is unlikely to be much later than *c.* AD 520, and the few amphorae also do not post-date the early sixth century. Four coins take occupation down to at least *c.* AD 550, about which time substantial falls of roofs and walls occurred, never to be cleared away. Thereafter, traces of structures are confined to some post-holes, and the latest 'Roman' presence is a burial (no. 53), assignable from a ceramic vessel and radiocarbon dating to the late sixth or early seventh century. Thereafter, for nearly 200 years, a human presence is essentially undetectable. Thus, the picture of decay and then demise, around the mid-sixth century, conforms remarkably closely with those derived from excavations at both San Vincenzo (Hodges 1993; 1995) and San Giovanni di Ruoti, near Potenza (Small and Buck 1994).

The broader economic and political background to this now well-defined watershed in the mid-sixth century has been much debated (for example, Barnish (1987)), and need not detain us here. In recent years, however, more data (albeit only summarily published) have become available for the late Roman period on both rural and urban sites in southern Etruria. They are principally reported by Gazzetti (1992). He has described how Lucus Feroniae was in decline in the fourth century, and in the following two centuries was used both for burials and as a quarry: contracting settlement seems certain, a picture matched by results from current investigations at Falerii Novi. Here, crudely built stone walls, with much reused material, have been revealed, resting upon silts overlying the paved streets to the east of the monastery of Santa Maria di Fálleri. They appear late Antique in date, and conform with a gradually emerging idea of the substantial changes that took place within many Roman towns and cities (not only in Italy) at this time (cf. Potter (1995) and the contributions in Francovich and Noyé (1994)).

It is three other sites investigated by Gazzetti (1992) that are of most interest, however. At a settlement beside the Via Amerina, near *Ad Baccanas*, it was found that structures described as shops had been rebuilt in the fifth century. They yielded various tools, including knives, picks and pitchforks, and a limekiln was also discovered. Nearby was a burial of the late sixth to early seventh centuries, with a wine flask, described as being of central European type (Gazzetti 1992: 92). Similarly, at Baciletti, a villa in the northeast Ager Capenas, iron agricultural tools were encountered in contexts datable to the fifth-sixth centuries, while another villa near Lucus Feroniae was rebuilt *c.* AD 400, and yielded a cemetery of the sixth-seventh centuries: one grave had a tile with a stamp of Theoderic (AD 493-526). Finally, we must recall the excavation of Pallottino (1937) at Monte Canino, also in the Ager Capenas, where an early Imperial villa was succeeded by a curious rectangular structure with an ambulatory, which became the focus for a cemetery in late Antique times. By AD 794, it may have become associated with a church of Santa Cristina (Tomassetti 1913 (1979): 286), although one can hardly postulate continuity of occupation without further evidence.

These analogies show that, whatever the status of the late Roman settlement at Monte Gelato, it is not alone in this region in demonstrating a revitalization at this time. Also striking is the occurrence elsewhere of iron tools, a limekiln and burials, a remarkable similarity of pattern. Likewise, none of these sites can be shown to extend much into the seventh century, although here we should note Gazzetti's interesting observation (1992: 25) that the castle at Scorano (just by Lucus Feroniae) overlies a Roman temple, and was apparently occupied from the seventh-eighth centuries. If correctly interpreted, this would be a most significant discovery, given the dearth of finds of this date in the region. Indeed, the degree to which this was frontier country between the duchy of Rome and the Lombards cannot be overestimated. Sutri, for example, was taken by the Lombards in both the late sixth century, and again by Liutprand in AD 728-9. The recent provenancing of a well-known

Fig. 255. Lombard tomb group of the late sixth-early seventh centuries, from Sutri (British Museum, registration number MLA 87, 1-8, 2-9).

Lombard tomb group in the British Museum to Sutri (Ciampoltrini 1993) is a further affirmation of this. Datable to the late sixth or early seventh century, the richness of the objects, several of which are in gold (Fig. 255), stands in some contrast with the bleak picture for this period derived from the present excavations. Indeed, Gregory mentioned Lombard incursions in the Rome area no fewer than seven times in AD 592-3 alone (cf. Brown 1984: 39-40). Given all this warfare in the locality, it is perhaps no wonder that so many rural sites were deserted by this time, even though we have little idea of the fate of the inhabitants.

THE *DOMUSCULTA* OF *CAPRACORUM*

We need not dwell in detail upon this episode at the Mola di Monte Gelato, for it has been discussed at length in both Chapters One and Three, and the broader context explored by Marazzi in Chapter Five. The construction of a new, larger and elaborately decorated church, *c.* AD 800, with a conjoined baptistery, can be safely ascribed to the period of the *domusculta* of *Capracorum* and, on documentary evidence, be regarded as one of its estate-centres. It is perhaps puzzling that, apart from a possible perimeter wall with a structure against it (neither necessarily of this phase), no other major buildings were encountered. Reused

Roman features, like the temple-tomb, and rock-cut caves apparently sufficed. But the animal bones (once again with pig predominant), and the plant remains, conform with the description of the produce of the *domusculta*, as described in the *Liber Pontificalis*, while the pottery kiln, making wares exactly paralleled in Rome, probably provided transport containers for these foodstuffs. The maintenance of the Roman paved road was here evidently of importance, and many of the blocks were relaid around this time.

Considerable attention has been paid in this volume to an analysis both of the extensive early medieval cemetery, and of the human remains themselves (Chapter Three). This was a normal population of men, women and children, with a clear hierarchy: the more elaborate graves clustered in or around the church and baptistery, while beneath the altar were two primary burials, which on radiocarbon dating must have been interred as relics. There were a few grave offerings, but little use of coffins. In general, the mode of burial was disorderly, propinquity to the ecclesiastical buildings being the prime concern. Study of the bones shows that this was a hard-working peasant population (including those buried in 'high-status' graves, and both men and women), with features indicating family links: the adjacent graves of two apparently related individuals, both accompanied by Roman coins, in pagan tradition, is here especially noteworthy. We infer that, between the foundation of the *domusculta* and the abandonment of the site some three centuries later, *c.* AD 1100, the community became ever more parochial and conservative, isolated from the outside world. The recovery of but a single medieval coin, of AD 884-5, is perhaps symptomatic of this.

The abandonment of the pottery kiln, in the mid- (or possibly late) ninth century may mark the demise of the *domusculta* of *Capracorum* (itself not heard of in the documentary or epigraphic sources after AD 846). This is in line with the evidence from the estate-centre at Santa Cornelia (Christie and Daniels 1991: 187), and reflects a gradual diminution of papal authority at the hands of the Roman nobility (and, too, the impact of raids by the Arabs). At neither Santa Cornelia or Monte Gelato, however, is it possible to say much about events between the late ninth century and the beginning of the eleventh century. Although there is some pottery of this period at Monte Gelato, significant stratigraphical deposits were lacking, and only the sequence over the bath-house (Fig. 77) suggests unbroken occupation. On the other hand, many decorative elements in the church, including the very fine altar screen (if that is what is is) with the Agnus Dei, remained to be broken up *c.* AD 1000, and burials seem to have been made continuously: on balance, therefore, the indications are that the site remained in use over this time, albeit in a decaying state.

THE REBUILDING OF *c.* AD 1000, AND ITS DEMISE

There is unambiguous testimony to show that, in the late tenth or early eleventh century, the church was partly or wholly reconstructed; the baptistery was rebuilt on a much larger scale, with a rather grand font; and other rooms were added to the north of the baptistery, including an entrance. Although the work was relatively crude, and there is no surviving evidence for embellishment (which could, however, have been in perishable materials), the importance of the ecclesiastical complex would seem to have been strongly reaffirmed.

At first sight this is surprising, for it flies in the face of a rich vein of documentary sources, which shows that *incastellamento* in the Ager Faliscus was well under way by this time (Potter 1979: 164). The village adjacent to Mazzano, for example, is first heard of in AD 945 and Calcata, a little further down the Treia valley, in AD 974, and they were part of an extensive reorganization of the landscape. However, as Wickham (1979: 89) has pointed out, the term *fundus* commonly coexists with that of *castellum* in charters for the Ager Faliscus up to the twelfth century. Something of the late Antique arrangement of estates clearly survived well into

the Middle Ages, and the rebuilding of the complex at Monte Gelato may indeed reflect this.

If so, it was a short-lived revival. Around the beginning of the twelfth century the buildings were systematically demolished, and the materials carted away; even some of the post-holes for the scaffolding needed for this operation were identified in the baptistery. Occupation also ceased in the rock-cut cave and in the temple-tomb, and the impression is of a systematic and orderly evacuation. Indeed, some of the more important graves were emptied of the bones, and then reconstructed, which may well reflect the fact that the place was not forgotten. Burials continued to be made for a time, including those of children placed in graves cut into or across the demolished wall footings in the baptistery. Moreover, in the church a tufo block foundation was constructed, probably to support a wayside shrine or some other form of commemorative monument, such as a cross. Continued veneration of this long-lived focus of Christian worship and interment was clearly considered a matter of considerable consequence, hardly surprisingly in a small, close-knit rural community.

CASTELLACCIO: CASTRUM CAPRACORUM

That the population moved to the nearby castle site of Castellaccio (identifiable as *castrum Capracorum* from a bull of 1053) was, from the outset of our work, always seen as a likelihood. The juxtaposition of late Roman villas and medieval *castelli* is a striking feature of the Ager Faliscus, and a shift from one to the other has long seemed a probability (Potter 1975). While a view that this was the process that took place in the sixth-eighth centuries (Potter 1979: 165-7) is not supported by the present work, the occurrence in our trenches at Castellaccio of a little eleventh-century pottery and, overwhelmingly, of twelfth-century material, amply sustains this conclusion. Whether this was an enforced move (as the archaeological indications could well imply, given the signs of a reluctance to forget the site in the valley), or a voluntary decision to abandon an unprotectable location, is another matter. Perhaps the former is more likely, given the broader historical background (cf. Wickham 1979: 88-9).

The very limited scope of the excavations at Castellaccio (where heavy tree cover restricted trenching), allows few other conclusions. Unsurprising were the remains of a masonry curtain wall, with a building constructed behind it; nor the traces of timber structures, perhaps of the sort encountered at Ponte Nepesino (Cameron *et al.* 1984). More interesting were the signs from the animal bones that the stock economy had reverted to the rearing of sheep and goats, as in the late Roman period; once again, the traditional practices of the region since prehistoric times (Barker 1976), still current today, were being reasserted. No plant remains were recovered, but the present mill, itself likely to be of twelfth-century date, is surely testimony to the active cultivation of cereals. Even so, the dearth of refuse implies a relatively small community, and there is little evidence to show that Castellaccio was occupied much after the late thirteenth century. Indeed, the dearth of pottery other than sherds of the twelfth century suggests that a decline began soon after; a migration to Mazzano, which has traditionally included the Mola di Monte Gelato within its sphere of influence, is more than likely. Only the mill continued in use, exploiting its advantageous position on the river, and protected, it would seem, by militia based in an adjoining tower.

LATE MEDIEVAL AND POST-MEDIEVAL TIMES

Rome continued to exert a powerful influence in the region, whether through the Church or through noble families, for most of the later Middle Ages and post-medieval times. The Mola di Monte Gelato and Mazzano were both the property of the monastery of San Gregorio on the Coelian down to the early fourteenth century. Also Civita Castellana emerged as an important centre of papal power: this is symbolized by the construction of the monumental Porta Romana by Calixtus III (1455-8), and the papal fortress, started by Alexander VI (1492-1503) and completed by Sangallo the Elder for Julius II (1503-13). Likewise, Nepi was endowed with imposing fortifications by Duke Pier Luigi Farnese in 1540, and a papal aqueduct, built in 1727 (Tomassetti 1913 (1979): 150). The appearance of new road stations like Baccano and Settevene on the via Cassia, in the fifteenth-sixteenth centuries, further marks the re-establishment of papal authority. Some of the remoter medieval villages like Castel Porciano (Mallett and Whitehouse 1967) were abandoned, and many of the others demonstrate a conspicuous investment in new buildings from the sixteenth century onwards, Mazzano being but one example (Potter 1972). Indeed, in early post-medieval times, there was what seems to have been a significant spread of rural *casali*, perhaps indicating substantial changes in agrarian practices.

The continued importance of the mill in this period at the Mola di Monte Gelato is well documented (Fedeli, this volume). Yet, outside the major towns of the Ager Faliscus, and away from the main highways, one has the impression that a very ruralized existence, largely divorced from that of the city of Rome, persisted. This may well have become still more accentuated in the nineteenth century. Sadly, the journeys of George Dennis never took him to the area of Narce and Monte Gelato; but his evocative description of the view

from nearby Capena may well be apt: 'the bare swelling ground to the north with Soracte towering above: the snow-capt Apennines in the eastern horizon: the deep silence, the seclusion: the absence of human habitations (not even a shepherd's hut) within the sphere of vision, save the distant town of San Oreste .... compose a scene of more singular desolation than belongs to the site of any other Etruscan city in this district of the land' (Dennis 1878: I, 133). Similarly, the photographs of Thomas Ashby (1927; 1986), taken mainly in the first two decades of the twentieth century, depict an empty, desolate Campagna, despite the burgeoning of Rome at this time.

Even in the mid 1960s, when the writer first began to explore the Ager Faliscus, it seemed extraordinarily cut-off from Rome (Potter 1991). As a lengthy sojourn in Mazzano showed, considerations were above all parochial, and contact with Rome infrequent for many of the village populace. Equally, the region was seldom visited by outsiders, and tourism was non-existent. The Mola di Monte Gelato, then approached by a rutted *strada bianca*, was the preserve of local people, apart from visits from time to time by film and television crews. During the 1970s, however, as Rome dramatically expanded, this gradually began to change. With the construction of the Via Cassia *superstrada* (the Via Veientana) in the early 1980s, this part of the Campagna once again became much easier of access. The opening of the '*Parco suburbano della valle Treja*' in 1982 provided a further incentive for urban people to come to the area. Now the Mola is flooded with weekend visitors, new properties are rising everywhere, and the local dialect is almost submerged by a welter of non-regional and foreign tongues.

The story has therefore come full cycle. The city and its northern hinterland is once more fully integrated, as was the case in early Imperial times. The Latin, Greek and (probably) Faliscan, that will have been heard at the Mola in the first and second centuries AD, may have been replaced today by Italian, local and non-local, together with English, French, German and other languages; but the implication, namely of close links between the major international city of Rome and its *territorium*, is the same. Likewise, in the Carolingian era, a further period of prosperity in Rome (Delogu 1988), contacts were close. Only when Rome's power waned were these links reduced or severed, a matter put in sharp perspective by the results of the present investigation. In both late Roman and medieval times, considerations at the Mola became largely parochial; in the seventh and early to mid eighth centuries all contact was lost in what seems, at the Mola di Monte Gelato at any rate, to have been genuinely a Dark Age. We might with Krautheimer (1980: 93) recall that in Rome 'not a single building remains from the more than one hundred years between the construction of S. Agnese fuori le mura (625-638) and that of S. Angelo in Peschiera, 755'. To portray the settlements at the Mola as in some respects a mirror of the history of the city of Rome is assuredly to oversimplify: but to deny a series of persistent echoes of the fortunes of Rome, in this seemingly remote and rustic place in the Roman Campagna, would indeed be perverse. The waxing and waning of the city's power and influence is, it would seem, writ large upon its adjacent landscape.

REFERENCES

Adams, J.P. (1984) *La construction romaine*. Paris.

Albarella, U. (1993) The fauna. In U. Albarella, V. Ceglia and P. Roberts, S. Giacomo degli Schiavoni (Molise): an early fifth century AD deposit of pottery and animal bones from central Adriatic Italy: 203-22, 226-30. *Papers of the British School at Rome* 61: 157-230.

Albarella, U. and Frezza, A. (n.d. a.) I reperti faunistici di GI 52. Unpublished bone report for P. Arthur, Naples.

Albarella, U. and Frezza, A. (n.d. b) I reperti faunistici di via San Paolo. Unpublished bone report for P. Arthur, Naples.

Allason-Jones, L. (1985) Bell-shaped studs? In M.C. Bishop (ed.), *The Production and Distribution of Roman Military Equipment* (BAR International Series 275): 95-108. Oxford.

Allason-Jones, L. (1989) Roman and native interaction in Northumberland. In V.A. Maxfield and M.J. Dobson (eds), *Roman Frontier Studies 1989*: 1-5. Exeter.

Allen, H.L. (1974) Excavations at Morgantina (Serra Orlando), 1970-1972: preliminary report XI. *American Journal of Archaeology* 78: 361-83.

Almagro-Gorbea, M.J. (1982) *El santuario de Juno en Gabii*. Rome.

Alvarez, W. (1972) The Treia valley north of Rome: volcanic stratigraphy, topographic evolution and geological influences on human settlement. *Geologica romana* 11: 153-76.

Alvarez, W. (1973) Ancient course of the Tiber River near Rome: an introduction to the Middle Pleistocene volcanic stratigraphy of central Italy. *Geological Society of America Bulletin* 84: 749-58.

Amelung, W. (1908) *Die Sculpturen des Vaticanischen Museums. Belvedere. Sala degli animali. Galleria delle statue. Sala de' busti. Gabinetto delle maschere. Loggia scoperta* II. Berlin.

'Amr, A.-J. (1984) Some Ayyubid pottery lamps from Rujm al-Kursi and other related Mamluke examples. *Berytus* 32: 201-10.

Andreolli, B. (1981) I prodotti alimentari nei contratti agrari toscani dell'alto medievo. *Archeologia medievale* 8: 117-26.

Andrews, D. (1978) Medieval masonry in northern Lazio: its development and uses for dating. In H. Blake, T.W. Potter and D. Whitehouse (eds), *Papers in Italian Archaeology* I. *The Lancaster Seminar* (BAR International Series 41): 391-412. Oxford.

Andrews, D. (1982) L'evoluzione della tecnica muraria nell'alto Lazio. *Biblioteca e società* 1-2: 3-16.

Annechino, M. (1982) Suppellettile fittile per uso agricolo in Pompeii e nell'agro vesuviano. In *La regione sotterrata dal Vesuvio (Atti del Convegno Internazionale (Naples))*: 753-73.

Arnason, H.H. (1936) Early Christian silver in North Italy and Gaul. *The Art Bulletin* 20 (3): 193-226.

Arthur, P. (1983) The pottery. In E. Fentress, S. Judson, T. Blagg, M. de Vos and P. Arthur, Excavations at Fosso della Crescenza, 1962: 78-96. *Papers of the British School at Rome* 51: 58-101.

Arthur, P. (1993) Early medieval amphorae, the duchy of Naples and the food supply of Rome. *Papers of the British School at Rome* 61: 231-44.

Arthur, P. and Whitehouse, D.B. (1982) La ceramica dell'Italia meridionale: produzione e mercato tra V e X secolo. *Archeologia medievale* 9: 39-46.

Arthur, P. and Whitehouse, D.B. (1983) Appunti sulla produzione laterizia nell'Italia centro-meridionale tra il VI e il XII secolo. *Archeologia medievale* 10: 525-37.

Arthur, P., Caggia, M.P., Ciongoli, G.P., Melissano, V., Patterson, H. and Roberts, P. (1992) Fornaci medievali ad Otranto. Nota preliminare. *Archeologia medievale* 19: 91-122.

Ascadi, G. and Nemeskeri J. (1970) *History of Human Life Span and Mortality*. Budapest.

Ashby, T. (1927) *The Roman Campagna in Classical Times* (1970 reprint). Tonbridge.

Ashby, T. (1986) *Thomas Ashby. Un archeologo fotografa la campagna romana tra '800 e '900*. Rome.

Auth, S.H. (1976) *Ancient Glass at the Newark Museum*. Newark, N.J.

Avagnina, M.E., Garibaldi, V. and Salterini, C. (1976-77) Strutture murarie degli edifici di Roma nel XII secolo. *Rivista dell'Istituto nazionale d'archeologia e storia dell'arte* 23-4: 242-7.

Bailey, D.M. (1980) *Catalogue of the Lamps in the British Museum* ii, *Roman Lamps made in Italy*. London.

Bailey, D.M. (1988) *Catalogue of the Lamps in the British Museum* iii, *Roman Provincial Lamps*. London.

Baker, P. and Clark, G. (1993) Archaeozoological evidence for medieval Italy: a critical review of the present state of research. *Archeologia medievale* 20: 45-77.

Balsdon, J.P.V.D. (1962) *Roman Women*. London.

Baradez, J. (1957) Nouvelles fouilles à Tipasa. Les fours à chaux des constructeurs de l'enceiente. *Libyca* 5: 277-94.

Barker, B.C.W. (1975) Relation of the alveolus to the cemeto-enamel junction following attritional wear in Aboriginal skulls. An enquiry into the normality of cementum exposure with ageing. *Journal of Periodontology* 46 (6): 357-63.

Barker, G.W.W. (1973) The economy of medieval Tuscania: the archaeological evidence. *Papers of the British School at Rome* 41: 155-77.

Barker, G.W.W. (1976) Animal husbandry at Narce. In T.W. Potter, *A Faliscan Town in South Etruria. Excavations at Narce 1966-71*: 295-307. London.

Barker, G.W.W. (1977) L'economia del bestiame a Luni. In A. Frova (ed.), *Scavi di Luni. Relazione delle campagne di scavo 1972-1973-1974*: 725-35. Rome.

Barker, G.W.W. (1982) The animal bones. In D.B. Whitehouse, G. Barker, R. Reece and D. Reese, *The Schola Praeconum I: the coins, pottery, lamps and fauna*: 81-91, 96-9. *Papers of the British School at Rome* 50: 53-101.

Barnish, S.J.B. (1987) Pigs, plebeians and potentes: Rome's economic hinterland c. 350-600 AD. *Papers of the British School at Rome* 55: 157-85.

Barnish, S.J.B. (1995) Christians and countrymen at San Vincenzo, c. AD 400-550. In R. Hodges (ed.), *San Vincenzo al Volturno 2: The 1980-86 Excavations Part II* (*Archaeological Monographs of the British School at Rome* 9): 131-7. London.

Baroni, E. (1980) *Guida botanica d'Italia*. Bologna.

Baruzzi, M. (1987) I reperti in ferro dello scavo di Villa Clelia (Imola). Note sull'attrezzatura agricola nell'altomedioevo. In R. Francovich (ed.), *Archeologia e storia del medioevo italiano* (*Studi NIS Archeologia* 3): 149-70. Rome.

Bass, G.F. and von Doorninck, F.H. (1982) *Yassi Ada*. Texas.

Bass, W.M. (1987) *Human Osteology: a Laboratory and Field Manual of the Human Skeleton* (third edition) (Missouri Archaeological Association Special Publications). Columbia.

Bavant, B. (1979) Le duché byzantin de Rome. Origine, durée et extension géographique. *Mélanges de l'Ecole Française de Rome. Moyen Âge et Temps Modernes* 91: 41-89.

Becatti, G. *et al.* (1970) *Mosaici antichi in Italia. Regione settima. Baccano: villa romana*. Rome.

Beltran Lloris, M. (1970) *Anforas romanas de España*. Zaragoza.

Berry, A.C. and Berry, R.J. (1967) Epigenetic variation in the human cranium. *Journal of Anatomy* 101: 361-79.

Bertelli, G., Guiglia Guidobaldi, A. and Rovigatti Spagnoletti Zeuli, P. (1976-77) Strutture murarie degli edifici di Roma nel XII secolo. *Rivista dell'Istituto nazionale d'archeologia e storia dell'arte* 23-4: 160-4.

Bertolini, O. (1947) Per la storia delle diaconie romane dalle origini alla fine del sec. VIII *Archivio della Società romana di storia patria* 70: 1-145.

Bianchi, L. (1989) Roma: tessuto urbano e tipologie monumentali. *Studi romani* 37: 104-15.

Bird, J. (1993) The 1969 excavations. In J. Bird, A. Claridge, O. Gilkes and D. Neal, Porta Pia: excavations and survey in an area of suburban Rome, Part I: 52-100. *Papers of the British School at Rome* 61: 51-113.

Birley, A. (1971) *Septimius Severus. The African Emperor*. London.

Blake, H. McK. (1983) Sepolture. *Archeologia medievale* 10: 175-97.

Blake, M.E. (1947) *Ancient Roman Construction in Italy from the Prehistoric Period to Augustus*. Washington.

Blake, M.E. and Bishop, D.T. (1973) *Roman Construction in Italy from Nerva through the Antonines*. Philadelphia.

BMC = H. Mattingly (1923-) *The Coins of Rome and the Roman Empire in the British Museum*. London.

Boardman, J. (1974) *Athenian Black Figure Vases*. London.

Boessneck, J. (1969) Osteological differences between sheep (*Ovis aries* Linné) and goat (*Capra hircus* Linné). In D. Brothwell and E. Higgs (eds), *Science in Archaeology* (second edition): 331-58. London.

Bonanno, M. (1979) Tipi e varietà di lucerne arabo-normanne rinvenute a Palermo. *Archeologia medievale* 6: 353-8.

Bonatti, E. (1970) Pollen sequence in the lake sediments. In G. Hutchinson (ed.), *Ianula – an Account of the History and Development of the Lago di Monterosi, Latium, Italy* (*Transactions of the American Philosophical Society* 40/4): 26-31.

Bond, F. (1908) *Fonts and Font Covers*. London.

Bonifay, M., Paroli, L. and Picon, M. (1986) Ceramiche a vetrina pesante scoperte a Roma e a Marsiglia: risultati delle prime analisi fisico-chimiche. *Archeologia medievale* 13: 79-95.

Bosio, B. and Pugnetti, A. (1984) (eds) *Gli etruschi di Cerveteri*. Modena.

Bosman, F. (1993) Viabilità ed insediamenti lungo la via Flaminia nell'alto medievo. In L. Paroli and P. Delogu (eds), *La storia economica di Roma nell'alto medioevo alla luce dei recenti scavi archeologici*: 295-308. Florence, All'Insegna del Giglio.

Bovini, G. (1960) L'impiego di tubi fittili nelle volte degli edifici a culto ravennati. *Felix Ravenna* (3rd series) 30: 78-99.

Brants, J. (1913) *Antieke Terra-Cotta Lampen uit het Rijksmuseum van Oudheden te Leiden*. Leiden.

Broneer, O. (1930) *Corinth IV, 2, Terracotta Lamps*. Cambridge, Mass.

Broneer, O. (1947) Investigations at Corinth, 1946-1947. *Hesperia* 16: 233-47.

Brothwell, D.R. (1972) *Digging up Bones* (second edition). London.

Brothwell, D.R. (1981) *Digging up Bones. The Excavation, Treatment and Study of Human Skeletal Remains* (third edition). London and Oxford.

Brown, T.S. (1984) *Gentlemen and Officers: Imperial Administration and Aristocratic Power in Roman Italy, 504-800*. London.

Bull, G. and Payne, S. (1982) Tooth eruption and epiphysial fusion in pigs and wild boar. In B. Wilson, C. Grigson and S. Payne (eds), *Ageing and Sexing Animal Bones from Archaeological Sites* (BAR British Series 109): 55-71. Oxford.

Bullock, D. and Rackham, J. (1982) Epiphysial fusion and tooth eruption of feral goats from Moffatdale, Dumfries and Galloway, Scotland. In B. Wilson, C. Grigson and S. Payne (eds), *Ageing and Sexing Animal Bones from Archaeological Sites* (BAR British Series 109): 73-80. Oxford.

Burnett, D., Clark, G. and Sutherland, S. (forthcoming) The animal bones from the Mura di Santo Stefano (Anguillara). In *Excavations at the Mura di Santo Stefano (Anguillara)*.

Burzachechi, M. (1962) Oggetti parlanti nelle epigrafi greche. *Epigraphica* 24: 3-54.

Buxton, L.H.D. (1938) Platymeria and platycnemia. *Journal of Anatomy* 73: 31-6.

Camaiora, R. (1985) Suppellettile da mensa. Ceramica a parete sottili. In A. Ricci (ed.), *Settefinestre. Una villa schiavistica nell'Etruria romana. 2. La villa e i suoi reperti*: 166-73. Modena.

Cambi, F. (1990) *Paesaggi romani dell'Etruria meridionale*. Tesi di Dottorato di Ricerca in Archeologia, Università di Pisa, III Ciclo, 1987-1990.

Cameron, F., Clark, G., Jackson, R., Johns, C., Philpot, S., Potter, T., Shepherd, J., Stone, M. and Whitehouse, D. (1984) Il castello di Ponte Nepesino e il confine settentrionale del Ducato di Roma. *Archeologia medievale* 11: 63-147.

Cameron, J. (1934) *The Skeleton of British Neolithic Man*. London.

Capitulario Regum Francorum = A. Boretius (ed.) (1883) Capitularia Regum Francorum. In *Monumenta Germaniae Historica, Legum Sectio II, Capitularia Regum Francorum I*. Hannover.

Cappelletto, R. (1983) *Recuperi Ammianei in Biondo Flavio*. Rome.

Carandini, A. (ed.) (1985) *Settefinestre. Una villa schiavistica nell'Etruria romana. 1* La villa nel suo insieme, 1** La villa nelle sue parti*. Modena.

Carandini, A. (1989) L'economia italica fra tarda repubblica e medio impero considerata dal punto di vista di una merce: il vino. In *Amphores romaines et historie économique, dix ans de recherche* (*Collection de l'Ecole Française de Rome* 114): 505-21.

Carandini, A. and Panella, C. (1981) The trading connections of Rome and central Italy in the late second and third centuries: the evidence of the Terme del Nuotatore excavations, Ostia. In A. King and M. Henig (eds), *The Roman West in the Third Century*: 487-503. Oxford.

Carbonara, A. and Messineo, G. (1993) La Celsa. Il complesso delle fornaci. *Bullettino della Commissione archeologica comunale di Roma* 91: 542-8.

Carroll-Spillecke, M. (ed.) (1992) *Der Garten von der Antike bis zum Mittelalter*. Mainz.

Cassanelli, R. (1987) Materiali lapidei a Milano in età longobarda. In C. Bertelli (ed.), *Milano, una capitale da Ambrogio ai Carolingi*: 238-57. Milan.

Castagnetti, A. (1980) Continuità e discontinuità nella terminologia e nella realtà organizzativa agraria: 'fundus' e 'casale' nei documenti ravennati altomedievali. In V. Fumagalli and G. Rossetti (eds), *Medioevo rurali*: 201-19. Bologna.

Cecchelli Trinci, M.M. (1980) La chiesa di S. Agata *in fundo Lardario* e il cimitero dei SS Processo e Martiniano. *Quaderni dell'Istituto di archeologia e storia antica dell'Università di Chieti* 1: 85-111.

Ceci, M. (1992) Note sulla circolazione delle lucerne a Roma nell'VIII secolo: i contesti della Crypta Balbi, con Appendice di H. Patterson. *Archeologia medievale* 19: 749-66.

Celuzza, M.G. (1985) La ceramica invetriata. In A. Ricci (ed.), *Settefinestre. Una villa schiavistica nell'Etruria romana. 2. La villa e i suoi reperti*: 163-6. Modena.

Cherkauer, D. (1976) Site K. The stratigraphy and chronology of the River Treia alluvial deposits. In T.W. Potter, *A Faliscan Town in South Etruria. Excavations at Narce 1966-71*: 106-20. London.

Chevallier, R. (1976) *Roman Roads*. London.

Christie, N. (1991a) Three South Etrurian churches – an overview. In N. Christie (ed.), *Three South Etrurian Churches: Santa Cornelia, Santa Rufina and San Liberato* (*Archaeological Monographs of the British School at Rome* 4): 353-9. London.

Christie, N. (ed.) (1991b) *Three South Etrurian Churches: Santa Cornelia, Santa Rufina and San Liberato* (*Archaeological Monographs of the British School at Rome* 4). London.

Christie, N. and Daniels, C.M. (1991) Santa Cornelia: the excavation of an early medieval papal estate and a medieval monastery. In N. Christie (ed.), *Three South Etrurian Churches: Santa Cornelia, Santa Rufina and San Liberato* (*Archaeological Monographs of the British School at Rome* 4): 1-209. London.

Christie, N., Gibson, S. and Ward-Perkins, J.B. (1991) San Liberato: a medieval church near Bracciano. In N. Christie (ed.), *Three South Etrurian Churches: Santa Cornelia, Santa Rufina and San Liberato* (*Archaeological Monographs of the British School at Rome* 4): 313-52. London.

Ciampoltrini, G. (1993) La falce del guerriero, e altri appunti per la Tuscia fra VI e VII secolo. *Archeologia medievale* 20: 595-606.

Cianfriglia, L. *et al.* (1990) Roma. Via Portuense, angolo via G. Belluzzo – indagine su alcuni resti di monumenti sepolcrali. *Notizie degli scavi di antichità*: 37-154.

Ciarrocchi, B. (1993) Pianabella (Ostia Antica). Area 3000. In L. Paroli and P. Delogu (eds), *La storia economica di Roma nell'alto medioevo alla luce dei recenti scavi archeologici*: 215-19. Florence.

CIL = Corpus Inscriptionum Latinarum

Ciotola, A., Picciola, S., Santangeli Valenzani, R. and Volpe, R. (1989) Roma: tre contesti. 1. Via Nova-Clivo Palatino. 2. Crypta Balbi. 3. Via Sacra-Via Nova. In *Amphores romaines et histoire économique, dix ans de recherche* (*Collection de l'Ecole Française de Rome* 114): 604-7.

Cipriano, M.T., Paroli, L., Patterson, H., Saguì, L. and Whitehouse, D. (1991) La documentazione ceramica dell'Italia centro-meridionale nell'alto medioevo: quadri regionali contesti campioni. In *A ceramica medieval no Mediterraneo ocidental* (*Atti del IV Congresso Internazionale*): 99-122. Mertola.

Claridge, A. (1988a) Roman statuary and the supply of statuary marble. In J.C. Fant (ed.), *Ancient Marble Quarrying and Trade* (BAR International Series 453): 139-52. Oxford.

Claridge, A. (1988b) La scultura romana. In T.W. Potter and A.C. King, Scavi alla Mola di Monte Gelato, presso Mazzano Romano, Etruria meridionale: primo rapporto preliminare: 291-4. *Archeologia medievale* 15: 253-311.

Clark, G. (1984) La fauna. In F. Cameron, G. Clark, R. Jackson, C. Johns, S. Philpot, T. Potter, J. Shepherd, M. Stone and D. Whitehouse, Il castello di Ponte Nepesino e il confine settentrionale del Ducato di Roma: 127-42. *Archeologia medievale* 11: 63-147.

Clark, G. (1987a) Stock economies in medieval Italy: a critical review of the archaeozoological evidence. *Archeologia medievale* 14: 7-26.

Clark, G. (1987b) Faunal remains and economic complexity. *Archaeozoologia. Revue Internationale d'Archéozoologie* 1 (1): 183-94.

Clark, G. (1989) Faunal remains: faunal remains and historical archaeology; large mammals: discussion; conclusions. In G. Clark, L. Costantini, A. Finetti, J. Giorgi, A. Jones, D. Reese, S. Sutherland and D. Whitehouse, The food refuse of an affluent urban household in the late fourteenth century: faunal and botanical remains from the Palazzo Vitelleschi, Tarquinia (Viterbo): 204-32, 241-5, 255-79, 294-6, 302-18. *Papers of the British School at Rome* 57: 200-321.

Clark, G. (forthcoming) The faunal remains from Colle Castellano. In S. Coccia (ed.), Excavations at Colle Castellano. In R. Hodges (ed.), *San Vincenzo al Volturno 4.*

Clegg, E.J. (1978) *The Study of Man. An Introduction to Human Biology* (second edition). London.

CNI = Corpus Nummorum Italicorum, vol. XV (1934). Rome.

Coarelli, F. (1993) I luci del Lazio: la documentazione archeologica. In *Les bois sacrés* (*Collection du Centre Jean Bérard* 10): 45-52. Naples.

Coccia, S. (1993) Il "Portus Romae" fra tarda antichità ed altomedioevo. In L. Paroli and P. Delogu (eds), *La storia economica di Roma nell'alto medioevo alla luce dei recenti scavi archeologici*: 117-200. Florence.

Cochet, A. and Hansen, J. (1986) *Conduites et objets de plomb Gallo-Romains de Vienne (Isère)* (*Gallia Suppl.* 66). Paris.

Codex Carolinus = W. Gundlach (ed.) (1892) *Codex Carolinus* (*MGH-Epistolae* III). Berlin.

Coleman, M. and Walker, S. (1979) Stable isotope identification of Greek and Turkish marbles. *Archaeometry* 21: 107-12.

Collectio Canonum = P. Martinucci (ed.) (1869) *Le "Collectio Canonum" del cardinale Deusdedit*. Venetiis.

Collette, B.B. and Nauen, C.E. (1983) *FAO Species Catalogue Vol. 2: Scombrids of the World* (*FAO Fisheries Synopsis* 125). Rome, United Nations Development Programme.

Comstock, M. and Vermeule, C. (1971) *Greek, Etruscan and Roman Bronzes in the Museum of Fine Art, Boston*. Boston.

Comstock, M. and Vermeule, C. (1976) *Sculpture in Stone. The Greek, Roman and Etruscan Collections of the Museum of Fine Arts Boston*. Boston.

Conheeney, J.M. (forthcoming a) Ph.D. thesis on periodontal disease in archaeological populations.

Conheeney, J.M. (forthcoming b) The human bone in the Priory of St Mary Spital.

Conspectus = E. Ettlinger (ed.) (1990) *Conspectus formarum terrae sigillatae italico modo confectae.* Bonn.

Conti, S. (1980) *Le sedi umane abbandonate nel Patrimonio di S. Pietro* (*Commissione per la geografia storica delle sedi umane in Italia* 5). Florence.

Cook, R.M. (1972) *Greek Painted Pottery* (second edition). London.

Coppi, A. (1847) *L'album. Giornale letterario di belle arti* XIV. Rome.

Corbet, G.B. and Ovenden, D.W. (1980) *The Mammals of Britain and Europe.* London.

Corpus Ravenna = (1968-9) *Corpus della scultura paleocristiana bizantina ed altomedioevale di Ravenna,* 3 vols. Rome.

Cortonesi, A. (1988) *Terre e signori nel Lazio medioevale. Un economia rurale nei secoli XIII- XIV.* Naples.

Costantini, L., Costantini, L., Napolitano, G. and Whitehouse, D. (1983) Cereali e legumi medievali provenienti dalle mura di Santo Stefano, Anguillara Sabazia (Roma). *Archeologia medievale* 10: 393-414.

Cotton, M.A. (1979) *The Late Republican Villa at Posto, Francolise.* London.

Cotton, M.A. and Métraux, G.P.R. (1985) *The San Rocco Villa at Francolise.* London.

Cotton, M.A., Wheeler, M. and Whitehouse, D.B. (1991) Santa Rufina: a Roman and medieval site in south Etruria. In N. Christie (ed.), *Three South Etrurian Churches: Santa Cornelia, Santa Rufina and San Liberato* (*Archaeological Monographs of the British School at Rome* 4): 211-312. London.

Coudray, J. (1951) Fours à chaux gallo-romains de Saint-Martin-du-Tertre (Yonne). *Revue Archéologique de l'Est et du Centre-Est* 2: 196-9.

Coulon, G. and Fauduet, I. (1991) Un manche d'eventail en ivoire à *Argentomagus* (Saint-Marcel, Indre). *Gallia* 48: 337-43.

Coulston, J.C. and Phillips, E.J. (1988) *Corpus Signorum Imperii Romani* I.6. Oxford.

Cozza, L. (1972) Appendice. Storia della carta archeologica d'Italia (1881-1897). In G.F. Gamurrini, A. Cozza, A. Pasqui and R. Mengarelli, *Carta archeologica d'Italia (1881-1897). Materiali per l'Etruria e la Sabina* (*Forma Italiae* II, 1): 429-59. Florence.

Cozza, L. (1981) *Carta archeologica d'Italia. Materiale per l'agro falisco. By A. Cozza and A. Pasqui* (*Forma Italia* II, 2). Florence.

Craig, H. (1957) Isotopic standards for carbon and oxygen and correction factors for mass spectrometric analysis of CO2. *Geochim.Cosmochim.Acta* 12: 133-49.

Craig, H. and Craig, V. (1972) Greek marbles: determination of provenance by isotopic analysis. *Science* 176: 401-3.

Crozzoili Aite, L. (1981) I tre templi del Foro Olitorio. *Memorie della Pontificia accademia romana di archeologia* ser. III, vol. 13.

Crummy, N. (1983) *The Roman Small Finds from Excavations in Colchester, 1971-9.* Colchester.

CSA = Corpus della scultura altomedievale (1959-). Spoleto.

Cubberley, A.L., Lloyd, J.A. and Roberts, P.C. (1988) *Testa* and *clibani*: the baking covers of classical Italy. *Papers of the British School at Rome* 56: 98-119.

Cunliffe, B. (1988) *Mount Batten, Plymouth. A Prehistoric and Roman Port.* Oxford.

Curle, J. (1911) *A Roman Frontier Post and its People: the Fort of Newstead in the Parish of Melrose.* Glasgow.

Dain, A. (1933) *Inscriptions grecques du Musée du Louvre.* Paris.

Daremberg, C. and Saglio, E. (1877-1919) *Dictionnaire des antiquités grecques et romaines d'après les textes et les monuments.* Paris.

D'Arms, J. (1990) The Roman *convivium* and the idea of equality. In O. Murray (ed.), *Sympotica*: 308-20. Oxford.

Davidson, G.R. (1952) *Corinth* XII. Princeton.

Davis-Weyer, C. and Emerick, J. (1984) The early sixth-century frescoes at S. Martino ai Monti in Rome. *Römisches Jahrbuch für Kunstgeschichte* 21: 1-60.

Dawes, J.D. and Magilton, J.R. (1980) *The cemetery of St Helen-on-the-Walls, Aldwark* (*The Archaeology of York. The Medieval Cemeteries* 12/1). London, Council of British Archaeology.

De Caro, S. (1987) Villa rustica in località Petraro (Stabiae). *Rivista dell'Istituto nazionale d'archeologia e storia dell'arte* ser. III, 10: 5-89.

De Francesco, D. (1990) Le donazioni costantiniane nell'Agro Romano. *Vetera christianorum* 27: 47-75.

De Vos, A. and De Vos, M. (1982) *Pompei, Ercolano, Stabia* (*Guide archeologiche Laterza*). Rome/Bari.

De' Crescenzi, P. (1310) *Liber Ruralium* (translated as *Trattato della Agricoltura*). Milan.

Del Chiaro, M.A. (1989) A new late republican-early imperial villa at Campo della Chiesa, Tuscany. *Journal of Roman Archaeology* 2: 111-16.

Del Chiaro, M.A. (1990) Second interim report on the excavation of a Roman villa in Tuscany. *Journal of Roman Archaeology* 3: 155-8.

DeLaine, J. (1992) New models, old modes: continuity and change in the design of public baths. In H. von Hersberg, H.J. Schalles and P. Zanker (eds), *Die Römische Städt im 2. Jahrhundert n. Chr.: Der Funkionswandel des öffentlichen Raumes (Xantener Berichte* 2): 257-76. Xanten.

Delogu, P. (1988) The rebirth of Rome in the eighth and ninth centuries. In R. Hodges and B. Hobley (eds), *The Rebirth of Towns in the West, AD 700-1050 (Council of British Archaeology Research Report* 68): 32-42. London, Council for British Archaeology.

Dennis, G. (1878) *The Cities and Cemeteries of Etruria* (second edition). London.

De Rossi, G.B. De (1870) Di un'insigne epigrafe di donazione di fondi fatta alla chiesa di S. Susanna da parte del papa Sergio I. *Bullettino di archeologia cristiana*: 89-115.

Desio, A. (1973) *Geologia dell'Italia*. Turin.

Desse, J. and Desse-Berset, N. (1994) Osteometry and fishing strategies at Cape Andreas Kastros (Cyprus, 8th millennium BP). In W. Van Neer (ed.), *Fish Exploitation in the Past (Proceedings of the Seventh Meeting of the ICAZ Fish Remains Working Group / Annales du Musée Royal de l'Afrique Centrale, Sciences Zoologiques* 274): 69-79. Tervuren.

Desse-Berset, N. (1994) Sturgeons of the Rhône during protohistory in Arles (6th-2nd century BC). In W. Van Neer (ed.), *Fish Exploitation in the Past (Proceedings of the Seventh Meeting of the ICAZ Fish Remains Working Group / Annales du Musée Royal de l'Afrique Centrale, Sciences Zoologiques* 274): 81-90. Tervuren.

Di Vita, A. (1955) L'afrodite pudica da Punta delle Sabbie. *Archeologia classica* 7: 9-23.

Dix, B. (1981) A suggested reading of the word *fortax*. *Classical Philology* 76: 52-3.

Dix, B. (1982) The manufacture of lime and its uses in the western Roman provinces. *Oxford Journal of Archaeology* 1 (3): 331-45.

Dosi, A. and Schnell, F. (1984) *A tavola con i Romani antichi*. Rome.

Driesch, A. von den (1976) *A Guide to the Measurement of Animal Bones from Archaeological Sites*. Cambridge, Mass.

Driesch, A. von den and Boessneck, J. (1974) Kritische Anmerkungen zur Widerristhöhenberechnung aus Längenmassen vor- und frühgeschichtlicher Tierknochen. *Säugertierkundliche Mitteilungen* 22: 325-48.

Driver, J.C. (1982) Medullary bone as an indicator of sex in birds remains from archaeological sites. In B. Wilson, C. Grigson and S. Payne (eds), *Ageing and Sexing Animal Bones from Archaeological Sites* (BAR British Series 109): 251-4. Oxford.

Duchesne, L. (1973) Le sedi episcopali dell'antico ducato di Roma. *Scripta Minora. Études de topographie romaine et de géographie écclesiastique (Collection de l'Ecole Française de Rome* 13): 409-37.

Dumitraşcu, S. (1973) *Tezaurul de la Tăuteni-Bihor*. Bucharest.

Dunbabin, K.M.T. (1991) Triclinium and stibadium. In W.J. Slater (ed.), *Dining in a Classical Context*: 121-48. Ann Arbor.

Dunbabin, K.M.T. (1995) Scenes from the Roman *convivium: frigida non derit, non derit calda petenti*. In O. Murray and M. Tecuşan (eds), *In Vino Veritas*: 252-65. London.

Duncan, G.C. (1964) A Roman pottery near Sutri. *Papers of the British School at Rome* 32: 38-88.

Duncan, G.C. (1965) Roman Republican pottery from the vicinity of Sutri. *Papers of the British School at Rome* 33: 134-76.

Duncan-Jones, R.P. (1980) Length-units in Roman town planning. *Britannia* 11: 127-33.

Dyson, S.L. (1976) *Cosa: The Utilitarian Pottery (Memoirs of the American Academy at Rome* 34).

Emery, W.B. and Kirawn, L.P. (1938) *The Royal Tombs of Ballana and Qustul*. London.

Eydoux, H.P. (1962) *La France antique*. Paris.

Fabbricotti, E. (1976) I bagni nelle prime ville romane. *Cronache pompeiane* 2: 29-111.

Famà, M.L. (1985a) Elementi e rifiniture di infissi e di mobili: metallo. In A. Ricci (ed.), *Settefinestre. Una villa schiavistica nell'Etruria romana. 2. La villa e i suoi reperti*: 51-8. Modena.

Famà, M.L. (1985b) Oggetti per scrittura, culto, toilette, ornamento, farmacia e gioco. Metallo. In A. Ricci (ed.), *Settefinestre. Una villa schiavistica nell'Etruria romana. 2. La villa e i suoi reperti*: 233-40. Modena.

Famà, M.L. (1985c) Strumenti da lavoro domestico. Osso. In A. Ricci (ed.), *Settefinestre. Una villa schiavistica nell'Etruria romana. 2. La villa e i suoi reperti*: 69-71. Modena.

Famà, M.L. (1985d) Oggetti per scrittura, culto, toilette, ornamento, farmacia e gioco. Vetro. In A. Ricci (ed.), *Settefinestre. Una villa schiavistica nell'Etruria romana. 2. La villa e i suoi reperti*: 222-33. Modena.

Fentress, E., Clay, T., Hobart, M. and Webb, M. (1991) Late Roman and medieval Cosa: the Arx and the structure near the eastern height. *Papers of the British School at Rome* 59: 197-230.

Ferembach, D., Schwidetzky, I. and Stloukal, M. (1980) Recommendations for age and sex diagnoses of skeletons. *Journal of Human Evolution* 9: 517-49.

Fiesole = (1990) *Archeologia urbana a Fiesole, lo scavo di Via Marini-Via Portigiani.* Florence.

Finnegan, M. (1978) Non-metric variation in the infra-cranial skeleton. *Journal of Anatomy* 125: 23-37.

Fiocchi Nicolai, V. (1988) *I cimiteri paleocristiani del Lazio:* I. *Etruria meridionale.* Rome.

Fiocchi Nicolai, V. (1988-89) Scoperta della basilica di S. Ilario "ad bivium" presso Valmontone. *Rendiconti della Pontificia accademia romana di archeologia* 61: 71-102.

Fisch, T.G. and Toll, N.P. (1949) *The Excavations at Dura Europos. Final Report.* IV. Part IV. Fasc. I. *The Bronze Objects.* New Haven.

Francovich, R. and Noyè, G. (eds) (1994) *La storia dell'alto medioevo italiano (VI-X secolo) alla luce dell'archeologia.* Florence.

Fraser, P.M. and Matthews, E. (eds) (1987) *A Lexicon of Greek Personal Names* I. Oxford.

Frederiksen, M.W. and Ward-Perkins, J.B. (1957) The ancient road systems of the central and northern Ager Faliscus. *Papers of the British School at Rome* 25: 67-208.

Freed, J. (1982) *The Late Roman Pottery from San Giovanni di Ruoti and its Implications.* Unpublished Ph.D. thesis, Department of Classics, University of Alberta.

Freed, J. (1989) Late stamped Dressel 2/3 amphoras from a deposit dated post 200 AD at villa site 10 on the Via Gabina. In *Amphores romaines et histoire économique, dix ans de recherche (Collection de l'Ecole Française de Rome* 114): 616-17.

Frenz, H.G. (1985) *Römisch Grabreliefs in Mittel- und Süditalien.* Rome.

Frova, A. (1973) *Scavi di Luni.* Rome.

Fulford, M.G. and Peacock, D.P.S. (1984) *Excavations at Carthage: the British Mission* I, 2. Sheffield.

Gancarz, A.J. (1970) *Geology of the Volcanic Rocks of the Treia River Valley, Italy.* Unpublished B.A. dissertation, Princeton University.

Garcea, F., Miragllia, G. and Soricelli, G. (1985) Uno scarico di età Adrianea-Antonina da Cratere Senga (Pozzuoli). *Puteoli. Studi di storia antica* 7-8: 245-85.

Gazzetti, G. (1992) *Il territorio capenate.* Rome.

Gessner, A. (1907) Römischer Kalkbrennofen bei Brugg. *Anzeiger für Schweizerische Altertumskunde* 9: 313.

Gilbert, B.M. and McKern, T.W. (1973) A method for ageing the female os pubis. *American Journal of Physical Anthropology* 38: 31-8.

Gilliver, C.M. (1990) A *mercator bovarius* from Veii in a new inscription from the Mola di Monte Gelato. *Papers of the British School at Rome* 58: 193-6.

Ginatempo, M. (1988) Corpi e uomini tra scienze e storia: studi di osteo-archeologia umana per l'Italia medievale. *Archeologia medievale* 15: 7-64.

Giorgi, J. (1989a) *The Plant Remains from Montarrenti.* Unpublished M.Sc. dissertation, Department of Archaeology and Prehistory, University of Sheffield.

Giorgi, J. (1989b) *The Plant Remains from the Piazza Centro d'Italia, Rieti.* Unpublished report.

Giorgi, J. (1991) *The Plant Remains from the Regia Vesta, the Forum, Rome.* Unpublished report.

Giovenale, G.B. (1927) *La basilica di Santa Maria in Cosmedin (Monografie sulle chiese di Roma* 2). Rome.

Goudineau, C. (1970) Note sur la céramique à engobe rouge-Pompeien. *Melanges de l'Ecole Française de Rome. Antiquité* 82: 159-86.

Grassinger, D. (1991) *Römische Marmorkratere (Monumenta Artis Romanae* X). Mainz.

Gregorii Magni Papae = P. Ewald and L.M. Hartmann (eds) (1887-99) *Gregorii Magni Papae Registrum Epistolarum (MGH-Epistolae* I and II). Berlin.

Grierson, P. and Blackburn, M. (1986) *Medieval European Coinage 1: the Early Middle Ages (5th-10th centuries).* Cambridge.

Guidoboni, E. (ed.) (1989) *I terramoti prima del mille in Italia e nell'area mediterranea.* Bologna, Istituto nazionale di geofisica (SGA Storia-geofisica-ambiente).

Guyon, J. (1987) *Le cimetère aux Deux Lauriers: recherches sur les catacombes romaines (Bibliothèque des Ecoles Françaises d'Athènes et Rome* 264). Rome.

Guzzo, P.G. (1970) Sacrofano – ponte romana in località Fontana Nuova. *Notizie degli scavi di antichità:* 330-44.

Hagen, W. (1937) Kaiserzeitliche Gagatarbeiten aus dem rheinischen Germanischen. *Bonner Jahrbucher* 142: 77-144.

Hansen, P.A. (1976) Piethecusan humour. The interpretation of 'Nestor's cup' reconsidered. *Glotta* 54: 25-43.

Harcourt, R.A. (1974) The dog in prehistoric and early historic Britain. *Journal of Archaeological Science* 1: 151-75.

Harden, D.B. (1935) Romano-Syrian glasses with mould-blown inscriptions. *Journal of Roman Studies* 20: 163-86.

Harden, D.B. (1944-5) Two tomb-groups of the first century AD from Yahmour, Syria, and a supplement to the list of Romano-Syrian glasses with mould-blown inscriptions. *Syria* 24: 81-95 + plates.

Harden, D.B., Hellenkemper, H., Painter, K. and Whitehouse, D. (1987) *Glass of the Caesars*. Milan.

Harrison, G.A., Weiner, J.S., Tanner, J.M. and Barnicott, N.A. (1983) *Human Biology. An Introduction to Human Evolution, Variation, Growth and Ecology* (second edition). Oxford.

Hartmann, L.H. (1895-1901) *Ecclesiae S. Mariae in Via Lata, Tabularium*. Vienna.

Haseloff, A. (1930) *Pre-Romanesque Sculpture in Italy*. Florence.

Hayes, J.W. (1972) *Late Roman Pottery*. London.

Hayes, J.W. (1980) *Supplement of Late Roman Pottery*. London.

Hayes, J.W. (1983) The Villa Dionysus excavations, Knossos: the pottery. *Annual of the British School at Athens* 78: 97-169.

Hayes, J.W. (1985) Sigillate orientali. In *Atlante delle forme ceramiche* II. *Enciclopedia dell'arte antica*: 1-96. Rome.

Hayes, J.W. (1991) *Paphos* III. *The Hellenistic and Roman Pottery*. Nicosia.

Healy, J.F. (1978) *Mining and Metallurgy in the Greek and Roman World*. London.

Hencken, H.O.'N. (1950) Lagore Crannog: an Irish royal residence of the 7th-10th centuries AD. *Proceedings of the Royal Irish Academy* 53: 1-247.

Henig, M. (1983) *The Handbook of Roman Art*. Oxford.

Higginbotham, J.A. (1991) *Artificial Fishponds in Roman Italy during the Late Republic and Early Empire*. Unpublished Ph.D. thesis, University of Michigan.

Higginbotham, J.A. (forthcoming) *Piscinae: Artificial Fishponds in Roman Italy*. Princeton.

Hillman, G. (1981) Reconstructing crop husbandry practices from charred remains of crops. In R. Mercer (ed.), *Farming Practice in British Prehistory*: 123-62. Edinburgh.

Hillson, S. (1986) *Teeth*. Cambridge.

Hochuli Guysel, A. (1977) *Kleinasiatische Glasierte Reliefkeramik* (*Acta Bernensia* VII). Bern.

Hodges, R. (1988) Aspects of the decline and fall of the Roman Empire (Review of A. Giardina (ed.) (1986), *SRIT* III: le merci, gli insediamenti). *Journal of Roman Archaeology* 1: 215- 20.

Hodges, R. (ed.) (1993) *San Vincenzo al Volturno* 1. *The 1980-86 Excavations Part I* (*Archaeological Monographs of the British School at Rome* 7). London.

Hodges, R. (ed.) (1995) *San Vincenzo al Volturno* 2. *The 1980-86 Excavations Part II* (*Archaeological Monographs of the British School at Rome* 9). London.

Immerwahr, H.R. (1990) *Attic Script*. Oxford.

IPU (Istituto di Paleontologia Umana) (1968) Reperti osteologici e malacologici. In A. Carandini *et al., Ostia* (*Studi Miscellanei* 13): 122-4.

IPU (Istituto di Paleontologia Umana) (1970) Reperti osteologici e malacologici. In A. Carandini *et al., Ostia* II (*Studi Miscellanei* 16): 158.

IPU (Istituto di Paleontologia Umana) (1973) Reperti osteologici e malacologici. In A. Carandini *et al., Ostia* III (*Studi Miscellanei* 21): 649-50.

IPU (Istituto di Paleontologia Umana) (1977) Reperti osteologici e malacologici. In A. Carandini *et al., Ostia* IV (*Studi Miscellanei* 23): 275, 393-4.

Jackson, D.A., Biek, L. and Dix, B.F. (1973) A Roman lime kiln at Weekley, Northants. *Britannia* 4: 128-40.

Jackson, R.P.J. (forthcoming) The metalwork. In W.M. Widrig *et al., The Via Gabina Villas*.

Jacobi, L. (1897) *Das Römerkastell Saalburg*. Homburg.

Jashemski, W.F. (1979) *The Gardens of Pompeii, Herculaneum and the Villas Destroyed by Vesuvius*. New Rochelle.

Jeffery, L.H. (1990) *Local Scripts of Archaic Greece* (second edition, revised by A.W. Johnston). London.

Johnston, F.E. (1962) Growth of the long bones of infants and young children at Indian Knoll. *American Journal of Physical Anthropology* 20: 249-54.

Johnston, F.E. and Zimmer, L.O. (1989) Assessment of growth and age in the immature skeleton. In M.Y. Iscan and K.A.R. Kennedy (eds), *Reconstruction of Life from the Skeleton*: 11-21. New York.

Jones, A.H.M. (1973) *The Later Roman Empire 284-602*. Oxford.

Jones, G.D.B. (1963) Capena and the Ager Capenas, part II. *Papers of the British School at Rome* 31: 100-58.

Jones, M.K. (1985) I resti vegetali. In A. Carandini (ed.) (1985) *Settefinestre: una villa schiavistica nell'Etruria romana* II: 306-9. Modena.

Jones, P. (1966) Italy. Medieval agrarian society in its prime. In M. Postan (ed.), *The Agrarian History of the Middle Ages*: 341-431. Cambridge.

Joulin, L. (1901) *Les établissements gallo-romaines de la plaine de Martres-Tolosanes*. Paris.

Jourdan, L. (1976) *La faune du site gallo-romain et paléo-chrétien de la Bourse (Marseille)*. Paris.

Kahane, A., Murray Threipland, L. and Ward-Perkins, J.B. (1968) The Ager Veientanus, north and east of Rome. *Papers of the British School at Rome* 36.

Kammerer-Grothaus, H. (1974) Der Deus Ridiculus im Triopion des Herodes Atticus. Untersuchung am Bau und zu polychromer Ziegelarchitektur des 2 Jahrhunderts nach Christ in Latium. *Mitteilungen des Deutschen Archäologischen Instituts, Römische Abteilung* 81: 131-252.

Kapossy, B. (1969) *Brunnenfiguren der Hellenistichen und Römischen Zeit*. Zurich.

Kautzsch, R. (1939) Die römische Schmuckkunst in Stein vom 6. bis zum 10. Jahrhundert. *Römisches Jahrbuch für Kunstgeschichte* 3: 1-73.

Kehr, P.F. (1907) *Italia Pontificia* II, *Latium*. Berlin.

Kelley, M.A. (1979) Parturition and pelvic changes. *American Journal of Physical Anthropology* 44: 489-506.

Kenrick, P.M. (1985) *Excavations at Sidi Khrebish, Benghazi (Berenice)*. Vol III part 1. *The Fine Pottery*. Tripoli and London.

King, A.C. (1985) I resti animali: i mammiferi, i rettili e gli anfibi. In A. Ricci (ed.), *Settefinestre. Una villa schiavistica nell'Etruria romana. 2. La villa e i suoi reperti*: 278-300. Modena.

King, A.C. (1990) Animal bones. In E. Fentress (ed.), *Fouilles de Sétif 1977-1984 (Supplément à Bulletin de l'Archéologie Algérienne* 5): 247-58.

King, A.C. (1994) Mammiferi. In P. Arthur (ed.), *Il complesso archeologico di Carminiello ai Mannesi, Napoli (scavi 1983-1984)*: 367-406. Galatina.

King, A.C. (forthcoming a) Mammals. In W. Jashemski (ed.), *The Natural History of Pompeii*.

King, A.C. (forthcoming b) The mammal bones. In S. Keay *et al.*, *Report on Surface Survey and Excavations at the Site of Ancient Celti (La Vina, Penaflor) 1987-1992*.

King, A.C. (n.d. a) Mammal bones from the 'impianta elletrica' excavations at Pompeii, 1980-81. Unpublished bone report for P. Arthur.

King, A.C. (n.d. b) Mammal bones from Naples, Girolomini site. Unpublished bone report for P. Arthur.

King, A.C. (n.d. c) Mammal bones from Naples, Sta Patrizia. Uunpublished bone report for P. Arthur.

King, A.C. and Potter, T.W. (1990) A new domestic building façade from Roman Britain. *Journal of Roman Archaeology* 3: 195-204.

King, N. (1993) An archaeological field survey near Campagnano di Roma, southern Etruria. *Papers of the British School at Rome* 61: 115-24.

Kleiner, D.G. (1977) *Roman Republican Group Portraiture*. Ann Arbor.

Kockel, V. (1993) *Porträtreliefs Stadtrömischer Grabbauten. Ein Beitrag zur Geschichte und zum Verständnis des Spätrepublikanisch-frühkaiserzeitlichen Privatporträts*. Mainz.

Kraus, T. and von Matt, L. (1975) *Pompeii and Herculaneum. The Living Cities of the Dead*. New York.

Krautheimer, R. (1980) *Rome. Profile of a City, 312-1308*. Princeton.

Kutzli, R. (1974) *Langobardische Kunst*. Stuttgart.

Lamboglia, N. (1950) *Gli scavi di Albintimilium e la cronologia della ceramica romana. 1 Campagne di scavo 1938-1940*. Bordighera.

Lamboglia, N. (1958) Nuove osservazioni sulla "terra sigillata chiara". *Rivista di studi liguri* 24: 257-330.

Lamboglia, N. (1963) Nuove osservazioni sulla "terra sigillata chiara". *Rivista di studi liguri* 29: 145-212.

Lang, M. (1976) *Graffiti and Dipinti (Athenian Agora* XXI). Princeton.

Laplace, G. (1964) Les subdivisions du Leptolithique italien. Etude de typologie analytique. *Bullettino di paletnologia italiana* n.s. 73: 25-63.

Laubenheimer, F. (1985) *La production des amphores en Gaule Narbonnaise sous le Haut-Empire*. Paris.

Leese, M.N. (1988) Statistical treatment of stable isotope data. In N. Herz and M. Waelkens (eds), *Classical Marble: Geochemistry, Technology, Trade*: 347-54. Kluwer, Dordrecht.

LeGall, O. (1994) Quelques remarques sur l'adaptation à court et à long termes chez les poissons d'eau douce du sud de la France. In W. Van Neer (ed.), *Fish Exploitation in the Past (Proceedings of the Seventh Meeting of the ICAZ Fish Remains Working Group / Annales du Musée Royal de l'Afrique Centrale, Sciences Zoologiques* 274): 91-8. Tervuren.

Leggio, T. (1989) Forme di insediamento in Sabina e nel Reatino nel medioevo. Alcune considerazioni. *Bollettino dell'Istituto storico italiano e archivio muratoriano* 95: 165-202.

Leggio, T., Barker G., Moreland J., Clark G. and Giorgi J. (1988) Insediamento altomedievale ed uso della terra nei dintorni di Farfa: approccio storico archeologico. *Archeologia laziale* 9: 424-31.

Levi, D. (1935) Ruderi di edifici romane presso Massaciuccoli. *Notizie degli scavi di antichità*: 211-28.

Liber Pontificalis = L. Duchesne (1887/1957) *Le Liber Pontificalis*. Paris/Rome.

Liversidge, J. (1968) *Britain in the Roman Empire*. London.

Llewellyn, P. (1983) *Rome in the Dark Ages* (second edition). London.

Llewellyn, P. (1991) The historical record: the bishopric of *Silva Candida* at S. Rufina. In N. Christie (ed.) (1991), *Three South Etrurian Churches: Santa Cornelia, Santa Rufina and San Liberato* (*Archaeological Monographs of the British School at Rome* 4): 214-23. London.

Lloyd-Morgan, G. (1981) *Description of the Collections in the Rijksmuseum G.M. Kam at Nijmegen. IX. The Mirrors.* Nijmegen.

Loeschcke, S. (1919) *Lampen aus Vindonissa.* Zürich.

Lopez Mullor, A. (1989) *Las ceramicas romanas de paredas finas en Cataluna.* Zaragoza.

Lovejoy, C.O., Burstein, A.H. and Heiple, K.G. (1976) The biomechanical analysis of bone strength: a method and its application to platycnemia. *American Journal of Physical Anthropology* 44: 489-506.

Lovejoy, C.O. Meindl, R.S. and Mensforth, R.P. (1985) Multifactorial determination of skeletal age at death; a method and blind tests of its accuracy. *American Journal of Physical Anthropology* 68: 1-14.

LRBC = R.A.G. Carson, P.V. Hill and J.P.C. Kent (1960) *Late Roman Bronze Coinage.* London.

Lugli, G. (1957) *La tecnica edilizia romana.* Rome.

Luni I = (1973) *Scavi di Luni I. Relazione preliminare della campagna di scavo 1970-1971.* Rome.

Luni II = (1977) *Scavi di Luni II. Relazione delle campagne di scavo 1972-1974.* Rome.

Lupu, N. (1937) La Villa dei Sette Bassi sulla Via Latina. *Ephemeris Dacoromana*: 117-88.

Maccabruni, C. (1987) Ceramica romana con invetriatura al piombo. In P. Lévêque and J-P. Morel (eds), *Ceramiques hellénistiques et romaines* II: 167-89. Paris.

Macchiarella, G. (1976) Note sulla scultura in marmo a Roma tra VIII e IX secolo. *Roma e l'età Carolingia*: 289-99. Rome.

Macchiarola, I. (1989) Il sepolcreto sannitico di Gildone. *Conoscenze* 5: 37-79.

MacDougall, E.B. and Jashemski, W.F. (1981) *Ancient Roman Gardens.* Dumbarton Oaks.

MacGregor, A. (1985) *Bone, Antler, Ivory and Horn.* London.

Maioli, M.G. (1983) La ceramica invetriata. In G. Bermond Montanari (ed.), *Ravenna e il porto di Classe. Vent'anni di ricerche archeologiche tra Ravenna e Classe*: 113-17. Imola.

Mallett, M. and Whitehouse, D.B. (1967) Castel Porciano: an abandoned medieval village of the Roman Campagna. *Papers of the British School at Rome* 35: 113-46.

Manacorda, D., Paroli, L., Molinari, A., Ricci, M. and Romei, D. (1986) La ceramica medioevale di Roma nella stratigrafia della Crypta Balbi. In *La ceramica medievale nel Mediterraneo occidentale* (*Atti del III Congresso Internazionale*): 511-44. Florence.

Manchester, K. (1983) *The Archaeology of Disease.* Bradford.

Mango, C. (1972) *The Art of the Byzantine Empire, 312-1453* (*Sources and Documents in the History of Art*). Englewood Cliffs.

Manning, W.H. (1966) A hoard of Romano-British ironwork from Brampton, Cumberland. *Transactions of the Cumberland and Westmorland Antiquarian and Archaeological Society* 66: 1-36.

Manning, W.H. (1983) The cauldron chains of Iron Age and Roman Britain. In B. Hartley and J. Wacher (eds), *Rome and her Northern Provinces*: 132-54. Gloucester.

Manning, W.H. (1985) *Catalogue of the Romano-British Iron Tools, Fittings and Weapons in the British Museum.* London.

Marabini Moevs, M.T. (1973) *The Roman Thin Walled Pottery from Cosa* (*Memoirs of the American Academy at Rome* 32). Rome.

Marazzi, F. (1988a) L'insediamento nel suburbio di Roma fra IV e VIII secolo. Considerazioni a 80 anni dai 'Wanderings in the Roman Campagna' di R. Lanciani. *Bollettino dell'Istituto storico italiano e archivio muratoriano* 94: 256-313.

Marazzi, F. (1988b) Inquadramentro storico del sito di Mola di Monte Gelato: suoi legami con le vicende dei possessi fondiari della Chiesa Romana nell'alto Medioevo. In T.W. Potter and A.C. King, Scavi alla Mola di Monte Gelato, presso Mazzano Romano, Etruria Meridionale: primo rapporto preliminare: 301-9. *Archeologia medievale* 15: 253-311.

Marazzi, F. (1991a) Il conflitto fra Leone III Isaurico e il papato fra il 725 e il 733, e il 'definitivo' inizio del medioevo a Roma: un'ipotesi in discussione. *Papers of the British School at Rome* 59: 231-57.

Marazzi, F. (1991b) *Il Patrimonium Sancti Petri da proprietà fondiaria a entità politica.* Thesis for a *Dottorato di Ricerca* in medieval history, *IV Ciclo*, University of Turin, 1988-91.

Marazzi, F. (1993) Roma, il Lazio, il Mediterraneo: relazioni fra economia e politica VII-IX secolo. In L. Paroli and P. Delogu (eds), *La storia economica di Roma nell'alto medioevo alla luce dei recenti scavi archeologici*: 267-85. Florence.

Marazzi, F. (1994a) Le 'città nuove' pontificie e l'insediamento laziale nel IX secolo. In R. Francovich and G. Noyé (eds), *La storia dell'alto medioevo italiano (VI-XI secolo) alla luce dell'archeologia*: 251-77. Florence.

Marazzi, F. (1994b) Proprietà fondiaria nel braccianese durante il primo medioevo (secoli VII-IX). In *Atti del convegno "Antichità tardoromane e altomedievali nel territorio di Bracciano"*: 299-314. Rome.

Marazzi, F. (in press) I "Patrimonia" laziali della chiesa romana tra IX secolo e inizi del X: strutture amministrative e prassi gestionali. *Nuova studi storici* 37.

Marazzi, F., Potter, T.W. and King, A.C. (1989) Mola di Monte Gelato (Mazzano Romano – VT): notizie preliminari sulle campagne di scavo 1986-1988 e considerazione sulle origini dell'incastellamento in Etruria meridionale alla luce dei nuovi dati archeologici. *Archeologia medievale* 16: 103-19.

Marini, G. (1805) *I papiri diplomatici*. Rome.

Martin, A. (1992a) Ceramica fine a Roma e Ostia tra la seconda metà del I e il II secolo. *Rei Cretariae* 31-2: 91-104.

Martin, A. (1992b) La ceramica invetriata romano: la testimonianza dell'area NE delle Terme del Nuotatore ad Ostia. In L. Paroli (ed.), *La ceramica invetriata tardoantica e altomedievale in Italia*: 323-9. Florence.

Martinori, E. (1930) *Via Cassia*. Rome.

Mastroroberto, M. (ed.) (1990) *Archeologia e botanica. Atti del Convegno di studi sul contributo della botanica alla conoscenza e alla conservazione delle aree archeologiche vesuviane*. Rome.

Matheson, S.B. (1980) *Ancient Glass in the Yale University Art Gallery*. Yale.

Matthiae, G. (1952) La iconostasi della chiesa di S. Leone a Capena. *Bollettino d'arte* ser. IV, no. 37: 293-9.

Mattias, P. and Ventriglia, U. (1968) *Carta geologica – regione vulcanica dei Monti Sabatini e Cimini*. Florence.

Mattias, P. and Ventriglia, U. (1970) La regione vulcanica dei Monti Sabatini e Cimini. *Memorie della Società di geologia italiana* 9: 331-84, maps.

Mayet, F. (1975) *Les céramiques à parois fines dans la peninsule Iberique*. Paris.

Mays, S.A. (1991a) *The Burials from the Whitefriars Friary Site, Buttermarket, Ipswich, Suffolk (Excavated 1986-1988)* (*Ancient Monuments Laboratory Report* 17/91).

Mays, S.A. (1991b) *The Medieval Blackfriars from the Blackfriars Friary, Ipswich, Suffolk (Excavated 1983-1985)* (*Ancient Monuments Laboratory Report* 16/91).

Mazza, M. (1986) Organizzazione produttiva e forza lavoro nell'agricultura romana di età imperiale. Premesse economiche del colonato tardoromano. In *La fatica dell'uomo. Schiavi e liberi nel mondo romano*: 119-94. Catania.

Mazzucato, O. (1972) *La ceramica a vetrina pesante*. Rome.

Mazzucato, O. (1977) *La ceramica laziale nell'altomedioevo*. Rome.

McCarthy, M.R. (1991) *Roman Waterlogged Remains at Castle Street, Carlisle*. Stroud.

McCrea, J.M. (1950) The isotopic chemistry of carbonates and a palaeotemperature scale. *Journal of Chemical Physics* 18: 849-57.

McKern, T.W. and Stewart, T.D. (1957) *Skeletal Age Changes in Young American Males* (*Technical Report for the Headquarters Quartermaster Research and Development Command (Natwick, Massachusetts)*).

McMinn, R.M.H. and Hutchings, R.T. (1977) *A Colour Atlas of Human Anatomy*. London.

Meates, G.W. (1987) *The Roman Villa at Lullingstone, Kent*. Maidstone.

Mello, E., Monna, D. and Oddone, M. (1988) Discriminating sources of Mediterranean marbles: a pattern recognition approach. *Archaeometry* 30 (1): 102-8.

MIB = W. Hahn (1973) *Moneta Imperii Byzantini* I. Vienna.

Michellucci, M. (1985) *Roselle. La domus dei mosaici*. Montepulciano.

Mielsch, H. (1987) *Die Römische Villa: Architektur und Lebensform*. Munich.

Migliario, E. (1992) Terminologia e organizzazione agraria tra tardo antico e alto medioevo: ancora su *fundus* e *casalis/casale*. *Athenaeum* 80 (2): 371-84.

Miles, A.E.W. (1978) Teeth as an indication of age in man. In P.M. Butler and K.A. Joysey (eds), *Development, Function and Evolution of Teeth*: 455-64. London.

Modzelewski, K. (1978) La transizione dall'antichità al feudalesimo. In R. Romano and C. Vivanti (eds), *Storia d'Italia 'Einaudi', Annali, 2, Dal feudalesimo al capitalismo*: 3-110. Turin.

Monacchi, D. (1990) Lugnano in Teverina (Terni). Loc. Poggio Gramignano. Saggi di scavo di una villa rustica romana. *Notizie degli scavi di antichità*: 5-36.

Montanari, M. (1989) Campagne e contadini nell'Italia bizantina (Esarcato e Pentapoli). *Mélanges de l'Ecole Française de Rome. Moyen Âge et Temps Modernes* 101 (2): 597-607.

Montanari, M. and Andreolli, B. (1983) *L'azienda curtense in Italia.* Bologna.

Moore, W.J. and Corbett, E. (1973) The distribution of dental caries. In *Ancient British Populations* (*Caries Research* 7): 139-53.

Moretti, M. (1978) *Cerveteri.* Novara.

Moretti, M. and Moretti, A.M.S. (1977) *La villa dei Volusii a Lucus Feroniae.* Rome.

Munzi, M. and Crifani, G. (1995) Considerazioni sugli insediamenti in area falisca. In N. Christie (ed.), *Papers of the Fifth Conference on Italian Archaeology:* 387-94. Oxford.

Murray, O., Parsons P., Potter, T.W. and Roberts, P. (1991) A 'stork-vase' from the Mola di Monte Gelato. *Papers of the British School at Rome* 59: 177-95.

Neumann, G. (1988) Ein späthellenistisches Tondo-Bildnis. *Athenische Mitteilungen* 103: 221-38.

Neville, R.C. (1856) Description of a remarkable deposit of Roman antiquities of iron, discovered at Great Chesterford, Essex, in 1854. *Archaeological Journal* 13: 1-13.

Nichol, R.K. and Wild, C.J. (1984) "Numbers of individuals" in faunal analysis: the decay of fish bone in archaeological sites. *Journal of Archaeological Science* 11: 35-51.

Nicholson, P.T. and Patterson, H. (1989) Ceramic technology in Upper Egypt: a study of pottery firing. *World Archaeology* 21 (1): 71-86.

Nordhagen, P.J. (1976) Un problema di carattere iconografico e tecnico a S. Prasede. *Roma e l'età Carolingia:* 159-66. Rome.

O'Connor, T.P. (1986) The garden dormouse *Eliomys quercinus* from Roman York. *Journal of Zoology* 210: 620-2.

Oliver, A. Jr (1980) *Ancient Glass in the Carnegie Museum of Natural History, Pittsburgh.* Pittsburgh.

Ortner, D.J. and Putschar, W.G.J. (1981) *Identification of Pathological Conditions in Human Skeletal Remains.* Smithsonian Institute.

Orton, C. (1975) Quantitative pottery studies: some progress, problems and prospects. *Science and Archaeology* 16: 30-5.

Orton, C. (1982) Computer simulation experiments to assess the performance of measures of quantities of pottery. *World Archaeology* 14 (1): 1-20.

Ostia I (1968) (*Studi Miscellanei* 13).

Ostia II (1970) (*Studi Miscellanei* 16).

Ostia III (1973) (*Studi Miscellanei* 21).

Ostia IV (1978) (*Studi Miscellanei* 23).

Oxé, A. and Comfort, H. (1968) *Corpus Vasorum Arretinorum.* Bonn.

Pallottino, M. (1937) Capena – resti di costruzioni romane e mediovali in località 'Montecanino'. *Notizie degli scavi di antichità:* 7-28.

Panella, C. (1968) Anfore. In *Ostia* I (*Studi Miscellanei* 13): 97-135.

Panella, C. (1973) Appunto su un gruppo di anfore della prima, media e tarda età imperiale (secoli I-IV). In *Ostia* III (*Studi Miscellanei* 21): 460-633.

Panella, C. (1986) Oriente ed occidente: considerazioni su alcune anfore "egee" di età imperiale a Ostia. In J.-Y. Empereur and Y. Garlan (eds), *Recherches sur les amphores grecques* (*BCH* Supp. XIII): 609-36.

Panella, C. (1989) Le anfore italiche del II secolo d.C. In *Amphores romaines et histoire économique, dix ans de recherche* (*Collection de l'Ecole Française de Rome* 114): 139-78.

Parker, A. (1977) Lusitanian amphoras. In *Méthodes classiques et méthodes formelles dans l'étude des amphores* (*Collection de l'Ecole Française de Rome* 32): 35-40.

Paroli, L. (1986) Ceramiche a vetrina pesante e macchie. In D. Manacorda, L. Paroli, A. Molinari, M. Ricci and D. Romei, La ceramica medioevale di Roma nella stratigrafia della Crypta Balbi: 516-20. In *La ceramica medievale nel Mediterraneo occidentale* (*Atti del III Congresso Internazionale*): 511-44. Florence.

Paroli, L. (1990) Ceramica a vetrina pesante alto-medievale (Forum ware) e medievale (Sparse glazed). Altre invetriate tardo-antiche e altomedievale. In L. Saguì and L. Paroli (eds), *Archeologia urbana a Roma: il progetto della Crypta Balbi, 5. L'esedra della Crypta Balbi nel medioevo (XI-XV secolo)*: 314-56. Florence.

Paroli, L. (1991) I laterizi. In N. Christie (ed.), *Three South Etrurian Churches: Santa Cornelia, Santa Rufina and San Liberato* (*Archaeological Monographs of the British School at Rome* 4): 152-72. London.

Paroli, L. (1992a) Ceramiche invetriate da un contesto dell'VIII secolo della Crypta Balbi, Roma. In L. Paroli (ed.), *La ceramica invetriata tardoantica e altomedievale in Italia*: 351-7. Florence.

Paroli, L. (1992b) La ceramica invetriata tardo-antica e medievale nell'Italia centro-meridionale. In L. Paroli (ed.), *La ceramica invetriata tardoantica e altomedievale in Italia*: 33-61. Florence.

Paroli, L. (1993a) Ostia nella tarda antichità e nell'alto medioevo. In L. Paroli and P. Delogu (eds), *La storia economica di Roma nell'alto medioevo alla luce dei recenti scavi archeologici*: 153-65. Florence.

Paroli, L. (1993b) Porto (Fiumicino). Area II-2000. I. In L. Paroli and P. Delogu (eds), *La storia economica di Roma nell'alto medioevo alla luce dei recenti scavi archeologici*: 231-43. Florence.

Pasquali, G. (1985) I rapporti di lavoro: resistenze e cambiamenti nelle campagne romagnole del Medioevo. In B. Andreolli, V. Fumagalli and M. Montanari (eds), *Le campagne italiane prima e dopo il mille. Una società in trasformazione*: 69-94. Bologna.

Pasqui, A. and Cozza, A. (1894) Antichità del territorio Falisco esposte nel Museo Nazionale romano a Villa Giulia. *Monumenti antichi* 4.

Pasquinucci, M. and Storti, S. (1989) *Pisa antica. Scavi nel giardino dell'Arcivescovado*. Pontedera.

Patterson, H. (1991) Early medieval and medieval pottery. In N. Christie (ed.) (1991), *Three South Etrurian Churches: Santa Cornelia, Santa Rufina and San Liberato* (*Archaeological Monographs of the British School at Rome* 4): 120-36. London.

Patterson, H. (1992) La ceramica a vetrina pesante (Forum ware) e la ceramica a vetrina sparsa da alcuni siti nella Campagna romana. In D. Manacorda, L. Paroli, A. Molinari, M. Ricci and D. Romei, La ceramica medioevale di Roma nella stratigrafia della Crypta Balbi: 529-43. In *La ceramica medievale nel Mediterraneo occidentale* (*Atti del III Congresso Internazionale*): 511-44. Florence.

Patterson, H. (1993a) Pianabella (Ostia Antica). La ceramica altomedievale. In L. Paroli and P. Delogu (eds), *La storia economica di Roma nell'alto medioevo alla luce dei recenti scavi archeologici*: 219-31. Florence.

Patterson, H. (1993b) Un'aspetto dell'economia di Roma e della Campagna romana nell'altomedioevo: l'evidenza della ceramica. In L. Paroli and P. Delogu (eds), *La storia economica di Roma nell'alto medioevo alla luce dei recenti scavi archeologici*: 309-31. Florence.

Patterson, H. and Whitehouse, D. (1992) The medieval pottery from Otranto. In F. D'Andria and D. Whitehouse (eds), *Otranto: the Excavations of the British School, Vol. II. The Finds*: 87-196. Galatina.

Patterson, J.R. (1987) Crisis: what crisis? Rural change and urban development in Imperial Appennine Italy. *Papers of the British School at Rome* 55: 115-46.

Pavolini, C. (1980a) Appunti sui 'vasetti ovoidi e piriformi' di Ostia. *Melanges de l'Ecole Française de Rome. Antiquité* 92 (2): 993-1020.

Pavolini, C. (1980b) Una produzione italica di lucerne: le Vogelkopflampen ad ansa trasversale. *Bullettino della Commissione archeologica comunale di Roma* 85: 45-134.

Pavolini, C. (1982) *Itinerari ostiensi IV. Ostia, vita quotidiana II. L'edilizia – Le attività artigianali – Il commercio*. Rome.

Payne, S. (1990) Preliminary report on the animal bones from the Palatine East excavations, Rome, 1989-90. Unpublished bone report.

Peacock, D.P.S. (1977) *Pottery and Early Commerce*. London.

Peacock, D.P.S. (1982) *Pottery in the Roman World*. London.

Peacock, D.P.S. and Williams, D.F. (1986) *Amphorae and the Roman Economy*. London.

Peduto, P. (1984) *Villaggi fluviali nella pianura Pestana del secolo VI* (*Studi storici meridionali*). Salerno.

Peña, J.T. (1987) *Roman-period Ceramic Production in Etruria Tiberina: a Geographical and Compositional Study*. Unpublished Ph.D. thesis, University of Michigan.

Peña, J.T. (1990) Internal Red-Slip cookware (Pompeian Red Ware) from Cetamura del Chianti, Italy: mineralogical composition and provenience. *American Journal of Archaeology* 94: 647-61.

Penhallurick, R.D. (1986) *Tin in Antiquity*. London.

Pensabene, P. (1985) No. IV.3: tempietto tetrastilo di Torrenova (inv. no. 121509). In A. Giuliano (ed.), *Museo nazionale romano. Le sculture: I/8.I. Aule delle terme*: 170-7. Rome.

Penteriani, U and Penteriani Iacoangeli, M.P. (1986) *Nepi e il suo territorio nell'alto Medioeveo*. Rome.

Peroni, A. (1975) *Pavia: Musei civici del castello visconteo*. Bologna.

Perrino, P. and Hammer K. (1982) *Triticum monococcum* L. and *Triticum dicoccum* Schubler (syn. of *T. dicoccon* Schrank) are still cultivated in Italy. *Genetic Agriculture* 36: 343-52.

Peters, W.J.T. (1963) *Landscape in Romano-Campanian Mural Painting*. Assen.

Peterson, R., Mountford, G. and Hollom, P.A.D. (1979) *A Field Guide to the Birds of Britain and Europe*. London.

Pettinau, B. (1984) No. XIII, 8: Acroterion. In A. Giuliano (ed.), *Museo nazionale romano. Le sculture: I/7.II. Giardino dei cinquecento*: 398-9. Rome.

Phenice, T.W. (1969) A newly developed visual method of sexing the os pubis. *American Journal of Physical Anthropology* 30: 297-302.

Picard, C. (1910) A propos de deux coupes du Vatican et d'un fragment du Musée Mircher. *Mélanges d'Archéologie et d'Histoire* 30: 99-116.

Picard, C. (1913) Questions de ceramique hellenistique. *Revue Archéologique* 22: 174-8.

Pietri, C. (1966) Le sénat, le peuple chrétien et les partis du cirque sous le pape Symmaque. *Mélanges de l'Ecole Française de Rome* 78: 123-39.

Pietri, C. (1976) *Roma Christiana* (*Bibliothèque de l'Ecole Française d'Athènes et de Rome* 224). Rome.

Pietri, C. (1978) Evergetisme et richesses ecclésiastiques dans l'Italie du IVe à la fin du Ve siècle. *Ktema* 3: 317-37.

Pietri, C. (1981) Aristocratie et societé clericale dans l'Italie chrétienne au temps de Odoacre et de Théodoric. *Mélanges de l'Ecole Française de Rome. Antiquité* 93 (1): 427-67.

Pohl, I. (1978) Piazzale delle Corporazioni. Portico ovest, saggi sotto i mosaici. *Notizie degli scavi di antichità*, supplement: 165-443.

Potter, T.W. (1972) Excavations in the medieval centre of Mazzano Romano. *Papers of the British School at Rome* 40: 135-45.

Potter, T.W. (1975) Recenti ricerche in Etruria meridionale: problemi della transizione dal tardo antico all'alto medievo. *Archeologia medievale* 2: 215-36.

Potter, T.W. (1976) *A Faliscan Town in South Etruria. Excavations at Narce 1966-71.* London.

Potter, T.W. (1979) *The Changing Landscape of South Etruria.* London.

Potter, T.W. (1985) *Storia del paesaggio dell'Etruria meridionale.* Rome.

Potter, T.W. (1991) Power, politics and territory in southern Etruria. In E. Herring, R. Whitehouse and J. Wilkins (eds), *Papers of the Fourth Conference of Italian Archaeology 2. The Archaeology of Power:* 173-84. London.

Potter, T.W. (1995) *Towns in Late Antiquity: Iol Caesarea and its Context.* Sheffield.

Potter, T.W. and Dunbabin, K.M. (1979) A Roman villa at Crocicchie, Via Clodia. *Papers of the British School at Rome* 47: 19-26.

Potter, T.W. and King, A.C. (1988) Scavi alla Mola di Monte Gelato, presso Mazzano Romano, Etruria Meridionale: primo rapporto preliminare. *Archeologia medievale* 15: 253-311.

Poulsen, F. (1914) *Tillaeg til Katalog over Ny Carlsberg Glyptoteks Antike Kunstwaerker.* Copenhagen.

Poulsen, V. (1962) *Les portraits romains* I. Copenhagen.

Prina Ricotti, E. (1988) Cibi e banchetti nell'antica Roma. *Archeo* 46: 52-97.

Provoost, A. (1976) Introduction et essai de typologie générale avec des détails concernant les lampes trouvées en Italie. *L'antiquité classique* 45: 5-39, 550-86.

Purcell, N. (1983) The *apparitores*: a study in social mobility. *Papers of the British School at Rome* 51: 125-73.

Purcell, N. (1985) Wine and wealth in ancient Italy. *Journal of Roman Studies* 75: 1-19.

Purcell, N. (1988a) Le inscrizioni. In T.W. Potter and A.C. King, Scavi alla Mola di Monte Gelato, presso Mazzano Romano, Etruria Meridionale: primo rapporto preliminare: 284-91. *Archeologia medievale* 15: 253-311.

Purcell, N. (1988b) Review of A. Carandini (ed.) (1985) *Settefinestre: una villa schiavistica nell'Etruria romana. Journal of Roman Studies* 78: 194-8.

Quilici Gigli, S. (ed.) (1990) *La Via Appia* (*Archeologia laziale* 10, 1). Rome.

Quilici, L. (1974) *Forma Italiae I.x. Collatia.* Rome.

Quilici, L. (1990) Via di S Paolo alla Regola – scavo e recupero di edifici antichi e medievali. *Notizie degli scavi di antichità*: 175-416.

Radke, G. (1981) *Viae publicae romanae.* Bologna.

Rahtz, P. (1977) Late Roman cemeteries and beyond. In R. Reece (ed.), *Burial in the Roman World* (*Council of British Archaeology Research Report* 22): 53-64. London, Council of British Archaeology.

Ramfjord, S.P., Kerr, D.A. and Ash, M.M. (1966) *World Workshop in Periodontics.* Ann Arbor, Michigan.

Rathbone, D.W. (1983) The slave mode of production in Italy. *Journal of Roman Studies* 73: 160-8.

Rebuffat, R. (1991) Vocabulaire thermal. Documents sur le bain romain. In *Les Thermes romains*: 1-34. Rome.

Reece, R. (1982) A collection of coins from the centre of Rome. *Papers of the British School at Rome* 50: 116-45.

Reece, R. (1984) The use of Roman coinage. *Oxford Journal of Archaeology* 3: 197-210.

Reece, R. (1987) *Coinage in Roman Britain.* London.

Reynolds, J.M. (1966) Inscriptions from south Etruria. *Papers of the British School at Rome* 34: 56-67.

Reynolds, J.M. (1988) Commento alle iscrizioni. In T.W. Potter and A.C. King, Scavi alla Mola di Monte Gelato, presso Mazzano Romano, Etruria Meridionale: primo rapporto preliminare: 284-5. *Archeologia medievale* 15: 253-311.

Reynolds, J.M. (1991) Inscriptions. In N. Christie (ed.), *Three South Etrurian Churches: Santa Cornelia, Santa Rufina and San Liberato* (*Archaeological Monographs of the British School at Rome* 4): 137-52, 301-7. London, British School at Rome.

RIC = *Roman Imperial Coinage*, vols III-IX.

Ricci, A. (1985a) Ceramica a pareti sottili. In G. Pugliese Carratelli (ed.), *Enciclopedia dell'arte antica classica e orientale – Atlante delle forme ceramiche* II.

Ceramica fine romana nel bacino mediterraneo (tardo ellenismo e primo impero): 231-357 + tavv. LXXVIII-CXIV. Rome.

Ricci, A. (ed.) (1985b) *Settefinestre. Una villa schiavistica nell'Etruria romana. 2. La villa e i suoi reperti.* Modena.

Ricci, M. (1986) Ceramica da fuoco. In D. Manacorda, L. Paroli, A. Molinari, M. Ricci and D. Romei, La ceramica medioevale di Roma nella stratigrafia della Crypta Balbi: 529-43. In *La ceramica medievale nel Mediterraneo occidentale (Atti del III Congresso Internazionale)*: 511-44. Florence.

Richter, G. (1915) *Greek, Etruscan and Roman Bronzes in the Metropolitan Museum of Art, New York.* New York.

Richter, G. (1926) *Ancient Furniture.* Oxford.

Rickman, G.E. (1980) *The Corn Supply of Ancient Rome.* Oxford.

Riley, J.A. (1979) The coarse pottery from Berenice. In J. Lloyd (ed.), *Excavations at Sidi Khrebish, Benghazi (Berenice)* II (Supplement to *Libya Antiqua* V): 91-467.

Ritchie, J.N.G. (1971) Iron finds from Dùn an Fheurain, Gallanach, Argyll. *Proceedings of the Society of Antiquaries of Scotland* 103: 100-12.

Roberts, P.C. (1988) *Pottery and Settlement in the Province of Molise during the Roman Imperial Period.* Unpublished M.Phil. thesis, Department of Ancient History, University of Sheffield.

Roberts, P.C. (1992) *The Late Roman Pottery of Adriatic Italy.* Unpublished Ph.D. thesis, University of Sheffield.

Roberts, P.C. (1993) The pottery from the cistern. In U. Albarella, V. Ceglia and P.C. Roberts, S. Giacomo degli Schiavoni (Molise): an early fifth century AD deposit of pottery and animal bones from central Adriatic Italy: 163-203. *Papers of the British School at Rome* 61: 157-230.

Roberts, P.C. (forthcoming) The Roman pottery. In J. Lloyd (ed.), *Excavations at the Roman villa at Matrice.*

Robinson, D. (1941) *Excavations at Olynthus* X. Baltimore.

Robinson, H.S. (1959) *Pottery of the Roman Period (Athenian Agora* V). Princeton.

Roes, A. (1963) *Bone and Antler Objects from the Frisian Terp-mounds.* Haarlem.

Rösler, W. (1995) Wine and truth in the Greek *symposion.* In O. Murray and M. Tecuşan (eds), *In Vino Veritas*: 106-12. London.

Rogers, J. and Waldron, T. (1989) Infections in palaeopathology; the basis of classification according

to most probable cause. *Journal of Archaeological Science* 16: 611-25.

Rogers, J., Waldron, T., Dieppe P. and Waitt I. (1987) Arthropathies in palaeopathology; the basis of classification according to most probable cause. *Journal of Archaeological Science* 14: 179-83.

Romanini, A.M. (1971) Problemi di scultura e plastica altomedievali. *Artigianato e tecnica nella società dell'alto medioevo occidentale* (Spoleto): 425-67.

Romanini, A.M. (1991) Scultura nella "Langobardia Maior": questioni storiografiche. *Arte medievale* 5: 1-30.

Romei, D. (1986) Ceramica acroma depurata. In D. Manacorda, L. Paroli, A. Molinari, M. Ricci and D. Romei, La ceramica medioevale di Roma nella stratigrafia della Crypta Balbi: 523-9. In *La ceramica medievale nel Mediterraneo occidentale (Atti del III Congresso Internazionale)*: 511-44. Florence.

Romei, D. (1990) Ceramica acroma depurata II. In L. Saguì and L. Paroli (eds), *Archeologia urbana a Roma: il progetto della Crypta Balbi, 5. L'esedra della Crypta Balbi nel medioevo (XI-XV secolo)*: 264-87. Florence.

Romei, D. (1992) La ceramica a vetrina pesante altomedievale nella stratigrafia dell'esedra della Crypta Balbi. In L. Paroli (ed.), *La ceramica invetriata tardoantica e altomedievale in Italia*: 378-93. Florence.

Rösing, F.W. (1983) Sexing immature human skeletons. *Journal of Human Evolution* 12: 149-55.

Rossiter, J.J. (1978) *Roman Farm Buildings in Italy* (BAR International Series 52). Oxford.

Saguì, L. (1986) Crypta Balbi (Roma): lo scavo nell'esedra del monumento romano. Seconda relazione preliminare. *Archeologia medievale* 13: 345-55.

Saguì, L. (1991) Ceramica da fuoco. In M.T. Cipriano, L. Paroli, H. Patterson, L. Saguì and D. Whitehouse (1991), La documentazione ceramica dell'Italia centro-meridionale nell'alto medioevo: quadri regionali contesti campioni. In *A ceramica medieval no Mediterraneo ocidental (Atti del IV Congresso Internazionale)*: 102-5. Mertola.

Saguì, L. and Paroli, L. (eds) (1990) *Archeologia urbana a Roma: il progetto della Crypta Balbi, 5. L'esedra della Crypta Balbi nel medioevo (XI-XV secolo).* Florence.

Salter, M. (1984) Compilation of age of fusion data from twelve sources. Unpublished paper.

Salvatore, M. (1982) La ceramica altomedievale nell'Italia centromeridionale: stato e prospettive della ricerca. *Archeologia medievale* 9: 47-66.

Salvatore, M. (1983) La ceramica tardoromana e altomedievale in Basilicata alla luce delle recenti scoperte. In M. Gualtieri, M. Salvatore and A. Small (eds), *Lo scavo di S. Giovanni di Ruoti ed il periodo tardoantico in Basilicata*: 111-23. Bari.

Saunders, S.R. (1989) Nonmetric skeletal variation. In M.Y. Iscan and K.A.R. Kennedy (eds), *Reconstruction of Life from the Skeleton*: 95-108. New York.

Schiaparelli, L. (ed.) (1901) Il cartario di San Pietro in Vaticano. I parte. *Archivio della Società romana di storia patria* 24: 393-496.

Schinke, R. (1994) The amphorae. In O.J. Gilkes, S. Passigli and R. Schinke, Porta Pia: excavation and survey in an area of suburban Rome, Part 2: 117-22. *Papers of the British School at Rome* 62: 101-37.

Schour, I. and Massler, M. (1944) *Development of the Human Dentition* (second edition). Chicago.

Schubart, W. (1911) *Papyri Graecae Berolinenses*. Bonn.

Schuring, J.M. (1987) Supplementary note to the Roman, early medieval and medieval coarse kitchen wares from the San Sisto Vecchio in Rome. *Bullettin Antieke Beschaving* 61: 109-29.

SEG = Supplementum epigraphicum Graecum.

Seminario = (1976) *Seminario sulla tecnica e il linguaggio della scultura a Roma tra VIII e IX secolo. Roma e l'età Carolingia*: 267-88. Rome.

Sennis, A. (1996) Un territorio da ricomporre: il Lazio tra i secoli IV e XIV. In *Atlante storico-politico del Lazio*: 27-61. Rome/Bari.

Serafini, A. (1927) *Le torri campanarie del Lazio nel medioevo*. Rome.

Sereni, E. (1982) *Storia del paesaggio agrario italiano*. Bari.

Shelton, K. (1981) *The Esquiline Treasure*. London.

Silver, I.A. (1969) The ageing of the domestic animals. In D. Brothwell and E. Higgs (eds), *Science and Archaeology* (second edition): 283-302. London.

Siviero, R. (1954) *Gli ori e le ambri del Museo Nazionale di Napoli. Le Opera d'arte recuperate* II. Sansoni.

Small, A.M. and Buck, R.J. (1994) *The Excavations of San Giovanni di Ruoti 1. The Villas and their Environment*. Toronto.

Smith, R.R.R. (1990) Late Roman philosopher portraits from Aphrodisias. *Journal of Roman Studies* 80: 127-55.

Smith, W. (1865) *Dictionary of Greek and Roman Antiquities*. London.

Sölter, W. (1970) *Römische Kalkbrenner im Rheinland*. Düsseldorf.

Solin, H. (1982) *Die Griechischen Personnamen in Rom: ein Namenbuch*. Berlin.

Soricelli, G. (1988) Osservazioni intorno ad un cratere in ceramica invetriata a Pompeii. *Rivista di studi pompeiani* 2: 248-54.

Spurr, M.S. (1986) *Arable Cultivation in Roman Italy c. 200 B.C.-c. A.D. 100 (Society for the Promotion of Roman Studies, monograph 3)*. London.

Staffa, A.R. (1984) Villa romana presso la Torre di Rebibbia. *Bullettino della Commissione archeologica comunale di Roma* 89: 114-24.

Staffa, A.R. (1986) Località Rebibbia, via S Canizzaro. Un punto di sosta lungo la via Tiburtina fra l'età di Augusto e la tarda antichità (circ. V). *Bullettino della commissione archeologica comunale di Roma* 91 (2): 642-78.

Steele, D.G. (1983) The analysis of animal remains from two late Roman middens at San Giovanni di Ruoti. In M. Gualtieri, M. Salvatore and A. Small (eds), *Lo scavo di S. Giovanni di Ruoti ed il periodo tardoantico in Basilicata*: 75-84. Bari.

Steinbock, R.T. (1976) *Paleopathological Diagnosis and Interpretation; Bone Disease in Ancient Human Populations*. Springfield.

Stone, M. (1984) I laterizi. In F. Cameron, G. Clark, R. Jackson, C. Johns, S. Philpot, T. Potter, J. Shepherd, M. Stone and D. Whitehouse, Il castello di Ponte Nepesino e il confine settentrionale del Ducato di Roma: 108-21. *Archeologia medievale* 11: 63-147.

Stoppioni Piccoli, M.L. (1983) I materiali della fornace romana di Via della Resistenza, a Santarcangelo di Romagna. *Studi romagnoli* 34: 29-46.

Storz, S. (1994) *Tonröhren im antiken Gewölbebau*. Mainz.

Strong, D.E. (1953) Late Hadrianic architectural ornament in Rome. *Papers of the British School at Rome* 21: 118-51.

Strong, D.E. (1963) Some observations on early Roman Corinthian. *Journal of Roman Studies* 53: 73-84.

Strong, D.E. (1966) *Greek and Roman Gold and Silver Plate*. London.

Stuart-Macadam, P.L. (1989) Nutritional deficiency diseases; a survey of scurvy, rickets and iron deficiency anaemia. In M.Y. Iscan and K.A.R. Kennedy (eds), *Reconstruction of Life from the Skeleton*: 201-22. New York.

Sundick, R.I. (1978) Human skeletal growth and age determination. *Homo* 30: 297-333.

Svenbro, J. (1988) *Phrasikleia: Anthropologie de la lecture en Grèce ancienne*. Paris.

Swan, V.G. (1984) *The Pottery Kilns of Roman Britain.* London.

Tattersall, I. (1968) Dental palaeopathology of medieval Britain. *Journal of the History of Medicine* 23 (4): 380-8.

Taylor, L.R. (1914) Augustales, Seviri Augustales, and seviri: a chronological study. *Transactions and Proceedings of the American Philological Association* 45: 231-53.

Tchernia, A. (1986) *Le vin de l'Italie romaine: essai d'histoire économique d'après les amphores (Collection de l'Ecole Française de Rome* 261). Rome.

Thesing, R. (1977) *Die Grossentwicklung des Haushuhns in Vor- und Frühgeschichtlicher Zeit.* Dissertation der Universität München.

Thomas, R. and Wilson, A. (1994) Water supply for Roman farms in Latium and south Etruria. *Papers of the British School at Rome* 62: 139-96.

Thompson, D.W. (1936) *A Glossary of Greek Birds.* London.

Thompson, H.A. (1934) Two centuries of Hellenistic pottery. *Hesperia* 3: 311-480.

Threipland, L.M. (1968) Cogged ware. *Papers of the British School at Rome* 36: 199, figs 26 and 35.

Tomassetti, G. (1877) Mazzano. *Notizie degli scavi di antichità*: 262-3.

Tomassetti, G. (1882) Della campagna romana nel medioevo. *Archivio della Società romana di storia patria* 5: 67-156.

Tomassetti, G. (1883) Della campagna romana nel medio evo (cont.). *Archivio della Società romana di storia patria* 6: 173-222.

Tomassetti G. (1884) La campagna romana nel medioevo. *Archivio della Società romana di storia patria* 7: 183-258, 353-462.

Tomassetti, G. (1910) *La campagna romana antica, medievale e moderna* I. Rome.

Tomassetti, G. (1913) *La campagna romana.* Rome.

Tomassetti, G. (1913 (1979)) *La campagna romana, antica, medioevale e moderna* 3 (*nuova edizione aggiornata a cura di L. Chiumenti e F. Bilancia*). Florence.

Tortorella, S. (1981) Ceramica africana. Ceramica da cucina. In G. Pugliese Carratelli, *Enciclopedia dell'arte antica classica e orientale. Atlante delle forme ceramiche.* I. *Ceramica fine romana nel bacino mediterraneo (medio e tardo impero)*: 208-27 + tavv. CIV-CIX. Rome.

Tosti, A. (1835) *Rilevazione dell'origine e i progressi dell'Ospizio Apostolico di S. Michele.* Rome.

Toubert, P. (1973) *Les structures du Latium médiéval: le Latium méridional et la Sabine du IX siècle à la fin du XII siècle (Bibliothèque des Ecoles Françaises d'Athènes et de Rome,* 221). Rome.

Toynbee, J.M.C. (1973) *Animals in Roman Life and Art.* London.

Tozzi, C. (1981) L'alimentazione nella Maremma medievale: due esempi di scavi. *Archeologia medievale* 8: 299-305.

Tran Tam Tinh (1988) *La casa dei cervi a Herculaneum.* Rome.

Trotter, M. and Glesser, G.C. (1952) Estimation of stature from long bones of American whites and negroes. *American Journal of Physical Anthropology* 10: 463-514.

Trotter, M. and Glesser, G.C. (1958) A re-evaluation of estimation of stature based on measurements of stature taken during life and long bones after death. *American Journal of Physical Anthropology* 16: 79-123.

Turner, E.G. (1971) *Greek Manuscripts of the Ancient World.* Oxford.

Turner, E.G. (1987) *Greek Manuscripts of the Ancient World* (second edition). London.

Ubelaker, D.H. (1978) *Human Skeletal Remains; Excavation, Analysis and Interpretation.* Taraxacum, Washington.

Ubelaker, D.H. (1989) *Human Skeletal Remains. Excavation, Analysis, Interpretation (Manuals on Archaeology* 2) (second edition). Taraxacum, Washington.

Van Essen, C.C. (1957) Reliefs décoratifs d'époque carolingienne à Rome. *Mededelingen van het Nederlands Historisch Instituut te Rome* 9: 84-113.

Van de Noort, R. and Whitehouse, D.B. (1992) Le mura di Santo Stefano and other medieval churches in south Etruria: the archaeological evidence. *Archeologia medievale* 19: 75-89.

Van Neer, W. (ed.) (1994) *Fish Exploitation in the Past (Proceedings of the seventh meeting of the ICAZ Fish Remains Working Group / Annales du Musée Royal de l'Afrique Centrale, Sciences Zoologiques* 274). Tervuren.

Vassy, A. (1934) Découverte de deux estampilles de plombiers romaine et estampilles du Musée de Vienne. *Rhodania* 16: 159-77.

Vera, D. (1986) Forme e funzioni della rendita fondaria nella tarda antichità. In A. Giardina (ed.), *Società romana e impero tardoantico* I: 367-447, 723-60. Rome/Bari.

Vera, D. (1995) Dalla "villa perfecta" alla villa di Palladio: sulle trasformazioni del sistema agrario in Italia fra principato e dominato. *Athenaeum* 83: 189-211, 331-56.

Vermeule, C.C. (1965) A Greek theme and its survivals: the ruler's shield (tondo image) in tomb and temple. *Proceedings of the American Philosophical Society* 107: 361-97.

Verzone, P. (1945) *L'arte preromanica in Liguria.* Turin.

Voza, G. (1989) I crolli nella villa romana di Patti Marina. In E. Guidoboni (ed.), *I terramoti prima del mille in Italia e nell'area mediterranea*: 496-501. Bologna.

Waldbaum, J.C. (1983) *Metalwork from Sardis: the Finds through 1974.* Cambridge, Mass.

Waldron, T. (1991) Rates for the job. Measures of disease frequency in palaeopathology. *International Journal of Osteoarchaeology* 1: 17-25.

Waldron, T. (forthcoming) The human bone from St Mary Graces (the Royal Mint), London.

Walker, S. (1985) *Memorials to the Roman Dead.* London.

Ward-Perkins, J.B. (1955) Notes on southern Etruria and the Ager Veientanus. *Papers of the British School at Rome* 23: 44-72.

Ward-Perkins, J.B. (1961) Veii. The historical topography of the ancient city. *Papers of the British School at Rome* 29: 1-123.

Ward-Perkins, J.B. (1970) Introduction to T. Ashby, *The Roman Campagna in Classical Times* (1970 reprint): v-x. Tonbridge.

Ward-Perkins, J.B. (1971) Quarries and stoneworking in the early middle ages: the heritage of the ancient world. In *Artigianato e tecnica nella società dell'Alto Medioevo occidentale*: 525-44. Spoleto.

Ward-Perkins, J.B. and Claridge, A. (1976) *Pompeii AD 79.* London.

Wells, C. (1982) The human burials. In A. McWhirr, L. Viner and C. Wells, *Romano-British Cemeteries at Cirencester*: 135-201. Cirencester.

West, B. (1982) Spur development: recognising caponised fowl in archaeological material. In B. Wilson, C. Grigson and S. Payne (eds), *Ageing and Sexing Animal Bones from Archaeological Sites* (BAR British Series 109): 255-61. Oxford.

West, B. (1985) Chicken legs revisited. *Circaea* 3 (1): 11-14.

Wheeler, A. and Jones, A.K.G. (1989) *Fishes.* Cambridge.

Wheeler, A. and Locker, A. (1985) The estimation of size in sardines (*Sardina pilchardus*) from amphorae in a wreck at Randello, Sicily. *Journal of Archaeological Science* 12: 97-100.

White, K.D. (1970) *Roman Farming.* London.

Whitehead, P.J.P., Bauchot, M-L., Hureau, J-C., Nielsen, J. and Tortonese, E. (1989) *Fishes of the North-eastern Atlantic and the Mediterranean* I-III. UNESCO.

Whitehouse, D.B. (1965) 'Forum ware' a distinctive type of early medieval glazed pottery from the Roman Campagna. *Medieval Archaeology* 9: 55-63.

Whitehouse, D.B. (1980) The medieval pottery from Santa Cornelia. *Papers of the British School at Rome* 48: 125-56.

Whitehouse, D.B. (1982) The pottery. In D.B. Whitehouse, G. Barker, R. Reece and D. Reese, The Schola Praeconum I: the coins, pottery, lamps and fauna: 56-80. *Papers of the British School at Rome* 50: 53-101.

Whitehouse, D.B. (1983) Ruoti, pottery and pigs. In M. Gualtieri, M. Salvatore and A. Small (eds), *Lo scavo di S. Giovanni di Ruoti ed il periodo tardoantico in Basilicata*: 107-9. Bari.

Whittaker, D.K., Griffiths, S., Robson, A., Rogers-Davies, P., Thomas, G. and Molleson, T. (1990) Continuing tooth eruption and alveolar crest height in an eighteenth century population from Spitalfields, East London. *Arch.Oral.Biol.* 35 (2): 81-5.

Wickham, C.J. (1978) Historical and topographical notes on early medieval south Etruria (part one). *Papers of the British School at Rome* 46: 132-79.

Wickham, C.J. (1979) Historical and topographical notes on early medieval south Etruria (part two). *Papers of the British School at Rome* 47: 66-95.

Wickham, C.J. (1981) *Early Medieval Italy. Central Power and Local Society, 400-1000.* London.

Wild, J.P. (1970) *Textile Manufacture in the North West Provinces.* Cambridge.

Wilson, R.J.A. (1992) Terracotta vaulting tubes (*tubi fittili*): on their origin and distribution. *Journal of Roman Archaeology* 5: 97-129.

Winkes, R. (1969) *Clipeata Imago. Studien zu einer Römischen Bildnisform.* Bonn.

Wolters, P. (1913) Eingeritzte Inschriften auf Vasen. *Mitteilungen des Deutschen Archäologischen Institute, Athenische Abteilung* 38: 193-202.

Woolf, G. (1990) Food, poverty and patronage: the signficance of the epigraphy of the Roman alimentary schemes in early Imperial Italy. *Papers of the British School at Rome* 58: 197-228.

Zanker, P. and Fittschen, K. (1983) *Katalog der Römischen Porträts in den Capitolinischen Museen und den anderen Kommunalen Sammlungen der Stadt Rom III: Kaiserinnen- und Prinzessinnenbildnisse Frauenporträts.* Mainz.

Zevi, F. and Carta, M. (1987) La taberna dell'Invidioso. *Notizie degli scavi di antichità*, supplement: 9-164.

Zevi, F. and Pohl, I. (1970) Ostia – saggi di scavo. *Notizie degli scavi di antichità*, supplement.

INDEX

compiled by Gillian Clark